Building Utopia

The Barbican Centre

Building Utopia

The Barbican Centre

Edited by
Nicholas Kenyon

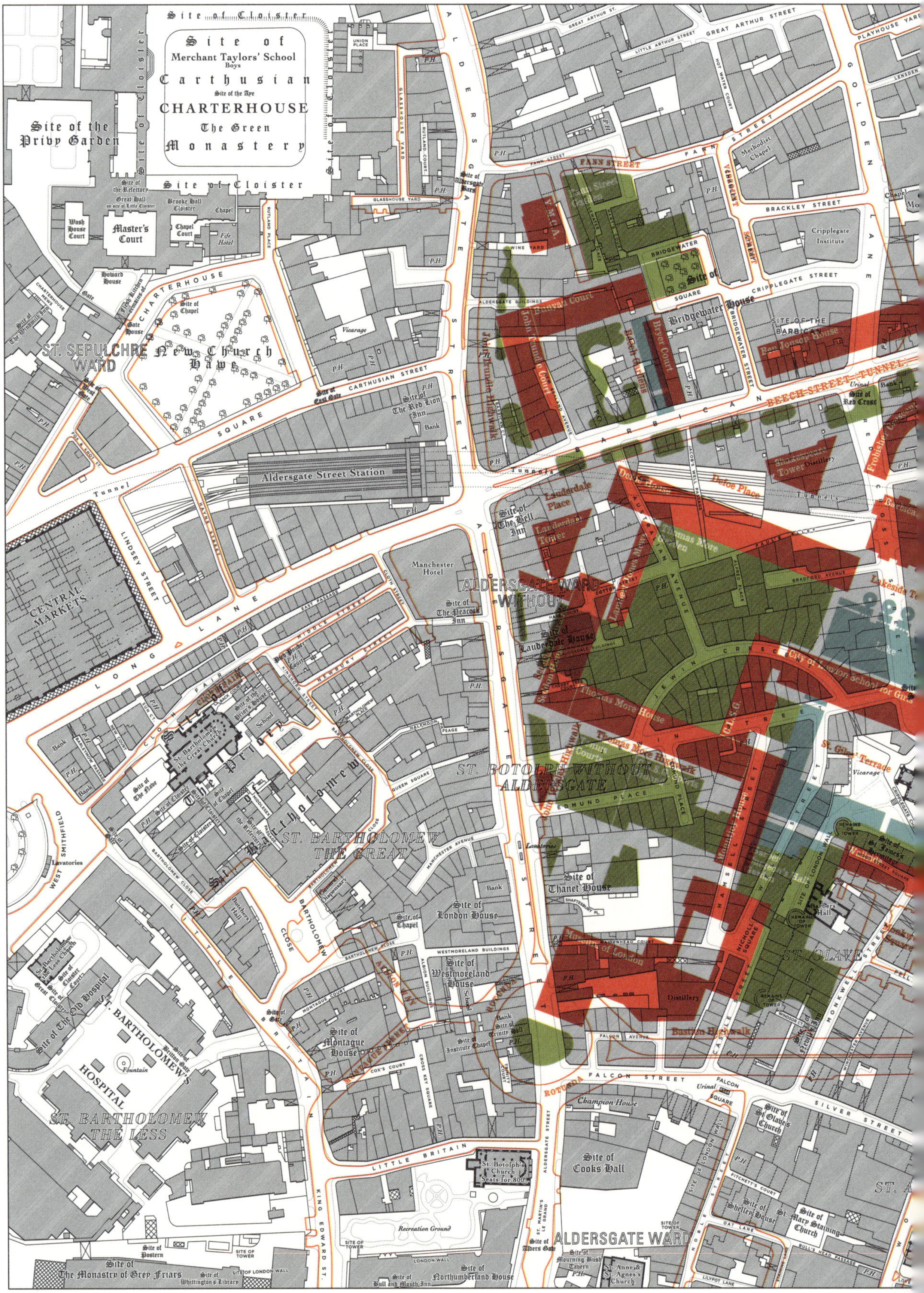

On the night of Sunday the 29th of December 1940, between 6pm and the early hours of the following morning, the area around what we now call Barbican in the City of London, saw one of the worst air raids of the entire Blitz. The Luftwaffe dropped around 24,000 high explosive and 100,000 incendiary bombs on the City that night. The area of destruction was vast, stretching from south of Islington to St. Paul's Cathedral. It was, at the time, called the Second Great Fire of London and actually caused more destruction than the Great Fire of London of 1666.

There were over 1,500 fires, many of which joined to form three major conflagrations, before becoming a firestorm that spread the flames towards St. Paul's Cathedral, which, Churchill had insisted, "must be saved at all costs". The Blitz, which had started on the 7th of September 1940, lasted until the 21st of May the following year and claimed the lives of over 40,000 civilians. Precious little remained within the present Barbican site after WWII, other than historic remnants of the Roman London Wall and the medieval St. Giles' Cripplegate Church.

This detailed map of the area shows how it would have looked before WWII. Redrawn from the Ordnance Survey of 1916, with the arts centre, residential towers and blocks, lakes and gardens of Chamberlin, Powell and Bon's hugely ambitious 40 acre Barbican Estate, overlaid on top; coloured, outlined roads, show the contemporary road network. The Barbican, once described by the Queen as "one of the wonders of the modern world", is now a Grade II listed site of special architectural importance and is home to some 4,000 residents.

BARB

BEFORE

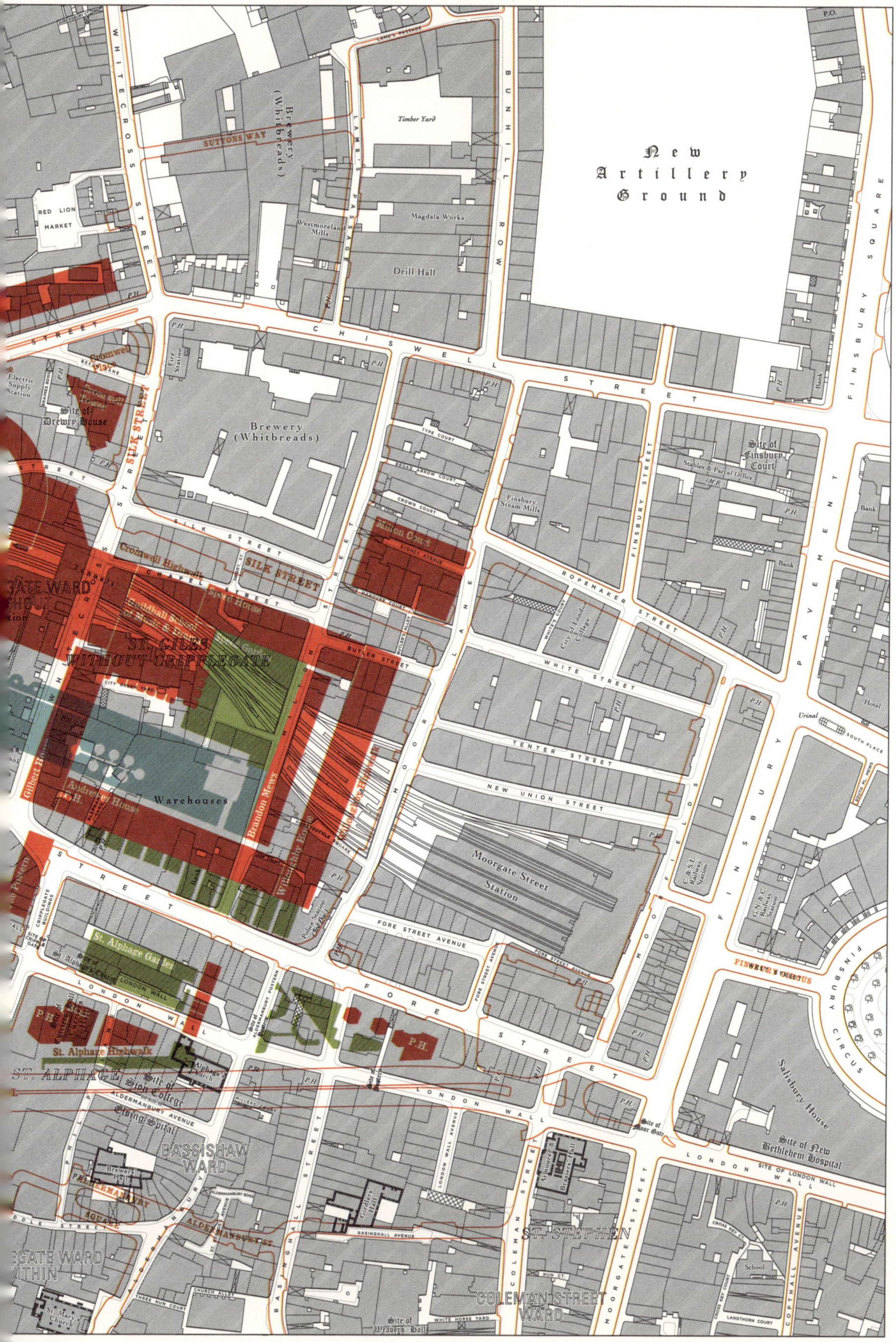

AN

0 10 20 40 60 80 100 120 140 160 180 200 Metres

0 50 100 200 300 400 500 600 Feet

KEY: P.H.: Public House, P.O.: Post Office, Site of: Roman site, Site of: non-Roman site.

Previous pages
Illustration by Russell Bell, 2014. This shows the Barbican development superimposed in colour on the Ordnance Survey map of the area before the Blitz of 1940/41. In the centre of the picture is the surviving church of St Giles Cripplegate, which provides the alignment for the whole estate. On the left is the semicircular shape of Jewin Crescent, echoed in the Barbican's new Frobisher Crescent.

Contents

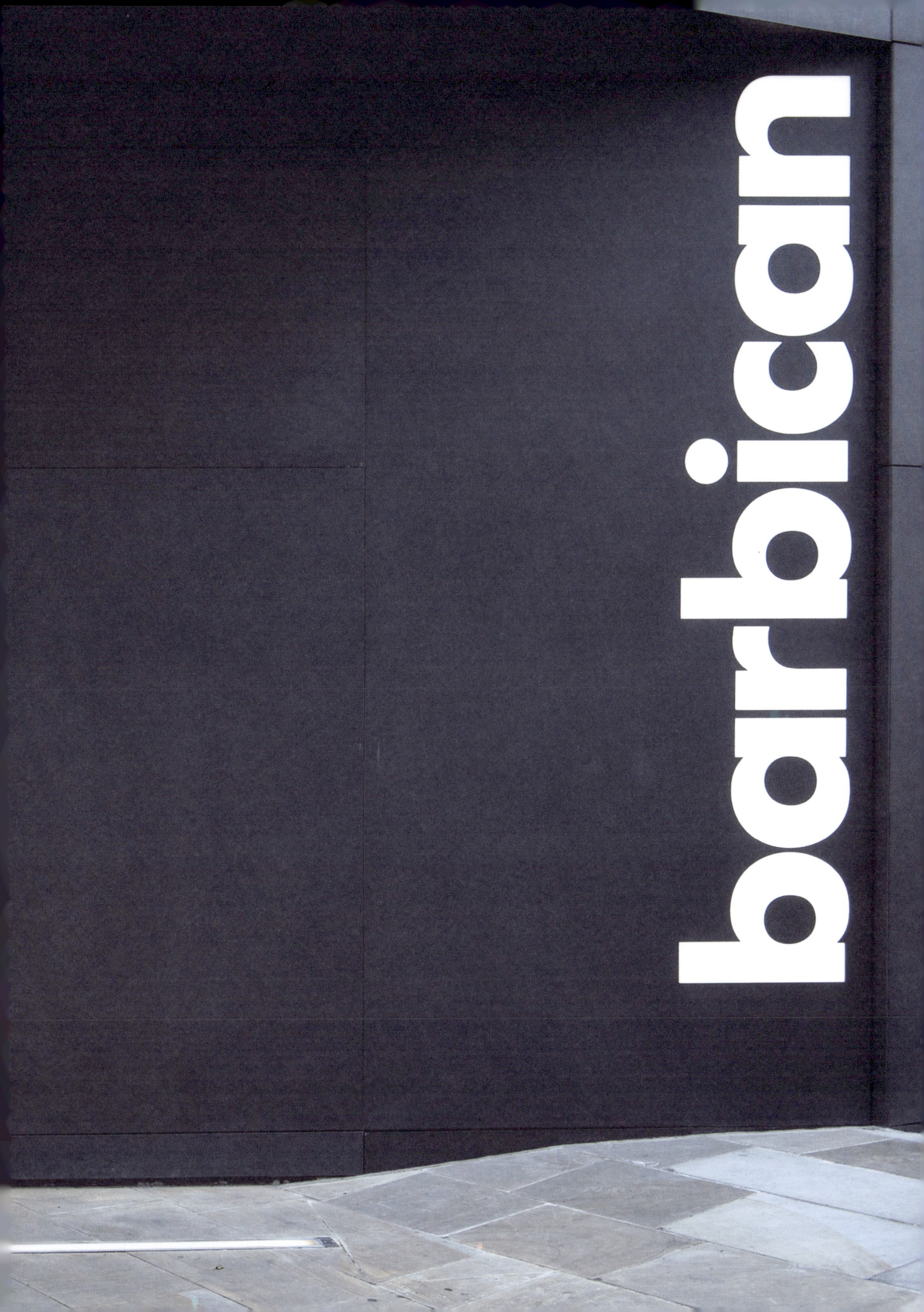
barbican

CITY OF LONDON

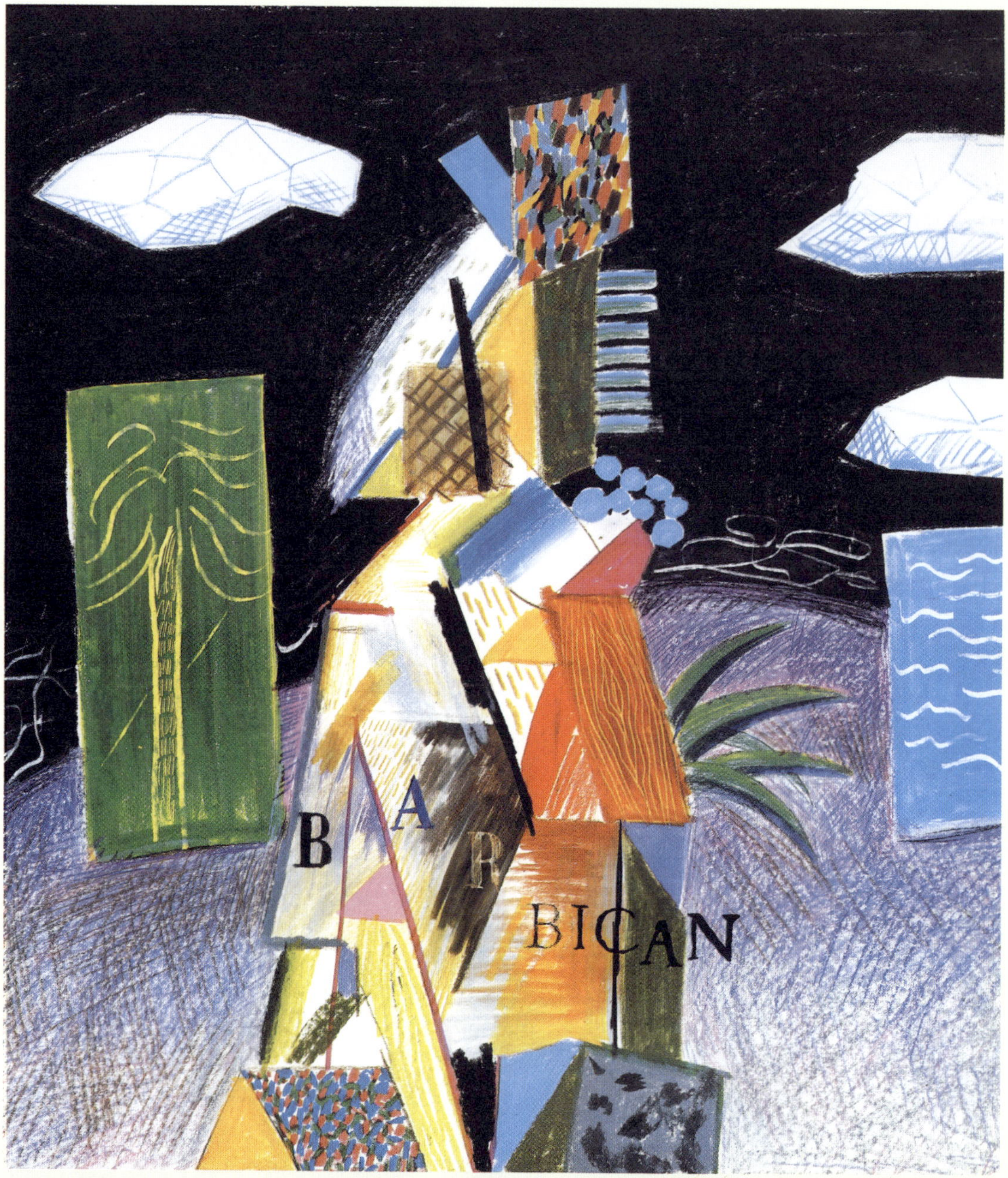

BARBICAN CENTRE FOR THE ARTS

March 1982

Preface

Nicholas Kenyon

There are many stories told about those who have lived the unique project that is the Barbican Centre: those who designed and re-designed it in its daunting scale and complexity; those who battled to construct it, often under dreadful conditions; those who argued for (and against) its large and seemingly ever-expanding funding; those who have created its vibrant artistic and dynamic commercial programme; those who have welcomed and guided audiences and visitors; and those who have worked constantly to maintain and enhance the building. Some have hated it, some have loved it, but millions have made use of the Barbican over four decades of near-continuous activity, and have come to value its profound contribution to civic and urban life.

We have sought to provide perspectives on why and how the Barbican was created, to give critics and writers free rein to assess the centre's programme across the years, and to provide a rich visual impression of this unique building, including much rare archive material. We do not tell a strictly chronological story, so there are repetitions and cross-references: there are accounts of the background by Robert Hewison, Elain Harwood and myself; conversations curated by Philip Dodd with those who have guided the organisation; studies of the art-forms by Fiona Maddocks, Lyn Gardner, Tony Chambers and Sukhdev Sandhu, which are interspersed with first-hand comments from some of those involved, from the plant room at the base of the building to the conservatory at the top. Roma Agrawal writes about the key building material, concrete; Theo Inglis considers the changing visual aspects of the distinctive brand.

We have not sought to impose any view, leaving authors free to make their own choices and to express their opinions. We cannot possibly cover everything that has happened; our chronology is a selective list of highlights. We take the story through the enforced closure of 2020, up to the re-opening in May 2021, to provide a context for the 40th anniversary in March 2022. The sheer diversity of the work and the contrasted approaches to the concept of an arts centre provide many different perspectives across the years, but through it all there shines one shared conviction: that any humane vision of the future must have the arts at its heart—that, if ever, is how we will build utopia.

Opposite
Poster by David Hockney for the opening of the Barbican, March 1982.

Following pages
Isometric drawing of the Barbican Arts Centre as built, by John Ronayne, August 1982.

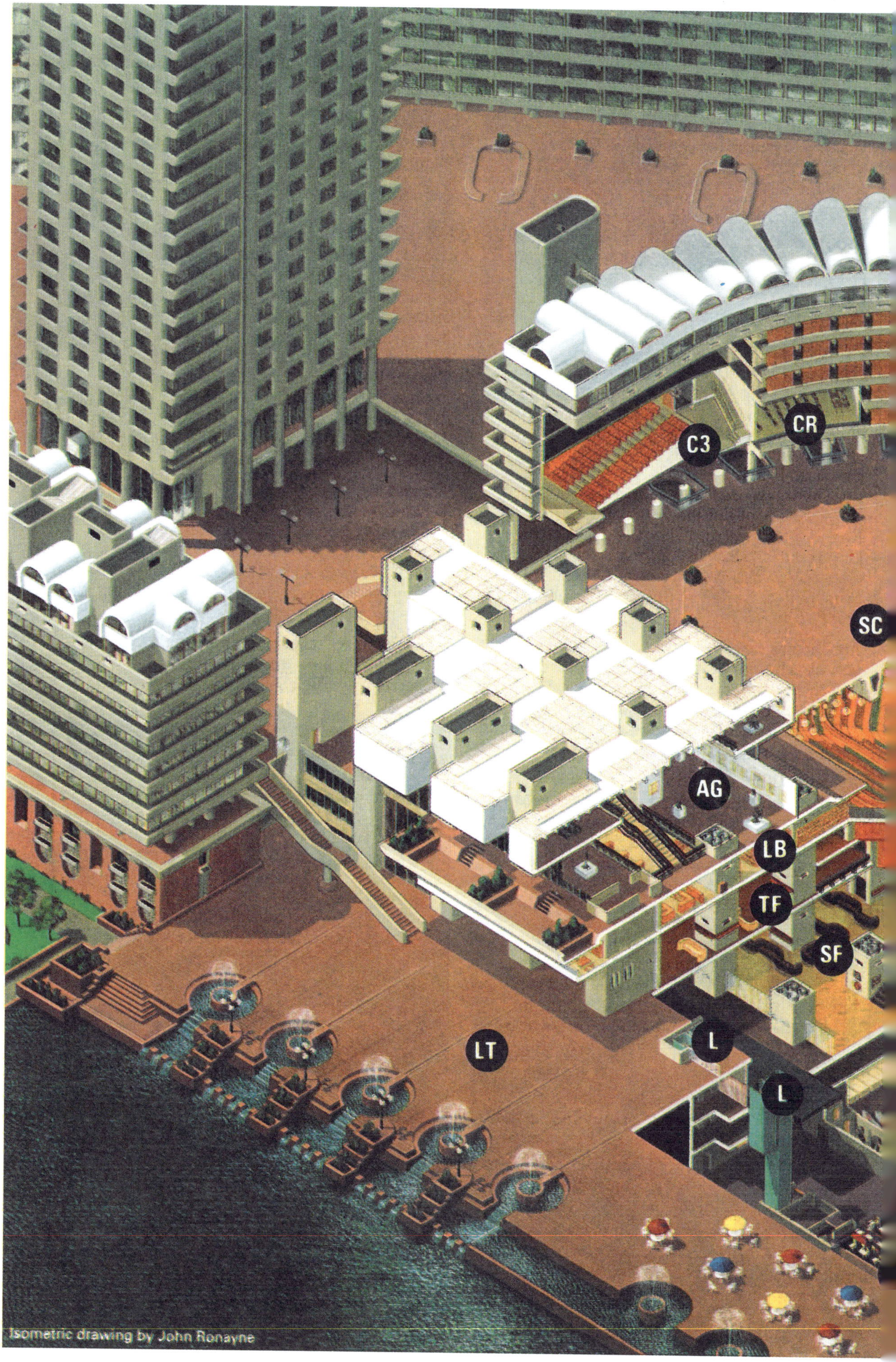

Isometric drawing by John Ronayne

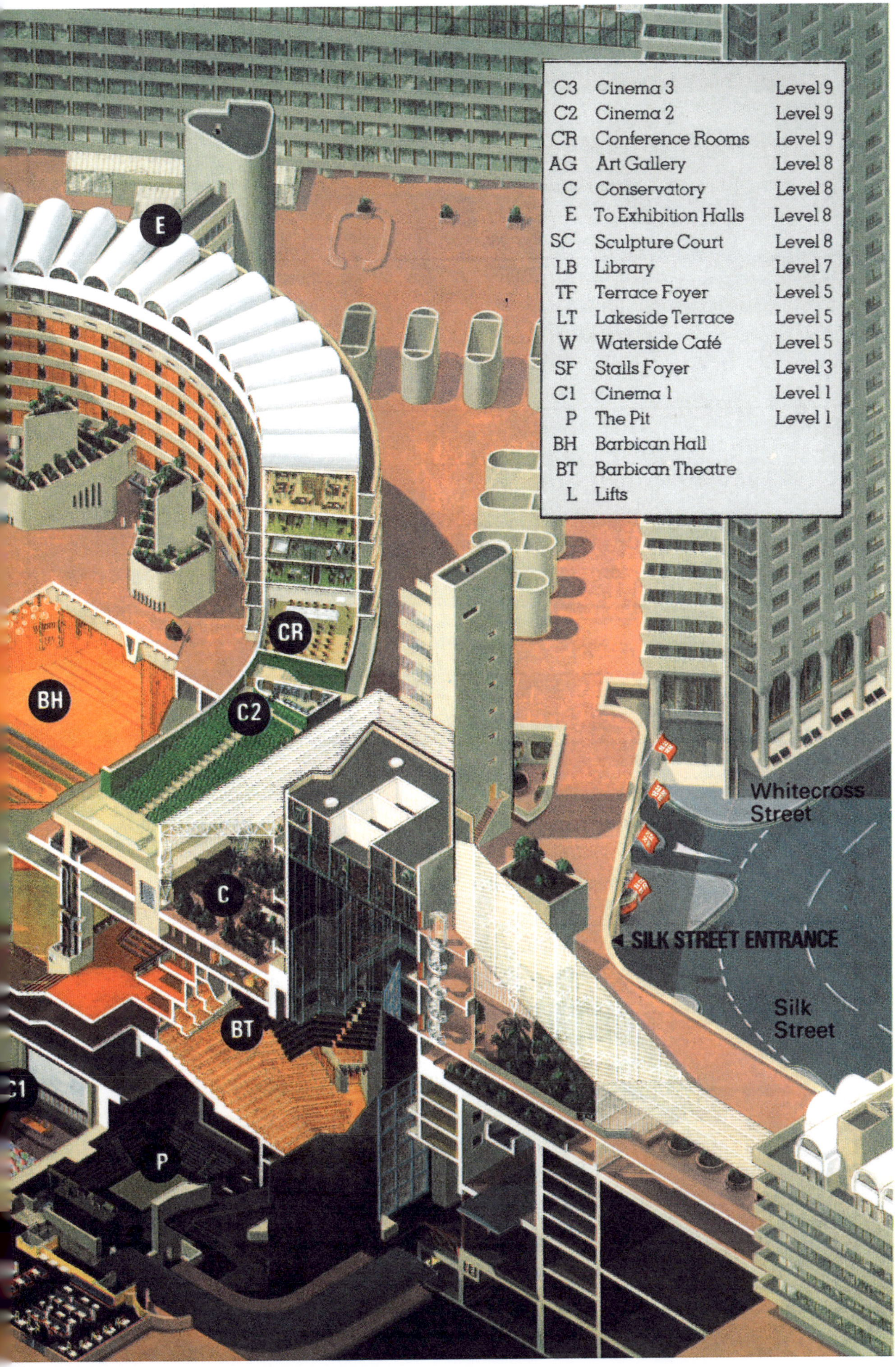

C3 Cinema 3 Level 9
C2 Cinema 2 Level 9
CR Conference Rooms Level 9
AG Art Gallery Level 8
C Conservatory Level 8
E To Exhibition Halls Level 8
SC Sculpture Court Level 8
LB Library Level 7
TF Terrace Foyer Level 5
LT Lakeside Terrace Level 5
W Waterside Café Level 5
SF Stalls Foyer Level 3
C1 Cinema 1 Level 1
P The Pit Level 1
BH Barbican Hall
BT Barbican Theatre
L Lifts
E
CR
BH
C2
C
BT
C1
P
Whitecross Street
SILK STREET ENTRANCE
Silk Street

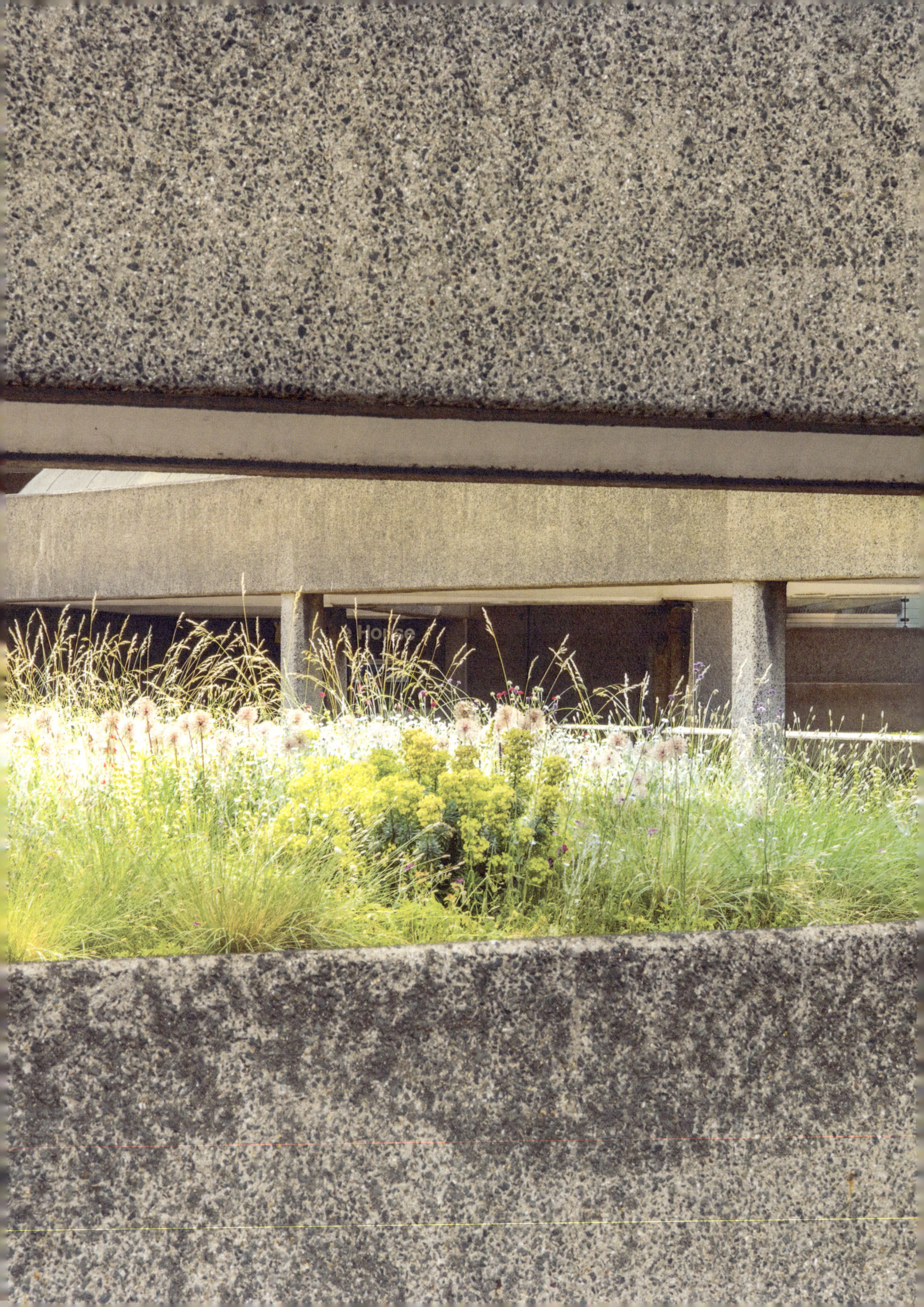

Foreword

Fiona Shaw

Barbican
'The outer defence of a castle or walled city,
A double tower above a drawbridge.'

It's not even a lifetime ago that the Barbican opened its invisible drawbridge to the public, yet in that time the Barbican has become as permanent as the ruins of the London Wall on which it stands. The building is enigmatic — a contradiction. It is a bastion protecting the many sources of energy that create pieces of performance; yet it opens outwards with a rare power and directness.

Theatre and the arts have radically changed their nature in the past 40 years, and the Barbican has been part of that change by gathering outside influences, inviting artists from all over the world, nudging local talent to expand the methods and the outcomes of the form, expanding the range of discourse and the meaning of our work.

In a world lately battered by economic inequality and pandemic, in a moment when we have become less international than at any time in memory, the Barbican is a preserver of the multinational democracy which is art.

This democracy has been delivered as a dazzling ongoing festival, thanks to the appearances of so many great artists of our time. In my world of theatre, Ninagawa has infused spectacle with scale and feeling, Shakespeare as owned by the world and redelivered to us by the innovation and intercessions of Ivo van Hove and Thomas Ostermeier.

For me, the greatest fundamental shift in approach should be attributed to Pina Bausch. She did this in dance, without spoken language — the lifeboat that has kept British theatre afloat. Like Peter Brook, her gift to the theatre will go on resonating over the next decades as the performances she brought to the Barbican transformed the approach to all theatre. She delivered the irony of the ordinary and the tragedy of the domestic. She slowed the moment down to its essence and we saw ourselves again. The North Americans too have told their story on this stage. Laurie Anderson with her music and hypnotic abilities, and Bob Wilson who has pushed aesthetic value towards a painterly meditation. Peter Sellars, who skims meaning in his semi-staged concert operas with Simon Rattle, shows how much can be expressed in a short time, just as Robert Lepage shows us what years of process can reveal in theatrical ingenuity.

It might seem naive now, but back in the 1980s we were very fired up. The RSC expanded from the country pleasures of Stratford and came to the Barbican. When I arrived it was only two seasons old, and its early reputation among the RSC actors was as a very luxurious, but terrifying building. It was daunting. The stage door hidden like an afterthought, a mouth halfway down the ramp to the car park. Backstage we were like colts, faltering and lost on the staircases and the inhospitable corridors. The theatre covers a depth of five floors that were arrived at by a lift that took us down underground to the Green Room with its dark floors, next to that the windowless rehearsal room where we spent so much time, like canaries in a mine.

But we produced living work. We believed we were challenging outdated attitudes. Feminism had finally begun to affect performances on stage. Language, and its male values, were being questioned. It felt like a structural shift; women characters could no longer be just in relation to men as daughters, wives or mothers. The frontiers of their possibilities were as infinite as for the men. This was challenging with Shakespeare, a writer who often makes his women characters silent once they have agreed to marry, so the actress heroines of the plays carried a huge responsibility in what we were reflecting during that shifting time; politically we were influenced by the recent miners' strike, which had left a wave of frustration and a need for rejuvenation.

The dressing rooms were luxurious, like hotel rooms. I remember in my second season some Russians were using my dressing room for a charity event. It was the day the rouble collapsed, and when I went in to see if they were all right, I discovered that in desperation they had broken my wardrobe door and liberated a bottle of whisky. They said they'd had to work hard as the wardrobe was so well made.

My first two seasons always remain with me. It was during those years that we performed *Les Liaisons Dangereuses* led by Alan Rickman, and *Electra* in the Pit — the small 160-seater that exploded with energy and brought in a new audience to discover the building with us. The seasons had other gems too. In the main house there was Ben Kingsley as Othello, and our controversial *As You Like It* with its abstract sets and discussions about gender and language. Who owned it?!

I remember the excitement of the first time seeing the golden mouth of the safety curtain in the main house as it opened. There is no central aisle, so there is a surprise in finding that the awe-inspiring view from the stage is reversed when in the auditorium. For the audience, the experience is one of intimacy. A season later when I was playing the 'Shrew', her controversial last speech — when some of the audience booed Kate's regressive capitulation — seemed very immediate for all of us.

Decades later I returned to play on stage alone, in the one-woman dramatisation of Colm Tóibín's *The Testament of Mary* — by then the theatre had the warm feeling of a much smaller house, a miracle of balanced architecture in a space that had settled into itself. I felt I was just talking with the audience. We were of one mind.

Last year, nearly 40 years since I first entered the Barbican building, I filmed in one of the beautiful hidden gardens — a secret place full of calm energy and peace. Like the theatre, music, art and cinema which it supports, it is becoming itself and transforming at the same time.

The Barbican looks to the future with that same openness and hope, not knowing what it may bring, ready to respond. It is observation and memory that makes for good theatre. The practitioners who have been able to capture their time and re-make it for audiences are the mappers of the way we see ourselves. In each time there will be new preoccupations. The theatre never lands, it just flows.

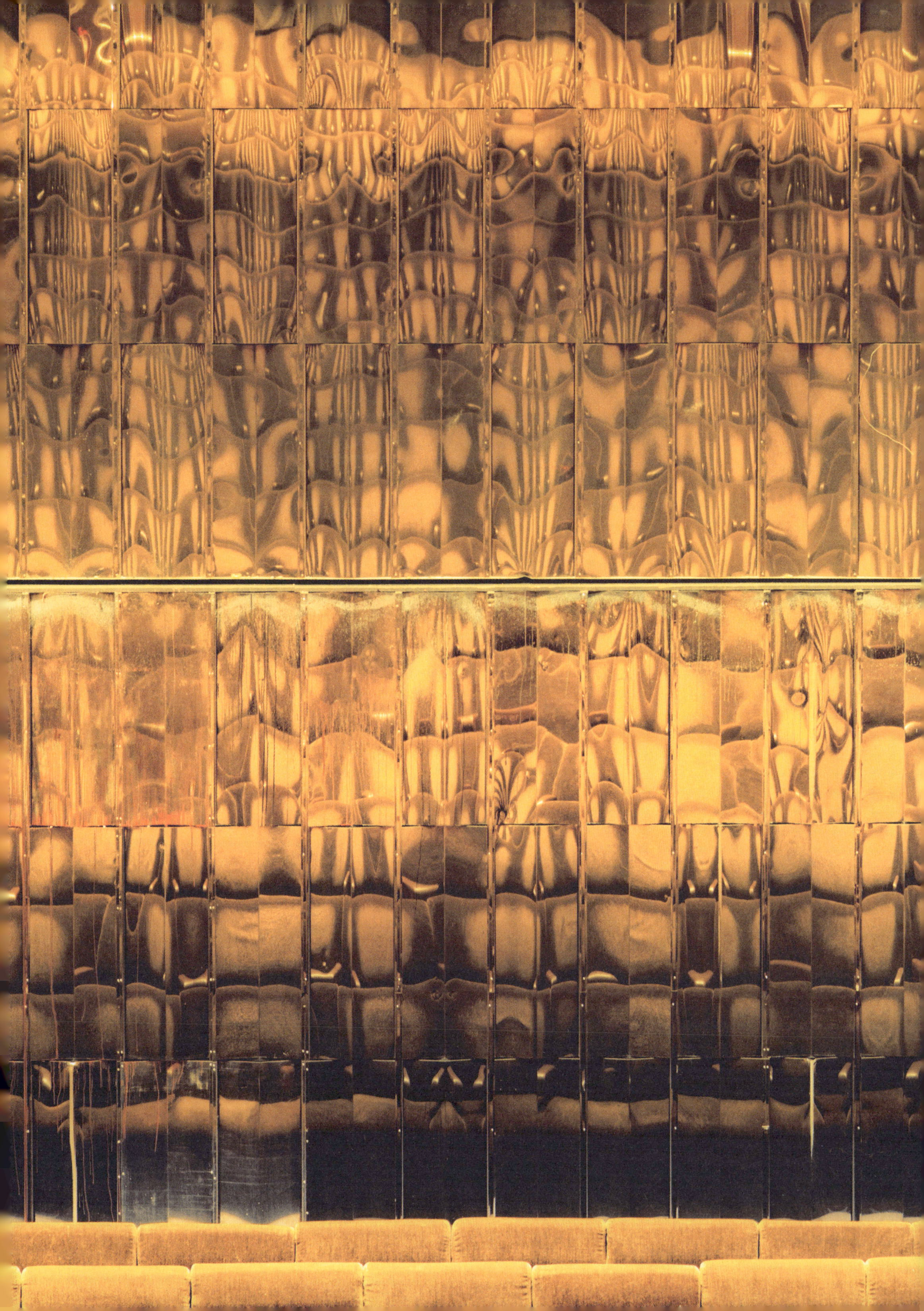

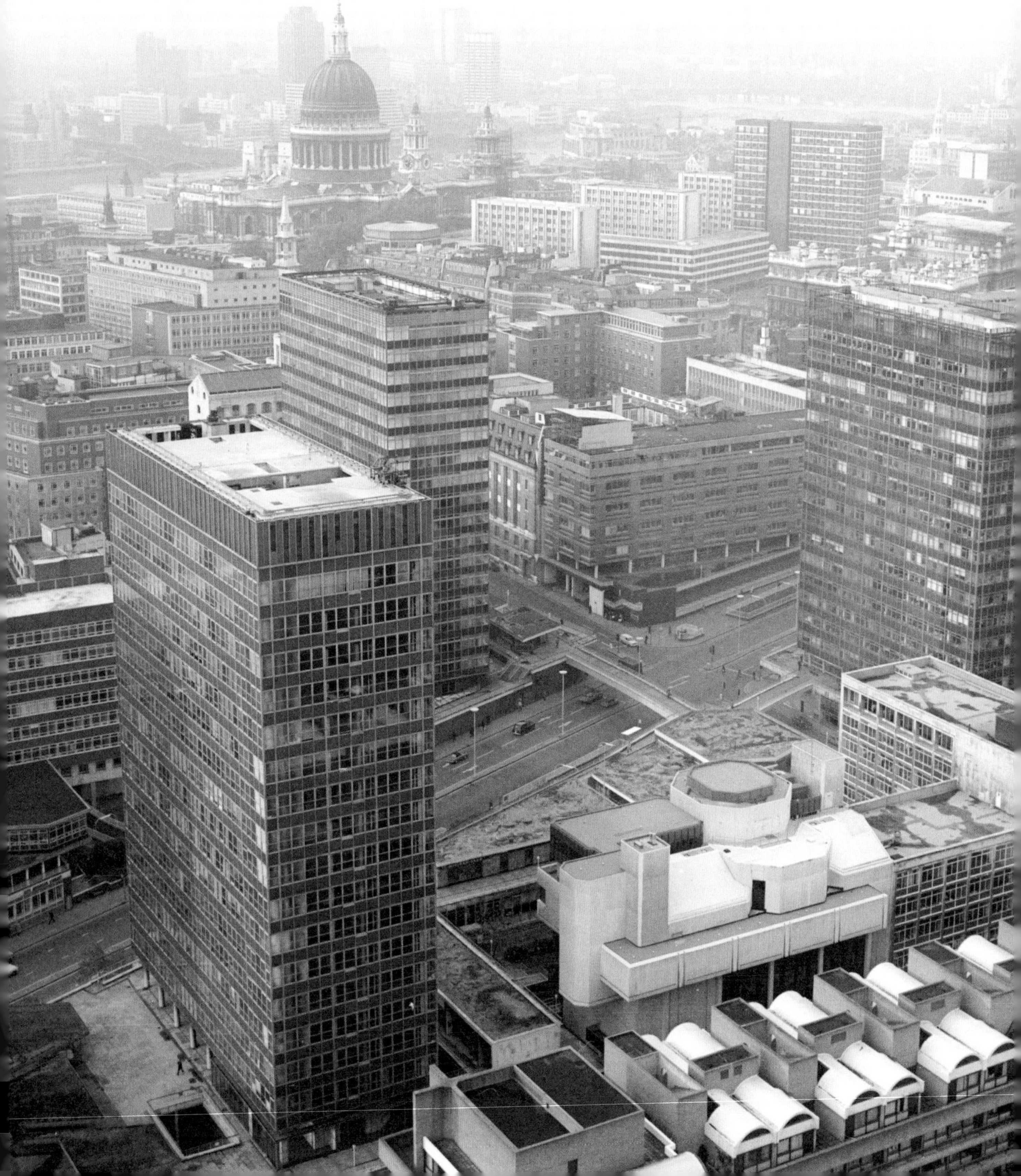

'Serious and fine entertainment': Creating an arts centre for the City

Robert Hewison

On 12 June 1945, in that strange space between the end of the war in Europe and the end of the war in Japan, when a Conservative government had taken over from the wartime coalition to prepare for a general election, the economist John Maynard Keynes gave a talk on the BBC Home Service, announcing the formation of the Arts Council of Great Britain (ACGB). Keynes was the architect of the United Kingdom's finances, but for the past three years he had also been chairman of the Council for the Encouragement of Music and the Arts, CEMA, now given a permanent role in the post-war settlement as the Arts Council of Great Britain. As Keynes remarked: 'I do not believe it is yet realised what an important thing has happened. Strange patronage of the arts has crept in. It has happened in a very English, informal way — half-baked, if you like.' The published transcript ironically does say 'strange', but he meant 'state' patronage, signalling that, just as they had raised morale during the war, the arts had a public role to play in post-war reconstruction. Keynes declared: 'Our wartime experience has led us already to one clear discovery: the unsatisfied demand and the enormous public for serious and fine entertainment.'

Keynes recognised that the destruction of wartime had only added to the cultural challenges the country faced: 'We shall have to solve what will be our biggest problem, the shortage — in most parts of Britain the complete absence — of adequate and suitable buildings. There never were many theatres in this country or any concert-halls or galleries worth counting.' He acknowledged the priority of housing, but, pointing to Russia, expressed the hope that in every blitzed town, 'the local authority will make provision for a central group of buildings for drama and music and art.' London, however, was a different case: 'It is also our business to make London a great artistic metropolis, a place to wonder at. For this purpose London today is half a ruin.'

Nowhere more so than in the square mile where the Barbican Arts Centre would be built. Nicholas Kenyon describes (p.31) the circumstances that led to the creation of this superb facility. Post-war reconstruction led the Corporation of the City of London to become one of the greatest patrons of the arts in the country. This chapter explores how the British concept of an 'arts centre' developed, and asks if the City foresaw its leading role in its development. Arts centres are not only a distinct kind of organisation, but a new building type. It is not clear that at first the City really did understand what it was doing, but the results are to be celebrated.

When Keynes spoke of a 'central group of buildings' as the basis of an arts centre, there were few precedents to go on. During the Depression, the American Federal Works Progress Administration had set up over a hundred 'arts centers', mainly in regional locations. In 1943 W E Williams, a future ACGB secretary-general, published an article in *Picture Post*, 'Are We Building A New Culture?', in which he proposed 'a national grid of cultural centres'. These would be 'civic centres where men and women may satisfy the whole range of educational and cultural interests, between keeping fit and popular argument.' He may have been thinking of the Peckham Experiment, a health and social centre established in a fine modernist purpose-built building in South London in 1935. In 1945 CEMA sent out a touring exhibition, *Plans for an Arts*

Centre, 'designed to show how the arts can be accommodated in a medium-sized town ... where it is not economically possible to run a separate theatre, art gallery and hall for concerts.' Despite Keynes's broadcast appeal to let 'every part of Merry England be merry in its own way', *Plans for an Arts Centre* did not have his elitist approval: 'Who on earth foisted this rubbish on us?' he asked.

At first ACGB supported some amateur-run arts clubs, and a single converted building as an arts centre in Bridgwater, Somerset, but as the Gulbenkian Foundation's report, *Help For The Arts*, warned in 1959: 'The terms arts centres and arts clubs can be misleading because they are used without distinction.' Only 1 per cent of ACGB's budget went on this area, and when W E Williams became secretary-general in 1951 and instituted his own elitist policy of selectively nurturing 'few, but roses', this funding ceased altogether. No one appears to have theorised much about what an arts centre might be, but in 1947 a different model was launched, the Institute of Contemporary Arts, which moved from the basement of London's Academy Cinema into a club-house in Dover Street in 1950. In its original form it was more think-tank than arts centre, until it expanded to its present premises in The Mall in 1968, by which time the combination of theatre, gallery, cinema, seminar room, shop and café under one roof had become the standard model. The Barbican, however, would be of a different scale and order.

In 1947 there was a warning of cultural conflicts to come when the Edinburgh International Festival opened with an upmarket programme. Provoked by the dearth of Scottish culture in the official Festival, eight theatre companies, six of them Scottish, independently organised their own theatre spaces and performances. People began to talk of a 'fringe' of events. That Fringe Theatre was born out of opposition to official culture, with its emphasis on new work and the often improvised nature of the spaces that it used, had a long-term influence on how theatre, indeed all culture, was thought about.

After a brief Labour dawn, in the 1950s Conservative retrenchment — symbolised by tearing down all but the Royal Festival Hall on the Festival of Britain's South Bank site — left ACGB to concentrate on 'few, but roses'. The arts centre movement would have to wait until the return of Labour in 1964 and Jennie Lee's appointment as the first minister for the arts. In 1956, however, the Conservative government set up an enquiry, serviced by ACGB, whose report would appear in 1959 as *Housing the Arts in Great Britain*. The London County Council (LCC), owner of the former Festival site, was quick to promote its plans for a National Theatre (mentioned in Keynes's 1945 talk) and other facilities, including possibly an opera house. ACGB supported the City of London's initiatives, and a notion of what the Barbican might be appeared in the 1959 report when it welcomed 'a carefully planned enclave of buildings connected with the arts as distinct from the haphazard growth of theatres, halls, and galleries on the North Bank'.

Housing The Arts proposed an almost Soviet hierarchy of provision on eight levels, rising from a town of 10,000 people, which would have amateur provision only, to a region of 10 million, with every facility, including a permanent professional opera company. But there was no money. The following year a more radical conception of what an arts centre might be began to develop when the Trades Union Congress passed Resolution 42 at its annual congress, committing it to encouraging the arts. The playwright Arnold Wesker gathered a group of

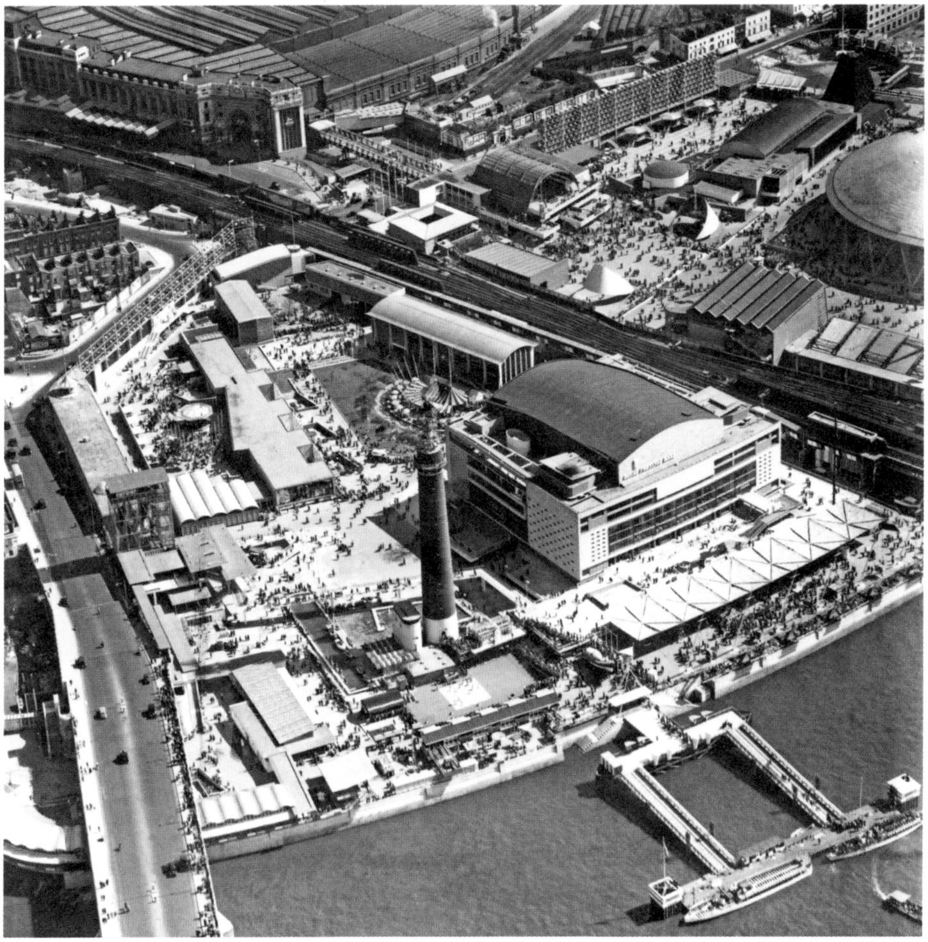

The Festival of Britain site on the South Bank in May 1951, of which only the Royal Festival Hall, designed by Leslie Martin and Peter Moro with the London County Council, was preserved for the future.

leftist, CND-minded supporters, including Jennie Lee (then an opposition MP) with the aim of establishing a 'cultural hub', Centre 42. In 1964 this turned out to be an 1847 former engine-turning shed in Camden, the Roundhouse. Wesker was unable to raise enough money and the partially converted Roundhouse had to be run on semi-commercial lines, supported by the Greater London Council, successor in 1965 to the LCC. Raves and radical theatre continued, to the delight of an audience unlikely to attend classical concerts. Centre 42 wound up in 1970, but the Roundhouse survived, undergoing its own successful transformation under the Roundhouse Trust in 1998.

Another approach to the idea of an arts centre was launched in 1964, the year that a truly imaginative conception was proposed by the theatre director Joan Littlewood, of Stratford East fame, and the experimental architect Cedric Price — the Fun Palace. This would be: 'a university of the streets. It will be a laboratory of pleasure, providing room for many kinds of action. But the essence of the place will be its informality; nothing is obligatory, anything goes.'

The roots of the Fun Palace idea may be found in 18th-century pleasure gardens, but this was the spirit of the 60s, and, like much of that spirit, it evaporated without becoming reality. It was not one that would appeal to the planners of the Barbican. Centre 42, however, did make an appearance when in 1965 Jennie Lee published a White Paper, the UK's first ever *Policy for the Arts*. The suggestion of a Centre 42 in every town echoes the Keynes broadcast of 1945, with a touch of Festival of Britain rhetoric on top: 'It is partly a question of bridging the gap between what have come to be called the "higher" forms of entertainment and the traditional sources … and to challenge the fact that a gap exists.'

In this policy document the arts centre concept ran from 'a single hall' to 'a long stretch of the South Bank', which must have gratified the GLC, but the Arts Council's *Directory of Arts Centres* continued to treat the facilities on the South Bank as 'highly specialised and discrete buildings'. The importance of *A Policy for the Arts* was that it came with a 30 per cent increase in the ACGB's government grant-in-aid, helping to establish a 'Housing the Arts Fund' for the first time. But this was only £250,000 to start with, far too small for a project like the Barbican. By 1970 £1 million had gone to new arts centres, which, with additional local authority funding, meant that £5 million had helped launch 125 arts centres and 26 regional film theatres. But the growth of arts centres was unplanned, usually in converted buildings, and always underfunded. At their zenith in 1986 it was calculated there were 242 arts centres in the UK; by 1996 some closures, and a narrower definition of the term, produced 129.

One centre, by then long gone, but which suggested another strand of thinking, was Jim Haynes's Arts Lab. After running a bookshop and founding the Traverse Theatre in Edinburgh — a key moment in the history of the Fringe — Haynes moved to the ACGB-funded London Traverse at the Cockpit Theatre. In 1967 he set up his decidedly *not*-ACGB-funded Arts Lab in Drury Lane. Focused on the avant-garde, not the Establishment, it descended into chaos and bankruptcy in the autumn of 1969, but its theatre was a launch pad for several fringe companies liberated by the abolition of theatre censorship in 1968. The idea of an arts centre had moved on a long way from Keynes's 'central group of buildings', and so had the nature and demands of the culture that enjoyed them.

In 1965 a less celebrated document than *A Policy for the Arts* proved of equal importance to the planners of the Barbican: a report for ACGB on the state of the London orchestras by the great panjandrum of cultural policy, Lord Goodman, who was about to become chairman of the ACGB. Although the blitzed Queen's Hall (by the BBC in Regent Street) had been replaced by the Royal Festival Hall, almost nothing had been done about providing suitable buildings for music, in London or elsewhere. Without naming them, W E Williams wrote in 1962 that there were 'only four genuine concert-halls' in the country. In most cities there was only 'an antiquated barn of a hall where a boxing-bout was held last night and where an orgy of jazz is billed for tomorrow.' This tells us something of the cultural values prevailing at the time, but the problem in London was not just too few halls, it was — in ACGB's view at least — too many orchestras, including, with the BBC's, five symphony orchestras. Goodman successfully proposed the creation of a joint ACGB-LCC London Orchestral Concerts Board to subsidise and supervise them, and declared that the Royal Festival Hall was insufficient to accommodate all their concert activity. One orchestra would have to find a proper home. This chimed well with the evolving thinking about the Barbican.

As Kenyon describes (p.38), Anthony Besch was asked by the City in 1963 to report. In the light of the City's hope that the Barbican hall and theatre could be 'commercially occupied', he recommended that both be increased in size, which inevitably affected their siting and design. The important question, from the point of view of this chapter, was who would occupy them, and on what terms? The only two viable candidates for the concert hall were the London Symphony Orchestra and the London Philharmonic, and subsidy would be needed. As we shall see, the obvious candidate for the theatre was the newly formed Royal Shakespeare Company, which might be able to cover its costs, but a subsidy should 'be envisaged' for visiting theatre companies if the resident went on tour.

In the context of creating an arts centre, Besch's report does not really conceive of the Barbican's various facilities as a cultural whole, nor do the City's documents at this period, but he was proposing to house companies of national status, a vision on a much grander scale than the mushrooming regional arts centres. Importantly, he was proposing that the City saw itself as a patron, spending between £100,000 and £150,000 a year on the arts. In March 1966 the Rates, Finance and Barbican Committees jointly responded to the Besch and Goodman reports, together with *A Policy for the Arts,* with this vision: 'a true arts centre, wholly in accord with the spirit of the White Paper; an arts centre which will be looked upon as an inspiration and a pattern of things to come by other cities and of which the citizens will have real reason to be proud.'

Aware of a strong body of opinion on the Court of Common Council that objected to wasting City rates on the arts, the report continued: 'We cannot believe that at this stage enlightened public opinion, let alone your Honourable Court, would contemplate mutilating such a fine conception by hacking off one of its two most essential elements.' The advocates of the arts centre must also have had an eye on rival developments on the South Bank. Just as the Barbican project was championed by Eric Wilkins, the South Bank had Isaac Hayward, leader of the LCC from 1947 until it became the GLC in 1965. The idea for a 'great cultural centre' went back to Abercrombie's *County of London Plan* of 1943, which answered the post-war Labour government's need for a main site for the Festival of Britain. A National Theatre was the presumed centrepiece, but its site kept moving around. Periodically, a proposed opera house appeared and disappeared. The Royal Festival Hall was unfinished when it opened in 1951; its acoustics were too 'dry', and the need for a smaller hall propelled developments, while the Arts Council recognised London's need for more exhibition space. In 1965 a revamped Festival Hall opened, and its audiences improved. In 1967 the Queen Elizabeth Hall and the Purcell Room opened, followed in 1968 by the Hayward Gallery. The architecture that emerged was in radical contrast to the Festival Hall, not least for being so 'opaque'. The architectural historian Christoph Grafe asks: 'Why was the building so heavy, so taciturn and, for many viewers, so hostile?' These new facilities shared two features with the future Barbican Arts Centre: brutalist poured concrete and a lack of transparency to viewers. Added to this, at the time the Festival Hall itself felt opaque, in that it was only open to ticket holders before a performance.

There was another serious complication in London's geo-cultural politics. In 1960, to the horror of ACGB and the embryonic National Theatre, Peter Hall had opened the Royal Shakespeare Company's first London season at the

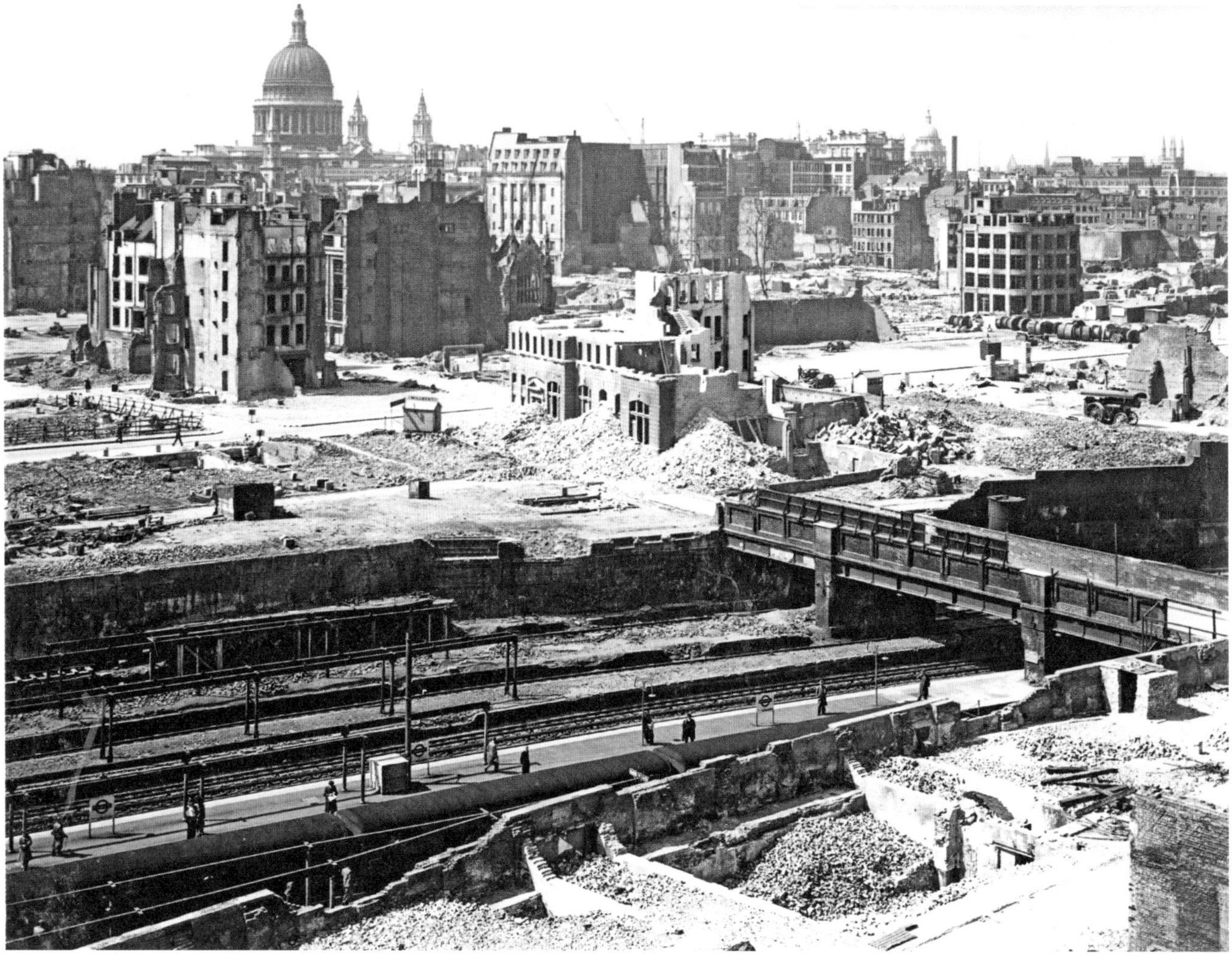

Looking across the future site of the Barbican from the north towards St Paul's Cathedral, 1942. Amongst the rubble the trains still run, and people can be seen on the platform.

Aldwych Theatre, in an apparently pre-emptive strike before the National Theatre company opened at the Old Vic in 1963. Lord Goodman was sent to Stratford to propose a merger between the RSC and the National Theatre. Although nothing ever came of it, the merger continued to be raised from time to time until 1972.

In February 1965 the RSC agreed in principle to become tenants of the theatre at the Barbican, paying a 'reasonable' rent. In 1968 this was set at £65,000 a year, considerably more than for the Aldwych, but regarded by the City as a form of subsidy, especially as a £12,000 remission was offered for the first five years. Hall and the theatre designer John Bury began to advise on the layout of the Barbican Theatre. The London Symphony Orchestra came on board in 1966, but as described elsewhere decided not to run the concert hall, but to be its resident orchestra. When Henry Wrong became administrator of the Barbican Arts Centre in 1970 (see Kenyon, p.43), he had a vision of which Keynes would have been proud: 'The Barbican will be competing with the capital cities of the world to present the highest standards of music, drama, cinema and visual art, as well as to play host to the world's major conferences.' Still a flexible concept, arts centres were now part of the international repertoire of cultural facilities. As Christoph Grafe writes: 'From the late 1950s until the mid-1970s they were the preferred solution for the state-administered provision of culture in Western Europe. By the end of this period ... most small or medium-sized towns in Sweden, Denmark, France, Holland, Flanders and England had obtained a new building housing a variety of cultural institutions, from performance spaces to galleries and libraries.'

The Barbican was different in two ways: the provider was not the state, but a state within a state, the Corporation of the City of London, a Venice of enormous financial power, with a very small residential population. Secondly, the scale of the Barbican put it on a par with the Lincoln Center in New York, opened in 1966 — imposing but uninviting — and the Kennedy Center in Washington, opened in 1971, which Peter Hall thought 'a pompous place, full of pretension, and *very* rich.' Under André Malraux, France had developed *Maisons de la Culture*, new buildings exporting Parisian culture to the regions. France's contribution to the major league was the Centre Pompidou, begun in 1971, that is to say, after the upheavals of 1968, and a building so transparent that it wears its inside on the outside.

Most large arts centres, planned in the 1950s, and long in the building, were made anachronistic by 1968. Peter Hall, having suffered a Calvary of delays and industrial disputes as bad as the Barbican's, finally got the National Theatre partially opened in 1976. He wrote it was achieved in the face of 'the swing against institutions, against large buildings and modern architecture, against nationalised art or industry of any kind, against expensive enterprises at any time.' That was an accurate reading of the times; and at this point in the mid-70s the Barbican Centre was yet to be completed.

In April 1971 the Court of Common Council was asked to approve the actual construction costs of the Barbican Centre. The joint report of the Barbican, Music and Library Committees pleaded: 'The vast amount of time and effort which has been spent on planning the Barbican Arts Centre cannot be undone ... To leave out the arts centre would create a void.' Yet they did not wish to be seen to be going too far in the cause of culture, and cautioned somewhat coyly: '"Arts Centre" is to some extent a misnomer'. Of the 14 elements in Phase V:

> The three elements which are essentially 'arts centre' in nature, as distinct from the activities of a library authority, are the theatre, the small studio-cinema, and the Hall, although the role of the last two as part of a conference centre is as important as their arts centre role.

In a revealing indication of the need to reassure those members of the Court who were sceptical about all spending on the arts, the report pretended that only half of the cost of Phase V, £8.4 million, should be attributed to the centre, while ingenuously suggesting that nonetheless '"Barbican Arts Centre" is a convenient and well-known description.' That compromise, or rather tacit concealment of the real purpose of the spend, was later echoed elsewhere when the City of Birmingham skilfully acquired European funding for its new Symphony Hall by referring to it only as Hall 2 of the Conference Centre.

In November 1972 the foundation stone was laid for the 'Barbican Centre for the Arts and Conferences'. Between 1968 and 1976 the anticipated costs rose from 10 to 20 million pounds. The addition of 'and Conferences' was significant, for as the costs of building and running the centre rose, so did the need to offset the expense. Henry Wrong was strongly committed to conferences, and a 'Trade and Exhibition Centre' was inserted into the undercrofts on the north side of Beech Street. It is revealing that even at this point the arts facilities were still being considered individually; Wrong's report suggests that such thematic planning as there might be would be driven by the need to service major conferences.

The Barbican Committee's next battle with the Corporation was over subsidy. In 1978 Henry Wrong warned:

> Experience elsewhere indicates that it can take up to ten years for a conference centre and arts centre to establish both reputation and audience to ensure the full use of the facilities ... it must be recognised that the centre, during its early years, will require financial support to supplement its earned income.

He was right. He forecast a deficit for five years, from nearly £2.9 million in year one to £1.85 million in year five, with no provision for debt charges. This excluded the library and the art gallery, where exhibitions were expected to make a profit. In November 1979 the City went ahead, anticipating completion some time after January 1982. The Royal opening in fact took place on 3 March 1982, with the theatre opening to the public on 7 May.

In the 1980s, the development of the arts centre concept received a boost from Ken Livingstone's Greater London Council. Responding to what he saw as an elitist and closed-door Royal Festival Hall next to the home of his administration at County Hall, Livingstone encouraged the opening up of the RFH. An 'open foyer' policy transformed its previously exclusive-feeling public spaces into an all-day thoroughfare and a welcoming place for cultural consumption, with a beneficial effect on the box office. The development continued even after the abolition of the GLC in 1986: handed over in 1986 to ACGB, who were already running the Hayward Gallery, the RFH, though still operating a 'garage' system that simply let its halls to visiting orchestras with their own programming, became more of a unit under the direction of a new South Bank Board. The Barbican responded with free foyer events at the weekends, but did not appreciate people bringing their own sandwiches.

As the 1990s opened, the City faced challenges, both as patron of a leading London venue, and as a financial institution. Mrs Thatcher not only closed down the GLC, that same year she also encouraged the 'Big Bang': the deregulation of the City's financial markets, which meant the traditional establishment centred on the Stock Exchange began to lose influence to more aggressive financial interlopers and foreign banks. Many of these moved east to a new, modern financial district, Canary Wharf. As César Pelli's 1 Canada Square began to rise in 1988, the City fathers came to see that one way to challenge this upstart was to re-assert its cultural clout. After all, after government and ACGB, it was now the third largest patron of the arts, prepared in 1990 to write off £20 million from the centre's building debt and commit

£10 million a year for running costs. Still, in the search for a more business-oriented approach to running an arts centre, in 1989 Henry Wrong was replaced as managing director by Detta O'Cathain, who had previously run the Milk Marketing Board.

Throughout this period, the art gallery was run by a separate committee. The centre's budget for its own arts activities was only £1 million, otherwise the art was supplied by the RSC and the LSO, when in residence, or by commercial hires to impresarios such as Victor Hochhauser and Raymond Gubbay, whose popular programming kept the centre busy and in business. To attract two million visitors a year could hardly be called a failure, but two and a half million were needed. The audience was fragmented. O'Cathain estimated that the 'crossover' between audiences that makes an arts centre a centre was between 20 and 25 per cent. She herself said that she did not 'quite understand what these words a "coherent artistic policy" mean.' It would have been difficult to achieve anyway, for neither the RSC nor the LSO were willing to co-operate. As far as Clive Gillinson, the manager of the LSO, was concerned: 'The health of the centre depends on the success of the individual constituents' parts.'

Unfortunately O'Cathain did not command the support of either the resident companies or many of the staff, and by 1994, press coverage of the centre's troubles was extensive. Baroness O'Cathain demanded a statement of confidence from her tenants and the Corporation. When she did not get it, she left. The City's town clerk and chamberlain, Bernard Harty, took over for a time, and the City then appointed John Tusa as managing director, a man of deep personal culture who understood how very large cultural organisations worked as a result of six years as managing director of the BBC World Service.

Having announced that from 1997 they would only play the Barbican for eight months of the year, in 2001 the RSC walked out completely, ready to pay £1.5 million on their broken 25-year lease. Their last performance as residents was on 25 March 2002. The Arts Council allowed them to take the Barbican element of their subsidy with them. John Tusa, who began his directorship of the centre in 1995, was bitter: 'Throughout my 12 years at the Barbican, the Arts Council never raised a finger or offered a single pound towards our buildings or arts programming.' The City, however, transferred their RSC funding to Tusa—and at last the Barbican began to be a coherent arts centre rather than a garage.

When a necessary plan to enhance the venues in the Barbican was refused Arts Council Lottery funding, Tusa and his team undertook a gradual redevelopment directly funded by the City to the tune of £35 million. It was not until 2013 that Arts Council England began to fund the centre's education and outreach work beyond the Barbican walls. Meanwhile the City, now operating through the Barbican Centre Board, continued to provide the underpinning funding in the Barbican's revenue, and gave the centre the widest artistic freedom.

The Barbican Arts Centre has emerged in a very English way: 'Half-baked, if you like', as Keynes described the evolution of state patronage during World War II, but organically. In spite of the time-lag between conception and construction, between construction and completion, there has been an informal development which, over time, has responded to the cultural changes between 1945 and 2022 that first built, then broke down, the Barbican's fortress walls. 'The post-war model has been turned on its head,' argues its director since 2007, Nicholas Kenyon. 'It is now much more participatory.' There may still not be a 'theory' about how to create the perfect arts centre, but today, with its architectural majesty and sense of cultural confidence, the Barbican is a pragmatic answer to what an international arts centre might be, as its individual spaces and art forms have come to be treated as a coherent whole. Just as the arts themselves have sought to become more democratic, offering 'serious and fine entertainment' to as many people as possible, and reaching out through integrated education programmes to all classes and ages, the Barbican has become more than an expression of civic pride: a genuine public space.

The blitzed site around the Barbican area, looking towards the church of St Giles Cripplegate at the top left.

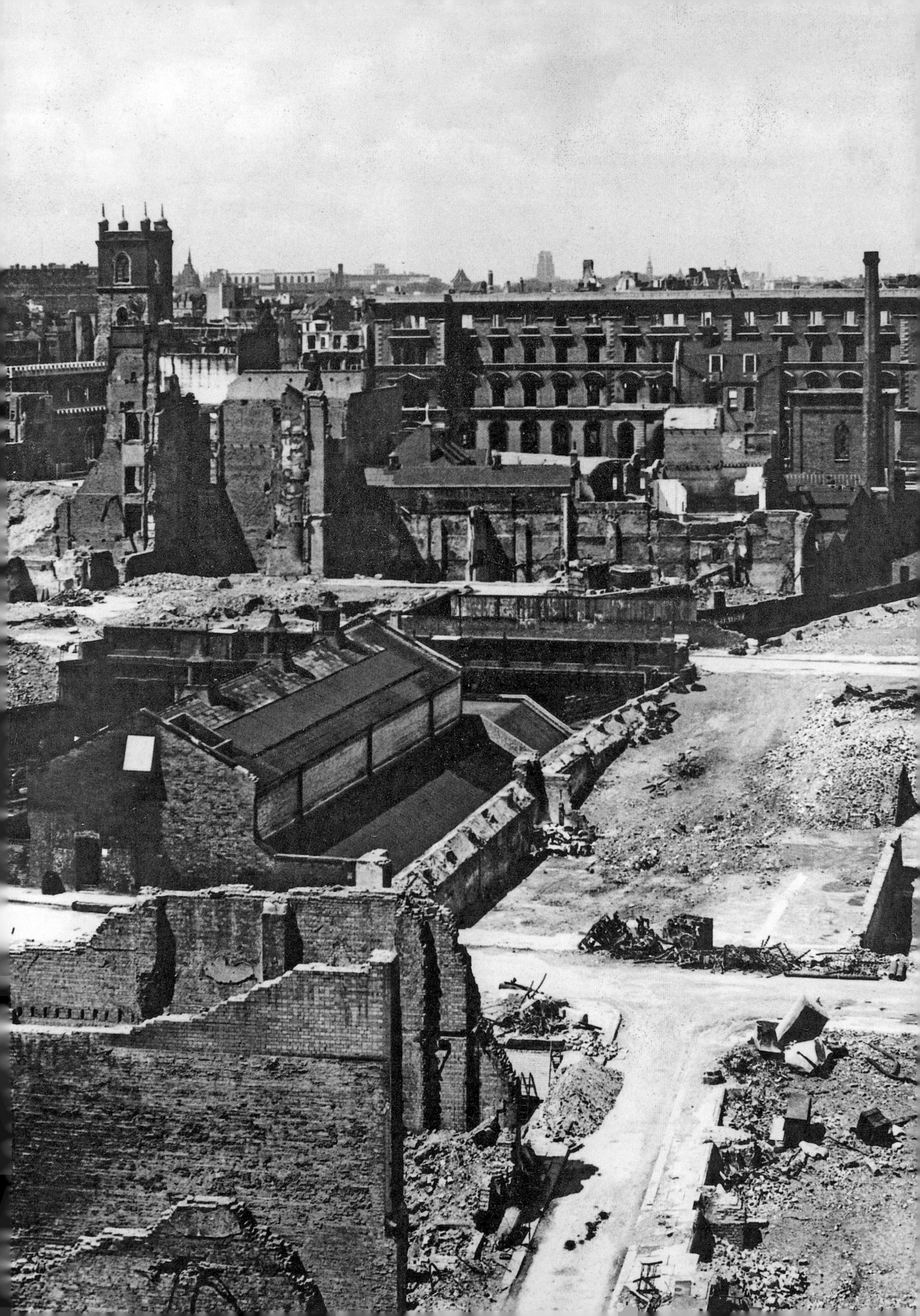

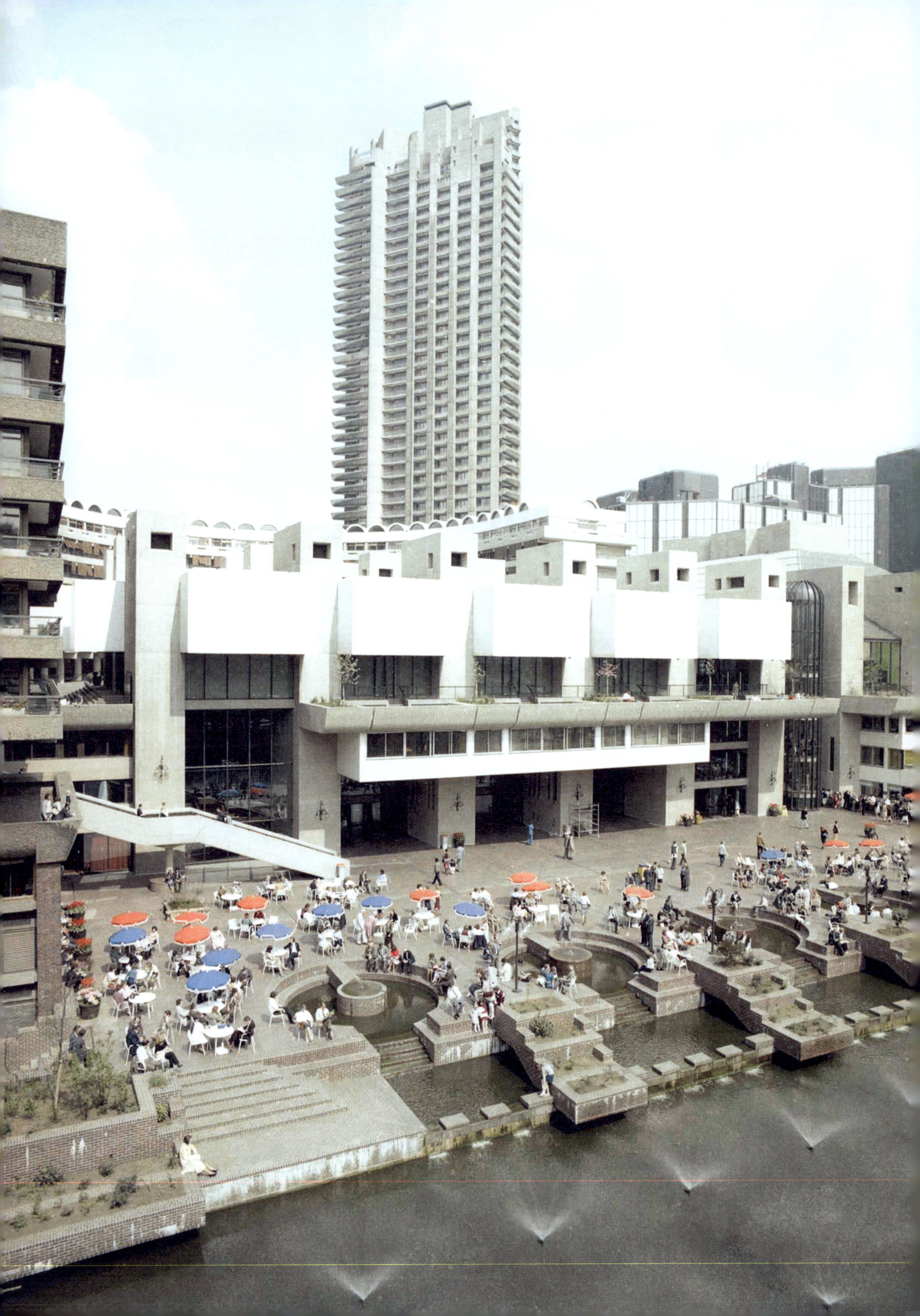

'A fuller way of life': The creation of the Barbican Arts Centre

Nicholas Kenyon

Why was the Barbican built? The answer is both very simple and very complex. On the simplest level, it was created from the devastation of the Blitz in order to ensure that the City Corporation had a future. The vanishing residential population of the Square Mile posed an existential threat to the survival of the Corporation, with its independent governance and long traditions, for there was a serious possibility in the post-war years that, without residents and voters, there might be a move to incorporate the City into the London County Council.

The complexities are more subtle. It would be wrong — though it makes a powerful narrative — to say that the creation of an international arts centre was part of the core concept of the Barbican from the beginning. In fact, the idea of providing world-class cultural amenities took a long time to become embedded in the thinking and planning of the scheme. Many elements came and went during that lengthy process. But eventually the commitment of the City ensured that the Barbican as a unique residential estate housed a magnificent collection of venues for culture and education: a utopian vision of living with the arts at its core.

As early as July 1952, the Public Health Committee of the Corporation was asked by the City's Court of Common Council 'to consider and report on the serious effects of the decrease of the resident population of the City'. The redoubtable figure of Eric Wilkins, then chairman of that Committee, had raised the spectre of the City losing its MP, and was determined to see off any threat to the Corporation. He became the leading, inexhaustible advocate for the Barbican as we know it. There were other interest groups: Sir Gerald Barry became head of an informal 'New Barbican Committee' to campaign for the more commercial development of the area, and the London County Council (which had acquired formal planning powers over the area in the post-war Town and Country Planning Act of 1947) was also active in making proposals. By October 1954 the New Barbican Committee had sponsored a gleaming futuristic plan by architects Sergei Kadleigh, William Whitfield and Patrick Horsbrugh; though this was rejected, it was influential on future plans as a comprehensive scheme for the area.

These were heady days for urban planning and cultural development. As Robert Hewison emphasises (p. 19), the growth of cultural venues and festivals including the creation of arts centres was a widespread phenomenon in this period, as the war-time Council for the Encouragement of Music and the Arts became the Arts Council in 1945. The opportunities offered by the widespread destruction of cities through bombing opened the potential for newly radical approaches to reconstruction, in particular for housing. In London, the City had been among the most severely damaged of all areas. The buildings around and to the north of St Paul's Cathedral, miraculously not including the Cathedral itself, had been comprehensively destroyed, which (as Pevsner noted) 'allowed one to walk for over half a mile without passing a single standing structure'. The question facing the City was whether to rebuild the area on the existing street plan, or to attempt a much more radical reimagining of the area. This was

The new Barbican Centre Lakeside Terrace entrance to the arts centre, with its pristine concrete, outdoor seating and cheerful umbrellas, in 1982.

a debate paralleled in many British cities after the war (and had also been a much earlier debate in the City after the Great Fire of 1666). A concern evident around many new city developments was whether those who were to live there actually wanted to be there, in new tower blocks rather than old terraced streets. But the Cripplegate area of the City had been reduced to a population of just 48 in 1951 (it had been 14,000 a century earlier in 1851), so public consent was less of a factor: it was the vision of the Corporation that would be the determining element here. Pevsner and Bradley write of 'the City's readiness to finance the costly new housing, schools and buildings for the arts, which did not falter in the quarter-century from conception to completion'; that is a somewhat generous interpretation of the long and fraught process that unfolded.

The tensions of the early years of designing the Barbican development were not around the arts. They were rather between the pressures for a major residential development and the provision of commercial office buildings that would earn income. In both the City and the London County Council there were progressive views and traditionalist approaches vying for dominance: already after the war the City's unimaginative planning officer had permitted, as Lionel Esher puts it, 'some fast movers to erect, luckily not on sites of major importance, old-hat buildings of quite incredible ugliness'. The LCC architects' department were committed modernists, especially interested in pedestrian-traffic segregation. City and LCC needed to come together in planning the new 'Route 11': a wide road running along the south of the blitzed site, it was to be a series of boldly angled 18-storey tower blocks of offices linked by walkways connected by bridges over the roadway. This concept could have been extended to the whole Barbican area, and an early model shows a bigger commercial development proposed by Charles Clore on the western, Aldersgate side of the site. Eric Wilkins had other ideas, and wanted to prioritise residential development.

Elain Harwood's piece later in this book gives Chamberlin, Powell and Bon's side of the long dialogue which brought the structure about. From the perspective of the City funders of the scheme, the New Barbican Committee in alliance with the LCC did not agree with the architects' June 1955 plan, and proposed an alternative scheme designed by Leslie Martin (co-architect of the Royal Festival Hall) and Anthony Mealand for warehousing, industrial and residential development, shopping and schools. Wilkins fought hard against this proposal, notably in a fierce address to the Court on 3 November 1955 denouncing the Martin/Mealand scheme as purely a project of the London County Council. 'Since when, my Lord Mayor, have we wanted the London County Council to ascertain our needs or plan for them? ... Barbican must be developed for the well-being of the citizens of London whose interests we are here to represent.' Wilkins's arguments won the day: the Court of Common Council turned the proposed scheme down on the grounds of over-development and excessive commercial provision, and Chamberlin, Powell and Bon responded with their first key proposal document in May 1956: Barbican Redevelopment.

The decisive intervention came from Duncan Sandys, Minister of Housing and Local Government, in a famous letter to the City on 28 August 1956: 'I am convinced that there would be advantages in creating in the City a genuine residential neighbourhood incorporating schools, shops, open spaces and other

Top
1956 sketch by Gordon Cullen showing a pyramid-shaped conservatory and garden layout.

Bottom
An early visualisation from the 1956 report of the potential landscape of the centre, with a lake at its heart. The architectural language changed, but the concept of an oasis in the City remained.

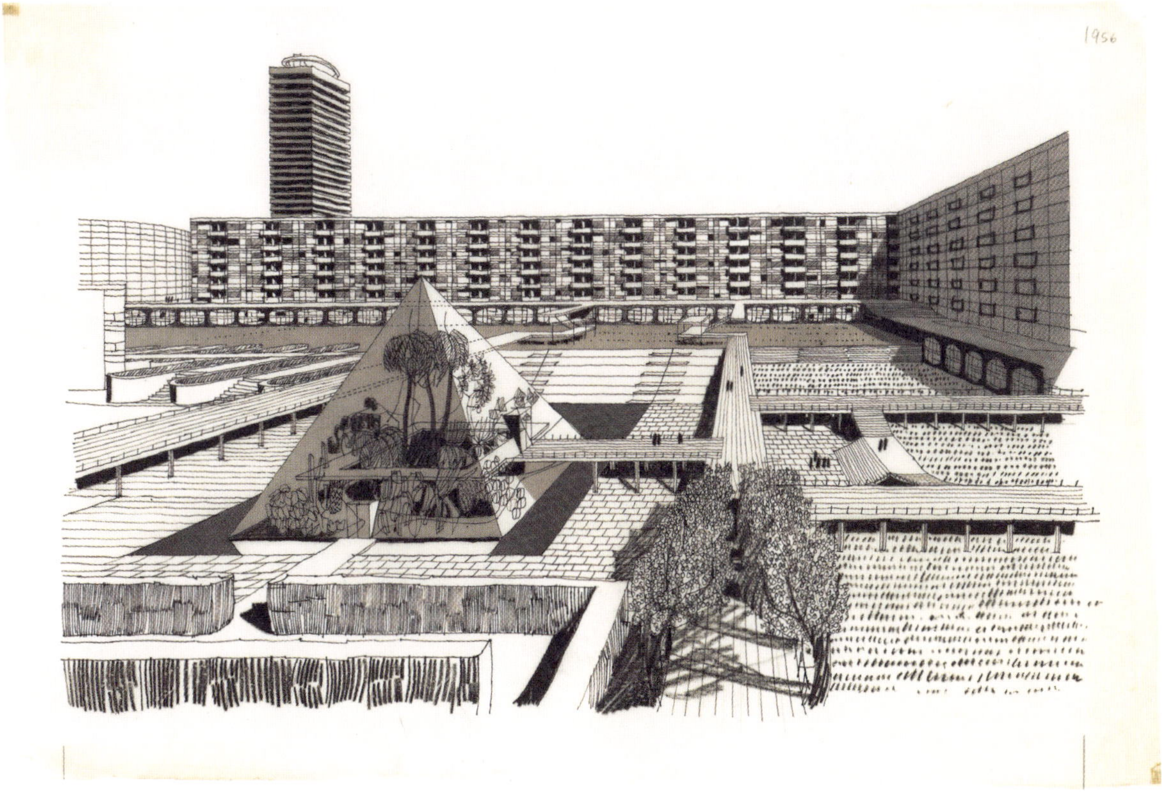
1956

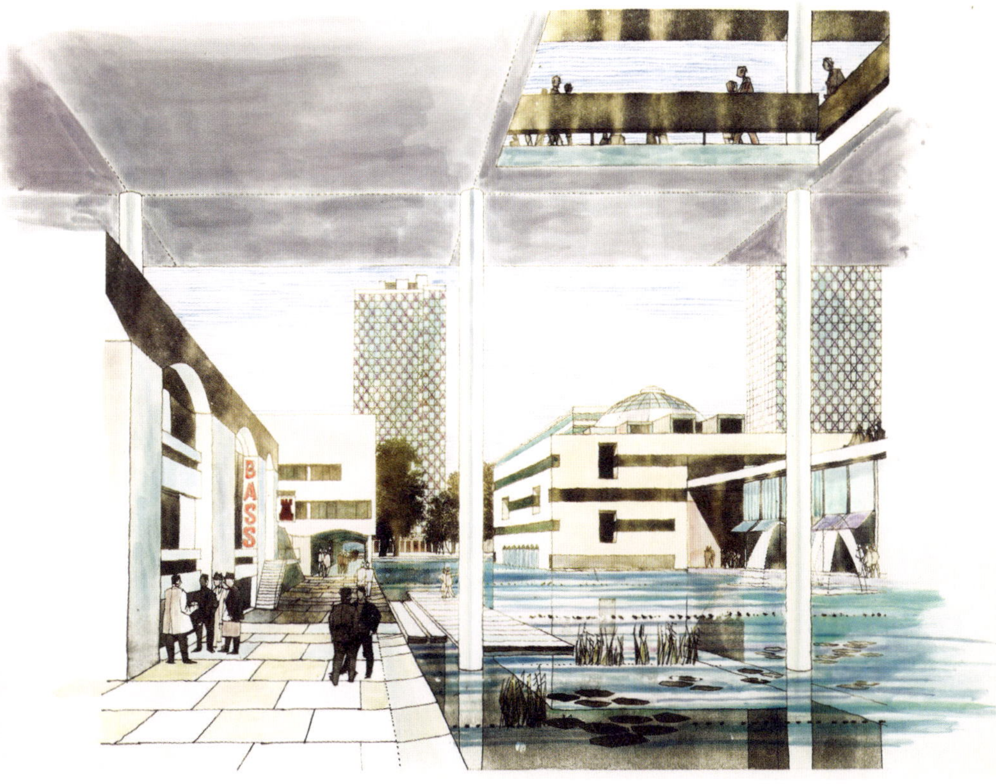
BASS

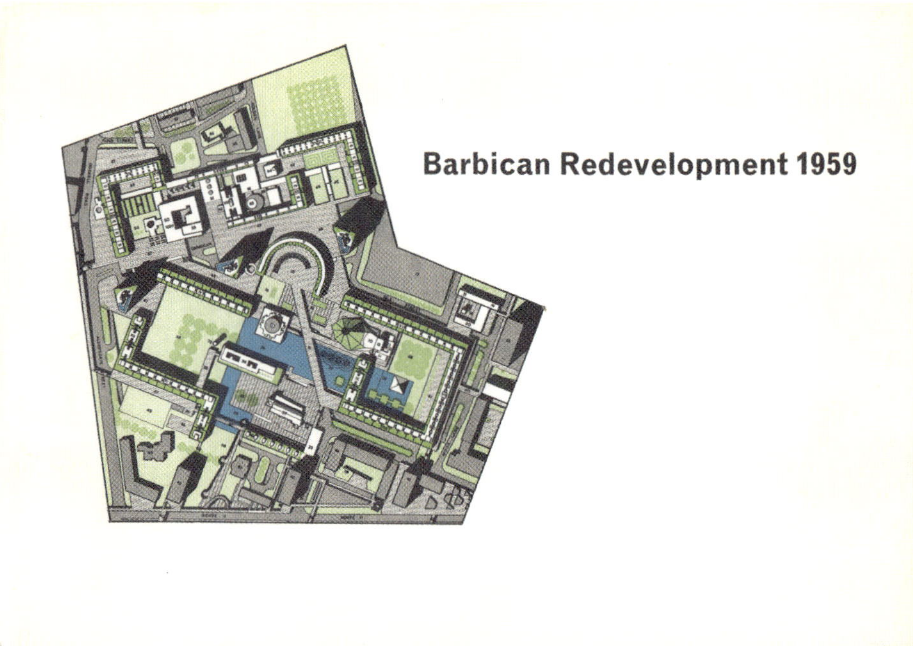

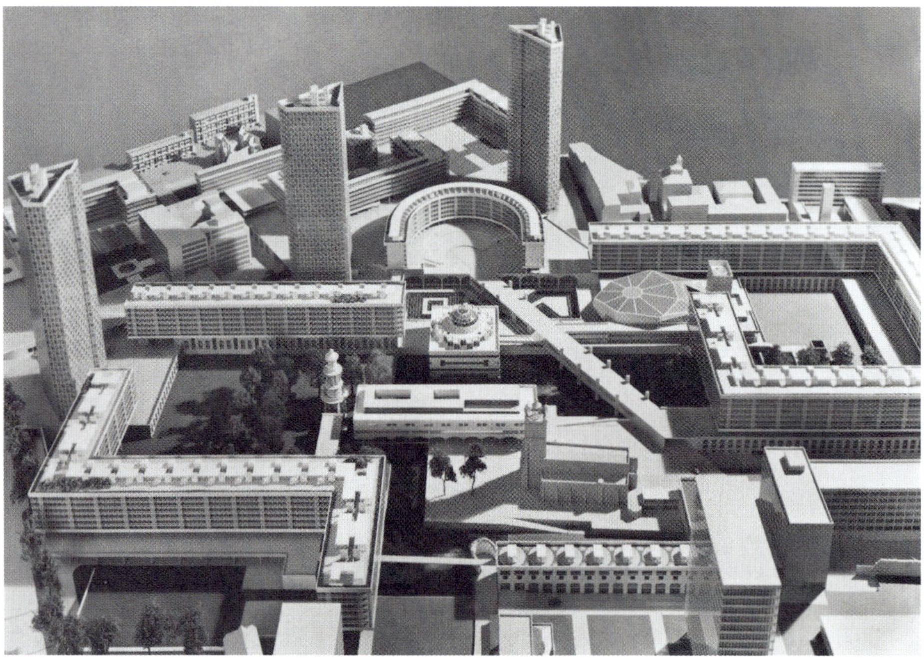

Top
Chamberlin, Powell and Bon's presentation document to the City, *Barbican Redevelopment 1959.*

Bottom
The model of the scheme, including a diagonal road across the site, and the proposed use of the circular Coal Exchange. Both were later taken out of the plans.

amenities, even if this means foregoing a more remunerative return for the land.' On that basis the town clerk of the City issued new guidance on 23 October 1956 with a view to finding a compromise between the City and the London County Council as planning authority: 'until that is done it is as though a dead hand lay over the area: nothing can happen'.

As they evolved, Chamberlin, Powell and Bon's plans looked back to history as well as forward, containing echoes of the landscape gardens of previous centuries and including a running track around a wooden area (almost exactly on the eventual site of the Girls' School); the emphasis was on 'quiet and sense of seclusion which should be characteristic of a residential neighbourhood'; shops were now omitted. This principle of seclusion might prove difficult to align with proposals for the arts, but it is an exaggeration for David Heathcote to write that the principle 'caused an irresolvable conflict with later plans for first a cultural centre and then an arts centre', since the two were eventually seamlessly integrated into a single estate.

In fact, it was exactly at this point that facilities for the arts quickly assumed a more central role in the scheme, and from the provision of some small venues that were essentially to serve the residents and the schools, the ambitions rapidly grew. In September 1957 a report to the Court by a 'Special Committee' led to the creation in October 1957 of the Barbican Committee, which met on 17 October and elected Wilkins as Chairman, and gave new terms of reference to Chamberlin, Powell and Bon. On 21 November CPB accepted the proposal to develop their plans without as yet being appointed architects. Ove Arup were appointed consulting engineers on 24 February 1958. The City of London [Boys] School was now omitted, and instead there was to be a theatre and a concert hall to serve the public as well as the Guildhall School of Music and Drama (GSMD): 'provided it could be arranged without detriment to the schools, both the theatre and the concert hall could be used by professional companies and orchestras'. The die was cast. It was optimistically thought that the cost of building a small concert hall would be £160,000 and a small theatre £175,000. Progress was at this point rapid, with the requirements of the City of London School for Girls and Guildhall School agreed in early 1958. As Elain Harwood explains, a number of foreign visits by the Barbican Committee took place that year to Stockholm, Malmö, Berlin, Zurich, Milan and Venice, where they saw new concert hall and educational facilities, including the large Hötorget district in Stockholm.

If there was a moment when the concept of the Barbican Arts Centre was firmly established, it was in April 1959 when the Barbican Redevelopment 1959 report by the architects was submitted to the Court of Common Council; this covered the whole residential development, and included initial thoughts on the arts venues. As David Heathcote notes, at this time 'the arts centre was a rising star in the Barbican project'. The main theatre and concert hall venues were to be above ground, and a lending library and gallery added to the scheme. Much was still in doubt: the cover of that elegant report shows the diagonal north–south road across the estate on which the City engineer insisted, potentially damaging the arts centre site. (After many arguments, and a visit from the Minister of Housing and Local Government, who said it was 'profoundly wrong', the road

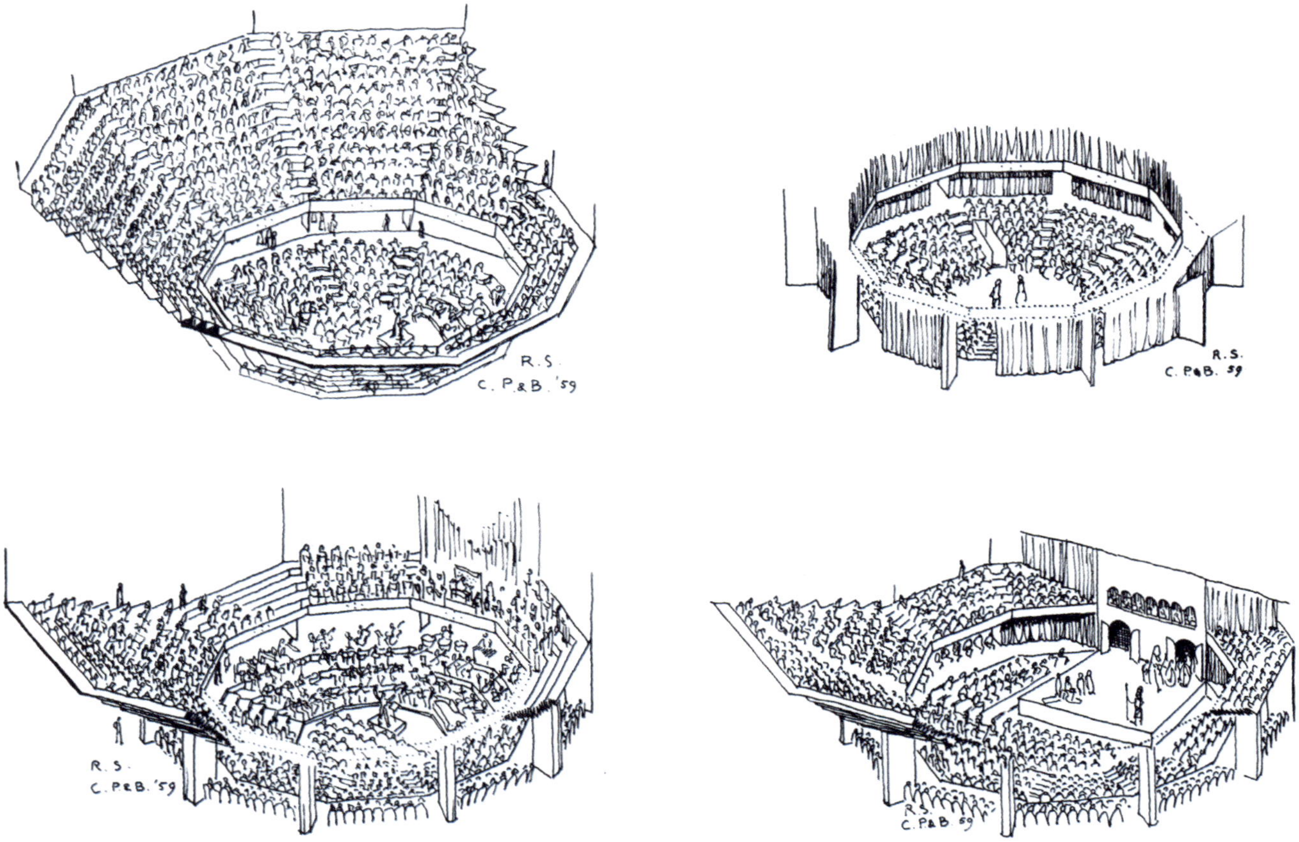

was subsequently excluded from the scheme, and that may have been related to the decision to retain Beech Street as an east–west traffic thoroughfare under the podium.) A small hotel had crept into the scheme, perhaps at the urging of one City member who noted that 'when in 1959 the transatlantic jet airplane passenger services come into operation … the existing hotel accommodation in and around London will be hopelessly inadequate'. There were to be conference facilities for 350–400, and an imaginative but unrealised concept to move the historic Coal Exchange from Lower Thames Street to form part of the GSMD; that building was finally demolished in 1962, despite an active campaign led by John Betjeman. (Temple Bar from Fleet Street, then languishing in a private estate in Hertfordshire, had also been proposed as a historic part of the scheme, but that was eventually restored in 2004 to Paternoster Square next to St Paul's.) A technical expert, Dr Richard Southern, had been retained as a theatre consultant, advising on the equipment needed for the GSMD venues 'if they are to be used for public performances by professional companies'. His concept was for a circular in-the-round concert hall for 1,000–1,100 that could double as a proto-Globe Shakespearian theatre, and a theatre that was also mixed use, with shared foyers. The prospect of potential income from these performing spaces, because of the shortage of such facilities in London,

Above
Richard Southern's sketches for a flexible theatre and concert hall in the round, 1959. Though superseded, these designs clearly influenced the future shape of the concert hall.

Opposite
As the theatre and concert hall were enlarged in size, Chamberlin, Powell and Bon sank them deep into the ground with retaining walls.

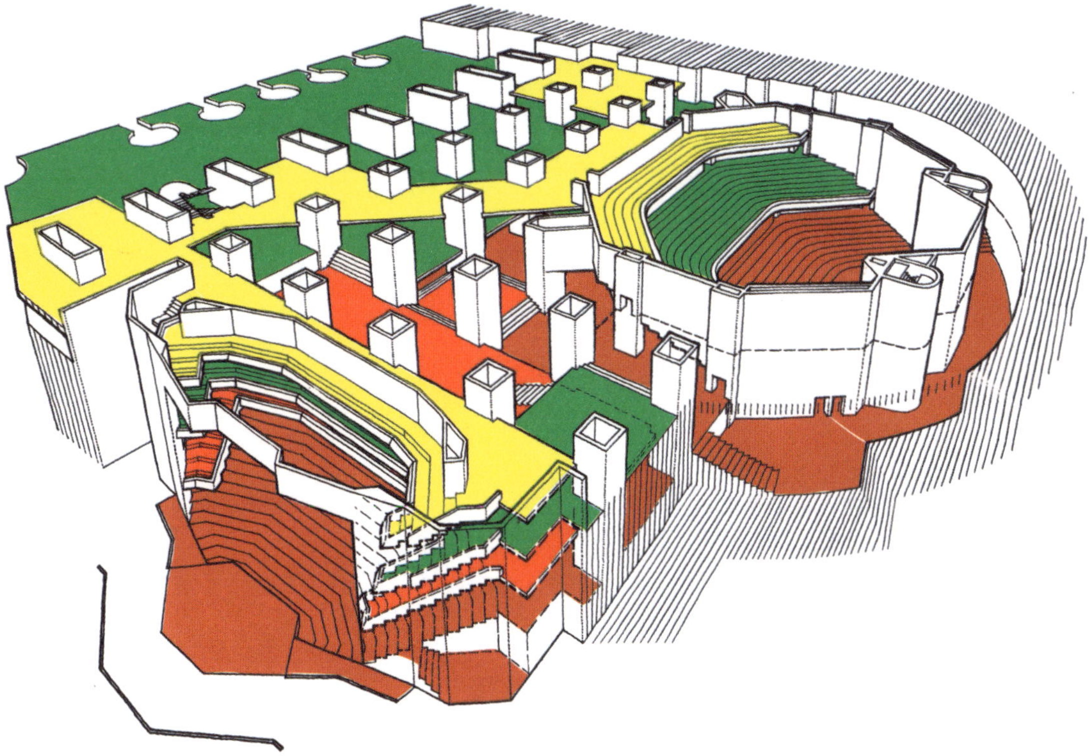

was attractive to the City, but there was still a huge commitment asked of the Corporation.

It was this bold and visionary scheme that was approved by the Court of Common Council on 11 November 1959. An enduring part of Barbican myth is that this approval was by a single vote, but there is no firm evidence for this in the Court minutes. Geoffry Powell later recalled that the vote 'was or was almost a dead heat'. What is clear is that there was then, and continued to be, fierce opposition to the scheme from some Court members. On this occasion an amendment was moved that proposed 'whilst approving the report in broad principle this Court is of the opinion that all buildings, other than Schools and the like, should be erected by private enterprise'. This was defeated, and the report was accepted seemingly without a division. Chamberlin, Powell and Bon were appointed architects in 1960, and the building of the residential estate could begin. The plans for the arts centre, however, were subject to a great deal of further work, and it was not until 1968 that a final proposal was submitted. There was widespread external support: the London Country Council saw the estate scheme as the first triumphant realisation of their modernist principles, with segregated movement supported by high walks for pedestrians, and the Arts Council supported the arts plans in its report on *Housing the Arts in Great Britain*

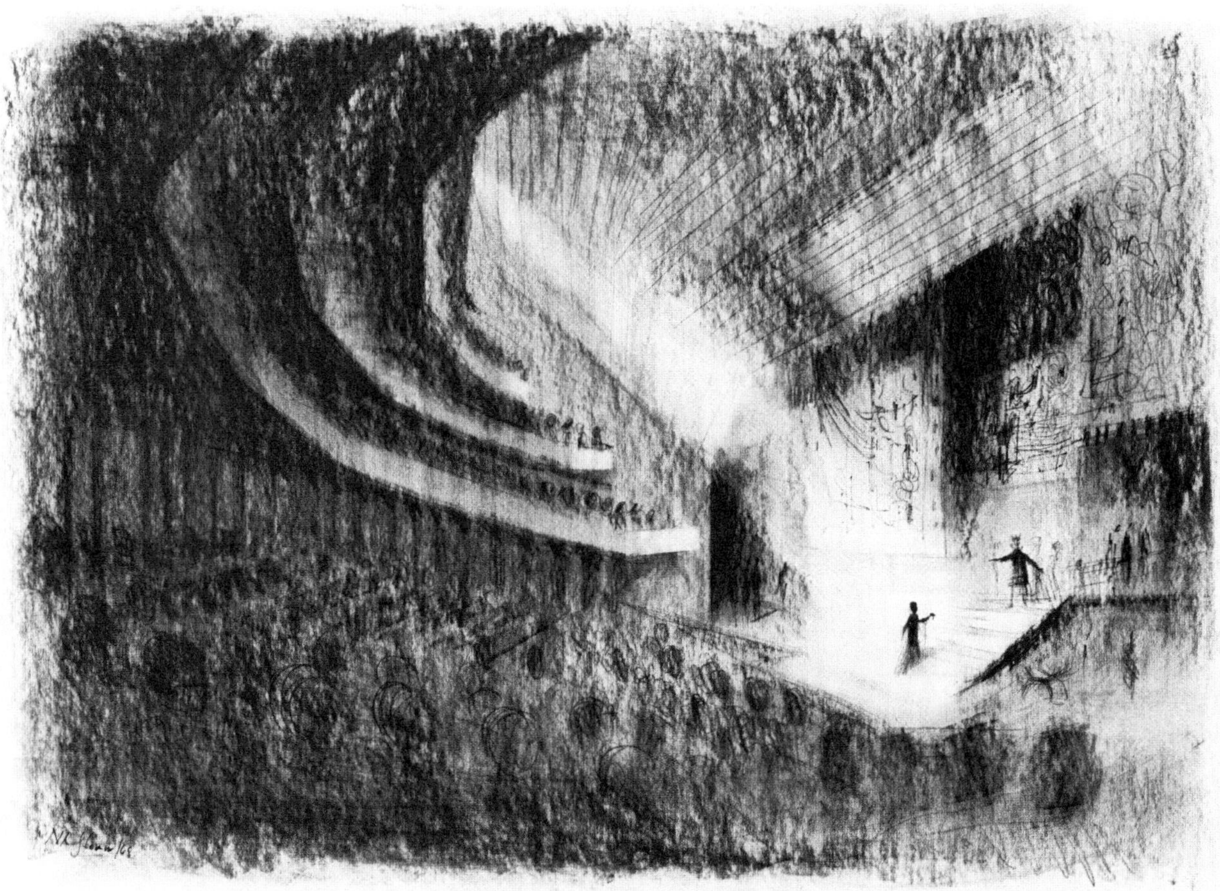

(see Robert Hewison, p.20) as part of the broader development of artistic facilities across the country. The City's commitment to investing in improving cultural provision had a following wind.

But who was going to occupy the spaces of the arts centre and how were they to be designed? CPB produced revised layouts during 1962 and by November 1962 it was accepted that the concert hall and theatre now had to be independent because of 'full-time occupancy by professional companies'. They were not just to be adjuncts to the Guildhall School but public venues in their own right. Because of the disappearance of the Coal Exchange from the plans, the GSMD was now to be a separate building on the east rather than the west of the arts venues, with its own smaller facilities.

What was urgently needed now was expert advice, and in March 1963 the City (in the imposing person of the Earl of Drogheda, Chairman of the City Arts Trust) turned to Anthony Besch, the opera producer and director, to produce a report with recommendations. Besch had already made a major tour of the United States in 1961–2, funded by the Ford Foundation and the English-Speaking Union, and had been able to visit a wide range of opera companies and conservatoires. He therefore proposed visits to Europe and the USA with Chamberlin, and took advice from a wide range of artistic figures.

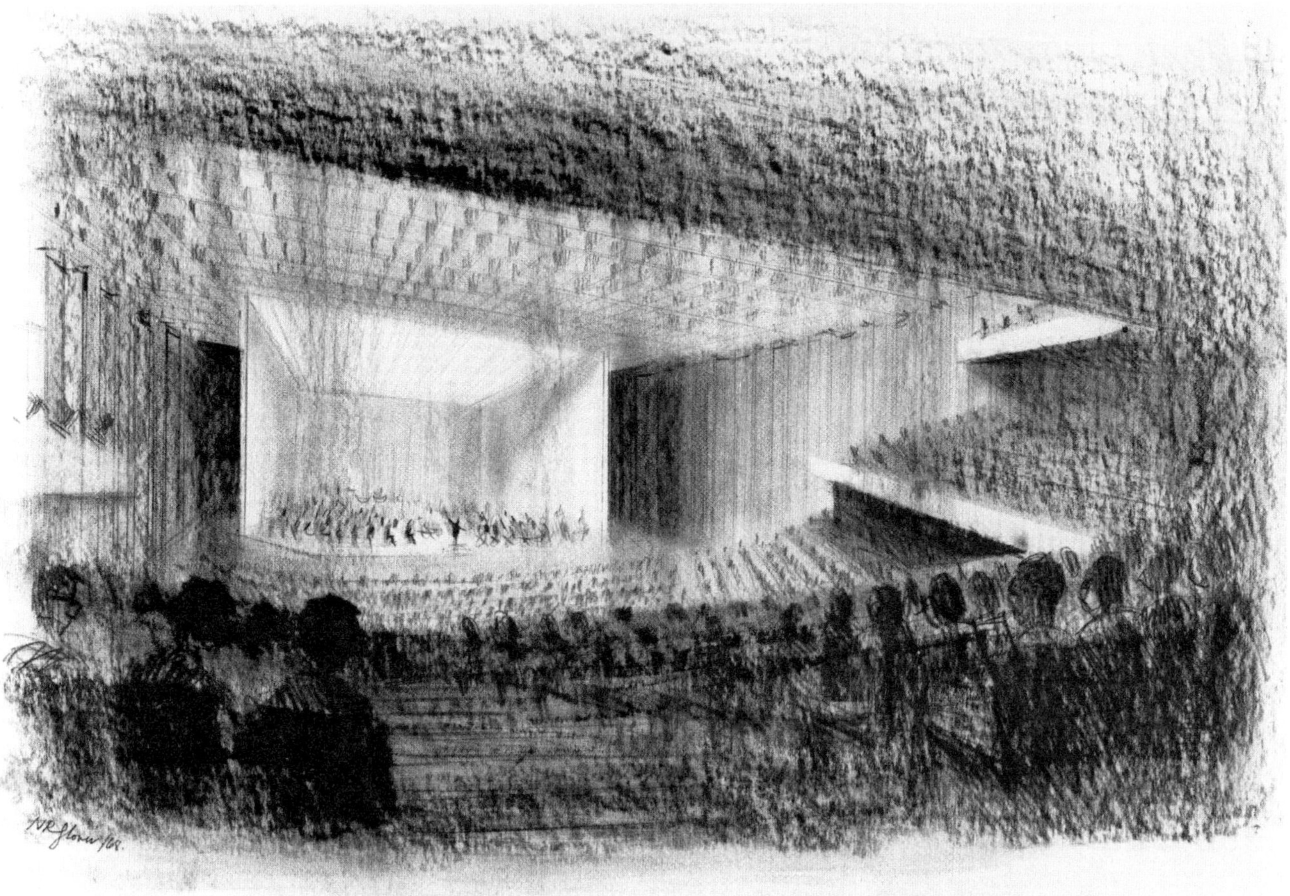

As the designs developed, these atmospheric, impressionistic sketches of the theatre (opposite) and concert hall (above) were created by Norah Glover, and appeared in the report *Barbican Arts Centre 1968*.

His circumspect and detailed report, delivered on 1 May 1964, makes fascinating reading.

Besch argued that the size of both concert hall and theatre should be increased to make them economically more viable. The plan before the City envisaged a hall of 1,300 and a theatre of 800; he estimated their annual running cost as £13,250 a year, whereas an increase to a hall of 2,000 and a theatre of 1,500 would return a modest surplus of £4,750. (Hope, as in so many artistic budgeting matters, sprang eternal.)

His convincing point about the concert hall was that 'the greatest anomaly in London musical life is that not one of its four leading orchestras has ever possessed a home of its own ... our London orchestras are compelled to lead a peripatetic existence, performing and rehearsing wherever they can find room, with the increased costs and general inconvenience and exhaustion which these conditions impose. The plans for the concert hall in the Barbican therefore present the attractive possibility of remedying this severe omission from the musical life of the Metropolis.' He recognised however 'that a considerable annual subsidy is necessary ... in effect, the City would be undertaking the role of patron'. Estimates varied from 'between £80,000–90,000' up to £120,000.

Besch received detailed proposals from the London Philharmonic and the London Symphony Orchestras; the Philharmonia, then under threat of disbandment by its founder Walter Legge, did not respond, and the Royal Philharmonic was regarded as in too precarious a financial state to be considered. For the theatre, the net was cast wider, to include ballet and opera as well as drama. The clear preference here was for the Royal Shakespeare Company, which did not have a permanent London home, and detailed discussions took place with Peter Hall, then its director. The RSC management was in the middle of negotiations around a project in Notting Hill, and could not at that point commit, but Besch said clearly that 'if this Company could be established in the City, the Barbican Theatre would become a centre of national and cosmopolitan importance'. The prospects for an opera season in the theatre were rather less appealing: Besch's whimsical suggestion was that Glyndebourne might 'be invited to mount a season of light or comic opera at the Barbican … a season of four to six weeks of light opera, beautifully presented in the Glyndebourne manner, could well be extremely successful'. This did not gain any traction with the Glyndebourne Board.

Anthony Besch's intervention in the planning of the arts centre was decisive. Clearly it could have led on to his appointment as the first director of the arts centre, should such a post be established, a possibility referred to in his report, but this did not happen. Besch helped to steer the negotiations for the Barbican's resident companies to a successful conclusion without having to deliver on the consequences. The negotiations with the RSC progressed once everyone had agreed they were the company of choice, and the RSC had abandoned their Notting Hill ambitions in exchange for the warm embrace of the City. For the concert hall, the LSO's entrepreneurial spirit won the day: according to Richard Morrison's history of the orchestra, the challenge brought out the best in managing director Ernest Fleischmann and player-chairman Barry Tuckwell who 'after a weekend of brainstorming in a proverbial smoke-filled room … had cooked up a brilliantly optimistic not to say pie-in-the-sky dossier about the orchestra'. The LSO would assume complete artistic and financial control of the hall, and pay the Corporation a rent somehow related to the as yet unfixed construction costs of the hall: an offer very difficult for the City to refuse.

Agreement with the RSC was reached in February 1965 and with the LSO in March 1966. The Court of Common Council signed off on the unanimous proposals from the Music, Barbican, and Rates Finance Committees (the concert hall was now to seat 'not less than 2,000 persons' at an estimated cost of £924,000, plus a possible extra £200,000 for conference facilities). The lending library had also grown significantly in size since being approved in principle in 1964. There was still an idea for a livery or banqueting hall, but catering consultants advised against that. However, the new developments meant that a far larger proportion of the estate was to be devoted to the arts, with the significant consequence that the main venues had to be taken underground: a major factor in their future design.

On 25 April 1968 Chamberlin, Powell and Bon submitted their report *Barbican Arts Centre 1968* to the Court, carefully noting that 'it will be appreciated that, in essence, as individual elements of the arts centre have grown in size, they have inevitably generated a major increase in the amount of space needed to accommodate the movement of a large number of visitors to the arts centre'. Or as Heathcote put it, 'by 1968 the design for the arts centre had grown like a cuckoo'. This fine report makes clear the expanded ambitions of the scheme for the arts centre, and the clarity with which CPB were undertaking the task; they now stated boldly that 'the Barbican Arts Centre forms the point of focus of the whole residential development ... to preserve the unity of the scheme as a whole, the visible structural elements will be built of reinforced concrete with a granite aggregate, the surfaces of which will be tooled or polished', a choice which was to be decisive for the look of the Barbican.

Among the specified elements were catering facilities on three levels, a 'first-class' restaurant seating 80, a medium-priced restaurant for 250, a cafeteria for 300 'and various bars'. Shops were back in, but 'primarily intended to serve the residential population'; these were to be grouped in the public highway around Frobisher Crescent. And consideration was given to car parking facilities and pedestrian routes in from the car parks and the underground stations, with the sadly unfulfilled promise: 'It is hoped that escalator connections between platform and podium levels will be constructed at both Aldersgate [now Barbican] and Moorgate stations.'

Crucially, the two main venues were now to be sunk below ground level (a design made possible only by the earlier decision to re-route the railway line between Moorgate and Barbican in a new insulated tunnel) and the entire building was re-conceived on some nine floors with many complex interactions of the levels: in the 1968 proposal, the main pedestrian podium level is somewhat alarmingly described as Level 68, while the concert hall and theatre area is Level 47. Pragmatism produced strokes of genius: the lack of scenery storage facilities for the theatre led to the creation of a double-height fly tower above the stage, whose bulk was to be concealed by a glass conservatory (possibly echoing a much earlier 1956 CPB idea for a Louvre-like glass planted pyramid at ground level), which became one of the most attractive spaces in the building.

In this proposal there were now, as the architects counted it, 'statistically speaking, about 560 rooms of assorted shapes and sizes planned'. Making a virtue of the time it had taken to arrive at this point, they concluded that 'it underlines the care which has been taken by the City Corporation to plan a centre for the Arts which can confidently be expected to thrive as soon as the buildings are available'. The 1968 plan was not, however, by any means the end of the story.

> *In a quirky 1969 City film about the Barbican development by Derek Stewart (with music by Elisabeth Lutyens, no less), the quizzical narrators perhaps represent the current 'man-in-the-City-street' point of view on the arts centre: 'I don't know. Times change, I admit, people too I suppose. An arts centre in the city — it's going a bit far isn't it? ... All I'm asking is — are we going to see a fair return? A fair return, hmm, that depends on how you look at it, but I think so. The arts centre is simply one part of the whole concept which couldn't truly flourish without the others. Together they'll make not just another place to live, but a fuller way of life'.*

The massive project proceeded, as ever with some scepticism but with an underlying confidence. At its December 1968 meeting the Court received

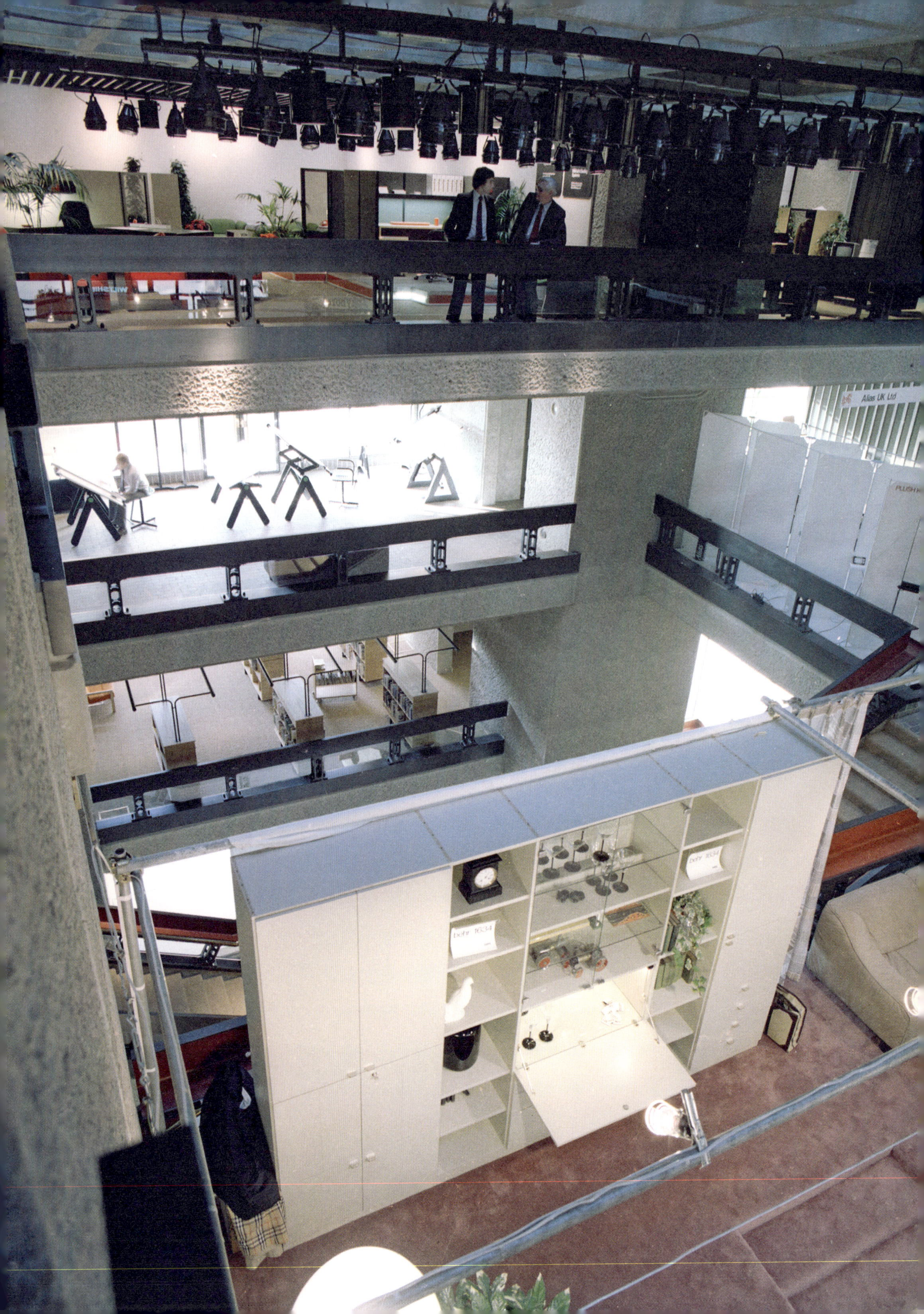
Alias UK Ltd

a joint report from three of its committees supporting the proposals. Once again, the opposition was out in force: a member proposed that the plan 'should not be proceeded with bearing in mind the present financial state of the nation and the need of local authorities to curb expenditure'. On division, that amendment was defeated by 57 votes to 48, quite a close-run vote. The Court endorsed the Chamberlin, Powell and Bon plan and rejected alternatives. Announcements and a public model for display were prepared: the machine was rolling.

One important development occurred in the process: while the RSC took on the running of the theatre as envisaged, the LSO decided that they did not wish to run the concert hall but would rather prefer to be its resident orchestra. This increased the imperative for a manager of the arts centre to be appointed to supervise both its construction and its programming. The post was approved in 1969, but because of continuing uncertainty about the status of the arts centre plans, an appointment was not made until July 1970: Henry Wrong was appointed administrator, initially for only 12 months. An ebullient Canadian who had worked for Rudolf Bing and managed the move of New York's Metropolitan Opera to Lincoln Center, he had been director of programming for the National Arts Centre in Ottawa; in 1967 he was responsible to the Canadian government for Festival Canada, involving 36 companies in 160 venues, and was thus experienced both in the managerial and programming aspects of the project.

The problems of realising the arts centre vision were only just beginning, however. Wrong faced an immediate backlash from members of the Court of Common Council who were beginning to realise the enormity of the financial commitments they were making. Building of the residential estate had already been taking place since 1963, interrupted by major strikes and disputes, written up by the press as 'the Battle of the Barbican'. Against this unpromising background, on 15 April 1971 the Court had to approve the construction cost of the arts centre (Phase 5 of the estate construction), tendered by John Laing Construction Ltd at £14.4 million. It was a daunting figure, and members realised that it was very unlikely to be the end of the story. (In fact, the final cost of the arts centre turned out to be around £150m.) A Capital Programmes Working Party of members was exploring cheaper options: there were alternative proposals at lower cost produced by the antipathetic City architect, doubtless to appease these more sceptical members of the Court, restricted to a hotel and the Guildhall School 'at a final cost not exceeding £9m including the cost of abandoning the present scheme'. This threatened 'either to kill off the centre entirely or to reduce it to such a limited conception that its success would be impossible', in the words of the *Evening Standard* arts editor Michael Owen, whose paper had been skilfully mobilised in support of the full Barbican scheme.

Fortunately, Eric Wilkins, now deputy chairman of the Barbican Committee, was still on hand to argue the case; as he put it: 'My Lord Mayor, I am thankful to have lived for this day.' He had to deal with the fact that the City's Coal, Corn and Rates Finance Committee had not concurred with the contractors' proposition, and 'the adverse vote by the narrow majority of one, of the Policy and Parliamentary Committee', possibly a contribution to the one-vote Barbican myth but one that could be overruled by the Court.

The original configuration of the art gallery, close to the library on lower floors, before the two were later separated for acoustical reasons.

In his address that April day, Wilkins powerfully captured a recurring theme of the City's deliberations on culture. 'I know there are still some who maintain that the City is no place for the Arts. I have many friends — and they are my friends — who have consistently opposed and even denigrated the whole Barbican project. I respect their right to be so critical: it would be a sad day for this Honourable Court if there were no opposition … The City of London is a tale of two Cities. Firstly … that intricate complex of Banking, Finance, Insurance and Exchange whose expertise and integrity produce those invisible exports without which this Country would be bankrupt … But there is another City. This other City has its own and no less important role. Its concern is for the whole of man: his mind and spirit and physical well-being. A living City. The Corporation of London can be proud indeed of its record … Those who see but one City … would have covered the Barbican acres with banks and offices and done so in spite of successive Government's advice to the contrary …'

It was reportedly the longest meeting ever of the Court of Common Council. Henry Wrong took refuge in prayer and avoided the proceedings. At the end of the day the motion to let the construction contract proceed was passed by 78 to 59 votes. The Barbican Arts Centre was on its way. On 20 November 1972 the Queen unveiled the foundation stone of what was by then described as 'the Barbican Centre for the Arts and Conferences', a mark of the evolving commercialism of the scheme. Wrong's time was to be absorbed by complexities and delays — in particular the underground location now added hugely to the cost and timescale of the construction. He did not form a productive relationship with the architects, and each regarded the other as unsympathetic, yet without his drive and persistence the centre could never have been built.

The long process of detailed design expanded further the range and contents of the arts centre. On the northern part of the site, where in the 1959 scheme there had been recreation areas and a swimming pool planned, those elements had been transferred to the second enlarged stage of the Golden Lane Estate. In the voids under the residential blocks on the north of Beech Street, built as storage areas, 'Display and Exhibition Areas' were established for commercial exhibitions, to increase income, and these flourished during the early years of the centre's operation. The roof of the concert hall was designated a Sculpture Court 'for temporary exhibitions of sculptures': this was supposed to be linked directly via doors to the art gallery, but that was impossible for security reasons, and nothing too heavy could be placed there.

The upper floors of Frobisher Crescent were let to the City University and used as offices, until they were much later converted to their original concept as flats. On the floors below in Frobisher Crescent, two smaller cinemas were established in the conference suites: they were later used as (rather inaccessible) public cinemas, until the residential conversion of the upper floors made them unviable, which led to the far better creation of Cinemas 2 and 3 in Beech Street. The enlarged Public Lending Library was defined, 'including a music and records section, fine arts section and children's library', this being (like the art gallery at that time) under the direct management of the City. Rather little thought seemed to have been given to the range of office accommodation needed to manage the whole complex, which was included among the backstage facilities of the concert hall.

An early, rare use of the Sculpture Court to actually display sculpture in 1982; the weight of loading heavy exhibits onto what is the roof of the concert hall prevented regular use, though the space has been used for outdoor events, including concerts, relays and cinema showings.

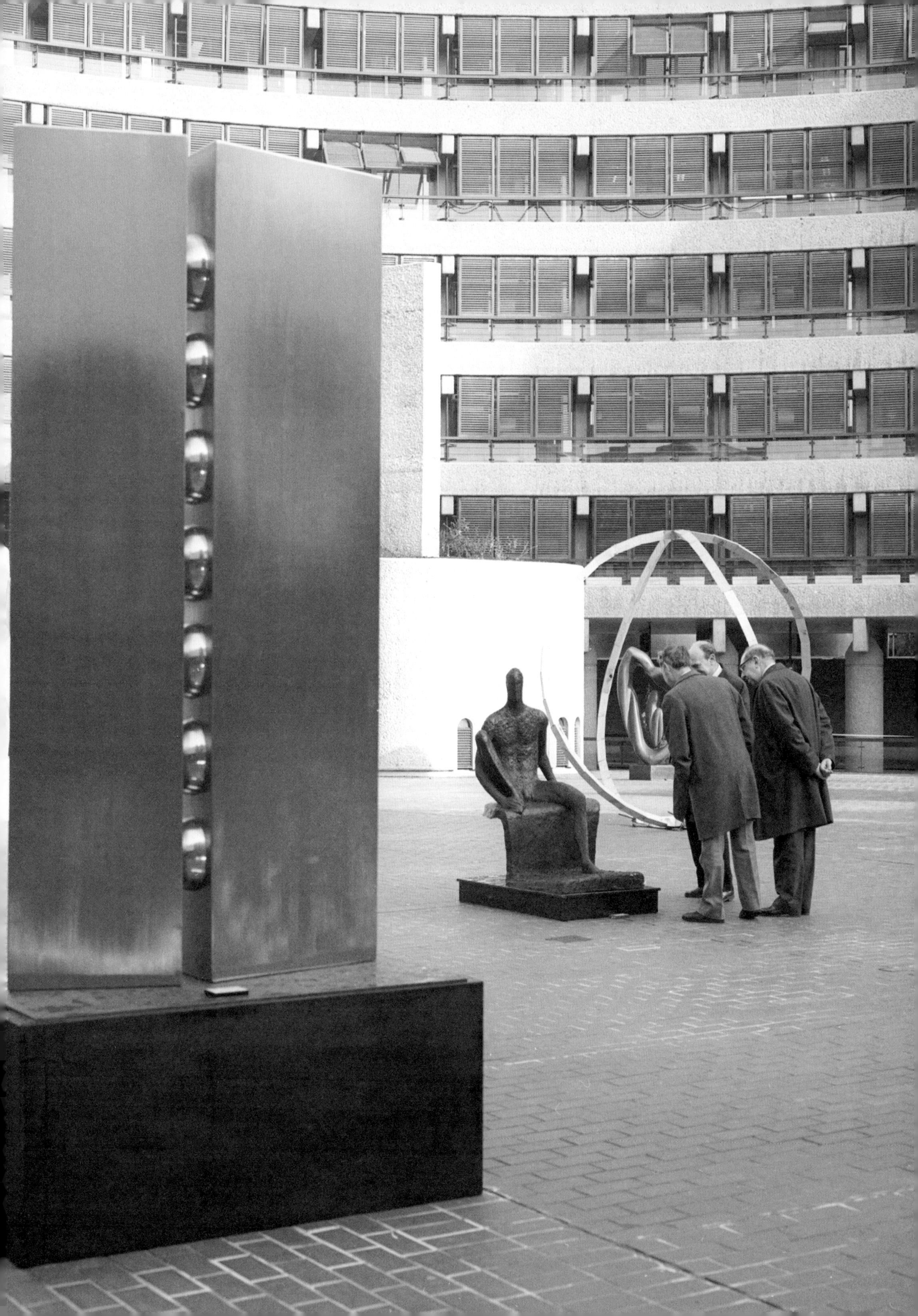

On 10 January 1978 Henry Wrong, having achieved earlier in the decade a status for himself as a chief officer of the City and for the Barbican as a separate department of the Corporation, produced his *Policy for the Future of the Barbican*, based on the premise that 'The Barbican Centre is unique in the United Kingdom in its combination of commercial and artistic facilities, all of which were conceived and are being built to the highest international standards.' That was a salient fact often ignored in assessments of the centre when it opened: the standards to which the building was built were extraordinarily high; the level of specially designed detail was impeccable – quite apart from the arts centre itself, if other tower blocks had been built to the exacting standards of the Barbican's three tall towers, there would have been far fewer causes of discontent in that area of urban planning.

Wrong's new emphasis on the commercial aspects of the activity doubtless reflected much budgetary work over the years to minimise the expected financial subsidy required from the Corporation, and the extent to which the centre, given the massive and escalating cost of construction, could expect to wash its own financial face through income generation activities once opened. As ever, this was certainly optimistic: Wrong suggested anticipated income for a first year's full operation, at 1977 prices, to be £4,989,000, while expenditure would be £2,850,800, a projected outcome which would have given great reassurance to the City but might just have fallen short of reality. However, Wrong realistically noted that the centre would be unlikely to produce a surplus on its operating account in the 'early years'.

While the relationship with the RSC was being deepened and strengthened, and the input of the RSC into the design of the theatre was extremely productive, the relationship with the LSO seemed to be stalled, doubtless partly because the orchestra realised that its original financial projections were now totally unrealistic. The LSO's long-time manager Clive Gillinson said that when he joined the orchestra as a player in 1970 'people were always talking about how we were going to move to the Barbican. But it was like a mirage … no one believed it was actually going to happen.' Wrong referred to 'indications that one other major London orchestra may be interested in a close relationship with the centre', and suggested a mixture of musical events in various genres that was rather distant from what was originally intended. Eventually via conversations between the Arts Council and the City, the plan reverted to the LSO as the sole resident orchestra, complemented by other more commercial concert programming (see Music, p.109).

If the centre had been designed more quickly and built promptly, without the many delays and strikes that overcame its progress, might its public reception have been different? By the time the arts centre was finally opened by the Queen on 3 March 1982, the public mood had turned against brutalism as an architectural style. So too had critical thinking. The architect Stephen Gardiner, a Le Corbusier disciple, was positive in *The Observer*. But in October 1981, prior to the opening of the theatre, Lance Knobel in *The Architectural Review* opined severely that the concept of an arts centre was one whose time had passed: 'The Barbican was planned to bring life to the City … Yet the notion of an arts centre, particularly one of this size in the middle of London, now seems

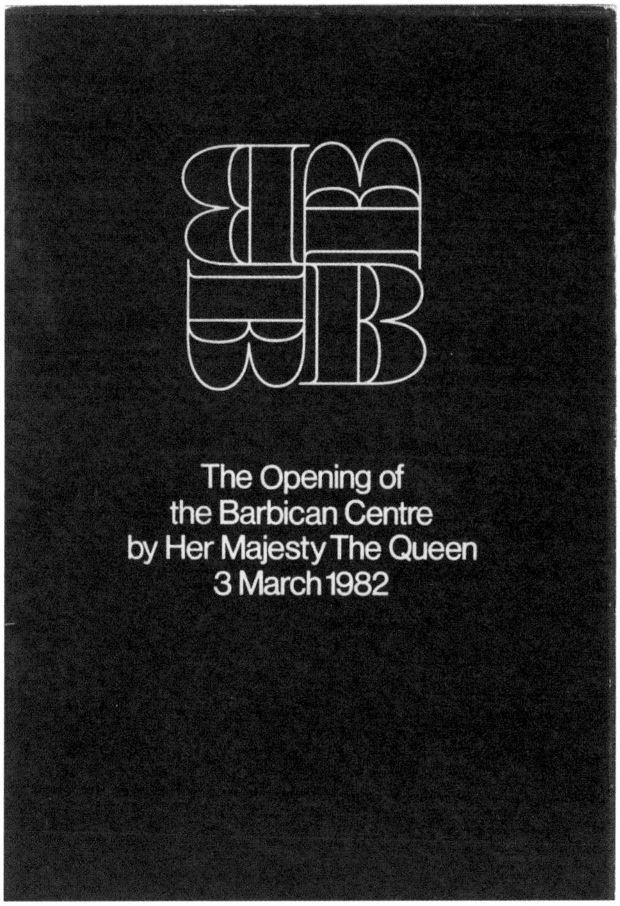

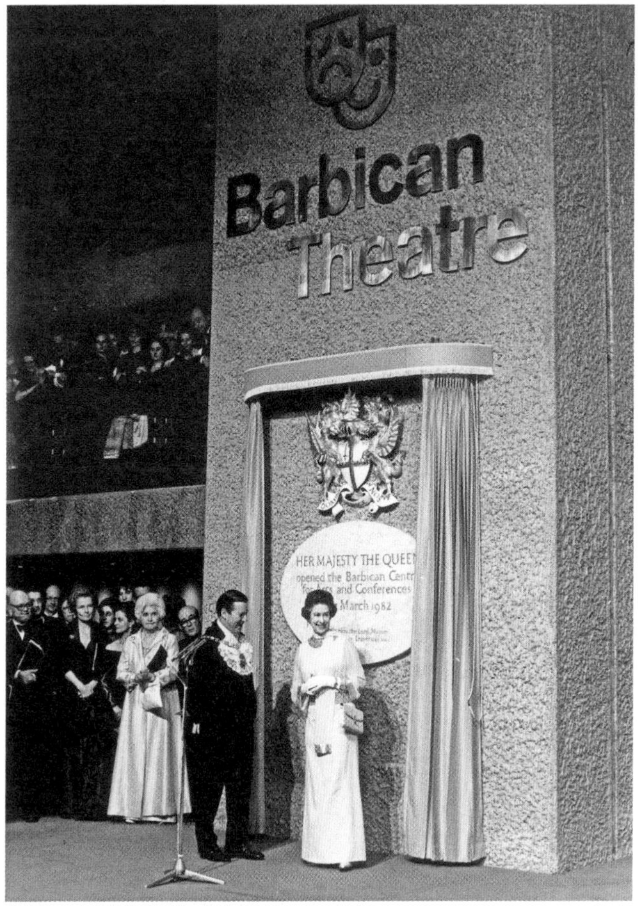

The opening of the Barbican Centre on 3 March 1982: the programme of the event featuring the LSO in the hall and the RSC in the theatre (left); the Queen unveiling the plaque in the foyer, accompanied by The Rt Hon the Lord Mayor Sir Christopher Leaver (right).

ill-judged. In the 80s, confronted by this 50s dream, one is made painfully conscious of the enormous changes that have occurred in planning thought, and more important, public awareness ... The Barbican would never be built today.'

That now reads like a very old-fashioned view of what an arts centre can be, and in the succeeding years the vision of the founding fathers has become ever more widely accepted. And now, as we look across 40 years to the way in which the Barbican has continually reinvented itself to prove the vital civic role and artistic international melting pot enabled by the concept of the multi-arts centre, selling over a million tickets a year and offering a diverse artistic programme in the heart of London, it is clear that neither the belief of the City nor the conviction of Chamberlin, Powell and Bon were misplaced.

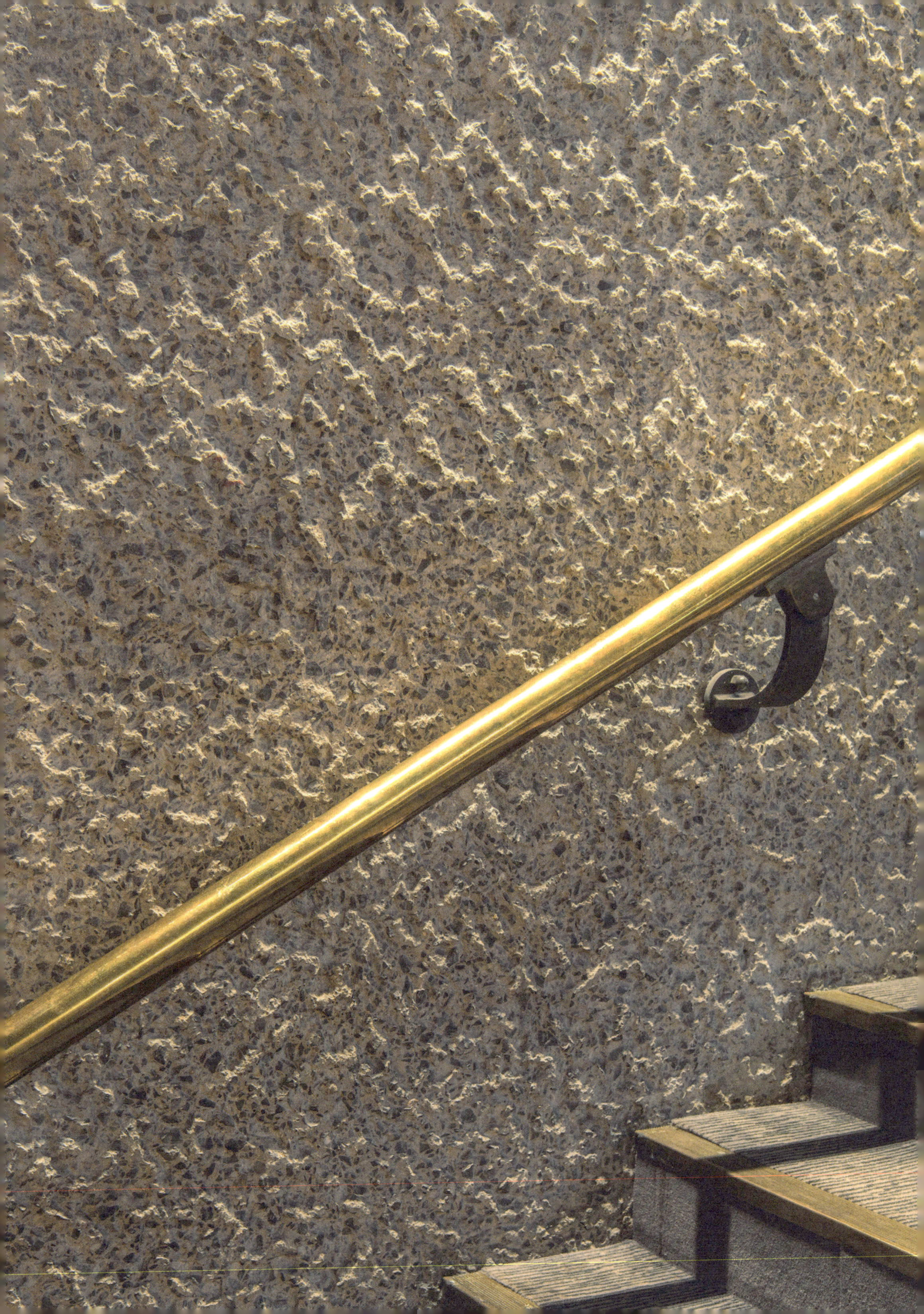

'A haven of cultural perfection': Chamberlin, Powell and Bon's design

Elain Harwood

Images of the Barbican are dominated by its flats, their dark, rocky aggregate uplifted by those soaring, aerodynamic ranks of balconies. By comparison the arts centre almost literally buried below is understated, the delights of its main spaces rarely commented on and appearing in remarkably few books on building for the arts. Commentators write about the huge hole that had to be dug, into which it descends well below sea level, or the strikes and rampant inflation that beset the building of the estate. (The estimated cost of filling in the hole if construction had been discontinued was so high that it was decided to continue building, it was claimed when the centre finally opened in March 1982.) Yet to venture into the foyers is an opportunity to admire the concrete up close, or to appreciate how every fixing, fire extinguisher station, speaker and vent had to be identified at the design stage of this uniquely complex three-dimensional design and cast in. The City Corporation's wealth and stability, compared to local authorities fraught by political changes, ensured that the project was realised, even though it took almost 30 years. Such a long time, with half of it devoted to the planning and building of the arts centre, ensured a far more ambitious complex than was initially intended, if also a building that seemed out of time on its completion.

The architects Chamberlin, Powell and Bon are not household names. Three men from very different backgrounds, they met in 1949 when teaching at the Kingston School of Architecture. Peter Chamberlin (1919–78, always known as Joe after the late-Victorian politician) had studied there in 1941–8 while working for the fire and ambulance services as a conscientious objector. His student drawings show a steady development of his craft, though not yet the outstanding ability to think through and expand a project that made CPB's work special. They include a school of art from 1942 and a theatre club from 1946, functional designs owing something to Walter Gropius's designs for Impington Village College, Cambridgeshire, built in 1936–9. Chamberlin stayed at Kingston to work with the course's founder, Eric Brown. Graeme Smart, a later assistant, described him as 'a giant of a man. He was very big physically and he had an amazing ability to persuade people to do things', a very necessary skill in such a large undertaking as Barbican. He gave his favourite occupations in 1953 as 'arguing with friends and travelling', but he also had a passion for the arts, particularly the theatre and cinema. Powell recalled that 'if he liked a film he did not mind seeing it again. He saw *Singin' in the Rain* over 30 times.'

Geoffry Powell (1920–99) had intended to enter the armed forces before contracting tuberculosis in his mid-teens. A talent for drawing led him instead to the Architectural Association in 1939, studying under Frederick Gibberd, whom he assisted on housing projects following his graduation. He then worked for Brian O'Rorke, who in 1947 was appointed to design the National Theatre on London's South Bank and made a study tour of Sweden. Powell never discussed his involvement in these early designs, and in 1949 lack of work led him to teaching.

Christof Bon (1921–99, who adopted the spelling Christoph later in life) was born at St Gallen, Switzerland, where his father and uncle were successful restaurateurs. He, too, was an outstanding cook but saw more opportunities in

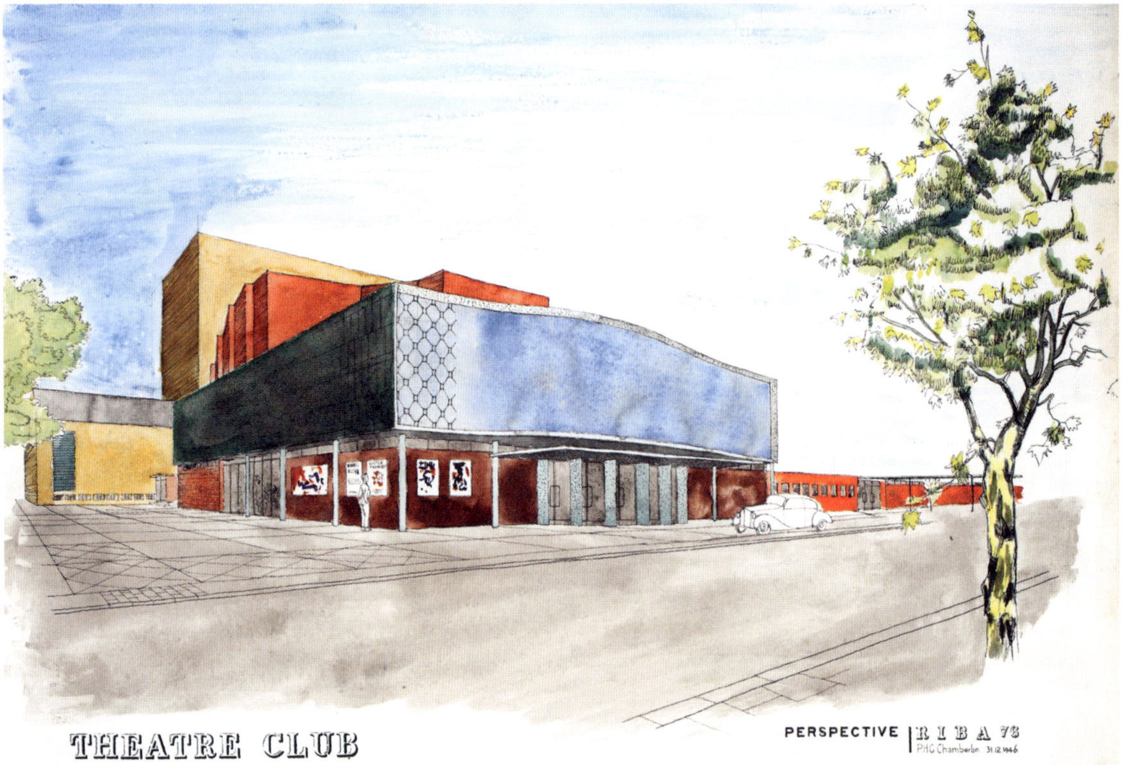

architecture, studying at the Swiss Federal Institute of Technology in Zurich. He first came to England in 1946, when he worked for three months on the City of London Plan under William Holford. He then ventured to Milan for two years until another Swiss architect, Alfred Roth, introduced him to Eric Brown, who invited him to Kingston.

A shared love of the arts drew these contrasting characters together. They also shared an urge to move on from Kingston, and a competition held by the Corporation of the City of London for public housing at Golden Lane offered an opportunity. At Powell's suggestion, each submitted an entry — thus increasing their chances — with the understanding that they would form a partnership should one be successful. Appropriately, it was Powell who was declared the winner in February 1952 with a scheme of ten, six and four-storey flats arranged around sunken courtyards. It had a high density and urban quality unmatched at a time when building in Britain was dominated by the new towns.

As the new partnership declared, 'we attempted to make Golden Lane truly urban as, for instance, Florence or Oxford City are truly urban. ... We strongly dislike the Garden City tradition with its low density, monotony and waste of good country, road, kerbs, borders, paths in endless strips everywhere.' The same philosophy informed their subsequent work next door at Barbican, as did a desire to include community buildings rather than simply erect housing. At Golden Lane they added a public house and shops in the last phase of the estate, and Powell designed a sports and recreation centre there, including a swimming pool, when in the late 1950s it was decided not to include one at Barbican.

Above
Perspective by Peter 'Joe' Chamberlin of a student design for a Theatre Club, 1947.

Opposite
Design sketch of the Golden Lane Estate, 1952. Geoffry Powell's successful competition entry led to the formation of the Chamberlin, Powell and Bon partnership.

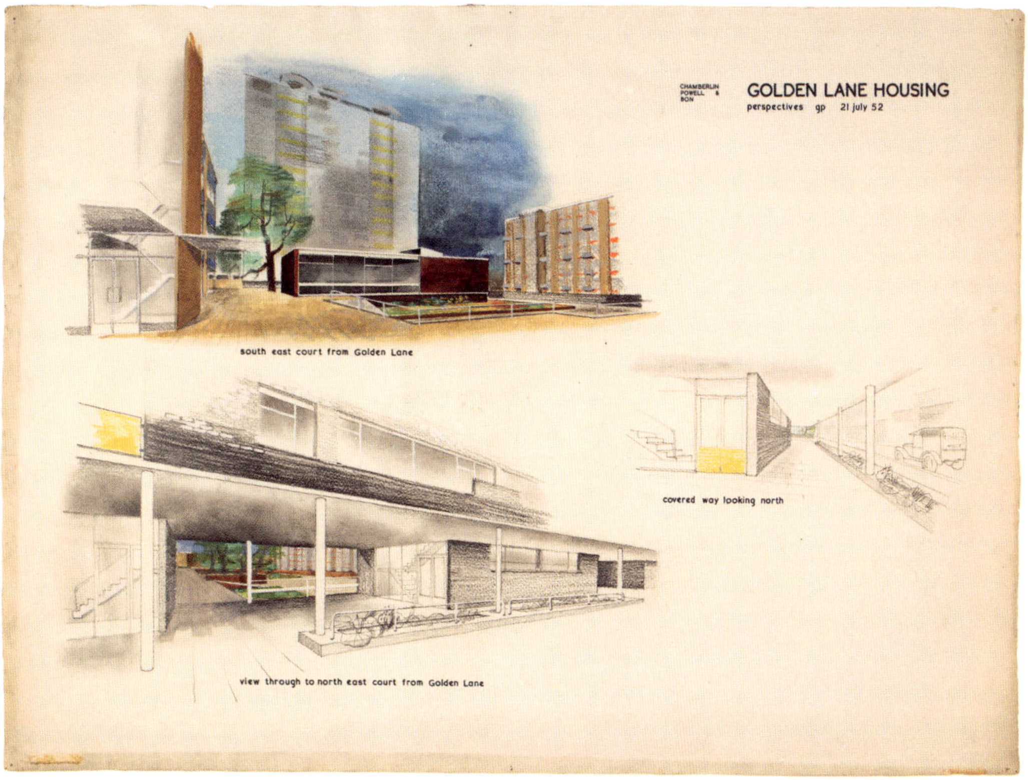

Nicholas Kenyon describes (p.32) how Eric Wilkins, the City councillor behind Golden Lane, promoted a residential scheme for the major part of the Barbican site, with Chamberlin working feverishly in the background. Their proposals displaced Holford's plan for offices and a subsequent, more detailed scheme by the London County Council under Leslie Martin and the City planning officer, Anthony Mealand. As Powell acknowledged in 1983, 'Essentially the Martin/Mealand plan was to cover the site with offices by individual developers, with the optional alternative of a few flats round the church. Without Joe's drive and enthusiasm both before we received any formal commission and after, I am sure it would have been like this and there would have been little for the Corporation to take pride in. No one deserves commemoration more than he.'

CPB's first proposals for Barbican in June 1955 proposed moving the Guildhall School of Music and Drama 'to its own advantage as well as to the benefit of the residential estate'. The Guildhall School's buildings included a theatre, used not only by the students but by amateur music societies and drama clubs from across the City. CPB proposed a small theatre, concert hall and gallery for temporary exhibitions gathered round the remains of St Giles Cripplegate, identified as a potential concert space but eventually restored as one of the City's working churches by Godfrey Allen in 1960. Additionally, CPB's scheme included facilities for conferences and physical recreation, mainly set in a strange, stepped pyramid. This was an exceptionally high-density scheme based around four-storey courtyards (like Golden Lane) with a line of tower

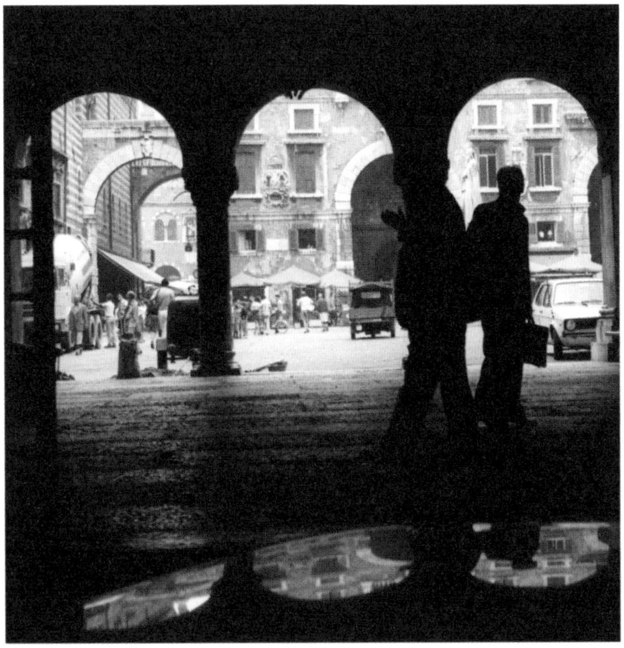

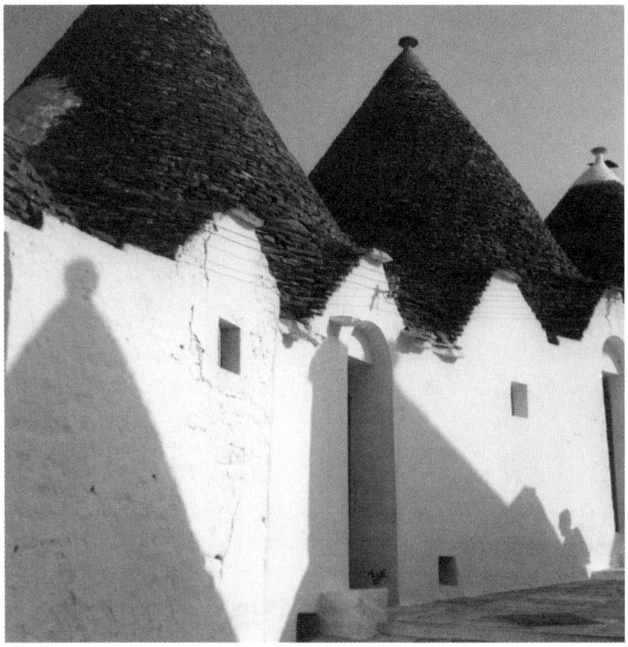

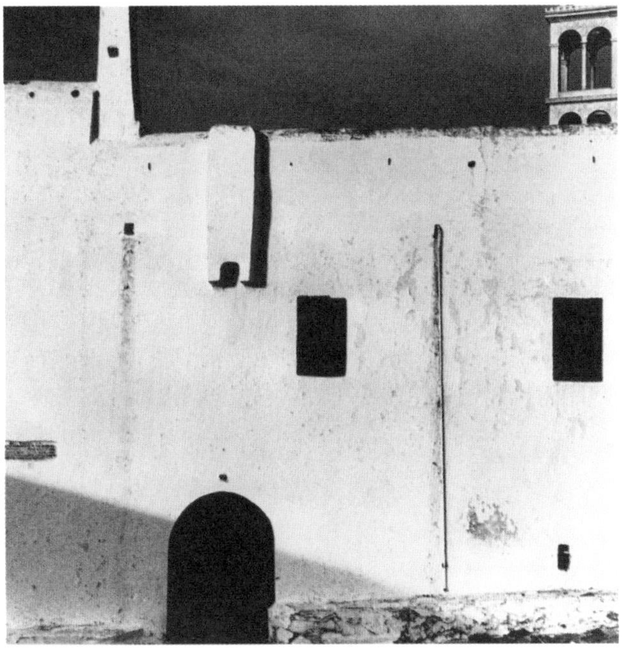

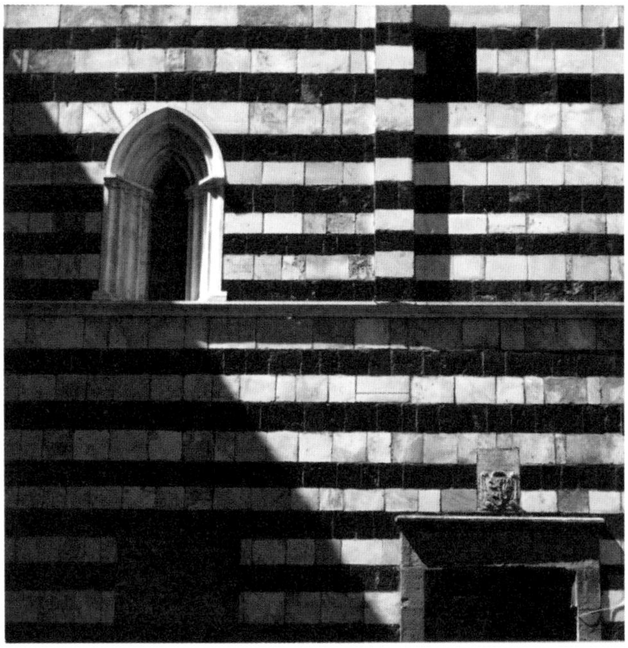

Chamberlin, Powell and Bon's annual Christmas cards from the 1950s and 1960s, showing their continental architectural inspirations.

blocks across the northern part of the site to answer the office towers along London Wall, the only part of the Martin/Mealand Plan to be realised. As a deeper reflection on London's history, CPB also sought to restore Christopher Wren's gateway of Temple Bar, which had been banished to Hertfordshire in 1878. The Corporation was unmoved: Temple Bar returned to the City only in 2004, while CPB secured only a handful of gas lights from Tower Bridge, set around St Giles Cripplegate.

The principle of a residential scheme was established, however, and in 1956 CPB proposed also moving the City's two secondary schools so that they could share modern facilities. The City of London School (for boys) deemed its premises near Blackfriars Bridge to be adequate and stayed put until the 1980s, but the City of London School for Girls shared an island site with the Guildhall School and had less room for manoeuvre; when the Corporation recognised its development potential it cajoled the girls' school to move.

In a detailed report and revised design made in 1956, CPB observed that 'the City offered virtually no opportunities for mental recreation in the evenings after the business life of the City closed down'. They argued that a 'small and compact cultural centre', offering repertory shows, temporary exhibitions, lectures and conferences, was more appropriate than a large concert hall or cinema for what was in essence an isolated town with a small population, but might encourage potential commuters to stay in London. They proposed a theatre, concert hall, art gallery and small halls suitable for lectures. Plans showed a theatre and concert hall set back-to-back, their foyers linked by an art gallery, with to the north a large open-air amphitheatre set across an ornamental canal and to the south a square flanked by the assembly halls and gymnasia of the two secondary schools; a swimming pool shared by the schools and public closed the fourth side. As built, the girls' school secured its own, exclusive pool while the public were directed to Golden Lane.

The venture had little precedent. The Arts Council of Great Britain had briefly continued the work of the wartime Committee for the Encouragement of Music and the Arts in encouraging local music clubs to acquire premises for performances and exhibitions. (See Robert Hewison, p.19.) A project by Geoffrey Jellicoe for Mablethorpe, Lincolnshire, remained unbuilt, but in 1946 the Arts Council took over an 18th-century house as the Bridgwater Arts Centre, installing gallery and concert facilities for a variety of professional events. Norwich's assembly rooms were privately restored as an arts centre and banqueting room for the Festival of Britain in 1951. However, from 1952 the Arts Council supported few save the most prestigious arts companies, and in 1954 the Ministry of Education suspended grants under the Physical Training and Recreation Act, which had supported the building of community centres, hugely important for amateur music and drama groups.

The County of London Plan, produced by the London County Council in 1943, had proposed building a theatre, concert hall, youth centre and swimming pool between Waterloo Bridge and County Hall. The Festival of Britain had hastened the building of the Royal Festival Hall and proposals for a National Theatre, only for momentum to cease when the government pulled out of an enabling development. Robert Maxwell (1922–2020), who revised the Royal Festival Hall's elevations for the LCC in the mid–late 1950s, considered the hall a 'Labour Party version of a People's Palace' and thus a multi-purpose building.

His quip is a reminder of the vast, popular halls of the 19th century such as the Crystal Palace, Alexandra Palace and the People's Palace in Bow, which were a source of inspiration for Joan Littlewood's Theatre Workshop, the cutting edge of drama in the mid–late 1950s along with the Royal Court Theatre. Yet, contrary to initial intentions, the Royal Festival Hall's foyers were closed during the day, though the building was used for popular dances and corporate functions long into the night after the evening concerts.

By 1955 the Royal Festival Hall sat bereft amid flowerbeds and Festival flagpoles. A theatre for amateur as well as professional drama and music had been cut from its design in the flurry to open in May 1951, leaving the landward façade unfinished. Now the LCC resolved to build a separate hall seating 1,000 for chamber music, together with an art gallery and conference centre, for which Leslie Martin cultivated a small team of young designers under his personal supervision. In 1956 the LCC addressed a Treasury committee appointed to investigate 'housing the arts' with the support of the Arts Council. It promised a centre providing 'opportunities for relaxation and enjoyment' that would contribute to the re-planning of post-war London and provide a wider range of activities after office hours, but without mention of amateurs. The Arts Council noted a visit to the South Bank led by John Rockefeller III ahead of plans for the Lincoln Center in New York; in turn Norman Engleback of the LCC Architect's Department made a study trip to Germany, Italy and Switzerland in 1960. It seemed natural for British architects looking to build for the arts to seek inspiration from Europe, selecting elements from a variety of sources to bring together on one site.

The Arts Council's report, *Housing the Arts in Great Britain*, published in 1959, welcomed the City's proposals for a theatre, concert hall and possible art gallery. 'It feels that, in addition to the importance of providing a close link between the academic training provided by the School and the field of professional practice, these buildings will go some way to serve a new audience drawn partly from the enormous daytime population of the city of London and partly from the growing residential population in the Barbican and neighbouring areas. The theatre could serve a particularly useful function in providing London with drama of the "off-Broadway" pattern, and also small-scale opera.' As Kenneth Cork, chairman of the City's Music Committee, later told *The Stage*, 'It is an intellectual kind of open space our present generation needs.' Thanks to CEMA and the Arts Council, access to the arts had become an accepted part of a general right to wider educational and opportunities, yet only that anachronistic, independent authority, the City of London, still suggested something of a 'bottom up' approach.

In October 1958 Chamberlin led a delegation from the City's Barbican Committee to Stockholm's post-war suburb of Vållingby, Malmö, Berlin, Zurich, Milan and Venice, with Cologne added at the committee's request. It visited the Berlin Academy of Music, where the war-damaged concert hall (now the UdK Concert Hall) had been rebuilt by Paul Baumgarten in 1953–4. Although only used for music, the hall was a useful comparison since it was used by both students and professional orchestras. CPB noted the generous size of the foyers, attempting a similar scale by designing a single foyer to be shared between the hall and theatre, with the performance times staggered accordingly.

CPB were not confirmed as architects for the schools until March 1960,

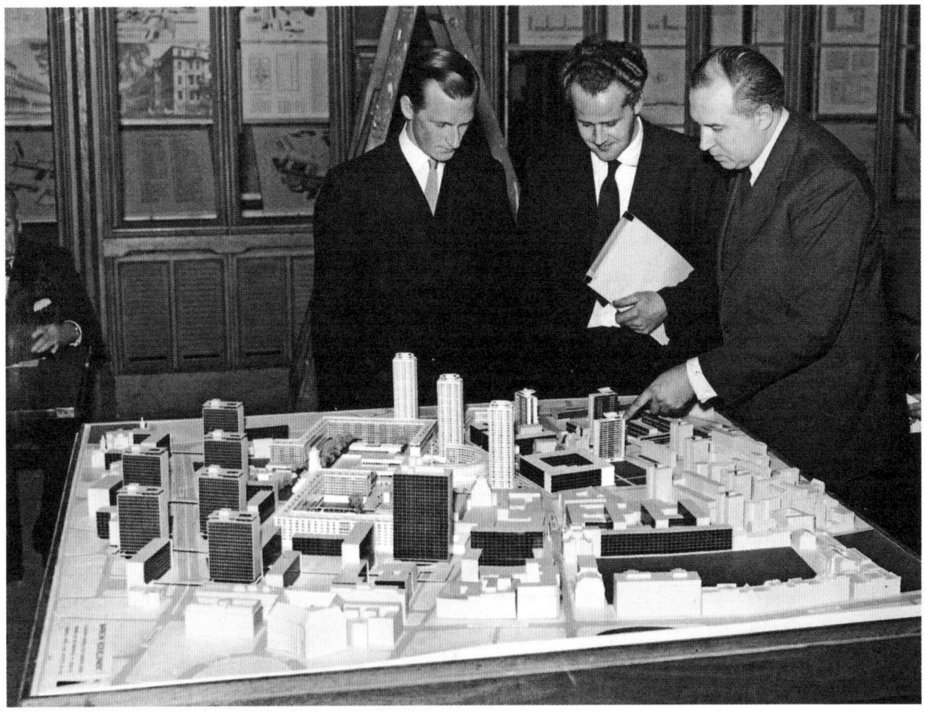

Geoffry Powell, Christoph Bon and Joe Chamberlin at a press conference at the Guildhall, London, with their model of an early scheme for the Barbican development. The Route 11 office blocks can be seen on the left. Chamberlin is pointing at a proposed hostel for the YMCA, then still in the style of the Golden Lane Estate.

the culmination of a stealthy manoeuvre in which they evolved their role from master planners to architects of the whole scheme; it was one they were to repeat at Leeds University. They also reversed the brief for Barbican when they established that the school needed a theatre and concert hall for only three months of the year. They therefore recommended building a larger theatre and concert hall aimed mainly at professional public performances, which would earn an income. CPB's third and most detailed report to the Court of Common Council, in April 1959, placed these buildings around a sunken garden court and alongside an open-air amphitheatre. They added a small art gallery for temporary exhibitions, pointing out their shortage in London and total absence in the City, highlighting the advantages for artists to have their work seen by a new audience of play-goers — an early awareness of the value of cross-fertilisation between disciplines.

The City's music committee sought reassurance that it was getting the best scheme possible, so in June 1958 it secured the appointment of Richard Southern (1903–89) as a specialist consultant, with CPB paying half his salary. Southern's career as a set designer had fostered an interest in historic staging, which in turn led to studies of theatre planning (published in 1953 as *The Open Stage*) and the building of a student theatre for the University of Bristol in 1951. He recommended building a conventional theatre with a proscenium stage and orchestra pit, with behind them a rehearsal stage that could house additional sets for elaborate productions. CPB followed his guidelines in designing an auditorium for 780 people, stacked as close to the stage as possible by the unusual device of cantilevering galleries forward rather than setting them back, and by omitting central aisles in favour of doors at the end of every row of seats

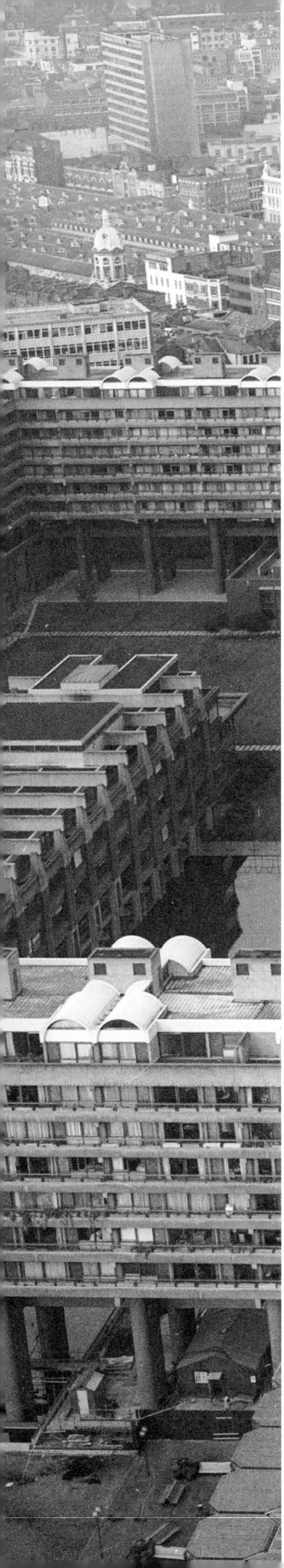

Frank Woods

What is the origin of the Barbican's architectural style? There is no simple answer. When the first ideas were being formulated for the Barbican in the late 50s, the whole of the site was a scene of total desolation, a bombed site, with St Giles Cripplegate as a sole beacon. It was a period of recovery from the war; there was a need to get rid of war damage and also old and supposedly useless buildings.

At that time there was no internet, no computers, but drawing boards, pencils and pens, slide rules and log tables. In our practice of Chamberlin, Powell and Bon we were all modernists. There was no spoken philosophy of or about style as such. A bright new world was coming, and this new world was about modern architecture — no decoration, no Victoriana or Edwardiana — it was more about the Bauhaus — clean lines and, most important, always involving a detailed analysis of the client's brief. Logic and reason were the rules of the day, out of which would emerge the answer.

The Barbican is a neighbourhood of the City. For the arts centre, place-making became an important factor. The houses and shops and offices within the streets and the squares make up the grain of a city, but there is always the need for features or icons such as churches or town halls that act as markers to help with way-finding. This was why the concert hall and the theatre volumes were differently coloured within the envelope of the foyers. Similarly, St Giles's church became the pivotal icon or marker for the whole development.

However, in our studios the phrase 'place-making' did not yet exist in our vocabulary. Nor did we use the word 'brutalism' to refer to concrete as a material. After the war concrete was readily available. As modernists we had an over-riding but unwritten belief in understanding the qualities of the materials we were using, concrete, steel, brick and wood, treating them as noble and not just utilitarian. For concrete we studied extensively the idea of carefully selecting the aggregates so that when the cast surface was pick-hammered the colour would show, displaying its own materiality. In the Barbican the tactility of the pick-hammered concrete and of the polish of the handrails and of the end grain of the wood block flooring are all examples of this materiality— an enjoyment and celebration of their innate qualities.

The phoenix that rose from that desolate site is the child of the late 50s and 60s. It took more than a generation and a half to be constructed, another generation to be absorbed into the culture and fabric of the City, and another to be regarded as an international model of its kind. A further generation yet to come will no doubt see many more changes, as the Barbican grows to match and reflect the society in which it will stand.

Frank Woods studied at Cambridge under Leslie Martin (formerly Chief Architect of the LCC) and Colin St John (Sandy) Wilson (later of the British Library) and then spent the whole of his career at Chamberlin, Powell and Bon, becoming a partner, working closely with the original partners and later inheriting the practice.

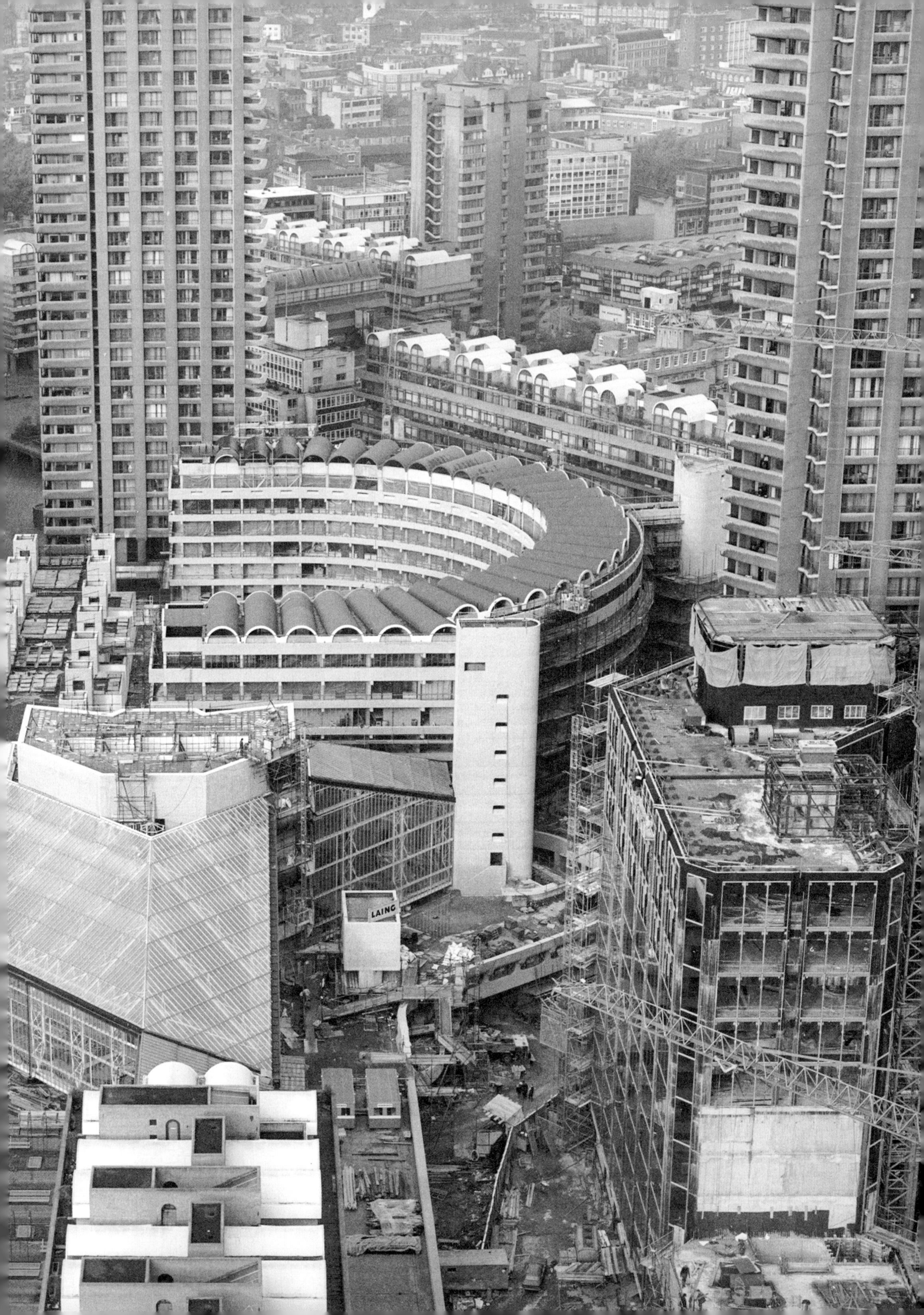
LAING

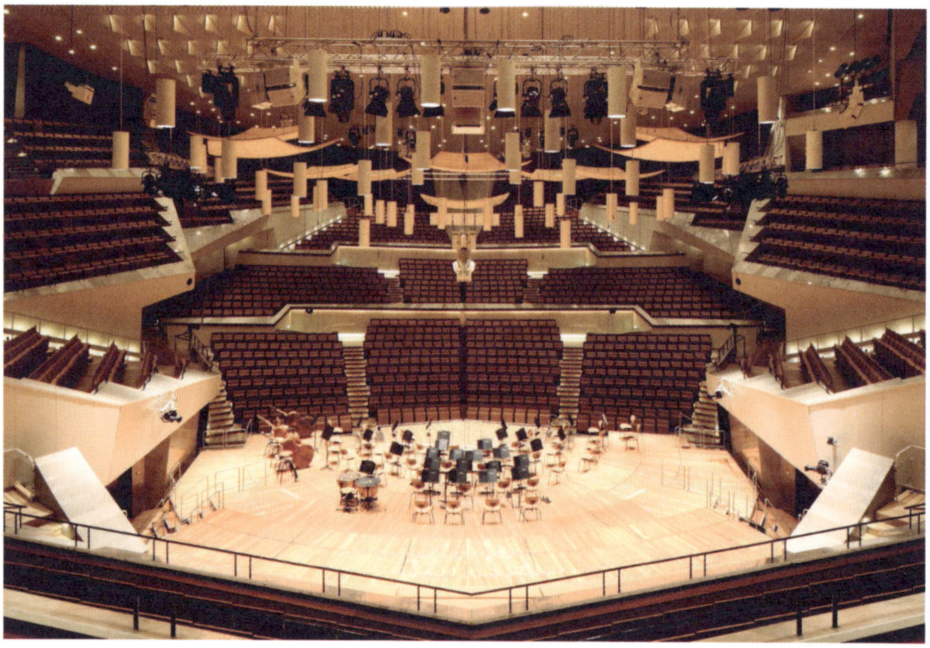

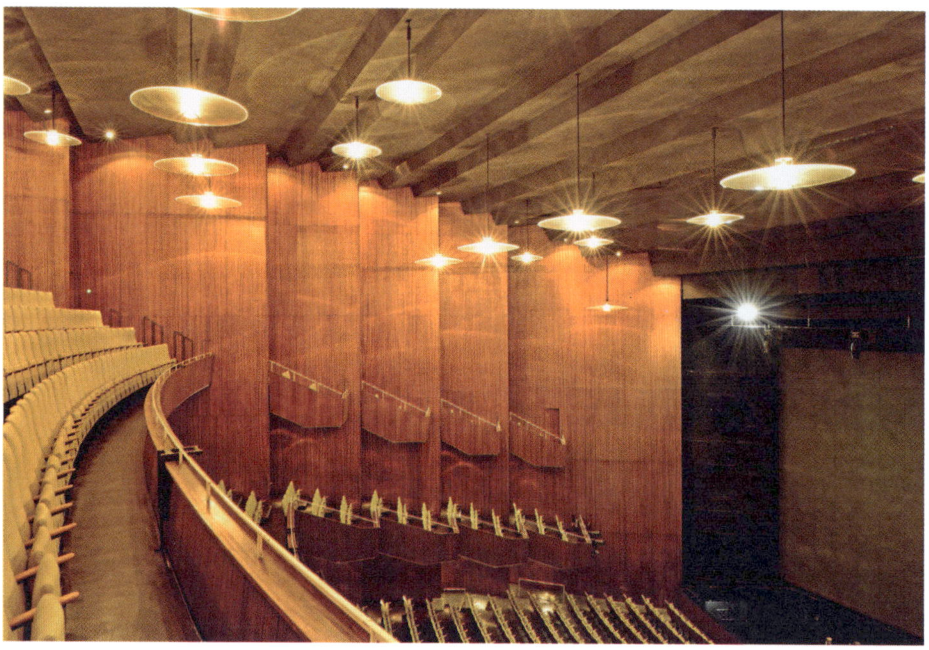

Berlin models for the Barbican: the Philharmonie, the pioneering concert hall in the round by Hans Scharoun, 1960–3 (top); the rebuilt Deutsche Oper by Fritz Bornemann, 1961 (bottom).

leading to large staircase areas. The theatre as eventually built substantially follows this design.

Southern's proposals were practical, but also suggested a larger agenda for theatre. They were made at a time of great debate over staging, led in Britain by the director Stephen Joseph, who in 1955 had created a temporary theatre at Scarborough where the audience surrounded the stage on all sides. He subsequently denounced the illusionist picture-frame theatre as irrelevant. At Barbican, Southern suggested that the concert hall, while to be used primarily for music, should be made octagonal so it could be adapted for theatre-in-the-round or Elizabethan drama. On its tour, the Barbican Committee visited the Teatro San Erasmo in Milan, a short-lived basement theatre of 1951–3 by Carlo de Carli that had a near-octagonal stage; it gave an indication of theatre-in-the-round on a tiny scale at a time when there was no similar permanent theatre in Britain. CPB included four of Southern's sketches illustrating the flexibility of the arrangement in their report of 1959. A crescent block of flats, inspired by Jewin Crescent previously on the site, determined the form of the outdoor amphitheatre rather than the concert hall, which like the theatre was treated as a separate building.

The City had never built a public library, its Library Committee providing a service through the Bishopsgate and Cripplegate Institutes. It agreed to support only an art gallery in Barbican (confirmed in 1962) but allowed CPB to leave a site where a library might be inserted later. One was duly included in the 1959 report, which illustrated Werner Düttmann's library of 1956–7 at Berlin's Hansaviertel seen on the 1958 tour, though its courtyard garden was described as an atrium, as was realised with the library and art gallery at Barbican. CPB gave form and character to the music school by setting its many identical practice rooms round the rotunda of the Coal Exchange, a cast-iron structure of 1847—8 they proposed unsuccessfully to relocate from Lower Thames Street where it faced demolition.

The 1959 plan had included a road, enclosed but raised on a bridge, which bisected the estate from Golden Lane to Wood Street and cut the arts centre site in two. Its elimination in 1960 enabled Chamberlin, Powell and Bon to refine their plans. From 1962 the concert hall and theatre were separated from the Guildhall School and became entirely professional. In March 1963, the Earl of Drogheda, chairman of the City Arts Trust, introduced Kenneth Cork to the opera director Anthony Besch. Besch assessed the practicality of the proposals for a concert hall seating 1,300 people and a theatre for 800, to be used almost exclusively by visiting companies. He found that no major companies had not been approached, and his investigations led to a detailed report presented to the corporation in May 1964 (see Kenyon, p.39). Agreements made with the RSC in February 1965 and the LSO in March 1966 allowed detailed accommodation schedules to be drawn up, but the bones of the two main spaces had already been substantially set out.

Also in 1964 the City appointed K G Hunt from the Association of Metropolitan Chief Librarians to advise on a library. He recommended a service for books and music on a larger scale than previously planned. CPB produced a new feasibility study showing how these larger facilities might be fitted into Barbican, where construction of the flats had finally begun, with two of the towers and Frobisher Crescent (part adapted to offices and conference facilities) awkwardly close at hand. It was made possible by tucking a semicircular concert hall on to the amphitheatre site below Frobisher Crescent. Lining up the concert hall, theatre and Guildhall School alongside the ornamental lake also meant placing them close to the railway tracks running between Aldersgate (now Barbican) and Moorgate stations, which the engineers Ove Arup & Partners recommended should be boxed in and the rails put on rubber anti-vibration mountings.

Besch and Chamberlin made a further study of new theatres and concert halls at home and abroad. They visited Nottingham Playhouse and Phoenix Theatre, Leicester, before heading to West Germany to study the more ambitious public theatres at Gelsenkirchen, Kassel and Hannover, and the Freie Volksbühne, Deutsche Oper and Philharmonie in Berlin. They then visited the Lincoln Center and the short-lived theatre of the American National Theatre Academy in New York, and the Arena Stage in Washington DC. They agreed that the most successful concert hall was Berlin's Philharmonie, built in 1960–3 by Hans Scharoun, which fulfilled a similar brief to Barbican but on a far larger scale. 'It seats 2,000 but seems much larger because of its great cubic capacity and technique of deploying the audience in height rather than depth. Like this a concert hall could also be used for some theatre in the round.' Of the theatres they most admired Gelsenkirchen, built in 1956–9 by Werner Ruhnau, and Berlin's Volksbühne, opened in 1963 to the designs of Fritz Bornemann. German cities had invested enormous sums in new theatres and opera houses since the early 1950s to affirm a positive cultural identity, with backstage areas and technical stage facilities that no British authority could match; the shallow side slips of the Barbican Theatre were a reinterpretation of a popular German device for stepped *schlitten* or sledges. Gelsenkirchen is the outstanding example, with vast foyers shared by two halls, but the Volksbühne is noted for its relative lack of gimmicks. Peter Rice of Arup's and Ralph Koltai of the Royal Shakespeare Company advised on the backstage and rehearsal spaces, while advice on staging from the RSC's John Bury led to a more open stage and large acting area, where Peter Hall emphasised the importance of 'the point of command'.

By 1967 multi-purpose arts centres were beginning to appear in great cities, but were still composed of individual buildings, as at the Lincoln Center (the Philharmonic Hall, New York State Theater and Metropolitan Opera House designed by a variety of architects using common materials in 1960–6), and the Canadian National Arts Centre built in Ottawa in 1966–9 to the designs of Fred Lebensold. Only the latest buildings of the South Bank suggested the artfully formless web to which architecture was turning. As strike action and violent demonstrations halted construction of the flats for a year, challenging even Barbican's most optimistic supporters, CPB worked hard on a detailed scheme for the arts centre. This they presented to the Court of Common Council in May 1968. It comprised buildings for the Guildhall School; a theatre seating about 1,250, which could be used as an open stage and for proscenium productions; a 2,000-seat concert hall; a public lending library with special collections devoted to music and the fine arts; an art gallery for travelling exhibitions; two restaurants and a cafeteria; a cinema, shops, foyers and car parking. The volume of the overall centre had trebled, and it was now 170 metres (560ft) long and 52 metres (170ft) tall, though sunk deep into the ground so as not to obstruct the luxury flats behind.

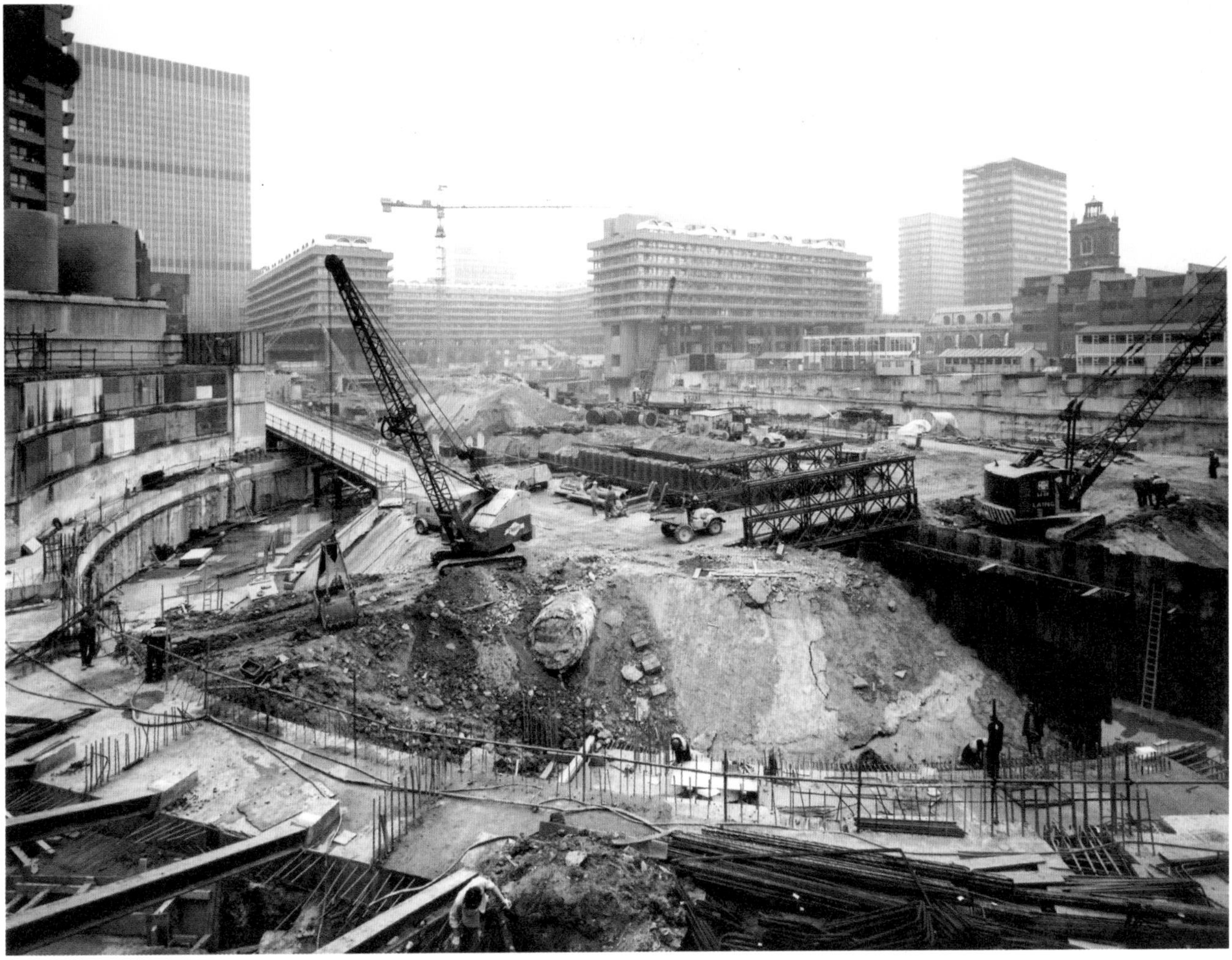

The sweep of the semicircular Frobisher Crescent, with the underground space of the concert hall being dug out, 1973.

In a heated Guildhall debate in 1971 (see p.43), Alderman Sir Edward Howard argued that money devoted to the arts would be better spent on prisons, but the centre's supporters secured a decisive if narrow victory by 78 votes to 59 and accepted a £14.4m tender by John Laing Construction. But it decided, at the suggestion of the centre's newly appointed administrator, Henry Wrong, to add conference facilities, hoping that by spending more money and squeezing in yet more accommodation, that in the long run it might approach financial viability. The cinema was originally designed with the projection box set at an angle within the middle of the 280-seat auditorium, which included a steep rake upwards towards the screen, which was exceptionally curved. It was an extreme version of the 'reverse rake' found in some 1930s cinemas where the throw of the projector demanded a very curved screen. Now it was made more conventional for use by conferences, and the Pit studio theatre was adapted out of a rehearsal space.

The Queen laid the foundation stone in November 1972, but inflation and further strikes (notably in early 1975) caused more delays. By 1976 the cost

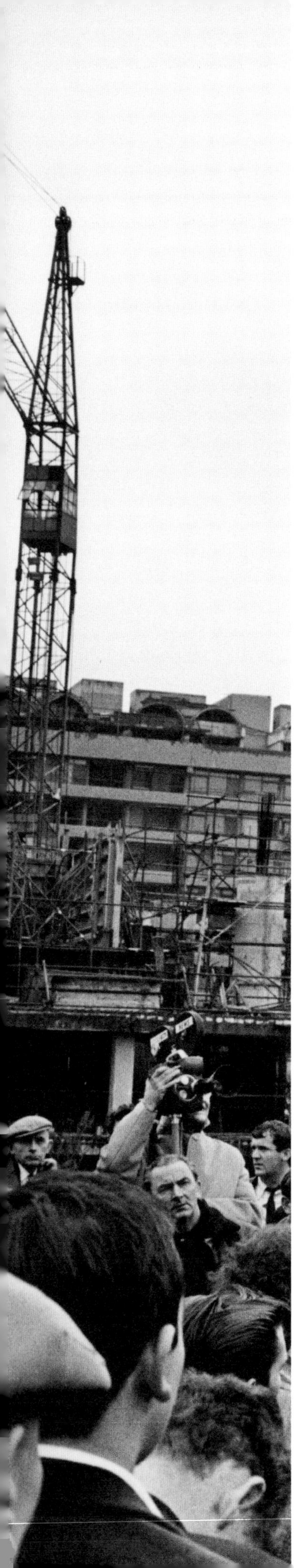

Workers' Stories

The workers engaged in the building of the Barbican Estate faced a wide range of problems, including major design flaws; an outdated industrial relations framework; a relatively untried payment system; a weak national trade union leadership; and health and safety hazards. Although engaged in the construction of a celebrated landmark of modern architecture they were subject to the most backward and dangerous of conditions.

This led to massive delays in the completion of the project; a huge escalation in costs; attempts by two major contractors to quit the site altogether, one of which was successful; strikes and a year-long lock-out, which resulted in a government Court of Inquiry and the blacklisting of many building workers. Many who built the Barbican responded to these difficulties with imagination and integrity. And in an industry that was notorious for its casualised, non-union nature, they tried to fashion a new way forward for trade unionism; one that was based on the principle of greater unity between all building workers; and one that was capable of providing for all building workers decent levels of pay, stable employment and good working conditions. Few who worked on the Barbican will ever forget it.

At the peak of the building process, the Barbican sites employed around a thousand workers. It was a diverse workforce, including workers from all parts of Britain, large numbers of Irishmen, Jamaicans and others from different parts of the West Indies, Sikhs from India and Eastern Europeans. Vic Heath was a scaffolder from Camden Town in his early thirties at the time. Here, Heath recalls the grim conditions faced by the workers in the early days and the struggle to improve them:

> Absolutely appalling. There were no toilets, no proper toilet facilities, the site was quite a big site, an enormous site really. It was covering a lot of ground, a lot of mud, and set in three different places on the site were toilets. That was wooden boxes with a toilet inside, with a chemical in the toilet, so you didn't have a flush ... So we said, well, alright then, if we're not going to have flush toilets, what we'll do is use the toilets at St Paul's. So, the management said, oh, you can't do that. I said, well, that's what we're going to f– have to do ... So the men started walking up towards St Paul's to go to the toilet, set up by us. So one lad would go off up the road towards St Paul's, and then one, after a short interval, would go behind him and so on, and so, within half an hour, near enough half of the men on the site was walking up towards St Paul's, and as they finished in the toilet and walked back down again, there was somebody to take their place.

Excerpted from *Constructing Post-war Britain: Building workers' stories 1950–70*, a research project led by Prof. Christine Wall, Prof. Linda Clarke, Charles McGuire and Olivia Muñoz-Rojas at the University of Westminster in the Centre for the Study of the Production of the Built Environment, 2010–12.

Image
Strike leader Lou Lewis talking to workers during the Barbican building site dispute, 16 October 1967.

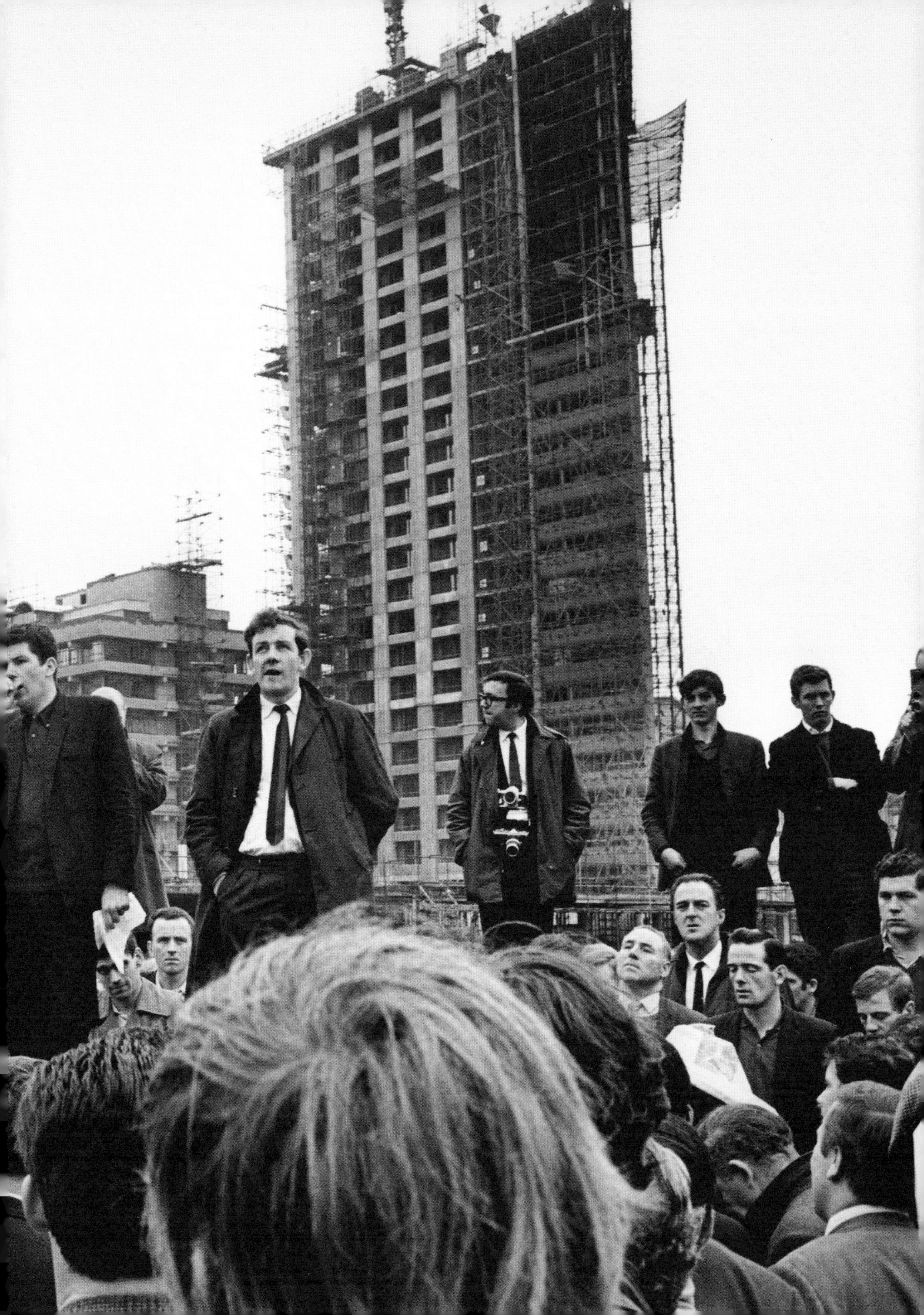

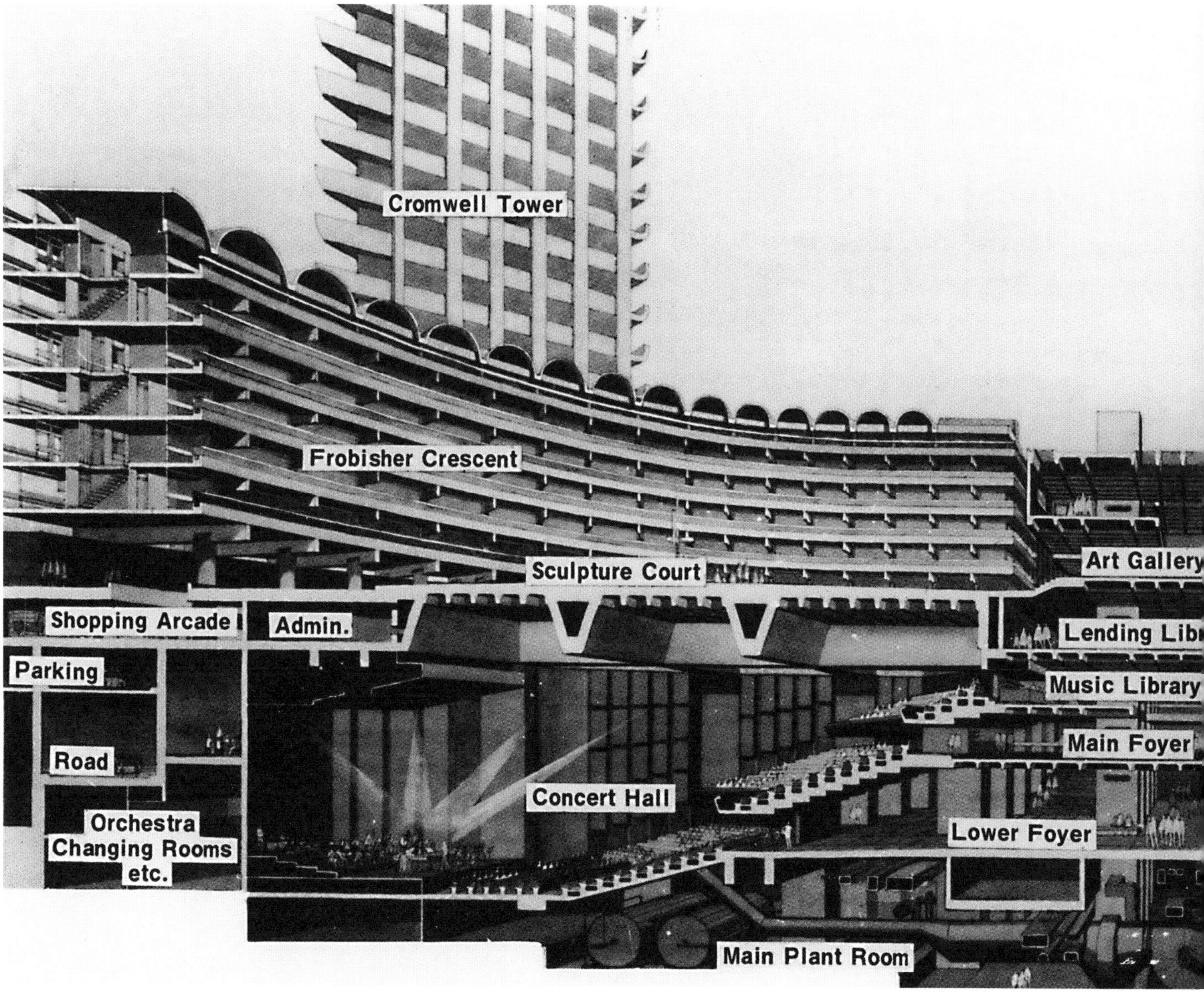
Cromwell Tower
Frobisher Crescent
Sculpture Court
Art Gallery
Shopping Arcade
Admin.
Lending Lib
Parking
Music Library
Main Foyer
Road
Concert Hall
Orchestra
Changing Rooms
etc.
Lower Foyer
Main Plant Room

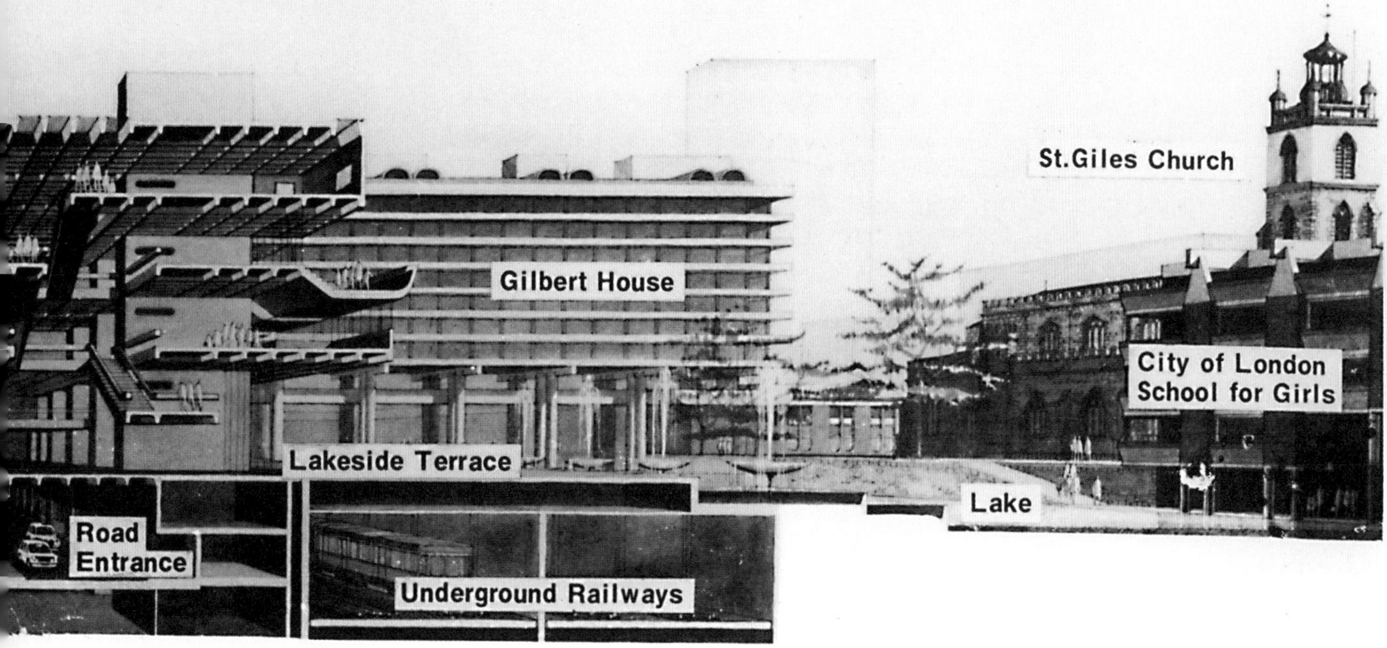

A detailed cross-section of the Barbican buildings, left to right roughly north–south, showing Frobisher Crescent (the shopping arcade planned there never materialised), the concert hall underground and the main plant room beneath, with Cromwell Tower behind. The gallery and library are stacked over the main foyer. The Lakeside Terrace with Gilbert House behind, the lake, St Giles Cripplegate and the City of London School for Girls are to the right.

of the development had risen to £50 million, blamed on the difficulty of the foundations and more industrial disputes, as well as inflation. The Guildhall School of Music and Drama finally opened in October 1977 with a small concert hall and flexible theatre. Final approval for the funding of an arts programme came in November 1979, after a last attempt by City councillors to control expenditure.

The Queen returned to open the centre on 3 March 1982. The publicity was big on statistics, claiming enough concrete to lay 19 miles of motorway; 5.3 acres of carpet, 1.7 acres of parquet flooring, 400 miles of electric cable and a roof weighing 6,000 tonnes. At the bottom of the iceberg, the cinema was 22 metres (72ft) below street level. The review of the *Aberdeen Press and Journal* (28 April 1982) was typical. 'From the outside, the much-publicised Barbican Centre for Arts and Conferences hardly looks like £152 million worth. On the inside, however, the overpowering imagination, skill and effort which has gone into the 25-year project becomes apparent immediately. It is engrained in the pine-clad walls, the polished teak flooring, the subtle lighting, the overall design. In fact, the Barbican has been described as "a haven of cultural perfection in the midst of the City of London".'

Other critics focused on the difficulties of finding their way round. However, they admired the novelty of the theatre with its forward-thrusting balconies and continuous seating rows, each with their own doors; these were tested in the lecture block CPB built in 1968–71 at Leeds University, where they were a boon for latecomers. The pyramid of the first Barbican scheme had evolved by 1956 into a conservatory; now a glasshouse wrapped itself round the fly tower, enveloping it. The concert hall faced more teething troubles. Chamberlin and Bon wanted leather seats, but were told that more absorption was needed, and the colours of Robin Day's upholstery resonate warmly with walls lined in pine. With a smaller volume than the Philharmonie came greater acoustic problems, while the relative width reduced early reflections. At the suggestion of the acoustician Hugh Creighton, Perspex spheres to diffuse the sound were suspended within the roof spaces, some of which also accommodated the house lighting and were exploited for decorative effect. These were soon removed and a canopy over the stage that reflected the sound towards the audience was renewed in 2002. Christoph Bon was anxious that the fittings in the public foyers should be as luxurious as possible, and there were artworks by Michel Santry and Gillian Ayres, whose husband worked for CPB. In 1999 Bon had two regrets, that the pedestrian routes were not as well signed as he had wanted, and that the communal nature of the complex was undermined by its partitioning between different organising bodies. He had also to quickly insert more ladies' lavatories.

Henry Wrong retired in 1989, and under a new managing director, Detta O'Cathain, in 1993–5 Theo Crosby of Pentagram and the artist Polly Hope introduced new lighting and pastel colours, and a temporary bridge across a void in the main foyer level. This work tried unsuccessfully to cloak the concrete in a pastiche of faded whimsy. Powell derided it as 'feeble tinkering'. It did not last long. O'Cathain was succeeded in 1995 by John Tusa, who met Bon shortly before his death in 1999 and embarked on a more sensitive scheme. Caruso St John and Kirkegaard Associates made alterations to the concert hall in 2002 to improve its acoustics, and the foyers and entrances were remodelled by

Allford Hall Monaghan Morris in 2005–7 at a cost of £12.25 million, with a new entrance from Silk Street and a permanent bridge.

Geoffry Powell acknowledged Le Corbusier to be the greatest inspiration for Barbican, suggesting that the Unité d'habitation in Marseille, which he had visited soon after its completion, was the only language of architecture at the time. The expressive shapes of the structure and textures of the concrete had given birth to the term brutalist, picked up by the Smithsons from an article in *The Times* that had anglicised the French term Art Brut. A younger partner, Frank Woods (see p.56), considered the technical reports and visits organised by the Cement and Concrete Association offered important guidance as the firm pushed to extend its knowledge of the material in the late 1950s. Yet there are also historical references in the housing, from the stark medieval towers of San Gimignano that were a model for urbanism in the 1950s to the repeated barrel-arched roofs to the churches on Mykonos, also visited by the partners on their extensive Mediterranean holidays, while brick at the lowest levels acknowledges the warehouse basements left by the Luftwaffe. Most importantly, perhaps, it is the ultimate expression of the Modern Movement's 1960s search for a monument, as the *Architects' Journal* recognised. 'The Barbican, now it is completed, has all the aspects, gigantisms, singleness of purpose — of that bygone age when architects had the confidence (or naivety) to believe that monumentality had a place in architecture and that part of [the architects'] job as designers was the imposition of a discipline and order on the users of the buildings.' Here is the timeless, sublime quality that characterises the Barbican; it is a reminder that the building has worn its 40 years remarkably lightly.

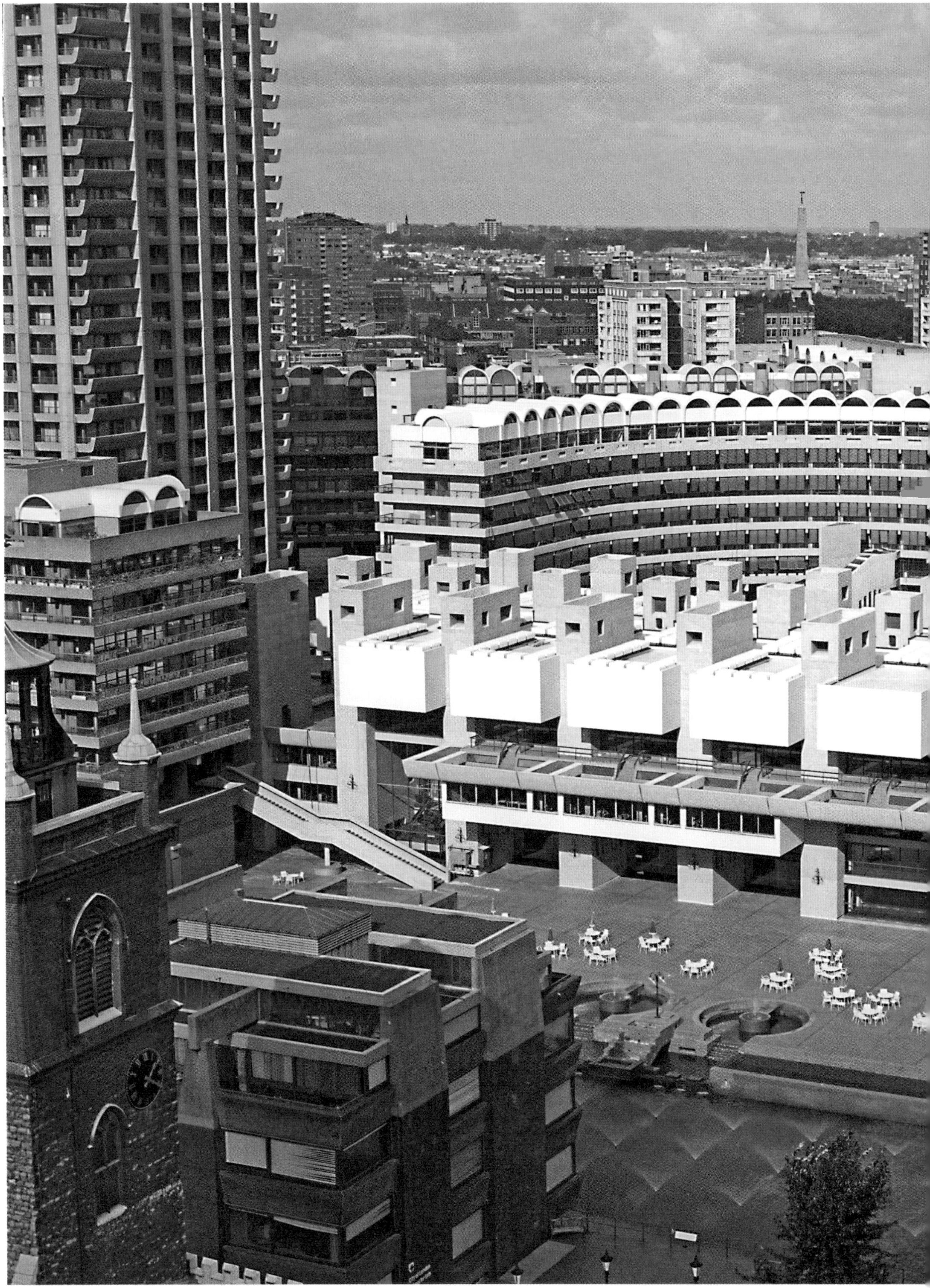

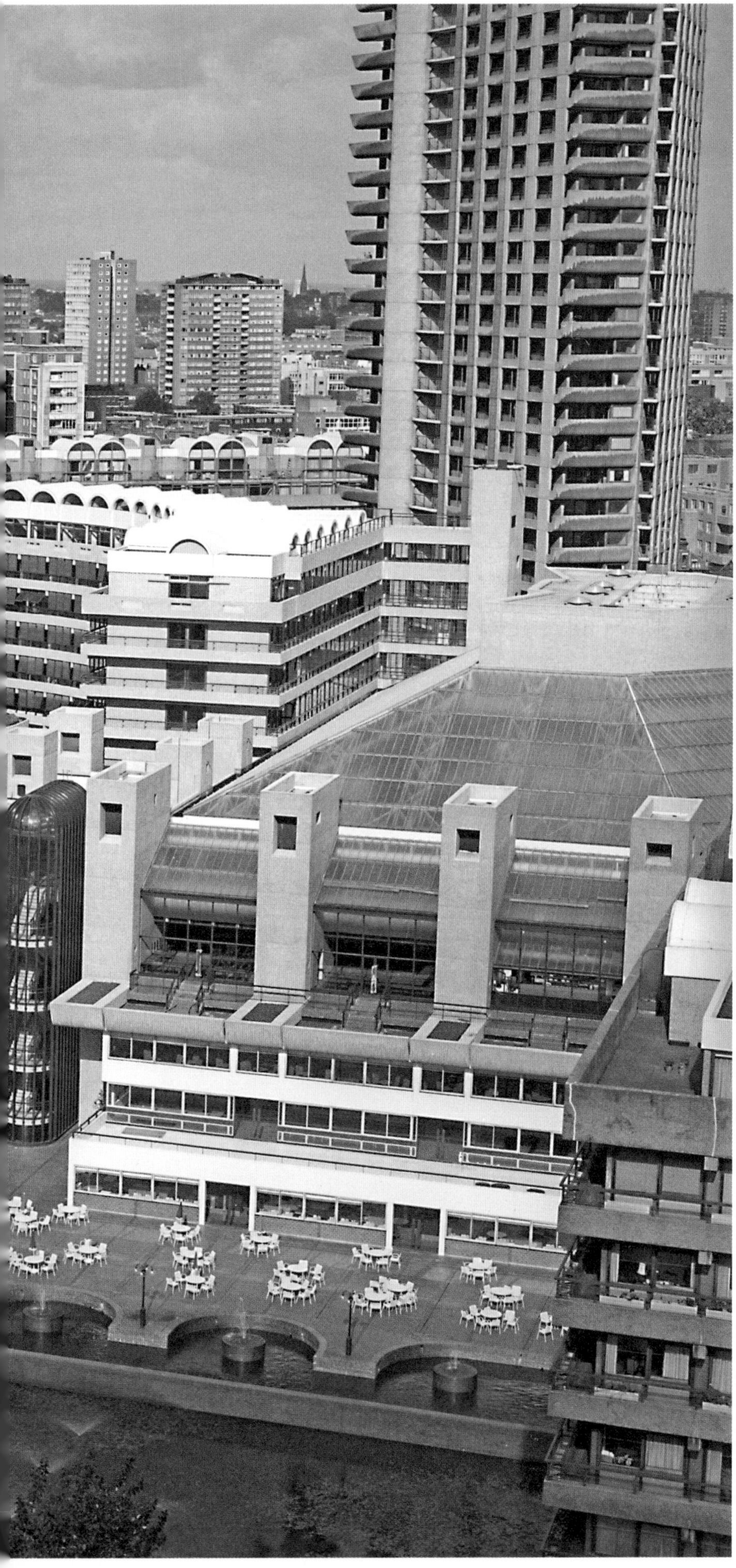

The Lakeside Terrace of the newly completed Barbican building, with its shining concrete and Frobisher Crescent behind, in Peter Bloomfield's photograph, 1982.

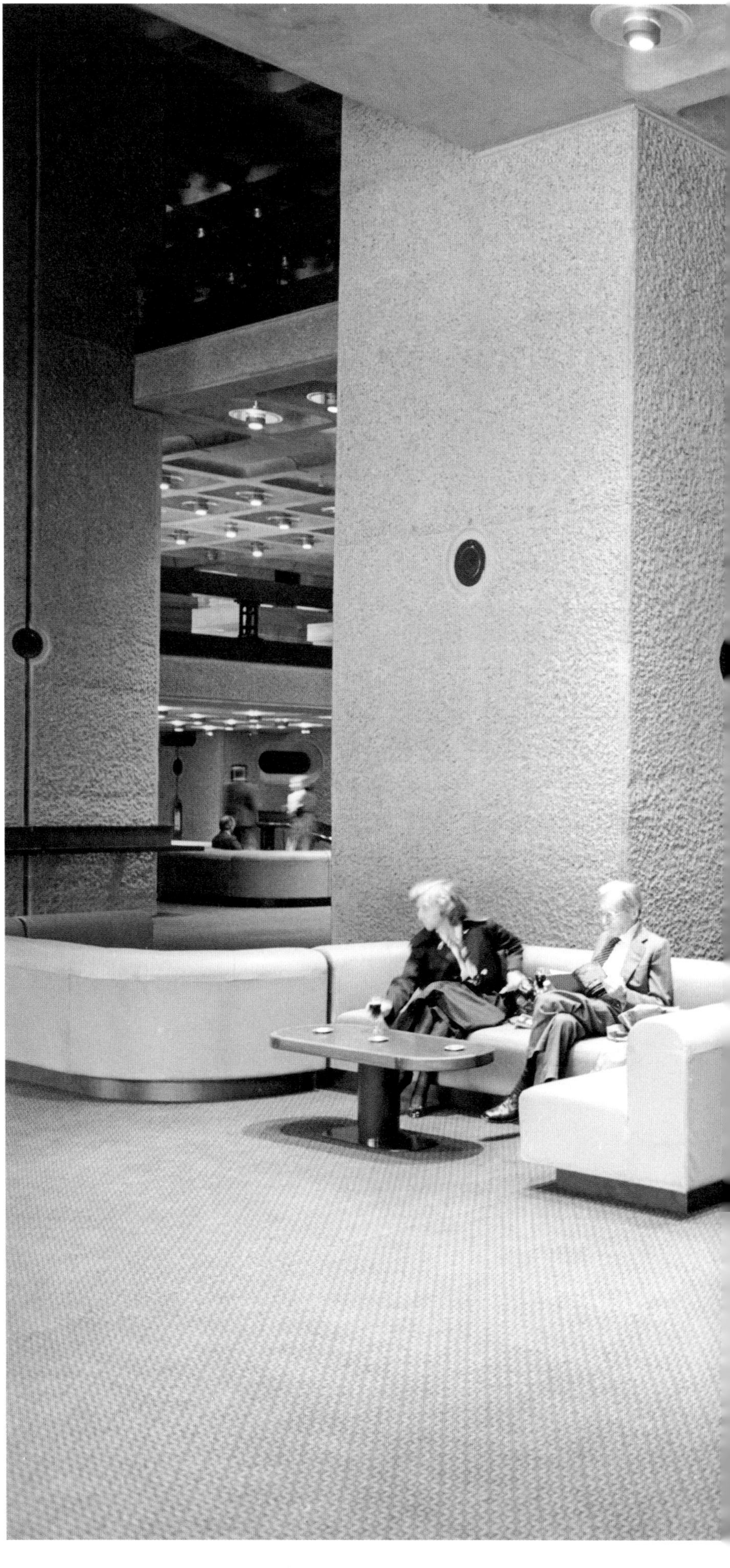

The interior foyer spaces of the Barbican, somewhat underpopulated by today's standards, with its distinctive original 'Hadrian' seating by the leading designer Robin Day (1915–2010).

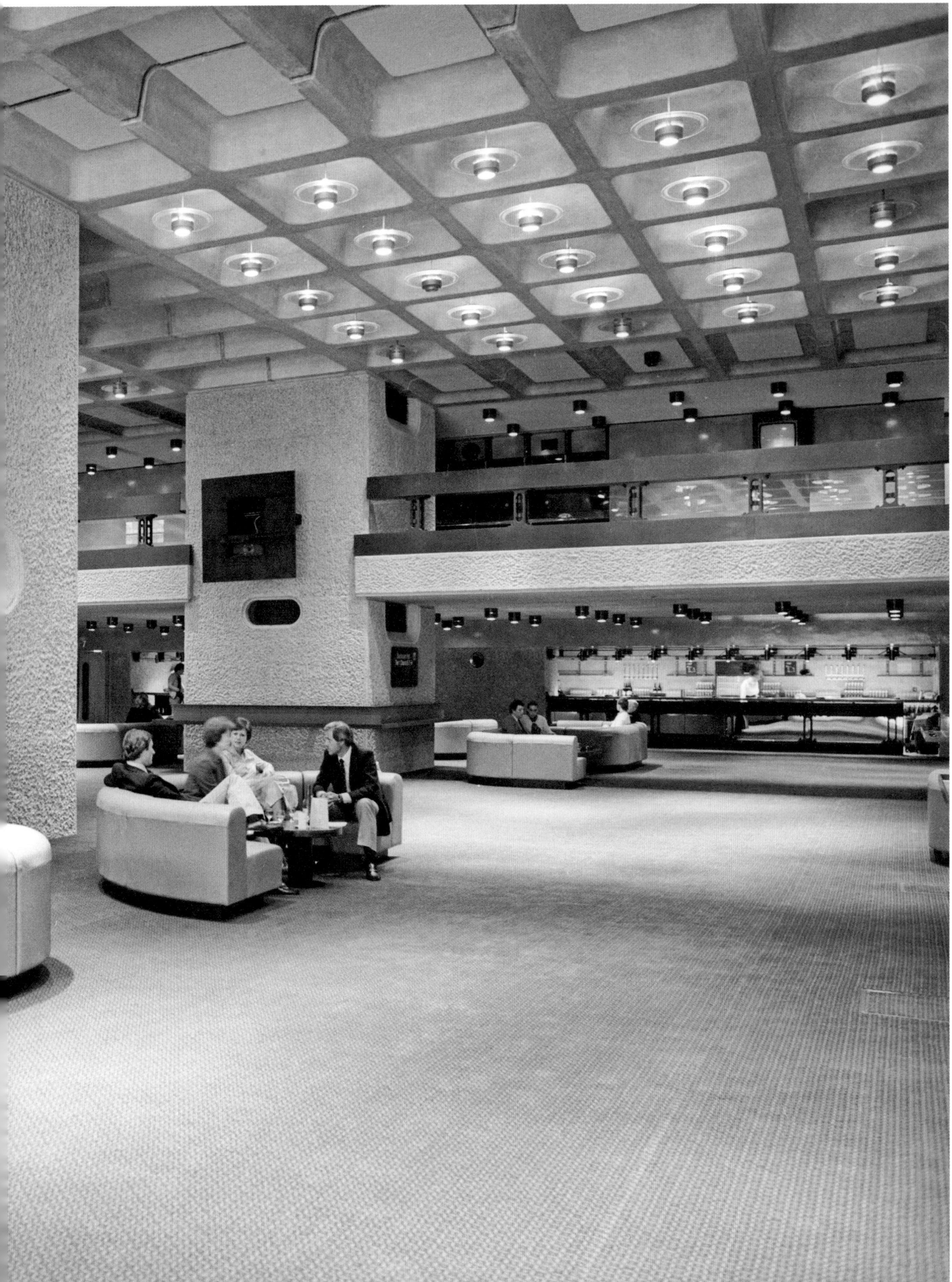

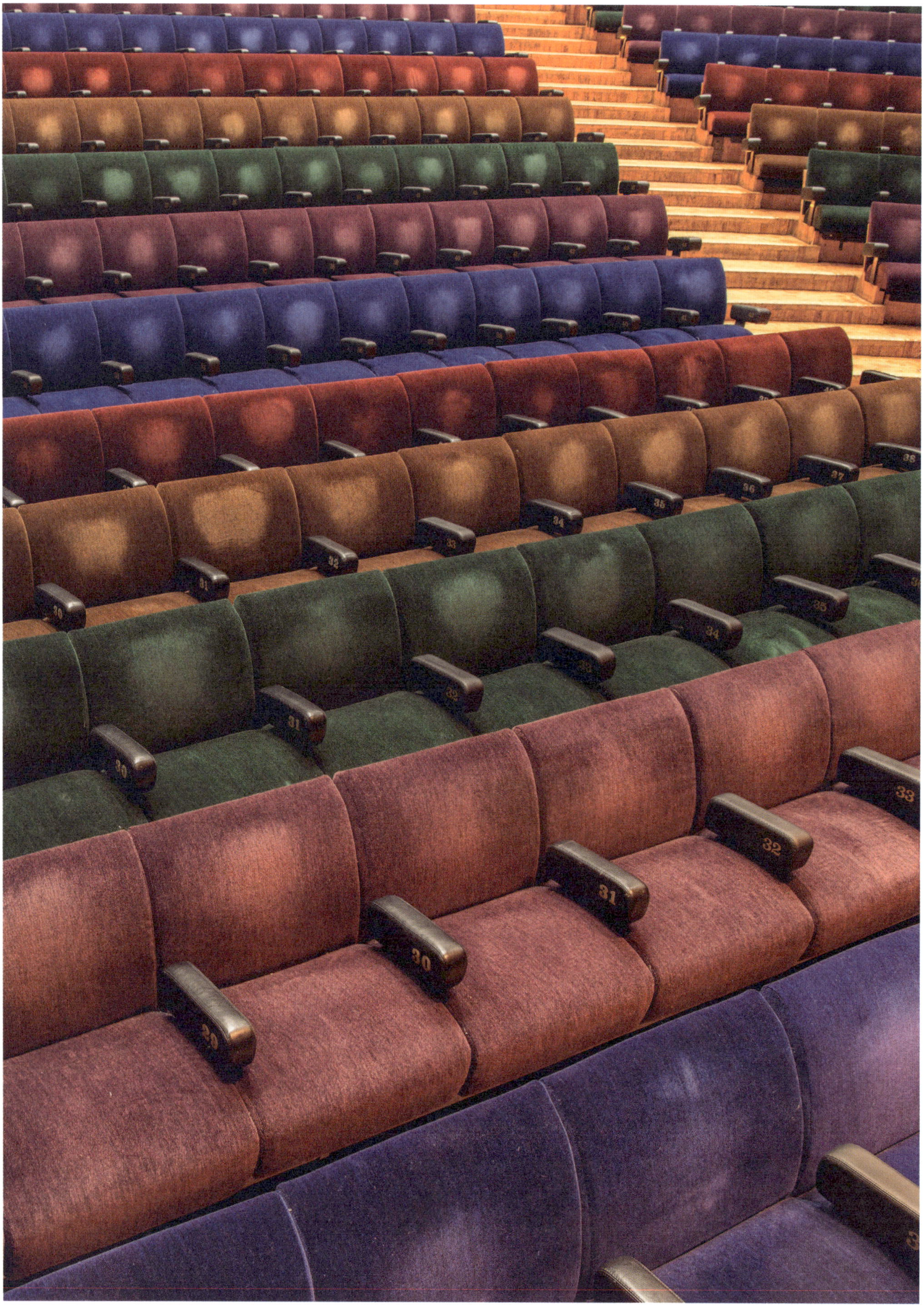

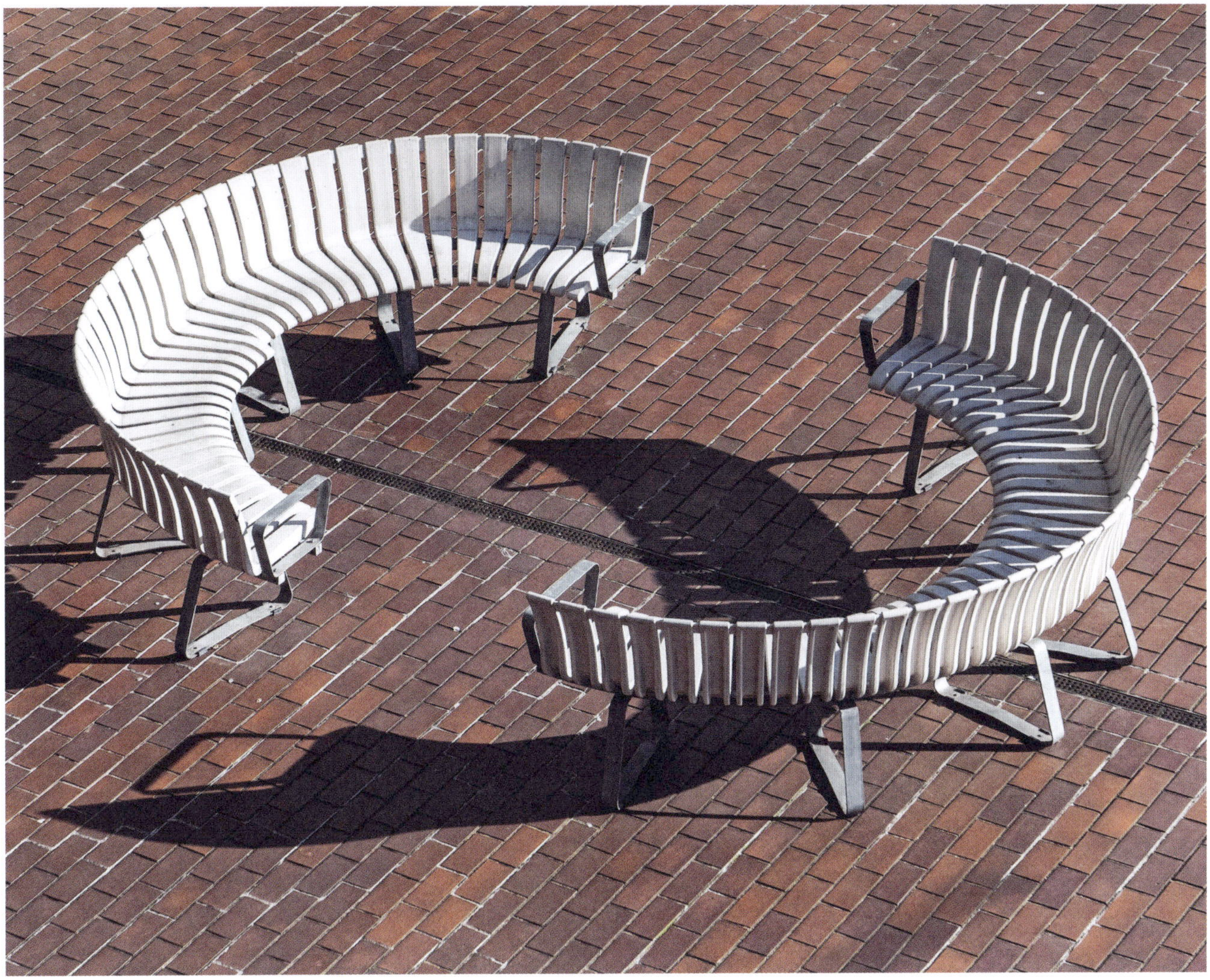

Opposite
The seating for the concert hall by Robin Day, who had worked on the Royal Festival Hall seating and for John Lewis. Colourful, spacious and comfortable, it has stood the test of time.

Above
In 2005 Day was brought back to the centre to renew the exterior seating on the Lakeside Terrace. His economical and elegant use of simple, moulded slats of plastic fits the cool, modernist aesthetic of the centre.

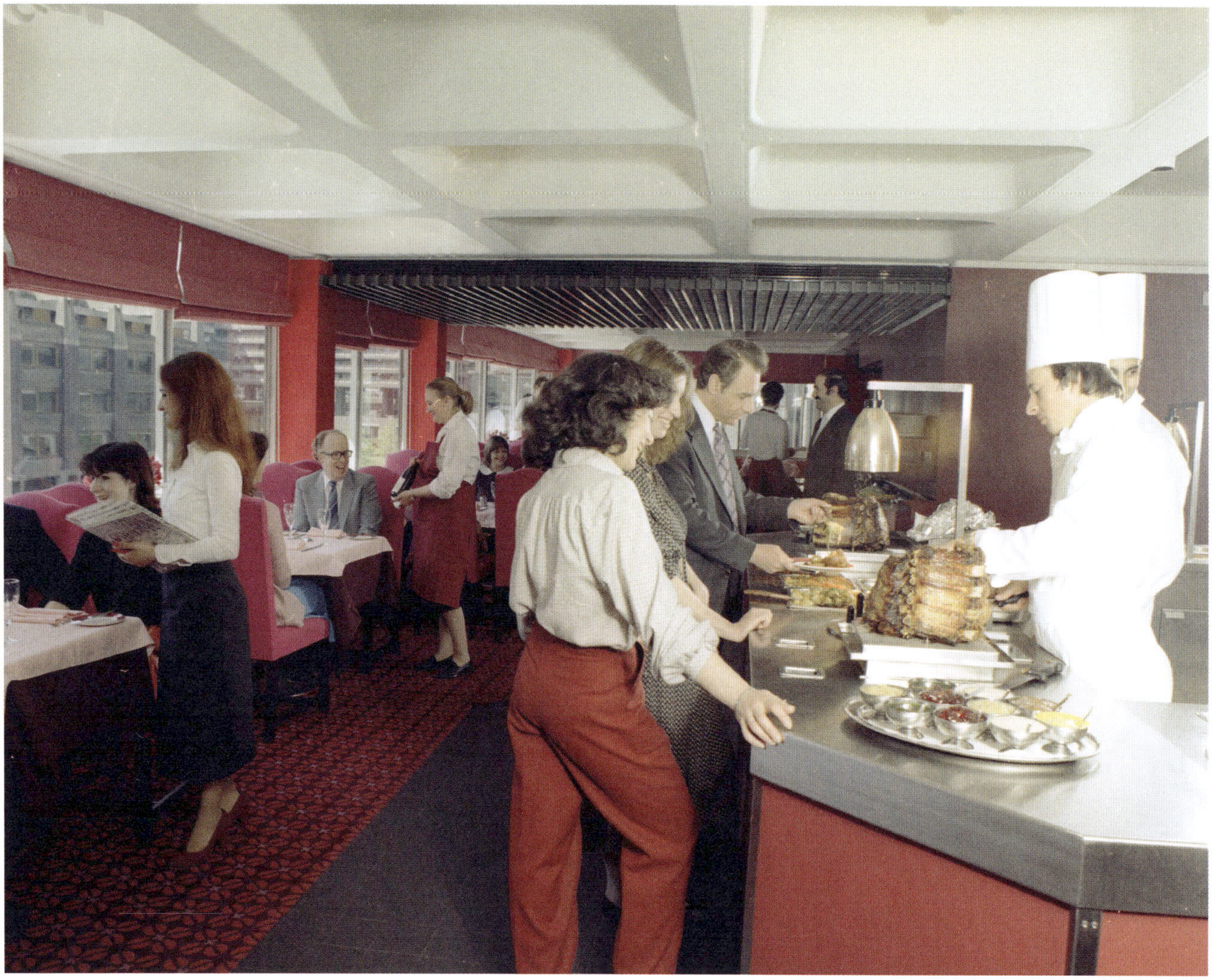

The commercial activities of the Barbican have been an essential part of its model from the start, with cafés and restaurants on the three floors facing the lake, providing fine views of the City from an urban oasis.

The designer David Hicks (1929–98) was a distinguished and innovative interior designer of restaurants and private houses for the aristocracy, the media and fashion worlds. He was noted for his boldly individual colour schemes and designed carpets, clothes and jewellery. He claimed his skill was to show people 'how to use bold colour schemes, how to use patterned carpets, how to light rooms and how to mix old with new'. He was commissioned to design the interior for this restaurant at the Barbican, which was originally named 'Cut Above'.

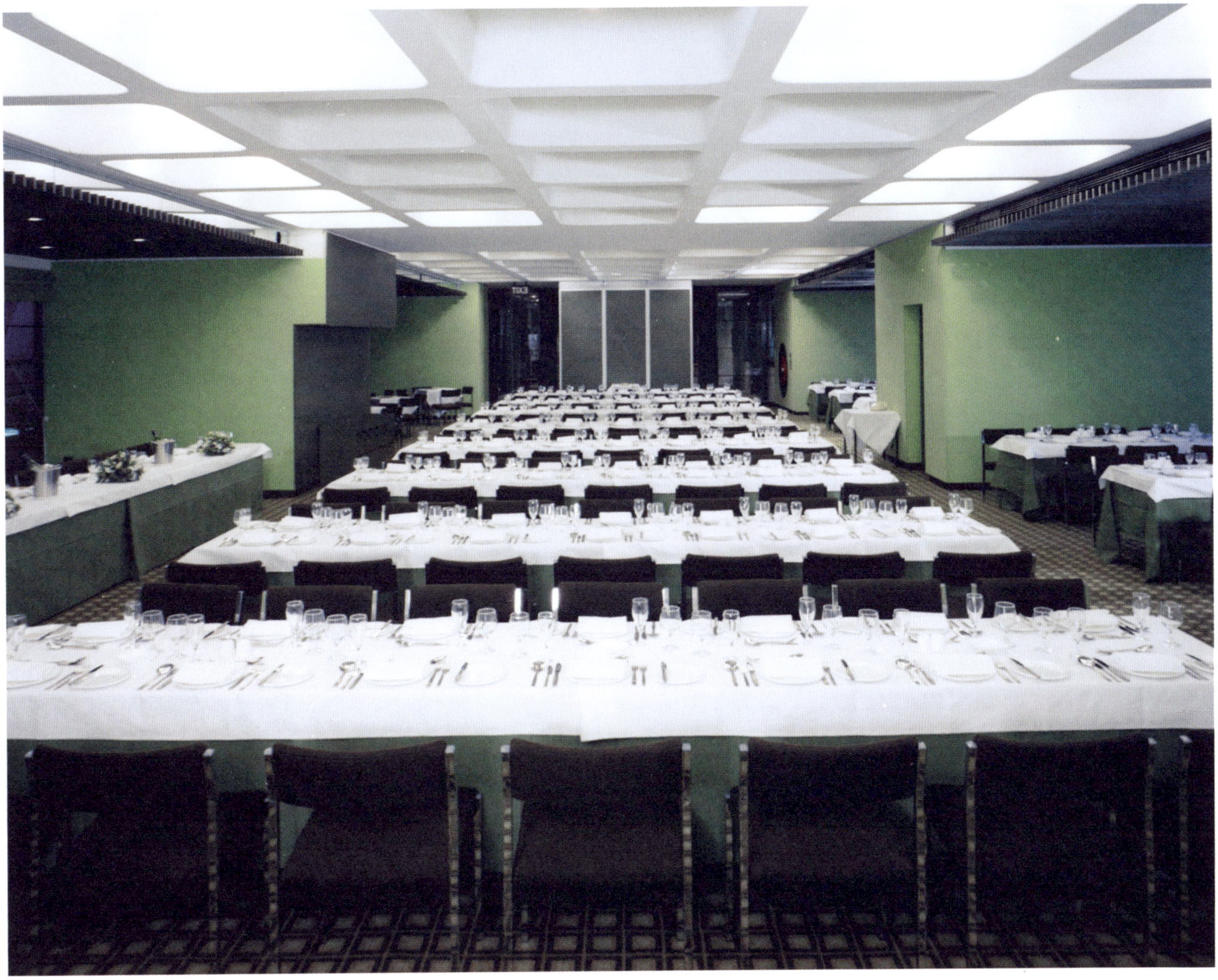

The Garden Room, linked to the conservatory, has been through many incarnations as a conference room and entertaining space. Today its many uses include wedding receptions after ceremonies in the conservatory.

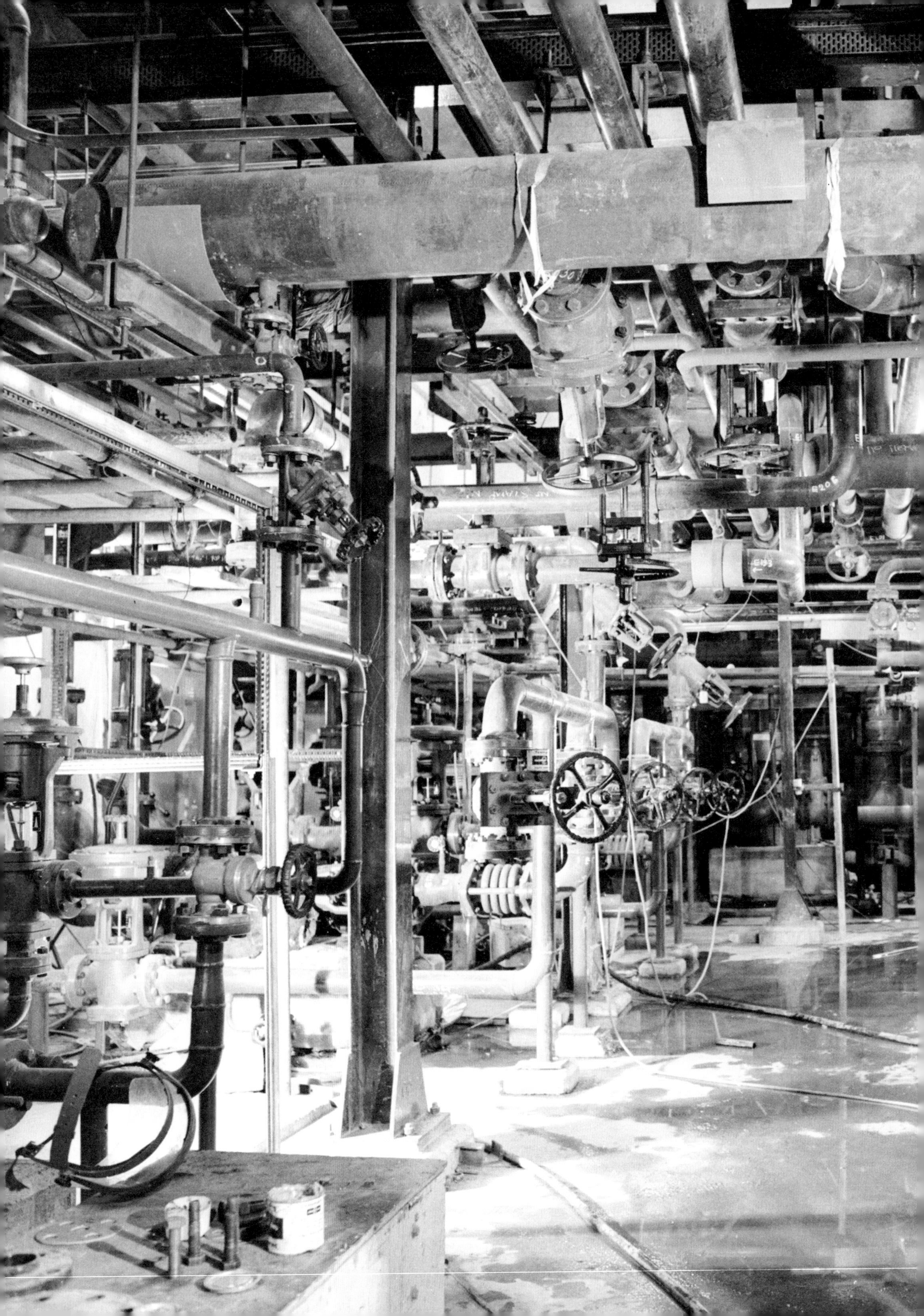

Cornell Farrell

Built by Arup and thousands of contractors and subcontractors, the Barbican building is a work of art in its own right. Whilst its purpose is to deliver a vision of community, the reality is hundreds of kilometres of cables, pipes and optic fibres. The Barbican is a 24/7 operation with over 50,000 hours of engineer time on site every day of the year, with more than 100 different plant rooms and 200 different distribution boards across the estate with literally thousands of electrical circuits.

All of this has to be tested and maintained to a compliant standard and must work first time and every time, in order to keep shows up and people safe. We have more than 30 lifts in the building, the biggest of which is large enough for a 20-tonne lorry. The fire alarm is so complicated that there are approximately 20 panels around the centre, and corresponding numbers of detectors and sounders. There are over 400 fans supplying or extracting air, some of them bigger than a person. To keep all this going, in order to provide a stage upon which our business performs, requires both art and science. Maintaining and operating one of the world's most iconic buildings is a pleasure and an honour for all of us.

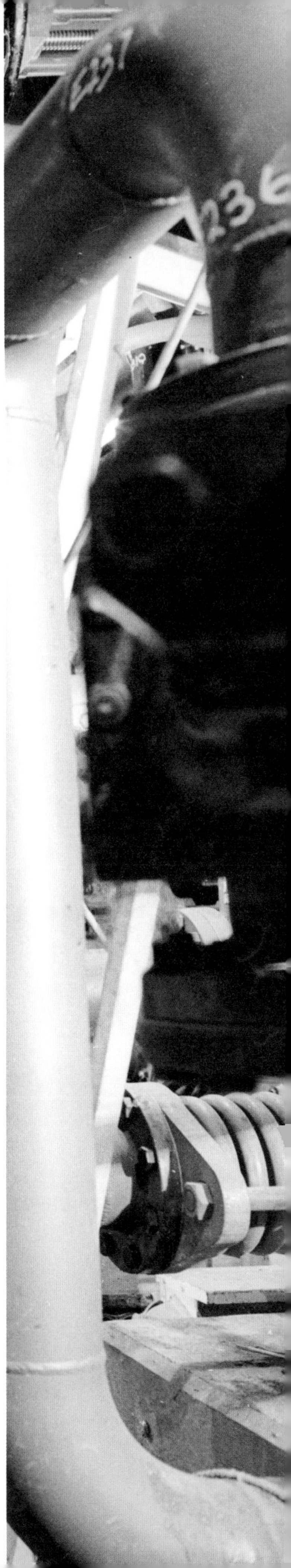

Cornell Farrell is the Barbican's head of engineering and projects.

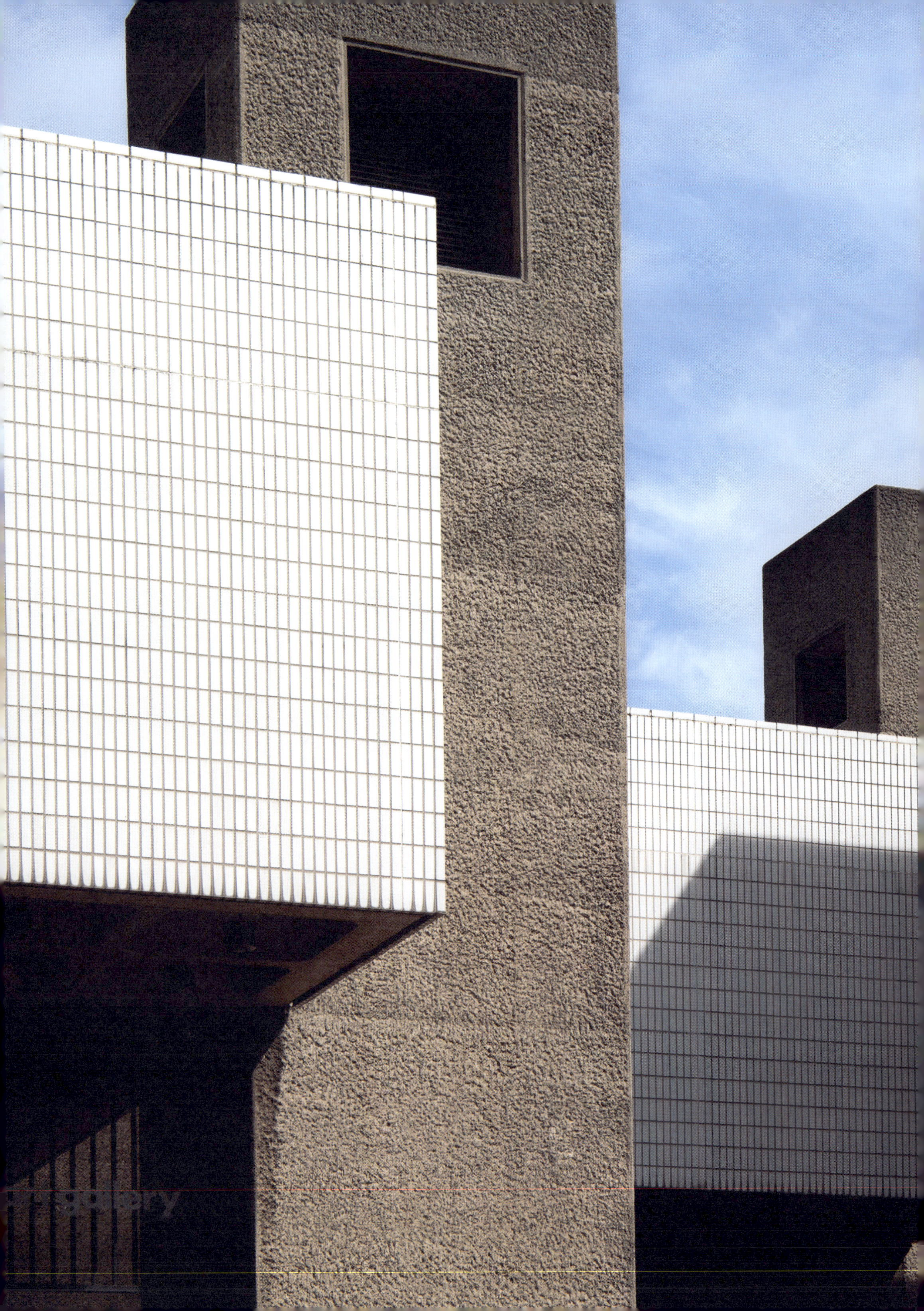

Concrete

Roma Agrawal

A man stands in front of a wall wearing ordinary khaki trousers and a cardigan as he goes about his work. I can't see his face clearly; it is partially hidden by a handkerchief around his nose and mouth, and the rest of it is blurred behind a plastic visor attached to a hard hat. His hands are protected by heavy-duty gloves. He holds a tool — cylindrical, as long as his forearm — and the front end of this is also blurred, by its rapid movement. The wall he is working on is made from concrete. There is a large, smooth patch, but around it is the ultimate goal, a textured finish that exposes small stones within the body of the material.

One of the first words that pops up in my mind every time I hear the word 'Barbican' is concrete. Perhaps that would be less surprising if you knew me; I'm a structural engineer, and am known for being obsessed with the material. Concrete is a rock, which through scientific processes is turned into a liquid, which once again hardens into a rock. It finds it magic in that intermediate liquid state, an indeterminate form which we designers can mould into anything we want (well, within reason).

I've received confused stares by passers-by who catch me stroking the surface of concrete buildings when walking around cities. The man with the visor is creating one of those finishes which so fascinates me. He is in a black and white image that was recorded 40 years ago, during the construction of the arts centre at the Barbican Estate. It's clear it's an old photograph, because today, he would be wearing a high-visibility jacket, a purpose-made facemask, and would be unlikely to be carrying the tool he does in the image. It's a vibrating hammer. Its end jabs the smooth concrete finish with such force as to break small pieces of it away in order to roughen it up, in a process called bush-hammering.

This manual process is slow and expensive. Using such powerful tools for long periods of time can lead operatives to suffer a condition called vibration white finger, which can cause poor circulation, loss of strength and numbness and pain in the hands and fingers. Today, such finishes are used less often, or if imperative to the aesthetic, created by using safer machines. The bush-hammered finish in the arts centre, tinged with some human cost, is therefore unique.

I visited the centre while researching this piece, and was shown around the usual places — the concert hall (where the concrete is hidden behind panels for acoustic reasons), the outdoor water and the exhibition space. But my favourite area was one that most people can't access. Hidden in a long corridor near the entrance to the loading bay are panels of concrete, lined up in a row. They each have a different finish — some have large, smooth pebbles embedded into the surface, others have chiselled-out chunks. These form a palette from which the architects chose the final finish for the centre, which was this hammered one, with exposed aggregate.

While we can easily see this aggregate, these little stones, when we look at the surface of the concrete, they actually form an essential part of the concrete itself. They are there for strength, not for design, and are present throughout the body of the structure. To understand its purpose, we need to explore the story and science of concrete, one which has its origins in ancient civilisations.

If you crush most types of rock into a powder and add water, you end up with an uninteresting sludge, the two parts don't hold together. But something strange happens when you heat certain rocks up to really high temperatures. Take a mixture of limestone and clay, for example, and fire them in a kiln at about 1,450 degrees Celsius, and they will fuse into small lumps without melting. Grind these lumps into a very fine powder and you've got the first ingredient.

The powder is called cement. It's a dull grey colour and might not look particularly impressive. But because it's been burned at very high temperatures, the parent materials are chemically changed. If you add water to this powder it doesn't turn into a sludge — instead, a reaction called hydration begins. The water reacts with the calcium and silicate molecules in the lime and clay to create crystal-like rods or fibres. These fibres give the material a jelly-like structure — a matrix — which is soft but stable. As the reaction continues, the fibres grow, and they bond to each other. The mixture becomes thicker and thicker until, ultimately, it solidifies.

So water + cement powder = cement paste. Cement paste hardens into a rock incredibly well, but it has its drawbacks. For a start, making it is expensive. The process also uses a large amount of energy and is carbon intensive. And importantly, hydration releases lots of heat. Once the chemical process finishes, the cement cools down, and as it cools it shrinks. And cracks. Fortunately, engineers realised that cement paste binds solidly to other rocks, and began adding aggregates (small, irregular pieces of stone and sand of varying sizes) to the mixture. The aggregates help to reduce not only the amount of cement powder being used (and hence the amount of heat being released), but also the energy consumption and hence cost. The cement paste undergoes the same chemical reaction, creating fibres that in turn bind strongly to other fibres and the aggregates — and the whole mass solidifies to give us the concrete we are familiar with today. So water + cement powder + aggregate = concrete.

To make good concrete, the proportions of this mix need to be right: too much water, and not all of it will react with the cement powder — and the concrete will be weak. Too little water and all the powder doesn't react and, again, the concrete ends up weak. For the best result, all the water needs to react with all the cement powder. And the mixing itself needs to be right too: concrete can end up poorly if it isn't stirred properly. The larger, heavier stone aggregates settle to the bottom, leaving the fine sand and cement paste at the top, making the concrete inconsistent and weak. That's why concrete trucks have giant rotating drums — the mixture is continually sloshed around so that the aggregates are nicely distributed throughout.

Ancient engineers didn't have such trucks, but their formula for concrete was pretty similar to ours. They too burned limestone and powdered it, then added water to create a paste with which to bind stones, bricks and broken tiles. However, their mixture was much lumpier and thicker than ours is today. But then the Romans found something even better. In the land around Mount Vesuvius was an ash they called *pozzolana*. Instead of using burnt limestone as a cement, they tried this ready-made ash. When they mixed it with lime, rubble and water, their resulting concrete hardened as they expected. But this mixture also hardened underwater. That's because the pozzolanic chemical reaction did not need carbon dioxide from the air to help it along: the mixture could harden without it.

The treatment of the concrete walls of the centre is one of its most distinctive features: each panel was individually treated to create a bush-hammered finish, a slow and expensive process ensuring a textured feel to the concrete.

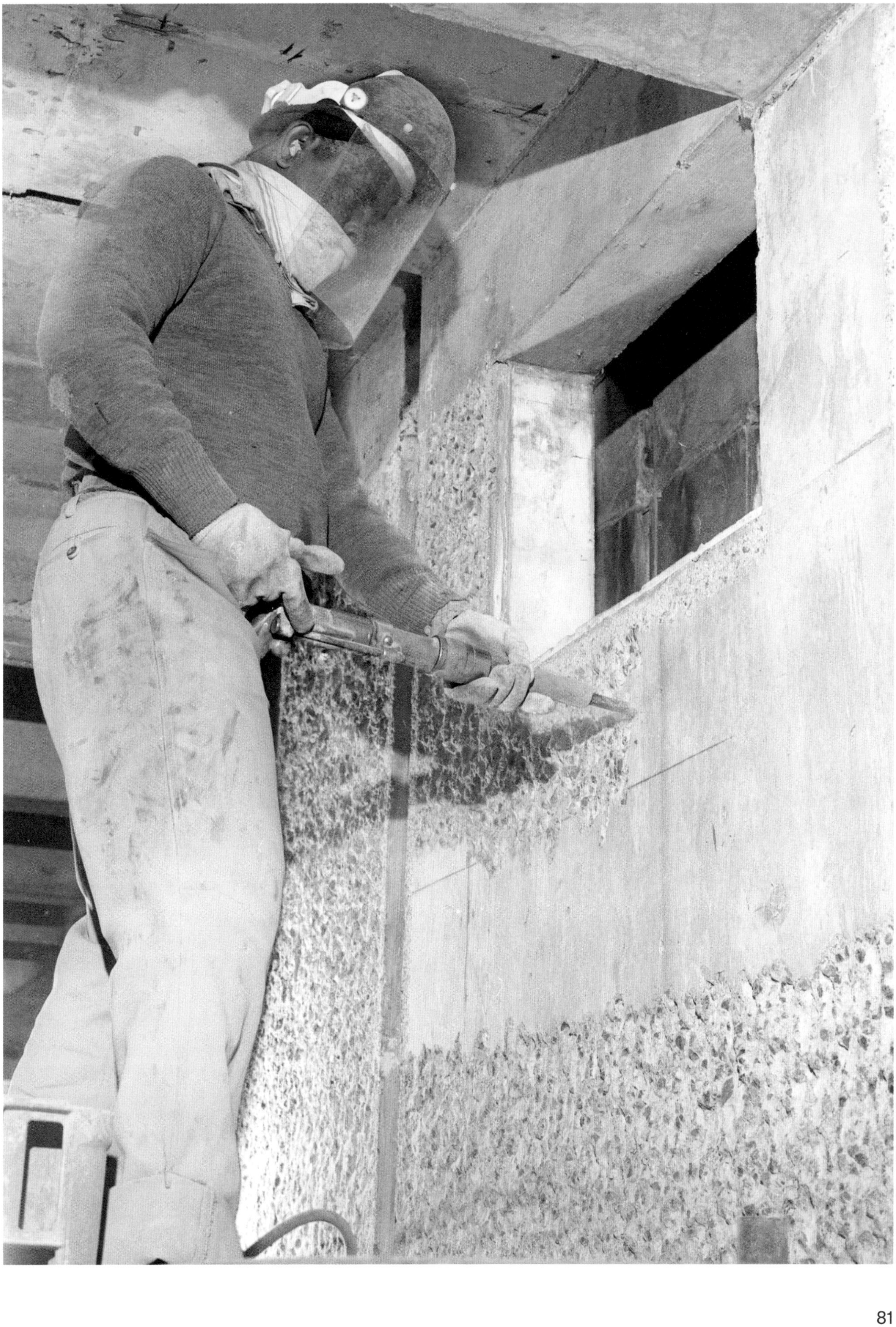

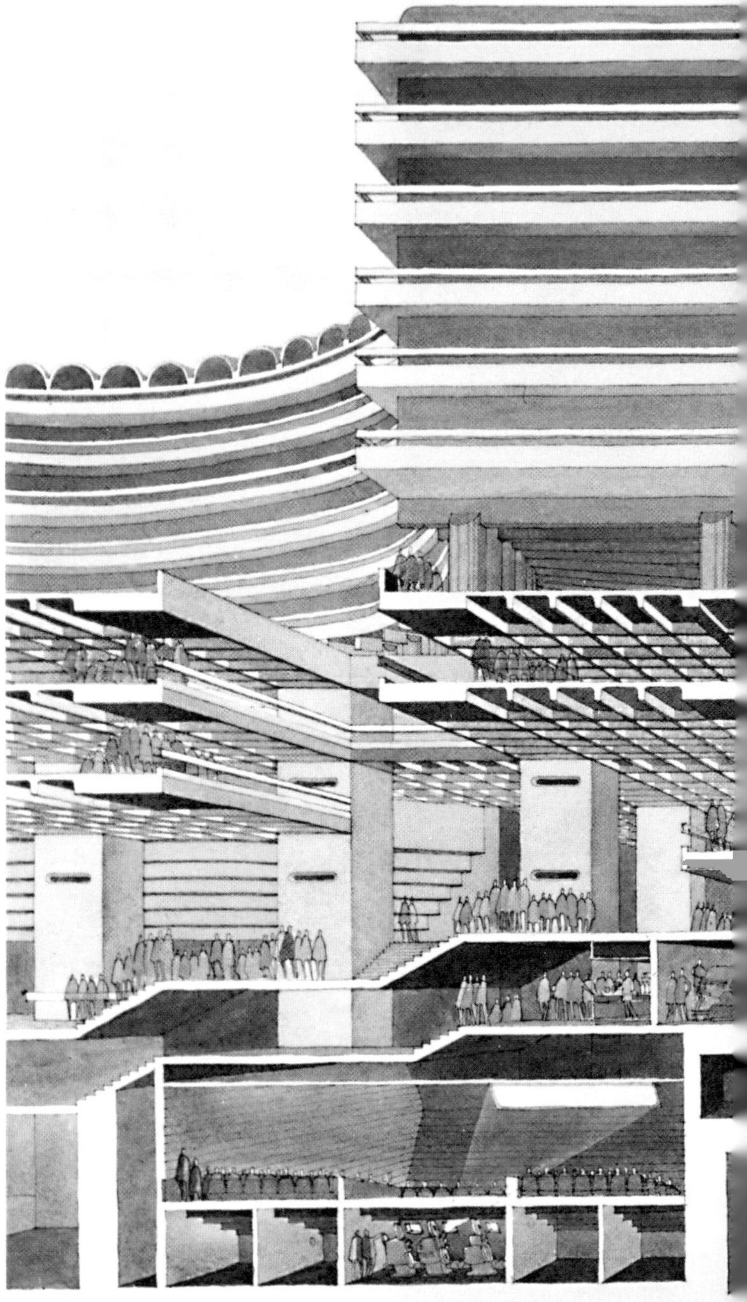

This early cross-section of the centre venues from the document *Barbican 1971* features the theatre as designed and built, and also shows (bottom left) the cinema with its proposed reclining seats and high-level projection, subsequently changed, and the creation of the conservatory around the theatre fly tower.

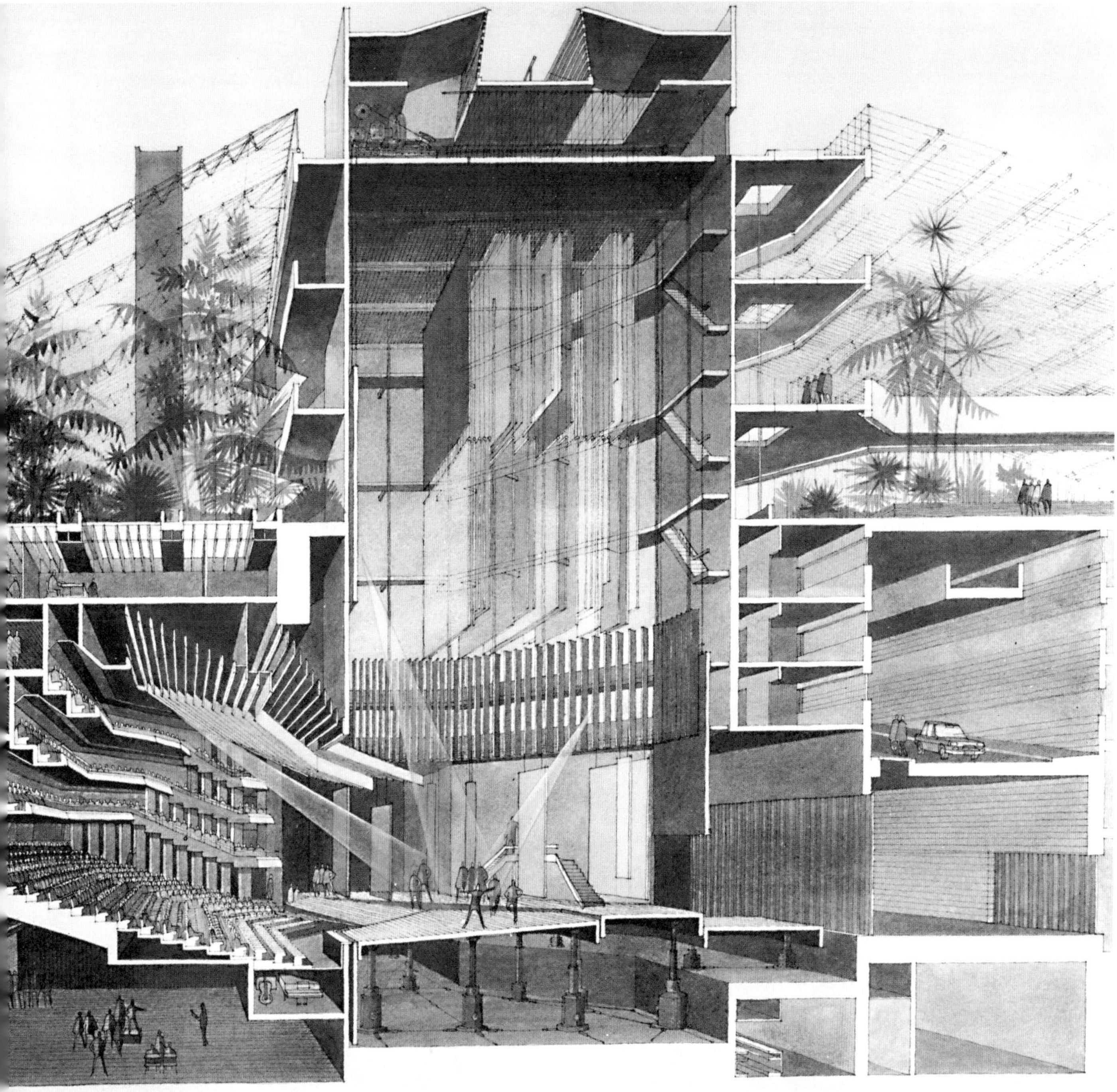

Concrete is, however, a fussy material. It loves compression, and for millennia it was used this way, being squashed in foundations or walls. But it dislikes being pulled apart. Its resistance to tension is minimal; in fact, it cracks if tested at loads less than one-tenth of what it can resist in compression. In the 1860s, French gardener Joseph Monier became fed up with the fact that his clay pots would constantly break. He tried making pots out of concrete instead but found that they fractured just as much. Randomly, he decided to reinforce the concrete by embedding a grillage of metal wires within it. This experiment could have failed for two key reasons: first, the concrete might not have actually bound to the metal reinforcement (there was no reason to think that it would), so the metal would only create more weak points in the pot. Second, during the change in seasons, the metal and concrete would expand and contract at different rates, creating yet more fissures. Unwittingly, Monier created a revolutionary pot that remained solid and barely cracked.

Like most metals, iron and steel are elastic and ductile, and they're good in tension: they don't crack when pulled. Metals aren't brittle like brick or concrete. So by combining concrete (which breaks in tension) with iron (which can absorb tension loads), Monier had created a perfect marriage of materials. In fact, an ancient version of this principle can be found in Morocco, where the walls of some Berber cities were made of mud with straw mixed in: a mixture known as adobe, also used by the Egyptians, Babylonians and Native Americans, among others. Straw fulfils a similar function to metal in concrete; it binds mud and plaster together and stops it from cracking too much because the straw resists tension forces. The plaster on the walls of my Victorian flat has horse hair mixed into it for the same reason.

Having exhibited his new material at the Paris Exposition in 1867, Monier then expanded its application to pipes and beams. Civil engineer Gustav Adolf Wayss from Germany saw the material and had visions of building entire structures with it. After buying the rights to use Monier's patent in 1879, he conducted research into concrete's use as a building material, and went on to build pioneering reinforced concrete buildings and bridges across Europe.

Concrete was coming towards the end of its fashionable status in the 1970s when the arts centre was constructed. And from a technical point of view, I sometimes wonder whether it would have been constructed from steel if designed today. It is a complex building that has large, tall, open atriums for transporting theatre equipment, long unsupported spans that hold up the seats in the concert hall, as well as mezzanine levels and a maze of rooms that form offices, a library and many more rooms. Steel is a light and versatile material that seems a good choice. But materials aren't chosen in isolation. The arts centre was part of a larger estate, where concrete was certainly the right choice. And in this building, it works. The countless hours of effort put in by men in visors to give the building its look have endured, and I can't imagine it any other way.

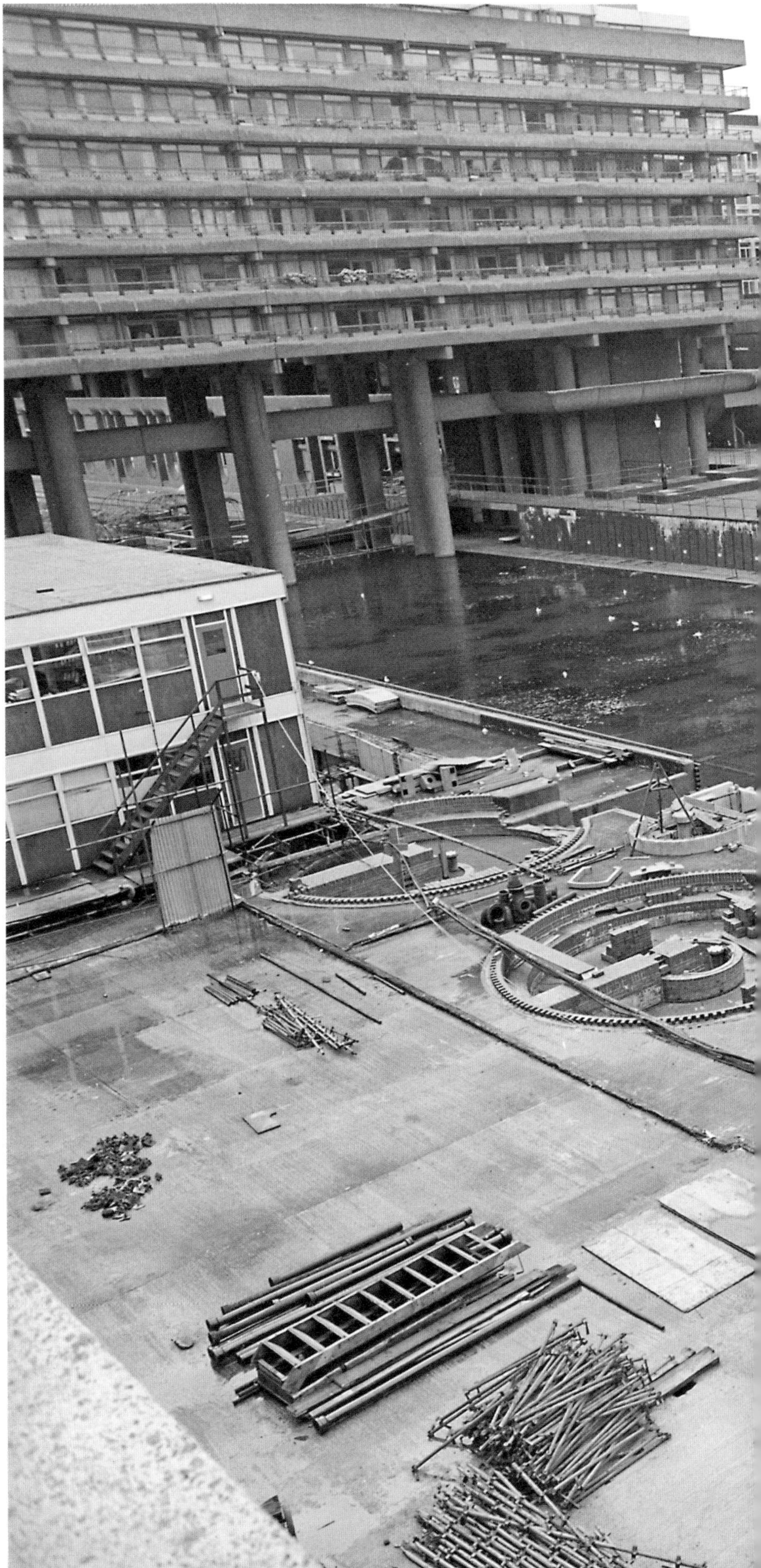

This historic series of photographs by Peter Bloomfield was commissioned by Henry Wrong, the first managing director of the Barbican, to show the completion of the building project in 1979–82.

The lakeside fountains begin to emerge from the concrete.

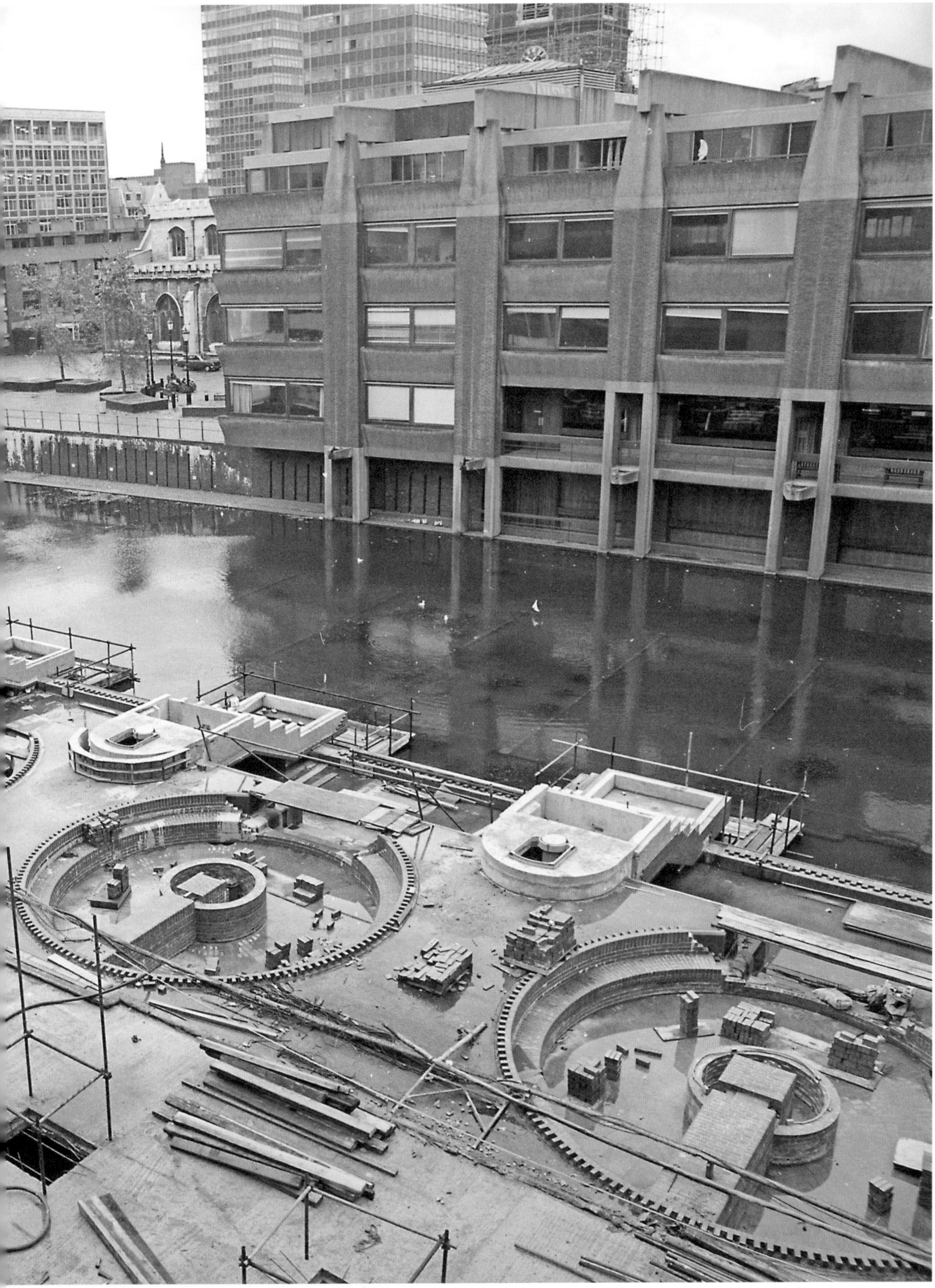

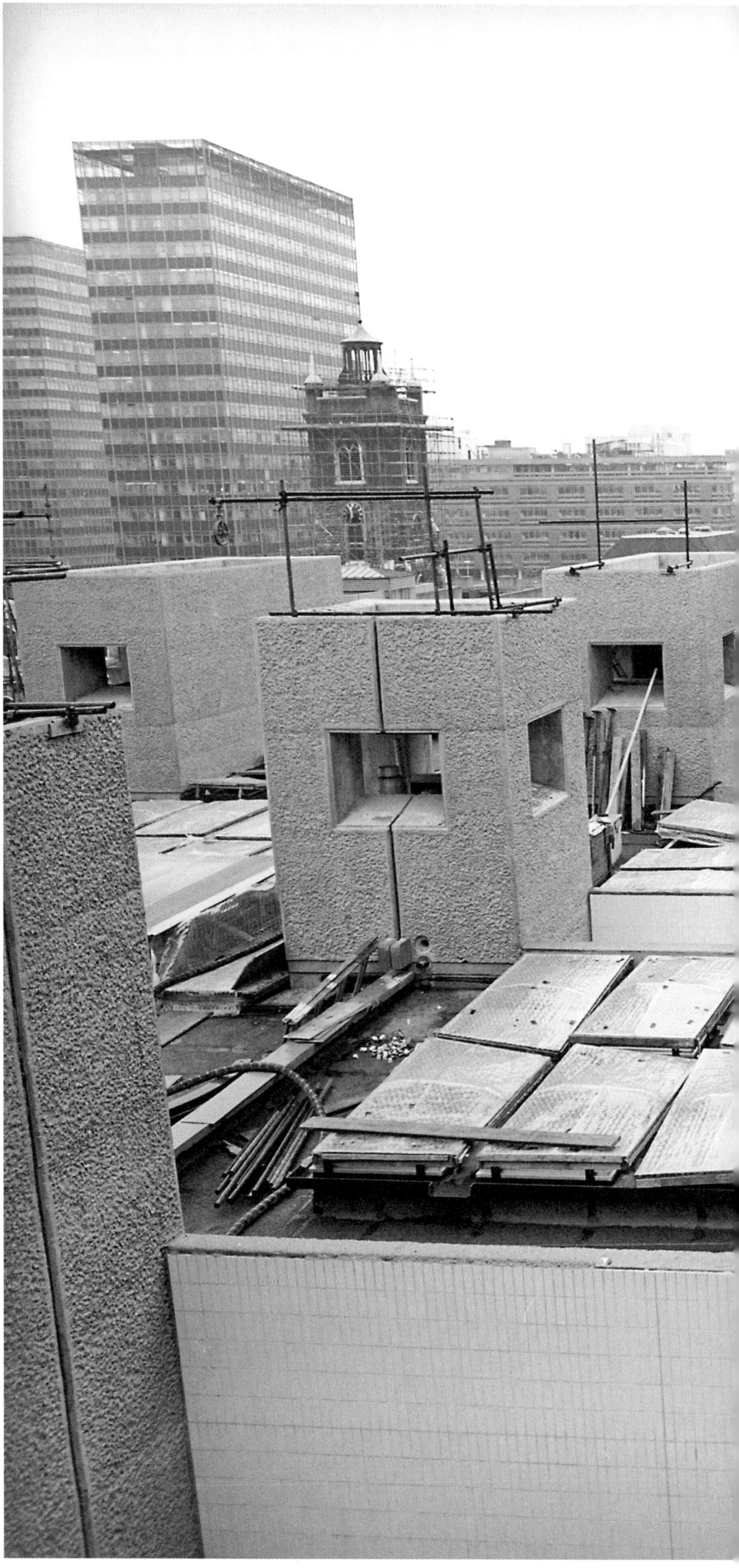

The roof of the building being assembled.

Following pages
Trees lifted by crane to be planted in the conservatory.

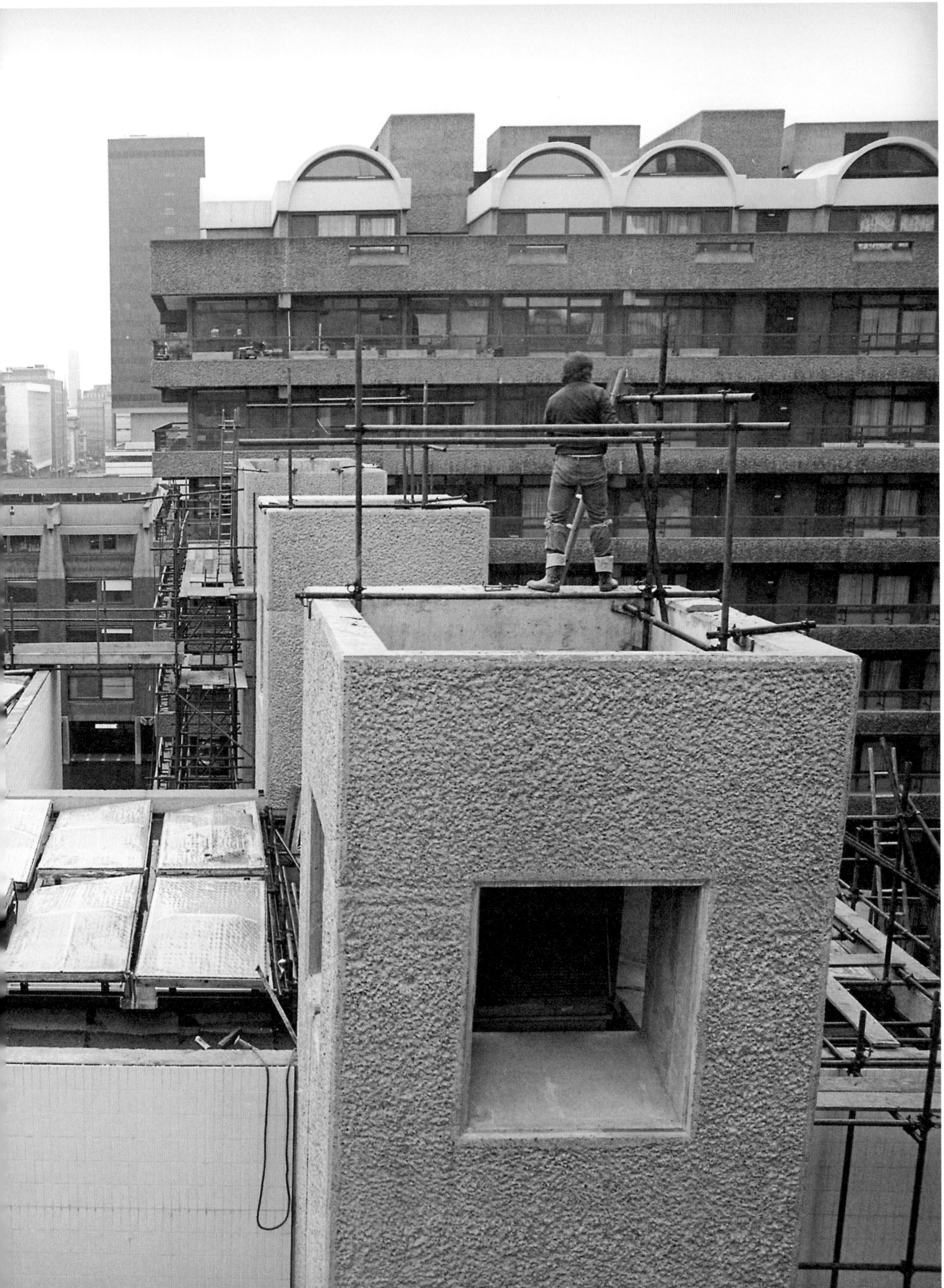

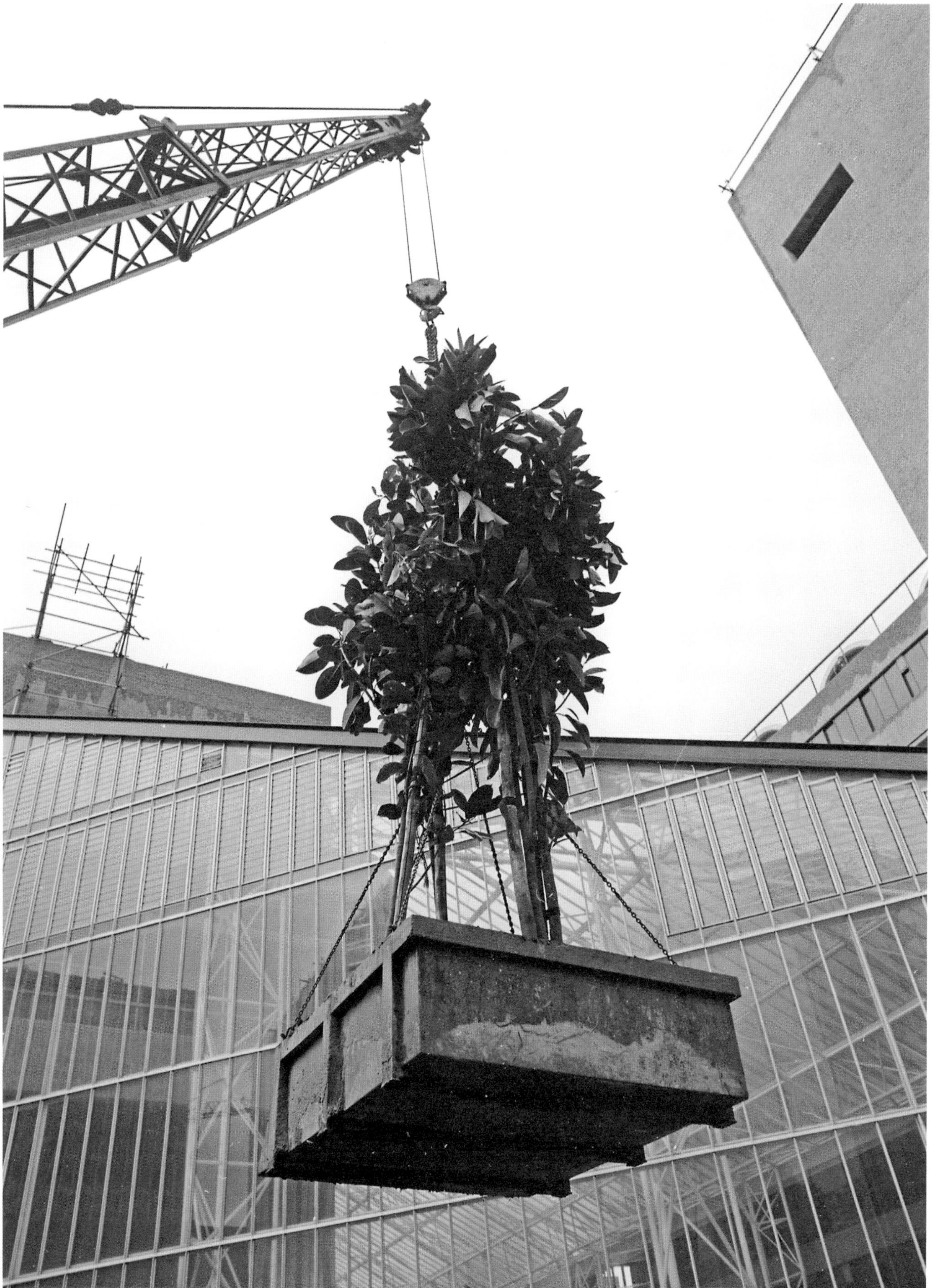

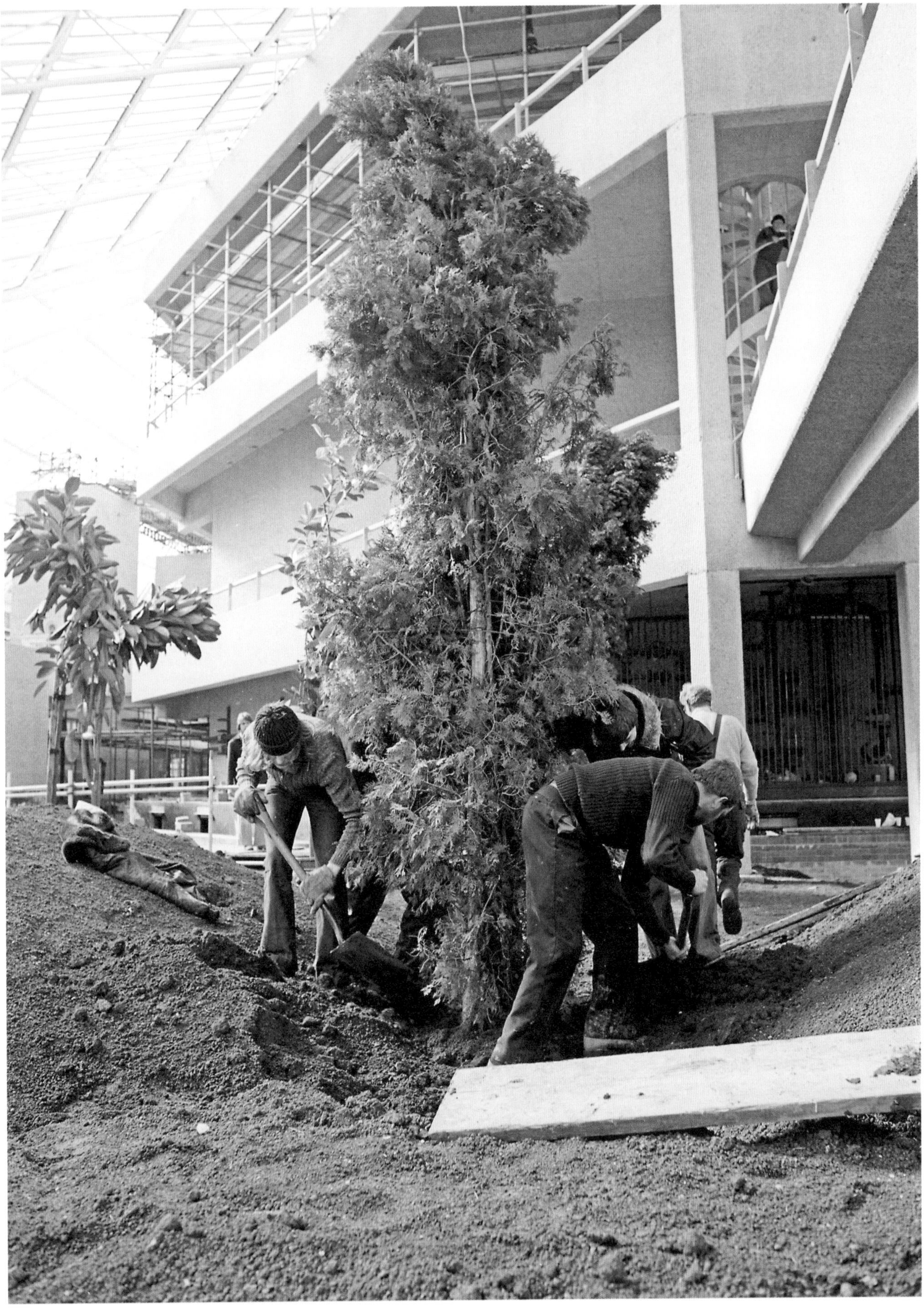

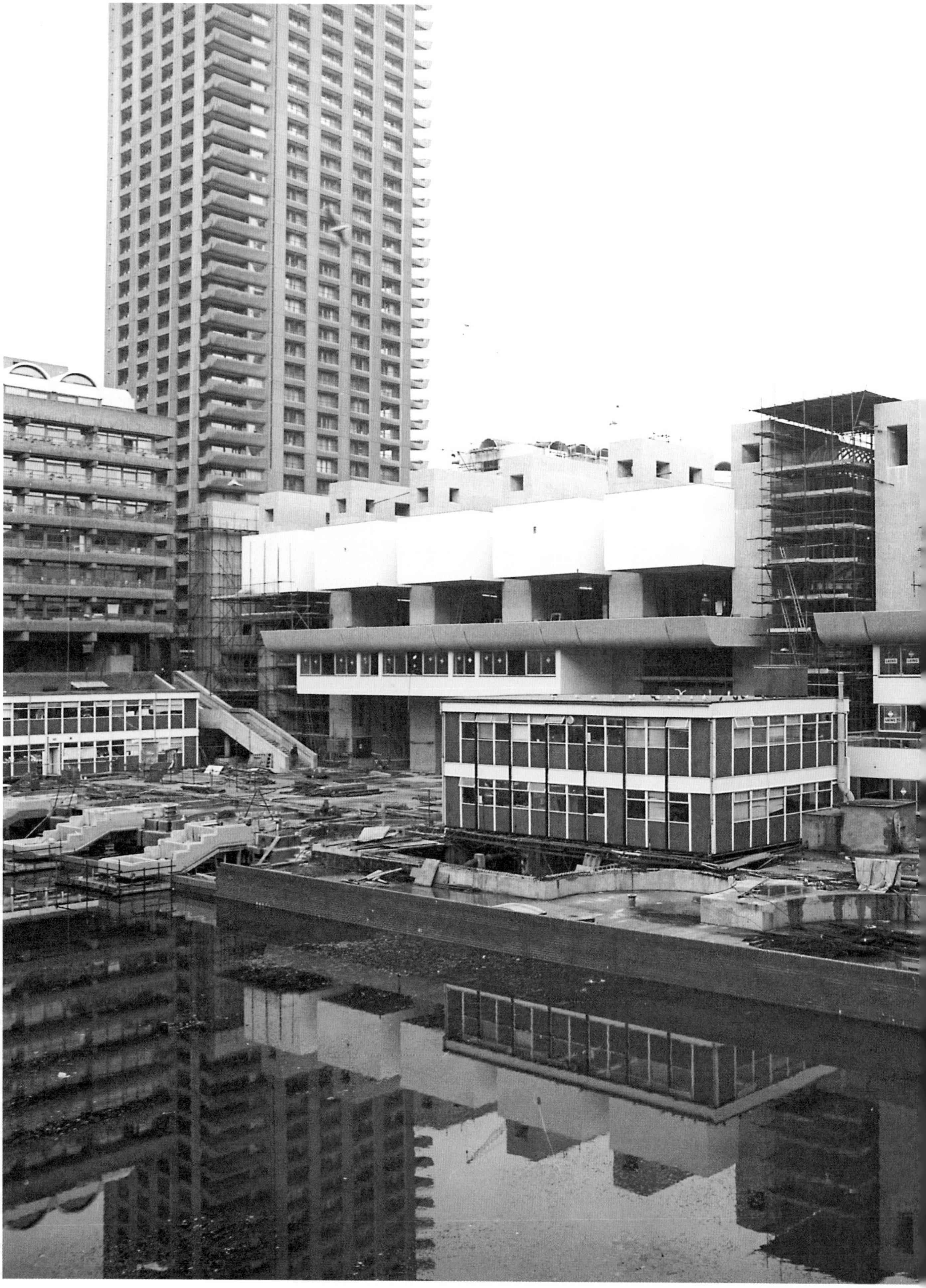

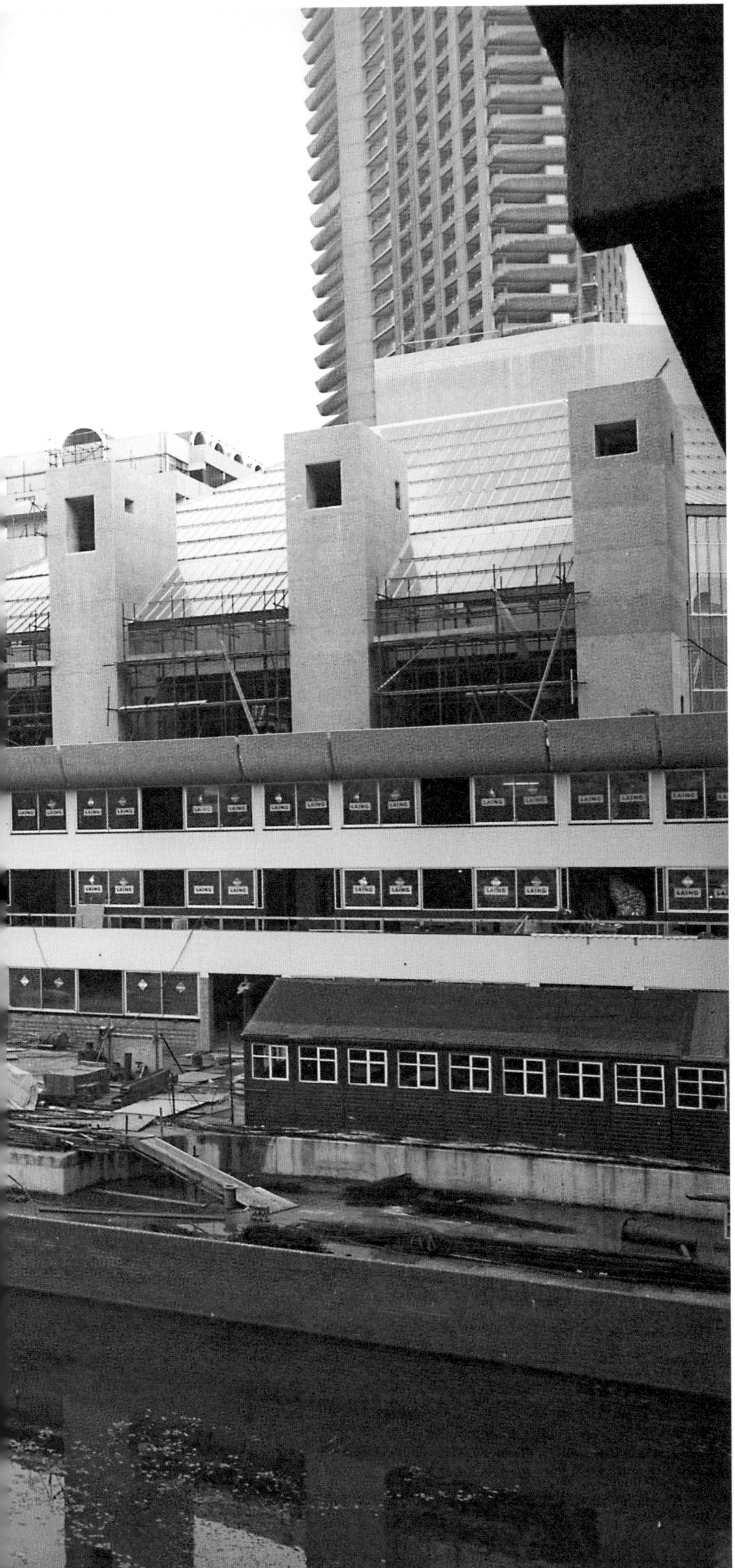

Temporary buildings for the construction on the Lakeside Terrace, reflected in the lake.

Following page
Frobisher Crescent and the Sculpture Court during construction.

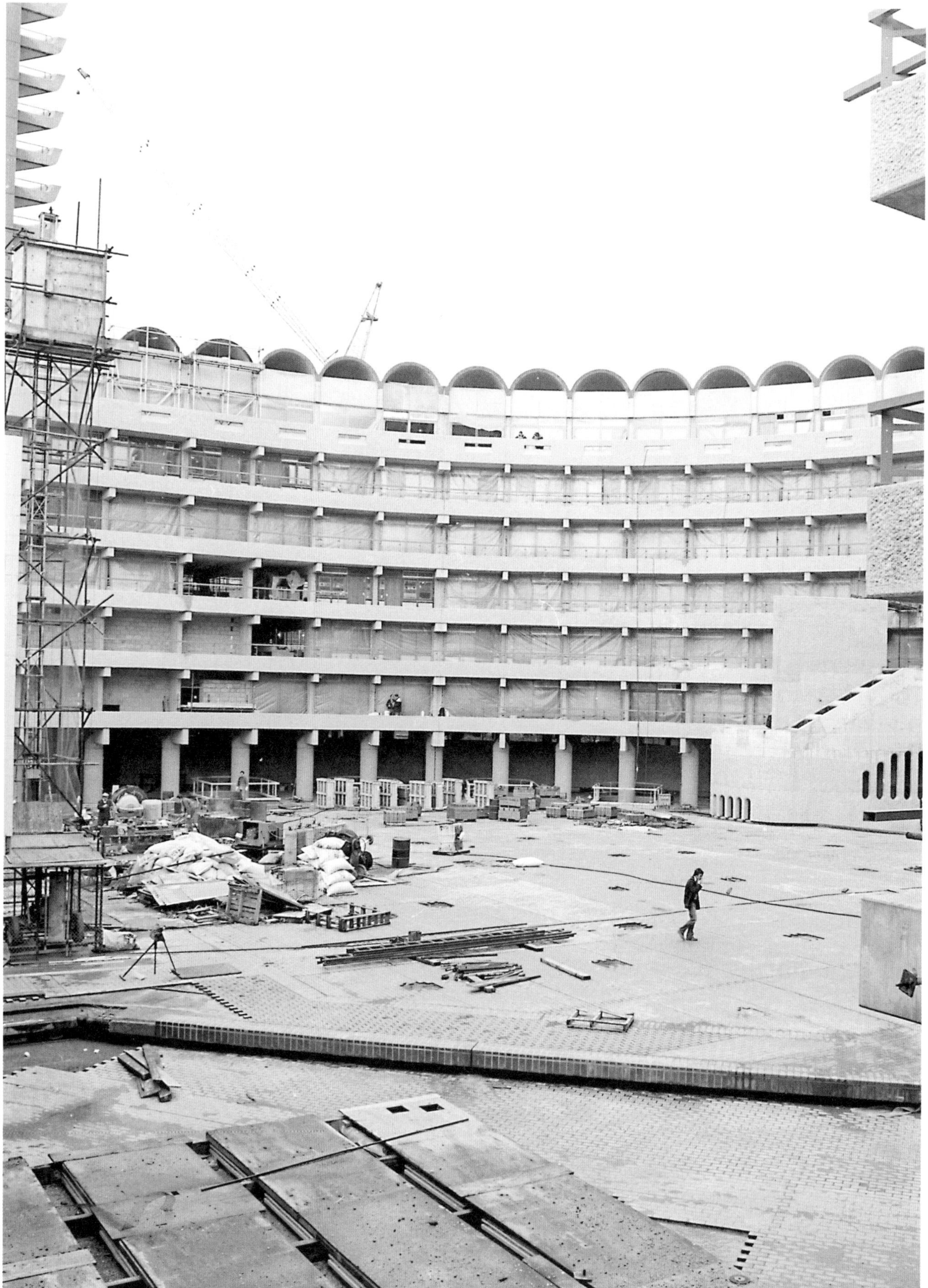

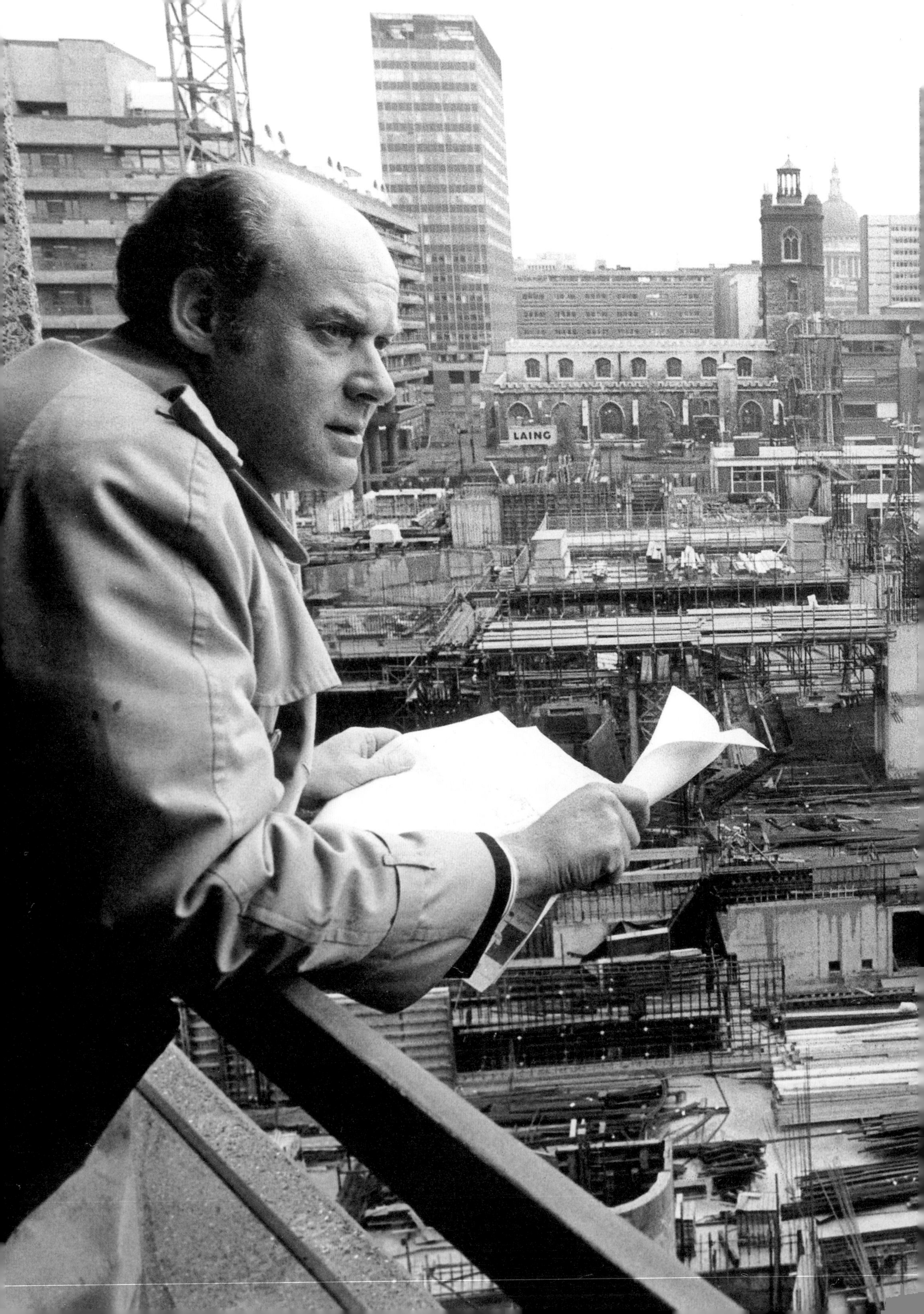
LAING

Henry Wrong

The Barbican Centre owes its existence to the foresight and generosity of the City of London Corporation. In the 19th century, local governments built monuments to civic pride. Yet this was not the City's main motivation; rather it wanted to create an artistic amenity for the country. Never before had a local authority so ambitiously planned an arts centre capable of providing a permanent home for a renowned orchestra and theatre company (the London Symphony Orchestra and the Royal Shakespeare Company), as well as an art gallery, library, cinemas and one of the foremost colleges of music and drama, the Guildhall School. Once the centre was completed, however, the Corporation could indeed be proud of its achievement, described as the 'City's gift to the nation'.

It was originally envisaged that the centre would house an orchestra that would assume responsibility for the running costs of the hall. As reality dawned, however, it became evident that this would not be viable. The Corporation took over the centre's overall management and, after considerable discussion, the Arts Council agreed to the partial support of two resident companies. All this meant that office space had to be found for both the LSO and the RSC, as well as the centre's own administration. In the end, Frobisher Crescent, planned as flats, was cannibalised to create offices, making a large quantity of curved bath fittings surplus to requirements.

Rising building costs forced the City to look for additional income. As London was fast becoming a centre for important conferences and exhibitions, new conference rooms were created and two exhibition halls were carved out of an area initially designated for warehousing. The design of the concert hall was adapted to accommodate conferences, with interpretation booths in the rear wall of the auditorium.

As the building programme progressed, so the artistic planning began, and the inter-relationship between the RSC and the LSO became very important. The idea that events could incorporate all parts of the centre appealed to the staff, who soon developed a wonderful esprit de corps. Our aim was to promote the new arts centre on an international as well as national level. The Foreign Office, through the British Council, brought it to the attention of a number of foreign embassies, in particular that of France.

In 1982, promoting and selling the arts, and indeed conferences and exhibitions, was a very different undertaking from today. Back then, the new centre was pursuing a course through uncharted waters in stormy conditions. Both the centre and the LSO were forced to develop a new marketing strategy. In doing so, we were enormously helped by the young impresario Raymond Gubbay, who worked with the centre to create a more popular level of musical promotions. At the same time, the LSO successfully challenged the Arts Council and the Corporation for a considerable rise in subsidy. This enabled the orchestra to introduce a breathtaking new series of events, beginning with Mahler, Vienna and the 20th Century and followed by the Rostropovich 60th birthday series in 1987. These two events set the tone of what the Barbican could offer and established a blueprint for years to come.

Excerpt from Henry Wrong's memoir in *Barbican at 25*, 2007.

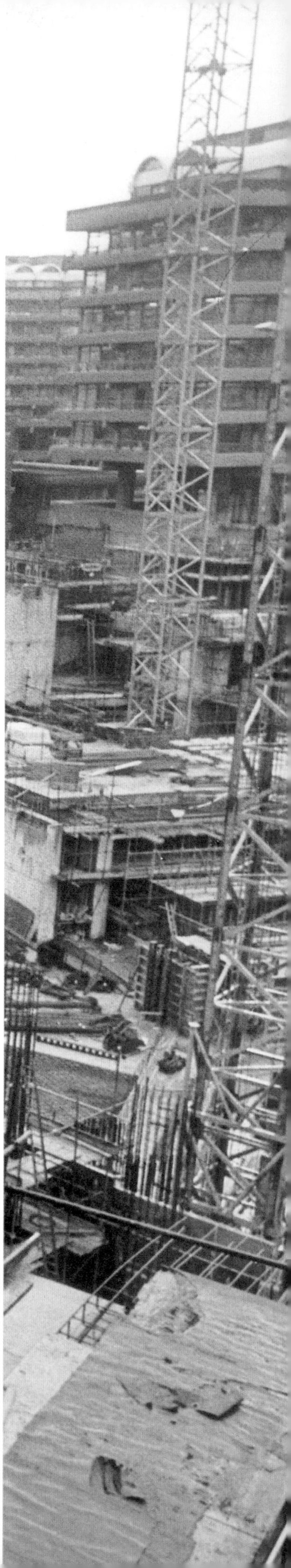

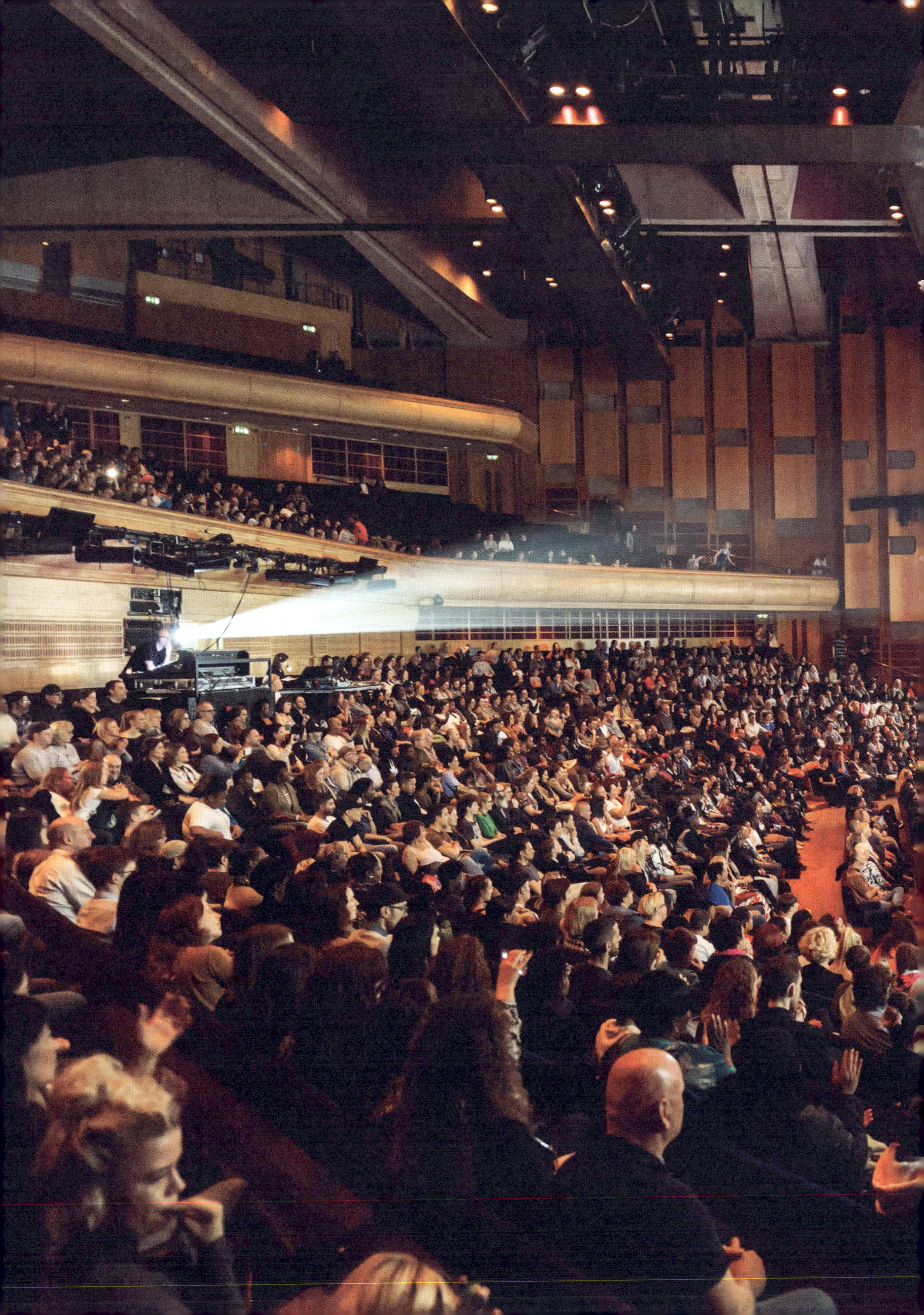

Raymond Gubbay

After a succession of delays, by 1979 it looked as though the Barbican Centre would be opening two years later and so I wrote to Henry Wrong to introduce myself and to express an interest in promoting concerts in the new concert hall. My first visit to the Barbican followed a few weeks later when I met Henry for the first time. Wearing boots and a hard hat, we made our way into the centre. Although it was unfinished, all the main features were in place with the roof on and so it was possible to visit every part of the building and to begin to imagine how it would look when it was fully fitted out. The sheer size and scale of the project made a deep and immediate impression on me and I realised at once that nothing on this scale was ever likely to be built again in London in my lifetime. So I resolved on the spot to take dates there.

The planned opening for 1981 was later put back a year with the new opening date set for 3 March 1982, and I reserved a few dates in April and May to follow the opening concert season by the London Symphony Orchestra. In February, tickets for the April dates went on sale. A few days after the tickets had gone on sale, I telephoned the box office for the sales reports; the initial figures were not bad but neither were they overly encouraging. Two days later, I rang again for an update and discovered that the figures had shot up. So I called the box office manager to make sure there had not been a mistake. No, not at all, he said, it was just that they had been overwhelmed by the amount of postal bookings and it was taking them some time to process all of these. Within a few days, all three concerts had sold out and I found myself having to schedule extra performances – and all of this before the centre had actually opened.

My relationship with the centre blossomed almost immediately. I suddenly found myself with sold-out concerts, and offers to take on more and more dates. The symphony concerts that I organised seemed to sell out quickly and there were often queues waiting for return tickets. In the first year, I promoted over 50 concerts with average attendance of over 90 per cent. The Barbican was clearly working for me and working well – at a time when concerts elsewhere in London seemed to be getting more difficult to sell. Quite why I had struck gold when others had failed was never absolutely clear to me. I was described later as the man who pre-packaged concerts, doing for music what Marks and Spencer did for food – I was never quite sure whether that was intended as a compliment. I took risks and developed new ideas. Whatever it was, it certainly put me well and truly on the map.

Within 18 months of the Barbican's opening, I was promoting about 125 concerts and events a year. This even included some lunchtime concerts, which proved very popular at the time and one actually sold out, which was amazing for a venue seating more than 2,000. Turning people away at lunchtime was an entirely new sensation which I rather enjoyed.

Raymond Gubbay was one of London's most active independent concert promoters, whose popular events did much to attract audiences in the early years of the Barbican. Now mainly retired, he has published a memoir, *Lowering the Tone and Raising the Roof*.

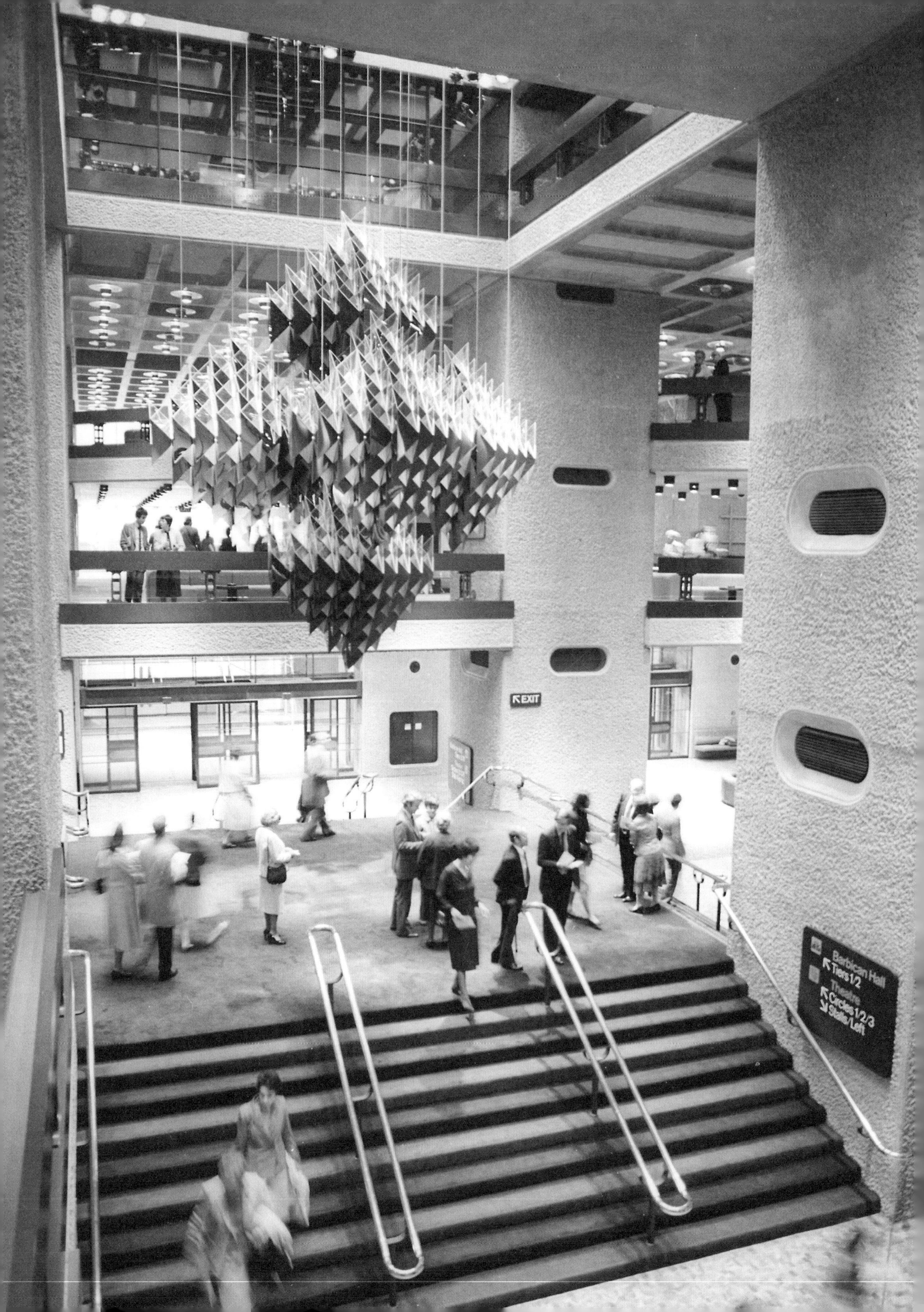
EXIT
Barbican Hall
Tiers 1/2
Theatre
Circles 1/2/3
Stalls/Left

Running the Barbican 1
A conversation with Philip Dodd

Richard York, Caroline York and Antony Lewis-Crosby

The first administrator of the Barbican Centre, appointed in October 1970, was Henry Wrong, who guided the enterprise through its protracted building programme in the 1970s up to its opening in March 1982, and ran the centre until 1989. He assembled around him a senior team including Richard York, Caroline Phillips (now York) and Antony Lewis-Crosby. Wrong remained a passionate enthusiast for the Barbican, cultivated good relations with his later successors John Tusa and Nicholas Kenyon, and felt that he had never received his due from the City for the commitment he had shown to the institution. Henry Wrong died in August 2017.

PD *The Barbican opens in 82: the Thatcher government is vigorously shaking up the thorny relationship of the public and the private, privatising public assets; and Channel 4 is launched, with a public service remit yet commercially funded. The Barbican enters this maelstrom — funded not by the Arts Council but by the City Corporation, a local authority like no other, driven by the wealth and power of the private City of London. How would you describe the Barbican's early relationship with the Corporation?*

CY It was a great shock. I'd worked in institutions where those who governed it were there to support the organisation. In the Corporation initially there was no real idea of what it wanted from the Barbican, nor experience of an arts centre, nor how to incorporate it into its usual way of working. Many Common Councillors thought it a monumental waste of money, and there had been repeated attempts to scale it back in the previous years. The resulting Committee of over 20 Common Councillors appointed to oversee the centre's management comprised perhaps around 50 per cent who were anti the organisation and 50 per cent who thought they were pro, but who could easily be blown off course.

RY Looking back, I now realise that I thought of myself as working for the Barbican, but I actually needed to know much more about how the Corporation worked. The Corporation provided no induction for new senior employees, and handed a new member of staff a diary which included a set of Standing Orders. Not something common in arts organisations! We were working within a very unusual, rather special local authority.

ALC From my point of view we were just expected to get on with it by the Corporation. It's thought they provided all our necessary income but that wasn't entirely the case: box office income and private support were also vital. I was often asked to go to beg for money. I remember we began to develop a series of big international festivals which needed serious funding. I was sent off to ask the Corporation for an extra quarter of a million pounds to mount the French Festival in 1988. Henry [Wrong]was flabbergasted when I came back with the money. He then took on a sponsorship consultant, Moira Bennett, whose role was to increase corporate support, which began to work well.

PD *The City was globalising during the 80s. Were the Barbican's international ambitions attractive to the City? Compared with other cultural institutions, the Barbican was very global — Brazilian art, Japanese culture, American folk art …*

ALC Yes. The Corporation slowly did begin to

understand the Barbican's value — that it could play an international role, a significant role in the world for the City. We were already linking up with cultural centres across Europe, particularly on the music side, making connections that really helped the work of the City.

RY There was the Hungarian festival in 1989, attended both by Margaret Thatcher and the Hungarian Prime Minister, and subsequently they met on a government level. The Barbican opened doors — that was invaluable to the City.

PD *In its early days the Barbican was described as an arts and conference centre — was there tension between the two imperatives? After all, the Barbican opened during the early Thatcher years. She wanted to rethink the culture/commerce relationship …*

RY The push for conferences was quite a late development in the Barbican plan when it became evident how much money the arts centre would cost to run. The slightly unrealistic idea was that conferences would significantly reduce that cost. But when I arrived, there was a very small team marketing the building as a conference centre with very little work done on the arts beyond keeping the LSO and RSC warm — arts events and conference were often vying for the same spaces and it was only when the two departments had achieved comparable weight that a way of working emerged. The timetables of arts events and conferences did not always complement one another!

ALC From 1985, when the London Symphony Orchestra programmed in the concert hall across the 12 months, there were problems between the arts programme and conferences, not least because the Corporation saw the conferences as money generators, and orchestras as money spenders; it wasn't at all as simple as that, especially when you had potential income-earning concerts for example in the Christmas period, up against commercial lets for graduations: that was a nightmare!

RY Yes, in the end, the Corporation's finance people were surprised to discover that the subsidy to conference attendees was around the same as for concert-goers — however, trade exhibitions did produce a real surplus to the centre's finances.

PD *Am I right to think that originally the LSO and the RSC were givens — and the rest of the programme had to develop around them?*

CY The two organisations were independent and separate. It was hard in the early days to persuade the RSC to think of the Barbican as a whole. It said, 'This is our theatre; this is what we are doing'. The LSO negotiated periods when they had the use of the Barbican Hall and in which they were free to programme as they wished.

PD *So the Barbican had no artistic say with the RSC, whether it was* Henry IV Part I *or* Les Misérables?

RY No, but one of the interesting things about the first seven years is that the RSC was a real success — a considerable one. People liked the theatre, similar in size to the Aldwych where the RSC had been, the box office was very strong. On the other hand, the LSO struggled in the early years — with early evening concerts which simply did not work. It was only by 1985 things began to change. As the LSO picked up, and became well-established and successful, the RSC started to fall back. I don't think there was ever a moment, in my time anyway, when the two were equally successful at the same time.

ALC And for the concert hall there were acoustic problems from the start, rather public criticism from Claudio Abbado and others … In the opening year '82 I programmed a Haydn festival — the conductor John Eliot Gardiner was involved in the programme — it turned him against the Barbican. He hated the acoustic. It wasn't until the early 90s and after that the acoustic problems were dealt with and Gardiner returned to conduct the LSO regularly.

PD *Was the BBC important to the music programme? After all, the BBC has had a long relationship with the Barbican — its last two directors are ex-BBC people?*

ALC Well, the first big BBC connection was in 1985 — a Stockhausen festival with BBC funding. After initial tiny audiences, it became a sell-out success and was the foundation stone for the BBC composer-led festivals ever since. But it is not as if the BBC was the first to bring modernist music into the Barbican. The LSO had similar interests and played Webern very early on with mixed results. Then Abbado brought his friend Hans Landesmann in to advise them, and they did a big series, *Mahler, Vienna, and the 20th Century*, which included recent music. It was a huge risk, and a big success. As a result of that, we retained Hans as an artistic advisor and he made many valuable European connections for us with major musicians. The Corporation's attitude? Well at that time it cared only about the bottom line — if a small number of people had paid huge sums of money for Stockhausen that would have been fine. The size of audiences as such did not matter to it, whereas we had the desire to attract people to the widest range of music, from Stockhausen and Gorecki to Nina Simone and Victor Borge.

PD *So you have a programme with Stockhausen in the concert hall and* Les Misérables *in the theatre — high and low, avant-garde and popular — how did you imagine the Barbican in the existing ecology of London's arts venues?*

ALC There are a number of different answers — one involves remembering what happened at the opening. We decided that the building should have a foyer full of activities — predating the Southbank's actions in that area. There was a lot of jazz and children's activities, building tours, small informative exhibitions — and people poured in, partly just to experience the building.

RY You have to remember that these were also the days of Ken Livingstone and the GLC, which wanted culture for the people: they wanted to open up the Festival Hall and get rid of champagne bars. For us, to be honest, I think there was lot of pragmatism in those early days about what you now would call the positioning of the Barbican.

CY Yes, I don't think we ever sat down as a team and said there will be x of this and y of that. There were Raymond Gubbay popular concerts as well as John Lill performing the Beethoven sonatas at lunchtime. We didn't want too much of this or that, because it needed to be a mixed model and we had to keep a close look at the money coming in. But I do remember that around early 1980, when the senior team were all in post, a group of 17 of us wrote a policy paper, each one addressing a separate economic activity, for the Barbican Centre Committee. This paper described a plausible mix of events for a model financial year (which would be some years after the opening), providing a basis for calculating potential income and quantifying the resources needed to support the programme. In the event the management team was necessarily pragmatic.

PD *The early days of the Barbican were prior to the moment when education became prioritised in arts and culture …*

RY The element of education certainly hadn't become so prominent. That was part of the whole change of giving funding with strings strongly attached: when people would say, 'We'll give you a grant, but you have to do X, Y, and Z with it.'

ALC … but I do remember making a proposal for an education officer to come in to work in the arts department in the late 80s. Henry rejected it, partly because he couldn't see its value to the centre and partly just for financial reasons. Clearly one of my less successful bids!

RY At that time there was also a growth in sponsorship and the pursuit of sponsorship: one of the elements in that was the realisation that education is attractive to sponsors because the shareholders are more likely to back that than a Chairman's party.

PD *There was a major change in 1989 — a sign of the Thatcherite times. When Henry Wrong stepped down, Detta O'Cathain, formerly managing director of the Milk Marketing Board, was appointed managing director. I know the Barbican invited her to participate in these interviews before her death in 2021, and I am personally sorry she did not do so.*

RY She was brought in because the Corporation made the mistake that many other organisations have made: that somebody from industry or commerce would get a grip on this place and reduce the costs.

PD *Were the financial circumstances of the Barbican dire before she was appointed?*

RY In a financial sense, in 1989 to 1990, we actually returned significant unspent subsidy to the corporation—a combination of better than projected business in a number of areas, some rationalisation of revenue projects mainly to do with the building, and the savings arising from an eight-month vacancy in the managing director's office. I think she inherited a very robust organisation.

PD *If she were sitting here, do you think she would agree?*

ALC No. She had been told quite clearly that the Barbican could be improved, so she came in with that view. I mean, to be fair, she didn't block any of the artistic schemes that we were already brewing, such as the big international festivals. To an extent she probably revelled in the Scandinavian Festival, *Tender is the North*, the biggest of them all. We had a massive gathering of prime ministers, presidents, Scandinavian royalty and the Queen. I think those occasions suited her very well. I just wish she had had a greater ability to talk to the arts world. Some performers found her impossible to deal with.

PD *I want to ask you whether you think the ability of the arts world to speak the language of commerce is as weak as the business world's capacity to speak the language of the arts?*

ALC I think the old comment is still true: when you have a Board, with a mix of artists and business people, the business people tend to leave their brains at the door.

RY Business sponsorship became a critical component from around '85 onwards. In this bit of London, you are very immersed in money and sponsorship and as the relationships between the Corporation and Barbican developed, things got better. I think the arts world of the 1980s and since has been at great pains to learn the language of the business world and indeed, reverting to the beginning of this discussion, to learn the language of local government!

PD *If I may say so, I am not sure that those responsible for the early period of the Barbican history have done themselves or the history any favours. Certainly, in the ecology of the arts in 80s London, the Barbican is a shining light of internationalisation.*

ALC I take your point. To some extent, our successors wanted to put across the view that they were rescuing the Barbican artistically in every way. I don't enjoy reading about that! They were building on and developing what we had put in place.

PD *What would you have done differently with the Barbican that succeeded you?*

ALC In terms of the artistic programme, probably nothing. But I still believe its roots were in what we did in the first decade, that our programme was very important in allowing our successors to do what they did.

RY I think the way the world changed also helped the Barbican. The evolution of the conference business was rapid, and the exhibition business soon found better places in London to do their things. The pressure to produce a vast quantity of events diminished. It made it easier to raise the quality, at least in those days when funding was sufficient. Looking back, we spent too much of our time writing papers to committees—which I'd quite like to re-read actually.

CY So would I.

PD *I can recommend more exciting reading.*

CY Yes, quite.

Richard York
Richard York joined the Barbican in 1977 as assistant administrator, number two to Henry Wrong. After a number of changes of job title, he became deputy director to Wrong as director. He left in 1991, shortly after the arrival of Wrong's successor Detta O'Cathain. Raymond Gubbay describes Richard York as 'the unsung hero of the Barbican who dug Henry out of many holes both before and after the centre opened'.

Caroline York
Caroline York, then Caroline Phillips, joined the Barbican in 1979 as head of finance, managing the finance structures, budgets and longer-term forecasts of the centre as part of the central management team. She left in 1988.

Antony Lewis-Crosby
Antony Lewis-Crosby joined in 1979 initially as head of planning; the job developed gradually into arts director. The role of the arts team included planning the international cross-centre festivals, programming the music in the Barbican Hall, cinema, foyer music and exhibitions programme including what is now the Curve, and co-ordinating programme planning with the LSO and later on with the RSC. He left in February 1994 to manage the Royal Liverpool Philharmonic Orchestra.

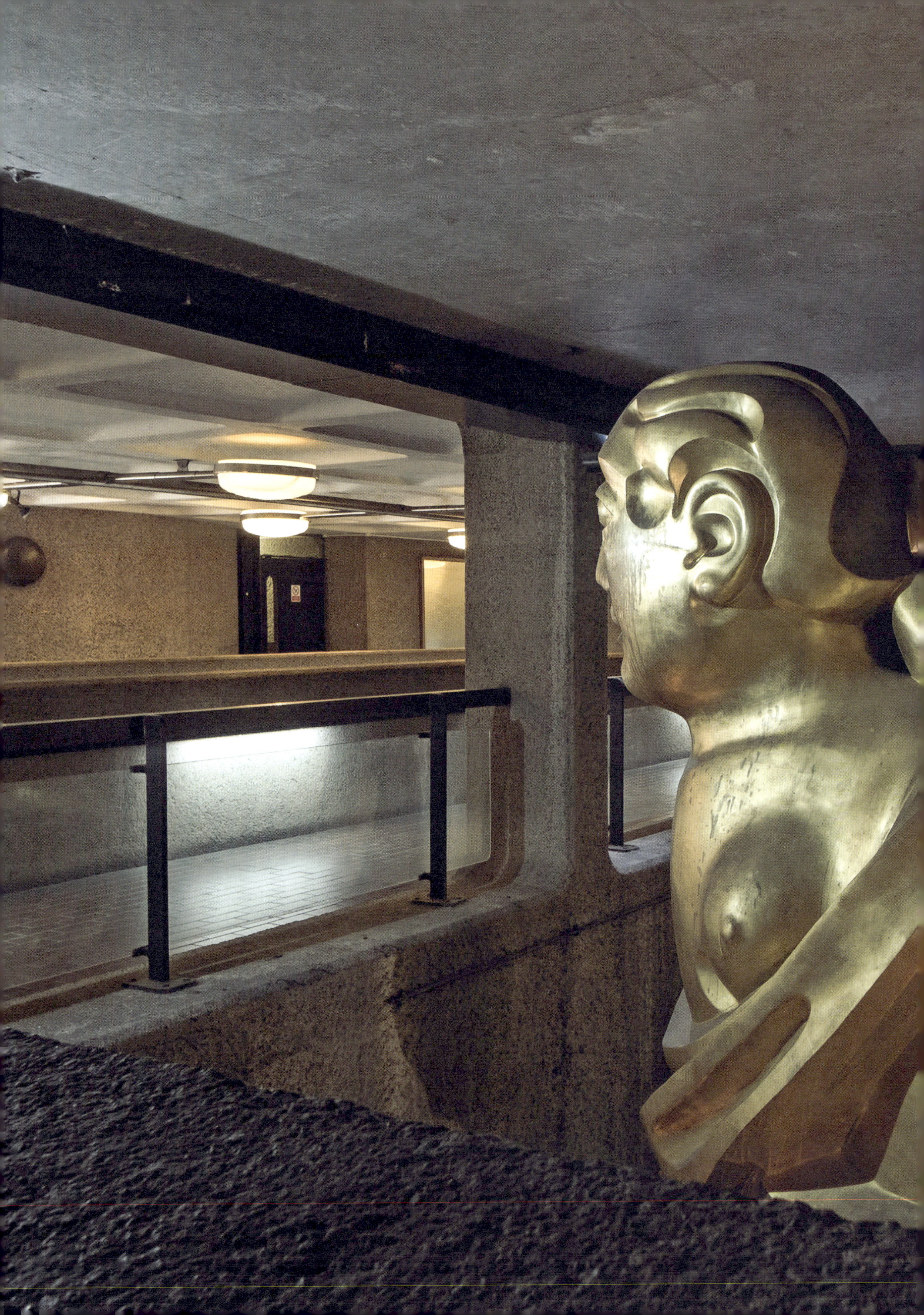

Detta O'Cathain

When Detta O'Cathain died in April 2021, *The Irish Times* described her as 'the most successful Irish woman there had ever been in the business and political life of Britain'. She had created her success in business not by abandoning her Irish heritage (her surname a Gaelic form of the name Kane) but by recognising that she would have greater opportunities in the UK and that if she had stayed in Ireland she might have, as she crisply put it, 'remained a grade 3 clerk at Aer Lingus' where she had worked since leaving school.

She progressed through businesses (applying to one while protesting against its advert which read 'the man appointed will be …'), working for Unigate, and then moved to a managing role at the Milk Marketing Board, establishing herself on the boards of Midland Bank and Tesco, and making regular appearances on BBC TV's *Question Time*. She was approached to take over the Barbican Centre in succession to Henry Wrong in 1990, at a Thatcherite moment when the perception of the City Corporation was that its spending needed to be reined in, and should be run by a manager with a firm cost-control background.

She supported the major international arts festivals that were already in the planning, and relished the political profile these provided, much increasing the visibility of the Barbican. She brought *Question Time* to the centre, and made improvements to the building. But the relations with the resident companies and the staff were very difficult, and her impatience for change, allied to a lack of understanding of the art forms, created a rapid turnover of staff. The City renewed her contract in 1994, but there was then a public campaign in the press against her leadership led by the artistic partners including the RSC and LSO. When she insisted that the City ask them for their support, they declined and she left the organisation.

She remained 'Baroness O'Cathain of the Barbican in the City of London' (though always referred to as Detta), moved from the cross benches to the Conservatives, and established a prominent and often controversial presence in the House of Lords until her recent illness.

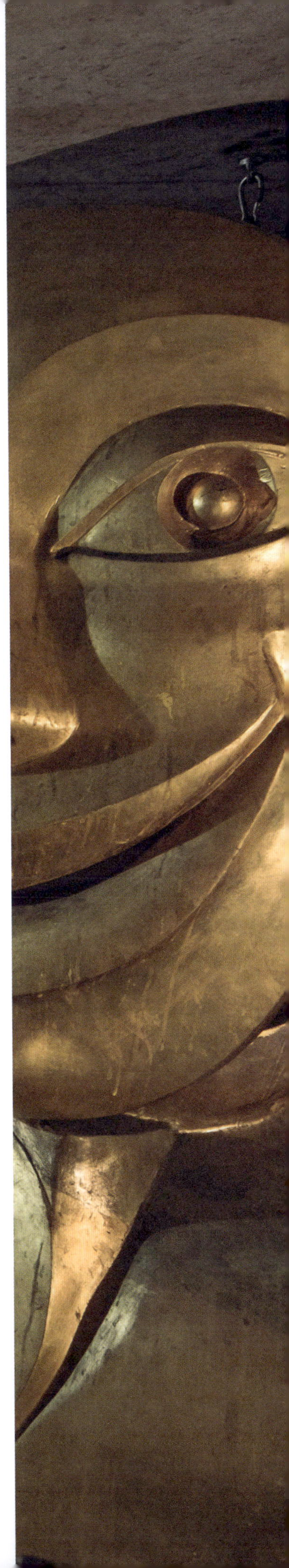

The Barbican Muse: the sole remaining survivor of the golden muses installed as part of Pentagram's redesign of the building for Detta O'Cathain (see Theo Inglis, p.176). A woman holds the masks of comedy and tragedy; designed by Matthew Spender and installed in 1994, it sits in the walkway to the centre at highwalk level.

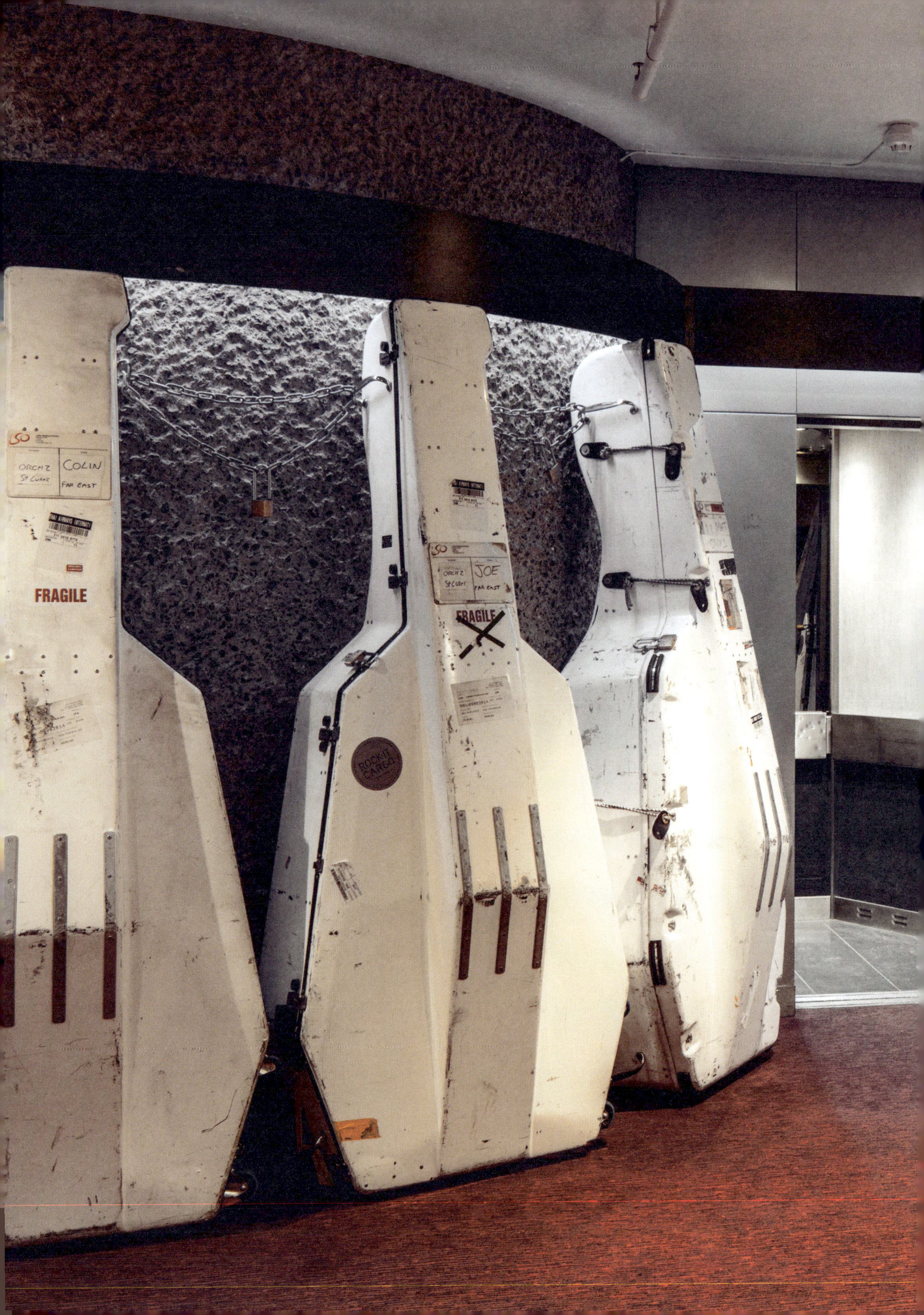

COLIN
FAR EAST
FRAGILE
JOE
FAR EAST
FRAGILE
ROCK-IT CARGO

Music

Fiona Maddocks

'What a fantastic shape ...
'It's very wide this hall ... fantastic stage.'
'The audience is very close from any seat.'
'A lot of wood ... should be good for sound.'

This enthusiastic exchange, between members of the Philip Jones Brass Ensemble, was recorded by BBC TV cameras when the illustrious group was invited to inspect the Barbican Centre in 1982, ahead of its official opening. As the brass players set down their instruments, making various popping and tapping noises to test the acoustic 'ping', their brilliant, chirpy leader, trumpeter Philip Jones, pointed up to the ceiling.

'What are those long black things?'

'Egg nishner' replied the tuba player, John Fletcher, quoting *Let Stalk Strine*, the dictionary of Australian usage, basis of cult jokes (in some quarters) in the early 1980s.

Whether the 'long black things' were air conditioning as Fletcher suggested or, together with thousands of plastic globes in varying sizes, part of the acoustic design, need no longer concern us. The globes soon disappeared, the distinctive canopy has gone, revamped by the Chicago-based acoustician Larry Kierkegaard in two stages: first in 1994 and then, more extensively, in 2001. Much happened before those transformations. Even more has happened since: a host of events far too many to itemise in a short survey, but a thrilling journey of cultural discovery, and musical achievement, which continues apace, 40 years on.

One of the first questions, and the hardest to answer, is what the Barbican concert hall sounded like in its earliest days. Despite all the science, acoustics is a quixotic art, as elusive and personal as scent or flavour. Some listeners claim not to notice acoustics at all. Yet for music professionals it's the one question that occupies pole position in assessing a venue. The issue was highlighted at the Barbican from the start. The Queen, attending the inaugural concert given in the hall by the London Symphony Orchestra as part of the opening event on 3 March 1982, may not have worried about the acoustic, but Edward Greenfield, music critic of *The Guardian,* writing the next day, certainly did: 'After all the flummery of publicity, our big question was just how well the music would sound.'

Greenfield's initial judgement, coming as it did from a legendary record collector, sounded like a thumbs-up: 'This, I suspect, is a hall which will please record collectors rather than concert-goers, for the sound is immediate and rounded, and in these days that is no bad thing.' Immediate? Rounded? What could be better. Consider what the antonyms might be. Then he swivels back on himself. 'My expectation was that the LSO, the loudest orchestra in London if not the world, would be too aggressive for comfort. Not so. The effect of the lateral shape seems to be to diffuse the sound. Even the soloists in the two concertos — Vladimir Ashkenazy in Beethoven's Fourth Piano Concerto and Yo-Yo Ma in the Elgar Cello Concerto — came over in a slightly disembodied way, the piano in particular a little too clangy.' From immediate and rounded, the new hall is now diffuse, disembodied and 'clangy'. He concluded: 'The Barbican is certainly an attractive place to go to, but judgement on its acoustics has to be reserved for the time being.' This jury of one *Guardian* critic was still out.

In *The Times* (4 March 1982), William Mann was more circumspect, first praising the leg room ('ample for a tall person'), the upholstery and the width of the seats, 'wide enough for this fat Englishman's hips'. Mann complained about the hum of the air conditioning (which would take many years to solve), but acknowledged a warmth in the opening bars of Wagner's *Meistersinger* overture, which sounded 'more appetising than they would in the Royal Festival Hall'. However, Mann made a separate point: that none of the music was new and the only involvement of a living composer was programme notes by, of all people, Michael Tippett who could, surely, have been invited to write a fanfare instead? *The Times*'s subeditors knew what the story was, and headlined the review accordingly: 'Acoustics prove tricky'.

Once a hall has a particular reputation, it tends to stick: Amsterdam's Concertgebouw, Vienna's Musikverein, Berlin's Philharmonie: good. Countless others, including some in London except the chamber-sized Wigmore Hall, bad. The Barbican quickly joined that second category, often condemned in contradictory language, from dry to noisy, patchy to diffuse. There are no absolutes with acoustics. Just absolute attitudes. Yes, there were difficulties, which would soon be addressed. For example, the shining Perspex globes in the ceiling that William Mann had likened to 'inverted brandy balloon glasses' were soon recognised as a problem and removed under the direction of acoustician Derek Sugden of Arup. But far more interesting was what took place inside this new hall: the musicians who came, and the music that was played, in all its stupendous variety.

How had decisions about the hall come about? The shape, capacity, seating design; the crucial lack of an organ (despite, as was frequently pointed out, having a decorative wooden panel at the rear of the stage that looked exactly like a set of organ pipes). Some of these issues are detailed by Elain Harwood in her article on p.49. The essential issue was that by the time the arts centre took shape, the footprint of the main venues on the crowded site was already fixed. The person who initially steered so many of the artistic decisions was Anthony Besch, the concert and opera impresario, who was introduced to the project in 1963 and had a decisive effect on the planning of the venues (see Nicholas Kenyon, p.38).

Besch took soundings from orchestras and established an initial, vital, relationship with the London Symphony Orchestra. Together with Chamberlin, he visited venues across Europe and America, including New York's Lincoln Center and the radically designed, recently built Berlin Philharmonie. All talk — at least among that specialist breed preoccupied with designing concert halls — was of the Philharmonie's pentagon shape, its tent-like canopy, its 'vineyard-style' seating, in which terraces fan out around the stage. Out with

Top
Creating the concert hall: inside the model. From left to right: Hugh Creighton, Henry Wrong and Anthony Camden of the London Symphony Orchestra.

Bottom
Site visit. From left to right: Henry Wrong, Anthony Camden, LSO chairman, Claudio Abbado, LSO principal conductor, and Sue Mallett, LSO administrator.

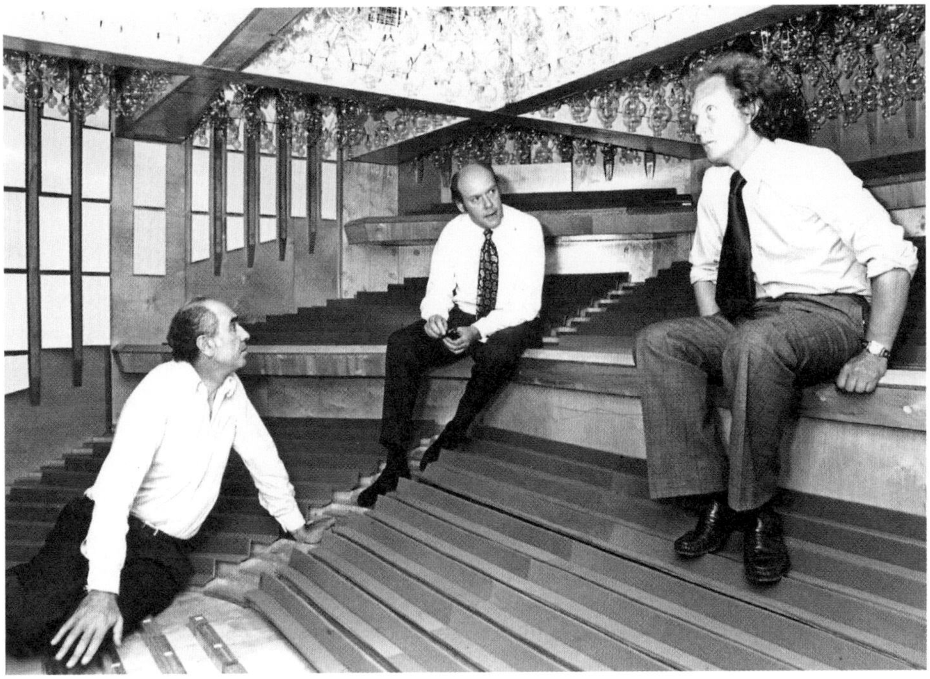

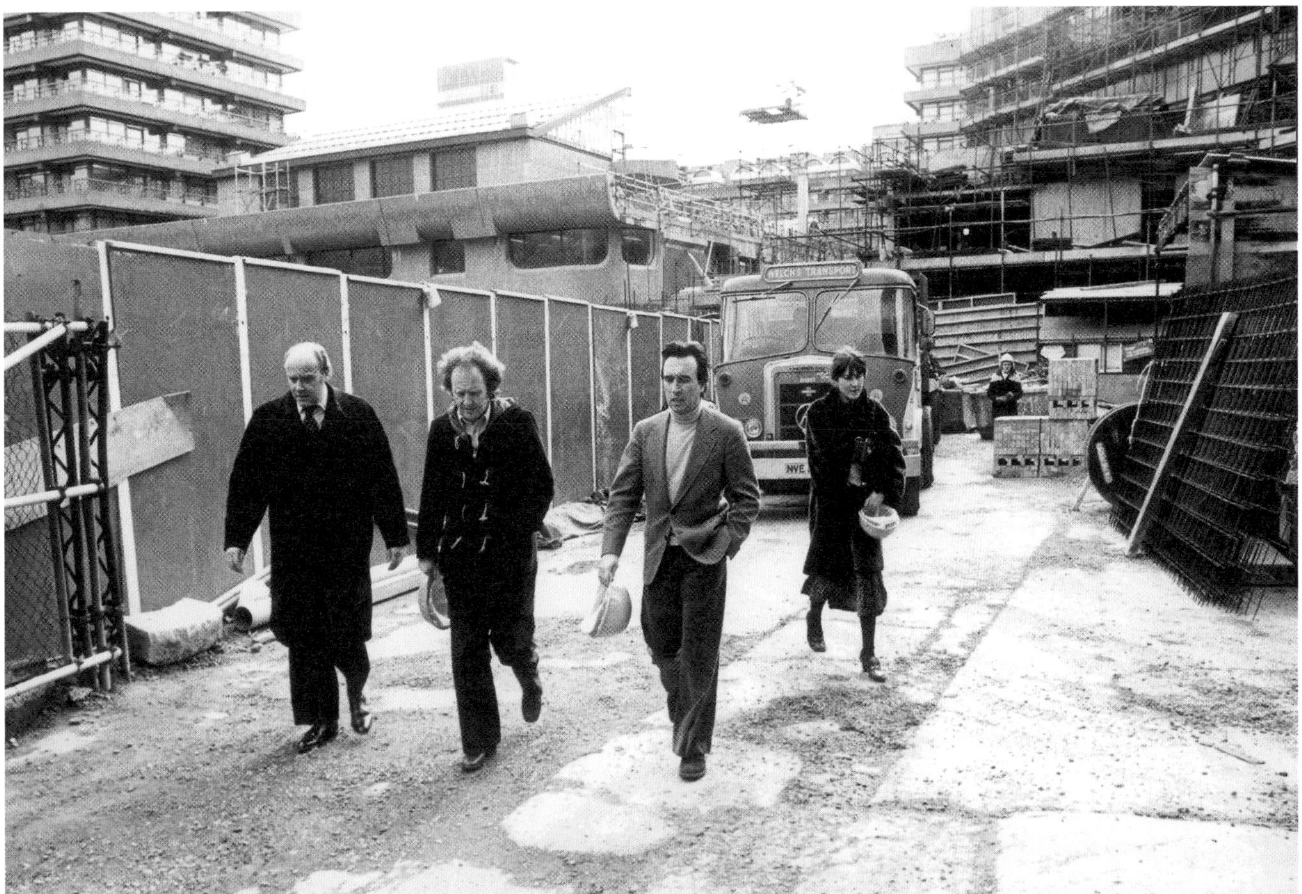

shoebox halls (conveniently, since the Barbican site could not accommodate one large enough), in with this brave new architectural solution. Could the Barbican achieve something similar?

Using the Philharmonie as a useful prototype, the hall's shape would mimic that of the semicircular sculpture court within Frobisher Crescent, directly above. The stage was designed for an orchestra of 120, with, in theory, space for a chorus of 200 — a moot point since, to this day, choruses always seem cramped when there's a full orchestra on stage. Seats were capacious and, as William Mann implied, big enough for portly bottoms. Fabric upholstery was chosen over leather, all part of trying to provide the LSO with the 'rich' acoustic they wanted. 'The overall sound is one of the warmest that I've heard for a long time,' observed Anthony Camden, then chairman of the LSO and principal oboe, fiercely defending his orchestra's new home against the comments in the press.

'Look, not enough attention was paid to the acoustic at the start,' Clive Gillinson recalls, speaking from New York in 2020. 'It had to serve other purposes — as a conference centre too. A lot of money was spent in improving it. Like many places, it's wasn't a great hall, but it's now certainly a good hall.' He adds: 'Some artists, especially singers, objected to the design. [The American soprano] Jessye Norman told me that when she went out on stage she had to swivel from right to left, so she could beam her sound out to the entire audience like a lighthouse.' That issue remains, but the sense of communication in the hall is close and vivid, and it remains a valued venue for chamber and song recitals for artists with the stature of the trio of Leonidas Kavakos, Emanuel Ax and Yo-Yo Ma who opened the 2018–19 season to a packed hall, and for outstanding singers such as Joyce diDonato and Jonas Kaufmann who have made it their London venue of choice for recitals.

The initial concert programmes sowed the seeds of the Barbican's future, even if not all bore early fruit. Some nights the hall, while never a receiving house as such, was available for hire, to help finances. Antony Lewis-Crosby, arts director from 1979 until 1994, established the parallel presence of the LSO and other visiting orchestras in the hall, as well as initiating major international festivals. Graham Sheffield as artistic director, with John Tusa as managing director, flung open the doors to embrace a wider world of music but some of that variety was there from the start. Tusa's successor, Nicholas Kenyon, and his team including heads of music Robert van Leer, Angela Dixon and now Huw Humphreys, have built on this progression, diversifying the output. They forged a strong relationship between the resident orchestra, the LSO, and its home base, as well as developing the idea of Associate ensembles, which allow the scope of the Barbican activities to grow wider still and wider in a way that reflects developments in the musical world, with more early music, more new music, more non-Western music. 'It's all music now!' says Kenyon.

In the opening weeks, many patterns were established. Major LSO concerts with Abbado were repeated, just as some of the orchestra's concerts are today. The mistake then, however, was that concerts would be played three, or even four times, using the American model of subscription tickets: workable in a US town with one orchestra and a guaranteed audience but hopeless for London, if not 'catastrophic', as Clive Gillinson, first a member of the cello section, then

The overhead installation of the concert hall takes place, with the seating waiting to be installed below. The glass ceiling globes were subsequently removed as unhelpful to the acoustic.

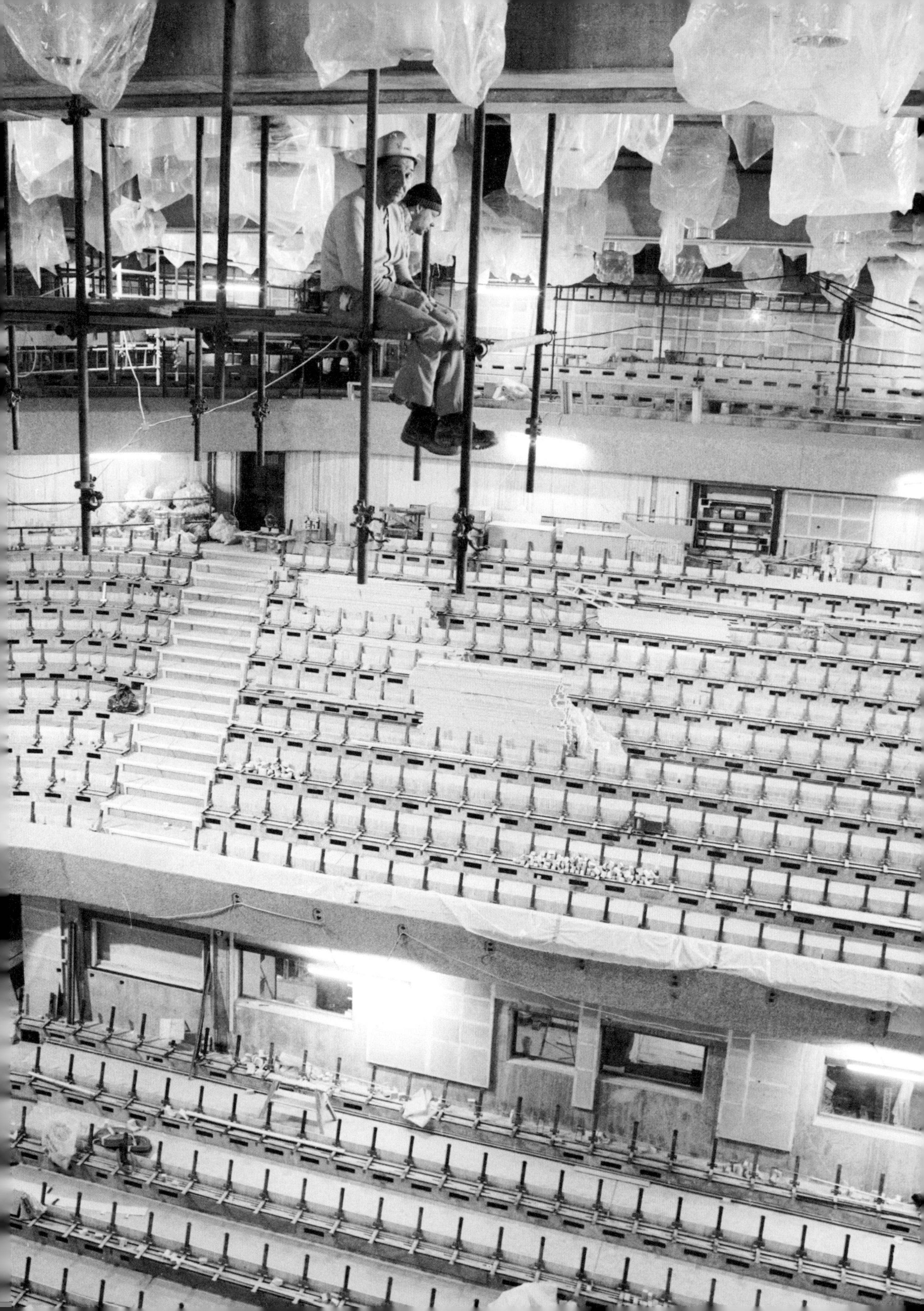

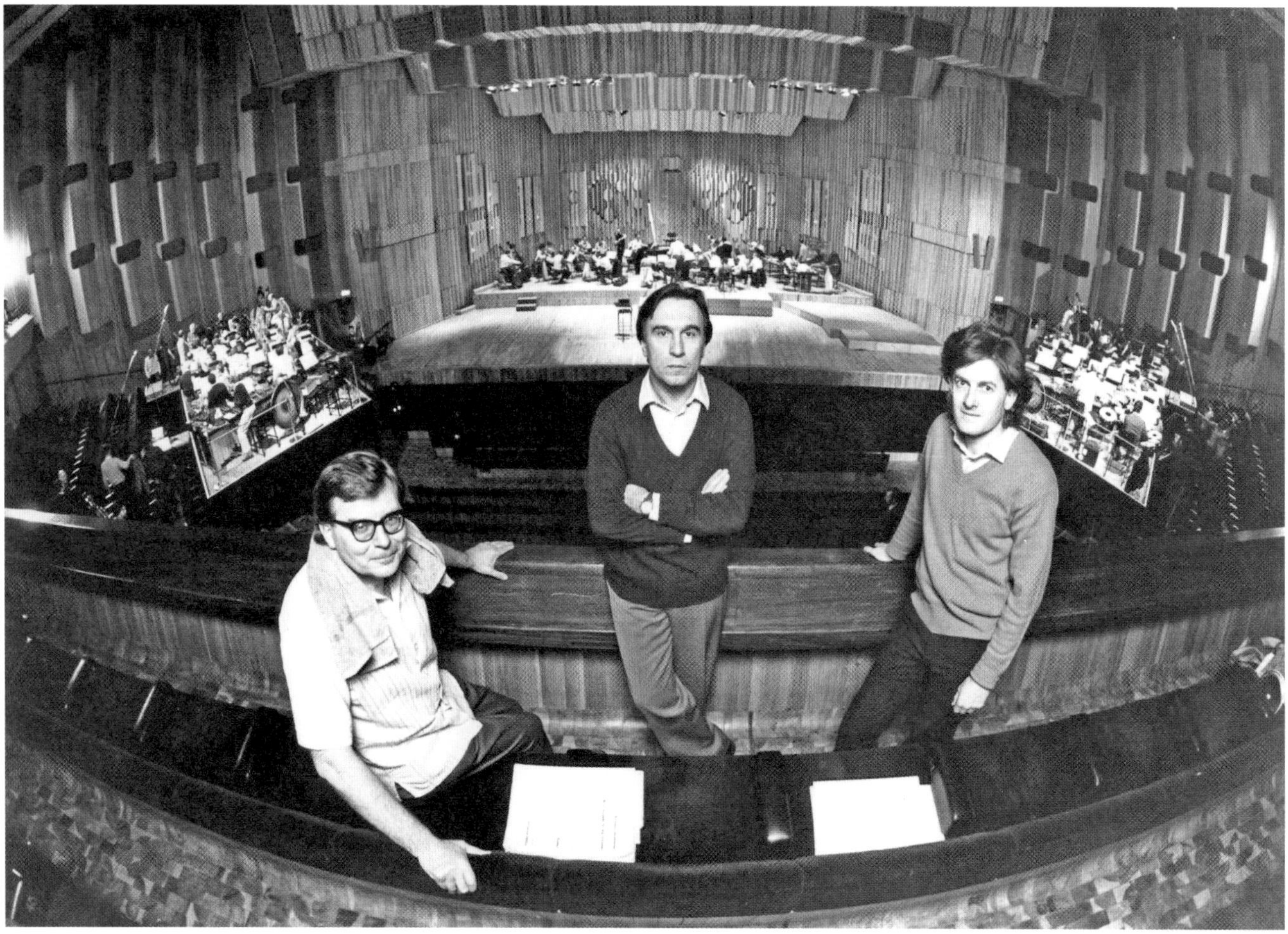

The challenge of mounting Stockhausen's *Gruppen* for three orchestral groups in the hall, with specially built stages left and right. The LSO was conducted by Edward Downes (left), Claudio Abbado (centre), and James Judd (right).

managing director of the LSO, puts it. 'As a musician, to come out into the hall and find it barely half empty was very demoralising.' The LSO, meanwhile, soon had its own acute financial difficulties. Within two years, Gillinson was managing director (1984–2005) with the task of rescuing the LSO's parlous finances: another story, told in full in Richard Morrison's history of the LSO, *Orchestra: A Century of Triumph and Turbulence*.

Smaller events took place at less conventional times (1pm, 6.30pm and mid-afternoon on a Sunday): John Lill playing Beethoven sonatas at lunchtime were sell-outs, but the 'rush hour' concerts did not catch on with City workers, especially with challenging repertory. The LSO would renew that idea, successfully, years later when Simon Rattle became music director. By 2018, working life and travel had changed: a short 6.30 concert with one of the world's favourite conductors had new appeal, with the snappy title of Half Six Fix. For the main evening concerts, top soloists and conductors, some of whom would return regularly over the decades, came: the pianists Murray Perahia, Krystian Zimerman and Stephen Bishop-Kovacevich; the conductors John Eliot Gardiner (who, according to Antony Lewis-Crosby, swore never to conduct there again, though eventually he did, regularly), Richard Hickox and Mark Elder. The

English Chamber Orchestra established itself as a regular fixture, complementing the LSO's four concerts a week.

Putting down an international marker, the Barbican welcomed the Orchestre de Paris on the opening weekend, with Daniel Barenboim conducting. Repertoire was not always safe or predictable. The LSO gave concert performances of Berg's *Wozzeck*; Hans Werner Henze conducted three programmes of his own music interleaved with Mozart, which must have been a hard sell. There were 'non-classical' events too: Chris Barber, Ralph McTell, Nina Simone and the Three Degrees played in the first few months. In a bank holiday weekend of jazz, 'informal events in the foyers and on the Lakeside Terrace' featured George Melly and Kenny Ball. The idea then, as now, was that the building was open all day and anyone could come in and sample whatever was on offer, from jazz on Sunday lunchtimes to weekday lunchtime concerts (an almost vanished genre now that lunchtimes are so short) and the annual fireworks display in the summer. 'What we really did in those first years was to build relationships,' Lewis-Crosby recollects, a factor perhaps not always appreciated in accounts of the period. Much of the programming was 'creative and experimental', he says, partly in repertoire, partly in seeking to establish how things might work in a new building which was still struggling to build audiences. Other collaborations were with the Chamber Orchestra of Europe, all too rare a visitor to the UK, who appeared with the inspiring conductor Nikolaus Harnoncourt. (Kenyon recalls a Beethoven Ninth Symphony in which the tenor was suddenly indisposed and Robert Tear had to be rushed to the hall, arriving just in time. As they walked on stage, Harnoncourt said to him: 'Like a madrigal!')

The saviour of those first years, however, came from an unexpected and exuberant quarter. Two photographs survive showing Henry Wrong, director of the Barbican from 1970 to 1990, with the concert promoter Raymond Gubbay. In one, their ties a jot askew, they jointly clutch a magnum of champagne. In the other they are wrapped around a giant furry cartoon animal. Months before the building opened Gubbay, a great showman who surely has 'can do' tattooed on his chest, had toured the Barbican site in a hard hat. Spotting an opportunity, he booked more than 50 concerts in the first season. Their average attendance was over 90 per cent. Gubbay's special brand of classical concerts and opera galas were crowd-pullers from the outset. He helped the Barbican Centre find, and build, audiences.

As Lewis-Crosby points out, 'Raymond is seen as a populist, but he did some very serious, high-standard mainstream concerts and his enthusiasm got people in. Then he started the Christmas festivals at a time when the rest of concert life was dead.' Valentine's Day concerts followed, with roses and champagne 'for the ladies', and film nights with orchestra (such as Abel Gance's 1927 epic *Napoleon*). 'Raymond's a great friend,' remembers Clive Gillinson, laughing. 'But he was driving me nuts! He was successful and we weren't. He was raking in audiences and – until we started to recover by about 1985 – we were running ourselves into the ground, and risked facing oblivion.' Gubbay's open-minded, accessible approach changed the musical landscape as well as helping establish the Barbican. This was nearly a decade before the Three Tenors' 1990 World Cup 'hit', 'Nessun Dorma', or the advent of Classic FM in 1992. Gubbay, ever gracious in the face of media flak, was ahead of the game in realising the wider appeal of classical music if presented properly.

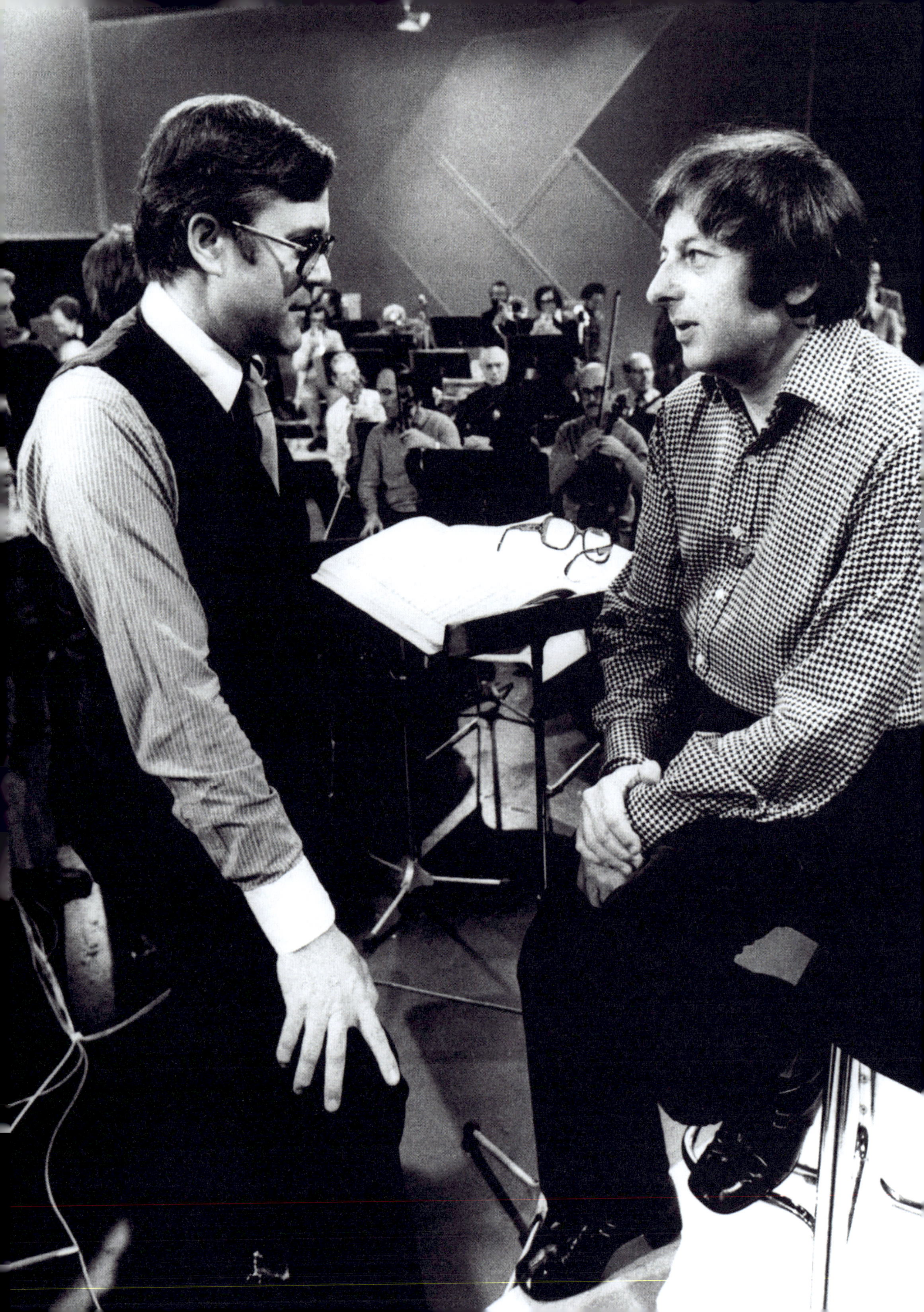

Sir Humphrey Burton

In 1988, out of the blue, Henry Wrong invited me to become artistic adviser of the Barbican Centre. A new post. I should have smelt a rat, given that it was to be a part-time job and nobody would report directly to me — that is, I had no budget and no troops. But I was intrigued: my role would be to watch over the entire output of the centre and look for synergies between the component parts, encourage everybody to work together, and make them all feel part of the same happy family. This was not as simple as it may sound. The centre is a warren of activity, but it's also a public thoroughfare next to a housing estate, and it was always going to be hard to create a sense of community.

This maze-like environment was matched by a mish-mash of governance. I discovered that Henry wasn't entirely master of his own house. The commercial exhibition spaces, potentially more lucrative, had to be given precedence over the concert hall. The hall itself doubled as a conference centre, which made long-term musical planning difficult. The RSC's home at the Barbican was in effect an outpost of the company's Stratford-upon-Avon power base, and decisions about its repertoire were taken at what was, at least for the Barbican's planners, the eleventh hour. That the art gallery and library were financed by a different City of London committee also added complications.

It was my impression that the head of planning, Antony Lewis-Crosby, and his deputy, Cecile Latham-Koenig, were meshing effectively with the LSO to create a cohesive concert-hall schedule night after night. The Barbican was by no means just a receiving house, as some alleged, even though it did have to help balance the books with a steady flow of one-rehearsal concerts booked by that most astute of concert promoters, Raymond Gubbay.

Looking back, I have to admit that my personal contribution to the Barbican was unimpressive. My saving grace was to mastermind the all-embracing season dedicated to the arts of Scandinavia, *Tender is the North* (the phrase is Tennyson's). My colleague Cecile Latham-Koenig is part-Danish and I have a Swedish wife, and in 1989, with only a few qualifications to match our patriotic enthusiasm, we set about planning a month-long celebration that would involve all the centre's resources and everything Scandinavian from Icelandic textiles to Danish music. Three years later, the season finally began. At its heart were the complete Sibelius symphonies given by Colin Davis and the LSO, and the Finnish choir that flew over to take part was a knock-out. Another coup was to persuade Simon Rattle and the manager of the City of Birmingham Symphony Orchestra, Ed Smith, to bring down the CBSO to perform the six Nielsen symphonies. Gallery, library and cinema all played their part. We were all very proud when *Tender is the North* won a Sony Award for Best International Festival of the Year. The collaboration of the Barbican's different parts through this project has been built on ever since — the promised land is now at hand. But it was fun to be a pioneer.

Sir Humphrey Burton is a television producer, director and presenter, seen here with André Previn, who had been principal conductor of the LSO 1968–79. Burton worked closely with Leonard Bernstein, and was the co-originator of the award-winning Barbican festival *Tender is the North.*

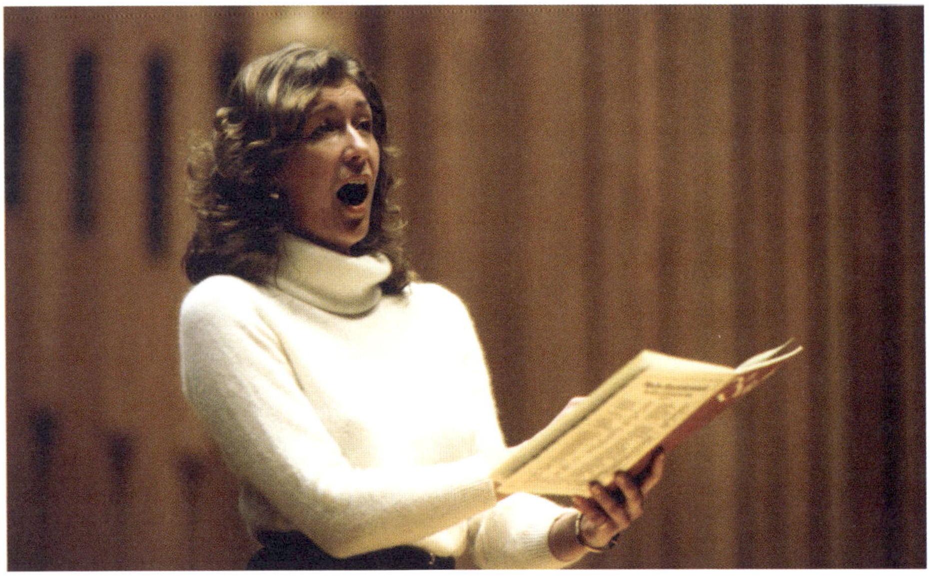

Felicity Lott sings Bach: a distinguished and popular soprano who alongside her colleagues has made many appearances in concerts and recitals at the Barbican.

One of the turning points to which Gillinson refers was the LSO's stupendous 1985 festival with Claudio Abbado: *Mahler, Vienna and the 20th Century* explored the idea of Vienna as the crucible of modernism in art and music and was complemented by Barbican events. Its success, despite frayed nerves and high costs, encouraged ambitious thinking, and led to increased cross-centre working. 'The relationship with the LSO was fairly strong, certainly in comparison with the RSC in that first phase, and musically the Barbican and the orchestra were ready to support each other. Musically, their plans and ours were very close.' That festival benefitted from the close involvement of the Austrian Hans Landesmann, a colleague of Claudio Abbado, who was a part of the Barbican's increasingly international thinking and became an artistic advisor to the centre. The LSO's two-week Bernstein festival from 29 April to 11 May 1986 was another pivotal event. There were screenings of *On the Waterfront* and *West Side Story*; an exhibition of photos and memorabilia; and a performance of *Mass* by students at the Guildhall School. The violinist Gidon Kremer, pianist Krystian Zimerman and the 15-year-old treble Aled Jones were among the soloists. Patricia Routledge, as *The Stage* reported, reminded us of her fine voice 'in a song from Bernstein's monumentally unsuccessful *1600 Pennsylvania Avenue*'. In addition to ten works by Bernstein, the programmes featured music by those he admired—Mahler, Stravinsky, Ives, Britten, Blitzstein and Shostakovich. Bernstein's presence, and charisma, added precisely the air of glamour the Barbican needed. *The New York Times* reported on the celebrations at length: 'Leonard Bernstein has few fond memories, musical or otherwise, of his first visit to London 40 years ago.' But Bernstein's relationship with Britain softened over the years. 'There was nothing like the high point reached Tuesday night at the Barbican Center when the composer and conductor came together with the London Symphony Orchestra for a nationally televised all-Bernstein gala concert designed to be the centerpiece of the most extensive celebration of his music and career ever mounted anywhere. Standing

Ovation.' Everyone in the packed hall rose to their feet when Bernstein brought his 'Age of Anxiety' Symphony 'to its thunderous climax with a mighty leap and stamp of his right foot' — a vivid reminder of Bernstein's thrilling all-body, all-emotions conducting style.

That festival established the Barbican's international credentials, as well as Bernstein's double genius as composer and conductor. The LSO was coming out of its financial doldrums. Bernstein became president of the orchestra from 1987 until his death in 1990, shortly before which the LSO, Bernstein and Michael Tilson Thomas founded the Pacific Music Festival in Sapporo, Japan. The LSO's particular talent for forging close relationships with artists flowered, too, in a festival with the Russian cellist-conductor Mstislav Rostropovich.

The Barbican's own international clout was sealed by events such as the four-week-long Hungarian Festival *Magyarok — Britain Salutes Hungary* in 1986. The composer György Kurtág came. So too did the Budapest Festival Orchestra with conductor Iván Fischer and a stream of dignitaries, confirming the political significance of a venue so closely tied to the mighty City of London. There were satellite events, including a Haydn series at the Wigmore Hall curated by a certain Nicholas Kenyon, then a music critic. The Prime Minister, Margaret Thatcher herself, came to the Barbican. Clive Gillinson remembers attending a gala dinner: 'It was a novelty that she was there. She wasn't scheduled to speak. But then someone persuaded her and she gave a 20-minute eulogy to Hungary and the power of the arts. Quite frankly we were all astonished.'

At the far end of the repertoire spectrum, a new relationship with the BBC was triggered by the success, in 1985, of a festival of music by Karlheinz

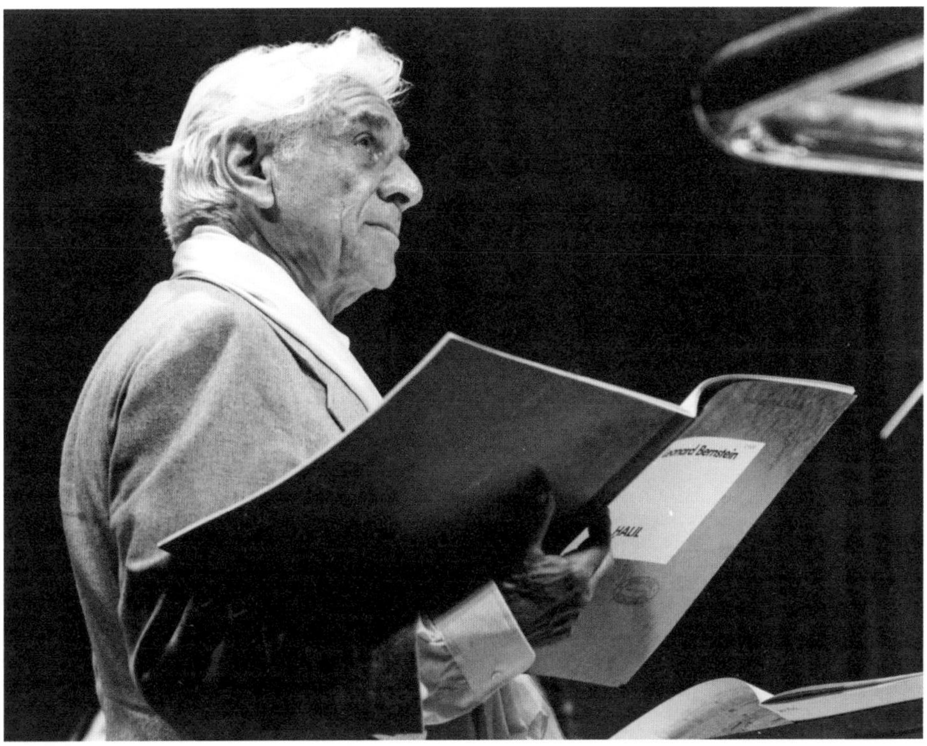

Leonard Bernstein, the conductor and composer whose hugely successful festival with the LSO in 1986 led to his being appointed president of the orchestra in 1987.

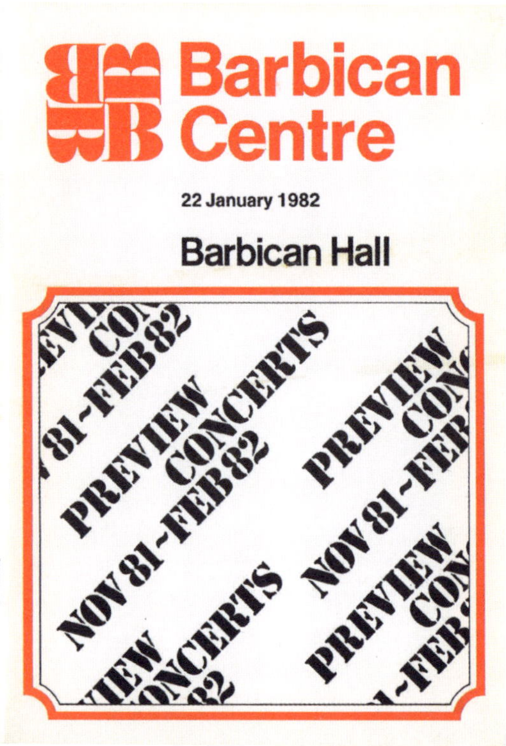
Barbican Centre
22 January 1982
Barbican Hall
PREVIEW CONCERTS NOV 81 - FEB 82

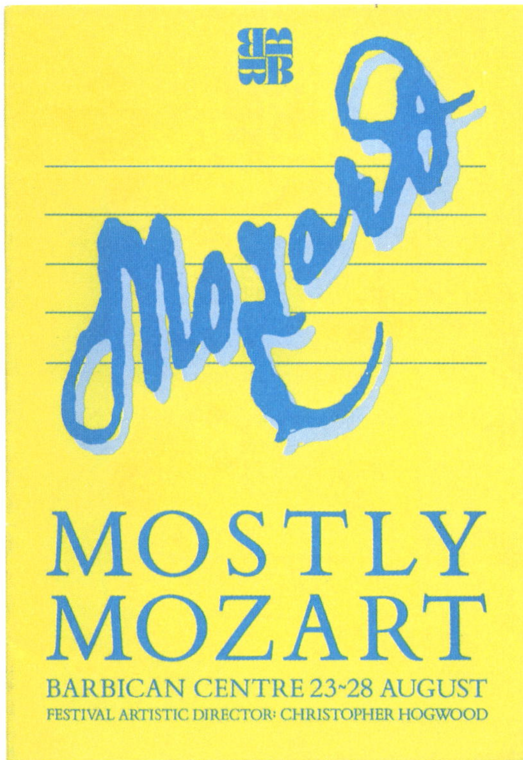
Mozart
MOSTLY MOZART
BARBICAN CENTRE 23-28 AUGUST
FESTIVAL ARTISTIC DIRECTOR: CHRISTOPHER HOGWOOD

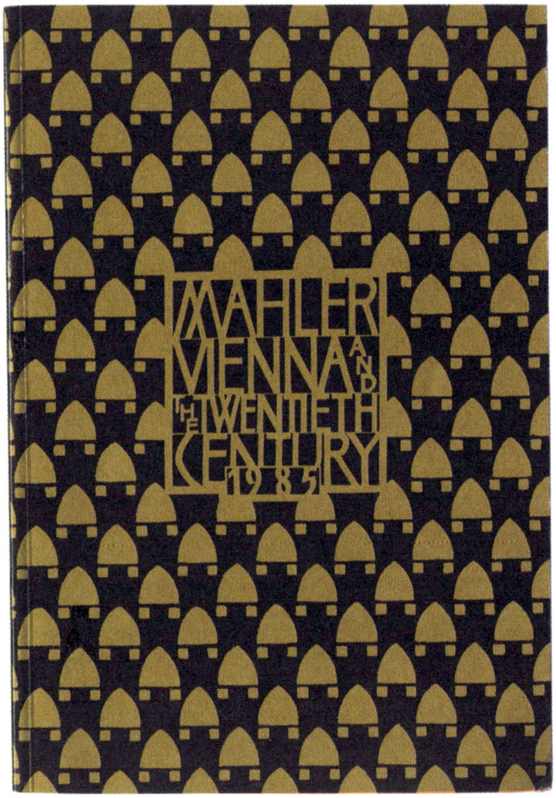
MAHLER VIENNA AND THE TWENTIETH CENTURY
1985

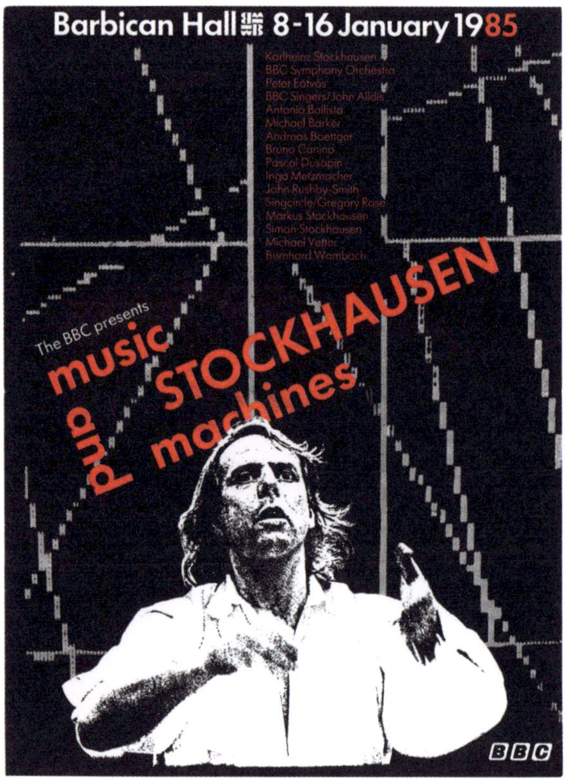
Barbican Hall 8-16 January 1985
Karlheinz Stockhausen
BBC Symphony Orchestra
Peter Eötvös
BBC Singers/John Alldis
Antonio Ballista
Michael Barker
Andreas Boettger
Bruno Canino
Pascal Dusapin
Ingo Metzmacher
John Rushby-Smith
Singcircle/Gregory Rose
Markus Stockhausen
Simon Stockhausen
Michael Vetter
Bernhard Wambach
The BBC presents
music and machines
STOCKHAUSEN
BBC

Stockhausen, *Music and Machines*. This was a major, ground-breaking collaboration with the BBC, using all its strengths in contemporary music, that later led to the BBC Symphony Orchestra taking up the role of Associate Orchestra of the centre alongside the LSO as Resident. Slowly but surely, in the mid-1980s, the Barbican's programme was acquiring international stature. The partnership with the BBC led to a series of celebrated single Composer Focus weekends in January from 1988. These were unforgettable experiences: adventurous, strange, round-the-clock (nearly), exhausting, absorbing and all-consuming journeys into the heart of the mid–late 20th century avant-garde. Weekends of living composers, Berio, Lutoslawski, Schnittke, Messiaen, Ligeti, Harrison Birtwistle, Sofia Gubaidulina and others, left an indelible mark, as did encyclopaedic explorations of other 20th-century figures across a weekend: Berg, Ives, Janáček. The Total Immersion Days, which replaced these weekends from the 2008-9 season, may be more practical and aurally manageable but will they ever have quite that same magnetic draw?

Through the period of his directorship, Lewis-Crosby was supported by his deputy Cecile Latham-Koenig, together with two music advisors, Hans Landesmann who had come through his connection with Claudio Abbado, and Humphrey Burton, whose original link was with Leonard Bernstein. Burton proposed and developed the fifth, and most ambitious, international festival with Latham-Koenig: *Tender is the North*, an exploration of Scandinavian arts in the 1992–3 season, remains a landmark in British cultural life. It won awards and became a talking point. The first phase of the Kierkegaard acoustical changes had just been completed, boosting as it were the hall's own sense of confidence. Colin Davis established a new relationship with the LSO (he would become chief conductor in 1995) in an unforgettable Sibelius cycle while Simon Rattle and the City of Birmingham Symphony Orchestra performed a Nielsen cycle. Everyone worked together, and everyone was happy. The new managing director of the centre, Detta O'Cathain, gained great kudos for the festival, both politically in the City and through the cultural relationships with the Scandinavian countries. She had succeeded Wrong as director, but her approach to business now threatened a change of direction. There was anxiety that credit was given not just to one element of the festival, as Humphrey Burton pointed out, implying a number of cracks in the Barbican's artistic edifice at that time, in *The Independent* of 7 October 1994:

> Sir, … David Lister asserts (3 October) that the success of the 1992 Scandinavian arts festival, *Tender is the North*, was mostly due to the LSO's Sibelius. This is a ridiculously dismissive assertion: those five magnificent Colin Davis concerts formed a vital but small part of the festival, in which the Barbican's art galleries, theatres, foyers and cinemas were all involved.
>
> *Tender is the North* received almost universal praise in the press and went on to win the Sony international classical music award as the world's best festival in the 1992–3 season. It exceeded its target for sponsorship, attracted good audiences and gave the Barbican staff a sense of unity and purpose, invaluable when it comes to sustaining morale.
>
> Baroness O'Cathain says she is giving proposals for new festivals 'a long hard look': obviously she has to be convinced they represent

The range of the Barbican's music programme in the 1980s, from the Preview Concerts of 1981–2 and the Mostly Mozart Festival to the LSO's *Mahler, Vienna and the 20th Century*, and the BBC Symphony Orchestra's first composer focus, *Stockhausen: music and machines*, both in 1985 — a milestone year for the music programme.

> value for money. The LSO's artistic policy (and the Royal Shakespeare Company's) has proved that insistence on quality is the best way to get bums on seats. There are 280 nights a year when the LSO is not playing: this is the area where the Barbican has to have its own policy.

The balance between the artistic input of the Barbican and that of the LSO was skilfully held in check by Antony Lewis-Crosby and his colleagues with Gillinson for the LSO. Soon, however, Burton's association ended. And more dramatically, after highly public dissatisfaction from the resident companies and the staff, O'Cathain would go within a year (see p.107). Despite behind-the-scene rows in the higher echelons of management and boardroom, with copious departures by senior management, Antony Lewis-Crosby had kept the Barbican's artistic life on track. Now he too left, to take a job with the country's oldest orchestra, the Royal Liverpool Philharmonic. In 1995 John Tusa was appointed managing director, with Graham Sheffield as artistic director and Robert van Leer as head of music. A new era was about to begin.

Those first two decades of the Barbican's history merit the extended assessment given here, not least because that period is now fading from the collective memory. Much happened artistically in the final years of the 20th century. The Barbican was winning larger and more dedicated, as well as eclectic, audiences. The year-long Tusa and Sheffield season *Inventing America* in 1998 would prove a mind-opener with its range of avant-garde offerings. Resident companies and the centre's own promotions had equal importance, giving new coherence to these more ambitious ventures. Two changes in the Barbican

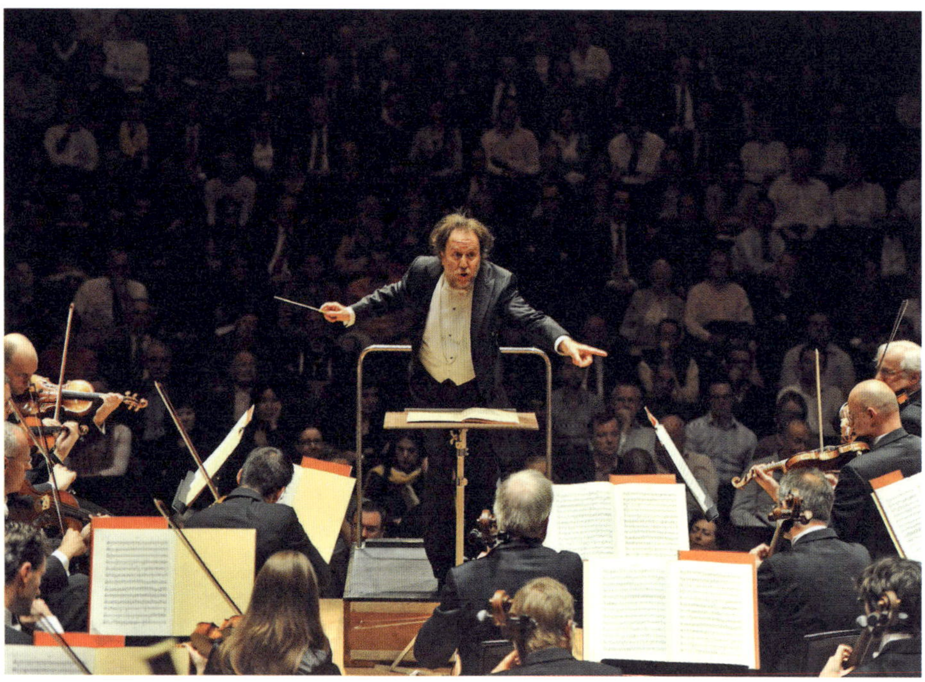

Riccardo Chailly conducted the Royal Concertgebouw Orchestra during the 2010s in powerful cycles of the Beethoven symphonies interwoven with specially commissioned new works, and the Brahms symphonies and concertos.

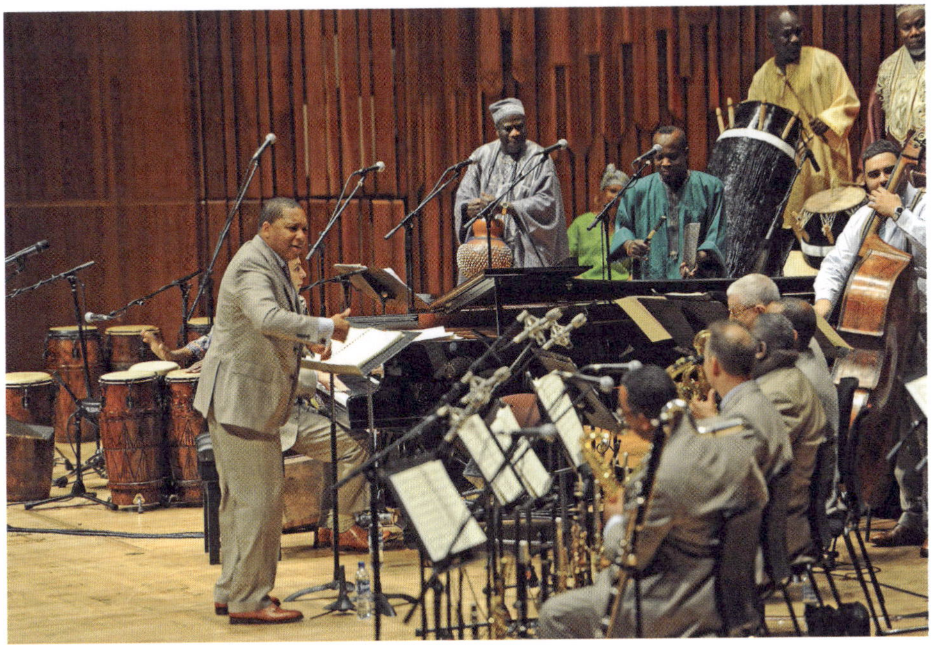

Regular residencies by the Jazz at Lincoln Center Orchestra with its charismatic director Wynton Marsalis have created special events including the premiere of his Swing Symphony with Simon Rattle and the LSO, for the Cultural Olympiad of 2012.

Centre, beyond the confines of the concert hall, had a radical effect: the Barbican took over control of the art gallery from the City (see p.195), and BITE (Barbican International Theatre Events), established as a year-round event in 2002 following the departure of the RSC, opened the doors to an exciting range of global theatre (see p.137). This was all part of a widening of ambition and perspective: 'cross-arts' under one roof. *Inventing America* set a trend. All the arts in one arts centre, iconoclasts, pioneers and rebels rather than only the mainstream: this was the innovative mood as the Barbican heralded the 21st century.

As Paul Keene, classical music programmer from 2012 to 2021, puts it, 'Just to rewind the clock as far back as I can, I'd say Robert van Leer basically moved the Barbican programme to the point where you have a standard model of high-impact international orchestras, and high-impact celebrity artists — the twin peaks of any venues programmes, plus everything else fitting around those peaks.' One essential element of these relationships with international orchestras was to involve the audience through a series rather than single concerts. Major highlights of that period included the Leipzig Gewandhaus under Riccardo Chailly in a hard-hitting Beethoven symphony cycle alongside contemporary scores, then Brahms symphonies and concertos, then Strauss. Mariss Jansons came regularly, and there were glamorous solo recitals. Keene says: 'There's a great consistency in the way things have developed, in maximising what an arts centre could do. From around 2010, there were many innovations, such as the International Associates scheme, as well as building up the baroque programme, semi-staging operas in co-production with the BBC, developing the masterclasses and understudy work with Guildhall students working alongside professionals — latterly with the Australian Chamber Orchestra, together with our other Associates.' In the 2020–21 season, the Associates

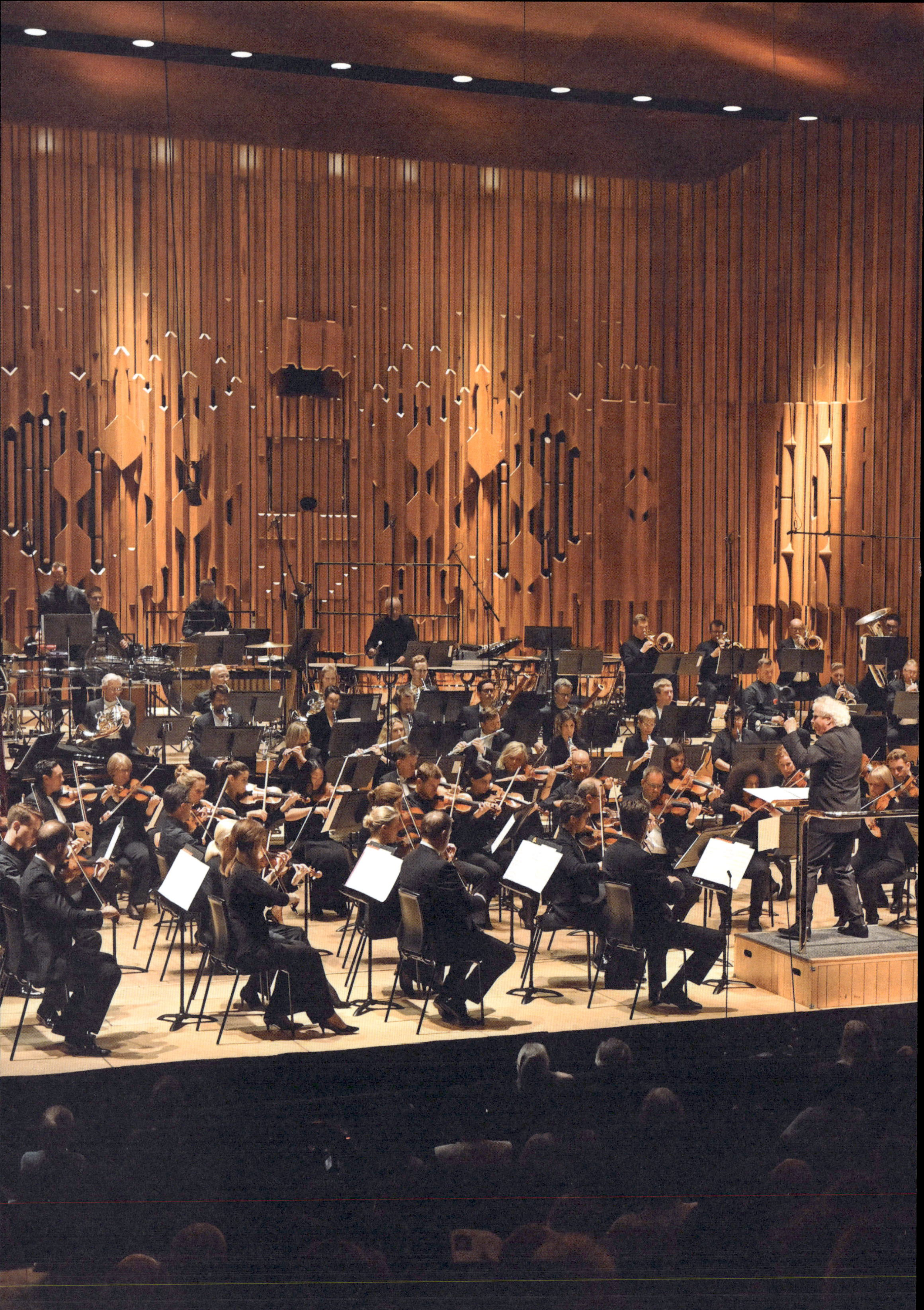

Rachel Gough

A tangle of brutalist corridors backstage and pillars outside, a kaleidoscopic riot of sounds and memories inside, this is our home. We have lived through much in this building, from expansive sweeps of Nordic landscapes with Sir Colin Davis, though cataclysmic renditions of Russian repertoire with Valery Gergiev and now with Sir Simon Rattle on to a spiral of music covering much of the available orchestral sound world.

This is a place of brutal honesty, with nowhere to hide. As a performer on the platform, waiting for the sickening silence before the conductor's hand signals that it's time to start *The Rite of Spring*, I wonder whether my heartbeats might be heard at the back of the auditorium.

Sitting in the audience during a schools' concert, the squeals of delight of the young child ring out across the hall, enhancing for us all the experience of sharing music. The LSO has travelled the world, performing in a mixture of esteemed, cutting edge, embracing acoustics, each with its own charm and challenge. But once we're here, we come back to the place we know and understand best, our home.

Rachel Gough is the principal bassoonist of the London Symphony Orchestra, which has been resident at the Barbican since it opened in 1982. She begins Stravinsky's *Rite of Spring* with a solo high in the bassoon's register, one of the most terrifying moments in any orchestral musician's life.

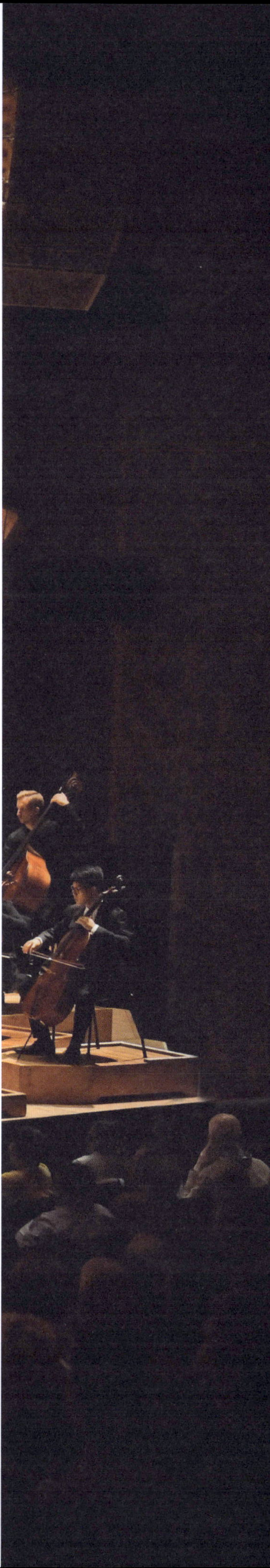

included Britten Sinfonia, Academy of Ancient Music and, a particularly fruitful connection among international orchestras, with the Los Angeles Philharmonic and Gustavo Dudamel, as well as the resident LSO and associate BBCSO. An especially strong collaboration came over several years with Jazz at Lincoln Center from New York, headed by the charismatic Wynton Marsalis, whose regular visits and outreach projects won a sell-out following.

In this period, the Barbican's resident orchestra, the LSO, was soaring: Colin Davis's musical love affair with orchestra and audience was richly captured in many recordings on LSO Live, its own label established in 1999. The LSO Discovery education programme had a new home in LSO St Luke's, once a derelict church, now a state-of-the-art multi-purpose hall. Opening in 2003, this exciting venue extended the Barbican out of the City and towards deprived communities in Islington and east London where vital links would soon be forged.

The surprise arrival of Valery Gergiev as Davis's successor, in 2007, secured by Gillinson but handed to his successor Kathryn McDowell to manage, may have given the LSO a switchback ride to set nerves jangling, but the musical fireworks sparked by this volatile and charismatic Ossetian ensured concert life was never dull. He was praised for his thrilling approach to Russian works but found wanting in other repertoire. 'Seat of the pants' and 'hair-raising' became bywords to describe the relationship, for better or at times worse. Reviews from his period with the orchestra, almost without exception, praise the excitement he can generate, while in the same paragraph worrying about his rehearsal style and, particularly, his political associations. 'I don't know of any case in musical history, except maybe for Wagner and mad King Ludwig of Bavaria, where a musician has been that close to a powerful ruler,' Richard Morrison, the chief classical music critic of *The Times*, told *The New York Times* in 2009. When Gergiev's term ended in 2015, a *Guardian* headline (9 October 2015) summed up the mixed emotions surrounding his departure: 'Gergiev and the LSO: fond farewells or sighs of relief?'

Simon Rattle, still at the Berlin Philharmonic, was able to consider offers from around the world. In a remarkable catch for the LSO, he was announced as Gergiev's successor (and the first principal conductor to hold the post of music director) from 2017. The wait seemed long, but when finally he arrived, the boost to the orchestra's, not to say the country's, musical morale was palpable. His first concert, on 14 September 2017, put British contemporary music centre stage, a habit which he has continued. The title of the opening series, *This is Rattle*, curated closely with the Barbican, caused wry smiles but the enthusiasm generated by his arrival was pretty much universal. *The Guardian*, somewhat pointedly, praised the LSO's new 'transparency and refinement which obviously were there already but waiting for the right conductor'. Under Rattle, the LSO's education programme expanded rapidly. The focus of repertoire shifted too: more Janáček, a composer Rattle holds dear, resulting in a superb concert performance and LSO Live recording of *The Cunning Little Vixen*. Many, with justification, regarded this as an Augustan age for the LSO — though Rattle, ever the down-to-earth Liverpudlian, might resist the imperial association. And it was not to last as long as some had hoped.

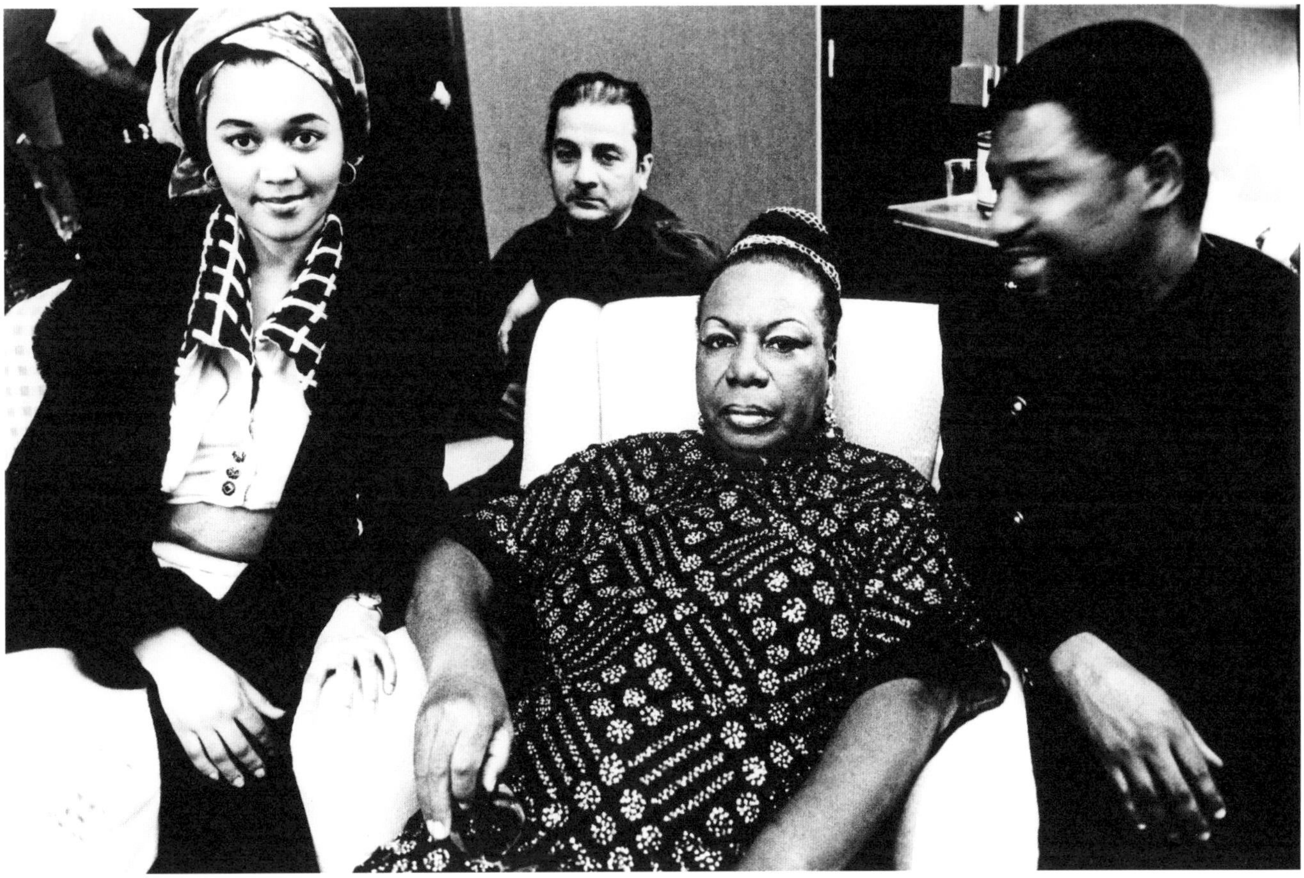

Nina Simone, photographed backstage at the Barbican by Peter Williams, who writes: 'The atmosphere is brooding. Dark, mesmeric, unsettling and powerful. Nina Simone. So charismatic. I turned on a couple of table lamps. She said "You may take my picture now, young man". ... It was one of the most enchanting and sensitive shoots I have ever done, one that has remained as a wonderful and privileged memory.'

Another aspect of musical life gave the Barbican new verve at the turn of the century. In 2000 the BBC Symphony Orchestra became an Associate, giving the orchestra a home away from the Proms, and a chance to develop its distinctive programming. With much fanfare, the concert hall was given a £7 million acoustic and aesthetic refurbishment. Once again, the Chicago acoustician Larry Kierkegaard, who had made significant adjustments in 1994, was there to advise. The canopy was replaced. Ceiling reflectors designed by Caruso St John, of adjustable height and tilt, were introduced. The air ventilation noise was silenced. As John Tusa wrote in his memoir *Making a Noise*, when Kierkegaard led him into the renovated hall, they stood for a moment, before Kierkegaard said 'Listen! I've given you a quiet room' — the proudest claim an acoustician could make. Despite a few complaints in the press of 'dryness', there was a universal sense that, at last, the hall's sound really had improved. It gave the centre new confidence, fresh impetus. The Great Orchestras of the World and Great Performers series presented a gilded lineup: from the Dresden Staatskapelle to the Cleveland Orchestra, and the best of the baroque ensembles, including Les Arts Florissants, Les Musicians du Louvre and Freiburg Baroque. A unique celebration of Bernard Haitink at 75, in 2004, merited first visits to the Barbican from the Berlin Philharmonic and the Vienna Philharmonic. For Huw Humphreys, the Barbican's head of music since 2014, this was a pivotal

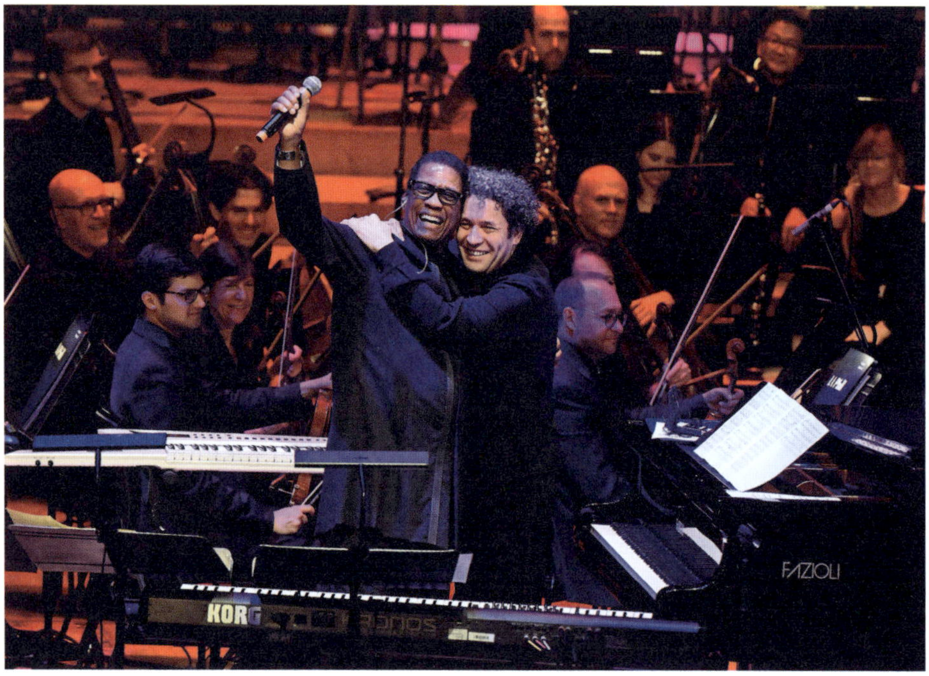

'A total love-in': veteran pianist Herbie Hancock and youthful conductor Gustavo Dudamel celebrate their collaboration with the Los Angeles Philharmonic Orchestra, now the centre's international orchestral partner.

moment: 'One of the greatest highlights I ever heard was Mahler 3, with the Berlin Philharmonic and Haitink. In that series there were seven international orchestras all harnessed under one conductor. That's perhaps something we wouldn't do now. We're more about in-depth relationships with particular ongoing groups and organisations. There's inevitably a financial element to that. We have to be much smarter, more quicksilver, more entrepreneurial. But it makes it more exciting, more coherent.'

He cites the Los Angeles Philharmonic's residencies as a prime example of an ensemble that not only visits, but unpacks its bags and settles into the Barbican's way of programming. 'What's special about the LA Phil is they don't think like an orchestra. They think more like a rounded cultural institution than an orchestra – perhaps because of their relationship to Disney Hall and the Hollywood Bowl. There's a great breadth to their thinking with Gustavo Dudamel at the heart of things. They don't want to bring two or three standard touring programmes. They bring, instead, ground-breaking concerts. So you get these extraordinary Peter Sellars/John Adams collaborations, as in *The Gospel According to the Other Mary*. Or the Messiaen *From the Canyons to the Stars* project we did, in 2016, with Deborah O'Grady's photography. Or the concert we did, in 2019, with the LA Phil and Herbie Hancock, a total love-in.'

In addition, a closer association with Guildhall School of Music and Drama, active but somewhat limited up till then, was fostered, and this benefitted greatly (in 2013) from the opening of the School's new building at Milton Court, a fine 600-seat concert hall and studio theatre close by in Silk Street. Humphreys stresses the mutual benefits, and importance, of this neighbourly exchange. 'Guildhall students perform in the Barbican Hall, they do their Gold Medal in the Barbican. The collaboration between Australian Chamber Orchestra and

Guildhall is extraordinary — players sit next to one another on absolutely equal terms. Meanwhile we curate 40 concerts in Milton Court each year, giving us an ideal smaller space with excellent acoustics. We've got a relationship that isn't one way. It's one of the joys of being here. Guildhall musicians aren't a spinoff to what we do. They're absolutely integral.'

When he arrived, Graham Sheffield immediately extended the somewhat rigid boundaries of music genres: Barbican Jazz was launched in 1996, and so too was the World Roots festival. With *Inventing America*, UK audiences embraced the American minimalists with open arms. Over the next two decades, the music of Philip Glass and Steve Reich would become a fixture in the Barbican season, with both composers being frequently in residence and, like John Adams, working with the LSO and the BBCSO. These charismatic stars still burn bright in the Barbican season, as Huw Humphreys warmly acknowledges: 'We have been very lucky indeed to have had long-term relationships with Steve Reich, Philip Glass and, more orchestrally mainstream, John Adams. They've been core to what the Barbican has done. Our reputation is also formed by this area between classical and contemporary which no one is quite sure what to define it as — people like Nico Muhly, Ólafur Arnalds, Daníel Bjarnason, Einaudi, Jóhann Jóhannsson. For some people it's classical music. For others it's veering off into non-classical and we've never sought to define it as one or the other.'

The person originally responsible for this area is Bryn Ormrod, who is now consultant creative producer at the Barbican while the programme is managed by Chris Sharp. 'I'm essentially the programmer of contemporary music,' says Ormrod, struggling to identify the boundaries of the wide-ranging terrain covered by Sharp and him. He arrived a year after Tusa and Sheffield and, in 2020, still advises on repertoire. 'It was an exciting time. I had no idea what to expect. Changes were just beginning. John brought Graham on board to broaden the programme beyond Western classical music and art. Graham hired me to help make it happen. My background was with a mainstream commercial music promoter, working at independent London venues like the Town and Country Club and the Jazz Café. I asked Graham want he wanted me to do. He said if there's anything that interests you, let's talk about it and see if we can bring it in, how it can work and attract audiences. It wasn't prescriptive. It was always carte blanche. Here's a magnificent concert hall, here's a budget, bring what you can. So we formed partnerships with festivals and presenters, and made a focus on different musical traditions, some geographic, some thematic: New Orleans jazz, blues, soul, electronica, Swing, Cuban, Buena Vista Social Club, Spanish flamenco, Brazilian avant-garde, Indian classical music — everything …'

All this had a radical impact on audiences that, in the 1990s, still divided broadly into classical, some jazz, some light entertainment. 'There was literally nothing else,' Ormrod points out. Suddenly new crowds were making their way to Silk Street, among them people from the very communities whose music was being played: followers of Gilberto Gil, Ali Akbar Khan, Ennio Morricone, Herbie Hancock; fans of music of Korea, Colombia, Chile. 'It was amazing. People came who knew this music, these artists, but couldn't hear them anywhere else. Others came because they were curious, catholic in taste, wanted

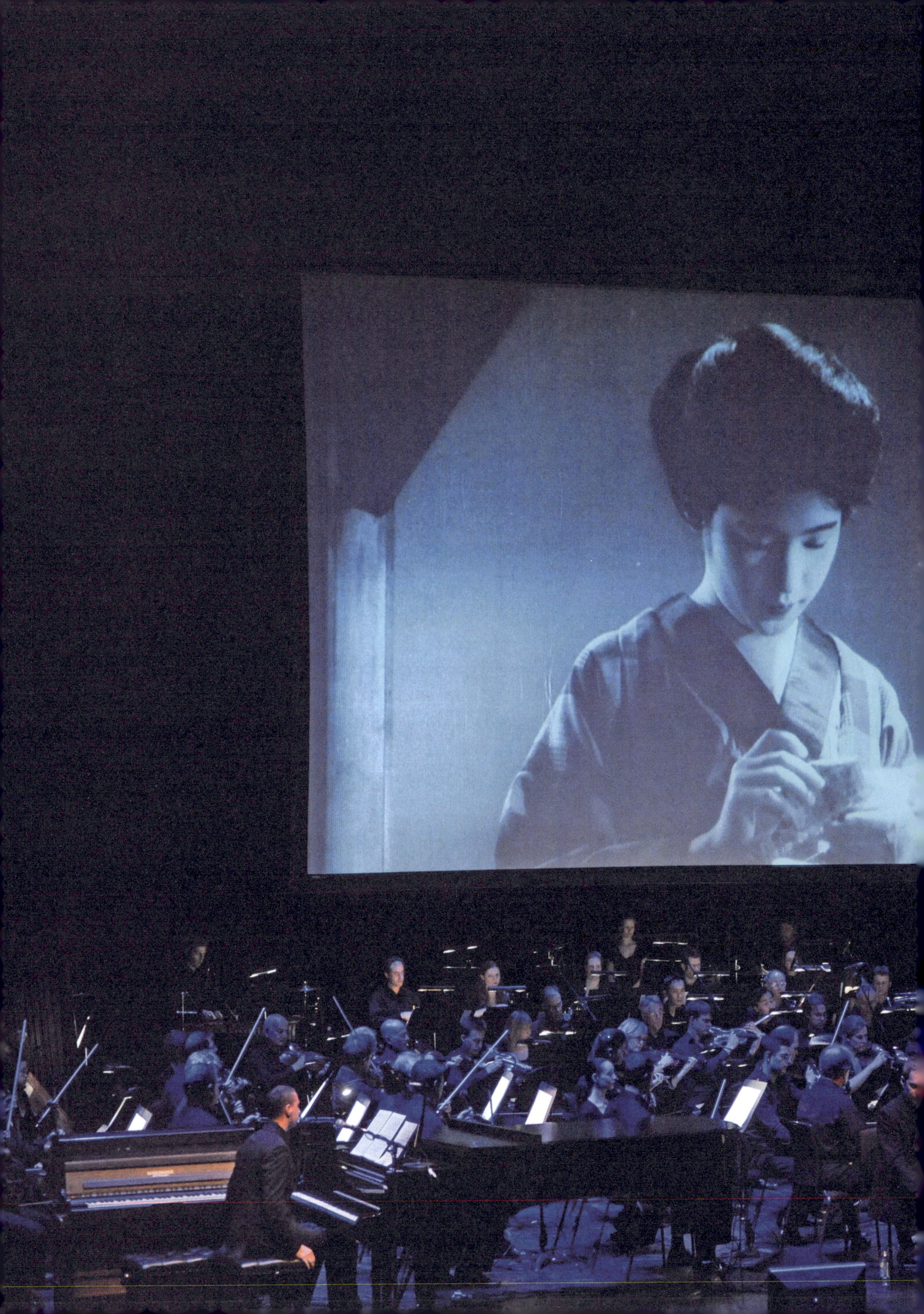

Nitin Sawhney

I have many powerful memories of working with the Barbican. Some of my fondest of these are in relation to the silent movies I composed for performance with the London Symphony Orchestra live at the Barbican. These were commissioned by the BFI, the first of which was a silent movie from 1929, by a German director called Franz Osten, entitled *A Throw of Dice*. This was loosely based on a tale from the Hindu scripture, the Mahabharat. Set in India, it was a beautiful story of the love rivalry between two kings. This was successively followed by my other two scores for the LSO, *Yogoto No Yume* by Japanese film noir director, Naruse, and finally my most challenging score for Hitchcock's 1927 silent movie *The Lodger*. It was an incredible pleasure to perform with the LSO as a pianist for all these productions but for *The Lodger* I actually conducted the LSO, which was a huge honour and privilege for me. Excited as I was to conduct such a renowned orchestra live at the Barbican, and despite our subsequent warm standing ovation, I was in a terrible state with pneumonia at the time and after a hastened conversation with the excellent film critic, Jason Solomons, afterwards I pretty much staggered into the wings.

Another fond memory of the Barbican is how open they were in supporting my work as a director when I conducted workshops for a play I had written about Albert Einstein's meetings with Rabindranath Tagore in Berlin in 1927 and 1930. I was joined for two weeks of workshops by the wonderful actress Natascha McElhone and two other superb actors. A final wonderful memory for me was working with theatrical company Complicité, whose performance of *A Disappearing Number*, which I scored, had its London premiere at the Barbican. This was a stunning theatrical performance based on the life, work and legacy of legendary Indian mathematician Srinivasa Ramanujan.

I feel that the Barbican is an incredible creative hub, supporting artists who want to challenge themselves and push the boundaries of creative exploration. I will always be grateful for how they have allowed me to do that.

Nitin Sawhney is a composer, musician and producer who has brought together many genres including Asian music, electronica, jazz and classical into his own distinctive mix in albums and concert performances, including at the Barbican with the LSO and Complicité.

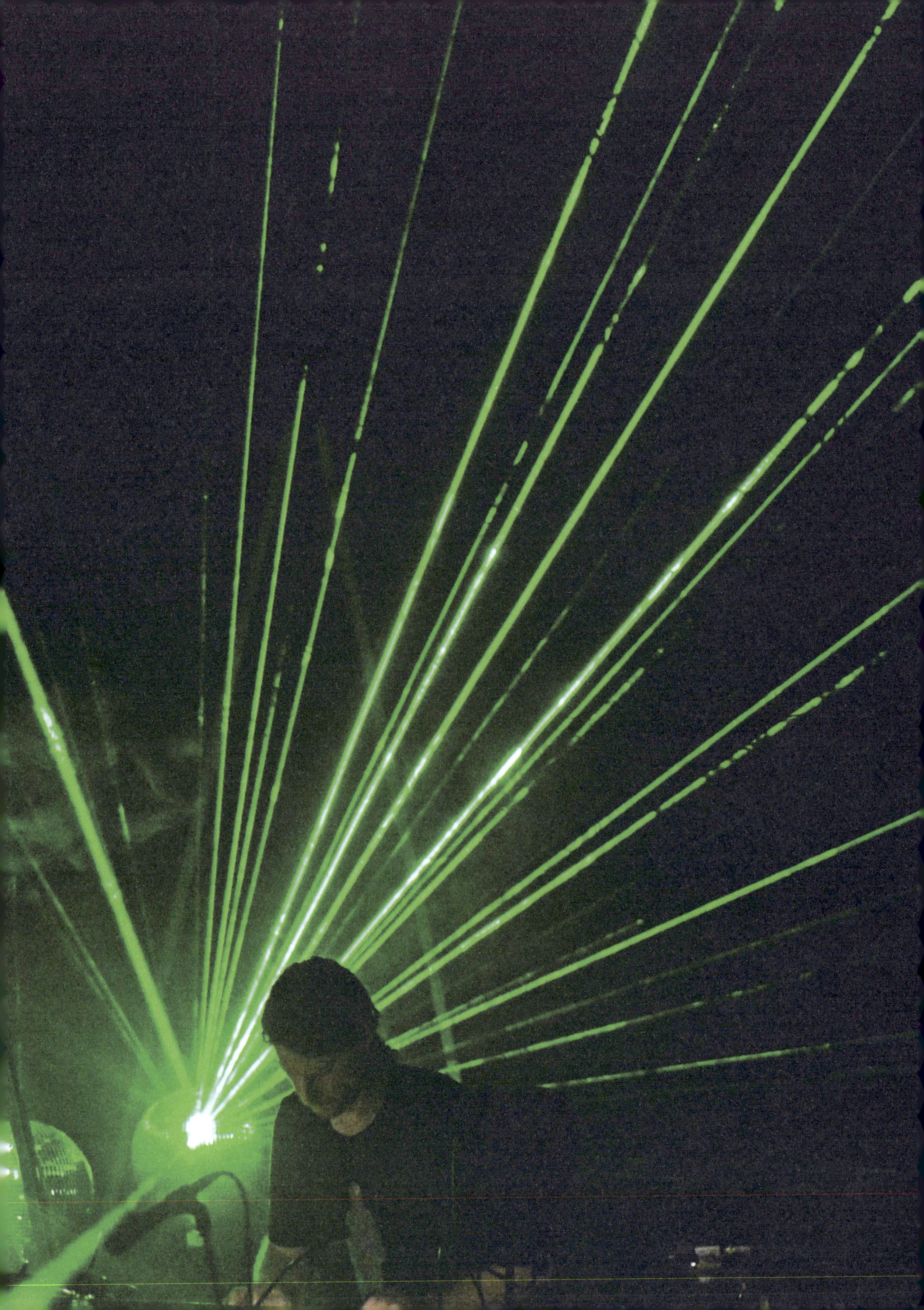

to experience music from other cultures. It was a unique mix of series, festivals, themes, mixed with film, theatre, visual art, dance, with lots of new commissions. We were always encouraged — by Robert van Leer, Angela Dixon and now Huw Humphreys — to see no emphatic dividing line between genres. To begin with we called our side of things 'non-classical' and then changed it to 'contemporary'. Neither term is perfect. There's been no master plan, but an incredible openness, and a confidence from the top to let us get on with it. Only many years later did I realise this. The Barbican was learning to improvise. That was a key to its success.'

An ability to improvise has been a lifeline not only to success but to survival for every artistic institution the world over: at the time of writing, London is still in the grip of the coronavirus pandemic and venues have once again shut down, after a year of cancellations globally and nationally. This was after 2020 had begun on a high, with a brilliantly devised Beethoven Weekender, in which five UK symphony orchestras shared out a cycle of all nine symphonies, the atmosphere one of friendship and excitement. As Humphreys says, 'It wasn't just the presentation of a Beethoven cycles. We had quartet concerts and Simon Callow reading Beethoven's letters to the Immortal Beloved, an exhibition with Beethoven's own ear-trumpet — that was the Barbican at its best, providing added value and supporting the best music-making of the UK.'

No one could foresee the catastrophe ahead which began in March. Following a closure period, there were a handful of concerts with socially distanced audiences and events streamed online, but a hoped-for re-opening in December 2020 with Krystian Zimerman and Simon Rattle was cancelled in a new lockdown. A ban on most international travel threw projects into disarray. Eventually in 2021 it also claimed the potential life of the planned new Centre for Music, intended as 'a world-class venue for performance and education across all musical genres, to inspire a new generation with a love of music', but in its place the City promised a comprehensive renewal of the Barbican's own building, which will be much needed over the decade to come.

Writing in the annual report, Nicholas Kenyon acknowledged the major impact the Covid year would have on future programming, not least via the power of digital transmission when we cannot be present in concert halls:

> Now we are considering how the digital offerings that have become so much a natural part of the audience's life during lockdown can be integrated into future blended models of presentation. With still limited numbers of live audiences in our theatres, cinemas and concert halls, work can be designed to communicate effectively through digital as well as live channels. One aspect of this will have to develop: the generous provision of much work online during lockdown was made freely, to maintain connections with audiences. This was a necessary and welcome initiative, but that work has a value that must now be returned to artists, performers and creative teams, so we have to work towards a model where those digital initiatives can earn a return to those who originated them.

Early electronic experiments: Aphex Twin, otherwise known as Richard David James, creating his unique musical mix in the conservatory at the Barbican.

The Barbican, like other arts institutions globally, found ways musically, via its Live from the Barbican series, to reach people in their homes, via their computers or smartphones. In December 2020, at the end of the hardest year ever for arts organisations the world over, one Associate, the Australian Chamber Orchestra, showed it had every intention of maintaining its relationship with London, carbon footprint and Covid-19 notwithstanding, and mounted an innovative digital residence. That spirit of inspired improvisation which characterises the Barbican's music is alive, and burns brightly. It was one of the reasons Huw Humphreys long dreamt of working there:

> I'm a Londoner. The Barbican was something I always aspired to, even when I worked on the other side of the world [with the Melbourne Symphony Orchestra]. It has an extraordinary resonance there for its curiosity of programming: striving, morphing, changing, never complacent. I think that's what I found most attractive.
>
> As head of music when you see an audience coming to a concert and it's an audience you weren't expecting, that's the best feeling. Especially when it's full! When the ACO presented their own film *Mountain*, I had the feeling there were a lot of hardcore mountaineers there in the Barbican, surely in most cases for the first time. I almost expected to see pulleys and crampons. That was just wonderful.

The ingenuity and determination which have kept artistic life going, through the silent year and more of the pandemic of 2020–21, deserve praise. Yet what a hall needs above all, to thrive, to breathe, to excite, is live audiences. Across the years, as the Barbican has offered its astounding range of music to audiences, curated with skill by different generations of programmers, and performed with passion by an ever-wider range of artists, the experience has been that nothing matches the joy of sharing music, for audiences and artists who are for that moment united in one place. A happy return to this precious shared experience will be the biggest cause of celebration for us all as the Barbican reaches its 40th birthday.

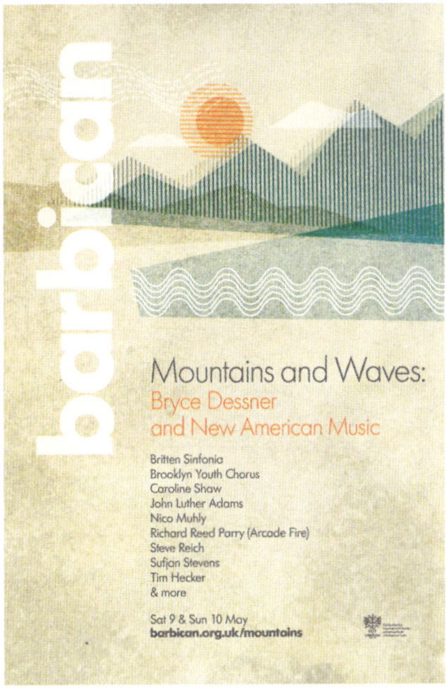

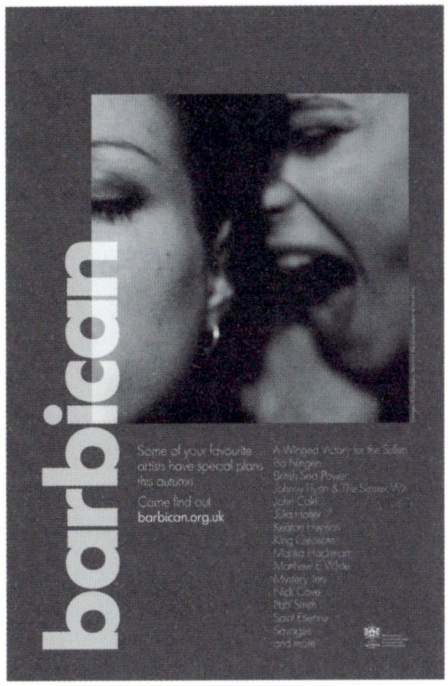

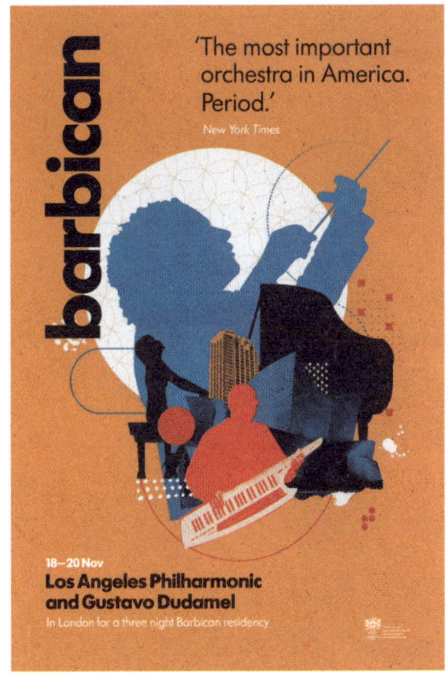

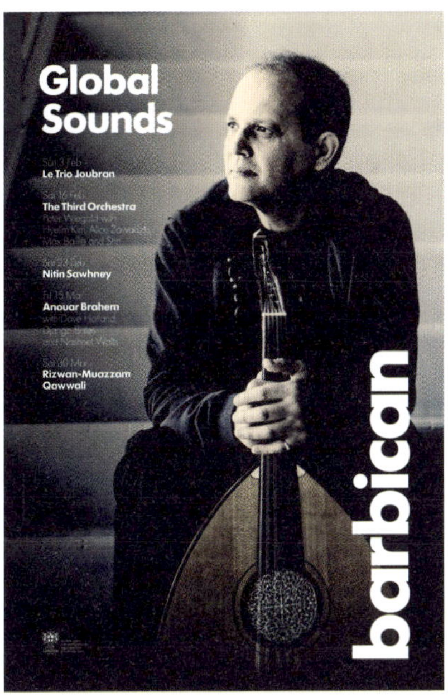

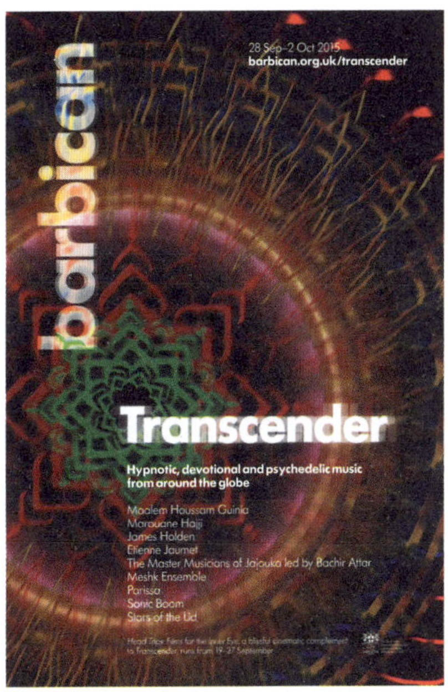

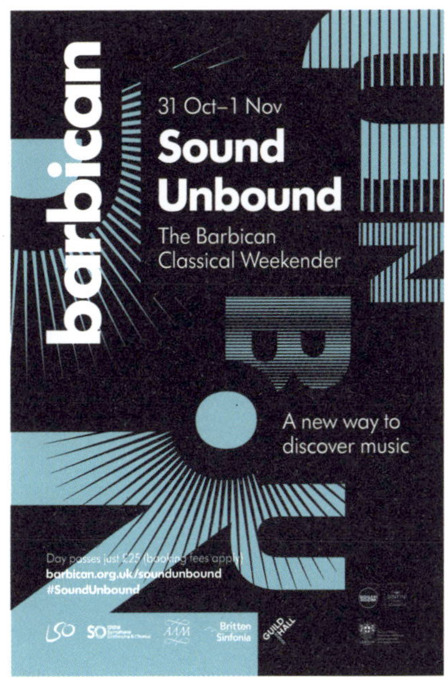

The sounds of the Barbican: music series across the genres including Global Sounds, Transcender, and the innovative Sound Unbound classical weekender.

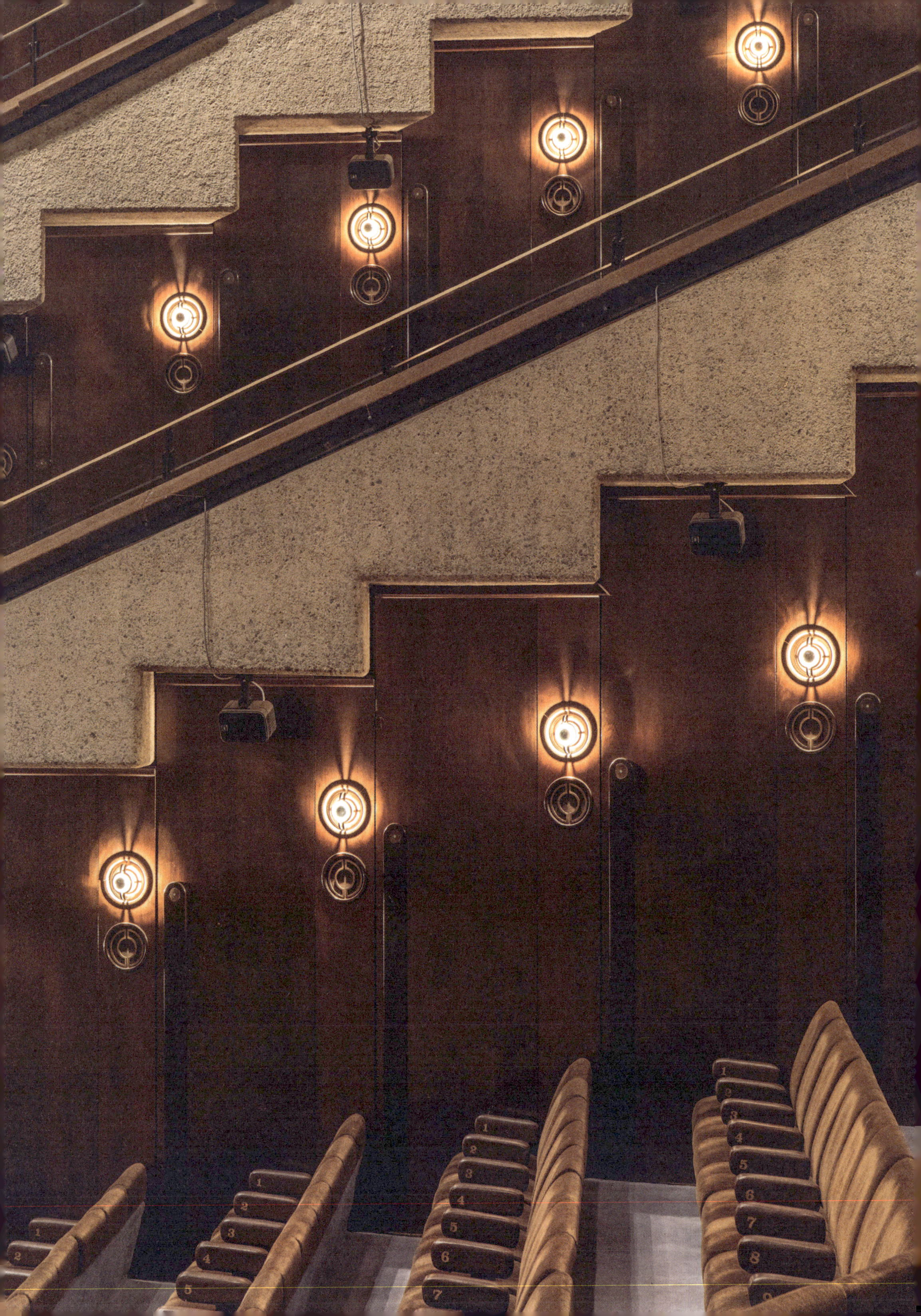

Theatre

Lyn Gardner

In theatre, the best place to start a play is often not at the very beginning of the story, but at the point when the plot thickens. So it is with the Barbican, when considering its considerable contribution to the theatre ecology of our time.

To begin in the middle of the drama, on 19 May 1998 Robert Wilson and Philip Glass's opera *Monsters of Grace* opened in the Barbican Theatre. Billed as a 'new digital opera in three dimensions', *Monsters* claimed to offer a signpost to the future of opera. More than one British opera critic trembled at the prospect it presented. *Monsters* may not have been a rip-roaring success, either with critics or audiences, but it signalled a significant change of direction for the centre. It was a change that would have lasting impact on the landscape of British theatre.

Over the following weeks, *Monsters* was swiftly followed by Stéphane Braunschweig's revival of *Measure for Measure*, and a seven-and-a-half-hour adaptation of Dostoevsky's satire on revolutionary zeal and human corruptibility, *The Possessed*, directed by the legendary Lev Dodin for the Maly Theatre of St Petersburg. The latter had been rehearsed over three and half years and came with the performances you'd expect from that investment of time. *The Observer* dubbed the acting 'a marvel'. It was: many of the ensemble stayed on stage almost throughout the piece and this was a masterclass in how in acting less is so often more, in a drama played out on a design of weathered timber and murky shadows that seemed to evoke secrets and suspicion.

There were also visits from Chicago's Steppenwolf Theatre with the 1930s comedy, *The Man Who Came to Dinner*, the Twyla Tharp Dance Company and the Merce Cunningham Dance Company. Yukio Ninagawa offered up a production of *Hamlet* with a forest of hanging lights, and the Romanian director Silviu Purcărete adapted the *Oresteia* in a production that shocked with its weirdly compelling mix of savagery and absurdity.

Some of these international shows were greeted with the same bewilderment as *Monsters of Grace*; others delighted audiences and were lauded by critics. Twyla Tharp's *The One Hundreds*, just one contribution in the Barbican's year-long thread of work across every art form entitled *Inventing America*, was acclaimed as the very best of the year. 'Brief but explosive,' was the verdict of the *Independent* about Tharp's piece in which 100 members of the public with no dance experience were each taught a single dance phrase lasting 11 seconds which they then performed simultaneously on the Barbican stage.

Tharp's piece was to herald many future projects with community involvement at the Barbican, including Deborah Warner's 2005 *Julius Caesar* that not only boasted Ralph Fiennes, Simon Russell Beale and Fiona Shaw in the cast, but also a hundred extras on the bare stage playing the volatile seething masses intent on popping both party balloons and political reputations. Or Nic Green's fiercely feminist hit, *Trilogy* (2010), in which groups of women enthusiastically accepted the invitation to strip off and join the naked cast on stage in a show which celebrated both women's achievements and their bodies — whatever their shape or size.

The significance of this first Barbican International Theatre Events (BITE) season was not in individual shows, however thrilling some of them were, but in the way that it offered a sustained window on the world. In this, and its subsequent iterations, it gave audiences a taste for international theatre and cross-art form practices and influenced rising generations of UK-based theatre-makers. The Barbican became a tastemaker. It continues to fulfil that role to this day.

For a British theatre culture that too often was navel-gazing, and which saw performance from beyond the UK as coming not just from another country but from another planet, this continuous programming of work from abroad, which would normally not be seen in the UK outside of festivals, was eye-opening. For increasing numbers of people — both audiences and practitioners — it was also exhilarating, making them redefine what they thought theatre and performance was and encouraging them to explore what it could be.

The first BITE season was hastily arranged to fill 22 weeks after the Royal Shakespeare Company's partial withdrawal from the building. Just how hastily is reflected in the testimony of Toni Racklin, now head of theatre, who when she first arrived at the Barbican to help set the season up, found 'six submission letters in a manila folder. We were pretty much starting from scratch, looking for companies who were making spellbinding work.' It was a challenge, but as a result the arts centre finally found its purpose and direction, and a compelling reason why audiences should find it. Almost two decades after it had opened the Barbican had not just put itself on the theatrical map but was invigorating that map itself.

The journey gained momentum when in 2002 the RSC left the Barbican completely, making room for the BITE seasons to become a year-round programme. That programme was constantly cross-fertilised by the activities in its galleries, its concert hall and its cinemas. It created, in effect, one Barbican and in the process transformed the place into one of most formidable arts centres in the world. 'Bringing the art forms together was transformative,' recalls Racklin, 'and it gave the Barbican its identity. It became a reference point for both artists and audiences. It was enthralling to see what happened when you offered Ninagawa alongside Merce Cunningham in the same programme and they bounced off each other. Often an audience comes out of the Barbican saying "I didn't expect that."'

Over the subsequent years the Barbican became the London home of international artists such as Robert Lepage and Ivo van Hove and also supported and nurtured UK-based artists including the great Fiona Shaw, and companies from Cheek by Jowl, Complicité and Duckie through to Boy Blue Entertainment and Ballet Black.

Racklin points out that while the Barbican has been able to attract the great names in international theatre, it has always understood that it has a responsibility to reflect a changing society, open up access and usher in the new. 'We've always been looking beyond the mainstream,' she says. The evidence of that has been in the way the Barbican has supported a company such as Ballet Black, the innovative company dedicated to bringing greater diversity to British ballet. Giving over the Barbican Theatre to Ballet Black has aided the company to become a major player, leading the way in innovation in an art form not known for diversity.

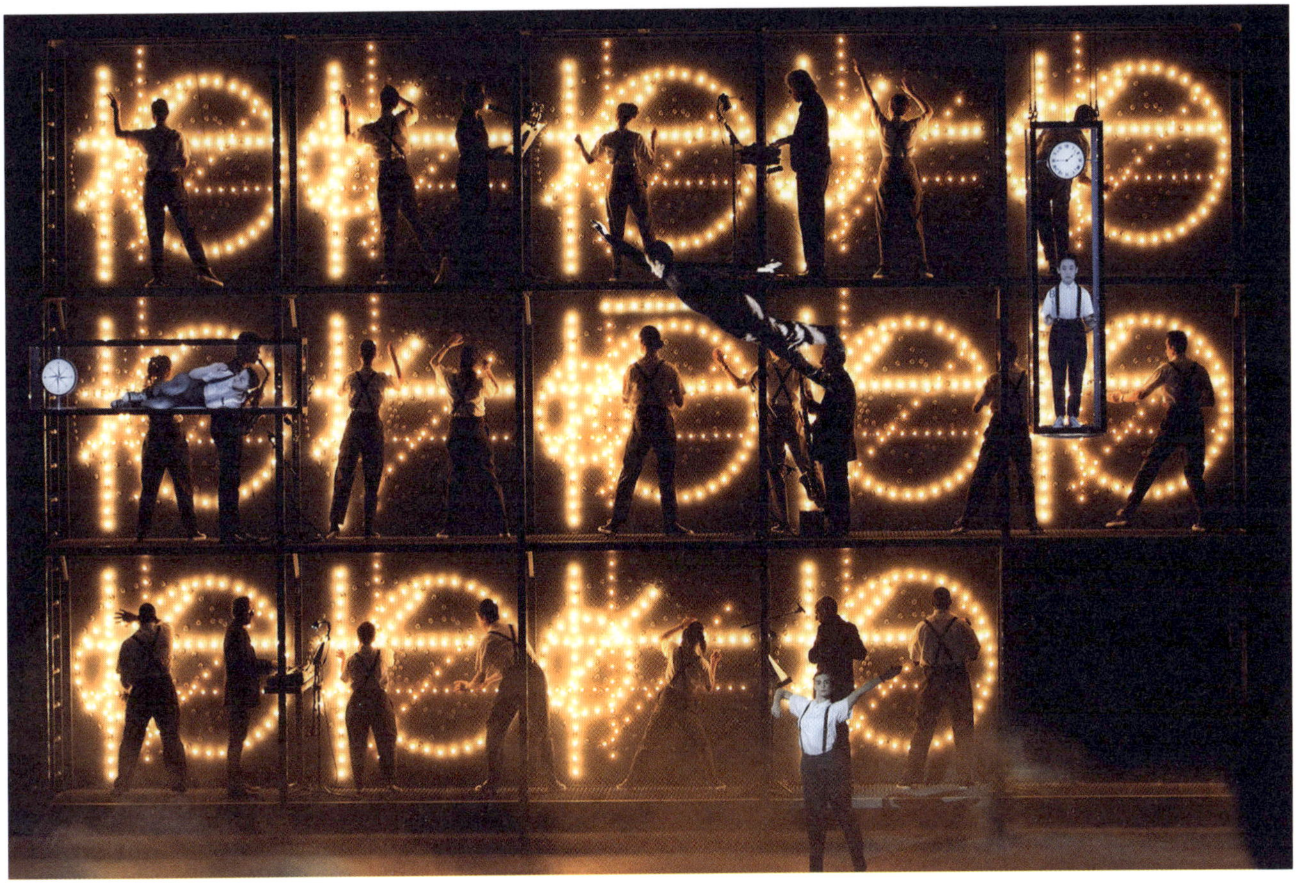

Einstein on the Beach, by Robert Wilson and Philip Glass, the classic minimalist music-drama, given its belated UK premiere in the Barbican Theatre in 2012.

In those days the Barbican became *the* place where you went to see the unexpected. You could see the Maly Theatre of St Petersburg put a swimming pool on stage as it did in 1999 for a revival of Chekhov's *Platonov*, a show that came complete with skinny-dipping and a jazz score, or the iconoclastic dance company, Fabulous Beast, updating a medieval Irish epic to 21st-century Ireland in *Bull* (2007). Or see regular visitor and Canadian theatrical wizard Robert Lepage in numerous shows including *The Far Side of the Moon* (2003), *The Andersen Project* (2006), *Lipsync* (2008), and *Needles and Opium* (2016) and *887* (2017). Or keep track of the work of Robert Wilson: when he returned to the Barbican in 2012 with the iconic Philip Glass collaboration *Einstein on the Beach* it was an Olympic-year event; music-theatre writ large. 'The Barbican space is an epic stage, and it needs work and artists who can fill it,' says Racklin.

The Barbican was, and remains, a place that revels in springing surprises. It was where London first saw the work of the German director Thomas Ostermeier with his shockingly explosive takes on both *Hedda Gabler* and *A Doll's House*. In the latter, Nora didn't just leave with a slam of the door but went out with all guns blazing. It was a rare example of finding yourself leaving the theatre after seeing a century-old play, seething with the same intensity and excitement that audiences must have felt when the play was first staged. There was a similar excitement in the work of Australian director Simon Stone, whose

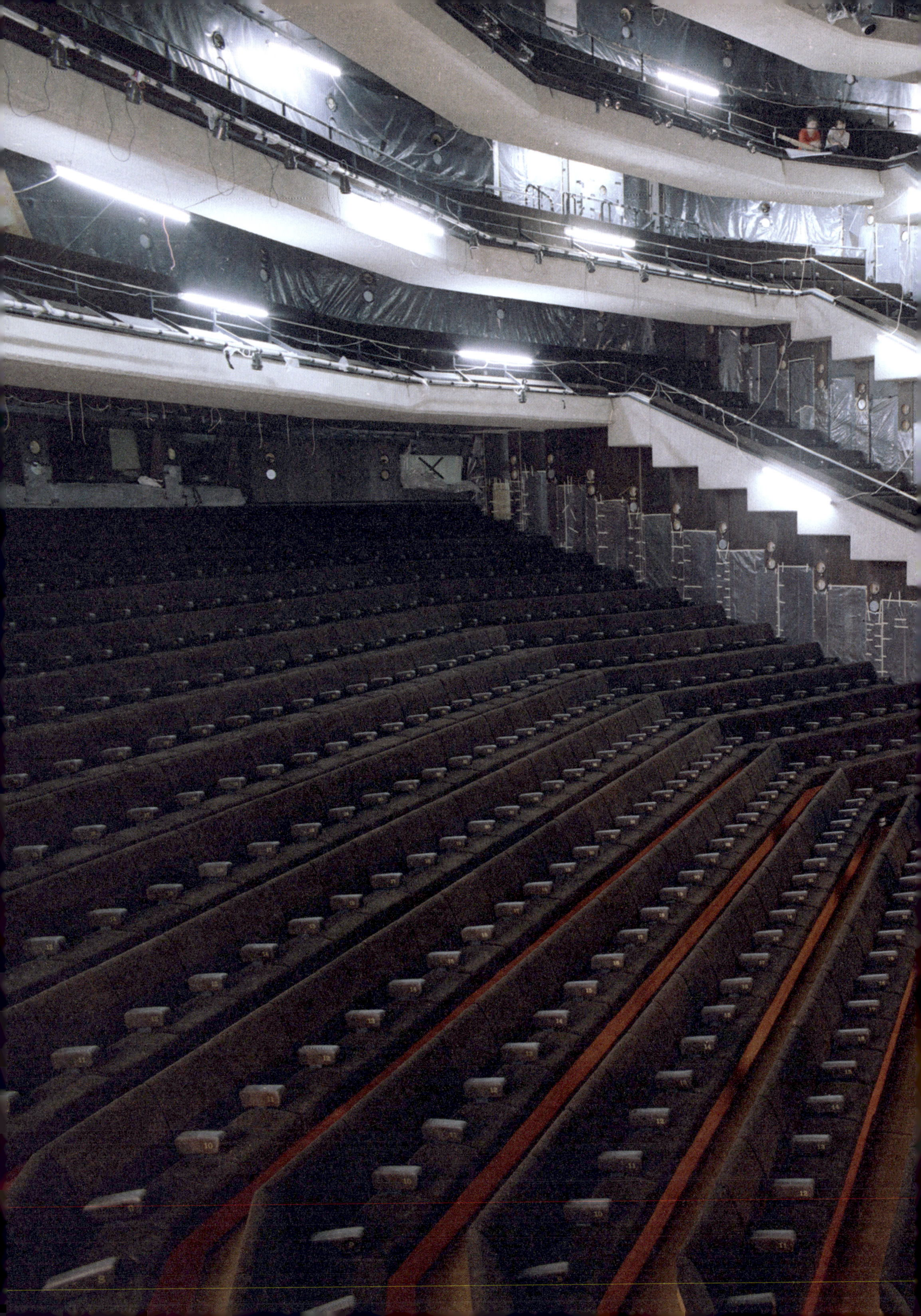

Kate Wood

We moved into the Barbican in February 1976. Very exciting, new home, new life, totally new place to live and the promise of the RSC and the library to come. At the time we moved in the arts centre was very much a work in progress. We came to Brandon Mews to find that what is now Speed Lawn was the builders' yard for the work going on at the arts centre and Guildhall School.

We watched with interest the growth of the fly tower, followed by the erection of the conservatory. By then residents had been invited to take part in various acoustic tests in the concert hall so we had had the opportunity to see how the centre was developing. I was hoping for similar invitations to the theatre but they were not forthcoming, so we had to wait until the RSC sent out the first invitation to members to book for the first season. I rapidly sent off for the first two productions, *Henry IV* on the main stage and *Our Friends in the North* to open the Pit. I got tickets for the first previews of both, including tickets numbered 1 and 2 for the Pit!

We entered the main theatre with great curiosity. The seats were well spaced and comfortable, and we looked up from the stall to see the remarkable raking of the seats on the higher levels. Then came the exciting moment when all those doors at the end of each row of seats slid into place and we were able to take in the full effect of the design – all this before the action started on the stage and the effect of that incredible rake became apparent. I can't pretend to have been over-impressed by the production, but that was not important. The great thing was that we now had the RSC only ten minutes away from where we lived, including the experimental excitement of the Pit.

So we had the enormous variety of the RSC repertoire to occupy us, not to mention the excitement of watching the start of the careers of most of the current elite of the British theatre. A browse through the programmes from those years really is a trip down theatrical history. We went to see every production and had some magical evenings, classic performances of Shakespeare, the Pit putting on obscure classics such as Fletcher alongside new works by Edward Bond.

Kate Wood is a retired librarian and theatregoer who moved into the Barbican in 1976, partly because she knew the RSC was planning to occupy the theatre.

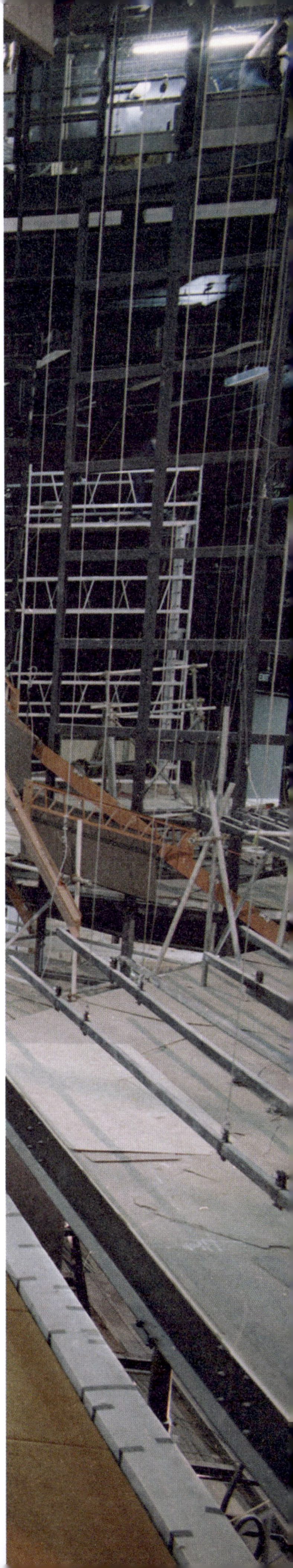

The Wild Duck (2014), set in the glass house of a modern Australian family, and *Medea* (2019) were both lessons in how to scrape the barnacles from classic works to reveal the unexpected truths lurking beneath well-known plays.

It was also where you might find U Theatre from Taiwan with *The Sound of the Ocean* (2002), a beguiling and utterly alien mix of meditative Buddhist ritual and explosive percussion. Or the South African director Yaël Farber exploring the legacies of truth and reconciliation in *Molora* (2008), a flinty, grief-filled version of the *Oresteia* that transposes the story to the present-day rural Xhosa community in South Africa to examine the cycles of violence and vengeance, and to ask whether forgiveness is ever possible. A trip to the Barbican could take you to the four corners of the globe and back again.

Innovation flourished and was constantly nurtured. It was at the Barbican that London audiences first saw the work of Ivo van Hove when in 2009 his *Roman Tragedies*, an extraordinary interval-less six-hour compression of *Coriolanus*, *Julius Caesar* and *Antony and Cleopatra*, first hit the Barbican stage, returning in 2017. The piece made the audience part of the action by including them on stage and allowing them to come and go, and in the process implicating them in an unfolding drama of private obsessions and political ambitions in a production of such dazzling stagecraft that, as *The Guardian* observed, it was as if 'Shakespeare is not only our contemporary but only finished writing the plays this morning'.

Indeed Shakespeare has become one of the Barbican's strongest and most enduring strands of programming, whether Calixto Bieito's Catalan version of *Macbeth* (2003), set in a gangland world where life is cheap and thuggery wins out, or Japan's Ninagawa Company's two productions of *Hamlet*, Deborah Warner's epic *Julius Caesar* in 2005, or the famous blockbuster show that was Lindsey Turner's 2015 staging of *Hamlet* at the Barbican with Benedict Cumberbatch in the title role. That instant sell-out *Hamlet* not only reached a live audience in EC2 but was also broadcast live over the entire UK and to audiences in 25 countries. The richness of the Barbican's classical and Shakespeare offer has been apparent not just in the large theatre but also in its use of the smaller Silk Street auditorium, which is part of the Guildhall School of Music and Drama. Here Cheek by Jowl have become regular visitors with their crystalline Shakespeare productions, including 2015's Russian language revival of *Measure for Measure* relocated to a shadowy place that suggested Putin's Moscow.

The basement Pit theatre, the Barbican's studio space, has also frequently hosted unexpected takes on the Shakespearian canon including Poland's Song of the Goat Theatre's *Macbeth* (2010), which treated Shakespeare's text like an orchestral score, and Forced Entertainment's *Complete Works: Tabletop Shakespeare* (2016) in which the plays were retold using only household utensils such as whisks and pepper pots. Both companies proved — as the Barbican so often demonstrated over the years — that when it came to Shakespeare what initially appeared like creative liberties often resulted in creative liberations.

This ability to make us look at Shakespeare differently, in different languages and through different lenses, was something of an irony given that the BITE seasons were conceived to plug the gap following the departure of the Royal Shakespeare Company for whom the Barbican had been intended as a year-round London home.

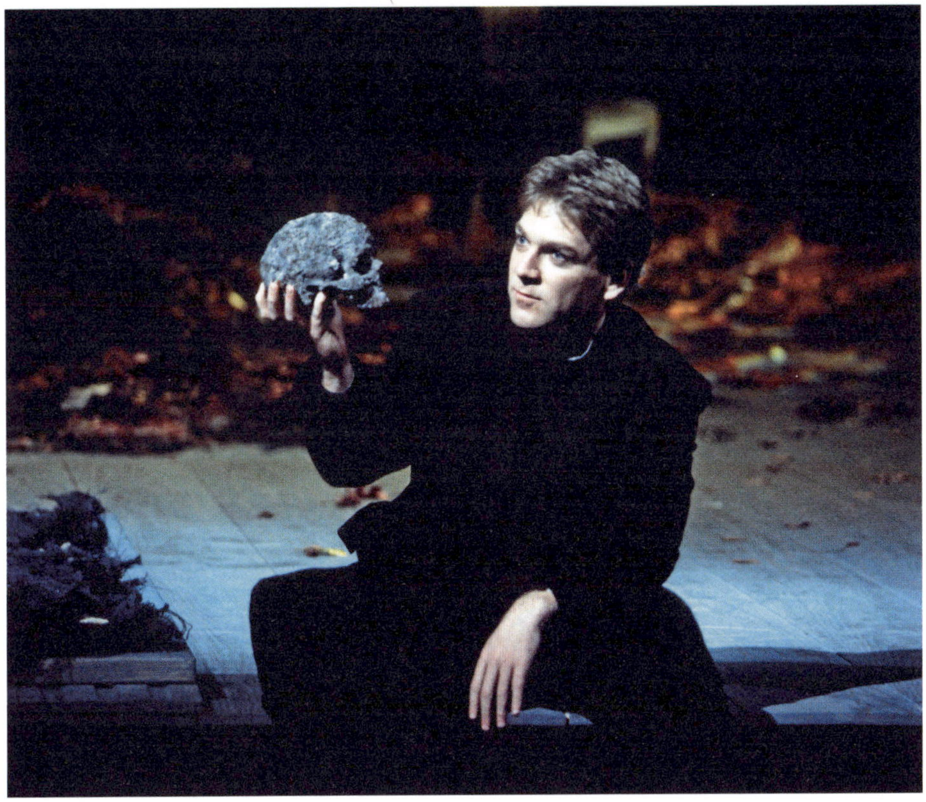

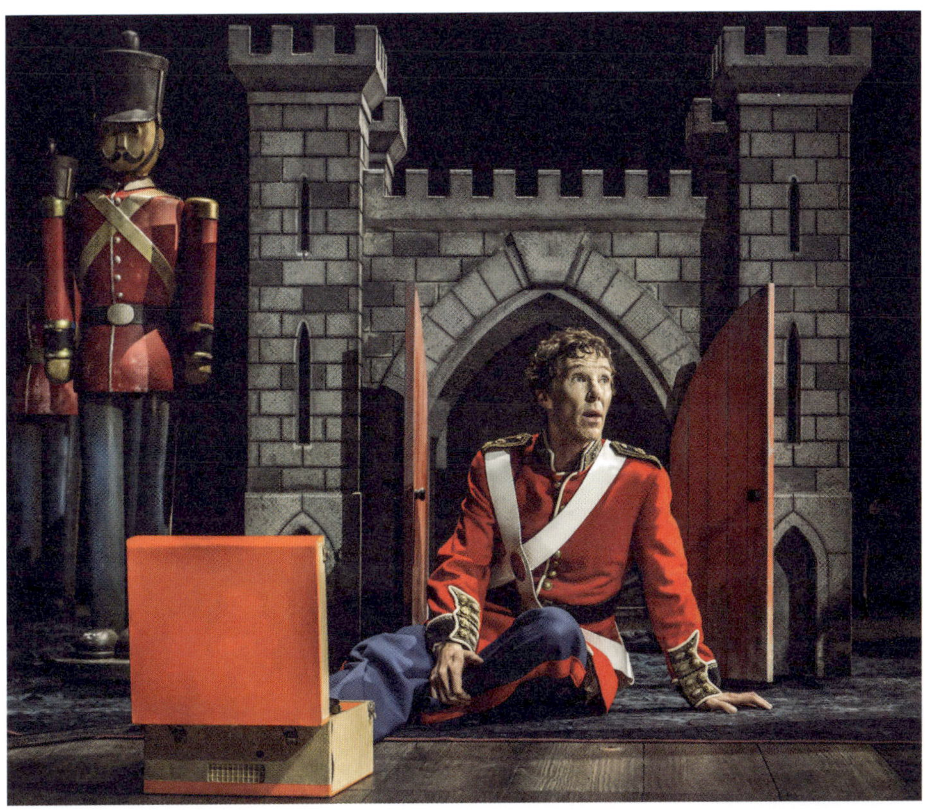

Hamlet across the decades: Kenneth Branagh with the Royal Shakespeare Company in 1992, directed by Adrian Noble (top); Benedict Cumberbatch in the instantly sold-out Sonia Friedman Productions presentation in 2015, directed by Lyndsey Turner (bottom).

Following pages
The multi-media, hi-tech, participatory staging of *Roman Tragedies* by Ivo van Hove and Toneelgroep Amsterdam, 2009, weaving together the texts of *Coriolanus*, *Julius Caesar* and *Anthony and Cleopatra* in an unbroken six-hour sequence, with audience encouraged to move around and sit on stage.

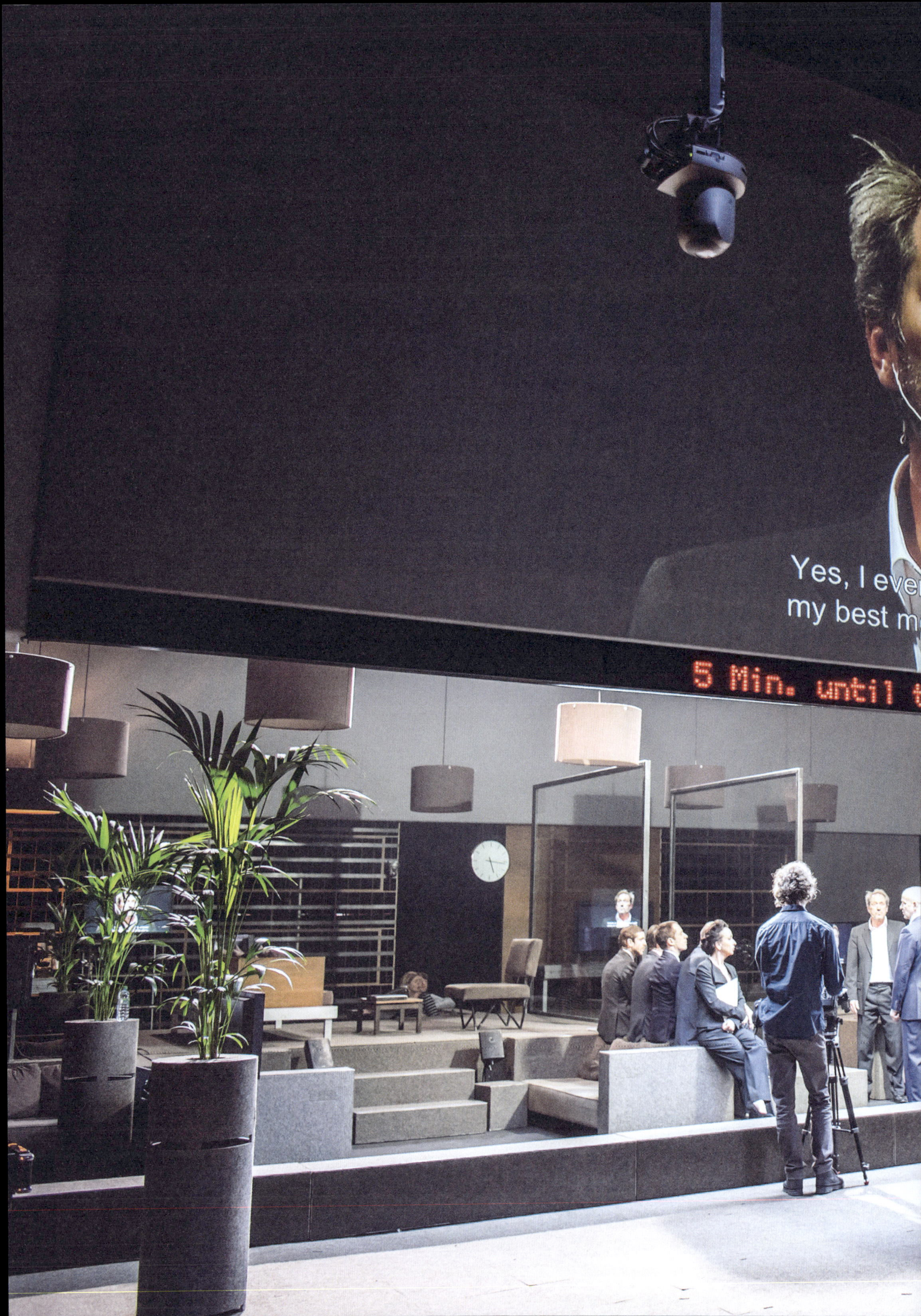
Yes, I ever
my best m
5 Min. until t

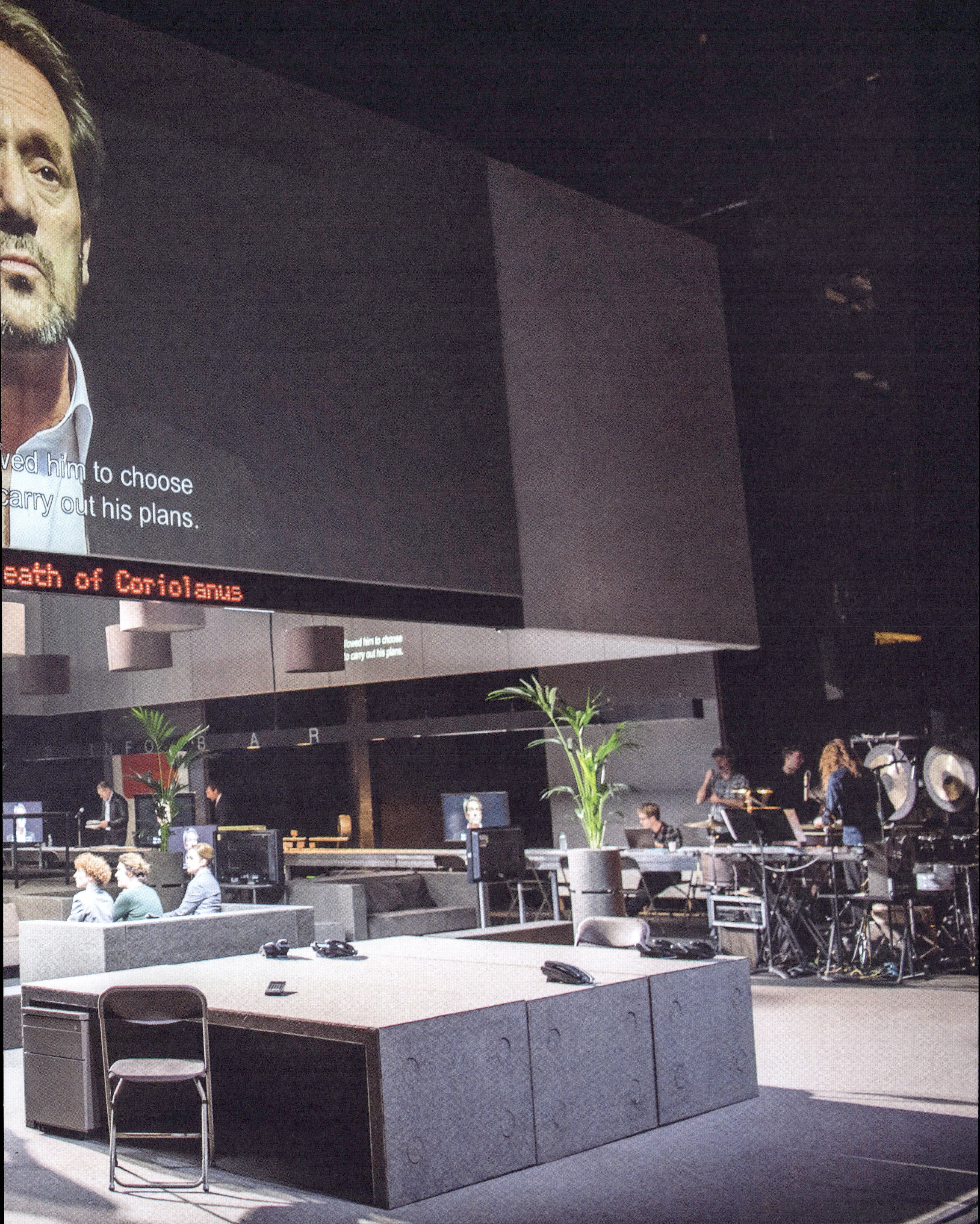
ved him to choose
carry out his plans.
eath of Coriolanus

When the Barbican Arts Centre opened in 1982 its theatre and studio space — the Pit — were the designated London residence of the Royal Shakespeare Company. It was the first time in the RSC's history that it was to have a permanent London base, and its new relationship with the Barbican should have been a marriage made in heaven.

The RSC had had a significant say in the design of the new Barbican Theatre and the then artistic director Trevor Nunn professed himself delighted with the result, calling the theatre 'a jewel in a sea of concrete'. The critics mostly agreed. The company's first production, a revival of *Henry IV* parts one and two, directed by Nunn himself, may have been dismissed as a little lacklustre, but most critics admired the theatre enormously, and not just for the novelty of the aisle doors that appeared to close like magic at the start of the performance. On the opening night the audience applauded the doors enthusiastically.

For audiences, for whom London theatregoing of scale often meant spending time in cramped, uncomfortable conditions, the shallowness of the auditorium created a sense of intimacy and democracy, and the leg room brought much pleasure. In *The Observer*, Robert Cushman declared the Barbican Theatre 'a triumph', writing that 'in the fanned auditorium you are excitingly aware of being part of a large house in contact with both actors and fellow spectators'. At last the RSC had a London home that was fit to produce 20th-century Shakespeare and take it into the 21st century.

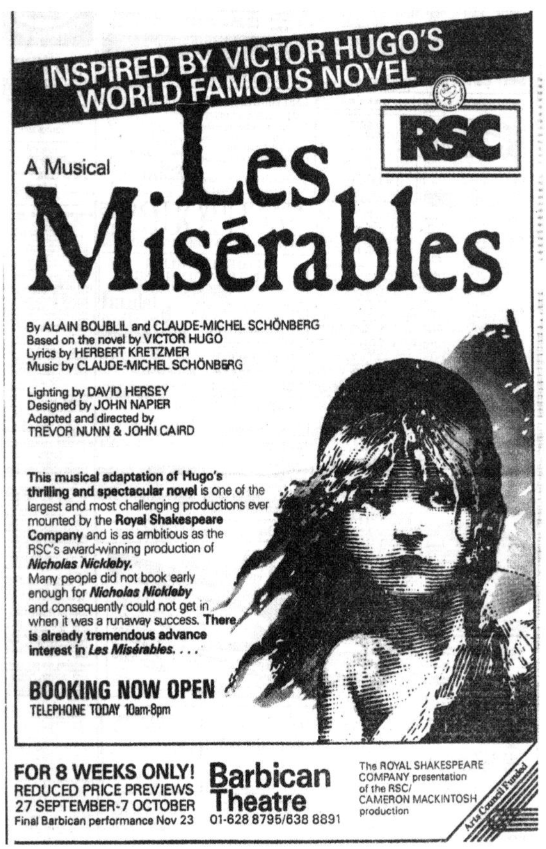

The slow start of a huge success story: the English-language premiere of *Les Misérables* by the Royal Shakespeare Company at the Barbican in 1985.

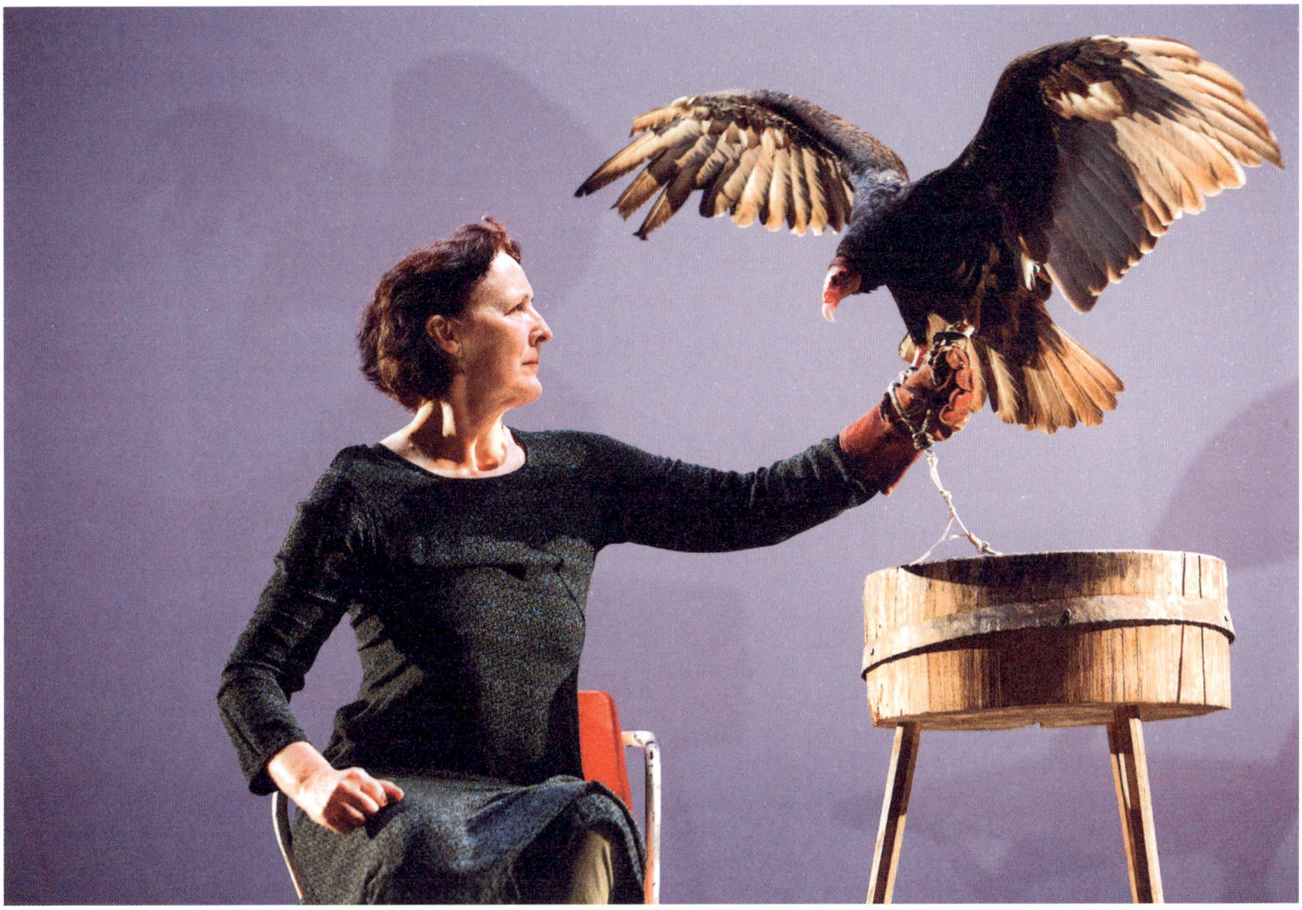

Fiona Shaw in the one-woman dramatisation of Colm Tóibín's *The Testament of Mary*, directed by Deborah Warner, 2014.

But the RSC was in deep financial trouble when it arrived at the Barbican, and only the surprise success of *Nicholas Nickleby* in its final season at the Aldwych saved it from imminent ruin. Its financial difficulties were to continue for many years despite the commercial success of the musical *Les Misérables*. This international mega-hit premiered at the Barbican in 1985 to indifferent reviews, before transferring to the West End where it triumphed and has been running ever since, interrupted only by the pandemic.

There were other difficulties with the RSC's tenure. The company disliked the lack of natural light in rehearsal spaces, the box office systems of the Barbican and the RSC's Stratford operation were not immediately compatible, and it was tricky to fit work from the Swan Theatre in Stratford into the Barbican because the theatre stage was too big for it and the Pit too small.

There were many very fine non-Shakespeare plays brought to the Barbican by the RSC over the years including Christopher Hampton's version of Laclos' *Les Liaisons Dangereuses* with Alan Rickman, Juliet Stevenson, Lindsay Duncan and Fiona Shaw, Peter Flannery's *Singer* with Antony Sher, and David Edgar's *Maydays*. But in originating at the Barbican, *Les Misérables* was the exception rather than the rule, with the majority of the work starting in Stratford and then being moved to London.

This was not itself an issue for the Barbican, but the RSC — used to the bright lights of the West End for its London seasons — missed the glitz and tingle of being in central London, and some audiences who had loved the RSC's annual residence at the Aldwych proved reluctant to beat a path to the Barbican. The relationship turned increasingly fractious, as the RSC's financial situation became ever more fraught: as John Tusa, who took over as managing director of the Barbican in 1995, subsequently remarked, 'The RSC were reluctant tenants. We were grumpy landlords.' The relationship was heading for breakdown. In 1998 the RSC withdrew for 22 weeks of the year, ushering in the first BITE season, and in 2002, amidst much acrimony, the RSC artistic director, Adrian Noble, pulled the company out of the Barbican altogether.

The wounds took some time to heal, but heal they did, not least because the RSC never found a satisfactory alternative London base. Eased by the smooth 2013 transfer from Stratford of the box office success of *Richard II*, starring former Doctor Who David Tennant, and realising that this was a production that otherwise Londoners would have missed out on, the RSC eventually returned to the Barbican to take up an annual London residency in 2014. Appropriately, it was the year that marked the 450th anniversary of Shakespeare's birth.

The new relationship was very different from the one that existed when the RSC had departed over a decade previously. The Barbican had turned itself into a much appreciated and loved theatre and performance destination for audiences, the RSC leadership had changed, and the new connection was a warm one and on an entirely different footing. The RSC were welcomed back as honoured guests and the Barbican, with a new managing director and supportive arts and theatre heads, were helpful and gracious hosts. It was a win-win for everybody, particularly when the two organisations agreed to partner on a creative learning programme together. The relationship continues to thrive to this day.

Back in the late 1990s and early 2000s, the withdrawal of the RSC, at first partially and then completely, could have been a major crisis for the Barbican. But as Graham Sheffield, who from 1995 was the artistic director of the arts centre, observed: 'What on the face of it appeared to be a liability we managed to turn to our advantage.'

Aided by a substantial 1997 theatre refurbishment that opened up the theatre space to the world's leading dance companies and large-scale productions, Sheffield started to turn the Barbican into a home for both international companies and artists but also for British companies. A lot of the success that followed had to do with the quiet brilliance of head of theatre Louise Jeffreys (who went on to succeed Sheffield as artistic director of the Barbican), and Toni Racklin, who both had a sharp eye not just for the shimmering blockbuster international show but also for the mavericks and rising stars of both international and British theatre. They were as eager to present Canada's Cirque Éloize as they were to co-produce Laurie Anderson. They recognised that there was not just one Barbican theatre audience but many audiences whose journeys would intersect and cross over.

The first all-year-round BITE season in 2002 included Robert Wilson's production of *Woyzeck* for Denmark's Betty Nansen Theatre, a contemporary

Duckie, who described themselves as 'purveyors of Progressive Working Class Entertainment', presenting the raunchy *C'est Barbican!* in the Pit, 2003–4, which created a cabaret-style dive mocking conventional theatrical convention, and won an Olivier Award for Best Entertainment.

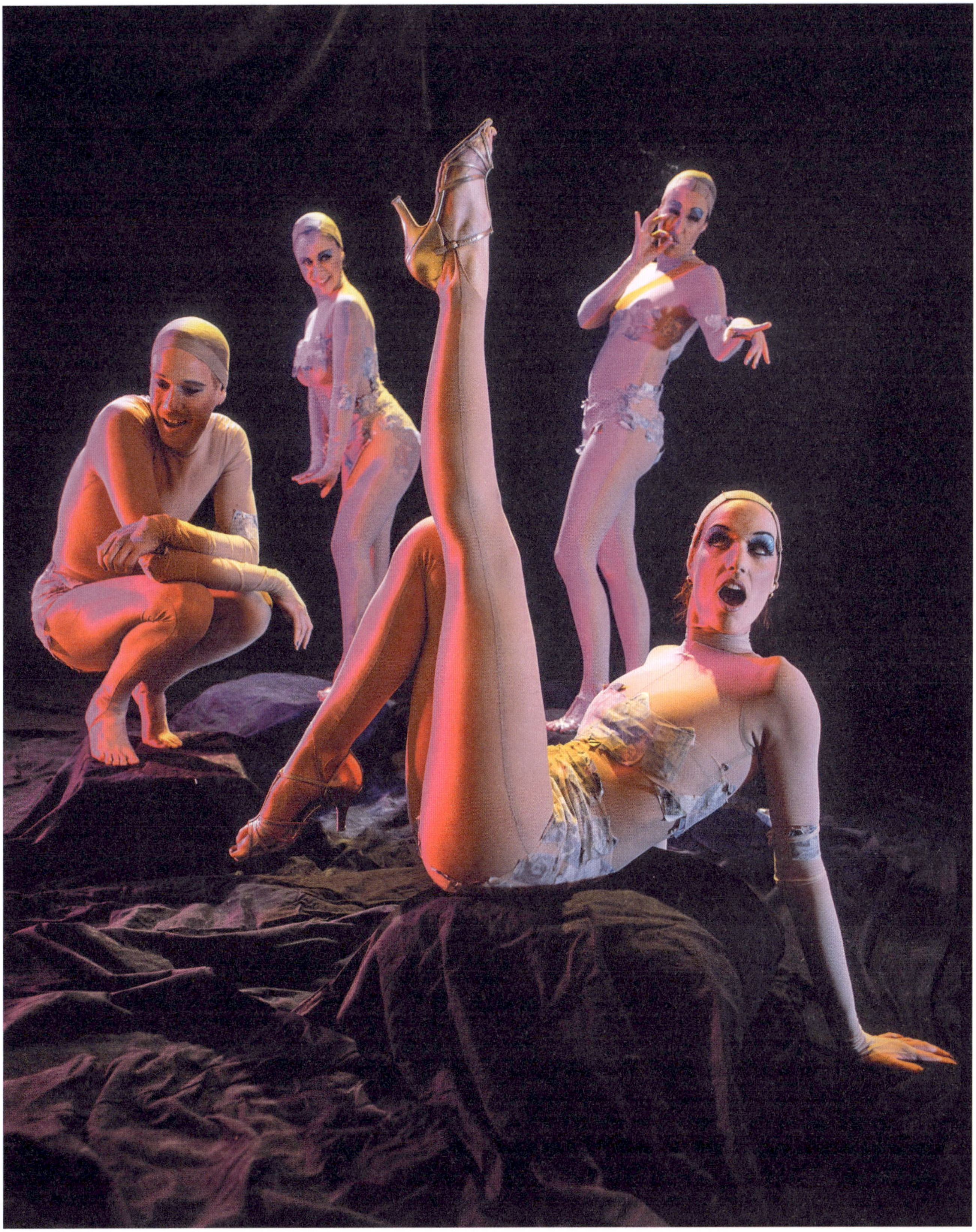

response to Georg Buchner's 1837 text, that came with a score by Tom Waits. There were dance offerings from Pina Bausch, Merce Cunningham and Deborah Colker. But the season also included the Tbilisi Marionette Theatre's *The Battle of Stalingrad*, a 70-minute puppet rendition of one of the bloodiest battles of World War II, and Ridiculusmus's *Say Nothing*, a seriously funny riff on the Northern Irish peace process.

Tusa firmly believed that 'if you programme with ambition and imagination your audience will find you'. Slowly, he began to be proved right. Audiences started to look to the Barbican not just to deliver high-gloss international productions but also to deliver surprises, whether it was Forced Entertainment's 24-hour marathon *Quizoola* (seen at the Barbican in 2013), or Duckie inviting audiences to get into their pyjamas and bed down in the Pit overnight for *Lullaby* (2011). The latter is quite possibly the only show ever made whose intention was to send the audience to sleep.

One of the things that has distinguished Barbican programming since the late 1990s has been the way that it has embraced all performance forms with unusual gusto, with a special focus on dance alongside theatre. It has fulfilled the true function of an arts centre not just by its cross-art form approach but also by siting circus alongside the contemporary dance of Michael Clark, mixing puppetry with plays, and catering for children and young people with the same care as it attended to work made for adult audiences.

At the Barbican, alongside the Royal Dramatic Theatre's revival of Ibsen's *Ghosts* you would also find the imaginative artfulness of Canadian puppeteer Ronnie Burkett whose gorgeous, gaudy and heart-breaking *Memory Dress Triology — Tinka's New Dress, Street of Blood* and *Happy* — offered minute observations on the best and worst of human behaviour, despite the fact no character was more than 75cm (2.5 ft) tall and all came with strings attached.

The Barbican championed great work from the classical canon brought by the great theatre companies from all across the world, but it also took a chance on rude upstarts like Duckie, the self-styled 'purveyors of Progressive Working Class Entertainment' whose gloriously sleazy 2002 interactive Christmas entertainment at the Royal Vauxhall Tavern, *C'est Duckie!*, was repackaged as *C'est Barbican!* the following year. In a savage satire on conspicuous consumption, designer Simon Vincenzi transformed the Pit into a cabaret-style dive where audiences could order a series of personal shows for their table — including Nacho Snatcho and Miss High Kick Does Seven Cocks — selected from an *à la carte* menu of acts.

Critics commented that it was quite a turn-up for the books to find this offering in the Pit, which so recently had been the home of that bastion of British theatre establishment, the RSC. Cocking a snook at traditional theatre practice and convention, *C'est Barbican!* went on to win Duckie an Olivier Award for Best Entertainment. It also signalled that the Barbican's artistic team could recognise a great popular show as a great show and had no time for the outmoded notions of high and low art that still beset British culture.

Duckie went on to make several other shows under the auspices of the Barbican and some of those involved in *C'est Barbican!* have continued relationships with the venue as solo artists, including Ursula Martinez, whose trilogy *Me, Me, Me*, and shows such as *My Stories; Your Emails* and *A Family Outing — 20 Years On* (2019) have found a regular home there.

Becoming a home for individual artists and companies has become an important function of the Barbican, whether they were uncategorisable maverick talents such as Lone Twin, who in 2007 spent a week making *Spiral*, an impossible journey through the Barbican Estate in which they attempted to navigate a spiral path from the Barbican tube station to the heart of the arts centre, or the mighty Schaubühne theatre from Berlin. It makes it unique in the British theatre landscape.

The urge to be a home rather than just a venue may have resulted partly from the lessons learned from the breakdown in its relationship with the RSC. But it was also about recognising the importance of nurturing longer-term relationships and lending artists support over many years and not just a single production. It is a distinctly different approach from the mentality which infects so much British theatre culture, which often reverts to the idea that you are only as good as your last show. The Barbican team understood that while perhaps an artist's last show might not have lived up to expectation, the next one might be a real beauty.

Long-term relationships have another benefit: they allow audiences and critics to start learning the vocabulary of artists with which they might be initially unfamiliar. It affords audiences the opportunity to expand their notions of performance, and over the years they can see developments in an artist's practice and also spot and make connections with other artists. Over the last 20 and more years, the Barbican has not just been developing artists but developing audiences too.

Richard Maxwell's 2001 visit with *House* and *Boxing* — the former played out in the Pit; the latter in the wings of the theatre, a space where actors linger awaiting their cues — offered a counterbalance to the great American dramas of the mid-20th century with which British audiences were so familiar. Instead of high drama there was deadpan mundanity. Even when the characters were experiencing high emotion, the actors delivered their lines with all the animation of the speaking clock. The result was curiously moving — as if language has suffered a catastrophic haemorrhage that leaves it bleached and exposed. Maxwell's subsequent visits allowed audiences to see a body of work that offered a very different slant on contemporary American life and culture.

The American avant-garde has often found a place at the Barbican whether it was the Wooster Group with *The Town Hall Affair* (2018), reconstructing and deconstructing one of the most notorious intellectual slug-outs of the 70s between Norman Mailer and feminists Jill Johnston and Germaine Greer, or Taylor Mac's fabulous and fabulously camp *A 24-Decade History of Popular Music* (2018). Mac's piece drew on 246 songs to chart the making of modern America from 1776 to the present day.

The Barbican has also supported those areas of British performance such as live art, and more recently spoken word and poetry, that for too long were ignored or overlooked by the mainstream. It has done so without trying to limit the scale on which artists operated. In 2004 Bobby Baker played the Pit with *Box Story*, an extraordinary meditation on the invisible domestic lives of women wrapped around a family tragedy. But in the same year Baker also single-handedly commanded the large stage in the quirky solo show *How to Live*, a gentle spoof on self-help and attitudes to mental health, which so won hearts it returned in 2006. Crossing the art forms with vigour, Circa's 2014 *Opus*

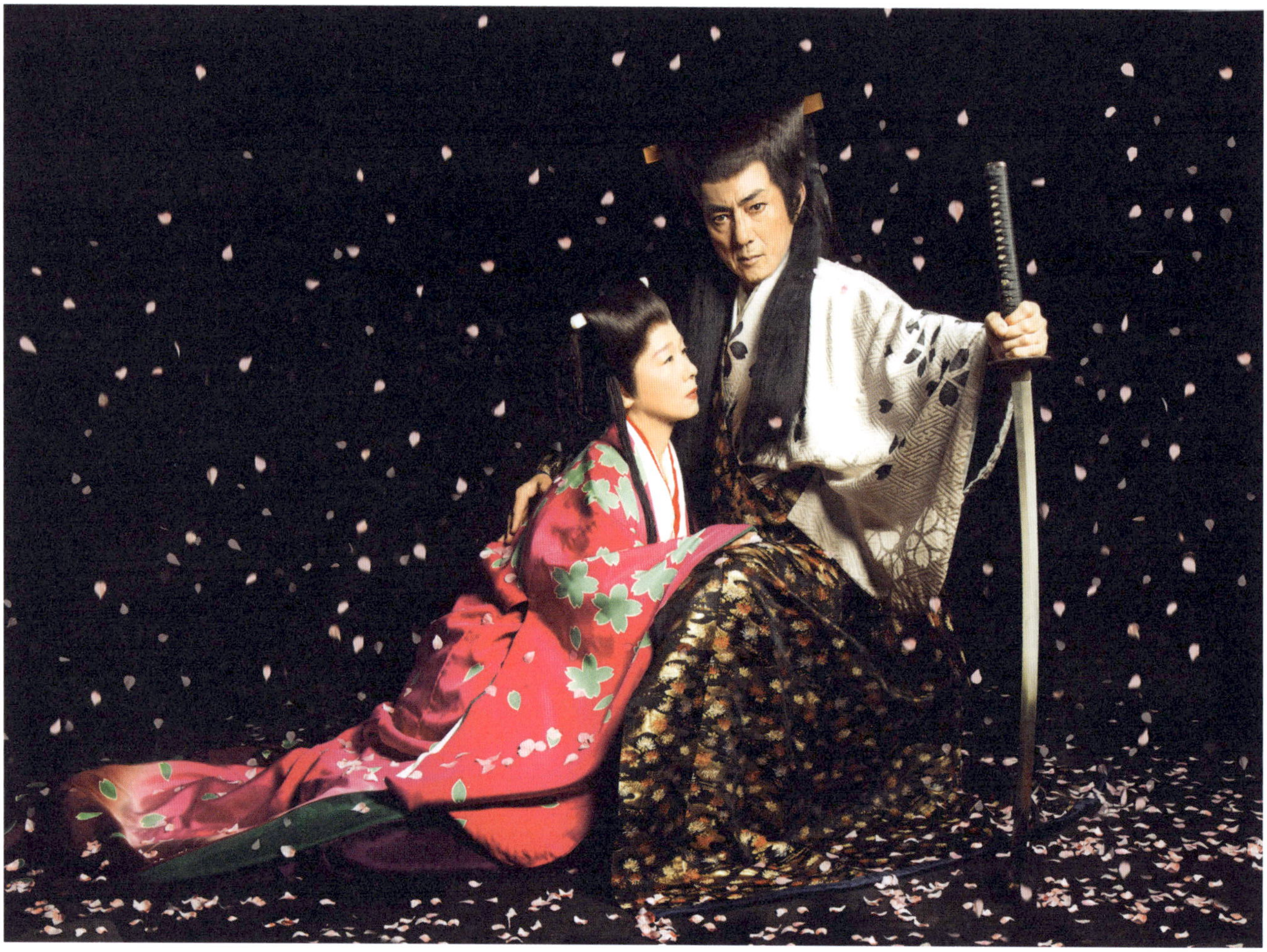

International exchange at the heart of the Barbican theatre programme:

Above
The Ninagawa Company's regular visits to the Barbican produced unforgettable visual theatre, here in *Macbeth*, 2017.

Opposite
Cate Blanchett with the Sydney Theatre Company in the adaptation of Botho Strauss's play *Big and Small, Gross und Klein*, 2012.

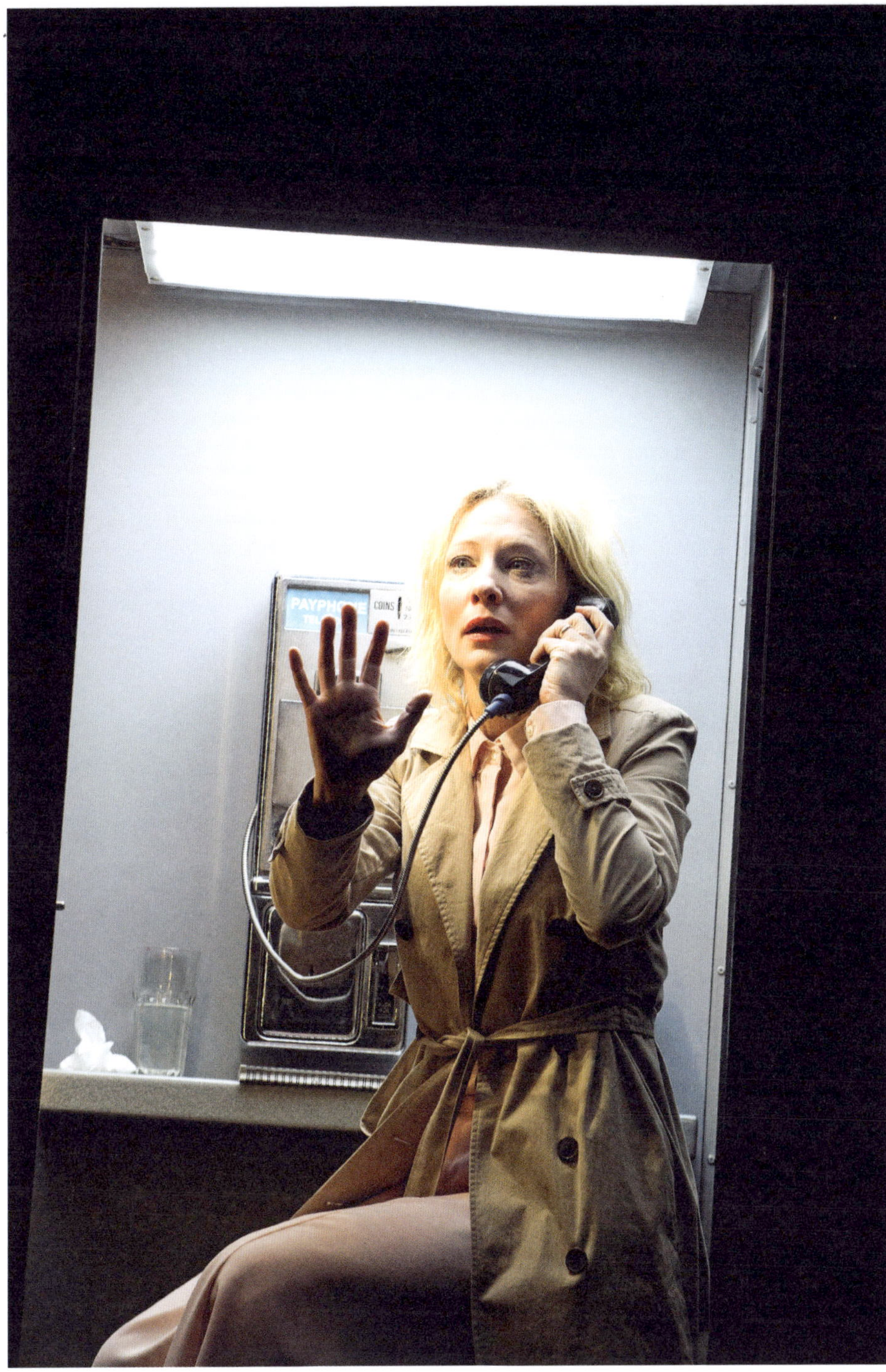

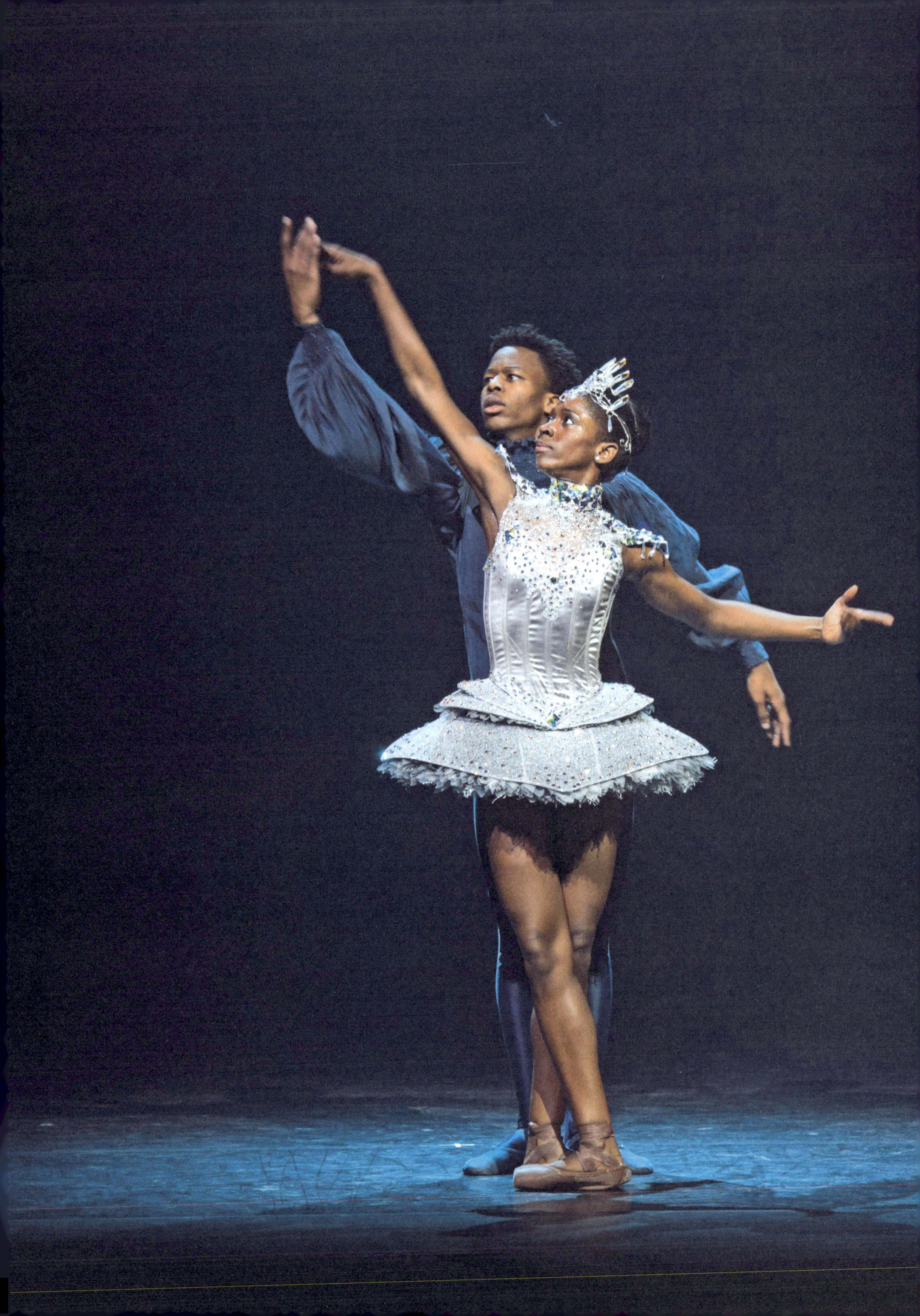

Cassa Pancho

My first experience at the Barbican was seeing a ballet company perform on the main stage. I hadn't been before; I immediately fell in love with the welcoming atmosphere and had never had such a comfortable seat at a theatre before. A couple of years later, our usual London venue closed for refurbishment, and, without much hope of hearing back, I sent an email to Toni Racklin, head of theatre and dance, about the possibility of Ballet Black moving its annual season premiere to the Barbican.

My presence in this book probably tells you the rest: Toni did reply, and I attended one of the most energising programming meetings I've ever had in 20 years of running Ballet Black. Toni and her team were excited at the prospect of us being on their stage! If you know anything about touring as a visiting company, you may appreciate that it can often be a bitter battle over every last light and photocopy, and can cause you to forget about the art. At the Barbican, the art was at the forefront of the discussion, even as great care was taken over the technical details. Since our first performance there, we have felt that we have come home.

Today we are in our fifth year of collaborating with Barbican (four live, one digital), and I hope the association continues for many more. On behalf of everyone at Ballet Black, we want to wish the Barbican a very happy 40th anniversary. You don't look a day over ten!

Cassa Pancho is the founder and artistic director of Ballet Black.

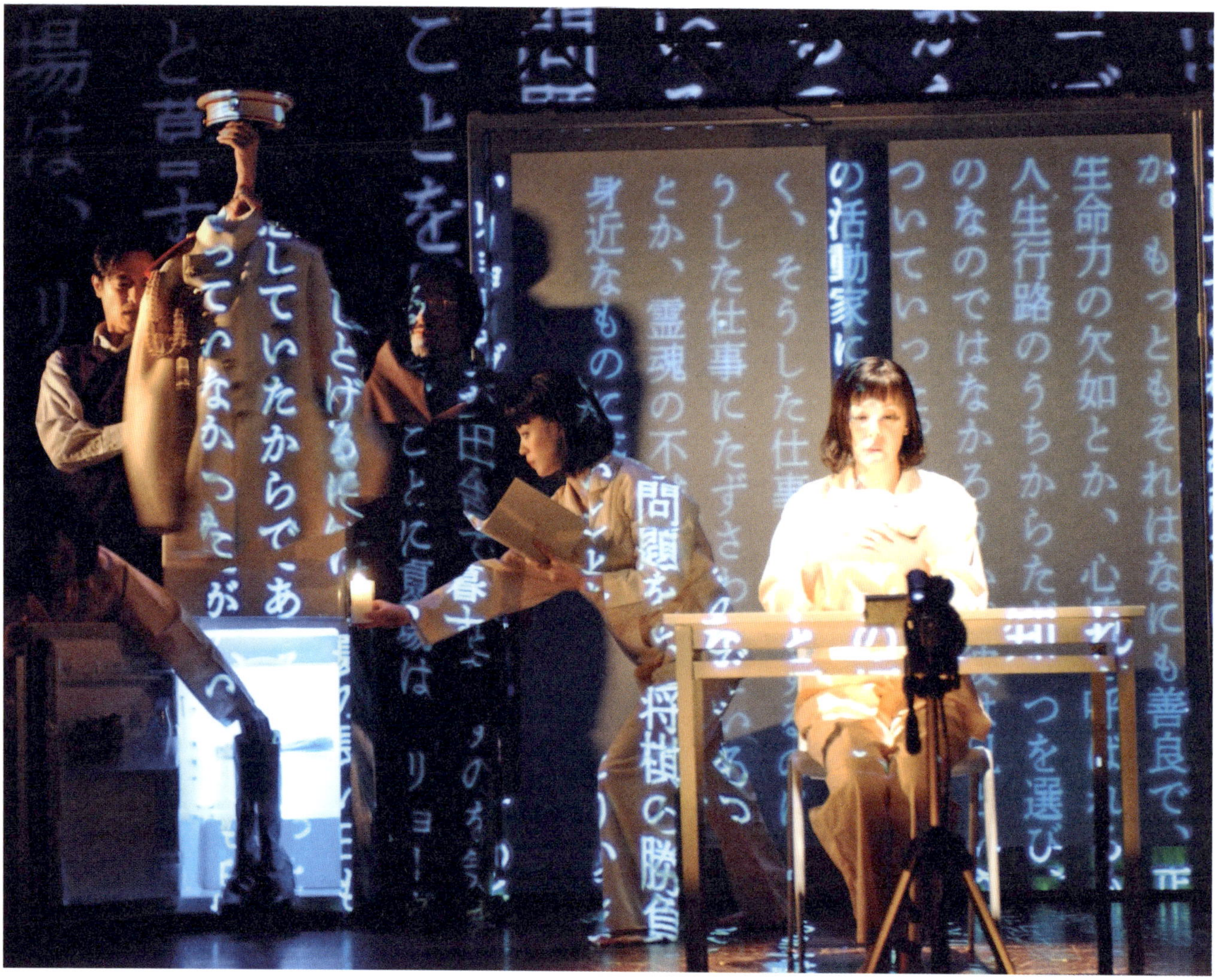

smashed classical music into circus, while Katie Mitchell's experiments with live action and live streams including 2013's *Fräulein Julie* and *The Forbidden Zone* (2016) have explored what we watch and what we see when we look at a stage and interrogated the notion of hyper-liveness.

Simon McBurney and Complicité's most enduring relationship with a building has been with the Barbican, which from *The Noise of Time* (2001) onwards has presented and sometimes co-produced much of the company's most innovative and spell-binding work. *The Noise of Time*, perched adventurously on the borders between traditional play and concert and which stared into the hidden depths of Shostakovich's 15th and final string quartet, was another path-breaking show which trampled across the artificial boundaries of art forms. The ongoing relationship with McBurney and his company has birthed some of Complicité's greatest shows and some of the Barbican's greatest hits. Complicité's bond with the Barbican has helped extend its reach and audience, both nationally and internationally. It offers a reminder that in an

Complicité's innovative staging of *A Disappearing Number*, 2007, which led onto their production of *The Master and Margarita*, 2012, and then to Simon McBurney's one-man journey *The Encounter*, 2016.

arts world full of short-termism, being prepared to take a longer-term approach often pays dividends not just for those who make the work but also for those who see it. It is the difference between grabbing and presenting the show that is making a stir and claiming ownership over it, and understanding that the best work requires support and nurture. It is the difference between being a house and being a home. In the case of Complicité it has produced some of the company's most enduring shows, including the mathematical wizardry of *A Disappearing Number* (2007), and *The Encounter* (2016). The latter makes such radical theatrical use of binaural sound to get right inside the heads of a headphone-wearing audience that we could have all sworn we had been transported to the Amazon rainforest.

The Barbican has not just been a refuge for companies with international clout. Graduate company Non Zero One made their professional debut at the Barbican, not on its stages but within public spaces and backstage areas, with its walkabout headphones show, *Would Like to Meet* (2010). The centre also supported the early theatrical experiments of Slung Low, including 2009's *They Only Come at Night*, a show about vampires and how fear infects our minds that played out in one of the centre's underground car parks. As the host venue of the Oxford Samuel Beckett Theatre Trust, an award aimed at expanding innovative theatre practice, it has supported numerous emerging companies and artists from Slung Low through to Rachel Mars with *Roller* (2018) and SUPERFAN with *Nosedive* (2019). Several years of hosting the Best of BE Festival, an initiative aimed at supporting cross-border collaboration and breaking down the boundaries between the artist and the spectator, also brought small-scale and often deliciously quirky European experimental performance to the Barbican.

Long before co-production and collaboration became buzz words in British theatre, the Barbican understood the need to work with others. Over the years there have been significant partnerships not just with individual arts companies but also with other producers including Dance Umbrella, the London International Festival of Theatre (LIFT), the Spill Festival and the London International Mime Festival. The latter's annual sojourn at the Barbican has produced some astonishing work from Mathurin Bolze's dizzying *Du Goudron et des Plumes* in 2011 to Peeping Tom's *32 rue Vanenbranden* (2015), a dance-theatre show which combined surreal cinematic spectacle with physical comedy to weirdly compelling effect.

Recognising that London is a series of diverse villages, not a single conglomeration, the Barbican has worked with other venues in the area to co-present work such as that made by Jess Thom of Tourette's Hero or Nic Green and Inua Ellams so that it can be seen more widely across London and not just in a single place. This generosity of spirit pays long-term dividends in terms of nurturing new audiences and broadening reach. Most recently the Barbican worked with the new Bridge Theatre on the intimate show *Flight*, a miniature miracle from Glasgow-based company Vox Motus that placed the audience in individual booths to watch an unfolding diorama that crossed the boundaries between theatre, installation and graphic novel and brought an entirely new and moving perspective to a refugee story.

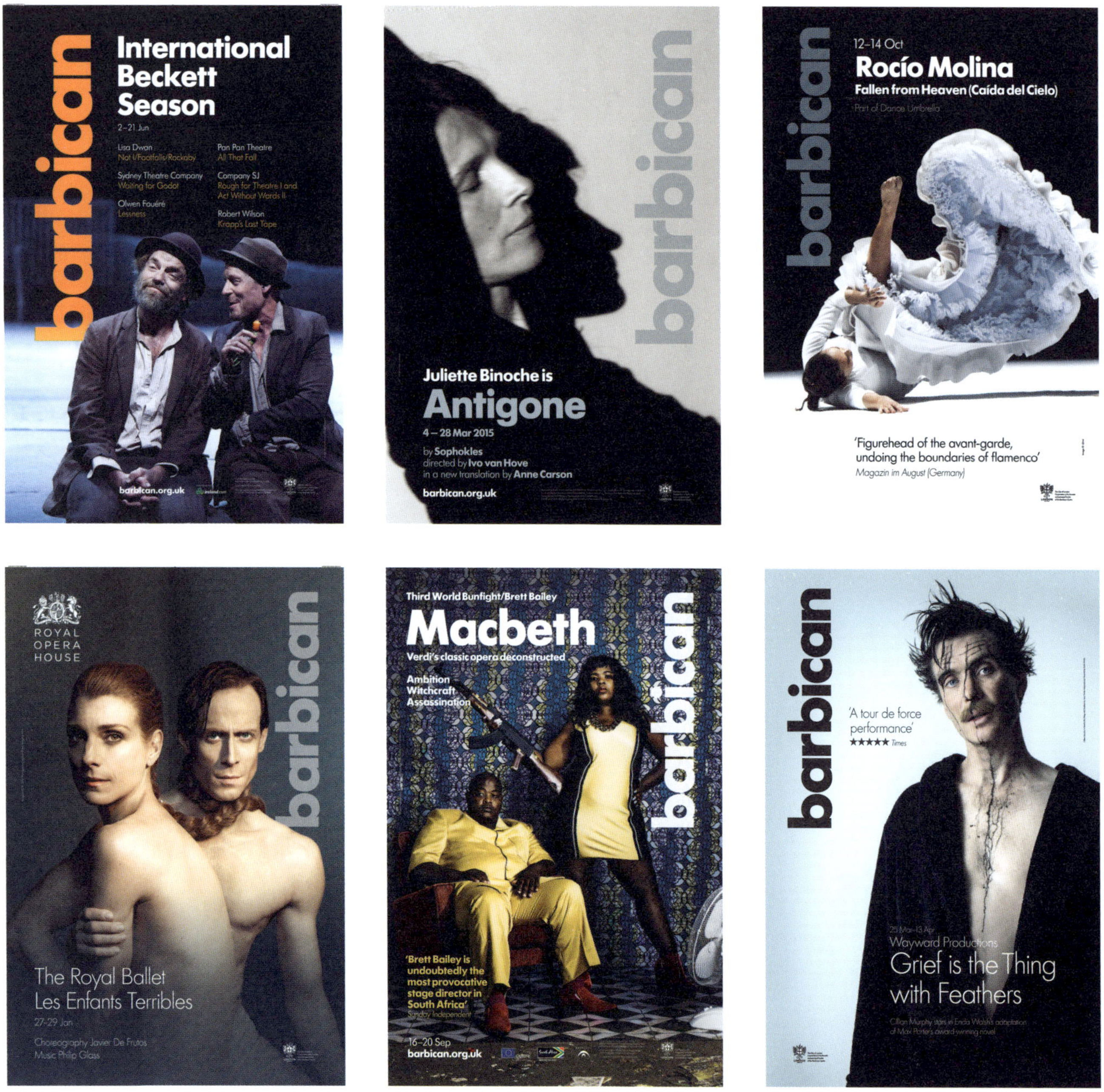

The range and diversity of the Barbican's theatre programme: visiting companies and original productions presented within a single brand.

Over the last 40 years the Barbican has had a unique role in British cultural life, and it has stretched out its tentacles across the world. The cross-border and cross-art form connections have led artists and audiences on a merry dance, expanding notions of what theatre and performance can be. As it looks to the future, particularly in the wake of the pandemic, the challenge facing the Barbican is the same as that facing any major arts organisation: how can it fully embrace its civic responsibilities? The Barbican has long been a space for debate, empathy, understanding and a place where artists and audiences can meet to interrogate the past and imagine the future together. The organisation's efforts in the last few years to face up to criticism, increase diversity, encourage different voices telling different stories and seek far wider engagement is proof that it refuses to stand still and welcomes change. An organisation that understands that art and civic responsibility are not binary opposites but can walk hand in hand is one that will remain relevant for the next 40 years.

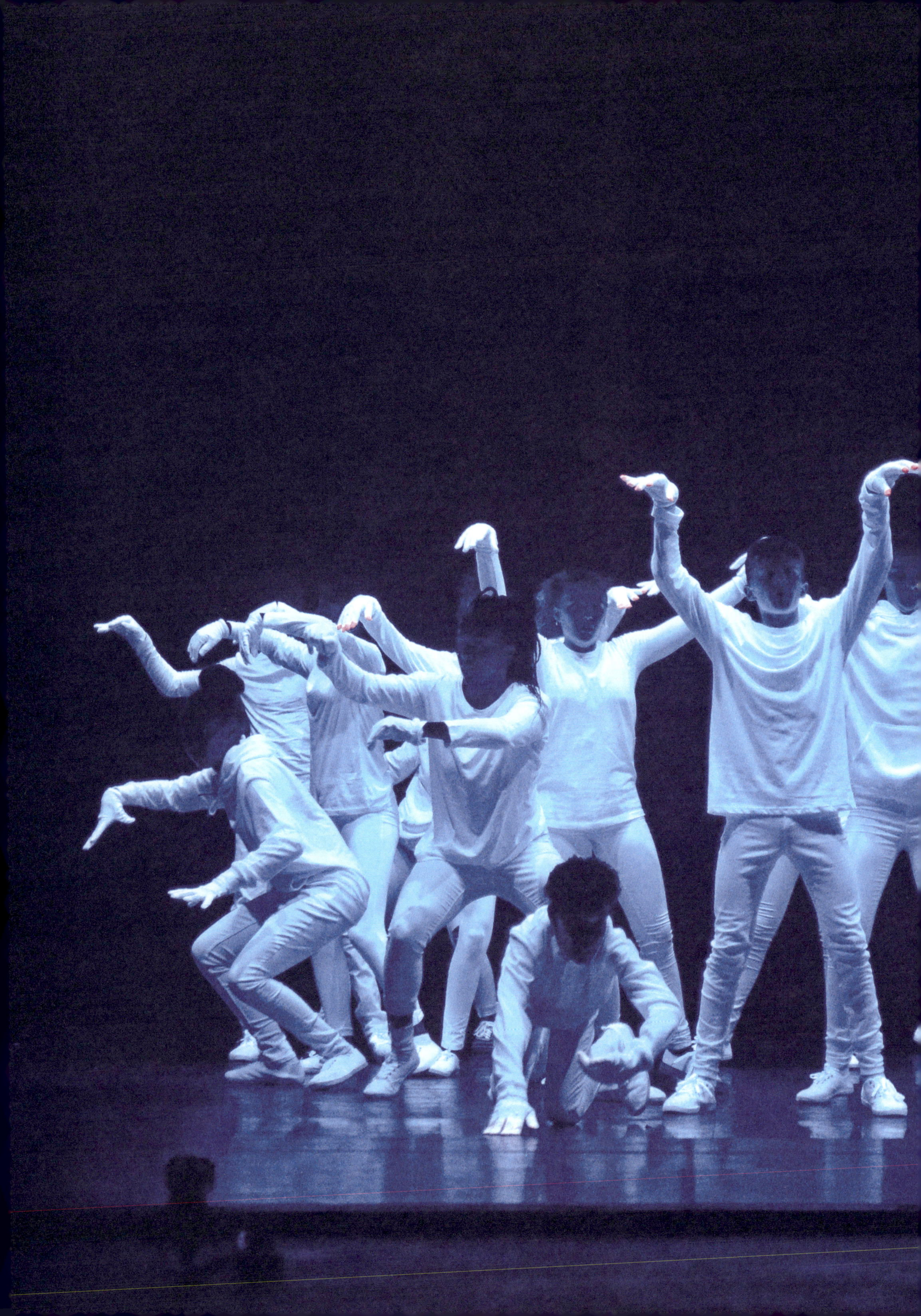

Boy Blue

Founded in London in 2001, Boy Blue, the award-winning brainchild of producer Michael 'Mikey J' Asante and choreographer Kenrick 'H2O' Sandy MBE, encapsulates the pulse of the city it was born in.

Weaving their frontline stage and screen work around the elevation of hip-hop culture, Boy Blue became an associate artist of the Barbican in 2009, having won an Olivier Award for their show *Pied Piper*, seen at Theatre Royal Stratford East and the Barbican. They went on to present *Touch* (2011), *The Five & the Prophecy of Prana* (2013), *A Night With Boy Blue* (2013, 2015, 2016, 2018), the Olivier-nominated *Blak Whyte Gray* (2017 & 2018), *Outliers* (2018) – Asante's musical debut in the Concert Hall – and *REDD* (2019). In 2018, Asante and Sandy co-directed their first film, *R.E.B.E.L.*, a Sky Arts / Art 50 commission.

Boy Blue contributed to the Opening Ceremony of the London 2012 Olympics, where in collaboration with Danny Boyle, Sandy choreographed hundreds of young dancers for the segment 'Frankie and June say thanks Tim', as well as staging the handover of the Olympic torch and the lighting of the Olympic cauldron.

With a long-term commitment to education, Boy Blue run a highly respected dance programme in East London. Using a typically unique approach, they enable more than 100 young dancers to train weekly alongside professionals. In addition, their work, *Emancipation of Expressionism*, is a set work of the AQA GCSE Dance syllabus – the first hip-hop dance theatre piece to be included – and was filmed on the Barbican stage by Director Danny Boyle and screened on the BBC.

In 2018 Sandy and Asante were awarded Honorary Fellowships (HonFGS) from the Guildhall School of Music and Drama.

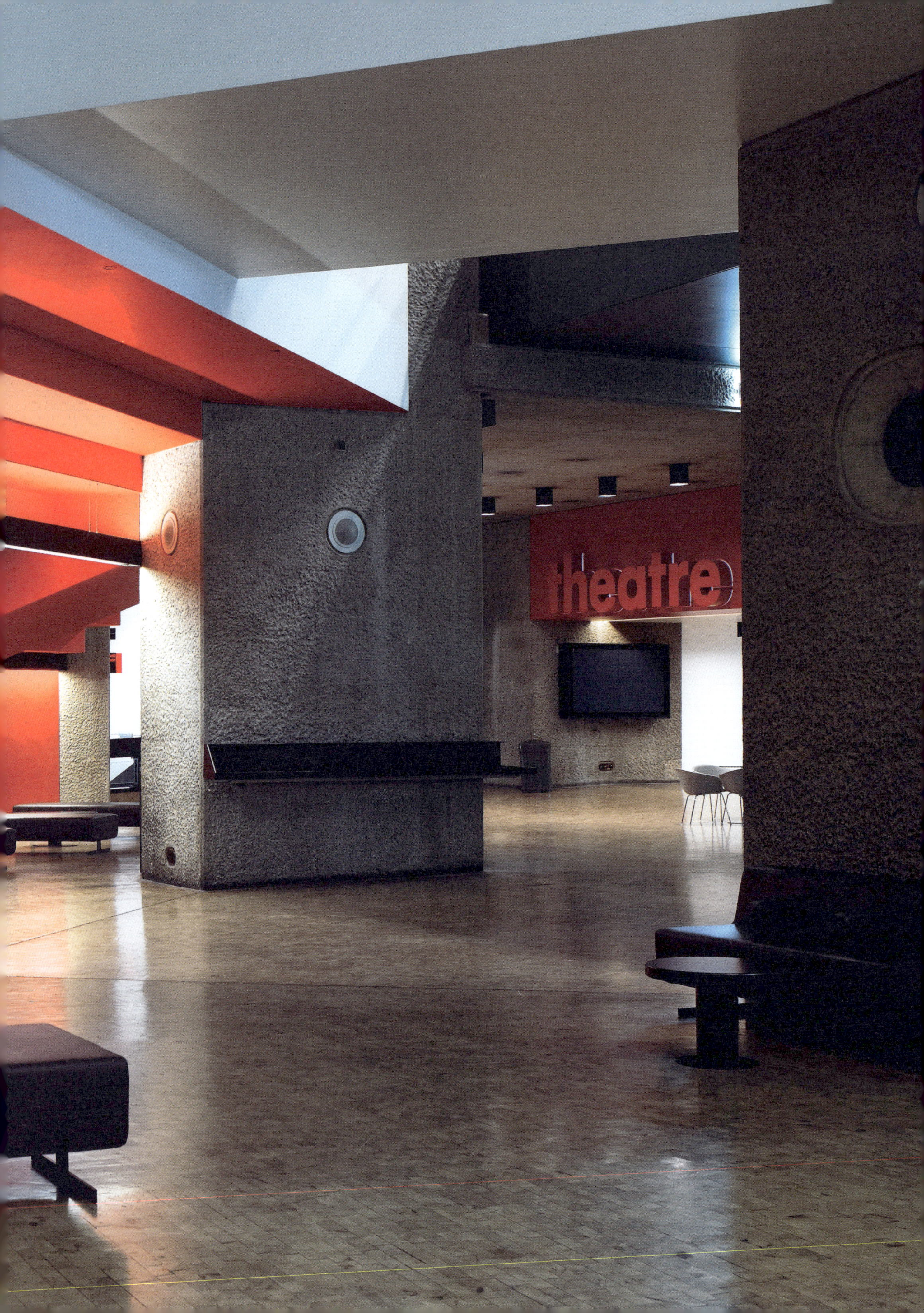
theatre

Running the Barbican 2
A conversation with Philip Dodd

John Tusa and Graham Sheffield

John Tusa was appointed managing director of the Barbican in 1995, and Graham Sheffield became artistic director the same year. They worked together until Tusa left in 2007; Sheffield moved on in 2010. When Tusa was interviewed and appointed in July 1995, he pointed out that 'there was one oddity about the selection process: Graham Sheffield had been appointed first'. However, 'at our first meeting we decided we would get on very well. We did for the next 12 years and do so to this day.'

PD *Did you know each other before you arrived?*

GS When I was approached, I said I would strongly consider taking the job, but I wanted some sort of say in who the managing director was going to be. I was told that 'we have got John in the frame'. Although I didn't know him, I knew him by reputation at the BBC. We had this kind of courtship meeting — at your old house in Hampstead Heath …

JT And I came to lunch in your house in Muswell Hill. I knew a lot of Graham's programmes from Radio 3 and they were absolutely professional — I like professional. One of the common things about working at the BBC and working at the Barbican is that you really try to do the very best with the material in hand, and it was clear this was what Graham did.

PD *Between you, there was the nod of recognition rather than the wink of conspiracy. Did you have a clear sense of what you felt needed to be done with the Barbican when you both arrived?*

JT A great deal. I remember somebody saying: 'You talk about the Barbican's arts programme, but you don't have one: the LSO does the music, the RSC does the theatre, so what arts programme do you have?' That was harsh, and at that time we didn't even manage the art gallery, and the cinema programme was very limited.

GS Yes, the perception, the reputation of the place was LSO, RSC and a plethora of Raymond Gubbay concerts to fill the gaps. Now we knew that wasn't the whole story at all. The previous administration *did* do international; the way they did it was to concentrate on those expansive, quality blockbuster seasons every other year, such as the Scandinavian *Tender is the North*. They put almost all their efforts into those big festivals. You wouldn't do it that way now, nor would you necessarily do my programmes that way now either! What we attempted was to create an overarching international framework but with a strong local context: it's a phrase that's been much used since but wasn't used then — 'local international'.

PD *That's been a common thread across the Barbican's history — irrespective of regime — a commitment to internationalism. It was certainly there in the 80s. What did the Tusa/Sheffield regime add?*

GS True, it has been a common thread, and local populations were also increasingly diverse and closer to us. But the creation of an international programme at least in theatre was very much linked to the departure of the RSC, and enabled by it — we'll come to that. In the concert hall it was a matter of attracting the top orchestras, ensembles and promoters, many of whom traditionally resisted the Barbican because of its poor acoustic reputation — we'll come to that too! The art gallery was hampered by being a very poorly designed space overlooking the library.

JT By the end of our time, our audience was 18 per cent BAME, a higher proportion than any other arts venue in London. People asked, 'How do you do it? Do you have special programming?' We didn't. The audience found us — they came to the range of the programme.

PD *The City had already gone through its Big Bang — it had already globalised. It was now international. Were you being pushed by a wind in the Corporation? Or was it indifferent?*

JT I don't think there was a direct link, because by this stage, the Corporation understood they could trust us. We weren't given artistic advice, other than from one person who said we should do more plays by Somerset Maugham! There was no great philosophical idea driving us. We didn't say, 'We must do more of this, that and the other.' Our question was, 'Where is the excellence?'.

PD *Both of you came from the BBC — as did Nick Kenyon after you. I am interested why there has been this railway line between the BBC and the Barbican.*

GS Let me have a go at this: I think it is partly a shared internationalism, and what I call the old-fashioned BBC virtues of high-quality editorial judgement about the arts. Like the BBC, authority doesn't always work here. It is not an authoritarian set-up — you have to influence people, to gain people's respect and trust through action.

JT The BBC breeds generalists. We are generalists — Graham is a specialist in the arts as well. And although people don't always associate this with the BBC, BBC generalists are also good with money. We are efficient, not ideologues. We never ran a deficit; Arts never ran a deficit …

GS One.

JT … one, OK, yes, but one in 12 years. We know that an organisation is made up of huge numbers of talented people who wouldn't like to be told what to do. That's why I think it works.

PD *Your regime also inherited the LSO and the RSC. Over your early years, the RSC began to back out. Did you think there was a danger that the cultural standing of the Barbican would be damaged?*

GS I think the reverse, personally. I mean I couldn't have been more delighted the RSC went, because most of their productions at that time were exceptionally dull. The danger with the LSO was that it felt the resurgence of an independently minded Barbican could become a threat to its hegemony. It took quite a bit of soft-shoe shuffling to convince the LSO that working together was a good idea. We were also able to attract the BBC Symphony Orchestra to become the centre's first Associate Orchestra.

JT We had a huge admiration for the LSO but in our earlier years the orchestra behaved as if it were a zero-sum game. Their view was that the moment another decent orchestra comes into the hall, they take away some of our audience — that was a difficult view to accept, because we wanted an outstanding programme of international touring ensembles alongside the LSO.

With the RSC, by the end, the Corporation was paying the Company £3.5 million each year to stay here. When they decided to leave, a decision that did them no good, the Corporation had been told nobody would want the theatre. The opposite happened. We went international: it was the obvious way to go, especially after the demise of Peter Daubeny's famous World Theatre season.

GS London saw relatively little international work in those days, apart from the biennial LIFT festival. We presented the blue-chip names and companies, including opera and dance, but also experimental work which we put in the smaller Pit theatre. In the same spirit, we started the world music and roots programme and a jazz strand to balance the LSO. Then we needed to position the cinema as a leading art house cinema in London — and to kick-start an education programme. That was the agenda, and we worked flat out to achieve it.

PD *Inevitably, internationally, some places mattered more to you than others. Louise Jeffreys who was running theatre at the time told me that as she looked back, her programme was more Anglo-American than she would have liked it to be.*

GS Well, the American emphasis was deliberate; 1998 was the first full year of our running the theatre, so we made a point of presenting many of the great American iconic figures — Philip Glass, Robert Wilson, Trisha Brown, Merce Cunningham, Laurie Anderson, Steve Reich — and constructed a year-long series across the art forms called *Inventing America*.

JT As Graham says, the sheer cornucopia from the US at that time was absolutely extraordinary — but then from Brazil as well …

GS … Brazil and Colombia, Argentina, Russia we explored extensively, and Japan. We were the regular London home of the superb Japanese company of Ninagawa. Many contemporary dance companies came here; it was about excellence and innovation, but I did crave a spread of quality international work that wasn't only from the Western canon. I wish there had been more in those days that we could have done at scale from the African continent. We did go out of our way, then, and this was Louise's achievement too, to find work in Europe and particularly Germany with the Schaubühne and all the places that were regularly on the co-production circuit. The early Barbican Theatre seasons (BITE) more or less defined the Barbican at the time.

PD *What about the political context you were working in? If the previous business-orientated administration was a product of the Thatcher years, you were surely a product of the Blair years?*

JT The Blairites didn't believe in the arts!

PD *Well, they believed in social engineering and the arts…*

JT Yes, but they were terrified of the arts as such. If you look at their first party in Downing Street after their 1997 win, everyone was there except anybody who had anything to do with the serious arts. The arts were elitist as far as they were concerned and actually, from that point of view, we could not have been more different from the spirit of Blair. We fought the Arts Council over instrumentalism and the creative industries. The creative industries were terribly important but not as a substitute for the arts, so we were regarded as anti-Blair. Chris Smith regarded me as the Antichrist and Christopher Frayling when he was chairman of the Arts Council called me 'that fucker Tusa' because we fought them all the way through. We never got any money from them.

GS John, to be fair, ACE did finally give us some support for our city neighbourhood programme — but that may have been after you'd gone!

PD *I remember talking to one of Blair's Number 10 team about the arts. What will you do with us? I asked. 'Kill you with cream,' he said.*

JT They never did.

PD *But they did provide the cream.*

JT After a huge fight.

PD *During the Blair years there was the consolidation of Cultural Studies with its celebration of popular culture and this helped to undermine the wall between high and popular culture. Despite what you say, John, surely the Barbican was part of that: you staged an exhibition on Harley-Davidson and one on Star Wars …*

GS *The Art of Star Wars* was the first deliberately commercial exhibition, and it gave us the idea to start the Barbican International Exhibitions programme, which would create shows initially for the Barbican, which would then tour and create a substantial income stream. Once the gallery had been redesigned and enclosed in 2004 (a bargain at just over £1m), it enabled us to be much bolder in our exhibition choices, because artists and curators could see the possibilities of the space. It was one of several brilliant architectural interventions by Allford Hall Monaghan Morris, which systematically overhauled and transformed the arts spaces and public areas.

PD *Another aspect of the Blair years was the slow merging of the commercial and the cultural — most arts organisations became much more dependent on commercial income.*

GS I think both John and I would admit that we did not maximise the potential of commercial income — and I think Nick Kenyon should take credit for enhancing the commercial opportunities for the Barbican, not least because his City funding has been reduced year on year. However, latterly we did take every opportunity of the potential for presenting high-quality shows, including two Christmas pantomimes authored by Mark Ravenhill!

PD *But were there limits? I heard that you said you'd only have* Les Misérables *back over your dead body.*

GS I don't remember ever saying that … it was the 'then' RSC I didn't want back. But we did bring in Opera North with *Carousel* and we brought in the classic *South Pacific* from Lincoln Center. If you are going to put up a four-hour show of Shakespeare in Dutch directed by Ivo van Hove, which we did, and it was fantastic, you do need to balance the diet. It is always a matter of a balanced programme in a year-round venue.

PD *One way of putting the subsequent history of the Barbican and lots of others art institutions is they have gone over to what one might call the 'Blair side'. The arts are now often described in terms of civic virtue …*

GS Again it's a matter of balance; the danger is that it becomes all about relevance and social engineering, and nothing about the art itself. With the emphasis much more now on diversity and inclusion — and I wholeheartedly welcome this — it's important to keep antennae peeled for high artistic quality.

PD *I am not being sentimental, but during the Blair years arts financing was relatively generous — compared with the earlier years or now.*

JT Our money came almost entirely from the Corporation. We had a huge need for capital: we needed to remodel the theatre, to improve the acoustic in the concert hall, transform the Curve and gallery, modernise the cinemas, overhaul the public spaces and access, as well as to improve way-finding. It was a massive task.

At that time, the Arts Council were regularly giving clients around £30 million to do themselves up and improve their facilities — so we approached the Corporation and asked for £30 million for improving the building. Our committee just freaked! But then we got together, planned it, and we agreed to do it bit by bit with a sum set aside each year to deal with one of the spaces. As Graham mentioned, AHMM led on much of the later work — the gallery, the public spaces and the new entrance — but early on the concert hall had been radically improved by the Caruso St John practice, coupled with Larry Kierkegaard's acoustic ingenuity.

PD *Was there a sense of trying to collapse the walls around you?*

GS You talk about collapsing walls: towards the end of John's time, we made at least the first breach in the wall between the Barbican and its next-door neighbour the Guildhall School. I think that this has had the most profound effect on the nature of the Barbican — the conjoining of the music and drama educational institution with the multi-arts centre.

JT I wanted them to be merged into one institution — with one director. We were keen on knocking down walls, in all kinds of ways. I thought they would work together better, and I thought there would be all sorts of synergies of activity. Also there's the issue that if you don't have very strong common leadership then the dangers are that they actually diverge. The fact was that for what, 12 years, the doors between the Barbican Centre and the Guildhall School had been locked. They were glass doors, they were locked and we said, 'Why are they there?' and they said, 'Security' and we said, 'What security?' So I said, 'Would you kindly open them?' We were breaking down things like that, so we merged finance, we merged HR, and then we threw a lot of weight behind the new building the Guildhall was developing at Milton

Court. I'm less passionate now about the idea that it's necessary to have one single director but all I'll say is that if you ever had, for personal reasons, a director at the Guildhall School and a director at the Barbican who are not of similar mind, then you'd just waste a great deal of opportunity.

PD *That fitted with the idea of Barbican outreach generally?*

JT At one stage, knowing that we wanted to have a larger presence in London, Graham and I created the idea of 'Barbican without walls'. We went together to the LSO and the RSC and said, 'Why don't we, once a year, all decamp to one of the outer London boroughs, do all sorts of classes and then a three-day arts festival at the weekend?' The reaction was not great: the frost was severe. I think that was the occasion when the RSC's Adrian Noble said to Graham 'I think you don't understand, only artists can talk to artists.'

GS Yes, Adrian said that to me, and I never spoke to him again.

PD *What was the story about the Barbican you wanted to tell the world? In the* Radio Times, *one has to find a way of describing a programme in eight or nine words. What would have been the* Radio Times *billing for the Barbican?*

JT The best of the arts around the world for every audience.

GS What we actually came up with, with our marketing director Chris Denton, was the strap line 'Do something different': we used this in our marketing for some time. The phrase works because it's not art-form specific, it's to do with adventure and choice and discovery. You could come to the Barbican and see an LSO concert, but also go to a fetish night in the gallery or a Kurosawa film or whatever it might be …

PD *I often think that the identity of the Barbican has been an issue. It's not Tate Modern, it's not the ICA …*

GS That's its strength, I think. For a building that continues to be much-loved and much-loathed by some, it has a very distinct personality and an unmistakable brand.

PD *The Barbican needs to continue to be reinvented. What should it be like in 2030?*

JT All I do know is that change has to be dramatic. You can do what you can in the environment that you live in, and somebody else comes along and does it differently. That's a strength, the place can absorb it, the institution can welcome it.

GS I agree with you, and the recognition that what you put in place has to change is something that all too many people never admit. I think there is a continuity between what we did and the present — the learning element has grown in an inspired way, and so has the locally based participatory work, which we made a start on. I think that's all good. I think the biggest change might come because you always have been hemmed in here by the exigencies and limitations of the spaces you're performing in. If there is one thing I hang my hat on, it's that there will be a major change in the influence of virtual reality and the digital element in the Barbican programme, some of this brought on by Covid restrictions. And social media is transforming so much. The new technologies allow people to participate without coming into the building. I think virtual reality will be a major way of transforming people's perception of this place. How, I have no idea. But nor yet does anyone else.

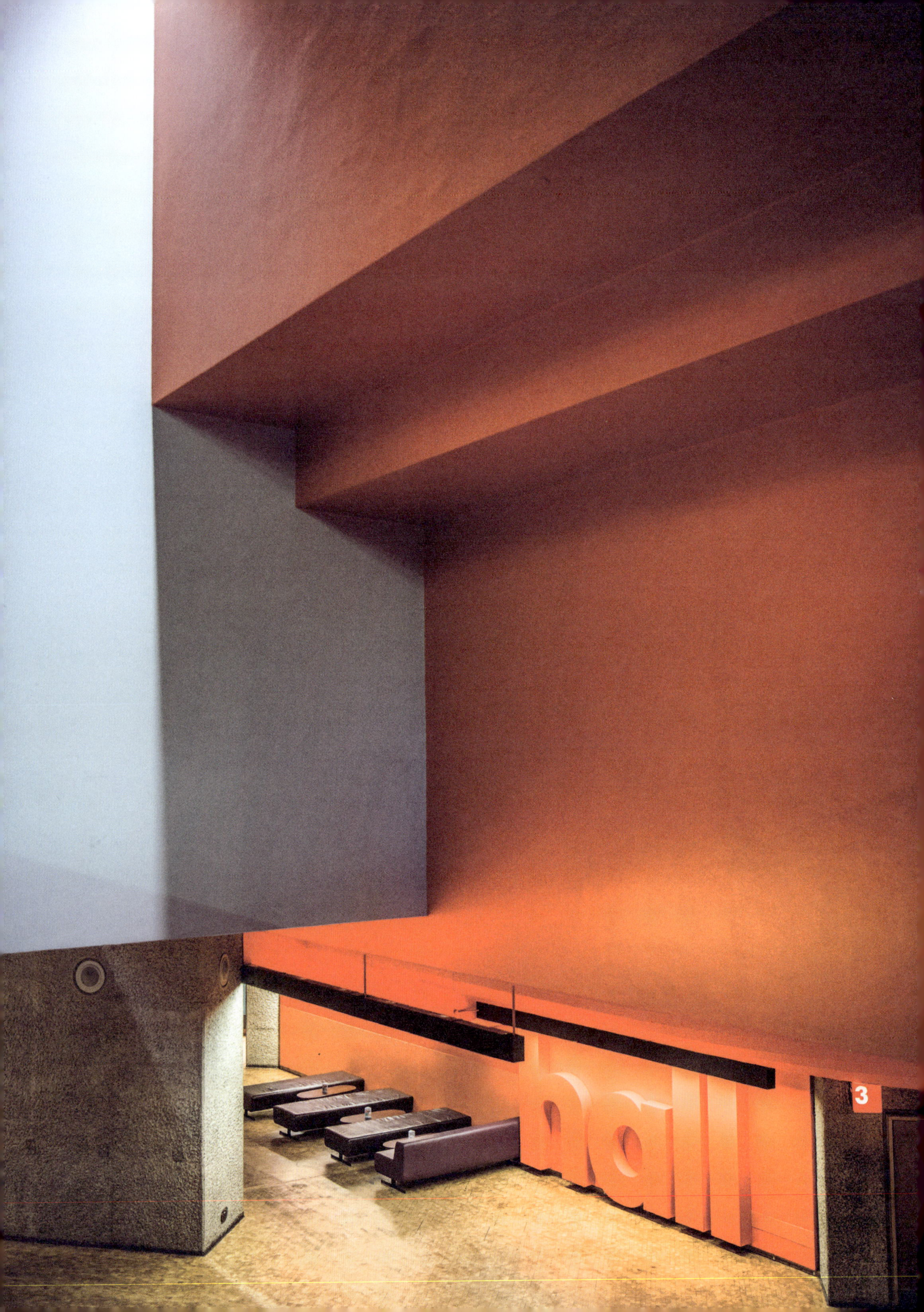
hall
3

Brand Barbican: Changing graphic design for a changing centre

Theo Inglis

The idea of a cultural venue as 'a brand' is something the Barbican — like all arts institutions — has had to reckon with over the last 40 years with ever-increasing urgency. The inherent problem is finding an appropriate fixed visual analogue for a venue whose output is eclectic and ever-changing. As architect George Perkin wrote in an article about the opening of the centre for *Concrete Quarterly*: 'the Barbican is a "complex" in more ways than one.' Notwithstanding the difficulties and compromises inherent in all cultural branding, the Barbican has had some unique complexities because its name has multiple interpretations. Barbican could refer to the arts centre, or the estate, or the whole combined site, or even the entire area of London known by that name for hundreds of years. The Barbican is also both a part of 'The City' and its property. The City of London Corporation's heraldic badge, serif typography and Latin motto — *Domine Dirige Nos* ('Lord Guide Us') — sit in stark contrast with Barbican's modernist walls throughout the complex. The City's corporate identity also mingles awkwardly with the Barbican in the signage dotted throughout the Corbusian high-walks.

For the Barbican itself, such contrasts between old and new came mostly from the choice of name and its associated symbolism; a 'barbican' was a fortified defensive outpost, usually near a gate in city walls. Various iterations of a castle tower icon, complete with crenellations and arrow slits, serving as the estate's logo can be seen in the marketing materials that promoted flats before a final version was settled on. Architects Chamberlin, Powell and Bon (CPB), keen to avoid signage inconsistency, turned to typographer Herbert Spencer. He had previously designed the 1959 *Barbican Redevelopment* report that CPB presented to the Corporation. As the Barbican's 'Lettering and Signposting Consultant' Spencer developed a 'new distinctive alphabet and "vocabulary" of letter sizes, symbols and layout' as well as a rationale for the identification of the Barbican's many floors. It was predicted in 1970 that such colour-coding would be 'particularly important in the Arts Centre, where the multiplicity of levels below the podium might otherwise be very confusing to people unfamiliar with the building'.

This statement hints that the huge development was always going to be a difficult beast to navigate, especially the still-under-construction arts centre. By the time the centre opened, the Barbican had already garnered a reputation as a maze, to the extent that an official advertising poster joked in its headline that 'If Helen Mirren can find the new Barbican Centre before it opens in March, she will be appearing there in *Midsummer Night's Dream*'. Navigation issues aside, Spencer's modern sans-serif lettering and simplified iconography were arguably a perfect visual fit for the estate and are now protected as part of the complex's Grade II listing. Spencer was an ideal choice for the estate: by the time the Barbican Estate was ready for residents, tastes had evolved in many circles of British graphic design; away from the 1951 Festival of Britain era's nostalgic and eclectic approach favouring Victorian typefaces, towards a more rational modernism, for which Spencer was an advocate.

Spencer's work for the estate set a precedent, but a more detailed identity system of lettering, logo, signage and iconography was later developed by Ken Briggs & Associates (KB&A) for the Barbican Centre before its 1982 opening. Ken Briggs, born in 1931 in Derbyshire, was educated at London's

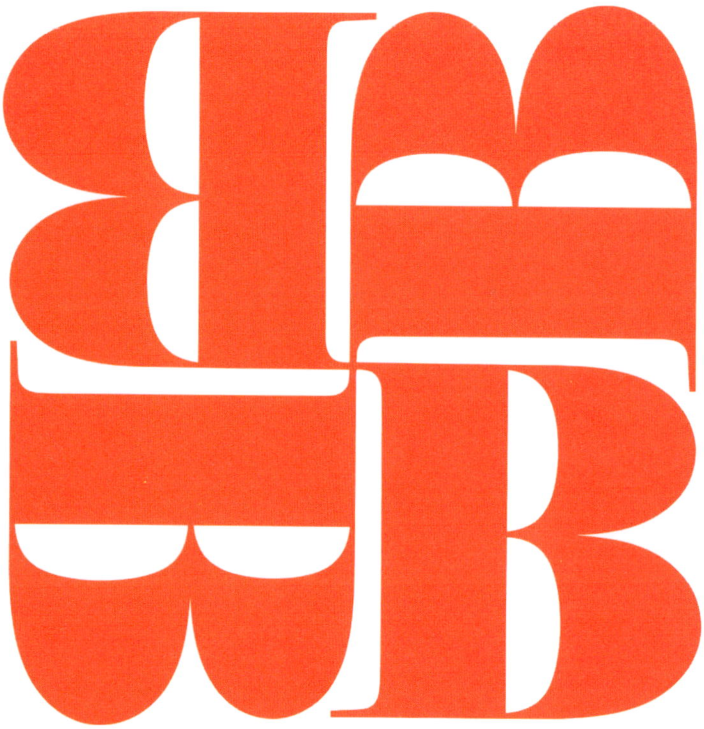

The classic four Bs logo devised by Ken Briggs & Associates for the opening of the centre. Designed to show the conjunction of the art forms, it was criticised as suggesting a lack of a single direction. It is preserved by the listing on the exterior of the building, but has since been replaced by new wordmarks to communicate the Barbican brand.

Central School of Arts and Crafts, as part of a talented cohort who would go on to define the graphics scene of 60s London. The Central at the time was a progressive place, thanks to teachers like Eduardo Paolozzi, Victor Pasmore, Nigel Henderson and the architect Peter Smithson, who with his wife Alison had popularised the term 'brutalism'. Briggs, thanks to exposure to the magazine *Neue Grafik,* became a devotee of the systematic, high modernist method of graphic design coming out of Switzerland. He soon put this serious, grid-based approach to work in the sector he would become best known for: the theatre, first at Sadler's Wells from 1959–60, then with the National Theatre, a career-defining client, into the mid-70s. For the NT, Briggs designed posters, publicity and economically produced programmes. These are some of the best examples of Swiss influences showing in British graphic design. After leaving the NT following their move to the South Bank, Briggs continued to have theatre clients and spent three years at the English National Opera. The waves he had made at the National, along with past experience working with the RSC and LSO, put Briggs on the Barbican's radar. Before Briggs's firm got to work, the centre was making do with his former teacher Herbert Spencer's castle icon as a logo, combined with various inconsistent typographic styles. Briggs's main point of contact was the centre's first head of publicity, Angus Watson, a former ENO colleague with whom he developed a close working relationship.

Like many visual identities at the time, Briggs's symbol for the Barbican Centre focused on initials; the letter B became key. It was Watson who had been behind this decision; upon joining in 1979 he felt the centre's name, in flux due to the late inclusion of a conference centre, should be reconsidered. He successfully argued for this system:

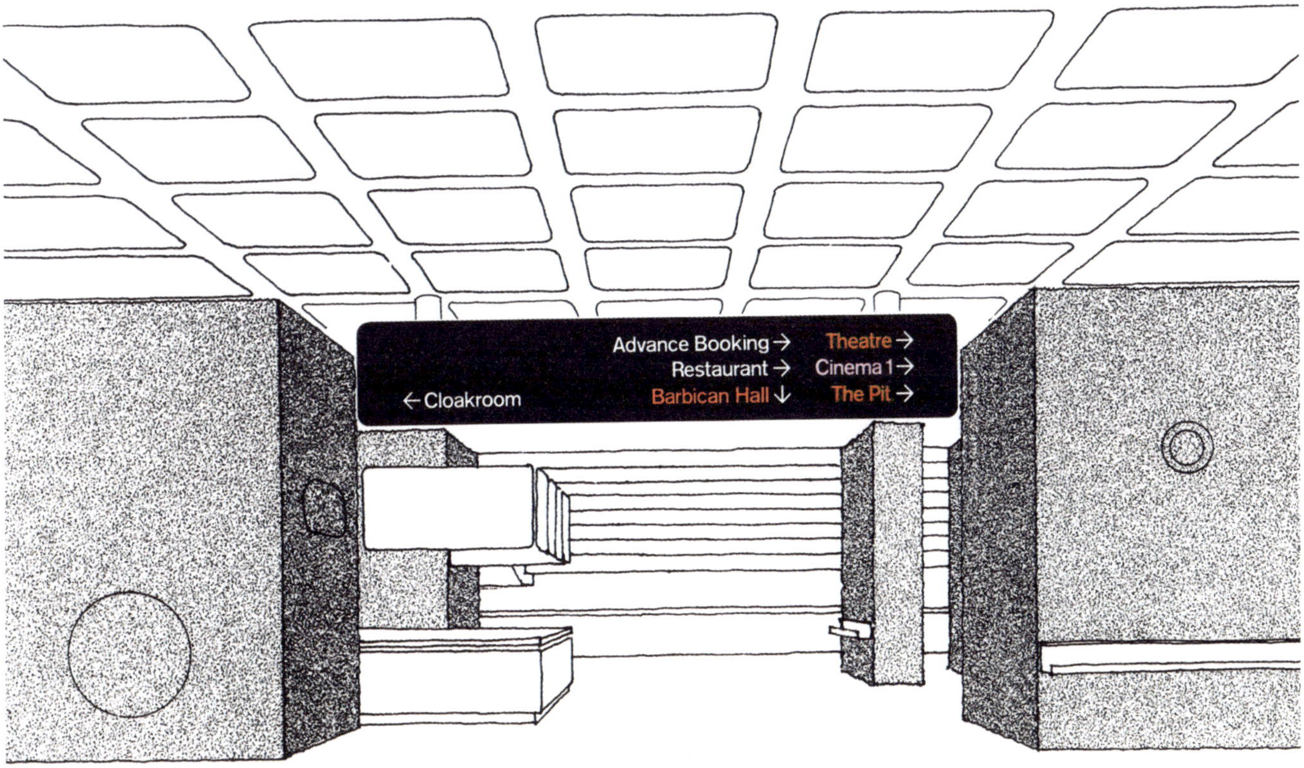

Early illustration by Ken Briggs & Associates from the Signs System Manual, visualising the signage system utilised throughout the centre, some of which survives today.

Full official name:	**Barbican Centre for Arts and Conferences**
Convenient abbreviation:	**Barbican Centre**
Colloquial name:	**Barbican**
Logo concept:	**B**

Briggs chose the typeface Annlie Extra Bold, designed for Letraset by his friend Fred Lambert in 1966, to set the letter B in, then arranged four of them, each facing a different direction, into a neat square. The lower-right B was correctly orientated and all four joined in the middle. Presumably, the Bs symbolised the coming together of the various arts the Barbican Centre would house. However, nowhere in the extensive identity manual was any rationale provided, which is indicative of Briggs's preference for the practical over the conceptual. According to Watson, it was much to everyone's surprise when Christoph Bon agreed to the logo appearing prominently on the centre's exterior, something he remembers hearing Denys Lasdun had objected to at the NT building, for which Briggs has also designed signage.

The Signs System Manual prepared by Briggs and his four staff was the key outcome of their work with the Barbican, even if the logo was the most visible. The idea of 'manuals' for visual identity schemes had grown out of the post-war modernist interest in systems and the desire for complete consistency. Alongside typography, KB&A also designed directional arrows and a library of graphic pictograms representing various aspects of the Barbican Centre. These icons all fit neatly into identical squares with rounded corners. Pictograms were used because,

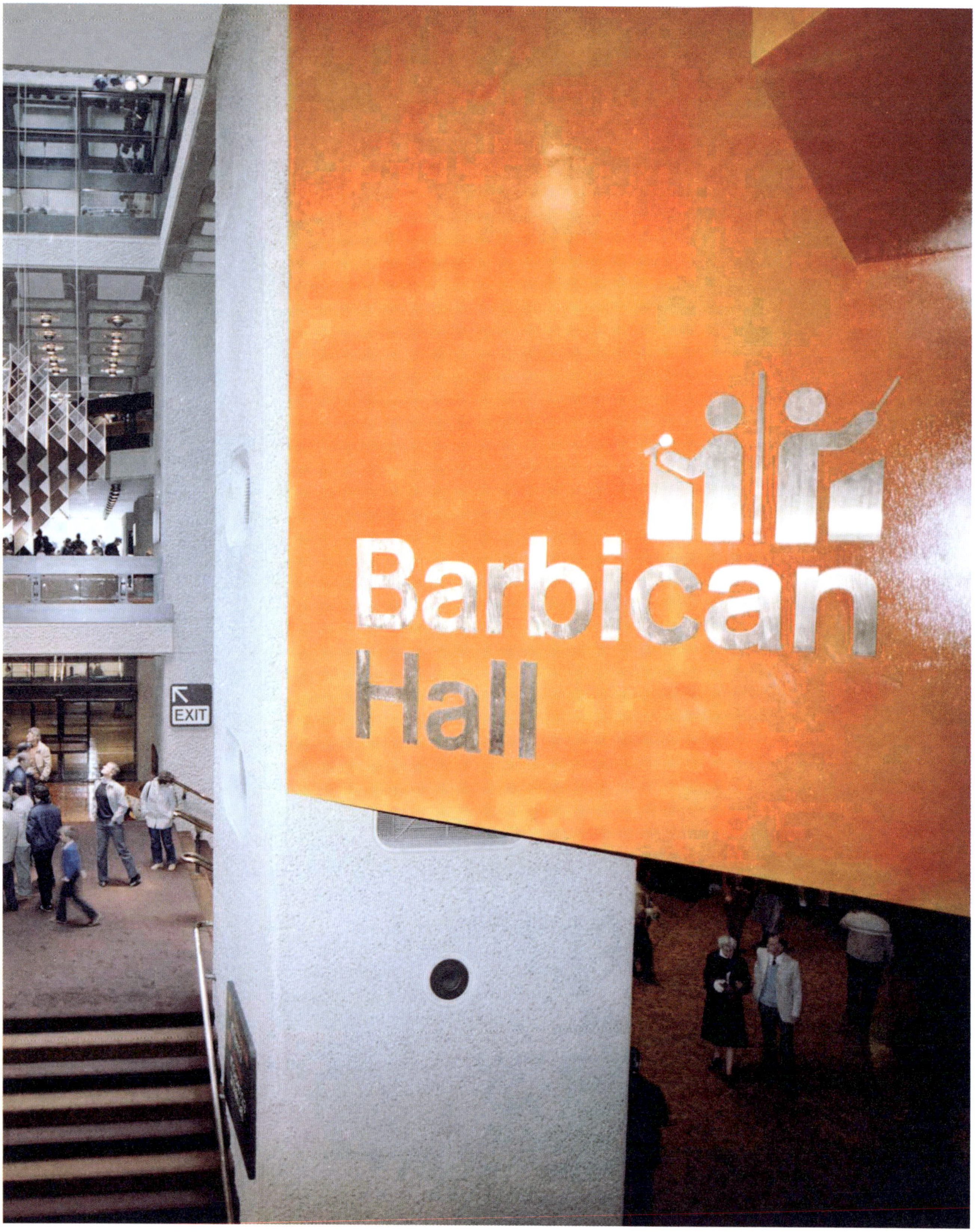
Barbican
Hall
EXIT

in Briggs's words, 'it is expected that many foreign visitors with language problems will use the centre'. Colour was likewise introduced to reinforce and signal various areas of the centre and the purpose they served, rather than using colour on a floor-by-floor basis. KB&A were following the lead of the interior designers here, the main hall was assigned bright orange — a colour used in Barbican branding ever since — because, as Briggs wrote, 'the outside of the Barbican Hall as seen from the stalls foyer and general circulation area is orange'.

Briggs's work for the Barbican had a brutal simplicity and clarity that suited the architecture. Stylistically however it represented a kind of civic modernism that, with postmodernism and privatisation on the march, and the rise of 'branding' shifting graphic design towards emotive 'marketing', didn't prove entirely timeless. Nor did it really communicate the Barbican's original positioning statement of 'Where the Arts Come to Life'. Since the Barbican's resident companies, the RSC and LSO, generated their own designs, and the art gallery was a separate entity, Briggs and his staff had little chance to design publicity, so Briggs's work for the centre didn't generate the exposure that his NT posters had. A former KB&A staff member remembers Briggs as shy, and not keen on self-promotion or the business side of running an agency. Subsequently, KB&A's work for the Barbican received little coverage in the design press and in discussions of Briggs's career rarely garners more than a passing mention.

After the 1982 opening KB&A did very little work for the Barbican; their only continuous project was the design of a few of the first monthly listings diaries. Following the end of Briggs's involvement, Barbican typography became increasingly inconsistent for almost two decades, muddying the centre's branding. The four Bs were one of the few elements that continued to be used, although it soon became only a small element on the diary covers. At times the top-left B was replaced by the shield of the City, as the Corporation sought to make its connection to the arts centre it was funding more obvious.

As for Ken Briggs's sign system, it suffered from the fact that it was limited to the arts centre itself, which the public often had trouble finding within the complex. Watson remembers that many of the limitations placed on KB&A by the architects before the centre's opening fell by the wayside once the 'realities of practical operation' became clear; throughout the 80s, the solution was the addition of ever greater numbers of signs, as well as the famous yellow lines painted on the floor to aid navigation from outside the centre.

Despite this, navigation issues long lingered. In 1993 managing director Detta O'Cathain, who had replaced Wrong in 1990, oversaw a £9.7 million refurbishment creating a 'new look' Barbican which, in her own words, was 'really on the move'. Theo Crosby of design agency Pentagram, chosen from 36 practices, was the mastermind of the scheme. His involvement focused on improving pedestrian access and creating a more inviting interior. Crosby wrote that they were creating a 'system to replace the enormous rash of signage which currently covers nearly every available piece of wall space'. His solution was the introduction of free-standing index signs featuring floorplans and maps with 'you are here' arrows.

The pictogram designed by Ken Briggs & Associates for the Barbican Hall illustrates the ambition that the venue would host conferences and lectures as well as music.

What Crosby didn't do was change the centre's graphic identity; he declared that Briggs's metal lettering 'read well on the concrete' and conveyed 'a sense of quality and style', adding that 'uncluttered relevant signage should, we hope, make moving about in the Barbican Centre a much easier and more pleasurable

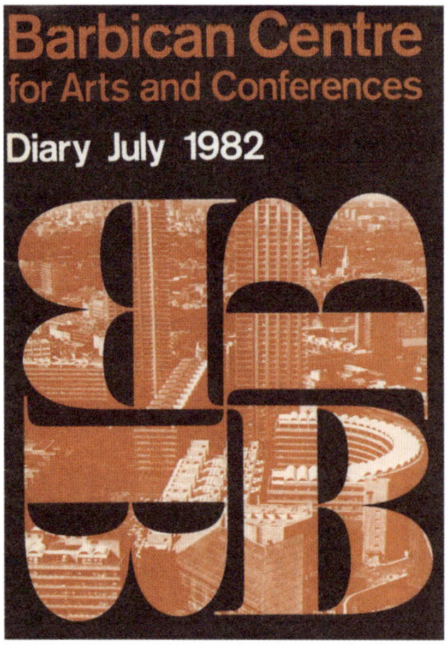
Barbican Centre
for Arts and Conferences
Diary July 1982

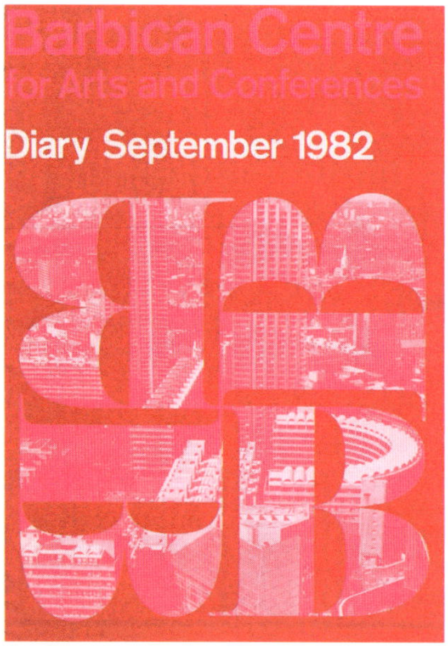
Barbican Centre
for Arts and Conferences
Diary September 1982

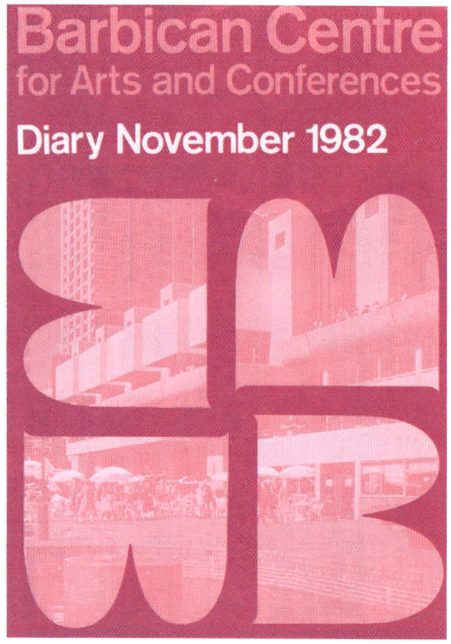
Barbican Centre
for Arts and Conferences
Diary November 1982

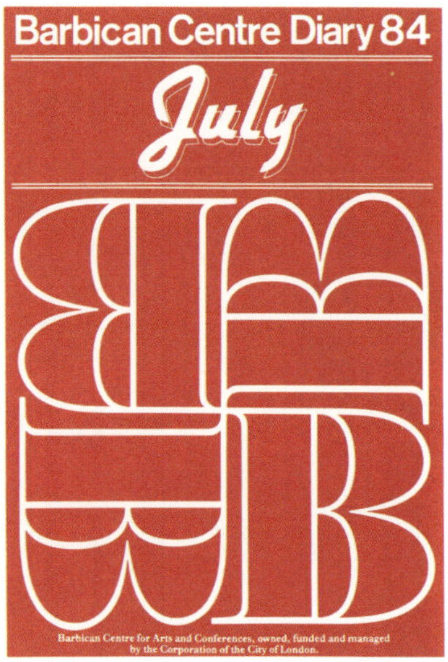
Barbican Centre Diary 84
July
Barbican Centre for Arts and Conferences, owned, funded and managed by the Corporation of the City of London.

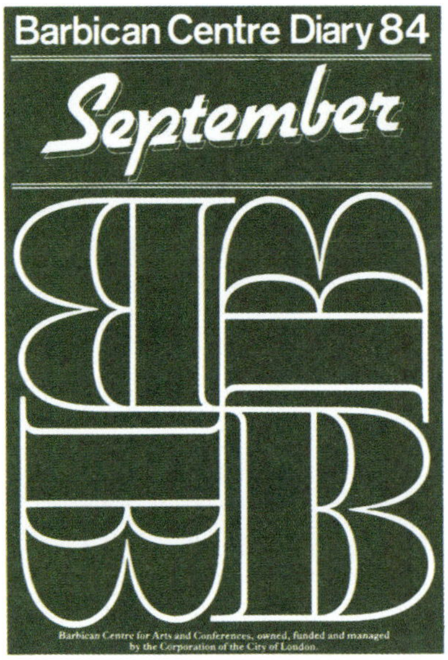
Barbican Centre Diary 84
September
Barbican Centre for Arts and Conferences, owned, funded and managed by the Corporation of the City of London.

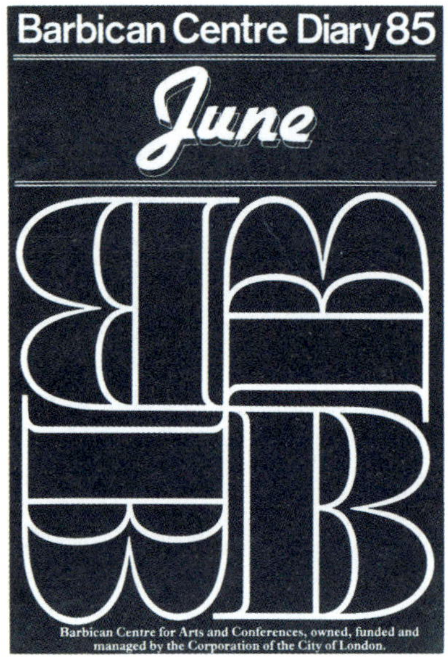
Barbican Centre Diary 85
June
Barbican Centre for Arts and Conferences, owned, funded and managed by the Corporation of the City of London.

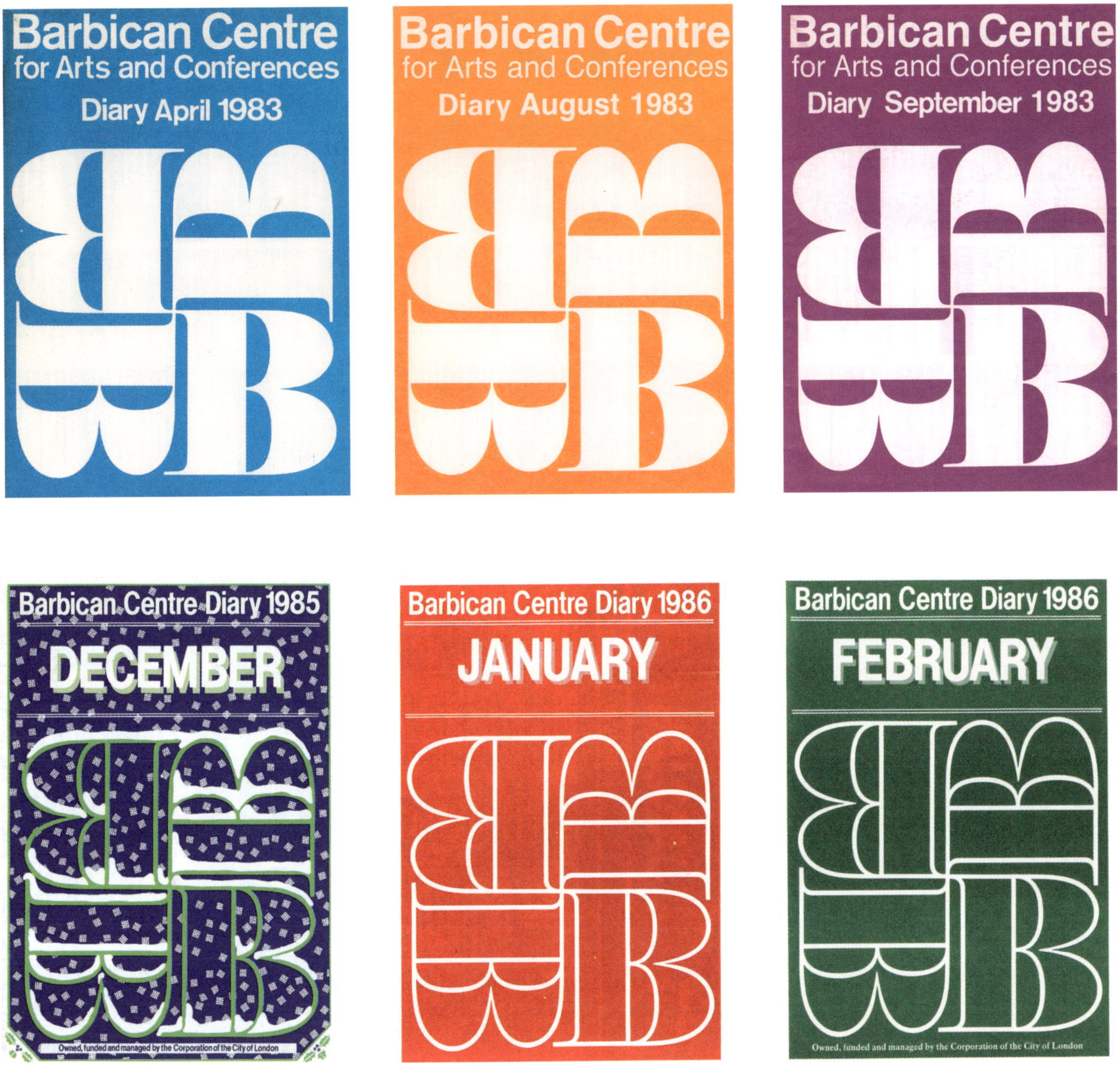

Evolving monthly guides in the 1980s show the process of Ken Briggs & Associates' strict modernist approach giving way to something more eclectic, still using the four Bs.

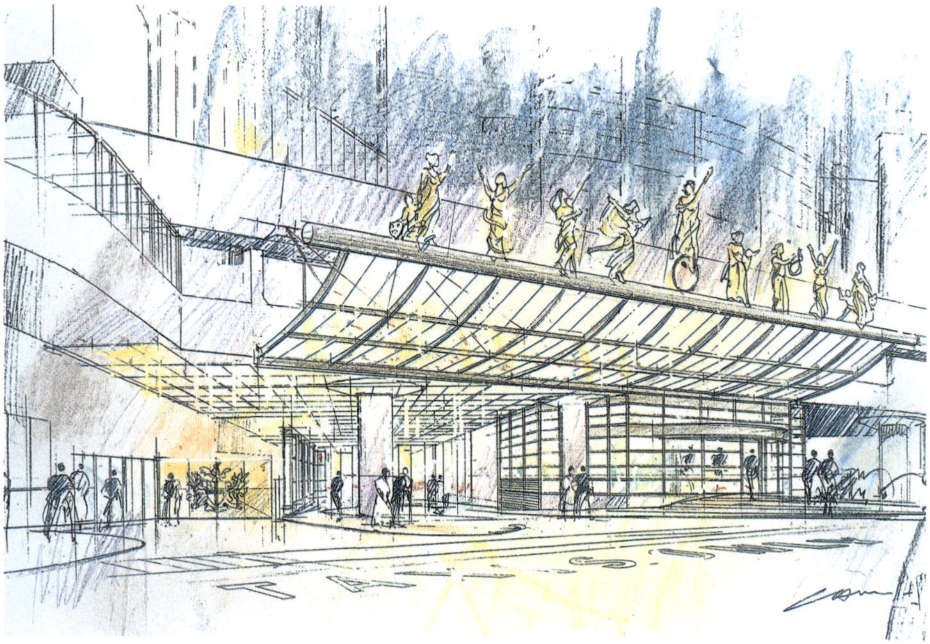

The controversial redesign of the front entrance of the Barbican by Theo Crosby of Pentagram, instigated by Detta O'Cathain from 1991, with Sir Bernard Sindall's gilded 'Nine Muses' above the entrance. They were removed by O'Cathain's successor John Tusa.

experience.' However, Briggs's identity for the Barbican wasn't universally loved. Discussing the upcoming revamp, a *Daily Telegraph* writer joked that the centre 'needs to find a new home for 4,000 square yards of that awful orange carpet they've had down since 1982 (...) it has one big flaw: there's no way of disguising its ghastly repeated BB logo'. Writing for *The Observer* in 1995, Christopher Middleton notes that the Barbican is 'sticking with its logo—four Bs following each other round in a square', implying that the Bs of the logo, like Barbican visitors, had no idea which way they should be going.

Theo Crosby's work at the Barbican is mostly remembered for the addition of artworks, including vast pointillist murals in the foyers by his wife, the artist Polly Hope, and gilded fibreglass statues over the Silk Street entrance by Matthew Spender and Bernard Sindall, whose 'Nine Muses' sculpture was derided as a deeply old-fashioned way of representing the arts. Gold statues by Hope also sat atop the new index signs placed on each floor. The sculptures and murals were removed when the centre's management changed, having lasted less than four years. The biggest success of Crosby's interventions was the rethinking of floor allocation. These were renumbered and each given a name relating to their main purpose, for instance Stalls, Library, Gallery. The lakeside floor where many visitors enter, previously level 5, logically became the ground floor.

Crosby's replacement carpets, which were patterned and colour-themed per floor, didn't fare much better than the originals, and were later described in newspapers as 'ghastly', 'a cacophony' and 'hangover coloured'. Gillian Darley in *The Observer* wrote witheringly about Crosby's scheme, noting that it was 'as if the designers suddenly turned against the building' and describing the art as 'far from top-quality'. Darley concluded that 'Crosby's peculiar attempts to jolly up the Barbican suggest a damp squib of a student project rather than a scheme drawn up by an international design group.' Crosby had made improvements to navigation, but it remained a problem which was tackled only by radical changes in a revamp by the centre's new management.

The same issues had been hampering the Barbican's visual identity. An absence of confidence in programming, which had been dependent on the RSC and LSO, as well as the now unfashionable architecture and interiors, were reflected in the lack of vibrancy in the Barbican's branding. Writing in *Arts Management Weekly* in 1996 following John Tusa joining as managing director and Graham Sheffield joining as artistic director, Simon Tait notes that the Barbican 'is at last, after nearly 15 years, emerging as an entity in itself. There seemed a determination to avoid that in the past, so that one didn't recognise a Barbican brand; only the brands, like the RSC and the LSO, within it.' By 2000, a *Guardian* article could lead with the headline 'It's farewell to the terminally lost visitor at Barbican mark two'. The piece included the line: 'The world's most bewildering arts centre is solving the problem of its notorious signs once and for all—by getting rid of most of them.'

A microcosm of the Barbican's identity problem was presented by the art gallery, which was for almost two decades run by its own separate team under

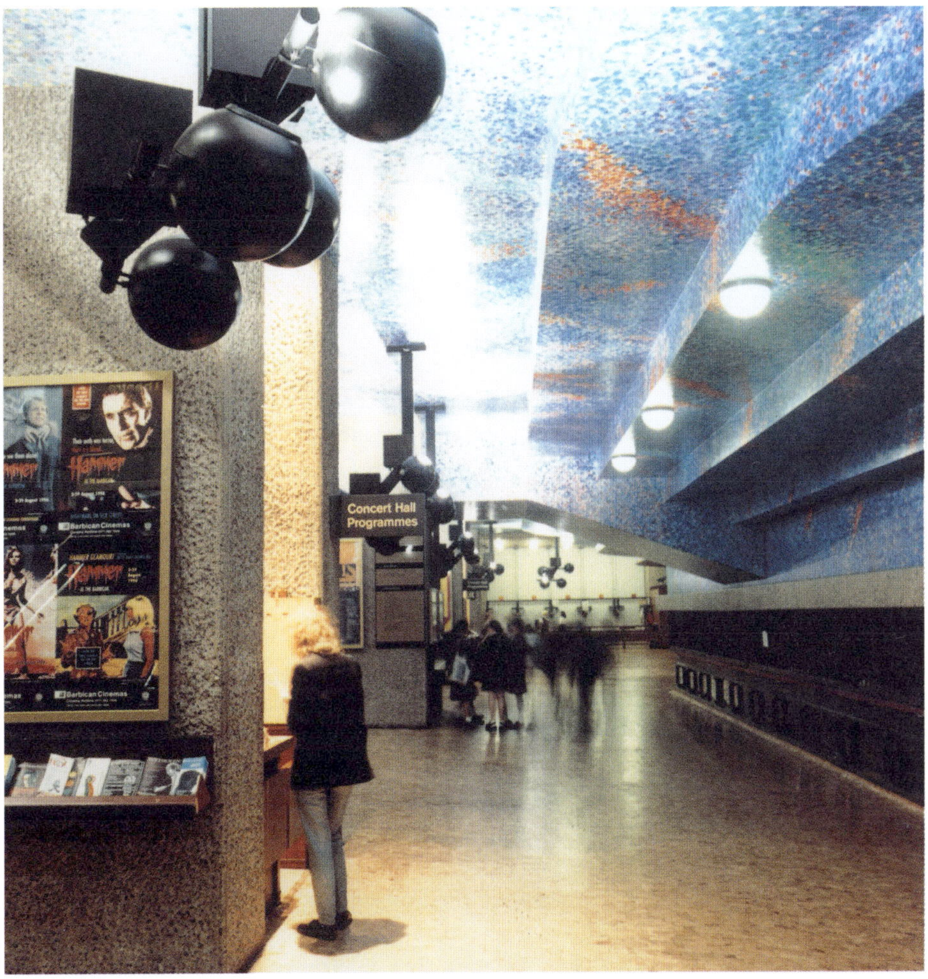

The interior foyer in the Pentagram redesign featured 1,400 square metres (15,000 sq. ft) of pointillist murals by Theo Crosby's wife Polly Hope. They divided opinion and were painted over within a few years.

the City's direct management and therefore had its own individual approach to graphic design. In 1990, they turned to Richard Hollis to develop a proper graphic style for the Barbican Gallery. Hollis, writing in a style guide prepared in August 1990, notes that the aim of his involvement was to 'make the Barbican Gallery identifiable and recognised by consistent graphics' and to 'reduce time and energy spent on print, design and promotion'. Hollis's identity, which exclusively utilised the typeface Gill Sans to create a unified voice, represented the gallery until 1999 when agency Lewis Moberly were behind a switch to the modernist sans-serif typeface Frutiger. This new identity, which was typeset in lowercase only, reflected the galleries' switch from 'Barbican Art Gallery' to simply 'barbican art'.

When Tusa took the Barbican's top job, the *Guardian* noted that the original four Bs logo was 'an image summing up for many the Barbican's problems' – everyone looking in different directions. Both Tusa and Sheffield had experience at the BBC, an organisation successful at integrating a varied output under a unified brand; they would do something similar at the Barbican. Their improved arts programme, facilitated by a large amount of creative freedom from the City, also fostered stronger links and integration between disciplines.

The withdrawal of the RSC, which became total in 2002, allowed for the creation of a new theatre festival, snappily named BITE (Barbican International Theatre Events), which ran from 1998–2011. Alongside a more vibrant overall programme, graphic design for the Barbican became more daring. BITE posters from 1998–2001 were designed by Why Not Associates, who utilised their trademark maximalist approach, blending typography with photography and digital techniques. Elsewhere, Jonathan Barnbrook, another typographic postmodernist, designed an eclectic campaign for a cross-arts celebration of Oscar Wilde that opened in 2000. Peter Saville, famed for his album covers for Factory Records, designed a poster for part of the *Inventing America* cross-arts programme in 1998.

At the turn of the millennium, John Tusa described the Barbican as 'a young organisation wearing very old clothes' and decided a corporate image change was needed alongside the planned architectural improvements. Much of the work, which would be undertaken by up-and-coming firm AHHM, focused on improved entrances and navigation, as well as removing the aesthetic missteps of the Crosby scheme. The design agency chosen for the rebrand, at a reported cost of £50,000, was Lloyd Northover Citigate (LNC), who won a competitive pitch to design both the website and identity, which was finally unveiled in October 2000 before being fully implemented.

According to a Barbican spokeswoman, LNC were chosen because they 'understood the nature of the problems we are facing in communicating the diverse and exciting nature of the Barbican'. The new branding was the biggest identity change in the centre's 18-year history. Most significantly the Barbican Arts Centre became simply 'barbican'. This newly shortened, lowercase name appeared in the centre of a holding shape, an incomplete flat-sided circle representing a spotlight. According to LNC co-founder Jim Northover, the cropped circle, which bled off the edge of the page, was a representation of the idea that 'there was always something more to discover' at the Barbican, something 'behind every corner'. It also referenced the building; seen from above, the area by Frobisher Crescent created a similar shape. Along with the logo, a new colour scheme was introduced, with three palettes: purple, orange and red, representing

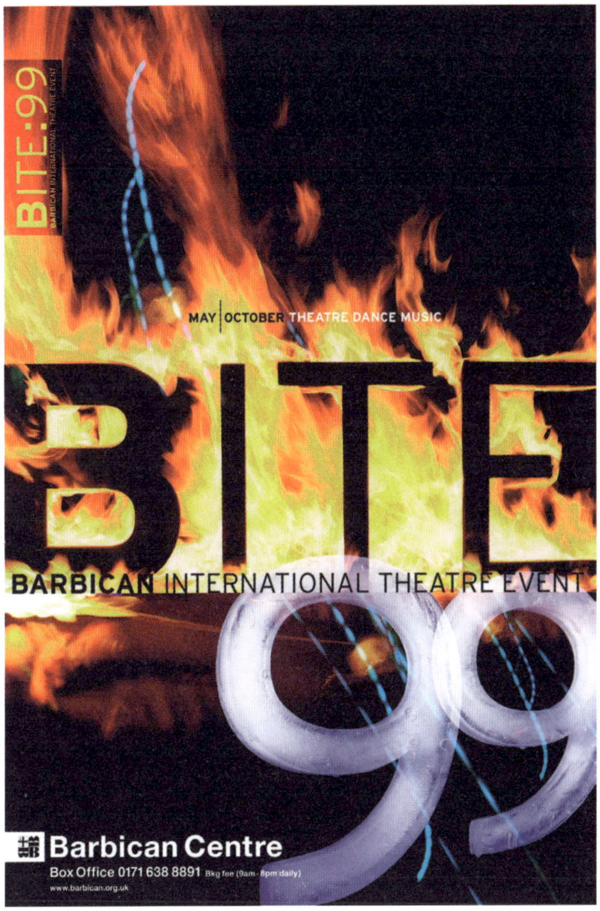

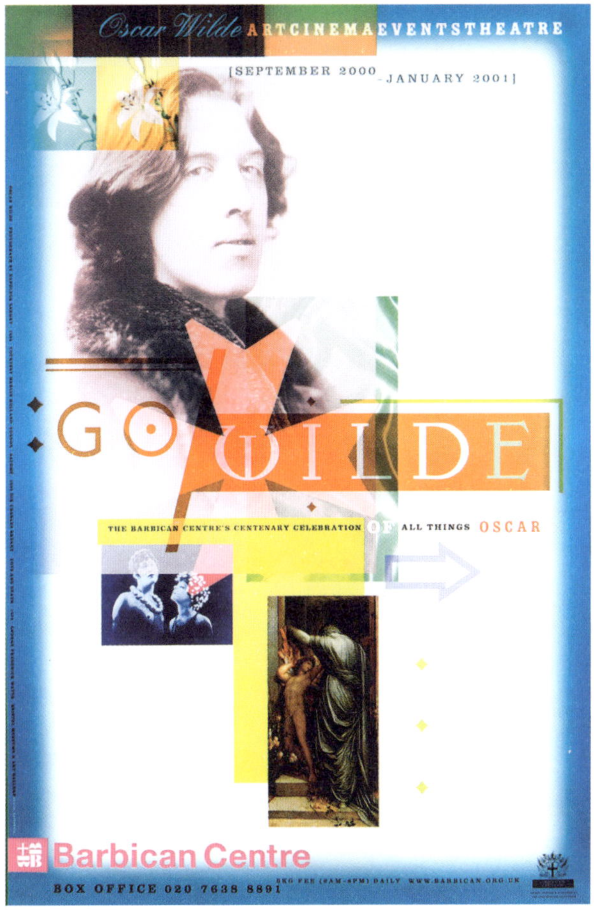

Design moves on: posters designed by Why Not Associates, for the 1999 Barbican International Theatre Events season, and by Jonathan Barnbrook, for the Oscar Wilde cross-arts programme in 2000–1. Here the description 'Barbican Centre' is still used in Ken Briggs' neutral typographic style, but the four Bs have been reduced to a tiny stamp and modified to include the City of London's shield in the place of the top left B.

the diversity of the Barbican's output. Sheffield noted that the centre wanted to 'achieve an aesthetic that communicates what we are – artistic and lively'.

Although the centre was rebranded in 2000, the four Bs logo was still up on external walls when the centre was included in the complex's 2001 Grade II listing. Subsequently, they remain up near two main entrances: Silk Street and on a large column next to Defoe House, although the original bronze has been painted in a more neutral grey. Attempts have long been made to update these signs to reflect the current identity, but the Twentieth Century Society object to their removal, as do many Barbican residents, in part because of the possibility of new signs being illuminated.

The dropping of the definite article from the Barbican was an idea that stuck. Following in the footsteps of Southbank Centre and Tate, this move reflected a trend which had many commentators bemoaning declining grammatical rigour. Philosopher Sir Isaiah Berlin had told John Tusa, 'You will not make the Barbican loved! But you can make it respected!' – the new identity by Lloyd Northover was a step in the right direction and definitely brought the centre urgently into the new millennium, but many aspects of it were short-lived. Design agency North, who were at the forefront of a neo-modernist wave of British graphics, were hired to create a new identity for the Barbican's art gallery in 2004. North's system,

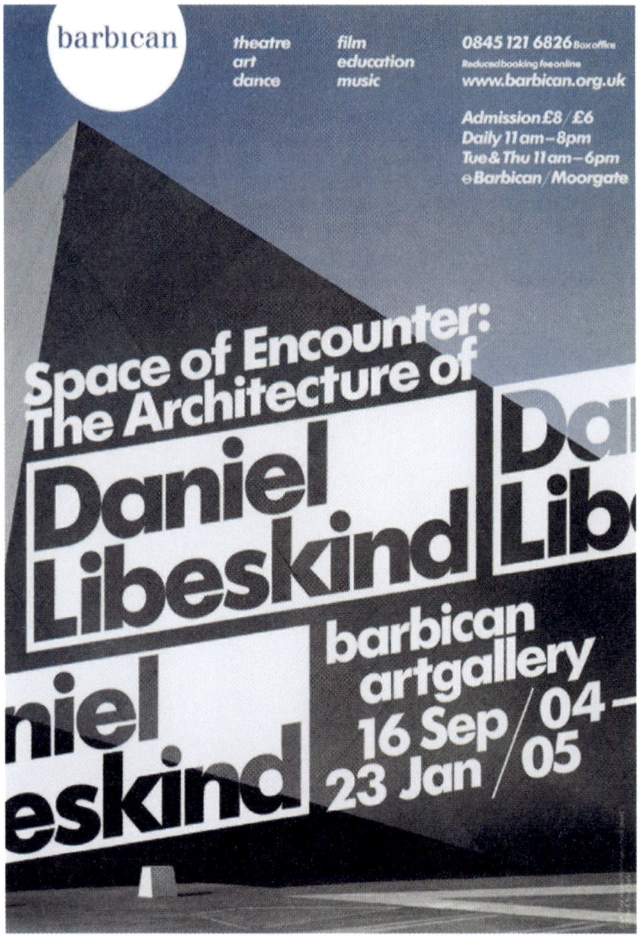

Poster by design agency North for the gallery's Daniel Libeskind exhibition, 2004. Here the use of the typeface Futura, soon to be applied to the entire centre, co-exists with Lloyd Northover's Barbican logo from 2000; a truncated circle, perhaps echoing the shape of Frobisher Crescent, with a lower-case serif wordmark in its centre.

which utilised the sans-serif typeface Futura inventively in a bold weight and italics set at dynamic angles, met with instant acclaim when it was applied to the recently refurbished galleries' marketing material. Branding designer Michael Johnson, writing for *Design Week* in 2004, concluded an article on the branding failures of many British cultural venues by suggesting that the new 'muscular' Barbican identity by North 'may be a sign that our institutions will finally get the graphic images that their programming suggests'.

The art gallery had only entered the fold of the overall Barbican Centre at last in 2001 and its long-standing identity problems hadn't been solved by simply placing 'art' next to the new circular Barbican logo on gallery posters. North had been brought in by gallery head Carol Brown and marketing director Chris Denton, who had joined from the South Bank in 2001 and was instrumental in the unification of the Barbican's disparate marketing teams.

Such was the success of North's initial design work for the gallery that Lloyd Northover's logo was soon updated to use Futura, which became the entire arts centre's brand typeface. Tusa recounted that there 'was no point shouting at the Barbican and ordering it to be what it could never be; it deserved to be listened to'; in a sense Futura reflected this belief, it spoke for the Barbican.

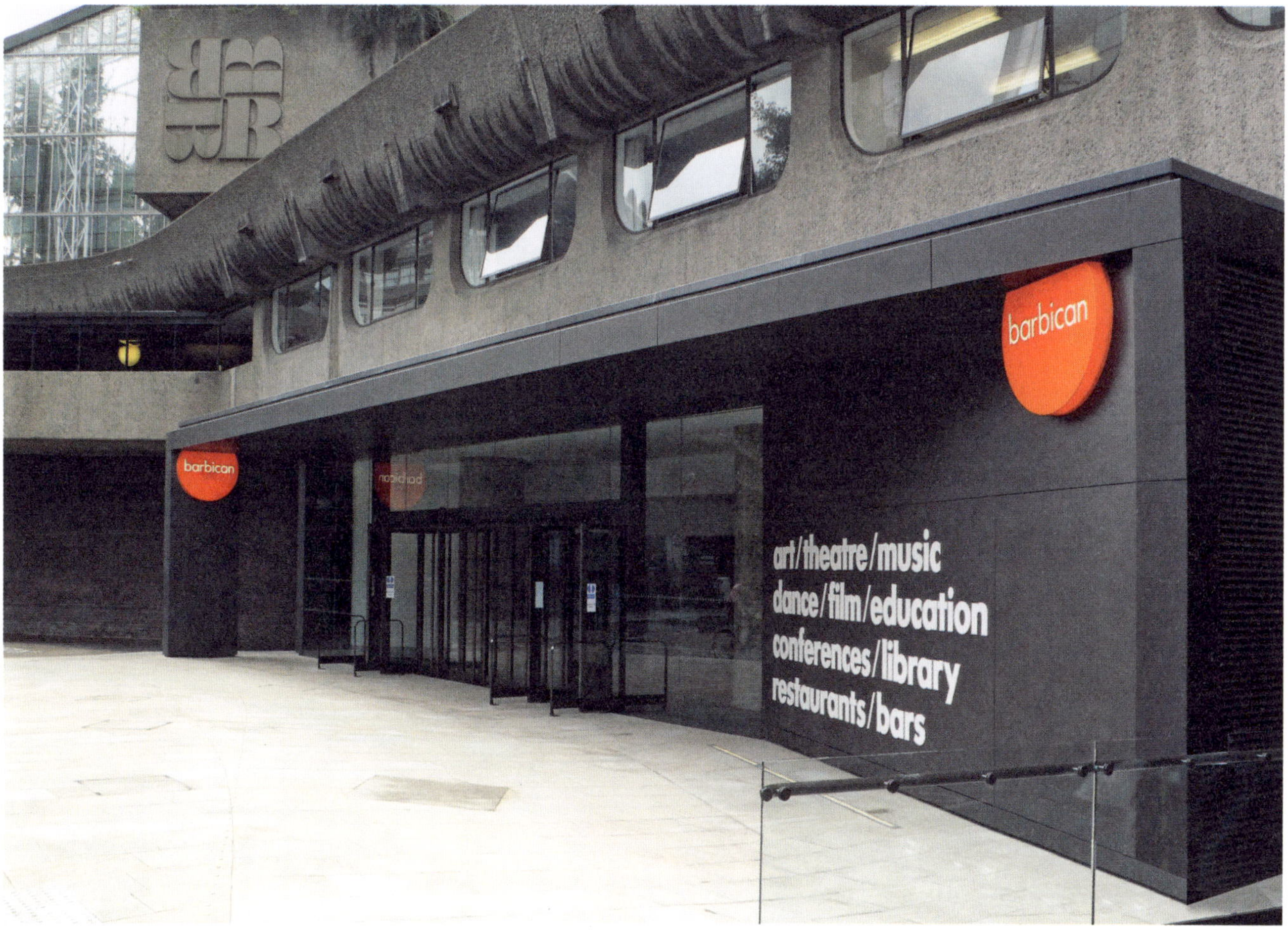

In the radical reworking of the entrance and interior spaces by AHMM, completed in 2007, the sans-serif typeface Futura dominates, and the semicircle symbol became a vibrant orange.

Futura had been designed by German typographer Paul Renner in 1927 using geometric, modernist principles combined with classical proportions, the same ideas espoused by CPB on the Barbican. The fact that Renner was responding to the same milieu as the pioneering figures who inspired the Barbican's architecture made Futura a suitable 'voice' for the arts centre. Although Lloyd Northover's Barbican identity turned out to be brief, many elements they introduced — such as the prominent use of bright orange, the flat-sided circle and switch to simply 'barbican' — remain important today.

Some observers worried that North's gallery identity would be restrictive due to its strict adherence to one typeface, however, subsequent creative uses of Futura have shown how a limitation can become a virtue. For instance, in 2009 Bibliothèque, an agency founded in 2004 by two former North staff, designed an identity for the Barbican's Le Corbusier retrospective, memorably creating a stencil version of Futura cast in concrete. The galleries' use of Futura has waned a little in recent years. Now that the centre's audiences are familiar with the overall Barbican brand not all art gallery exhibitions and publicity — designed by the likes of Fraser Muggeridge Studio, A Practice for Everyday Life and John Morgan Studio — use Futura exclusively.

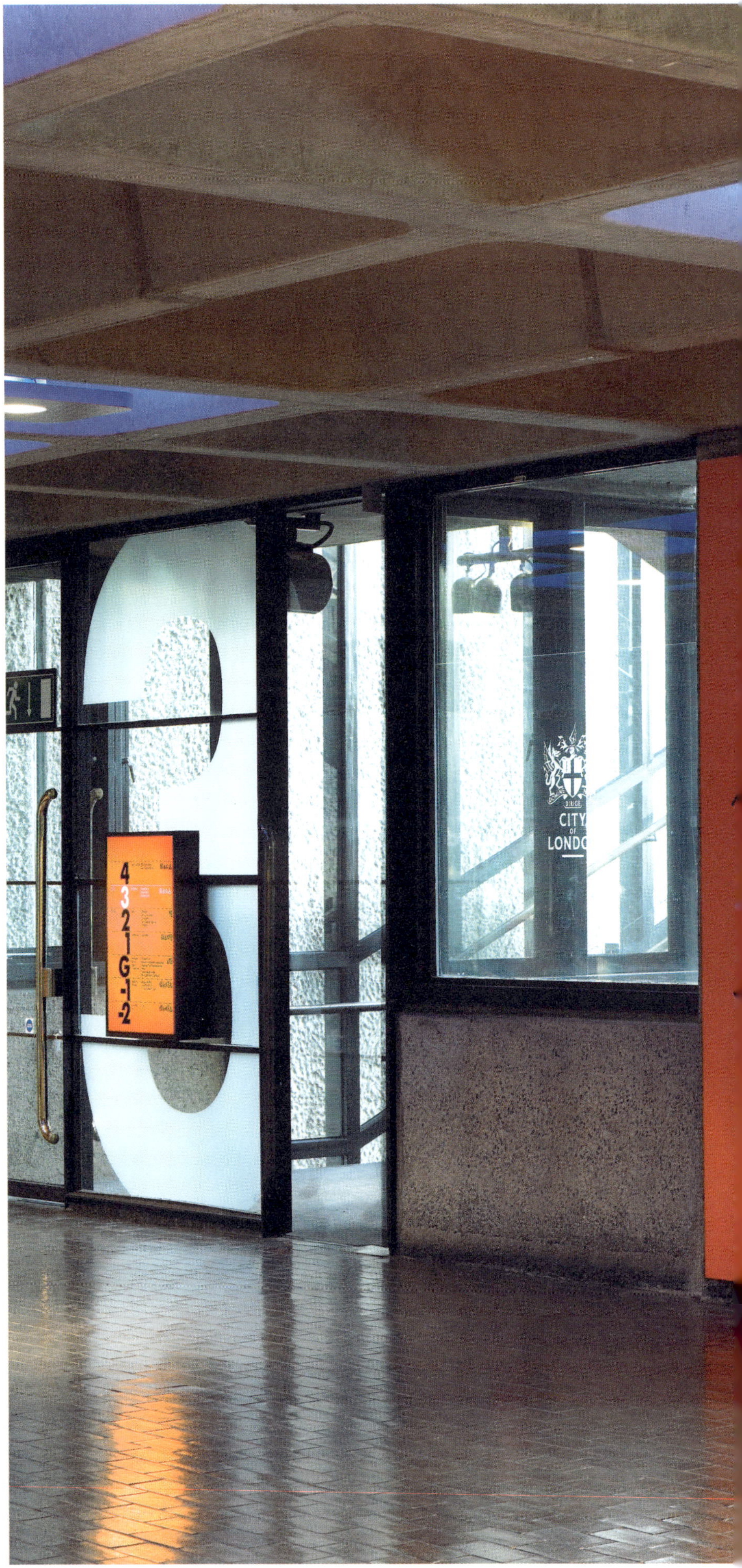

The AHMM interior redesign made a bold and successful graphic attempt to clarify wayfinding, with large, impactful numbered floor panels and signs designed as part of an award-winning scheme by Cartlidge Levene and Studio Myerscough.

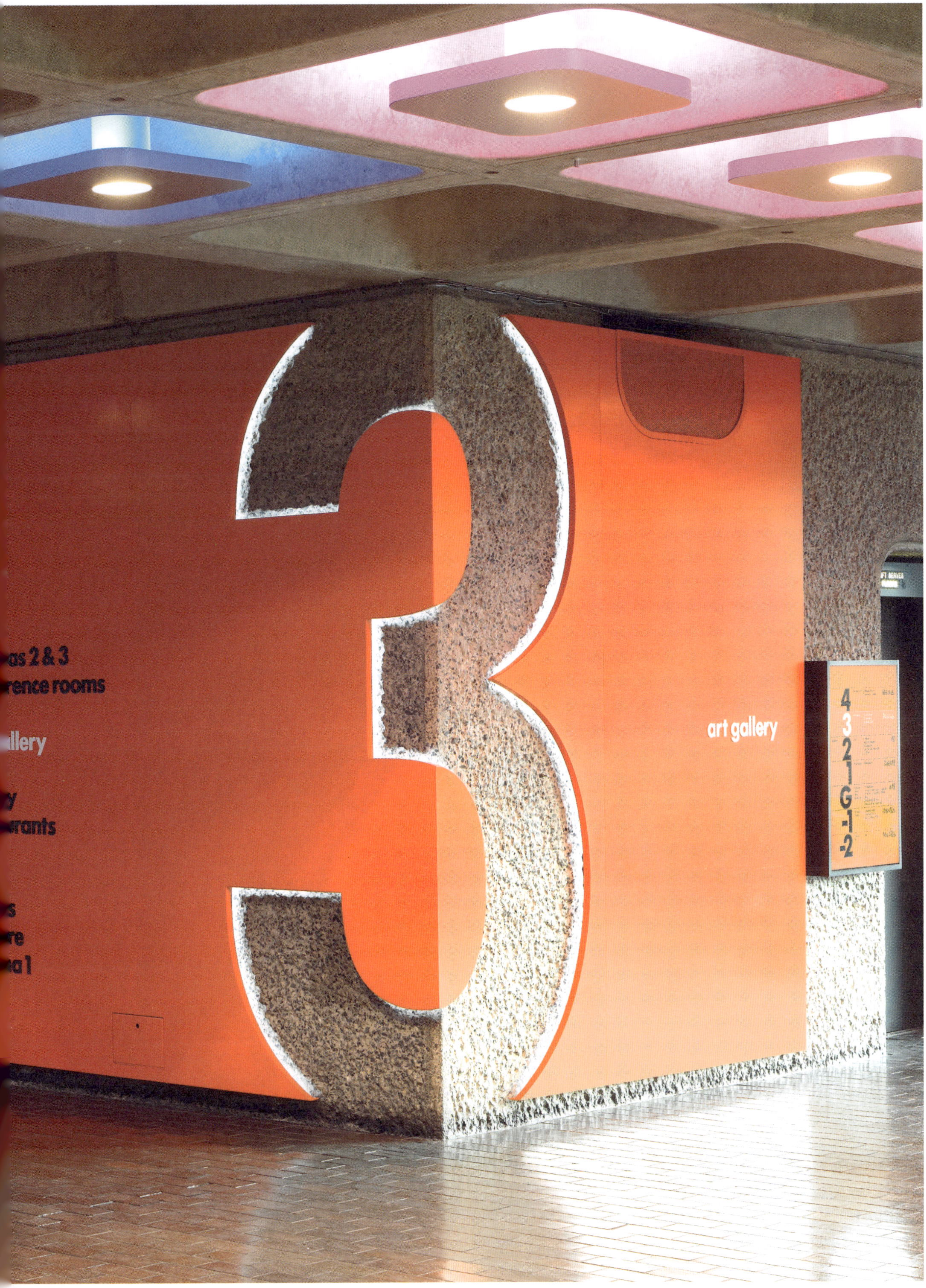
3
art gallery

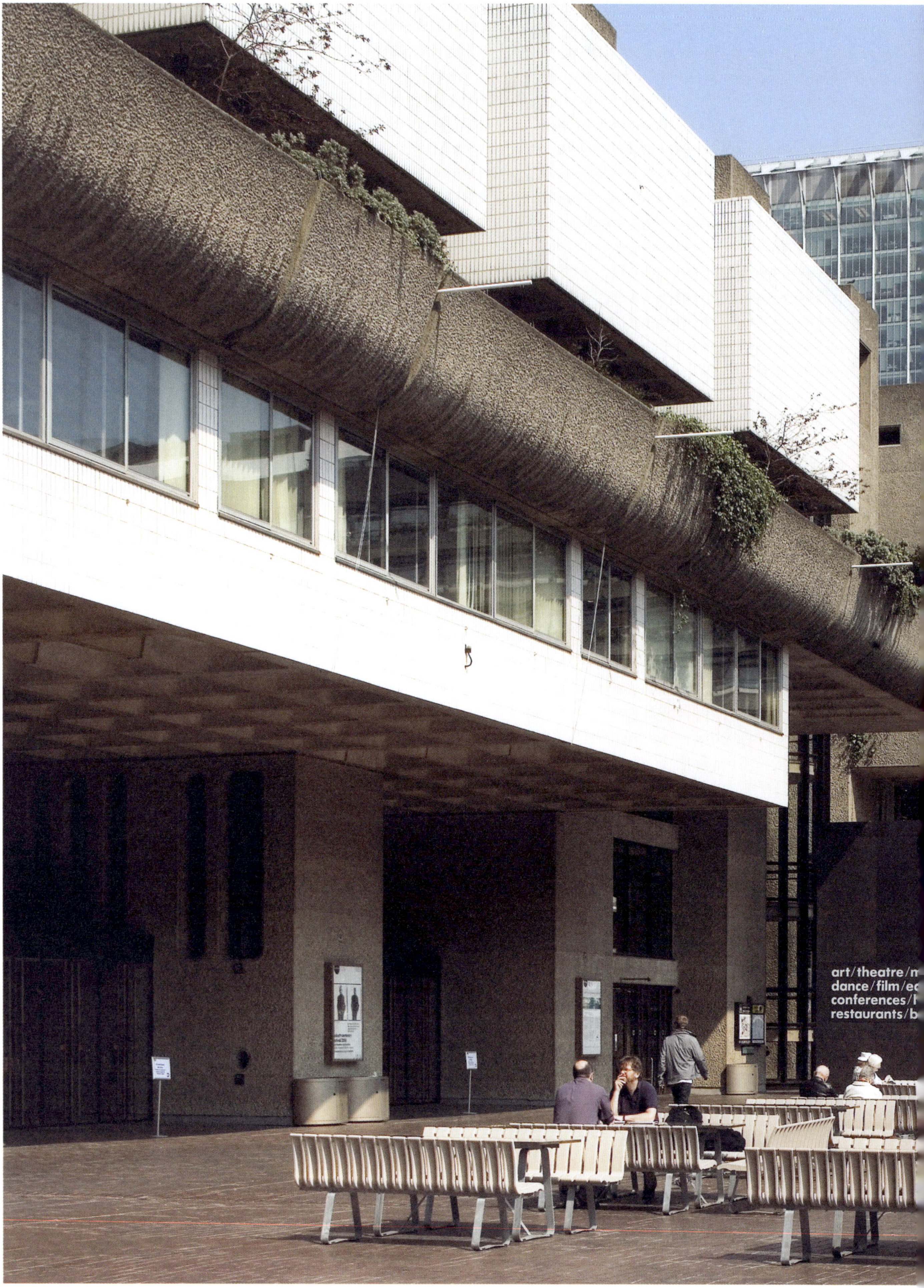
art/theatre/
dance/film/
conferences/
restaurants/

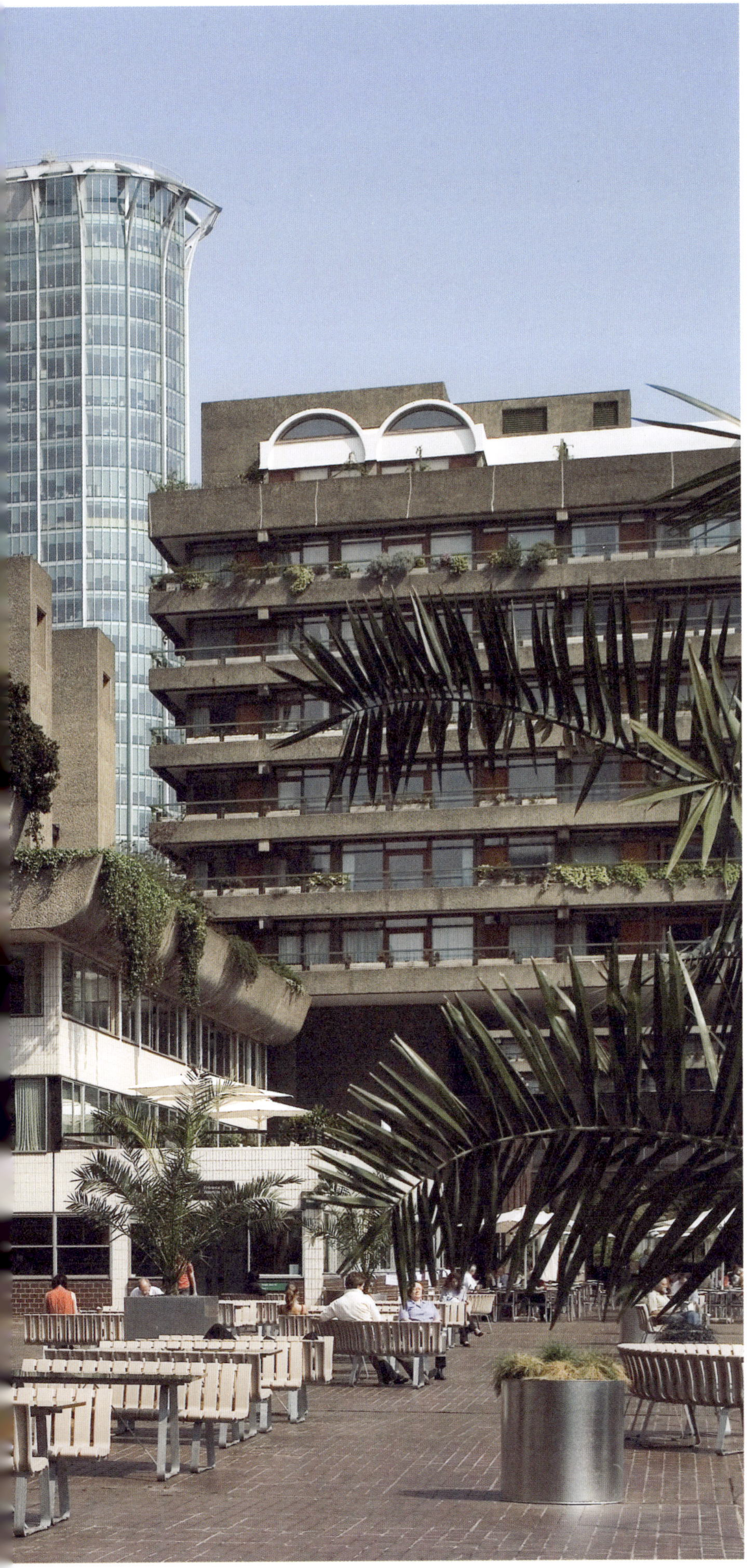

The Lakeside Terrace entrance with the new monolith sign introduced as part of the AHMM work, echoing the Silk Street entrance (p.181) and featuring the renewed seating by Robin Day (p.73).

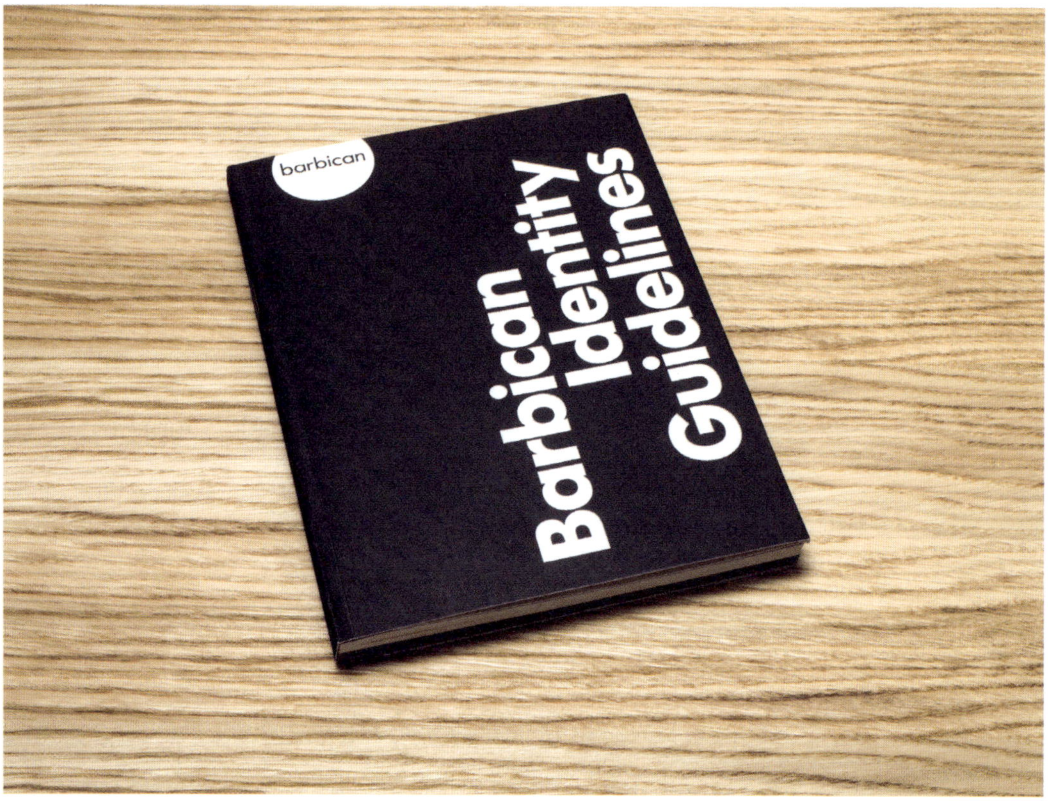
barbican
Barbican Identity Guidelines

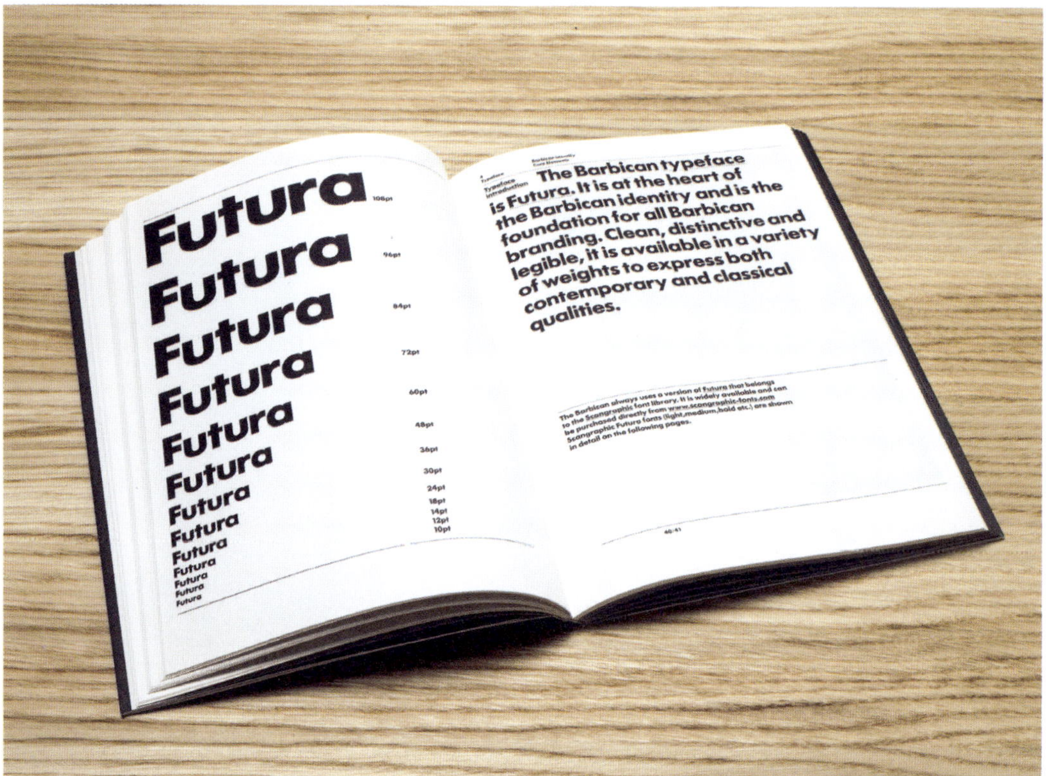
Futura
Futura
Futura
Futura
Futura
Futura
Futura
Futura
Futura
Futura
96pt
84pt
72pt
60pt
48pt
36pt
30pt
24pt
18pt
14pt
12pt
10pt
The Barbican typeface is Futura. It is at the heart of the Barbican identity and is the foundation for all Barbican branding. Clean, distinctive and legible, it is available in a variety of weights to express both contemporary and classical qualities.

An indication of the state of flux that the Barbican was in when North began their work is revealed by the wayfinding project that was happening concurrently. Architects AHMM had begun working on their refurbishment of the Barbican, described by Tusa as 'clearing out the crud', in 2003 and had brought in two of their long-standing collaborators to work together on the graphics and wayfinding elements of the project: Cartlidge Levene and Studio Myerscough. By the time it had been decided that Futura would become the Barbican's brand typeface, the wayfinding project had already reached the prototyping stage using Rockwell, a slab-serif font with some similar proportions to Futura. Ultimately, John Tusa made the final call and Cartlidge Levene and Studio Myerscough ended up using Futura rather than Rockwell.

AHMM's scheme resolved a myriad of longstanding issues — especially the entrances and overall navigation — and the bold graphic elements were an absolutely integral part of its success, something recognised when the project won awards from RIBA, *Design Week* and D&AD in 2007. D&AD described the project succinctly: 'Architecture, graphics and lighting have been designed together to bring clarity and cohesion to this once unnavigable space. Entrances have been created, routes have been rationalised, and the foyers have been de-cluttered with a bold, calm, confident approach that respects the original architecture. Key elements include supergraphic arrows at key decision points to direct flow and sculptural circular signs at circulation hubs.' The use of bright flat colour, particularly the orange, helped delineate different spaces and enliven the interior, while the appearance of Futura at gigantic sizes was eye-catching and helped reinforce it as the key element of the Barbican's visual identity. Lynda Relph-Knight, editor of *Design Week*, noted of the scheme: 'Not since the complex was launched in 1982 has wayfinding been as clear, despite various efforts over the years.' Quoted in 2011 Ian Cartlidge, the co-founder of Cartlidge Levene, would say the success of any wayfinding project was 'measured in a dropoff in complaints rather than a barrage of praise'; in the case of the Barbican, the scheme achieved both.

By the time the wayfinding was praised, North had fully implemented their rebrand of the Barbican in time for its 25th anniversary year and had produced an in-depth, 111-page brand-book explaining the correct use of the logo, typeface, grids, sub-brands and layouts. Not since Ken Briggs & Associates' Signs Systems Manual, produced before the 1982 opening, had the Barbican had such a complete grasp over its identity. In the annual report from 2007, Chris Denton notes that North's work 'represents the culmination of a project to re-energise the look and feel of the Barbican and further strengthens the Centre's identity as a dynamic place to experience the best of the arts from around the world.'

An aspect that made North's new branding successful in the long term was the fact that it was seen as an ongoing collaboration rather than something handed off to the client and forgotten about. As part of North's new look, a list of the areas represented by the Barbican — Art, Theatre, Music, Dance, Film and Education — frequently appeared alongside the semicircular logo to reinforce the full range of the centre's activities. This list, with the addition of Library, Conferences, Bars and Restaurants, also appeared in large Futura at the two improved main entrances: on a wall at Silk Street and on a new 'monolith' by the lakeside doors. North also developed distinct identities for the Barbican's different cultural outputs, each of which used Futura in inventive ways.

The Barbican Identity Guidelines by agency North in 2007 provided a rigorous, clear and sharp outline to the centre's communications, based on the typeface Futura as 'the heart of the Barbican identity and the foundation for all Barbican branding'. Though much has changed in its use, Futura remains core to the brand.

Following pages
The de-cluttered foyers of the AHMM renewal, with the new bridge connecting across the space, and the restrained use of posters with the North vertical wordmark branding.

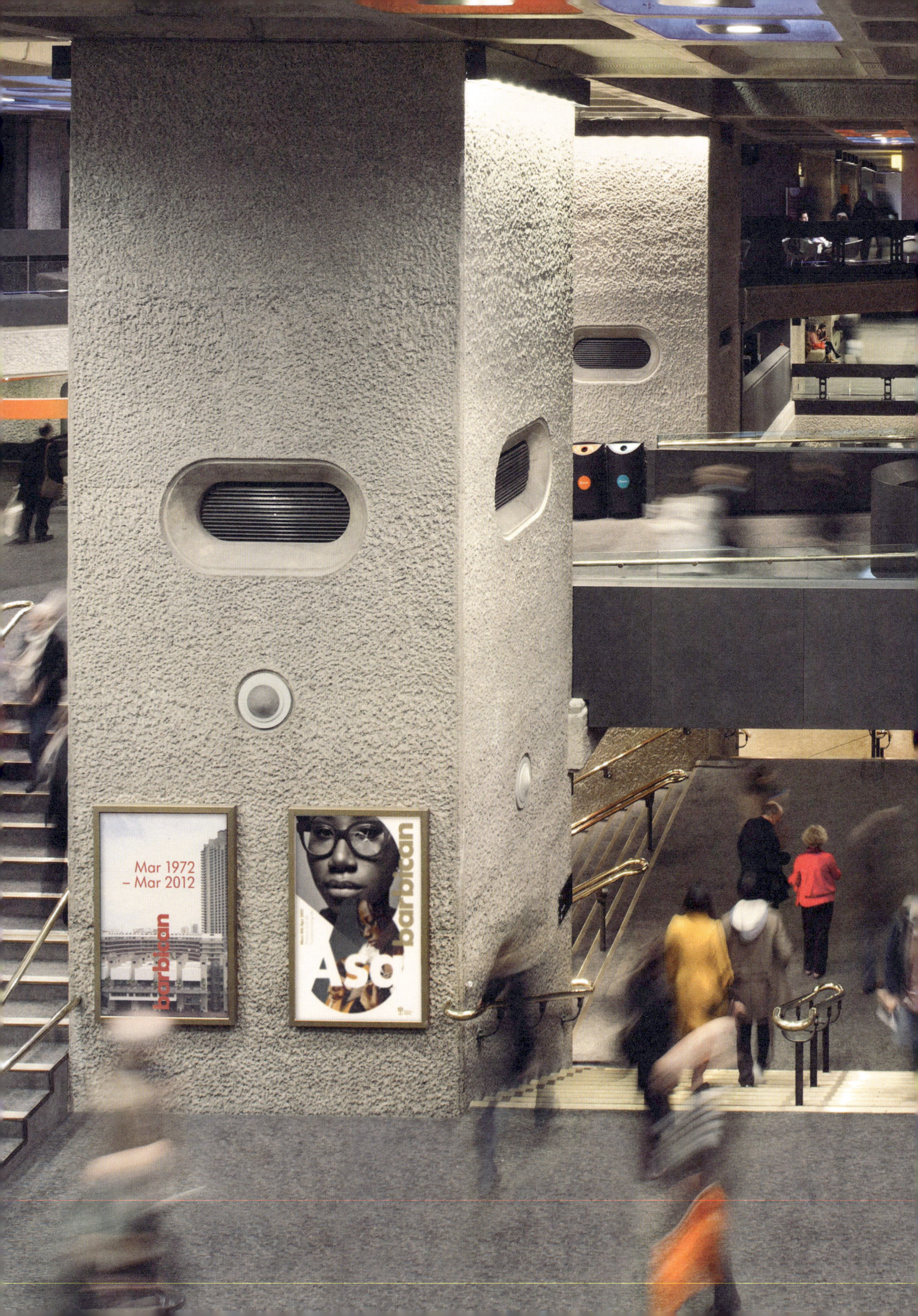
Mar 1972
– Mar 2012
barbican
barbican

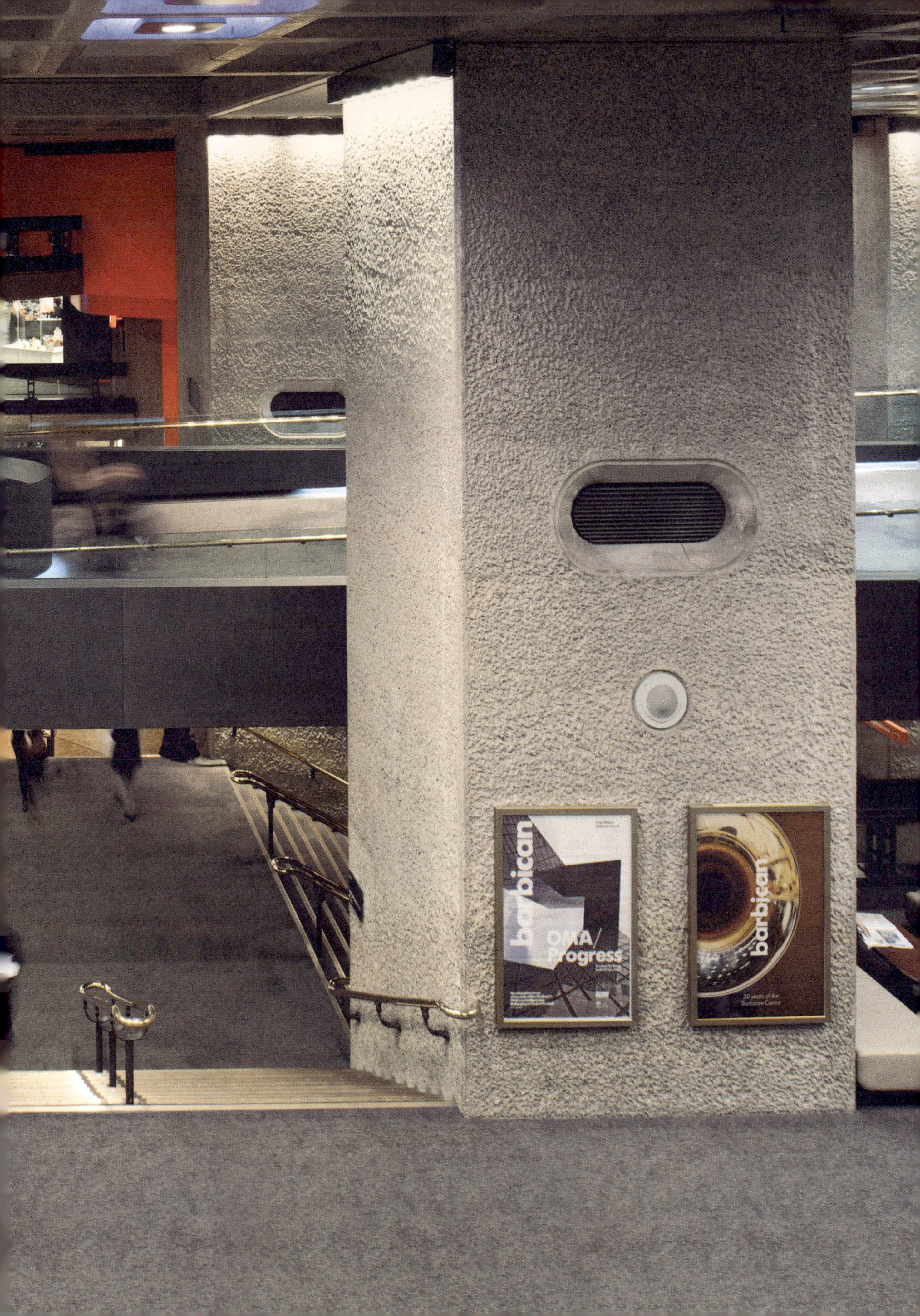
barbican
OMA/
Progress
barbican
30 years of the
Barbican Centre

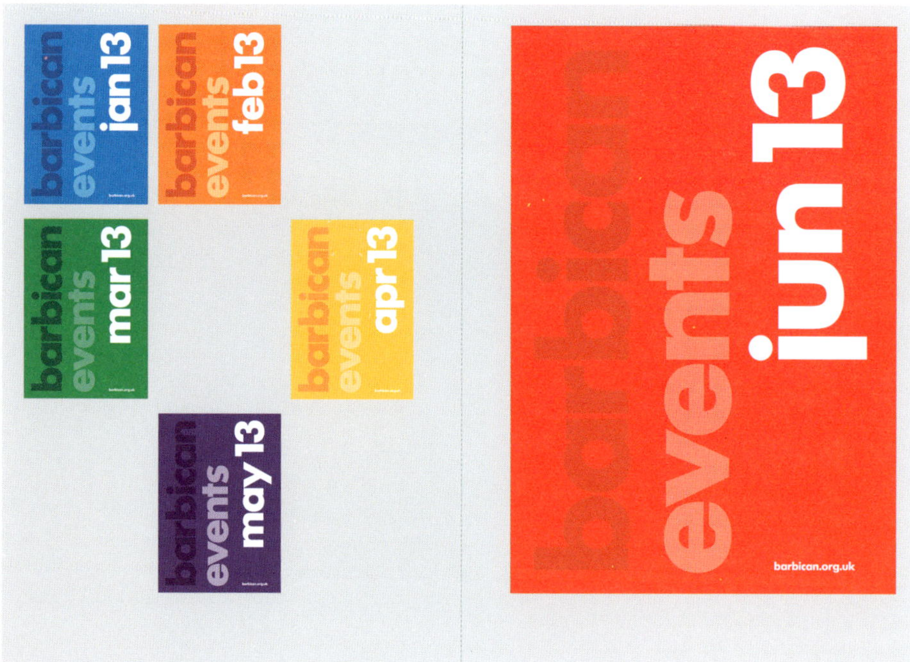

Graphic design for the monthly guides emphasises simplicity, clarity and impact through use of the Futura type family and Barbican brand colours, while leaflet and poster design (see pp.192–3) diversifies and enlivens the treatment within the brand.

After a quarter-century, the Barbican — once 'a byword for unfashionability' — had finally begun to shake off some of the negative associations that had plagued it since its launch. Writing in February 2007, Linda Sweet in the *Evening Standard* declared: 'The Barbican wins all round … For fans, the place remains true to its original and exciting Brave New World vision. Meanwhile, for anyone who has had past reservations, now is the time to visit — and prepare yourself for a concrete conversion.' Aside from improvements to its programming, navigation, brand identity and overall image, over the following years, with a new management regime in place, the Barbican benefited hugely in the new millennium from the redevelopment of East London as a creative hub, the buzz surrounding the upcoming 2012 Olympics and perhaps most of all from a renewed interest and appreciation of brutalist architecture. By the second decade of the 21st century concrete brutalism was an incredibly trendy subject and the subject of numerous popular blogs, books and social media accounts. North's identity felt like a manifestation of a confident, exciting arts centre and one which fully embraced its architecture.

In 2013, some ten years after they had first taken them on as a client, North were again tasked with evolving the brand, and the changes they implemented very much reflected a more confident Barbican. A major reason for the evolution was a strategy to further unify the centre under one umbrella; as North partner Gilmour put it, the Barbican wanted to 'move away from sub-brands' and focus on 'the centre as a whole'. As managing director, Nicholas Kenyon talked often of 'One Barbican' as his ideal; artistic director Louise Jeffreys, who had previously been the influential head of theatre under Sheffield, explained that the directors wanted to make sure 'the Barbican was the word that people think of first, rather than BITE, or Great Performers'. The refreshed rather than rebranded identity, which was unveiled in time for the centre to host the prestigious AGI graphic design conference, maintained the majority of the distinctive characteristics of the original North identity.

The most radical change was that the Barbican logotype, still in Futura, switched to a bolder cut of the font and was freed from its cropped roundel and usually appeared running vertically when space allowed. A hangover from the original Lloyd Northover identity, the circular carrier shape switched from being the key element of the logo to become a part of the brand's 'visual language'. The benefit of a vertical wordmark was that it could appear at much larger scales than a logo in a circle ever feasibly could, which, combined with the bolder weight, communicated a more assured and assertive arts centre.

The verticality of the new logo freed from its carrier shape, which Perkins explains was 'a slight nod to the tower blocks at the heart of the Barbican development', also fitted into the centre's new proposition; 'arts without boundaries'; it was determined rather than constrained and allowed for more dynamism and flexibility. As part of the shift, North again produced an in-depth brand book, and in recent years some of the content of this guide has been migrated to a digital version that lives on the Barbican website. The final aspect of the 2013 identity update was to extend it into the physical realm, a project created by North in collaboration with Endpoint, an agency specialising in signage and wayfinding. Endpoint describe the results of the project as a 'unified aesthetic; one that gave this eclectic arts destination a timeless, bold new placemaking identity that matched the freshly new visual language that's now instantly recognisable as "the Barbican"'. The vertical logo allowed the word itself to be more prominent, and in a way, when applied to the architecture, the current logo makes the most sense—like the brutalist concrete of the building it is pragmatic and matter of fact, perhaps even iconic.

What then does the future hold for the Barbican's branding as its 40th birthday looms? It is hard to imagine any radical changes now, given the success of the current Futura incarnation. As Perkins notes, the 40th anniversary 'may not be a bad time to give the identity an MOT, to go into the brand and figure out what is still great about it and what isn't working so well'. After all, the Barbican has succeeded in the new millennium thanks to a willingness to change with the times. With the memories of early tribulations fading fast, and a successful formula now in place, it is hard to imagine that the Barbican as a brand won't go from strength to strength.

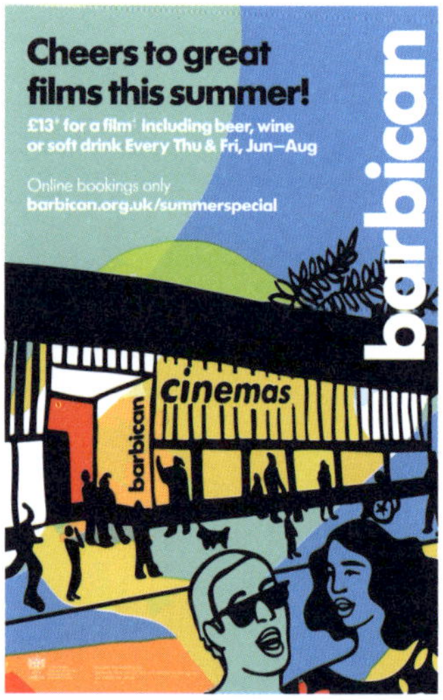
Cheers to great films this summer!
£13* for a film* including beer, wine or soft drink Every Thu & Fri, Jun–Aug
Online bookings only
barbican.org.uk/summerspecial
cinemas
barbican

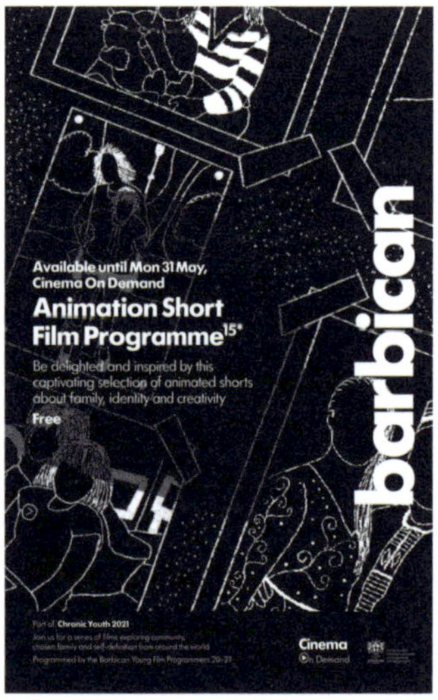
Available until Mon 31 May, Cinema On Demand
Animation Short Film Programme15*
Be delighted and inspired by this captivating selection of animated shorts about family, identity and creativity
Free
Cinema On Demand
barbican

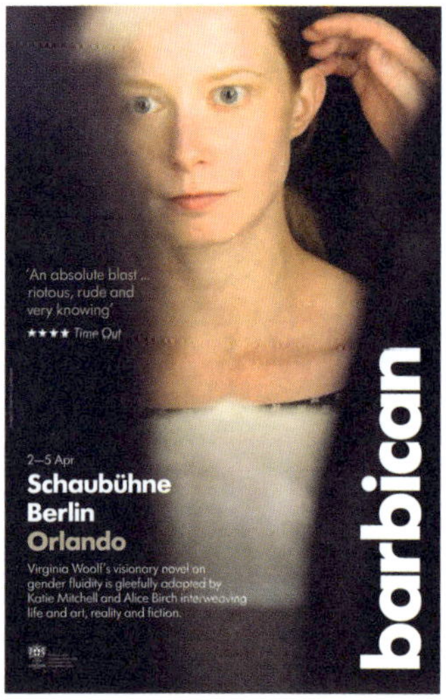
'An absolute blast … riotous, rude and very knowing'
★★★★ Time Out
2–5 Apr
Schaubühne Berlin
Orlando
Virginia Woolf's visionary novel on gender fluidity is gleefully adopted by Katie Mitchell and Alice Birch interweaving life and art, reality and fiction.
barbican

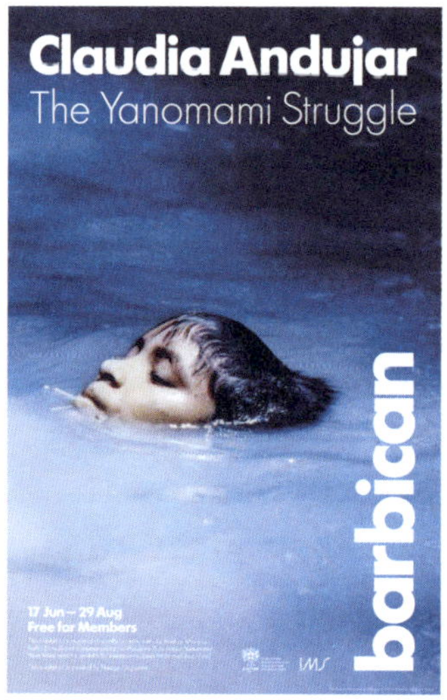
Claudia Andujar
The Yanomami Struggle
17 Jun – 29 Aug
Free for Members
barbican

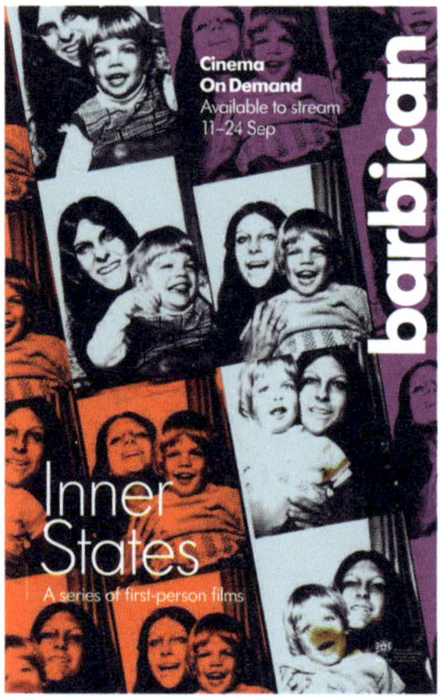
Cinema On Demand
Available to stream 11–24 Sep
Inner States
A series of first-person films
barbican

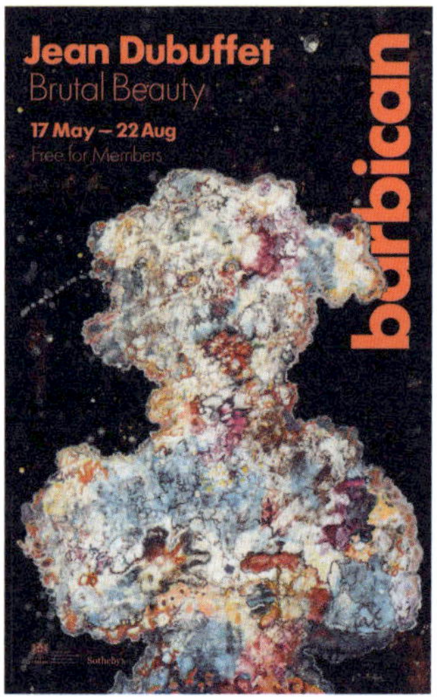
Jean Dubuffet
Brutal Beauty
17 May – 22 Aug
Free for Members
barbican

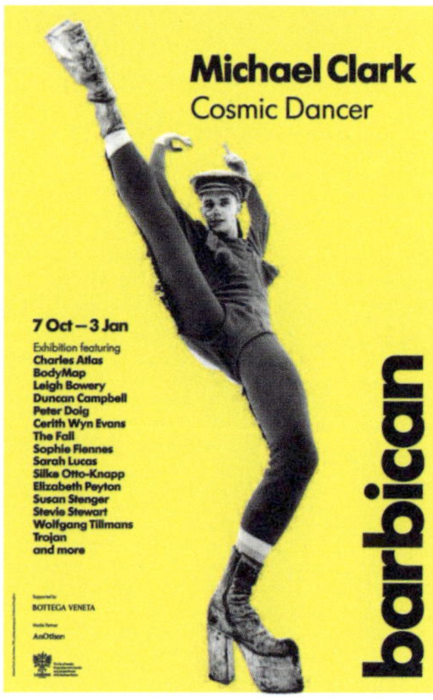
Michael Clark
Cosmic Dancer
7 Oct – 3 Jan
Exhibition featuring
Charles Atlas
BodyMap
Leigh Bowery
Duncan Campbell
Peter Doig
Cerith Wyn Evans
The Fall
Sophie Fiennes
Sarah Lucas
Silke Otto-Knapp
Elizabeth Peyton
Susan Stenger
Stevie Stewart
Wolfgang Tillmans
Trojan
and more
BOTTEGA VENETA
barbican

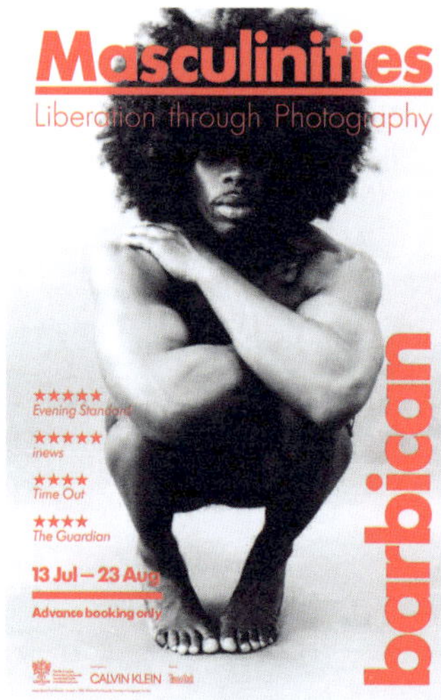
Masculinities
Liberation through Photography
★★★★★ Evening Standard
★★★★★ inews
★★★★ Time Out
★★★★ The Guardian
13 Jul – 23 Aug
Advance booking only
CALVIN KLEIN
barbican

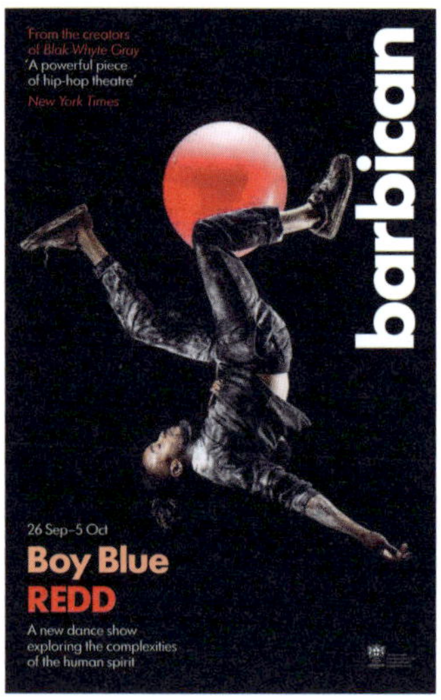
From the creators of Blak Whyte Gray
'A powerful piece of hip-hop theatre'
New York Times
26 Sep – 5 Oct
Boy Blue
REDD
A new dance show exploring the complexities of the human spirit
barbican

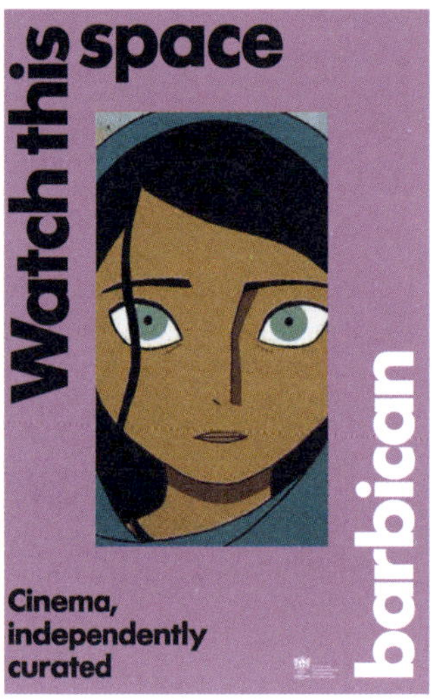
Watch this space
Cinema, independently curated
barbican

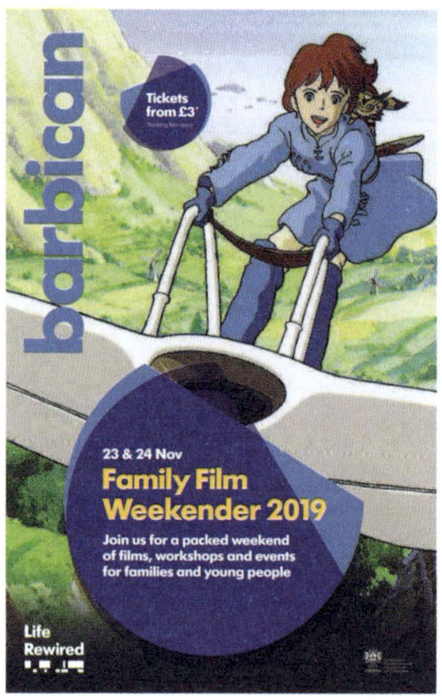
Tickets from £3*
23 & 24 Nov
Family Film Weekender 2019
Join us for a packed weekend of films, workshops and events for families and young people
Life Rewired
barbican

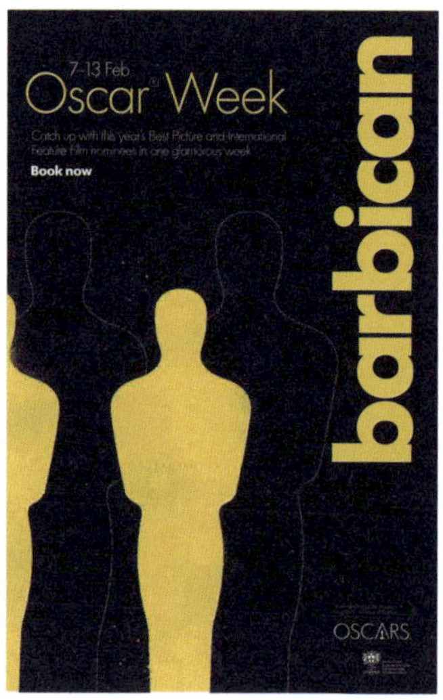
7–13 Feb
Oscar Week
Book now
OSCARS
barbican

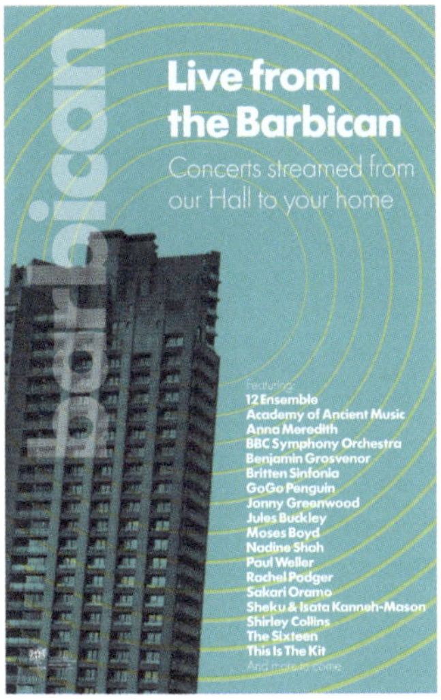
barbican
Live from the Barbican
Concerts streamed from our Hall to your home
featuring
12 Ensemble
Academy of Ancient Music
Anna Meredith
BBC Symphony Orchestra
Benjamin Grosvenor
Britten Sinfonia
GoGo Penguin
Jonny Greenwood
Jules Buckley
Moses Boyd
Nadine Shah
Paul Weller
Rachel Podger
Sakari Oramo
Sheku & Isata Kanneh-Mason
Shirley Collins
The Sixteen
This Is The Kit

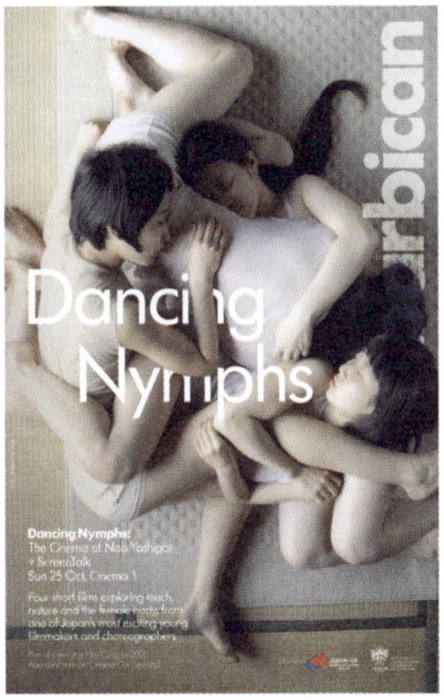
barbican
Dancing Nymphs
Dancing Nymphs:
Sun 25 Oct, Cinema 1

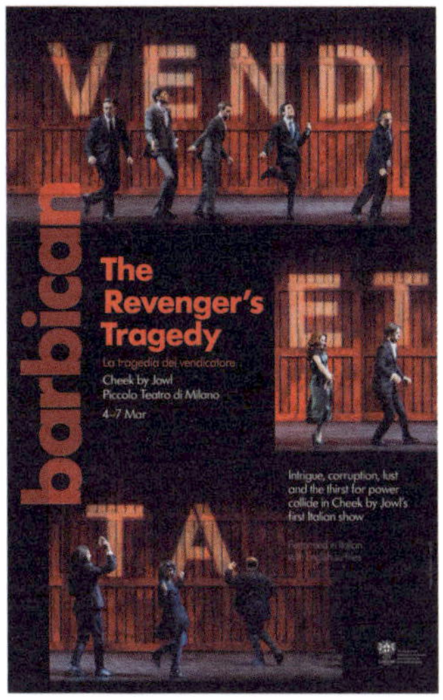
barbican
The Revenger's Tragedy
Cheek by Jowl
Piccolo Teatro di Milano
4–7 Mar

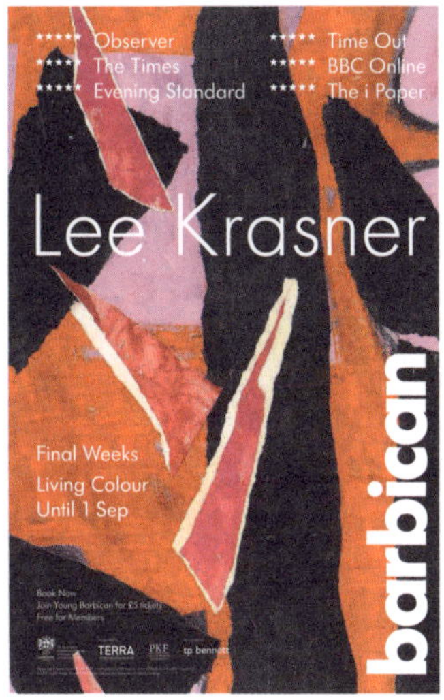
Observer
The Times
Evening Standard
Time Out
BBC Online
The i Paper
Lee Krasner
Final Weeks
Living Colour
Until 1 Sep
barbican

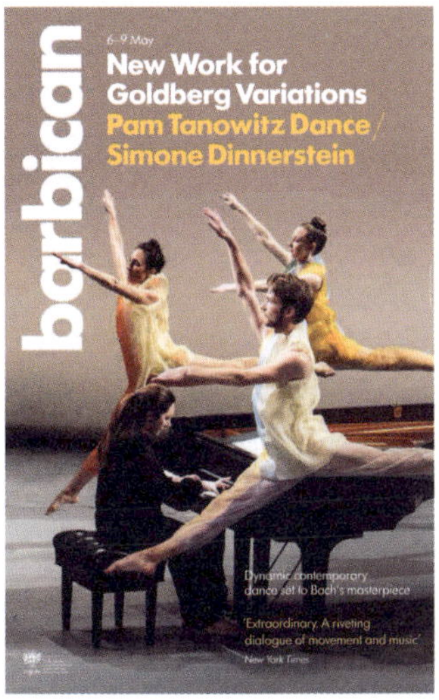
barbican
6–9 May
New Work for Goldberg Variations
Pam Tanowitz Dance/
Simone Dinnerstein
Dynamic contemporary dance set to Bach's masterpiece
'Extraordinary. A riveting dialogue of movement and music'
New York Times

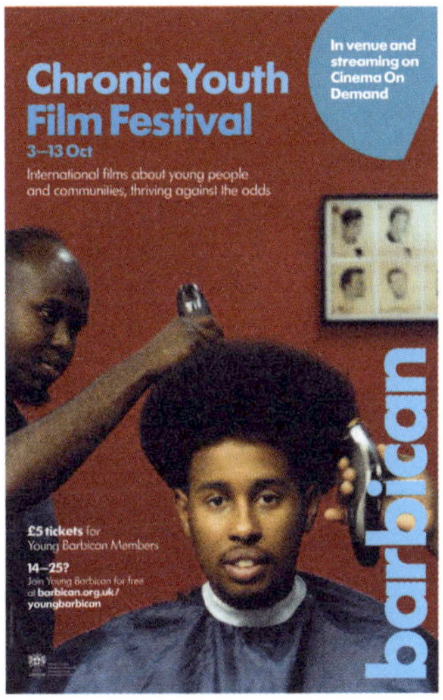
Chronic Youth Film Festival
3–13 Oct
International films about young people and communities, thriving against the odds
In venue and streaming on Cinema On Demand
£5 tickets for Young Barbican Members
14–25?
youngbarbican
barbican

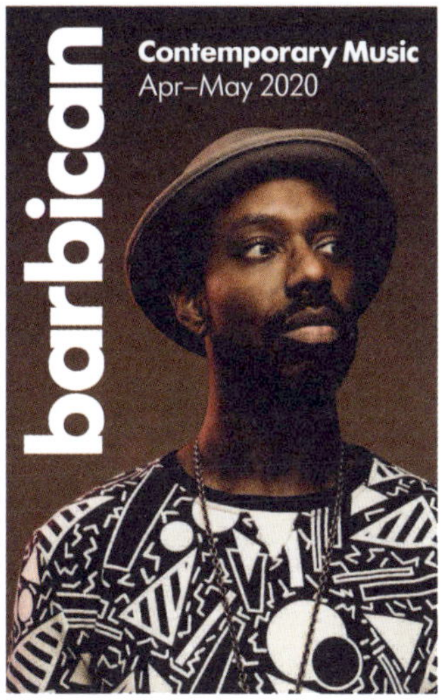
barbican
Contemporary Music
Apr–May 2020

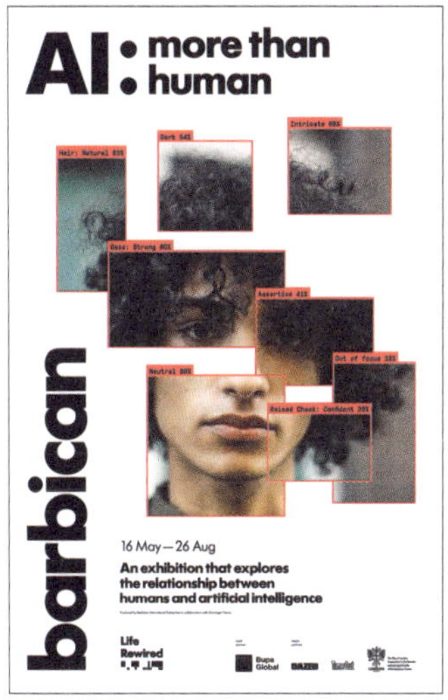
AI: more than human
16 May – 26 Aug
An exhibition that explores the relationship between humans and artificial intelligence
barbican
Life Rewired

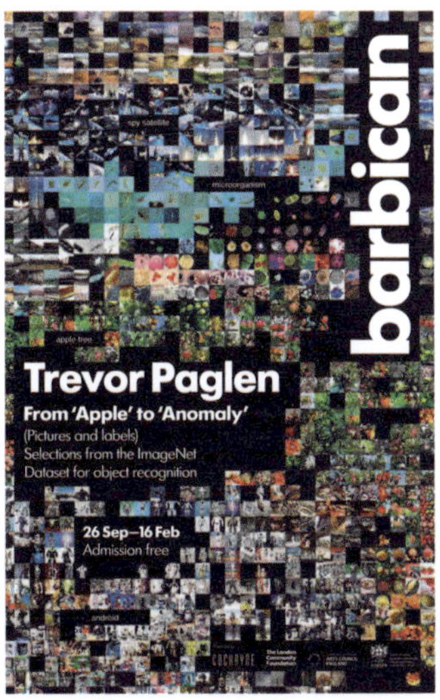
barbican
Trevor Paglen
From 'Apple' to 'Anomaly'
(Pictures and labels)
Selections from the ImageNet Dataset for object recognition
26 Sep–16 Feb
Admission free

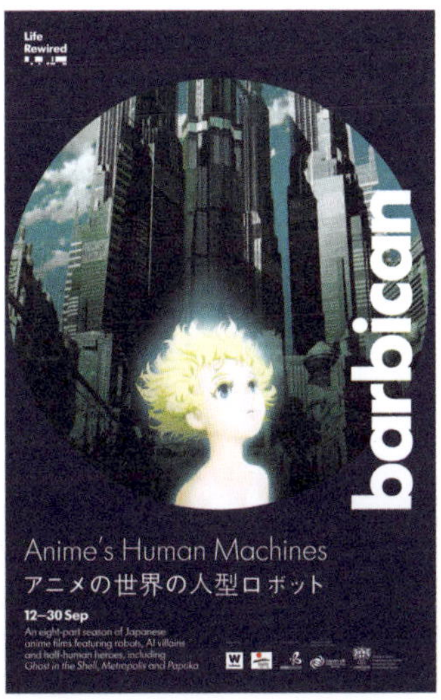
Life Rewired
barbican
Anime's Human Machines
アニメの世界の人型ロボット
12–30 Sep

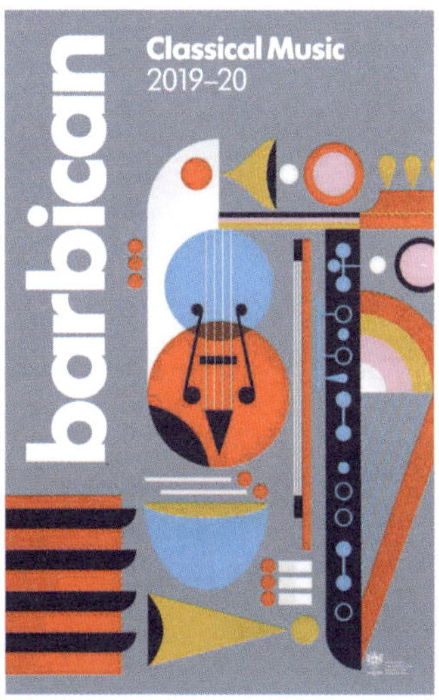
barbican
Classical Music
2019–20

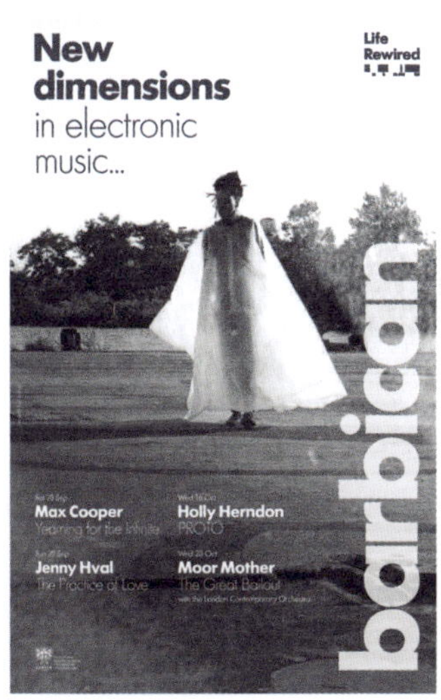
New dimensions in electronic music...
Life Rewired
Max Cooper
Holly Herndon
Jenny Hval
Moor Mother
barbican

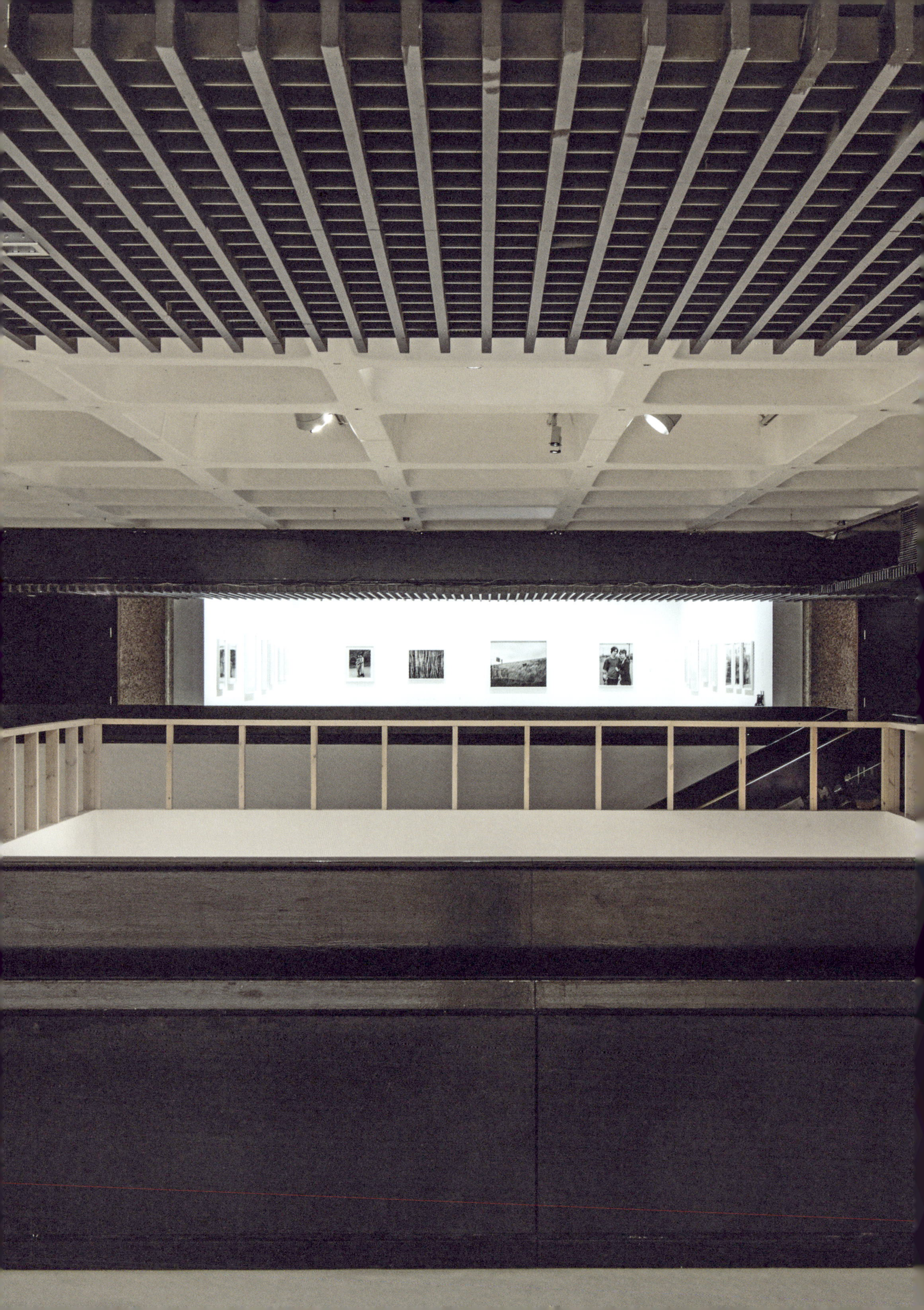

Art

Tony Chambers

The Barbican Arts Centre and I seem to be inextricably linked. I distinctly remember reading about the imminent opening of 'the largest single building for the arts in the Western world' in the 27 February 1982 edition of the *Radio Times*. I still possess a pristine copy. It may seem odd that a 17-year-old boy in Liverpool would treasure such an edition, so I will admit that I'd kept the copy not for the feature on the Barbican but because the cover was graced by my hero David Bowie, who was taking the title role in a BBC adaptation of Bertolt Brecht's play *Baal*.

I first visited the centre a year later, in the early summer of 1983, during a trip to London for my interview at the Central School of Art. This time there was a closer link to Bowie after being mesmerised by the closing scene of his just-released erotic vampire film, *The Hunger*. Susan Sarandon peering out across the metropolis from the distinctive balcony of this futuristic, brutalist Shakespeare Tower apartment was exciting, alluring and prescient (see p.254). I was blown away by the modernity and sheer un-Englishness of the arts centre and the surrounding residential estate: it had more in common with the Bauhaus architecture I'd recently been introduced to on my art foundation course in Liverpool.

The show at the gallery was equally inspiring. The work of the Austrian painter, ecologist and 'alternative' architect, Friedensreich Hundertwasser, was new to me — and to most people in Britain, I'd imagine. Covering the whole range of his work from the early paintings and sketches through postage stamps, tapestry, architectural models and graphics, the exhibition was something you'd never see anywhere else in the UK. My mind was made up — I had to move to London — it was where it was all happening.

A fellow student at Liverpool art foundation course, Neil McConnon, had also gained entrance to the Central to study textile design and he'd found cheap accommodation in a bohemian but grotty flat share in then-not-so-bohemian Stratford, East London. Two of the other tenants were final-year music students at the Guildhall School of Music and Drama. They taught me a lot about classical music and talked enthusiastically about the weird and wonderful Barbican Centre where their school was based. Neil was to go on to work for the centre, and my love of the Barbican was cemented in 1994 when I took the plunge and rented an apartment there. The flat in Gilbert House, which is still home, is about a two-minute walk from the art gallery. I've visited every exhibition held at the gallery since moving there — some multiple times, sometimes in my slippers. So, in short, I'm a huge Barbican fanboy — but I promise to try to be objective.

Barbican Art Gallery's inaugural exhibition, *Aftermath: France 1945–55, New Images of Man*, was a blockbuster. A Franco-British co-operation, with close ties to the Centre Pompidou's *Paris-Paris* show of 1981, it provided a unique appraisal of paintings and sculpture from France after the liberation of Paris. Bringing together outstanding works from artists such as Matisse, Leger, Bonnard, Braque, Giacometti, Picasso and Dubuffet, and covering Realism, Expressionism, Primitivism and Art Brut, the show sent out a powerful message that the Barbican meant business. Any confusion as to why a new British art centre should open with a collection of post-war art from France was explained, poetically, by the centre's administrator Henry Wrong: 'The theme of the exhibition is particularly relevant to the Barbican, which itself rose like a Phoenix from the ashes of World War II.'

However, this assured start masked a certain amount of turmoil behind the scenes. The gallery's first curator, Roger Took, had resigned before the opening, after only six months in the post. He was known to have had 'administrative headaches' — partly triggered by the curious situation that the gallery was not actually run by the arts centre, but fell under the administration of the department that ran the libraries and art galleries of the Corporation of London.

Took's long-serving successor, John Hoole, an art historian and curator, who joined from Oxford's Museum of Modern Art, inherited this unusual management structure and the inadequate budget that went with it. 'Henry Wrong understandably realised that the library's department wasn't really equipped to deal with what would be necessary to run a gallery that size in terms of staffing and financial resources,' Hoole recalls. 'There were only two and a half staff posts and for a gallery that was 14,000 square feet and expected to do temporary exhibitions, we had an annual budget for that first year of just £4,000.'

Sarah Wilson, now a professor at the Courtauld Institute of Art, was fresh out of university when she found herself assisting on the *Aftermath* show, having helped curator Germain Viatte with translations at the Centre Pompidou. 'That show was so very carefully arranged, superlatively selected and beautifully hung,' she remembers. 'But the administration had literally no concept of how such things worked or what they cost — they thought an exhibition could just fly over the Channel and stick on the walls and I was paid out of the petty cash.'

The design of the gallery space was also revealing teething problems. There were positive notes in the *Radio Times* article: 'the two tiers of the art gallery look down on to the library, intersected by a wide staircase with cast iron mouldings of a solidity rarely found in a contemporary building'. But others were not so kind. William Packer in the *Financial Times* (6 March 1982) judged that 'The sad truth is that the Barbican's gallery must count as a chance not missed entirely, but thoroughly bungled.' While conceding that the exhibition was 'strong, important, historic stuff', Packer hit out that 'something must have gone seriously wrong when works of such quality, by such artists of so many kinds, have to shift so desperately for themselves against their immediate physical surroundings'. He concludes: 'The implicit contempt of the administration for Visual Art in general, and the work in particular, is hard to bear.'

This view was compounded by art critic Richard Cork. He recalled in *The Times* in 1992 how a decade earlier, he'd joined a hard-hat tour of the nearly completed centre. 'Although the spaciousness of the arenas reserved for plays and concerts was generous, the art gallery felt like an afterthought.' Relegated to the top of the building, the main floor was unaccountably surrounded by large plate-glass windows. 'With considerable pride, our guide commented on the amount of light they admitted to the gallery. But when I asked him where on earth the pictures would hang, he looked puzzled and failed to supply a coherent answer.' The art gallery felt 'tacked-on' and was clearly 'never intended to stage events on the scale of the Royal Shakespeare Company or of the London Symphony Orchestra downstairs'. Perhaps this was a sobering symbol of British cultural priorities at that time. 'While generous provision is automatically granted

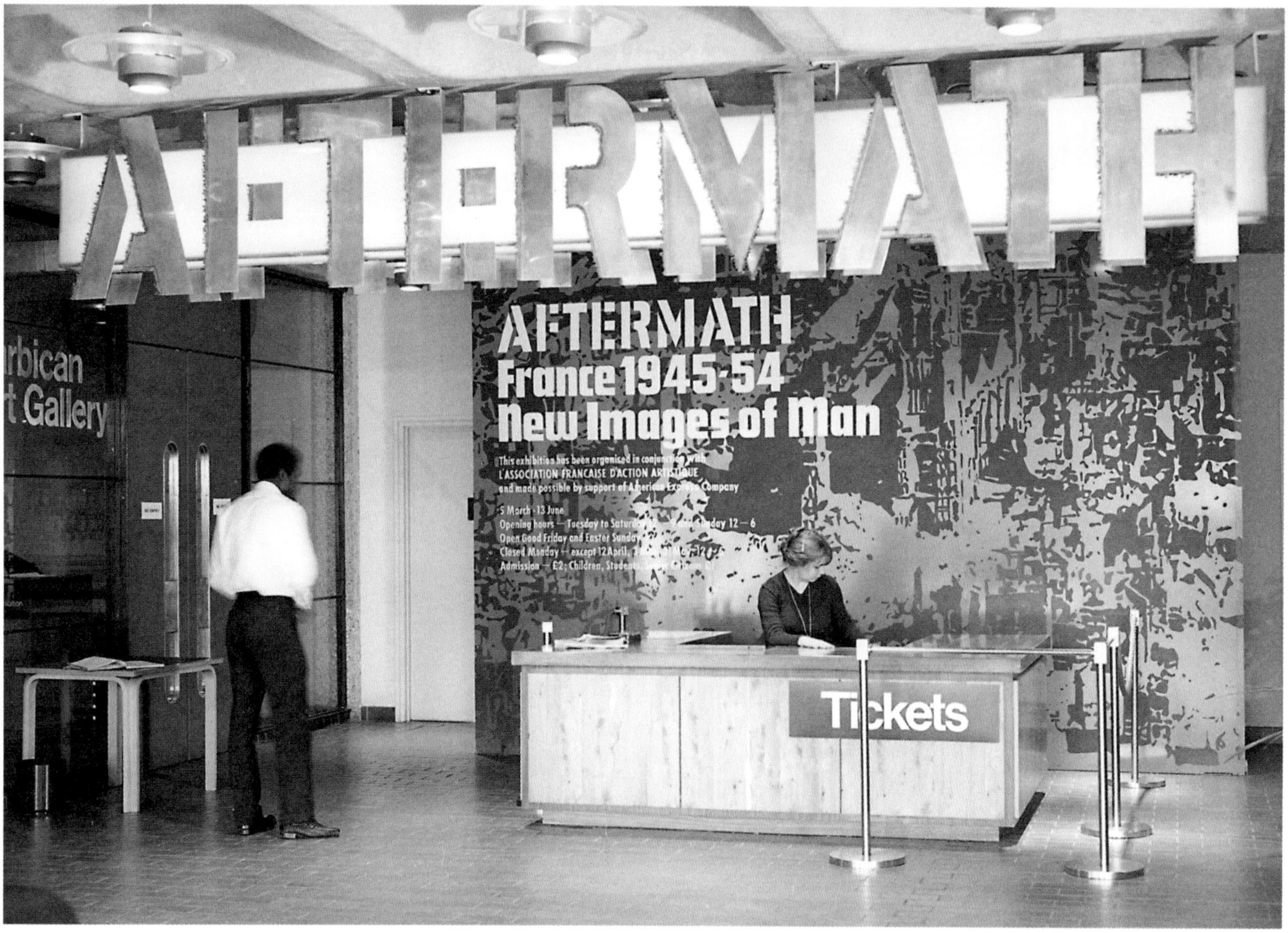

Entrance to art: the gallery ticket desk and design for the opening show in 1982, *Aftermath*. At this time the gallery was managed as part of the Corporation's Libraries department, transferring in 2001 to the centre management.

to music and theatre, visual art often finds itself treated with humiliating inadequacy,' Cork lamented.

So why did the Barbican's founders have such an apparent lack of ambition for the role of the art gallery? Perhaps it was because the gallery was a relatively late addition to the collection of venues, and perhaps it was also because the Corporation already had their own considerable collection which hadn't been seen since the Guildhall Art Gallery had been blitzed during the war. It was all in storage, so why not display it at the Barbican? Some at the time agreed passionately with this. Referencing the *Aftermath* show, Dr Celina Fox, curator of painting at the Museum of London, called it 'a disgraceful neglect of the Guildhall Art collection', while Jeffery Daniels, honorary secretary of the London Federation of Museums and Art Galleries, said 'the Barbican should have started with the Guildhall's superb collection—not a lot of Fifties French tat'.

'The first ten years were a real struggle,' says John Hoole, 'a matter of just seeing what one could do.' It was obvious to Hoole that they could not afford to stage shows as ambitious as *Aftermath* and he was aware that the Corporation had a collection in storage. 'I went to see it in the store and I just thought we could do something with this. We could actually show it and it wouldn't cost us much.'

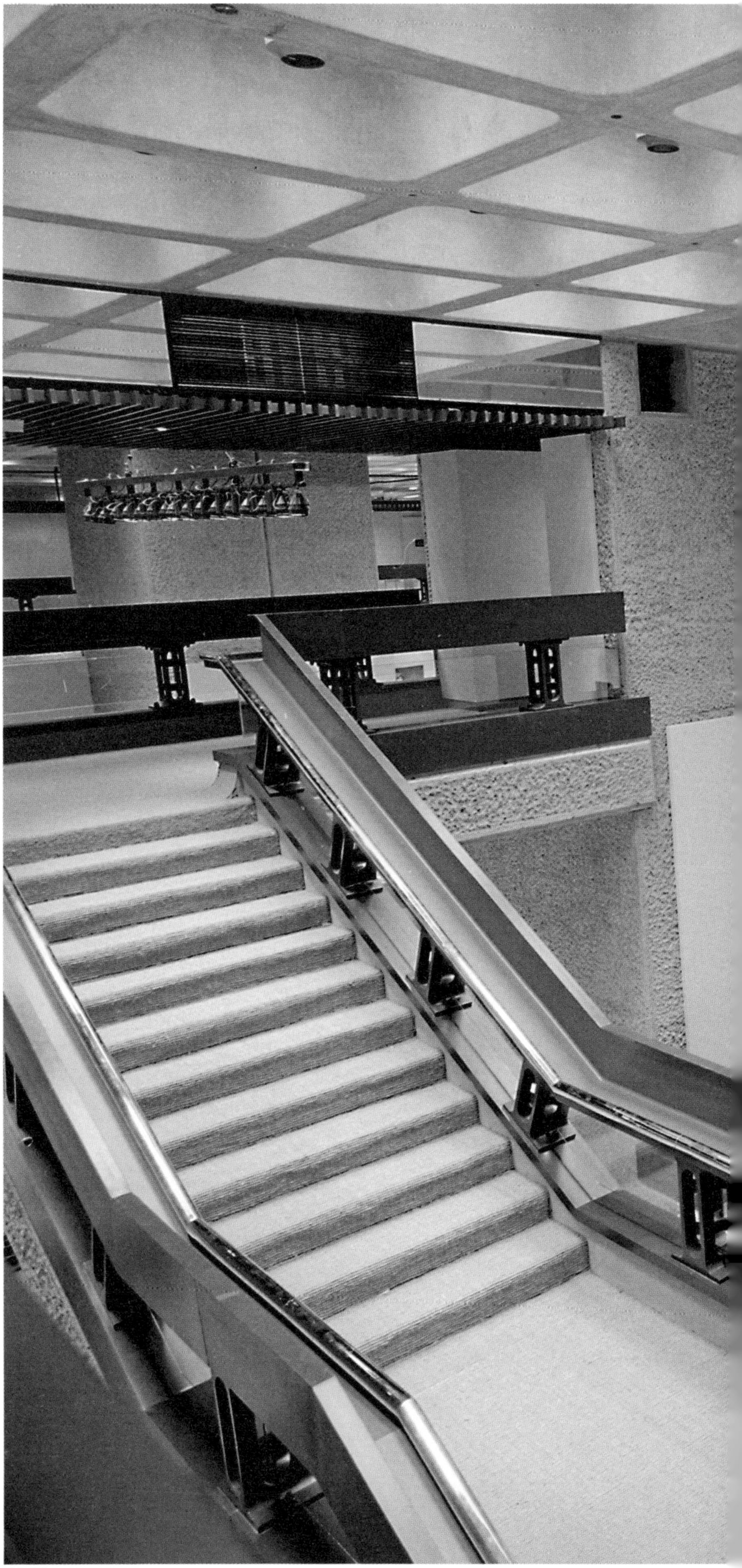

The open plan of the gallery in its early years, before a £1.2m refit in 2003–4 created better spaces and structure, acoustically contained.

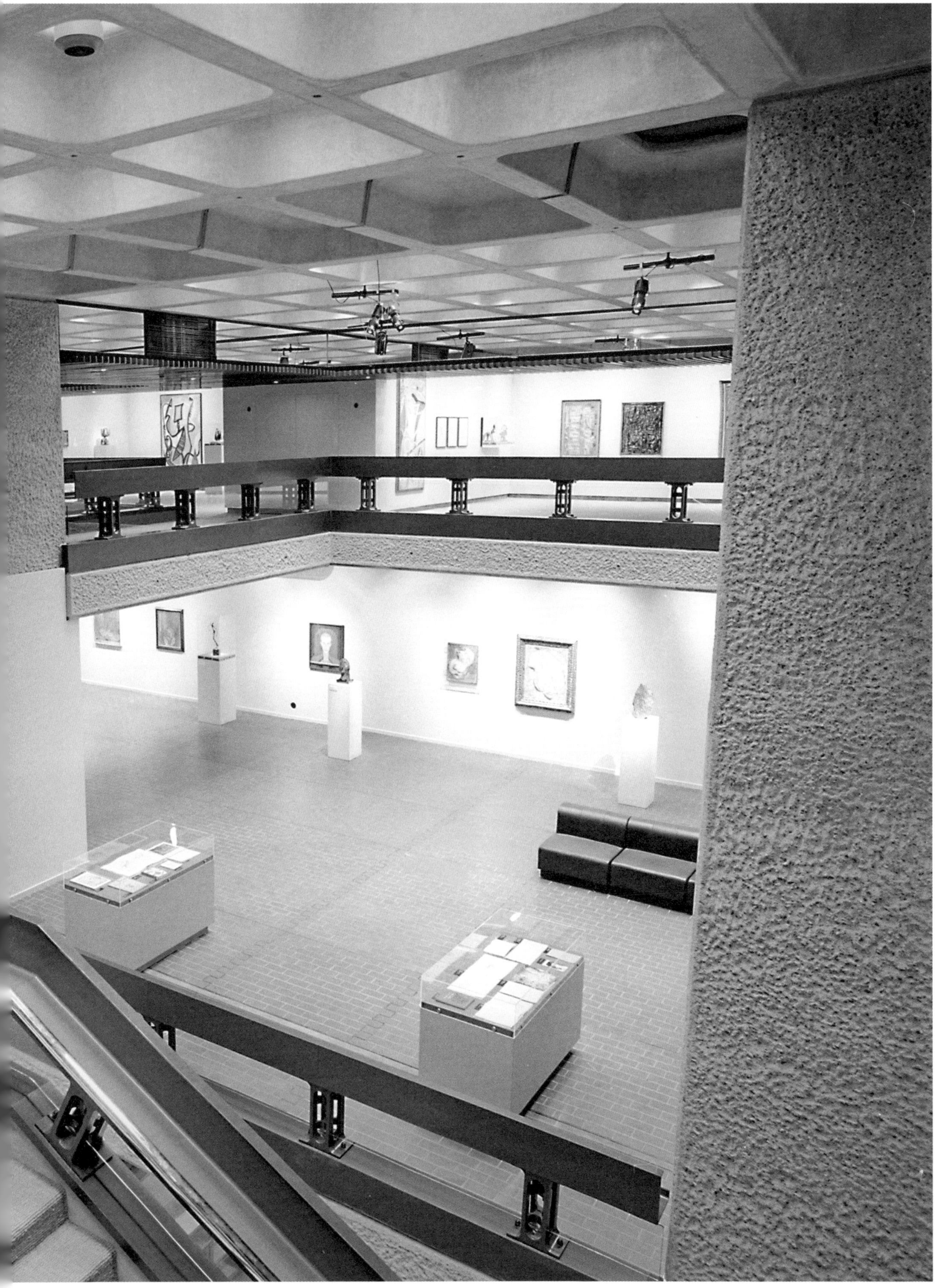

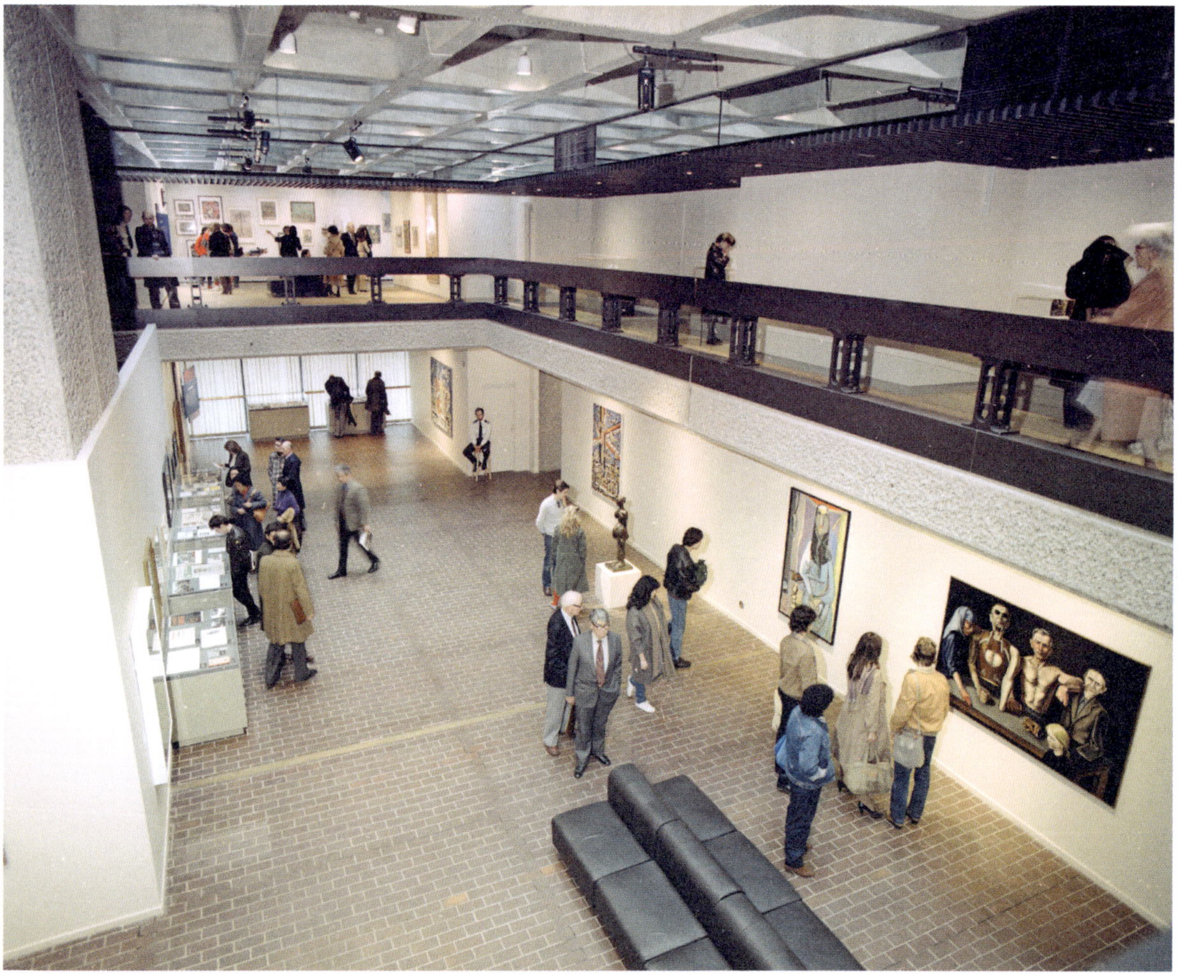

The opening exhibition in the gallery, *Aftermath*, 1982.

The Corporation were pleased, but the centre was not. 'Henry Wrong was dead set against it,' recalls Hoole. '[Wrong] thought the gallery had to be modern, exciting, international, and there was all this Victorian stuff coming out the cellars.' However, shows such as *The City's Pictures* (1982 and 1984) actually proved to be very popular. 'For one year, we put the Corporation's collections downstairs and did smaller temporary exhibitions upstairs.'

A couple of sponsored exhibitions, *Cadbury's Children's Art* (1982) and *That's Shell – That Is* (1983), helped with the coffers and were also popular with the public — but were not good for the reputation of an international gallery. 'The issue really was how to give the gallery's programme any sort of gravitas, given the competition in London,' Hoole concludes. At that time the Barbican couldn't compete with the scale of galleries like Tate, Hayward, or even Whitechapel. 'We couldn't do things like that — but there were things that we could do that they might not want to,' Hoole elaborates. 'The Hundertwasser exhibition was something that came as a package from Vienna, and I just thought, well, nobody else is going to show that … It might work.' *The Carpet Magic* exhibition (1983) also proved popular and economically savvy, due to the support of dealers, as did a Brazilian modern art show (1984). The *Getting London in Perspective* show (1984) was another that leant heavily on the Corporation's collection, but it also included some very early work by Zaha Hadid.

'We were able to scrape by initially doing things like this,' says Hoole. 'It took about four to five years before we were able to start doing things that might compete with the other galleries.' They also gained the confidence of the Corporation, and, in particular Melvyn Barnes, the City's director of libraries, art galleries and records: 'Without his support, it wouldn't have been possible to do what the gallery went on do,' says Hoole. Financial support for the gallery grew dramatically and within ten years, the staff rose from that initial two (and a half) to more than 30, and the annual exhibition budget grew.

It was a remarkable achievement in the circumstances — acknowledged by Richard Cork, who later described 'an impressive sequence of well-researched, stimulating and timely exhibitions'. The Gwen John retrospective (1985) he called a 'landmark in the reassessment of a grossly under-estimated painter', and the *Edwardian Era* survey (1988) 'opened up another neglected period of comprehensive exploration', as did *The Last Romantics* (1989). The survey of Hungarian art's 'golden age' (1990) 'introduced a British audience to the full range of the art, architecture and design in a then unfamiliar country'. Cork concluded ten years on in 1992 that the Barbican Art Gallery's programming 'has never been better'.

Photography shows became a regular and popular feature of the gallery's early programme, starting with the group survey *American Images* in 1985. A distinguished series of solo retrospectives followed: Cecil Beaton and W Eugene Smith in 1986, Ansel Adams in 1987, Karsh and Henry Peach Robinson in 1988. The group survey, *Through The Looking Glass* (1989), was ground-breaking. Selected by Jerry Badger and John Benton-Harris, and concentrating on photography as an art form rather than a commercial activity, it charted the rise of British contemporary art photography from the end of World War II up to the 1980s. Highlighting a wide range of inventive techniques and exploring areas of landscape, social documentary and portraiture, the show featured more than 70 artists, including David Hockney, George Rodger, Raymond Moore, Tony Ray-Jones, Don McCullin and Chris Killip. The work of a younger generation of influential artists such as Susan Hiller and Helen Chadwick, and the colourists Paul Graham and Martin Parr were also shown. Looking through the catalogue again recently confirmed that this was a show that would still look challenging and progressive today — in any gallery context.

Henry Wrong's retirement in 1989 saw the Corporation turn to an unlikely successor, former Milk Marketing Board managing director, Detta O'Cathain. A militantly Thatcherite businesswoman, O'Cathain did not endear herself to the artistic communities, launching a strident public campaign against 'unfettered expenditure by creative people'. John Hoole recalls that 'she had no notion as to how to encourage artistic output and no real sympathy for that at all'. Her legacy was the £9.5m refurbishment plan in 1993. She commissioned architect Theo Crosby, from design consultants Pentagram, to make a series of ill-judged postmodern interventions. I remember them all too well as they were being installed around the time I moved to Barbican. I still have the nightmares. They included a huge garish pointillist mural across the foyer wall, an internal bridge with handrails festooned with owl heads and the pièce de resistance — a kitsch parade of nine gilded eight-fee-tall Muses placed above the glazed canopy at the Barbican's entrance (see p.176).

Despite the tumultuous and divisive period under O'Cathain, John Hoole and his team (which included future gallery directors Carol Brown and Jane Alison) quietly got on with their business of mounting exhibitions of increasing depth and variety. Traditional surveys such as *Pursuit of the Real: British Figurative Painting fom Sickert to Bacon* (1990), Stanley Spencer (1991) and *Impressionism in Britain* (1995), contrasted with more progressive, atypical shows such as *African Textiles: Technology, Tradition and Lurex* (1995), which championed artists such as Yinka Shonibare and Chant Avedissian and began creative collaborations on the design of the shows — this one with Joe Casely-Hayford, while John Pawson produced an exquisite scenography for ceramics exhibition *The Raw and the Cooked* (1993). This was the start of a path-breaking collaboration with architects and designers that transformed the gallery for each show.

There was a new focus on contemporary photography including William Eggleston (1992) and the critically acclaimed group show *Who's Looking at the Family?* (1994), a cause of controversy at the time due to the inclusion of Sally Mann's images of her naked children. *The Cutting Edge* (1992) — a show of contemporary political cartoonists mounted to complement a retrospective of John Heartfield's anti-fascist photomontages — also ruffled feathers. 'We commissioned *Spitting Image* to make a contribution,' explains John Hoole, 'and they produced an extraordinary tableau depicting "Margaret Thatcher's Last Supper"' (Mrs T having been forced from office in 1990). 'I knew it would be controversial — Thatcher appearing as Christ with six of the apostles on either side — but it was too good not to include.' The press loved it, but it resulted in Hoole having to explain it to Lambeth Palace: 'The Archbishop had to make a statement as the ex-Bishop of London had accused us of blasphemy, which was a criminal offence at the time. I should've been kicked out,' Hoole admits. 'But my boss, director of libraries Melvyn Barnes, saw how popular it was, stood up for me and rode out the storm.'

1995 saw the resignation of Detta O'Cathain and the arrival of two cultural heavyweights: John Tusa as managing director and Graham Sheffield as artistic director, heralding a major turning point in the centre's fortunes, specifically in the future running of the art gallery. (The statues quickly disappeared, and all nine muses were sold to Dick Enthoven, owner of Nando's, and reside at his Spier estate in Stellenbosch, South Africa.) Tusa explains: 'If we were trying to run an integrated arts centre, and especially with the slogan "All The Arts Under One Roof", it simply made no sense if we didn't artistically run the art gallery as well.' However, this bureaucratic switch was not realised at once, as Tusa and Sheffield had other fires to fight first. Until it was achieved, Hoole's gallery department, as always, went about their work stoically — and continued to surprise with shows that can now be considered ahead of their time. *Serious Games* (1997), curated by Beryl Graham, was a critical look at artistic production related to computer-based technologies. Looking beyond the mere seductiveness of such media, it questioned the content and the issues being raised by artists working within these nascent forms. It even featured a contribution from the then little-known, now vaunted architects, Diller Scofidio. *Jam: Style + Music + Media* (1996), curated by

A younger generation finds the Barbican: viewing for *Jam: Style + Music + Media*, 1996, the first show curated by today's head of art galleries, Jane Alison.

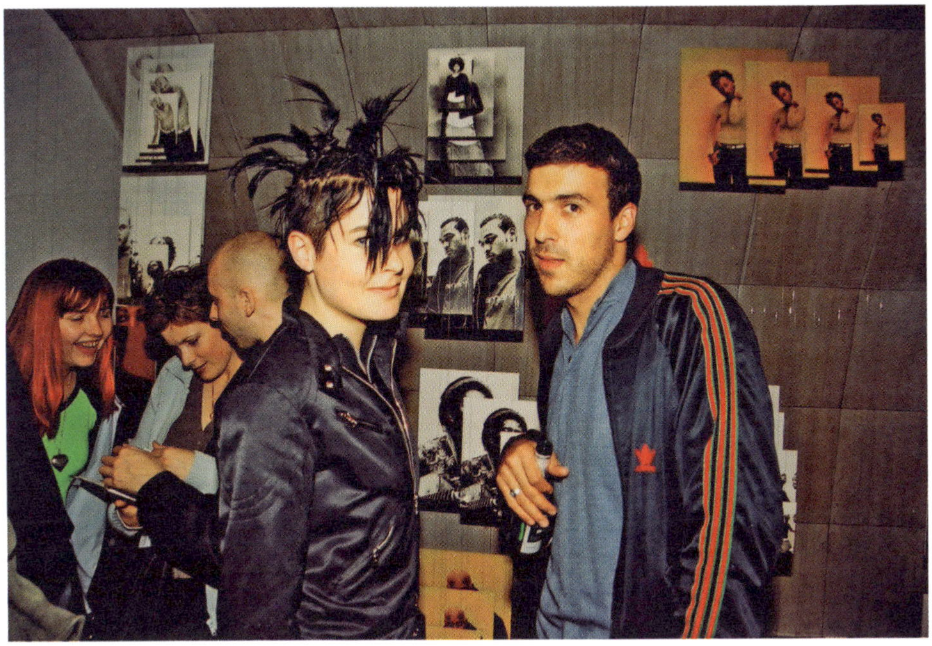

Jane Alison, who later became head of visual arts, was a celebration of innovation and eclecticism across art forms not usually seen in a gallery space. '*Jam* was the first show I actually curated. Previous to that I was just in a support role, so I was a little daunted,' says Alison. 'It was my concept, so I was told to just get on with it.' A response to the explosion of creativity at the cutting edge of urban style culture in 90s Britain, *Jam* included an installation from cult design outfit Tomato, some specially commissioned work from photographer David Sims and fashion from the then emerging designers Hussein Chalayan and Alexander McQueen.

By 1999, other aspects of Tusa and Sheffield's to-do list were in hand, enabling them to switch their focus to the visual arts. Graham Sheffield was adamant that the gallery had to come under the centre's jurisdiction: 'I was running an arts department which didn't have the art gallery in it,' he recalls. 'It just had a whole load of ancillary spaces. And with a small team of just three people, we could only run a very modest, low-key programme.' 'I said to John — we're not going to be the holistic centre that we want to be without control of the gallery.' When it finally happened, the transition was surprisingly smooth. 'I think this odd situation had become clear to the Corporation as well and they could see a switch made sense,' recalled Tusa. 'We inherited a pretty big deficit though,' he adds regretfully. 'Why I didn't insist that that deficit should be written off, I don't know.' Tusa had also managed to cleanse the building of the postmodern excrescences left by the previous director, and this enabled a new focus on the centre's architecture. Sheffield explains that this was not just a cosmetic exercise: 'Once we'd cleared out all the postmodern crud, we could clarify the building in a way that the original architects had been striving for — and really start to make the spaces work.' And with the art gallery now fully under the remit of the centre's artistic director, clarity of vision could also be applied to the whole of the visual arts programming.

Two physical spaces needed urgent attention: the ground-floor Concourse gallery and the main art gallery. The Concourse had always been part of the centre's remit but had not been given a serious, coherent programming vision. It was an unusual space, following the curvature of the concert hall above: William Packer described it in the *Financial Times* in 1982 as 'a very difficult, narrow, dark, high corridor of a space with continuously curving walls, an obvious left-over space, and what else to do with it but give it over to art'.

'It also had a ghastly carpet in it,' recalls Sheffield. 'No self-respecting artist wanted to exhibit in a gallery with a carpet!' There was a provincial quality to some shows — and the space could often be rented out. Sheffield, and the head of his own visual arts team, Ann Jones, brought in architect John Pawson to re-imagine the space — primarily to replace the carpet with the best possible concrete floor — and in March 2000, the Concourse was rebranded as the Curve. 'We asked John to do the floor and get rid of a load of stuff like extraneous electric sockets,' remembers Sheffield, 'to clean it up, apply his pared-back signature and really turn it into something — a place where we would curate single-artist, site-specific shows.'

Having the Curve become part of their remit was transformative for the gallery department, remembers current head of visual arts, Jane Alison. 'As our main gallery tended to focus on historical reassessments, this gave us a space to engage with emergent or mid-career artists and curate site-specific exhibitions.' They certainly hit the ground running with memorable shows by Andy Goldsworthy (2000), Andres Serrano (2001), Grayson Perry (2002 — a year before he won the Turner Prize), Toby Paterson (2005) and Lucy Orta (2005).

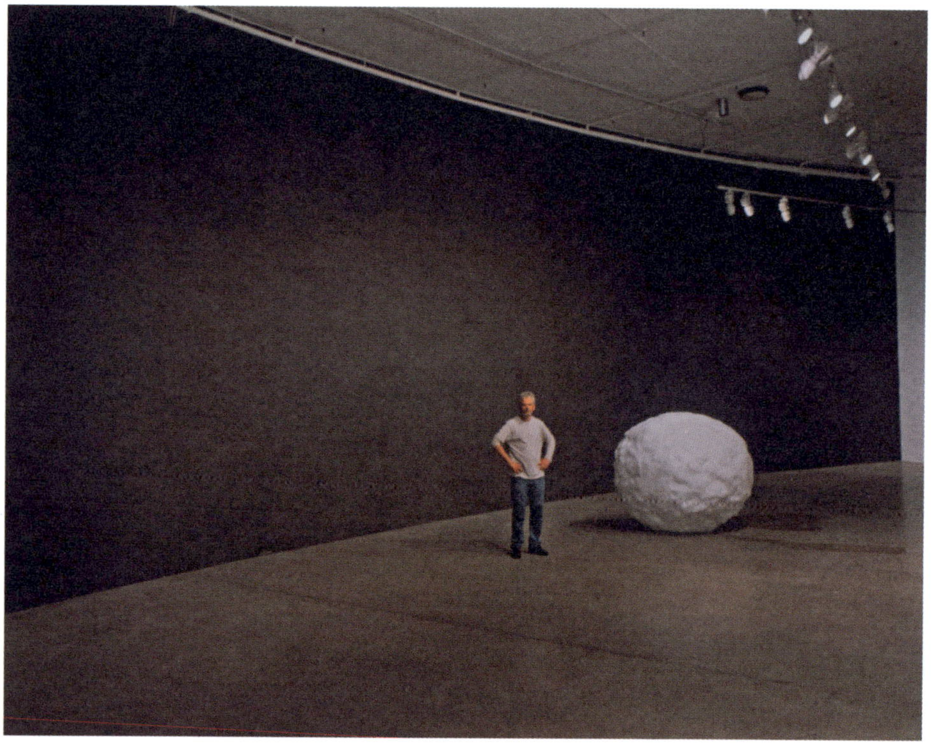

Andy Goldsworthy with his snowball installation in the recently renamed Curve gallery, which also reached beyond the Barbican and unloaded 13 huge snowballs around London just after midnight on Midsummer Day 2001.

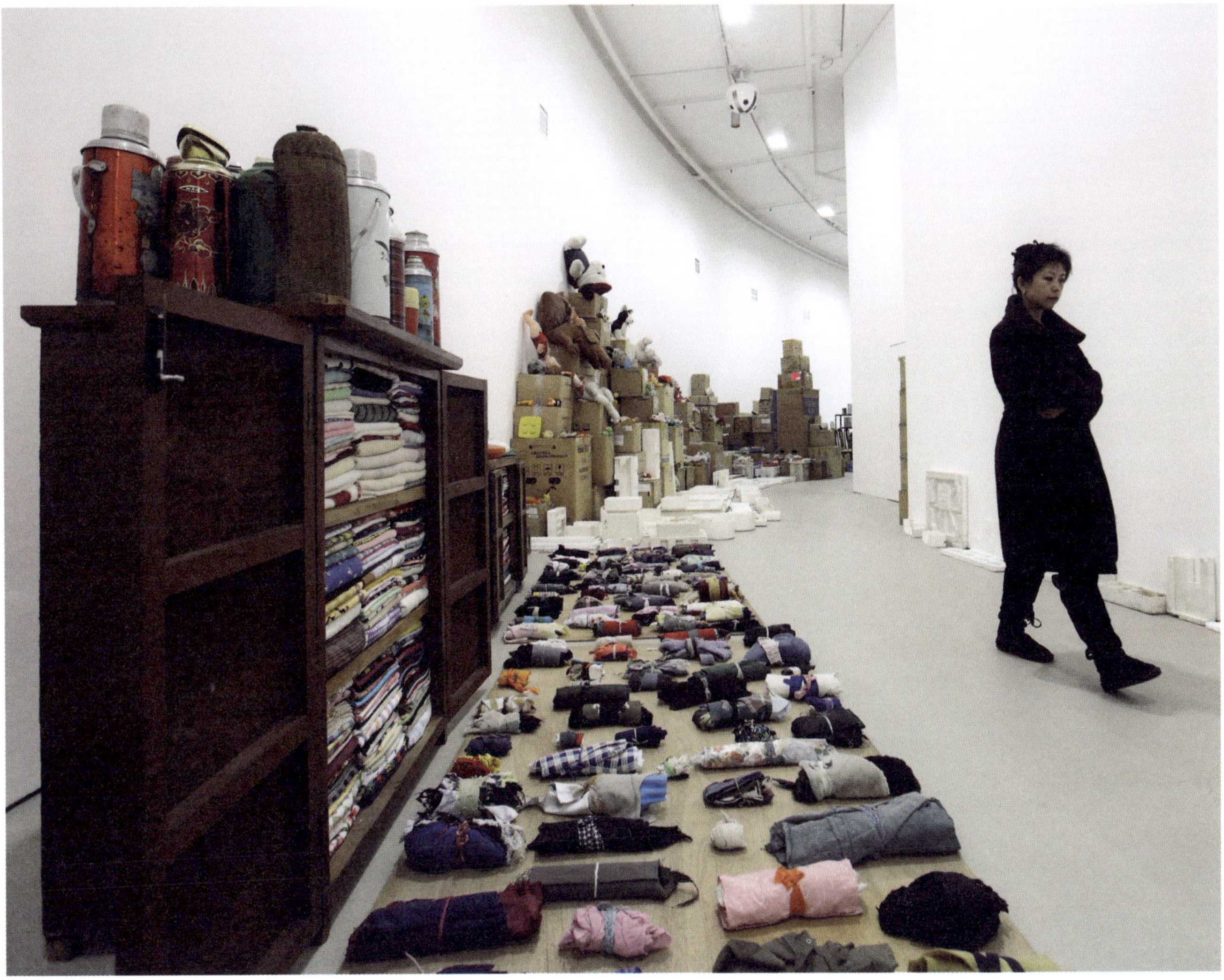

Waste Not, a 2012 installation in the Curve gallery by the Chinese artist Song Dong: 10,000 items collected by his mother, reflecting the artist's childhood during the Cultural Revolution.

The Curve also acted as the hub for the pivotal *Black President: The Art and Legacy of Fela Kuti*, a 2004 festival celebrating the life of the Nigerian multi-instrumentalist Afrobeat pioneer that spread across the whole centre. A series of film screenings, club nights and an impressive live music programme, headed by Fela Kuti's son Femi, illustrated the benefits of the cross-arts programming aided by the new administrative unity. 'Adding such diverse, contemporary and international cultures, we were able to substantially broaden the audience demographic and reduce the average age,' explains Sheffield. 'You only had to look at the foyers on a Fela Kuti night to know we were reaching audiences never known before to the Barbican.'

2001 saw the departure of John Hoole after almost 20 years at the gallery's helm and the baton passed to his long-time assistant Carol Brown, who had joined the team in 1988. Hoole's last few years introduced new exhibition ideas that still impact positively today. A show of customised Harley-Davidson bikes to accompany the *Inventing America* programme in 1998 and the phenomenally successful, if divisive, exhibition *The Art of Star Wars* in 2000 both further broadened the gallery's audience reach and opened a strand of commercially oriented programming that blossomed into what now operates as Barbican International Enterprises.

Championed further by Carol Brown after Hoole's departure, and managed by Neil McConnon (yes, the same art school colleague and my flatmate from 1983), BIE's aim was to develop large exhibition concepts that would not only be staged at Barbican but could have a subsequent life internationally. The first show in this mould was *Game On: The History and Culture of Video Games* in 2002. Incredibly, there's a version of it still touring now. *Watch Me Move: The Animation Show* launched in 2011, *Designing 007 — Fifty Years of Bond Style* was a huge success in the Olympic year 2012, then *Digital Revolution* in 2014, *Into the Unknown* in 2017 and *More than AI* in 2019. With more of a focus on moving image, digital and new technology, BIE shows serve as a strong counterpoint to the art gallery programming and are conceived as immersive exhibitions. 'We have the main narrative of the show in the Curve, but spill out into the foyers, the main entrance, sometimes out to the waterside, and take over one of the theatre spaces,' explains McConnon, who has now moved on to Tate. In these shows new works have been commissioned from figures such as will.i.am, teamLab, Conrad Shawcross, Umbrellium, Es Devlin and Universal Everything.

As head of exhibitions from 2001–4, Carol Brown steered the art gallery through a crucial transformative period. It was now fully integrated into the centre's arts division and Brown pushed the cross-arts agenda with energy and commitment. 'Carol was a wonderful curator,' recalls Graham Sheffield. 'Her vision was a genuinely international and diverse one, well before diversity became a political necessity.' Her superb Iranian contemporary show in the Curve in 2001 was a case in point. Brown was also central to Tusa and Sheffield's plans to significantly refurbish the main gallery space and eradicate a structural quirk that had impeded curatorial endeavours since the opening. 'It had a huge hole through the middle — like a Polo mint,' remembers Sheffield. 'You could look over the top and see into the library, so it felt like a municipal space, and it was difficult to put any decent art in it because there were no temperature or atmospheric controls,' he says. 'Any top-rate artists would not want to exhibit in that gallery.' This incongruous hole had long been a source of bemusement. Tusa can see why it was designed that way. 'It had a sort of heroic, Piranesi-type feeling to it,' he explains, 'but it was a very compromised space and the art gallery needed to be its own enclosed, coherent space.'

In 2003, work began with architects Allford Hall Monaghan Morris on a major remodelling scheme. In what sounds like a manifestation of the divorce from the libraries department, this involved taking out a very long, generally redundant, staircase leading down to the library. The central void could then be filled in — creating an extra 140 square metres (1,500 sq. ft) of gallery space. Finally, the brown terrazzo floor tiles, which had limited the display of sculpture, were replaced with a lighter, seamless concrete flooring. 'It was a serious bit of design and engineering considering the substantial heft of that Barbican concrete,' says Sheffield. 'And we did the whole project for about £1.2 million — which is amazingly good value.'

The reopening in April 2004 saw exhibitions on Tina Modotti and Edward Weston in the upstairs space and a retrospective of Helen Chadwick occupying the resplendent new, chasm-less, ground floor. Tragically, Carol Brown died in

The distinctive look of gallery artwork in the early 2000s, when it came under the centre's management, with the wordmark and Futura typeface treated at an angle.

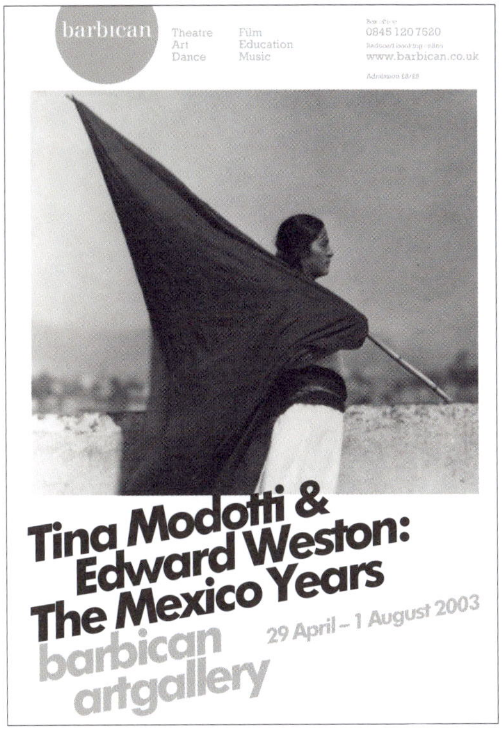
barbican
Theatre
Art
Dance
Film
Education
Music
0845 120 7520
www.barbican.co.uk
Tina Modotti &
Edward Weston:
The Mexico Years
barbican
artgallery
29 April – 1 August 2003

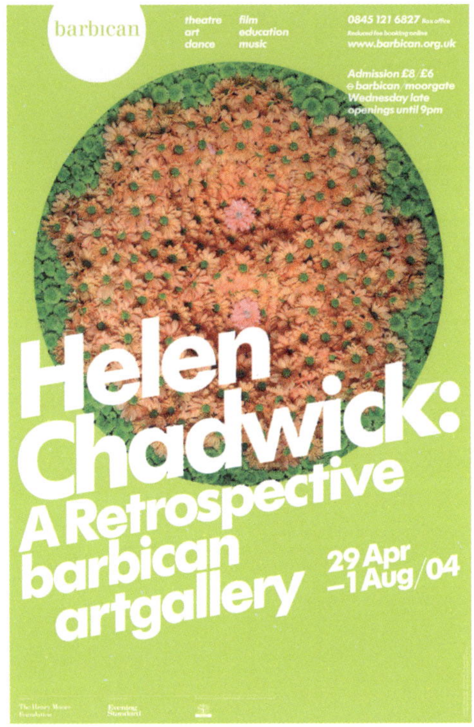
barbican
theatre
art
dance
film
education
music
0845 121 6827
www.barbican.org.uk
Admission £8/£6
barbican/moorgate
Wednesday late
openings until 9pm
Helen
Chadwick:
A Retrospective
barbican
artgallery
29 Apr
–1 Aug/04

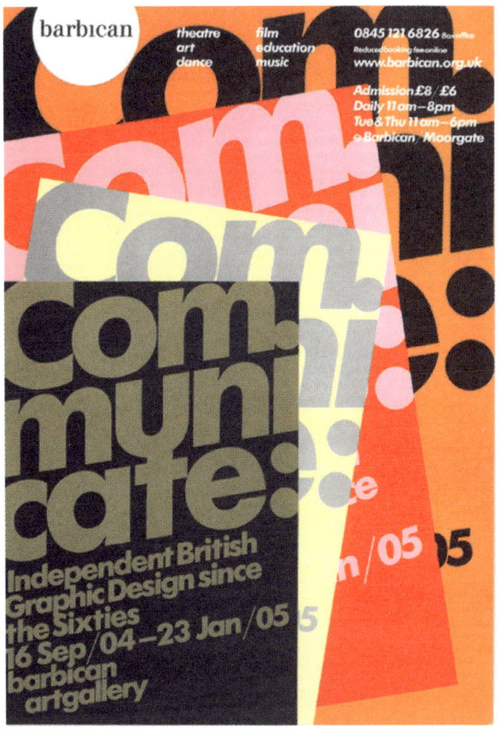
barbican
theatre
art
dance
film
education
music
0845 121 6826
www.barbican.org.uk
Admission £8/£6
Daily 11am–8pm
Tue & Thu 11am–6pm
Barbican/Moorgate
com
muni
cate:
Independent British
Graphic Design since
the Sixties
16 Sep/04–23 Jan/05
barbican
artgallery

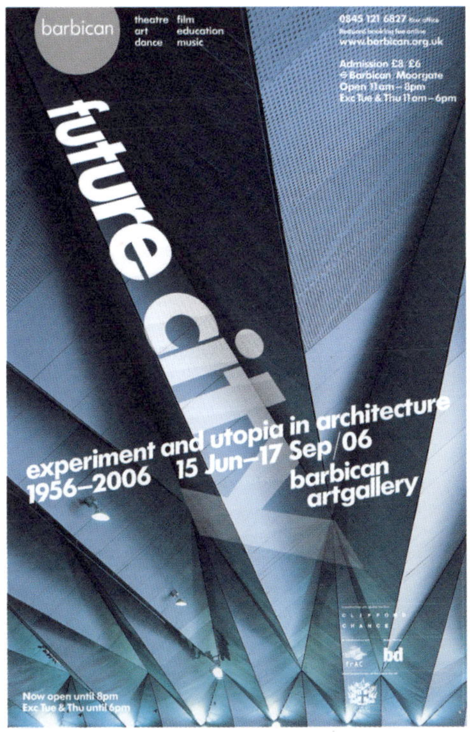
barbican
theatre
art
dance
film
education
music
0845 121 6827
www.barbican.org.uk
Admission £8/£6
Barbican/Moorgate
Open 11am–8pm
Exc Tue & Thu 11am–6pm
future city
experiment and utopia in architecture
1956–2006
15 Jun–17 Sep/06
barbican
artgallery
Now open until 8pm
Exc Tue & Thu until 6pm

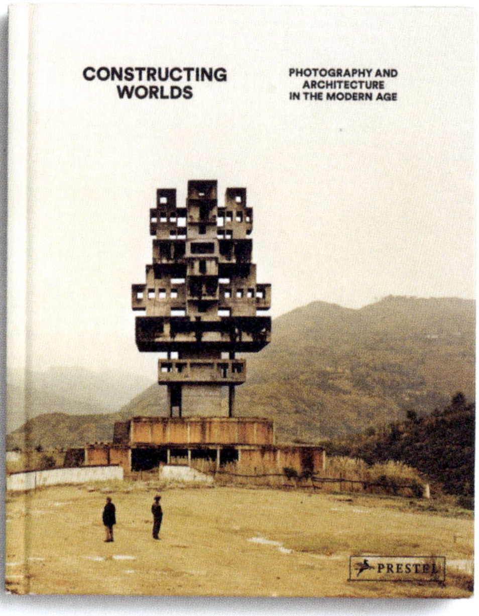
CONSTRUCTING
WORLDS
PHOTOGRAPHY AND
ARCHITECTURE
IN THE MODERN AGE
PRESTEL

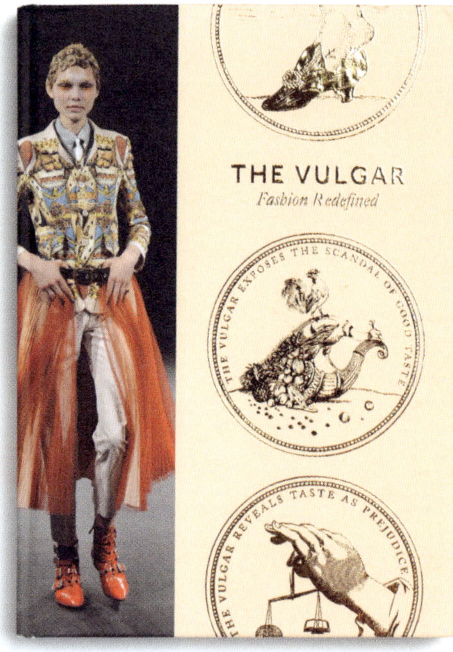
THE VULGAR
Fashion Redefined
THE VULGAR EXPOSES THE SCANDAL OF GOOD TASTE
THE VULGAR REVEALS TASTE AS PREJUDICE

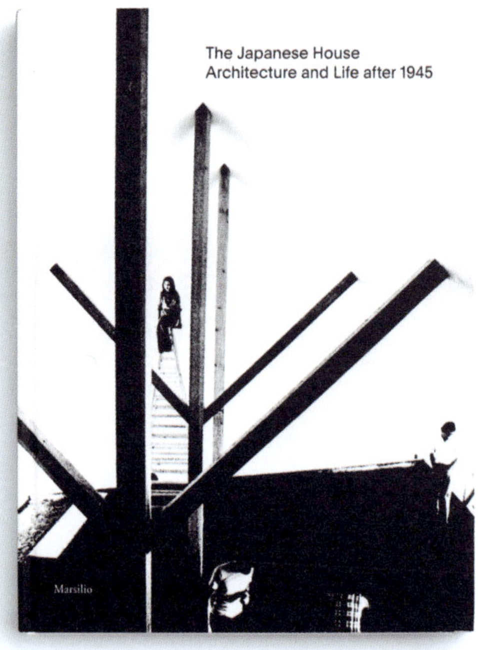
The Japanese House
Architecture and Life after 1945
Marsilio

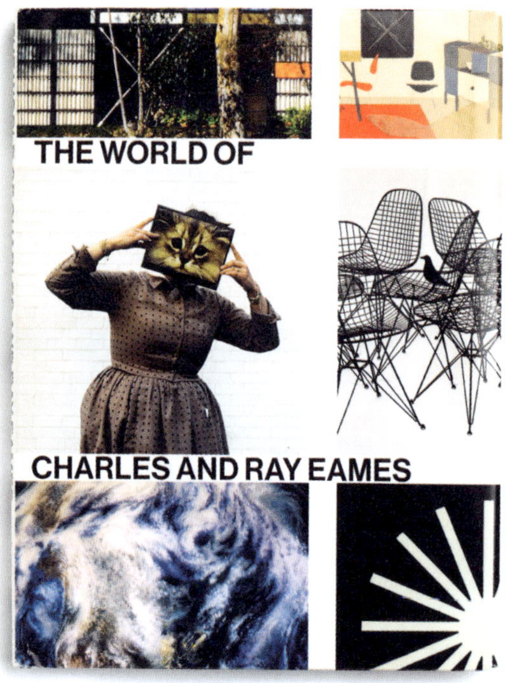
THE WORLD OF
CHARLES AND RAY EAMES

October 2004, so never fully witnessed the great benefits the refurbishment reaped. 'Her advocacy for the renovation of the gallery was a major factor in getting the job done. Its success stands as a testament to her work and character,' says Sheffield.

The Barbican was by now renowned for being London's primary venue for showing photography, and the arrival in May 2005 of Kate Bush as head of galleries strengthened this further. Formerly head of programming at the Photographers' Gallery, Bush was keen to develop something far broader at Barbican. Over her nine-year tenure, Bush and her team created a programme that was to exemplify what is now recognised as the unique Barbican mix: a deft fluidity across art, design and photography allied to performance.

Bush also pushed the programming of ideas-based exhibitions such as *Seduced: Art and Sex from Antiquity to Now* in 2007, and *Radical Nature: Art and Architecture for a Changing Planet* in 2009, and established a reputation for large-scale, authoritative architecture shows. *Future City: Experiment and Utopia in Architecture* 1956–2006, curated by Jane Alison and opening in 2006, was a show destined to be held at, and inspired by, the Barbican Estate with its own visionary, idealistic design. Including 70 radical projects by influential and ground-breaking architects, it was arguably the most comprehensive survey of experimental architecture to be held in the UK. The exhibition design, by Foreign Office Architects, amplified the message.

The prominence of design and architecture content in the programme grew significantly — *Alvar Aalto: Through the Eyes of Shigeru Ban*, 2007, *Le Corbusier: The Art of Architecture*, 2009, *Ron Arad: Rest*less, 2010, *The Surreal House: Architecture of Desire*, 2010, *OMA: Progress*, 2011, *Bauhaus: Art and Life*, 2012 (which ran alongside BIE's *Designing 007!)*, and *Pop Art Desig*n, 2013, all made the Barbican the go-to place for this rapidly growing area of interest. Performance-related exhibitions — a fitting reflection of the centre's core cross-arts identity — were another fruitful development. *Pioneers of the Downtown Scene: New York 1970s* (2011) scrutinised the working relationships of performance artist and musician Laurie Anderson, choreographer Trisha Brown and artist Gordon Matta-Clark. Daily performances in the gallery, including Brown's 'Walking on the Wall', were not-to-be-missed and never-to-be-forgotten. *The Bride and the Bachelors: Duchamp with Cage, Cunningham, Rauschenberg and Johns* (2013) was another examination of extraordinary creative relationships — featuring around 90 works reflecting Marcel Duchamp's engagement across art, music and dance. The dynamic experiential staging by contemporary artist Philippe Parreno brought it bang up to date.

The gallery's reputation for photography continued to be nurtured — with a particular attention on the artistic value of documentary photography. *In the Face of History* (2007), Robert Capa (2009) and *Everything Was Moving* (2013) were all prescient shows — elevating this form of image making into a gallery context. Kate Bush's most significant impact, however, was the further development and re-invention of the Curve space. Curve Art was launched in 2006 as a new venue for site-specific commissions for contemporary artists — with the primary brief that they must respond to the space and take advantage of its chapel-like height and the panoramic potential of its 90 metre (300 ft) curve. The genius of flipping

Catalogues from outstanding gallery shows in recent years: *Constructing Worlds*, 2014–15, curated by Alona Pardo and Elias Redstone; *The Vulgar*, 2016–17, guest curated by Judith Clark and Adam Phillips, *The Japanese House*, 2017, curated by Florence Ostende, and *The World of Charles and Ray Eames*, 2015–16, curated by Catherine Ince with Lotte Johnson.

Pages 210–11
A view of *Le Corbusier, The Art of Architecture*, 2009, with models, photographs and art brought together in illuminating juxtaposition.

Pages 212–13
Japanese House: Architecture and Life after 1945, 2017, which included a whole replica house designed by Lucy Styles in the gallery space.

Opposite
A view of *Le Corbusier, The Art of Architecture*, 2009, with models, photographs and art brought together in illuminating juxtaposition.

Pages 212–13
Japanese House: Architecture and Life after 1945, 2017, which included a whole replica house designed by Lucy Styles in the gallery space.

Pages 214–16
The Surreal House: Architecture of Desire, 2010, designed by Carmody Groarke with Jane Alison.

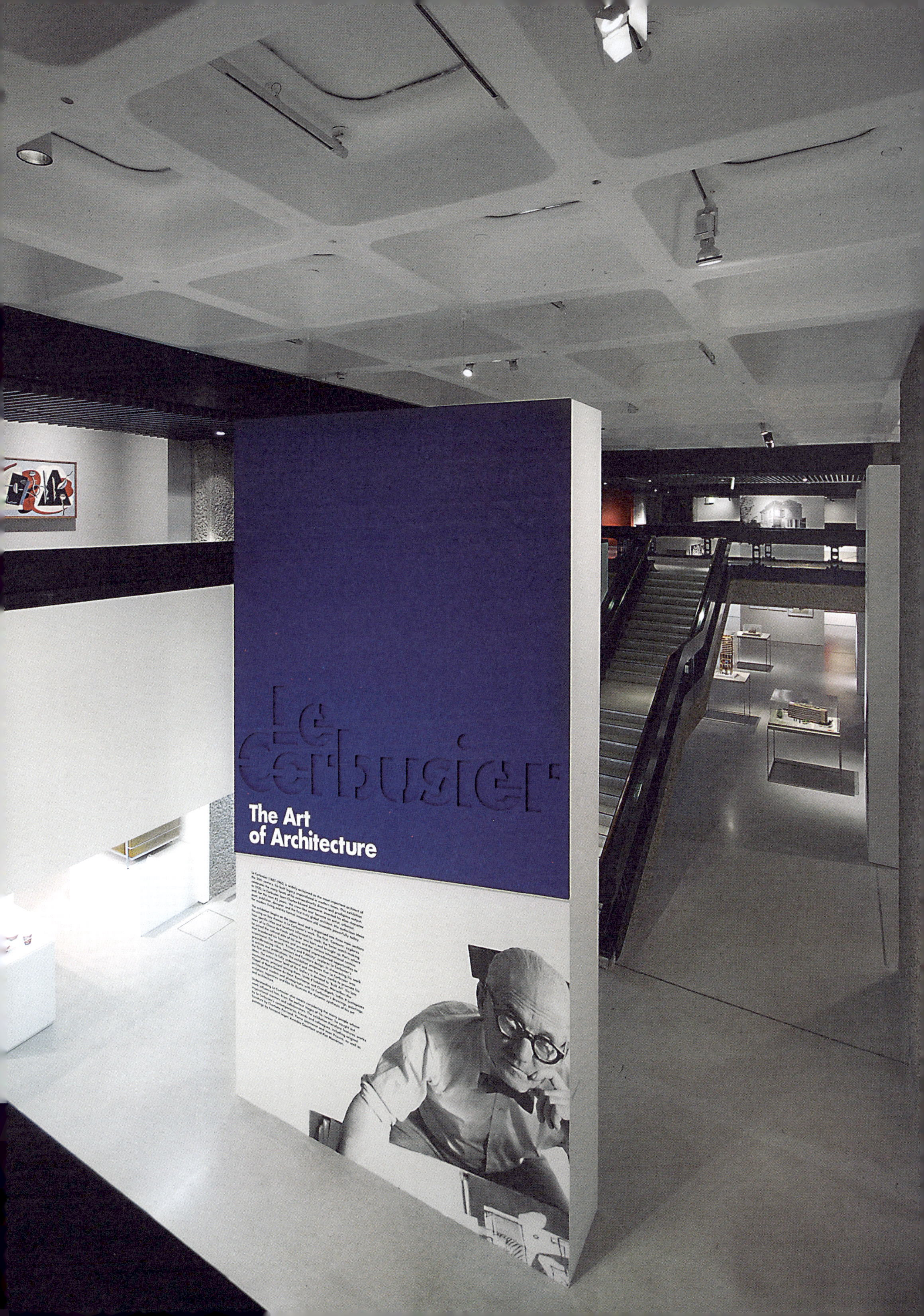
Le Corbusier
The Art of Architecture

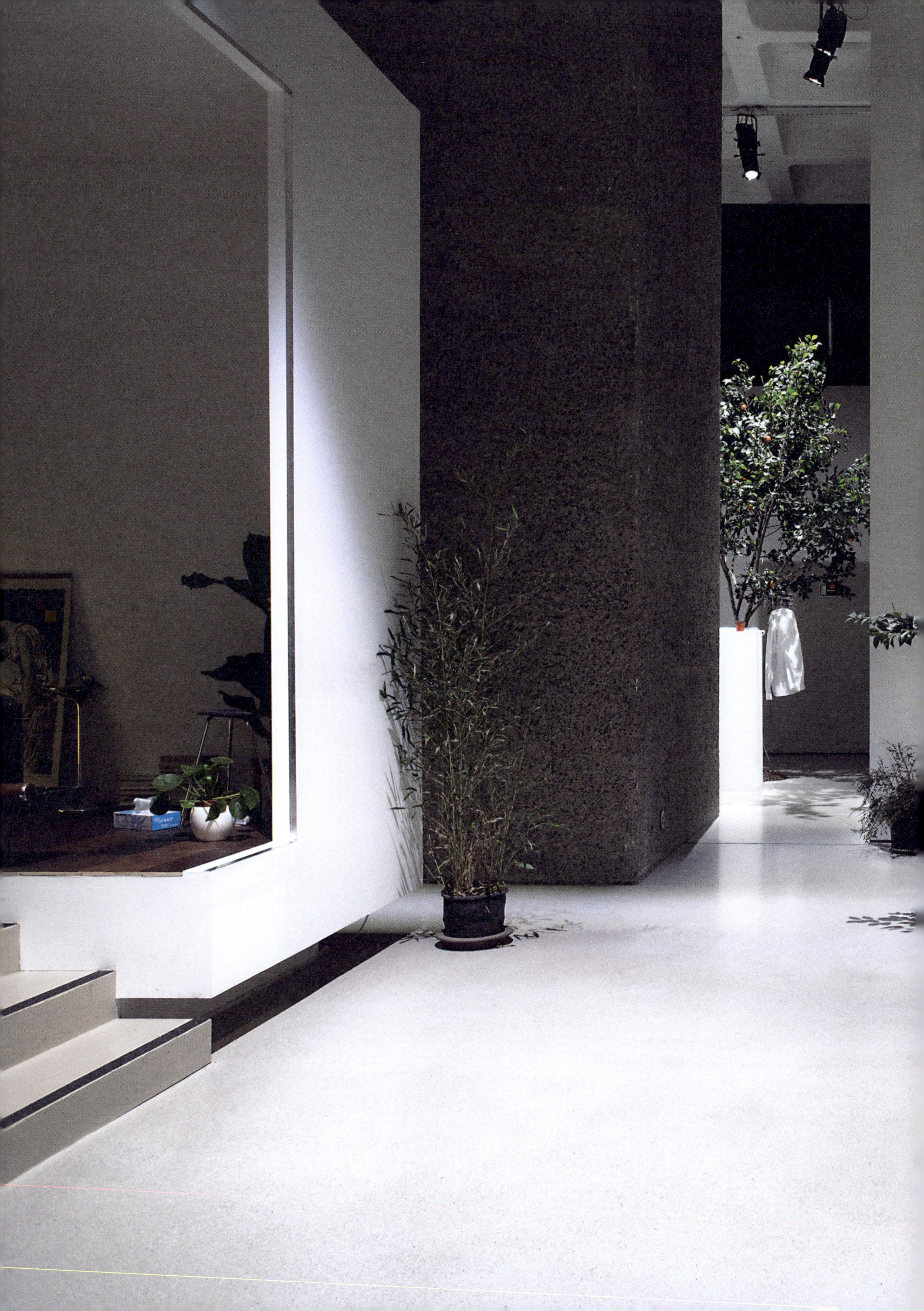

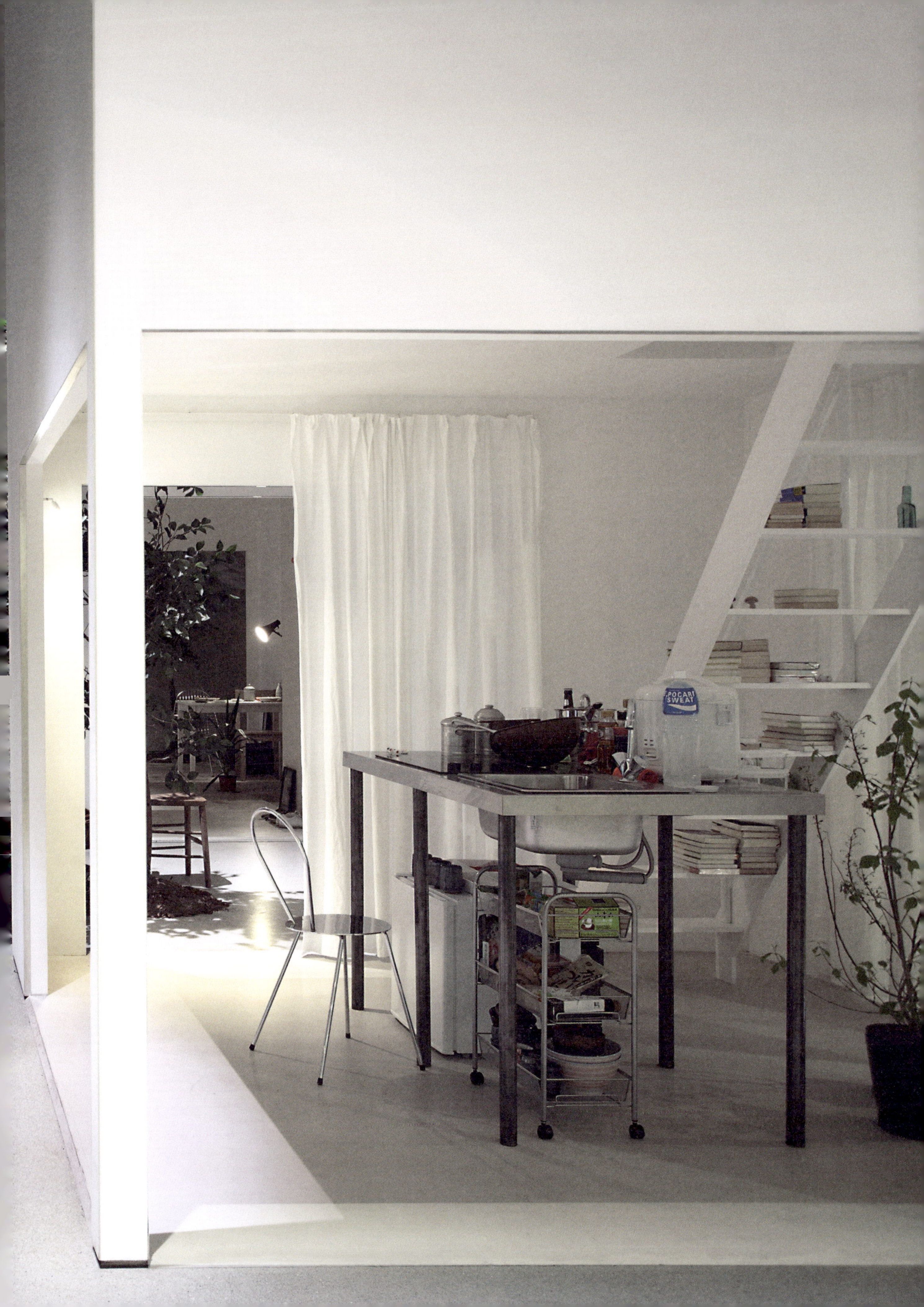
POCARI
SWEAT

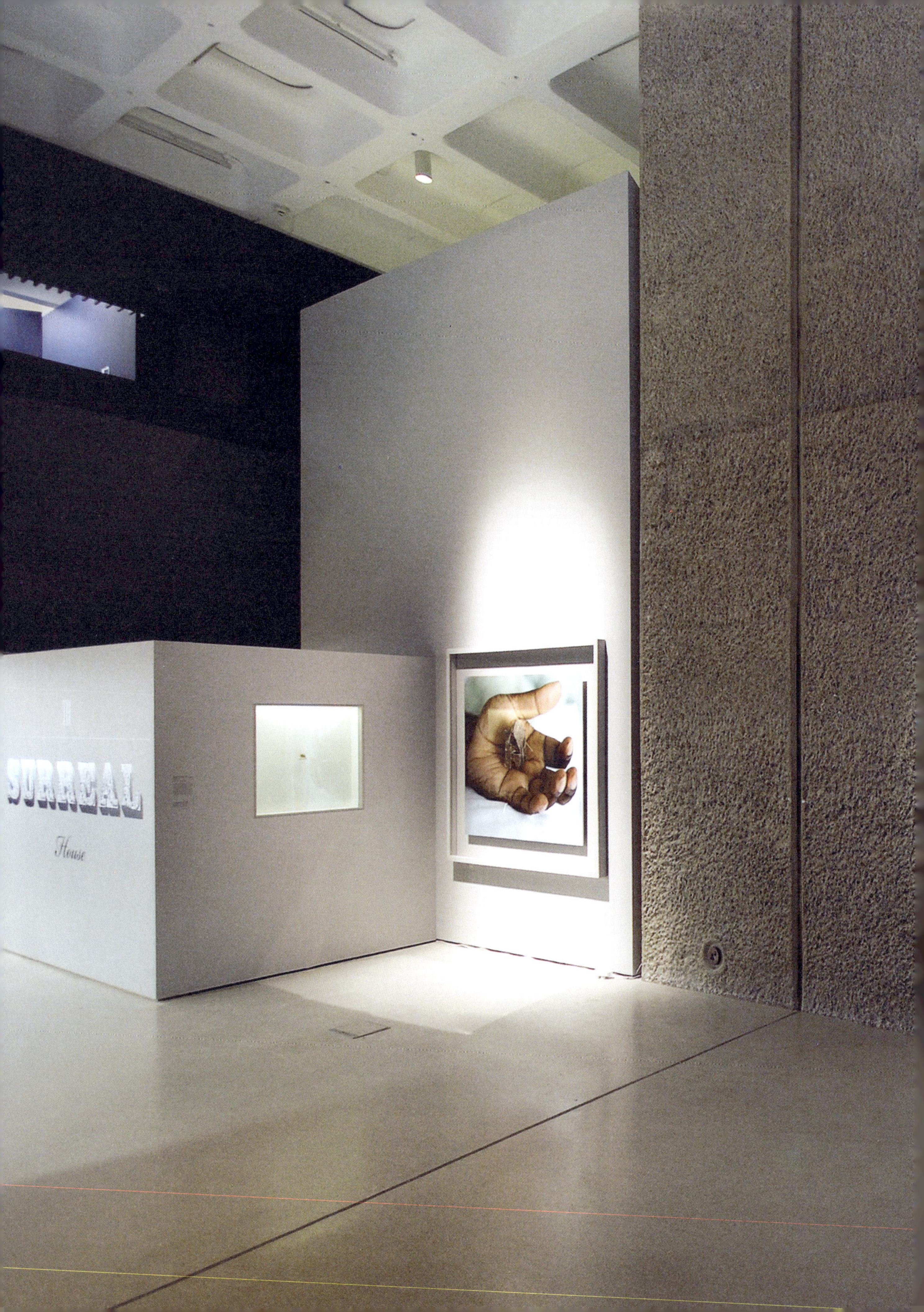
SURREAL
House

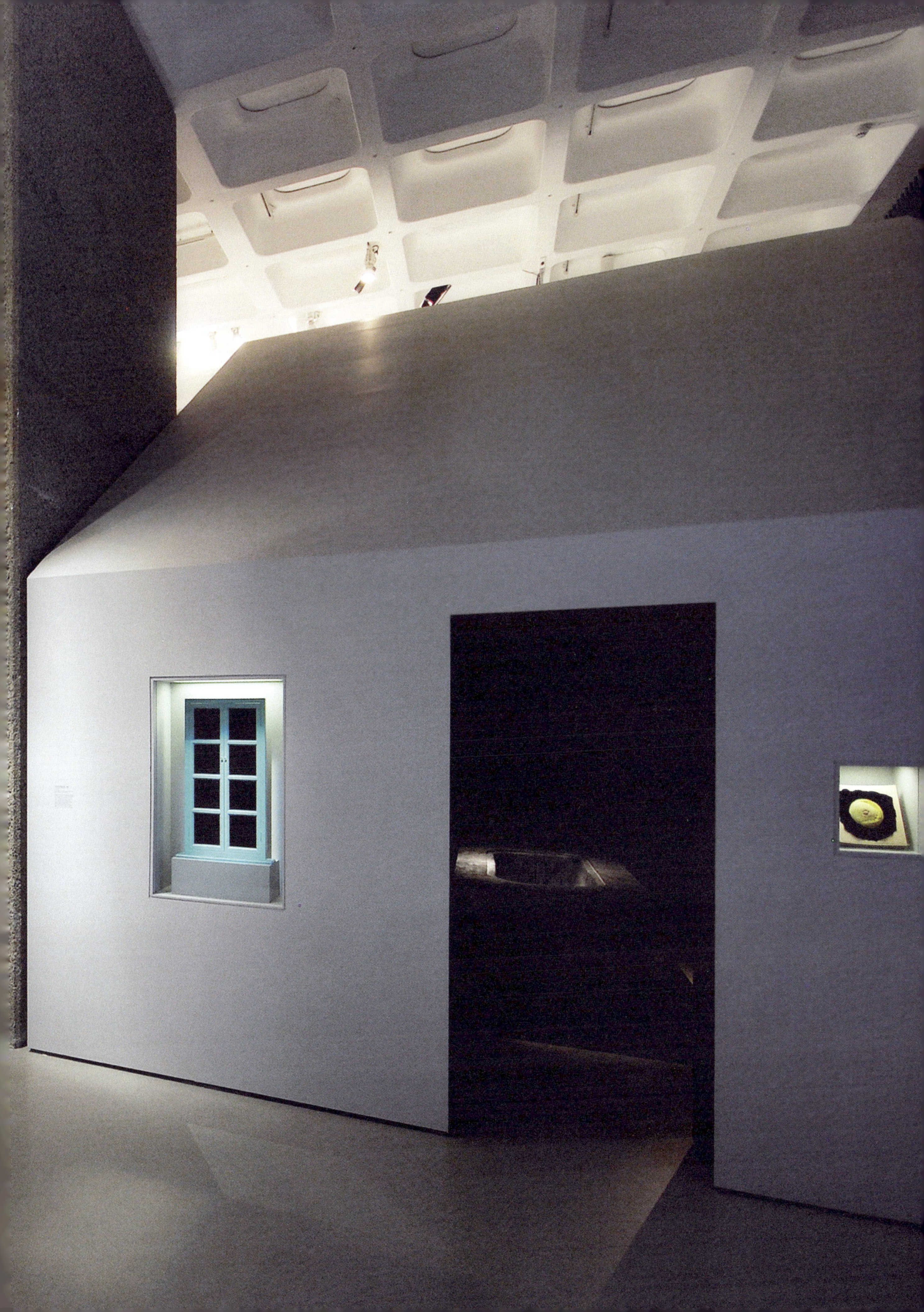

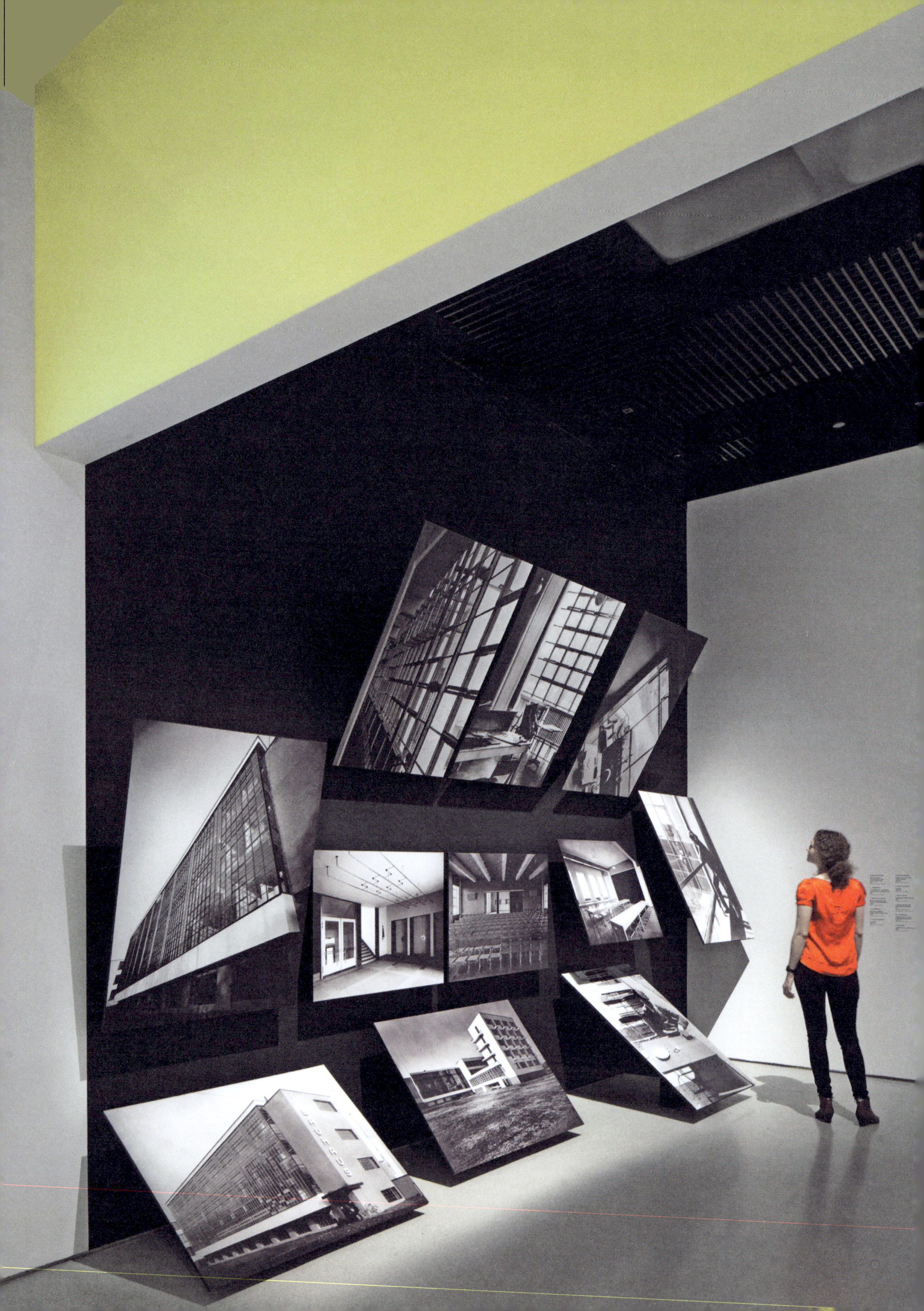

this once derided, problematic art space into one of the most coveted venues for contemporary commissions in the UK has resulted in shows that are both innovative and popular, both challenging and enjoyable. Céleste Boursier-Mougenot's 2010 installation of 40 zebra finches responding to pre-programmed electric guitars was an interactive highlight, while in terms of an appeal that caught the spirit of the moment, nothing matched the extraordinary success of Random International's technically sophisticated and truly immersive *Rain Room* in 2012, where audiences queued for hours to experience the excitement of the pouring rain drying up around them as they walked through the installation.

In 2007 Nicholas Kenyon succeeded John Tusa as managing director, and in 2010, former head of theatre Louise Jeffreys stepped up to the role of artistic director after the departure of Graham Sheffield. Consistency and shrewd judgement were the order of the day in 2013 when Jane Alison, who had joined as a curatorial assistant back in 1986, was promoted to head of visual arts. With Alison's unique perspective and years of experience in what makes a great Barbican exhibition, the art gallery programming exudes confidence and authority. Challenging shows in the Curve with political relevance, such as Richard Mosse's powerful *Incoming* (2017) and Toyin Ojih Odutola's award-winning *A Countervailing Theory* (2020), now went hand-in-hand with moving meditations like Ragnar Kjartansson's haunting exhibition (2016) or sophisticated whimsy like *The Fashion World of Jean Paul Gaultier* (2014).

The Barbican is now undoubtedly the go-to place for exploring the intersection of contemporary art, photography, design, architecture and performance; and the place where the design and presentation, the scenography, of an exhibition has become as memorable as the content on display. Relationships with architectural practices have flourished — with outstanding results such as *The Surreal House*, 2010, by Carmody Groarke, *Constructing Worlds*, 2014, by Office KGDVS, and *The Japanese House*, 2017, by Lucy Styles, which built a replica house within the structure of the gallery. London-based architectural practice Carmody Groarke have designed four shows over the last 12 years, including the sensationally successful *Basquiat: Boom for Real* in 2017. 'The Barbican has managed to forge an exhibition space which has become in many senses, a place for architectural experimentation — rather like the modernists used pavilions as the hotbed of architectural endeavour in the early part of the 20th century,' says Kevin Carmody. 'That's radical in its thinking and there aren't many galleries that start with that premise.' It gave them the opportunity to build things very quickly without the 'weight' of architecture: 'We could test a pure idea about what architecture should or could be,' Carmody continues. 'Our practice honed its skills in understanding a visitor experience in that space — which led to us winning and developing some big projects.'

Eleanor Nairne, one of the newest recruits in Alison's curatorial team, is an enthusiast for the building and the ways it can impact on the curatorial process. 'You always need to be thinking in response to the building and in a site-specific vein — what's going to be spicy in the Barbican context,' she says. 'I'm often thinking about an artist who's got a kind of muscularity to their practice, where they can really benefit from being in a space that is as strong as the Barbican is. I think you struggle with the space if you're trying to tell a story that's not well situated there.' The muscularity of artists such as Basquiat, Lee Krasner and

Bauhaus: Art and Life, 2012, mounted in collaboration with the Bauhaus archives and museums in Berlin, Dessau and Weimar, curated by Catherine Ince.

Pages 218–19
Rain Room in the Curve, by Random International, 2012–3.

Pages 220–21
Digital Revolution, an interactive show by Barbican International Enterprises, 2014, guest curator Conrad Bodman.

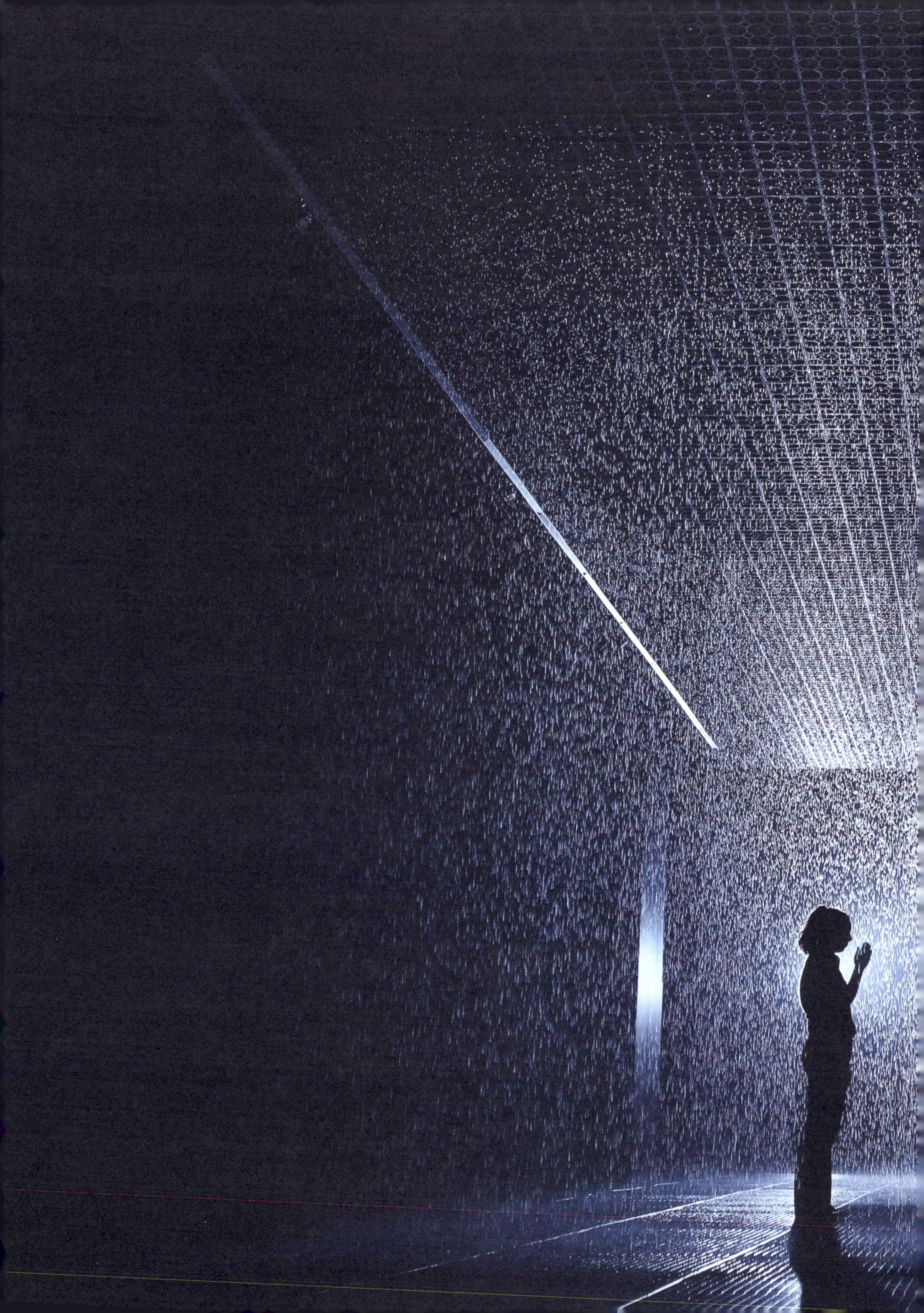

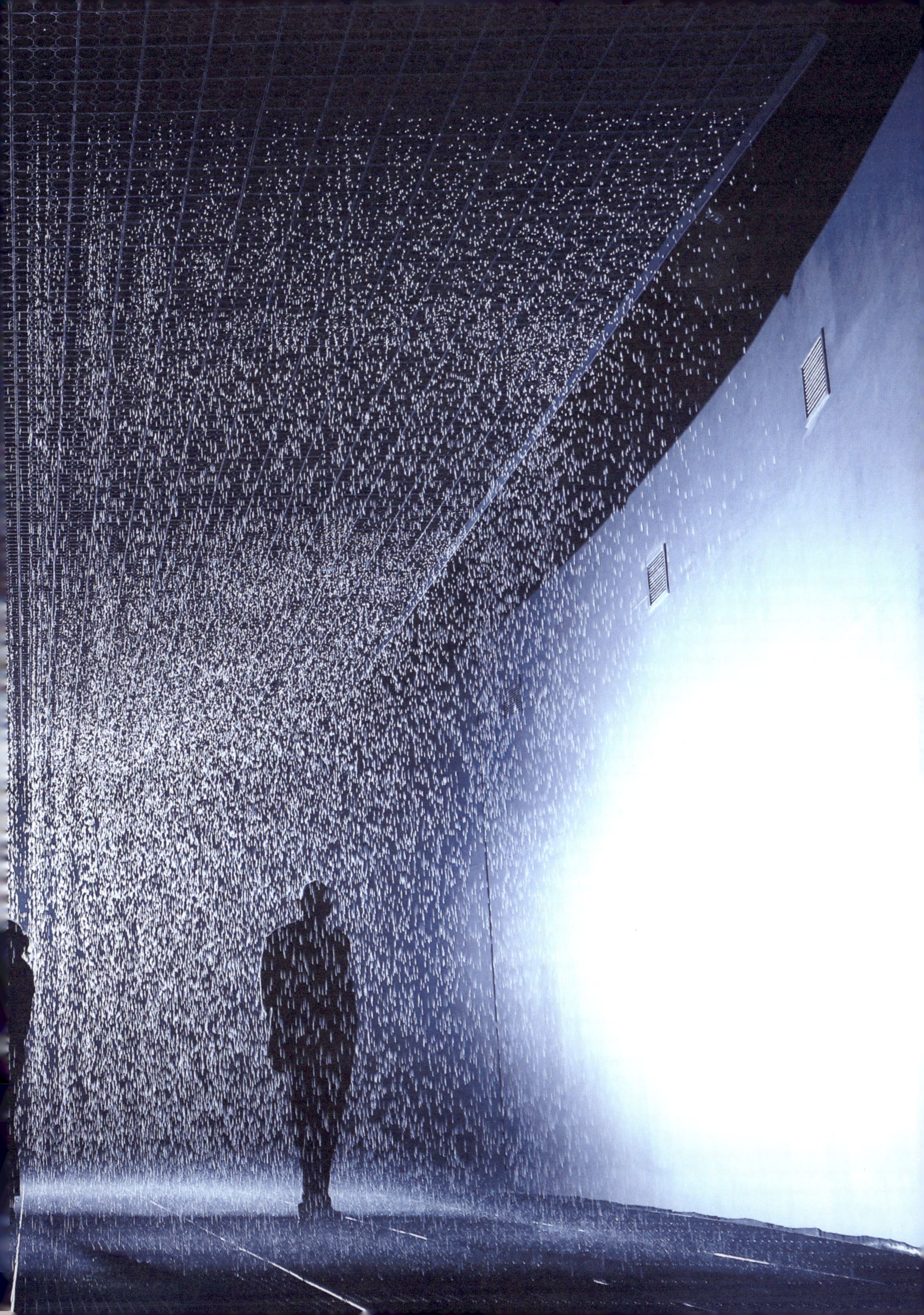

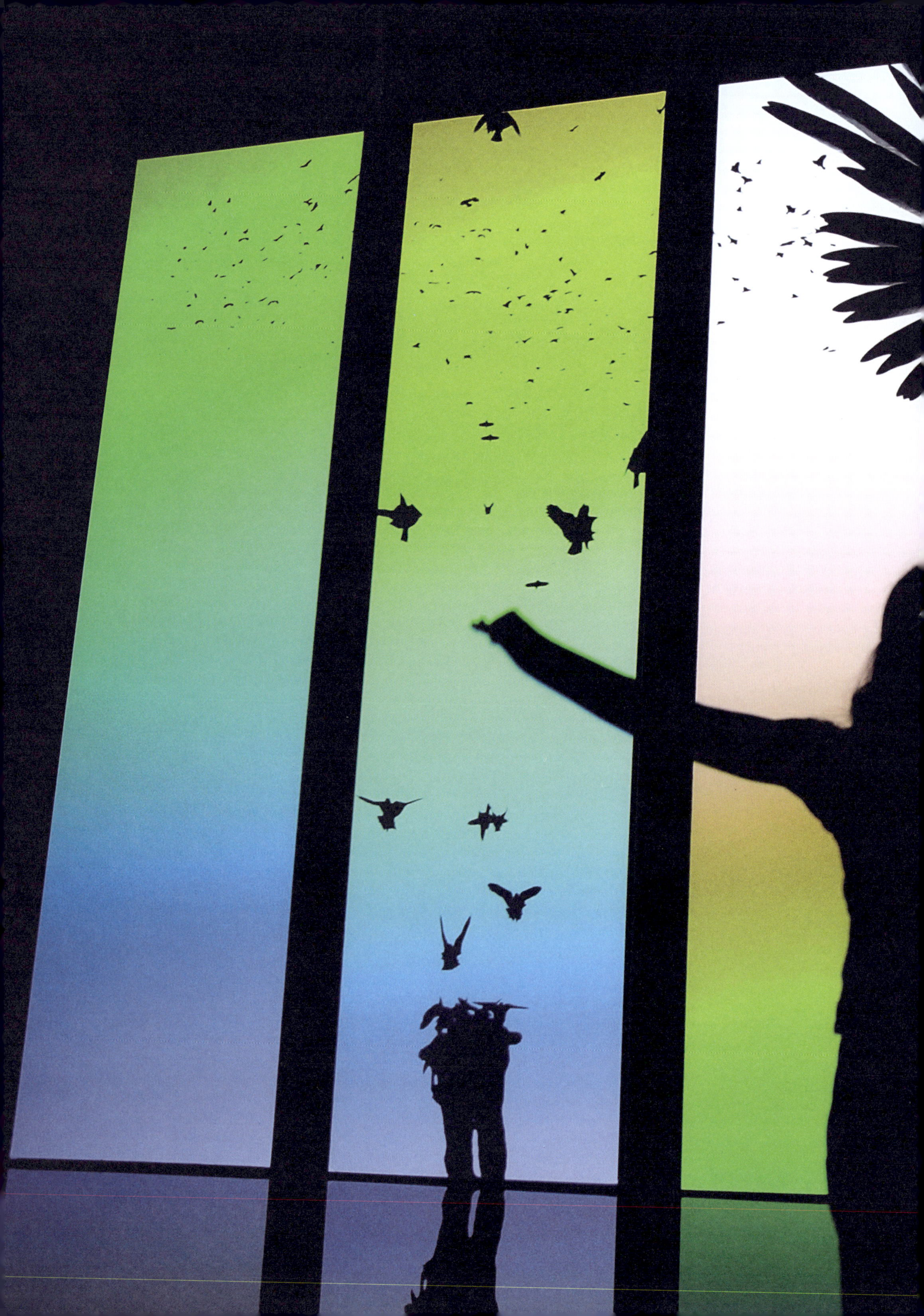

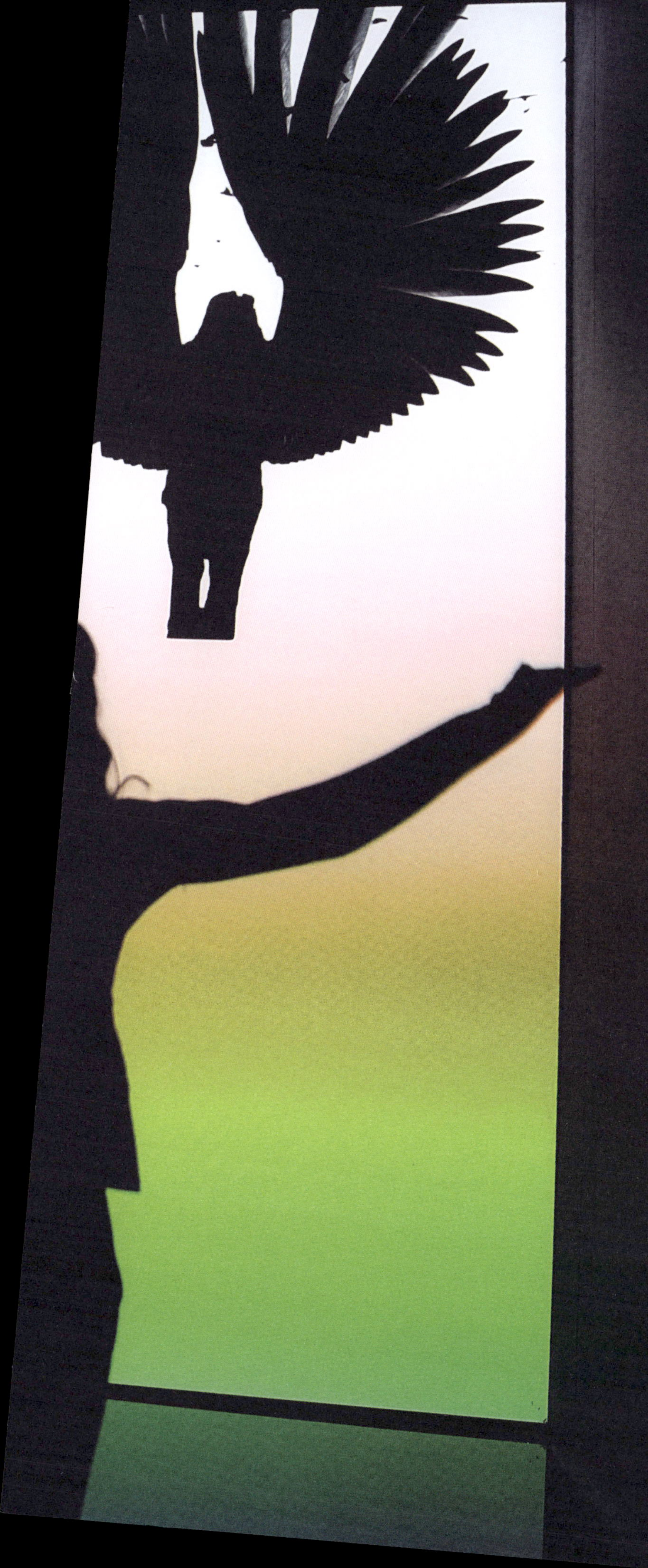

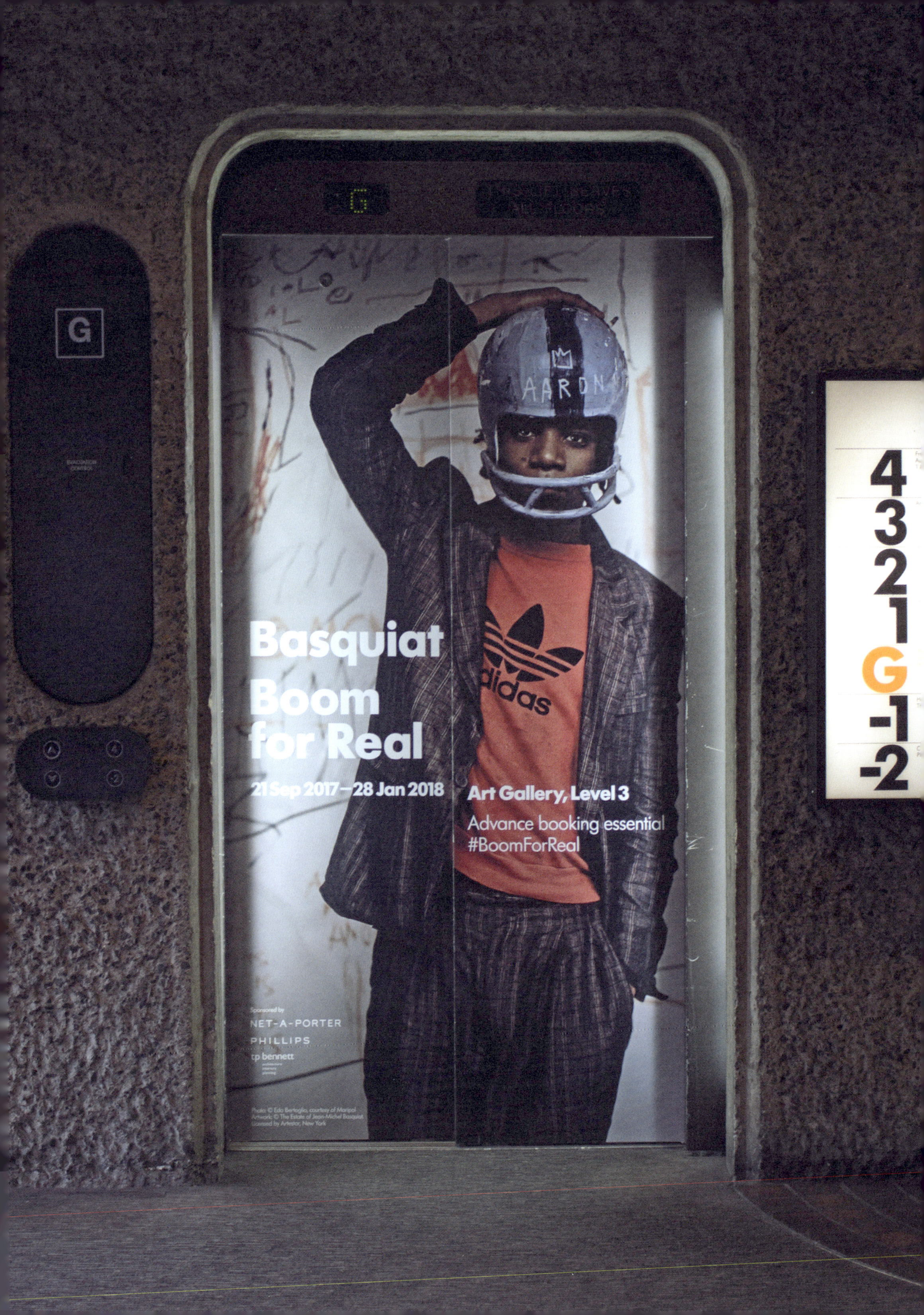
G
Basquiat
Boom
for Real
21 Sep 2017 – 28 Jan 2018
Art Gallery, Level 3
Advance booking essential
#BoomForReal
Sponsored by
NET-A-PORTER
PHILLIPS
tp bennett
4
3
2
1
G
-1
-2

Dubuffet are cases in point. All three of these recent shows were curated by Nairne and *Basquiat: Boom for Real*, 2017, was the best attended Barbican show ever — by some stretch. They also pointed to a new direction as Barbican art gallery was not renowned for tackling big solo surveys of painters. 'Everybody raised their eyebrows as there was a preconception that we would just do a certain type of show and would never take on something like Basquiat or Krasner — because we couldn't,' Alison explains. 'But evidently we could.' It was brave and a very important new direction — and it really made a mark.

Such risk-taking and avoidance of complacency bodes well for the future. But how is a gallery like Barbican's to stay relevant? 'It's about the shows being timely, scholarly but with a lightness of touch, and with a lot of attention on the visitor experience,' says Alison. 'We're a lot more personal in our telling of stories, looking at contextualising artists of the past with a contemporary lens. Asking what new story are we telling? What's not been done, what is waiting to be done? Why do we need to look at this person again? Always staying ahead of the game.'

The growing influence of social media and rapid developments in virtual and augmented reality will certainly be a major factor over the next ten years and the restrictions caused by the recent pandemic have been a catalyst to create new ways of helping audiences experience the content without physically attending. A series of in-depth films of curator-led tours of recent exhibitions such as Alona Pardo's *Masculinities* (2020) have been of the highest quality — and have reached a large global audience. But whatever the balance turns out to be between digital and live in the post-pandemic world, nothing will adequately replace our real-life experiences, and the Barbican experience is unique.

'We're really quite theatrical,' says Nairne. 'That's what comes from having concerts and theatres staged in the same building. It gives us a bit more of a sense of drama — creating a journey for a visitor. This, says Alison and Nairne, is very much the future of exhibition making. 'People come to exhibitions for an opportunity to be transported. They want to feel that they can be immersed in another world,' says Nairne. 'And that's something that the Barbican does particularly well, whether it's with scale-one models such as Mr Moriyama's home in *The Japanese House* show or Ragnar Kjartansson's troubadours singing in the gallery eight hours a day or Trish Brown's dancers *Walking on the Wall*. These are all opportunities to be immersed in a totally different creative landscape.'

The Barbican Art Gallery at 40 is a remarkable story: of how, despite modest beginnings and a difficult environment, a long line of dedicated curators and directors with brave and imaginative programming have established a world-renowned reputation and identity. The Barbican was built as a multi-arts centre, and although some believed when it opened that the very idea of a great arts centre had had its day, in fact the concept of truly concerted arts programming across the genres was not yet fully developed. Thankfully the thinking has caught up, and the astonishing building is reaching its full potential. The art gallery is in the right place at the right time.

The most successful show in Barbican history: *Basquiat: Boom for Real*, 2017, curated by Eleanor Nairne, which drew diverse London to fill the centre and hugely increased the numbers of Young Barbican members into the future.

The Barbican's commitment to adventurous art extends throughout and outside the centre, complementing the gallery shows and enlivening the spaces of the building.

Opposite
On the stairs down to Cinema 1 and the Pit on level –2, the original mural by the artist Gillian Ayres (1930–2018).

Following pages
On the walkway from the centre past the Guildhall School towards Moorgate, these panels by the artist Dorothy Annan (1900–83) were installed when the Fleet Building for which they were commissioned in the Farringdon Road was demolished. They are a depiction of technology: pylons, cables, telegraph poles, generators, a rare survival of 1960s mural art.

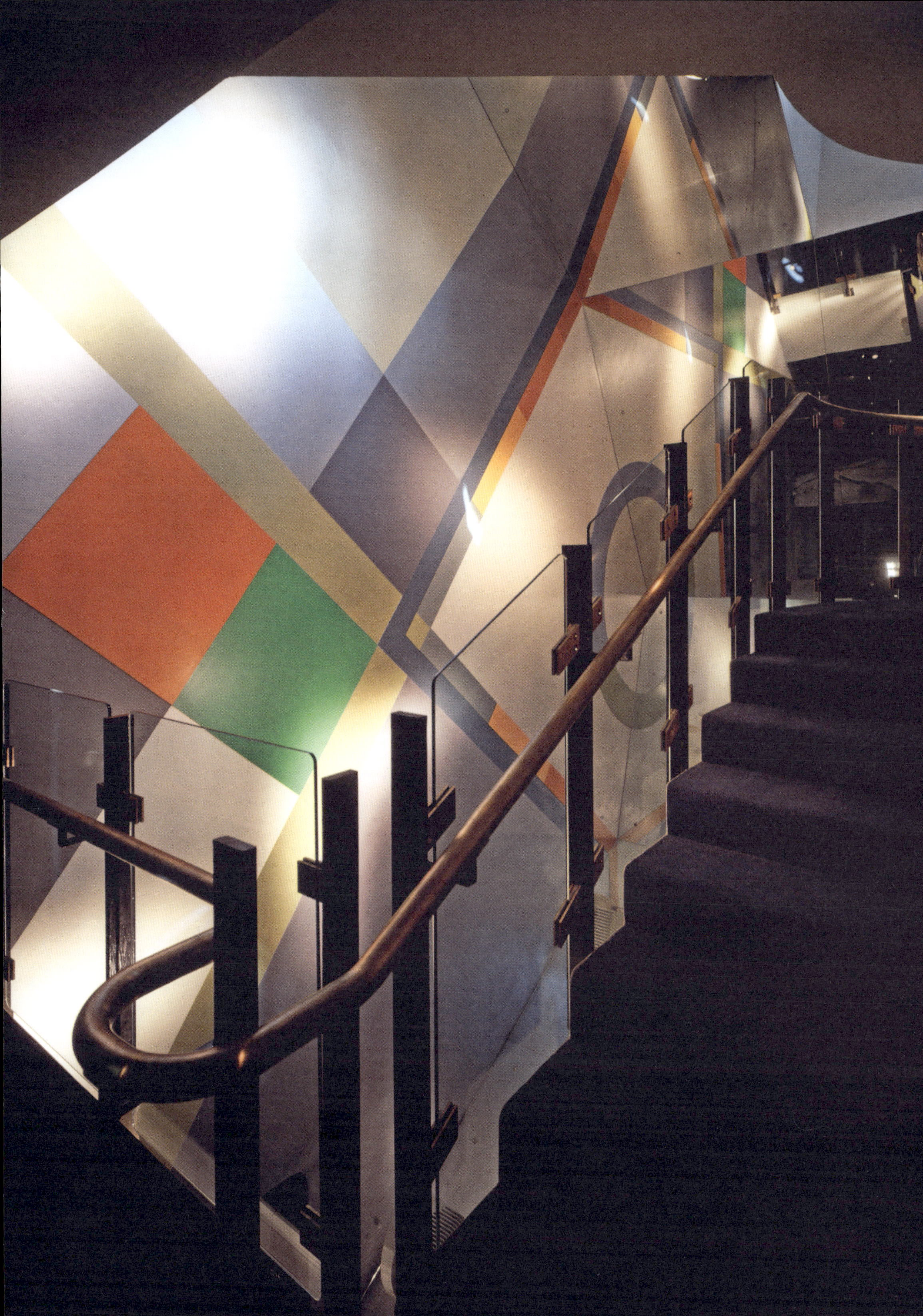

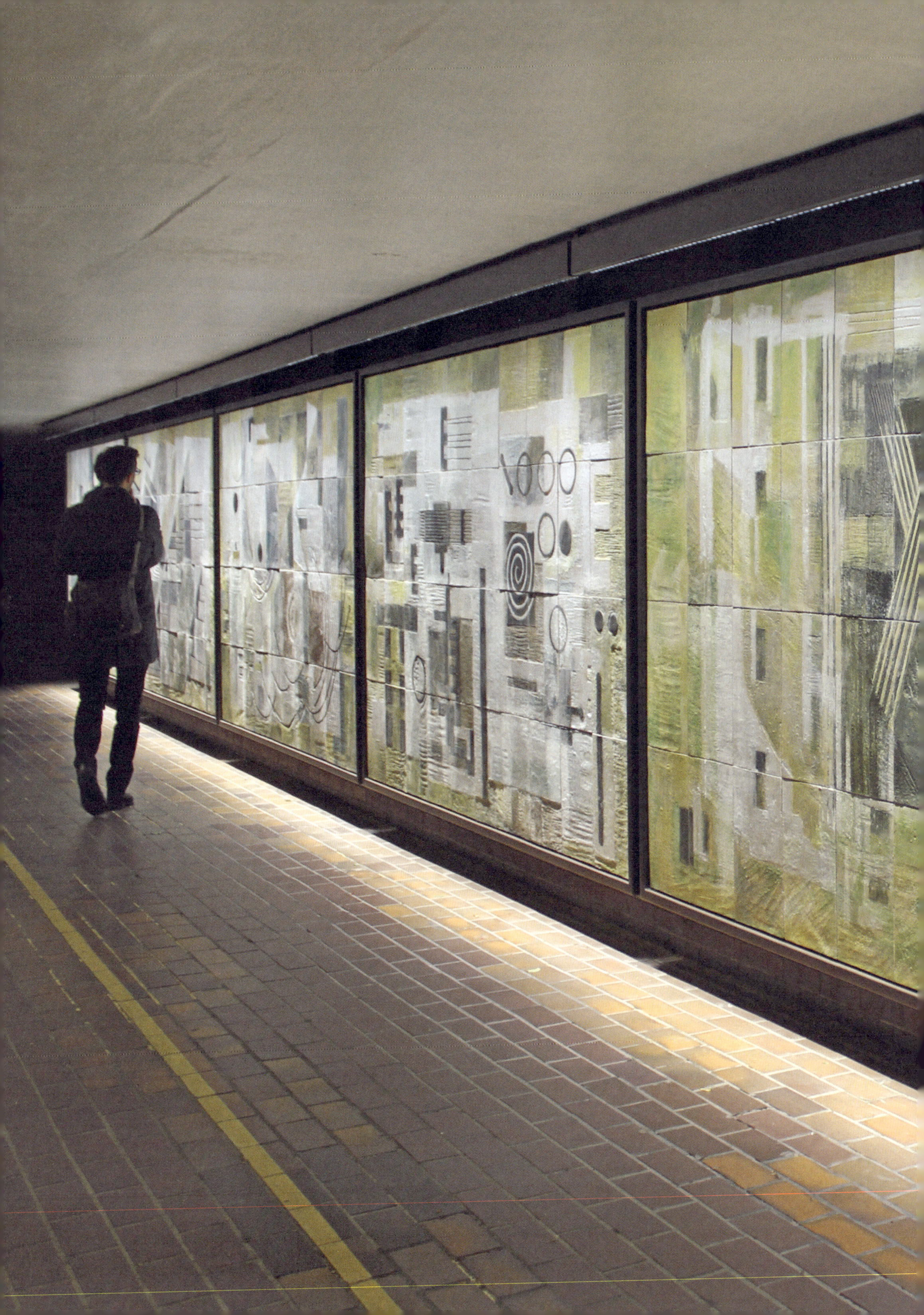

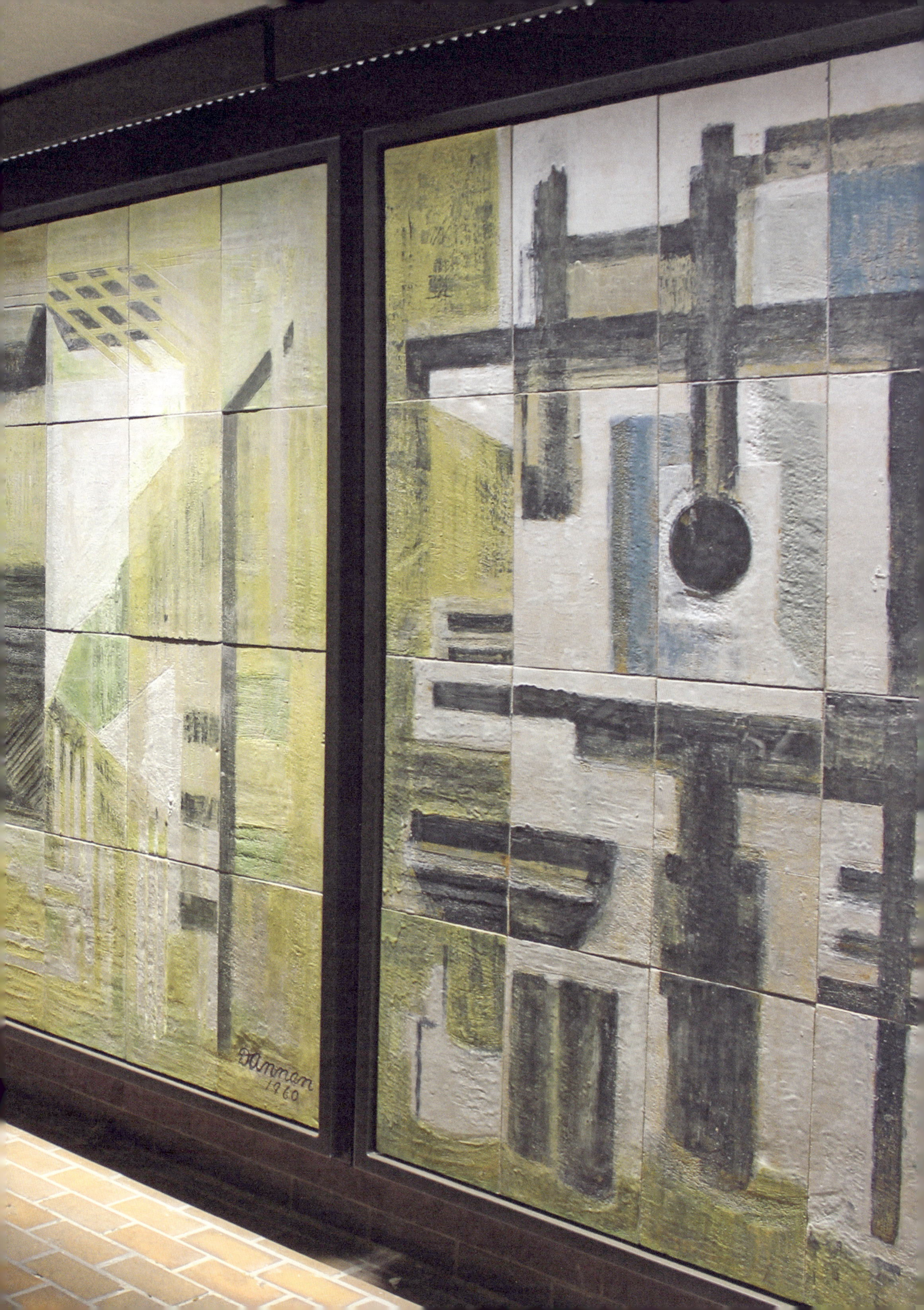
DAnnan
1960

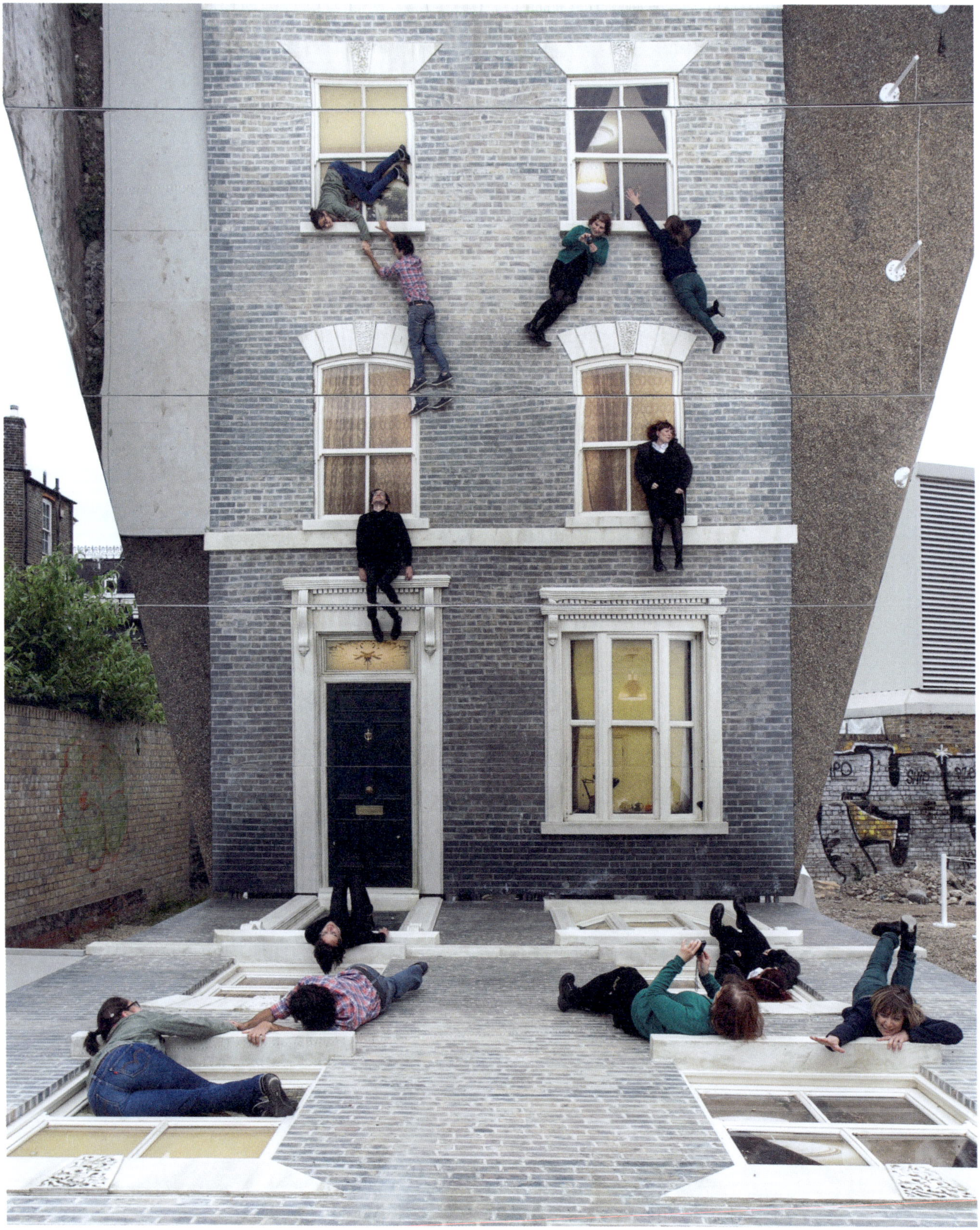

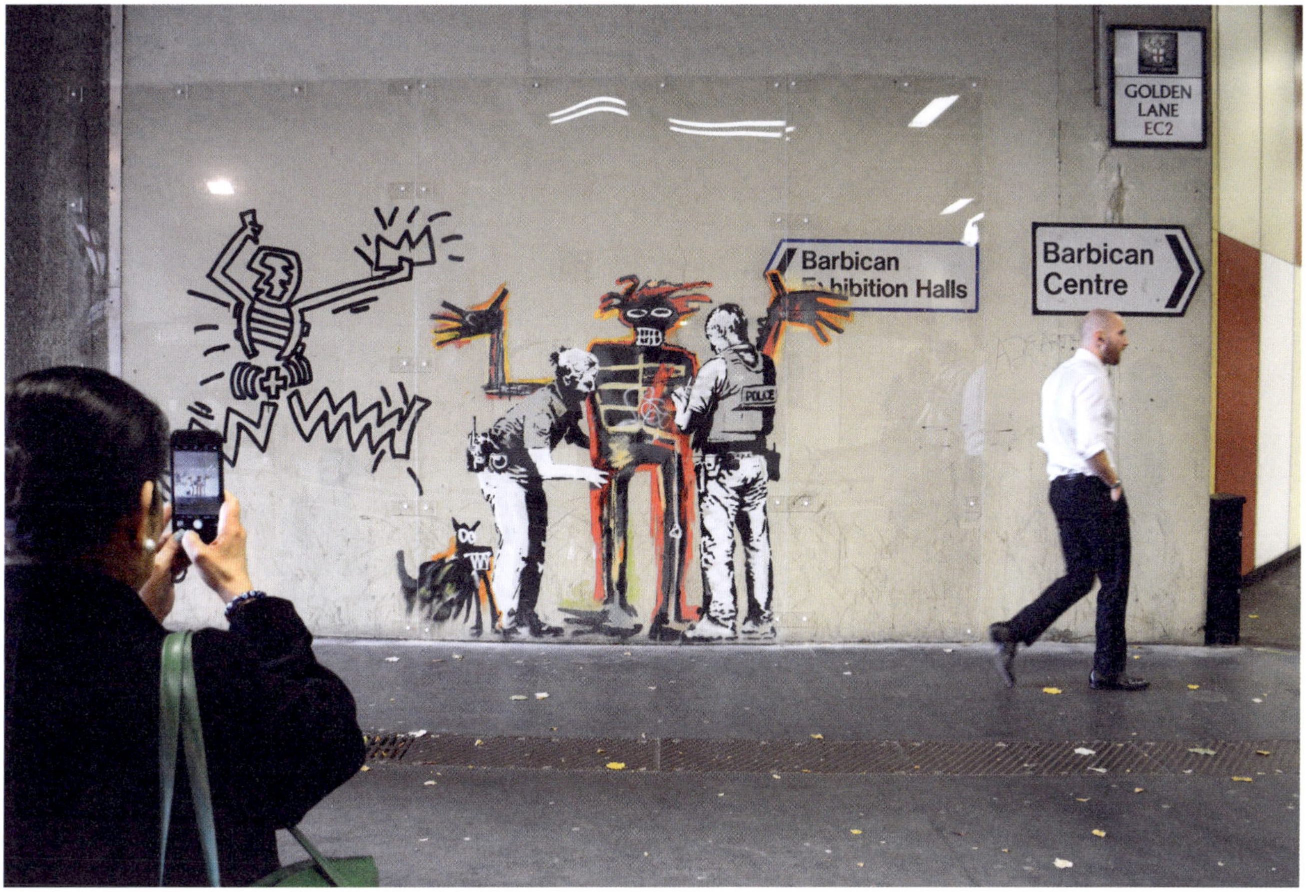

Opposite
Among the off-site installations by the gallery in East London, Dalston House was a takeover of a disused site by the Italian artist Leandro Erlich. A terrace house frontage laid on the ground was projected by a large angled mirror and turned into a visual illusion — a huge success with children and families and a hit on Instagram!

Above
The sincerest form of flattery: Banksy's overnight creation of a homage to the Basquiat exhibition on the outside walls of the Barbican Exhibition Halls in Golden Lane, joined by other admiring graffiti and providing a magnet for selfies.

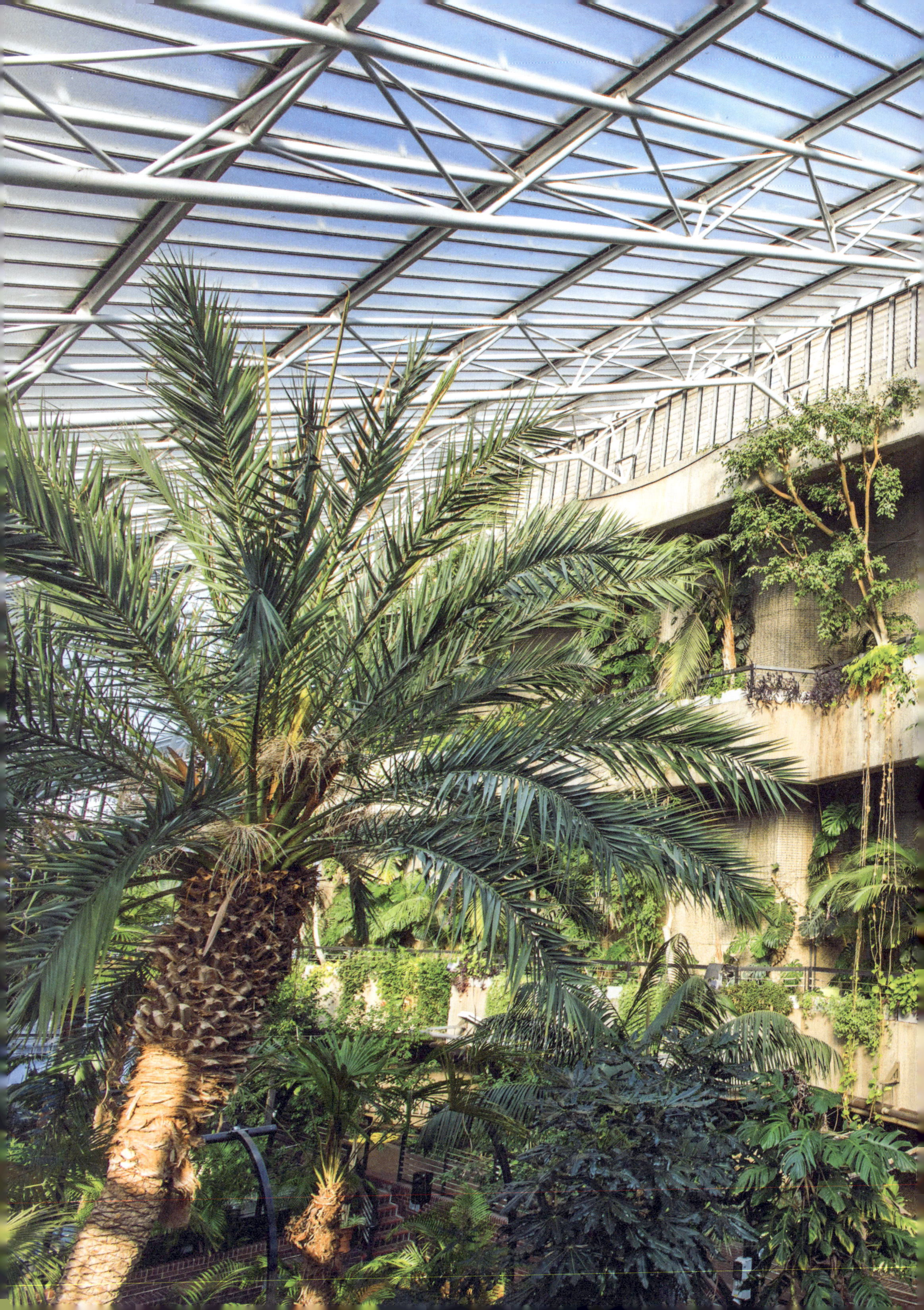

Marta Lowcewicz

What started as a temporary job for me has become a permanent part of my life. It is really hard to describe what the Barbican Conservatory is, and what it's like to work here. But let's start from the basics. Over the years there have always been two or three full-time gardeners and a handful of volunteers. Our working day starts at 6.30 am. While some people are still in their warm beds, we head to train stations or cycle to work. I must admit that after all these years this is still not an easy task ...

The conservatory is one of the largest spaces of this type in London. And over the last 40 years it has been and still is a labour of love, for many talented gardeners and plant enthusiasts. They all put their mark on this place: Neil, Dave, Sara and Silvia, who over years helped and are still helping to create this space. The 1,500 species of plants come from every continent except Antarctica. The quirky collection was started in the late 1970s and early 1980s, when the plants arrived from all sorts of places. Over the years many have been kindly donated to us as well. We house all types of temperate and succulent plants, from tiny *Tillandsia usneoides* (Spanish moss) that create long hair-like structures, to the gigantic leaves of *Monstera deliciosa*, which produce tasty edible fruits.

Plants are living matter. Hence no two days are the same in here, not to mention the seasons or even years. Plants 'come and go'. We do grow a lot of our own plants from seeds and cuttings, which can sometimes challenge your patience. But it also gives you enormous satisfaction, seeing them mature and reaching their full potential. We always try to update the collection by adding new and exciting species to the mix.

Quite a few of them have medicinal properties and some parts of them are edible like *Citrus* x *hystrix* (kaffir lime), *Psidium cattleyanum* (strawberry guava) or *Coffea arabica* (coffee plant). Some are endangered in native habitats, like *Lophophora williamsii* or *Obetia ficifolia*. Each plant is different, but to us each one is as important as any other.

The conservatory enables people to make the connection between the everyday cup of tea or coffee, and the plant that it's coming from. For some, it brings a happy memory of home: when among all those plants they spot an inconspicuous chilli plant, which their dad used to use in their favourite dish ... So many connections, so many wonderful stories, so many smiling faces. That is what keeps us going, and that's why we all do it.

Marta Lowcewicz has been running the unique glass-roofed Barbican Conservatory on the fourth floor for 12 years. Built around the fly tower of the theatre below, it houses rare plants and fish, and also welcomes visitors to weddings, parties and myriad events. During and after the pandemic it re-opened as a popular free offer to local communities, providing an oasis in the City.

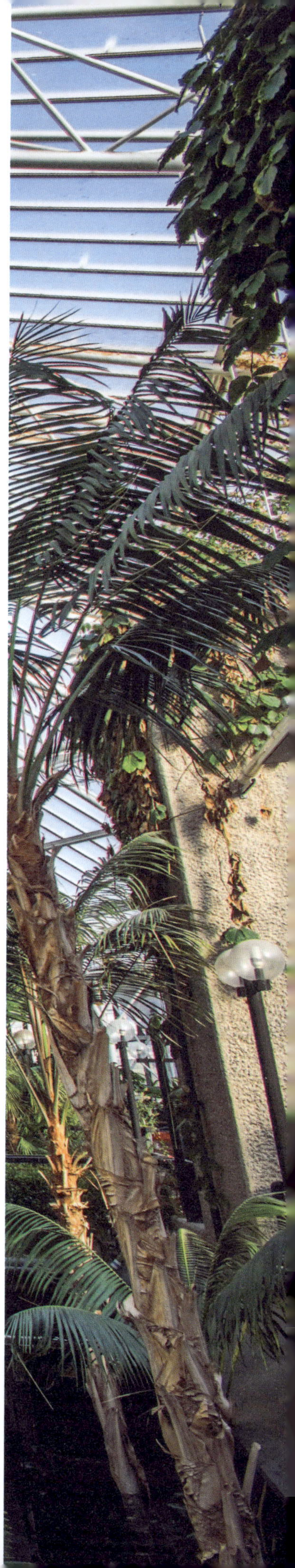

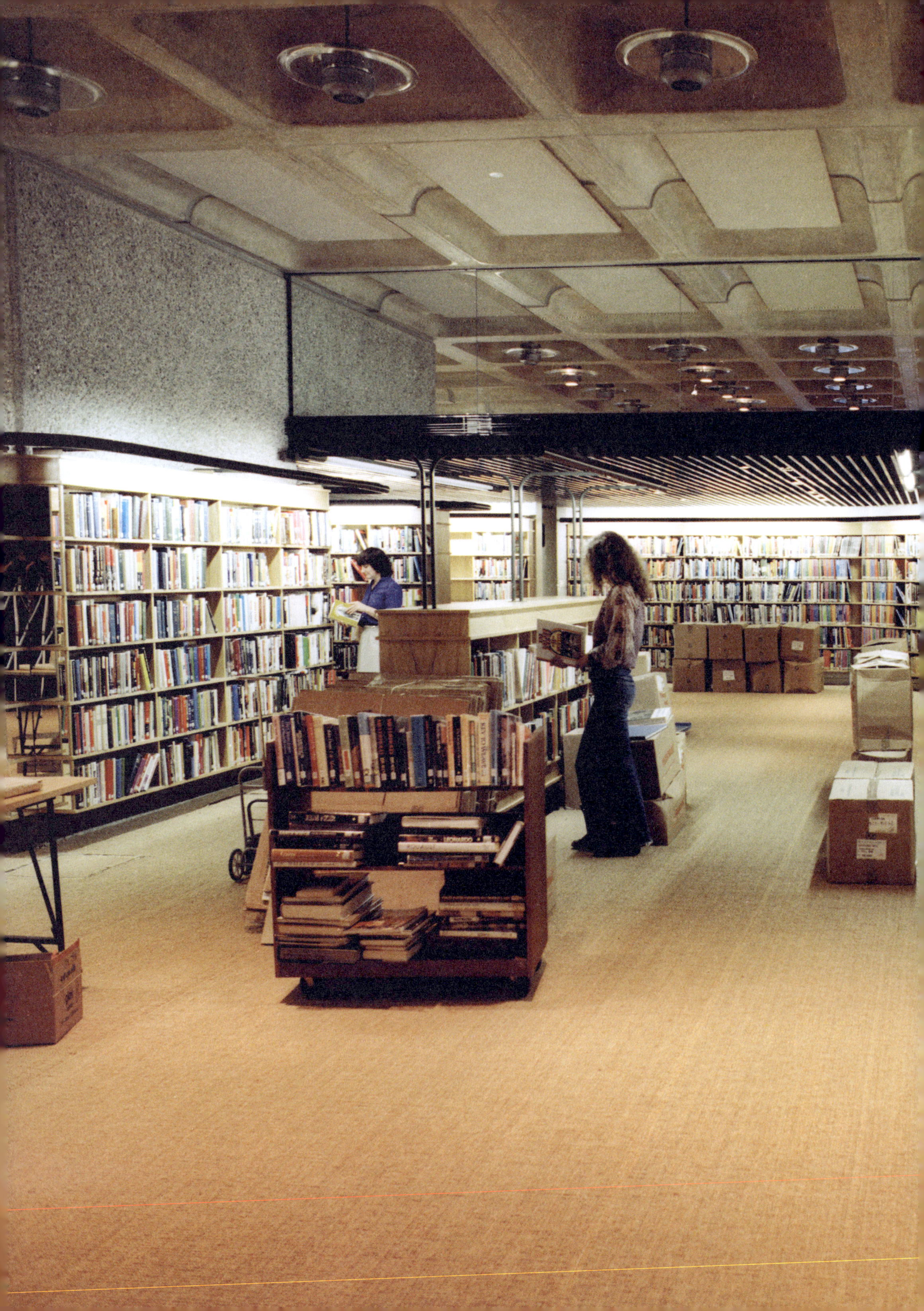

Carol Boswarthack

When Barbican Library first opened, I was still at library school studying for my Librarianship degree. I vividly remember visiting this brand new, iconic library building and feeling completely over-awed by it. Back then, I would never have guessed that nearly 40 years later, I would be head of Barbican and Community Libraries for the City of London Corporation and working in that incredible building.

It's so very different from most other libraries; the open-plan design creates an exciting buzz while sometimes that buzz from the surroundings can be a little challenging! One of my colleagues recalls that for seven months in 2000, the art gallery hosted a massive celebration of all things Star Wars. This pre-dated the enlargement and acoustical containment of the gallery – he remembers how exciting it was to look up and see Star Wars paraphernalia in the central well above the library. Unfortunately, the show also included 'The Imperial March' on a continuous loop, and library staff marched around to it!

On any given day, we can expect a variety of entertainment from elsewhere in the building. I remember coming back from an outside meeting one lunchtime and a really good salsa band was playing on the free stage in the foyer. They were joyful and accomplished but so loud that staff and customers couldn't hear each other, gave up trying to speak and decided to dance instead! Where else could that happen?!

One day, one of the library attendants noticed a young man unrolling a sleeping bag. He then produced a pillow, an alarm clock and a teddy bear. Then he stripped off his outer clothes to reveal … pyjamas! It turned out to be a BBC crew testing laws and byelaws – in this case the byelaw that says people must not sleep in the library.

The music library on the mezzanine floor has confused some visitors who look in vain for an entrance other than the one on level 2. As far as we know, the only people who have left the library via that mezzanine are parkour enthusiasts who jumped from the CD section for a Channel 4 show. Without the crash mats they used, this is definitely not something we would recommend! Our music library has hosted some amazing exhibitions and some very special guest artists from all musical genres including Peggy Seeger, Simon Rattle, Gerald Scarfe and most recently electronic pop pioneers, Tangerine Dream.

Many library staff (but not me) have heard what they call The Voice: a woman who just says 'Hello!' When they turn to see who it is, there is nobody there. It isn't in the least threatening and colleagues who have yet to hear this friendly vocal apparition are jealous! Perhaps it is the history of the Barbican following us …

Carol Boswarthack spent many years providing library services in various London boroughs before taking up her role as head of Barbican and Community Libraries for the City of London in 2011.

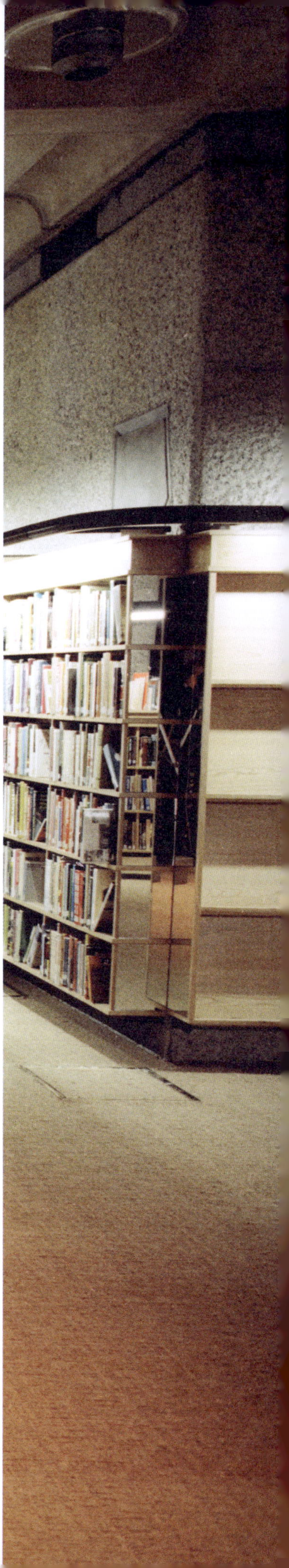

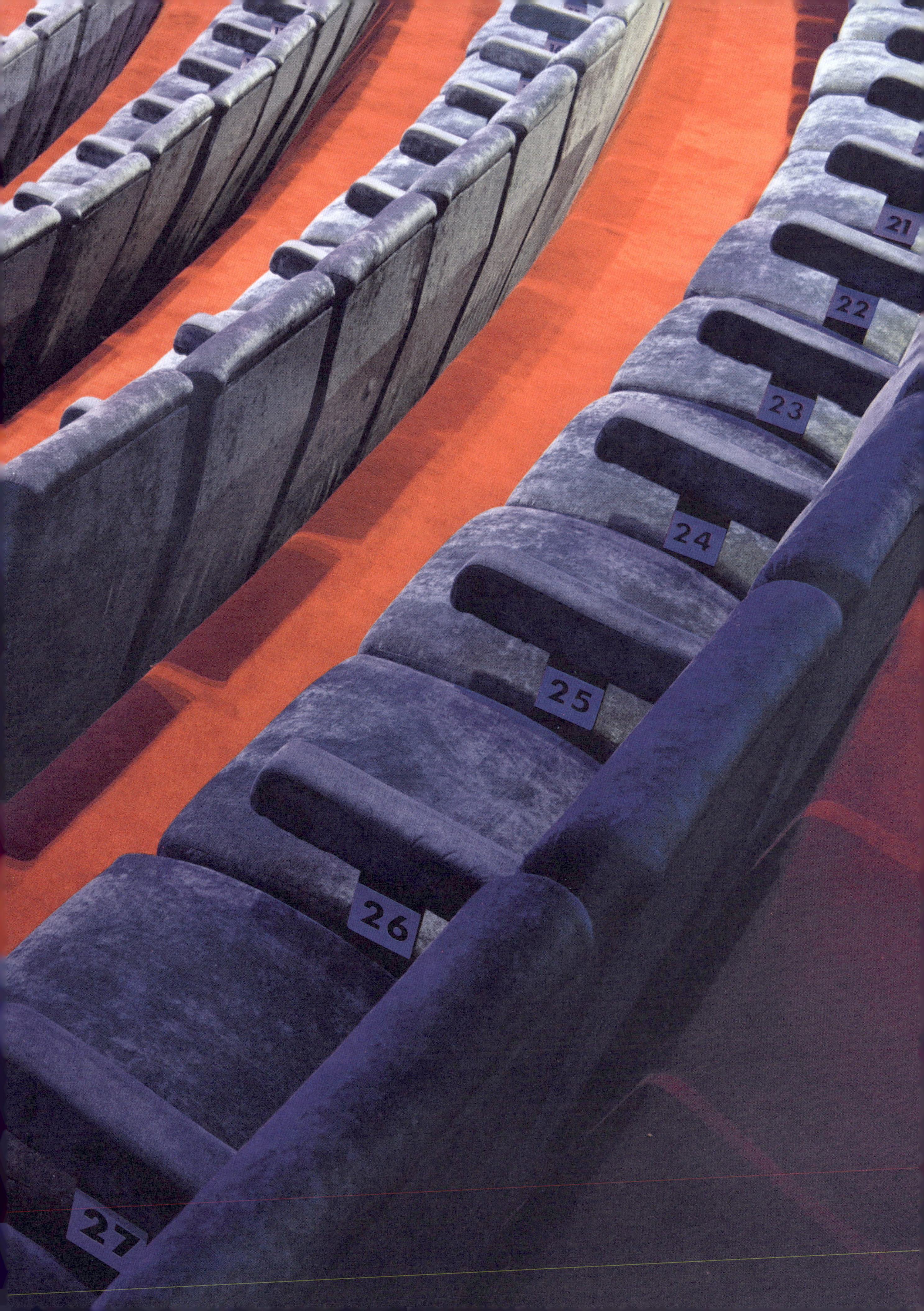
21
22
23
24
25
26
27

Cinema

Sukhdev Sandhu

The Barbican was a cinematic space long before it opened an actual cinema. In 1940 and 1941, when German bombs rained down on old Cripplegate, newsreel footage of burning London quickly travelled the world. Here were images — spectacular, compelling — of a Britain on the brink of being destroyed by fascism. And yet here too were images — heart-swelling, defiant — of a city that persisted, a city that refused to die even though its population has been decimated, its steeples and ancient courts blown away by firestorms.

On screen the Barbican has often been depicted as a place both of horror and of hope. It served as suitably spectral terrain in the video to The Specials' 'Ghost Town', a single that topped the pop charts during the week that riots broke out across Britain in the summer of 1981. In Skepta's 'Shutdown', it's a backdrop evoking a London version of the Parisian *banlieux*, a brutalist zone about which grime MCs can spit rhymes about inner-city resistance. In Saint Etienne's 'Side Streets', commuters fear to tread through its road tunnel, which attracts intimidating subalterns. Many readers of J G Ballard's 1975 novel *High Rise* (and viewers of Ben Wheatley's 2016 adaptation of it) assume its dystopian portrait of aerial living (opening paragraph: 'Later, as he sat on the balcony eating the dog, Dr Robert Laing reflected on the unusual events that had taken place within this huge apartment building during the previous three months.') is based on the Barbican.

At the same time, the Barbican, when it wasn't offered up as *neo noir*, represented an alternative to the kind of film, typified by Norman Cohen's James Mason-presented *The London Nobody Knows*, that might be described as Metropolitan Moribundia. These doleful documentaries, especially common in the 60s and 70s, portray the remnants of the Victorian capital, peasouper dark, all tenements and tears. Here are lamplighters, homeless men and women shuffling around, dirty-kneed urchins rough-and-tumbling on cobbled streets. The Barbican may not have been the white heat of technology rendered in concrete, but it was commonly portrayed, in news reports and promotional films, as a fresh new start for London, a beacon of hope.

One person to have been inspired by that vision was Ray Diehl. Born in Southampton, the now 87-year-old film buff and former National Film Theatre board member moved to Marble Arch in 1967. 'One day I went to the ABC on Edgware Road. The picture was *The Getaway* — the original with Steve McQueen. This was a time when cinemas showed supporting programmes and when double bills had finished you always got a travelogue or something. I often used to get a bus which went past this place called the Barbican when it was still like a disused building site. You can imagine I was taken by the ABC promotional film that showed how wonderful the Barbican was. It gave the impression — not entirely true — that you could play the trumpet there and nobody would hear it outside the flat. A quiet place, good soundproofing. It showed everything being of high quality, you know. The fittings. So I actually put my name down on a list, got called, liked it, and moved here in 1975. Haven't changed a thing. My flat is still in its original state.'

Yet when the Barbican Arts Centre opened in March 1982, cinema was low in its priorities. In a February 1982 edition of TV's *Omnibus* about the centre introduced by Barry Norman, there was plenty about music and theatre, architecture and nightlife, but not one of the interviewees mentioned film. There was no speculation about what Barbican Cinema might be screening, far less how it might contribute to the centre's mission in the years ahead.

The early 1980s was hardly an auspicious time to open a new cinema in London. Colin Welland may have roared, 'The British are coming!' when he picked up his screenwriter award for *Chariots of Fire* at the Oscars but, in the capital, as across the rest of the United Kingdom, audiences were dwindling and movie theatres were closing. Unemployment was rising steeply and many Hollywood companies had pulled out of British production. The Conservative government scrapped the Eady Levy that, since 1950, had subsidised British film production through a small tax on box-office receipts. The number of households owning video recorders was quickly rising and, with annual admissions in 1982 down to 64 million (in 1969, when Speed House, the Barbican's first residential building, went up, they had been 214.9 million), there was a fear that movies would permanently migrate to living rooms. Britain ran the risk of becoming *Das Land ohne Kinema*.

Liz Wrenn, the Barbican's first film programmer, had an unusual background. Born in Santa Barbara, California, in 1939, she had grown up in Alabama and Florida, and had escaped an increasingly volatile New York by decamping to Paris with her husband and young sons in 1970. In 1976 she moved to London where, living without legal papers, she got by working as a sub-editor at *Time Out* and teaching English as a foreign language. A property windfall back in the States meant she was able to invest in a project to transform the Other Cinema on Tottenham Court Road into the Scala. She insisted that, in return, she would have to be its programmer, but when the increasingly popular venue relocated to King's Cross in 1981, she was ousted and made ends meet by working as a booker at both the Ritzy in Brixton and the Everyman in Hampstead.

'I got a telephone call from Antony Lewis-Crosby who was head of planning at the Barbican Centre,' she recalls. 'He had asked the British Film Institute for recommendations of someone who might be able to programme. I hadn't been in this country very long. If there was a job coming, if someone wanted me to do something, I said yes. Only later did I worry about how I would fulfil it. I was self-employed while I was at the Barbican. Freelance. By 1982 I had five cinemas I was responsible for — the Roxy, the Everyman, the Electric Portobello Road, the Duke of York Brighton and the Barbican. I used to dedicate one day to each cinema. That's a lot of bookings!'

Wrenn found her new gig in EC2 to be particularly challenging. 'It was a big imposing thing. It was corporate. It's not like this now, but at the weekend the City closed down. There was no one on the street. Not a soul from Friday late afternoon until Monday morning. Also, the other places for whom I worked had their own character — the Ritzy was in Brixton, which had a big Afro-Caribbean population; the Electric Portobello had a large Spanish crowd — but the Barbican was a blank slate. It had difficulties. One was the building itself: people kept getting lost coming from the tube to the cinema. Moorgate was more convenient than the Barbican stop, but no one could even find their way from Moorgate.'

An Escher-like original concept model for the stairs down to Cinema 1 in the basement of the building. Compare the Gillian Ayres mural on p.225.

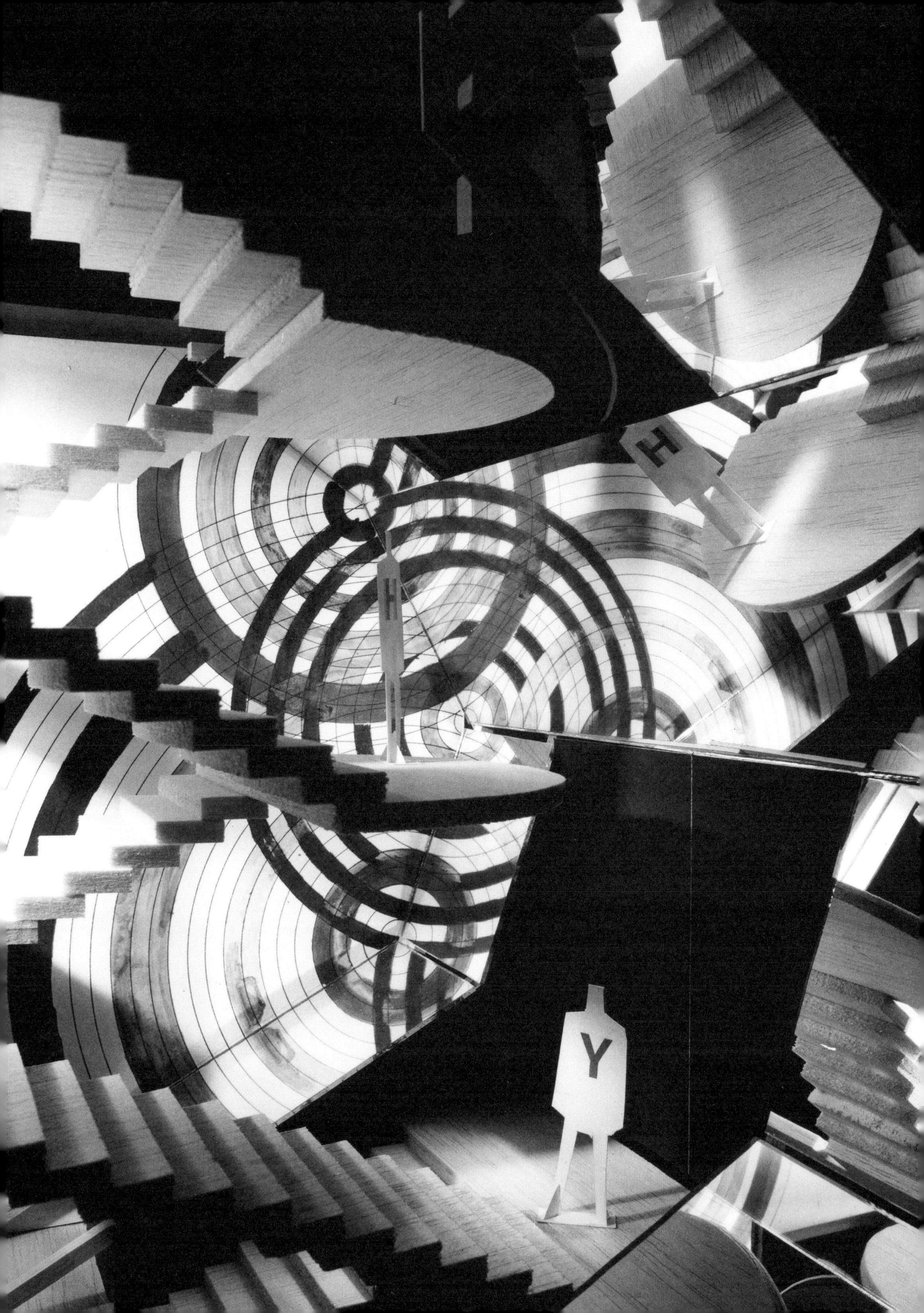
H
H
Y

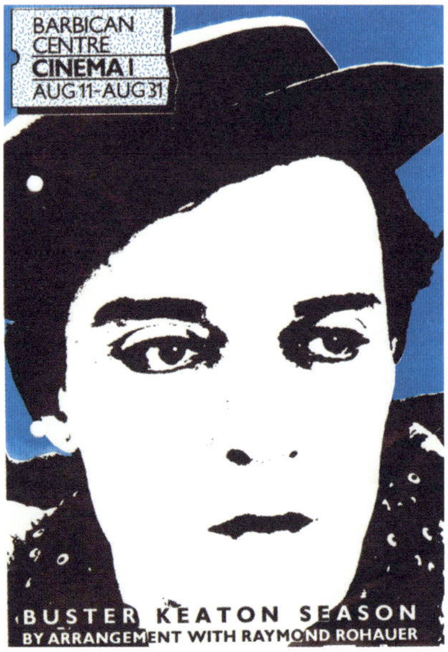

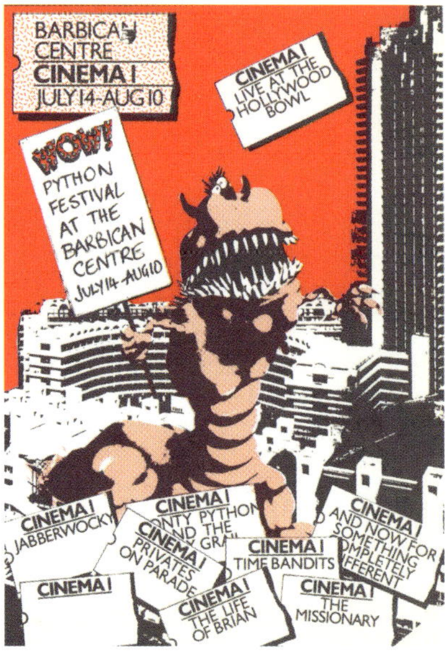

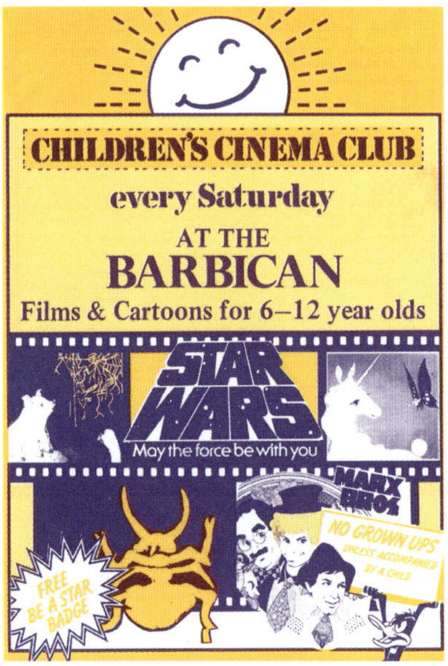

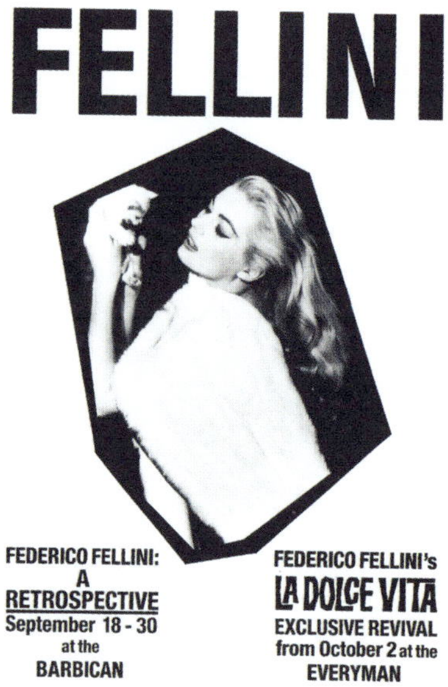

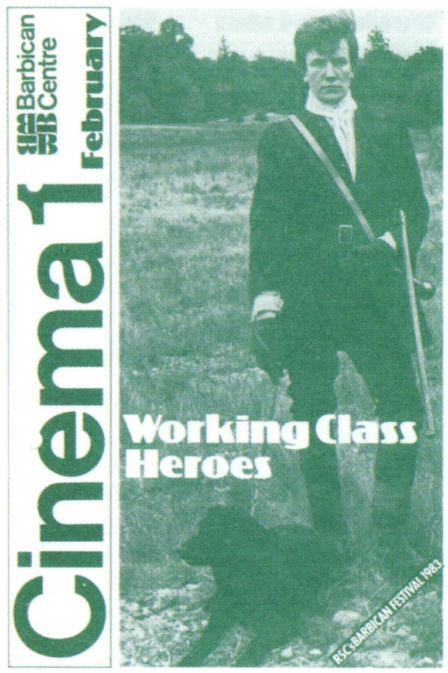

Early cinema brochures from the 1980s, from Buster Keaton and Monty Python to *Black Orpheus*, Fellini and *Working Class Heroes*. Children's cinema and family film clubs have always been a central part of the Barbican programme.

Would-be cinema-goers faced more problems upon arriving at the centre. 'The building was a nightmare! Really! Cinema 1, which had 300 seats, was two floors below ground. There were also two little cinemas up in the far reaches. If you came to the wrong cinema it could take up to 15 minutes to get to the right one.'

Wrenn had no prior experience of big organisations and says she found it hard to adjust to the Barbican's scale and structures. 'You had a technical department, a department that was in charge of people and ushers, a planning department: these departments didn't necessarily work harmoniously. It wasn't like at a cinema where there's a manager and a cashier and the coffee bar staff and there's the ushers and a programmer and everybody works together. In any large organisation there are teething problems where there are people who have been hired who really shouldn't have been hired. And it was too easy for people to get their noses out of joint.'

Wrenn's biggest problem was persuading exhibitors to allow her to screen their films in the first place. She craved new releases of the kind that were being reviewed in the broadsheets and London weeklies, that were neither too obscure nor too populist, that would appeal to the kind of people who lived in or worked near the Barbican. She knew too that going to the movies was more affordable than going to the theatre or to a concert; if she could cultivate regulars, they in turn would promote the centre to their friends and help make the place seem less rarefied. But, especially in its first 18 months, the film industry viewed it with suspicion, and it took time for the distributors to agree that it should have first-run films. 'The Odeon in Islington or the Screen on the Green would get everything. I didn't get any of the films I wanted. You had to prove to them that you could make enough money for them to let you into the club.'

Struggling to fill seats, Wrenn decided to stage themed seasons and retrospectives — on Hitchcock and Buster Keaton, Herzog on Film, tributes to Joseph Losey, Henry Fonda, Luis Bunuel, Jack Nicholson. These attracted those directors' and performers' fans as well as coverage in the press; as Wrenn recalls: 'You had to have something entirely different and not playing elsewhere for people to come to the Barbican.' Her own tastes were reflected in screenings of Godard's *Prenom*, Lizzie Borden's *Born in Flames*, Güney's *The Wall*, Trotta's *The Second Awakening of Christa Klages*. In January 1983 there was an event devoted to filmmakers who worked in exile in Paris. There were also appearances by radical journalists and filmmakers such as John Pilger, Anna Coote and Chris Reeves (the latter's *Cause of Ireland* had recently won an award at the Tyneside Film Festival).

Could the Barbican ever have been a hub for militant and independent cinema? It seems unlikely. The ability to properly promote its film offerings, experimental or otherwise, would have been helpful however. 'As an Arts Centre the Barbican wanted you to programme three months ahead,' remembers Wrenn. 'You can't do that with film. Even the distributors aren't at all sure what they're going to be showing. In the Barbican's own programmes, there was no more than an inch for cinema. Most films weren't listed at all.' Small wonder then that 'it was quite empty at the beginning. It had no built-in audience. At least we didn't have the pressure of having to pay rent and lighting like other standalone cinemas.'

It's hard not to chuckle at, or be puzzled by, the schedules for the early days of Barbican cinema. For every season on Russian Visionaries there's a book celebrating whales that's being launched. In one screening room a mini-series on Italian neo-realism, in another an LBC Celebrity Interview strand, hosted by Bob Holness (best known as presenter of children's TV quiz show *Blockbusters*), featuring guests such as Penelope Keith, Tommy Steele and ex-Goon Michael Bentine.

Most striking are the Cinema 2 slots occupied by John Huntley's Movie Memories. Huntley (1921–2003) started out as a Denham Studios teaboy, an assistant to conductor Muir Mathieson, and went on to become head of the National Film Theatre's Regional Unit. An enthusiast and a popular lecturer, he regularly put on all-day screenings devoted to Great Singers of the Silver Screen, Aircraft of World War Two, Best of the Musicals, London's Steam Railways. These attracted sizeable audiences. He was, in effect, Barbican Cinema's Raymond Gubbay. 'He would get these slots from Planning, fill them, and take whatever profit there was,' remembers Wrenn. 'I didn't mind so much as I was still struggling to get product from the distributors. But it did make it difficult for the programming to look coherent.'

There were some unexpected successes. Wrenn recalls: 'The first season that really did work was a Monty Python retrospective in August 1983. Their office in north London generously gave me rights to show all the TV products — plus the shorts, which are adorable. They even let us show two or three of John Cleese's management training films, which at that time he was selling to businesses for a lot of money. One of them was called *The Unorganized Manager*, which resonated with me enormously!'

Wrenn's persistence with distributors meant she sometimes snagged significant titles. 'A breakthrough that I was really, really happy about was the premiere of *Blade Runner* in September 1982. The head of Warner Bros, Sandy Lieberman, physically carried the reels over to the Barbican and stayed through the whole screening because of fears about piracy. The film had tanked in the US, but that wasn't true in Europe, and its success helped me enormously in my talks with the majors.' The following year, *Gandhi* helped attract older crowds not dissimilar to those who went to the centre's other arts offerings. There were more and more week-long runs of new films, which best suited the 300-seat Cinema 1. The marketing team was laying on early-evening screenings geared towards the range of City workers, and they broadened the reach and attracted a young, diverse audience the centre at that time found elusive.

By 1985 Wrenn had started her own distribution company called Electric; as that blossomed, snapping up future hits by the likes of Pedro Almódovar, Sally Potter, Mary Harron and even a young Christopher Nolan (*Following*, 1998), she wasn't able to commit as much of her time to the centre as she would have liked. In the end, she left in 1989 and handed over the reins to Robert Rider. Today, while she describes her departure as both inevitable and amicable, she characterises the early years of Barbican cinema in terms of a poor relation. 'Within the centre there didn't seem to be any cinephiles,' she believes. 'Cinema wasn't particularly their interest. It was very much something we did *as well*. There was one season related to Orwell's *1984* — Thought Crimes at the Barbican — where I sat down with the people in charge of the theatre and the art gallery and discussed ways in which we could collaborate. But that was one of the few times we did that. The directors must have felt the cinema was adding to the general business of the Barbican. But they didn't want it to be too off the wall.'

Wrenn's successor Robert Rider is the single most important figure in the history of Barbican cinema. He is responsible for raising its status in the arts programme. His background was as an academic – writing a PhD on railway workers in Derby and working part-time at cinemas in Bloomsbury and Camden to help make ends meet. In 1981 he became a joint-programmer at the Rio in Dalston, Hackney, freelancing at the Barbican from 1986 onwards, before being appointed head of cinema in 1989. His central challenge, he believes, was 'to raise the profile of film as an art form in its own right alongside the more established music, theatre and art departments.' Early in his tenure he persuaded marketing to fund a programme leaflet focusing exclusively on the cinema. Later he would inaugurate a no-popcorn rule, and argue against the food-at-your-seat tendencies of other art cinemas.

The centre as a whole aspired to world-class status, and Rider too was keen to 'develop and initiate a variety of World Cinema, alongside mainstream cinema, both through regular and one-off programmes.' His earliest series were devoted to Hungarian, Polish and Israeli film, and he would remain a committed anti-parochialist, recalling that many of his favourite programmes 'had an international outlook and included one-off special screen talks and events, not all of which were comfortable viewing – some include Screen Griots (on African Cinema, 1995), Black Films and Film Makers in the USA (1998), War in Iranian Cinema (2007), Cinema of Brazil: Urban Tales.' Later on the Barbican regularly hosted the Palestine and London Korean Film Festivals (starting in 2006 and 2007).

Rider regularly invited film critics to the Barbican as on-stage interviewers or discussants. For the venue's tenth anniversary in 1992 he had Barry Norman present his Top Ten movies. For its 20th anniversary, Norman's successor as *Film …* presenter Jonathan Ross chose his Top 20. In 2013, to celebrate the centenary of the London-based Critics' Circle, he asked a number of writers to introduce screenings in a series entitled The Film That Changed My Life.

More significant still was his emphasis on screen talks. A total of 673 were staged during his time – many of them under the popular stewardship of Beverley Silverstone. Guests included Charlton Heston, Bernardo Bertolucci, Ang Lee, David Mamet, Penelope Cruz, Cate Blanchett, Peter Brook, Harold Pinter, Laurie Anderson and Ousmane Sembène. (When Spike Lee presented *The 25th Hour* in 2003, he asked Silverstone and her team to find him a local pub where he and his friends could watch an Arsenal live game during the film's screening.) The centre's generous lobby also made it easy for audiences to hang around and continue discussions afterwards. 'What the Barbican does is invite discourse,' says filmmaker and producer Don Boyd. 'And discourse is what I feel the Barbican has always represented.'

Since the 1990s, Q&As and discussions have become ever more important as programmers, in competition with online platforms, emphasise the intimacy and communal aspects of the cinematic experience. Another opportunity to put on screenings that felt like events came about through Rider's passion for

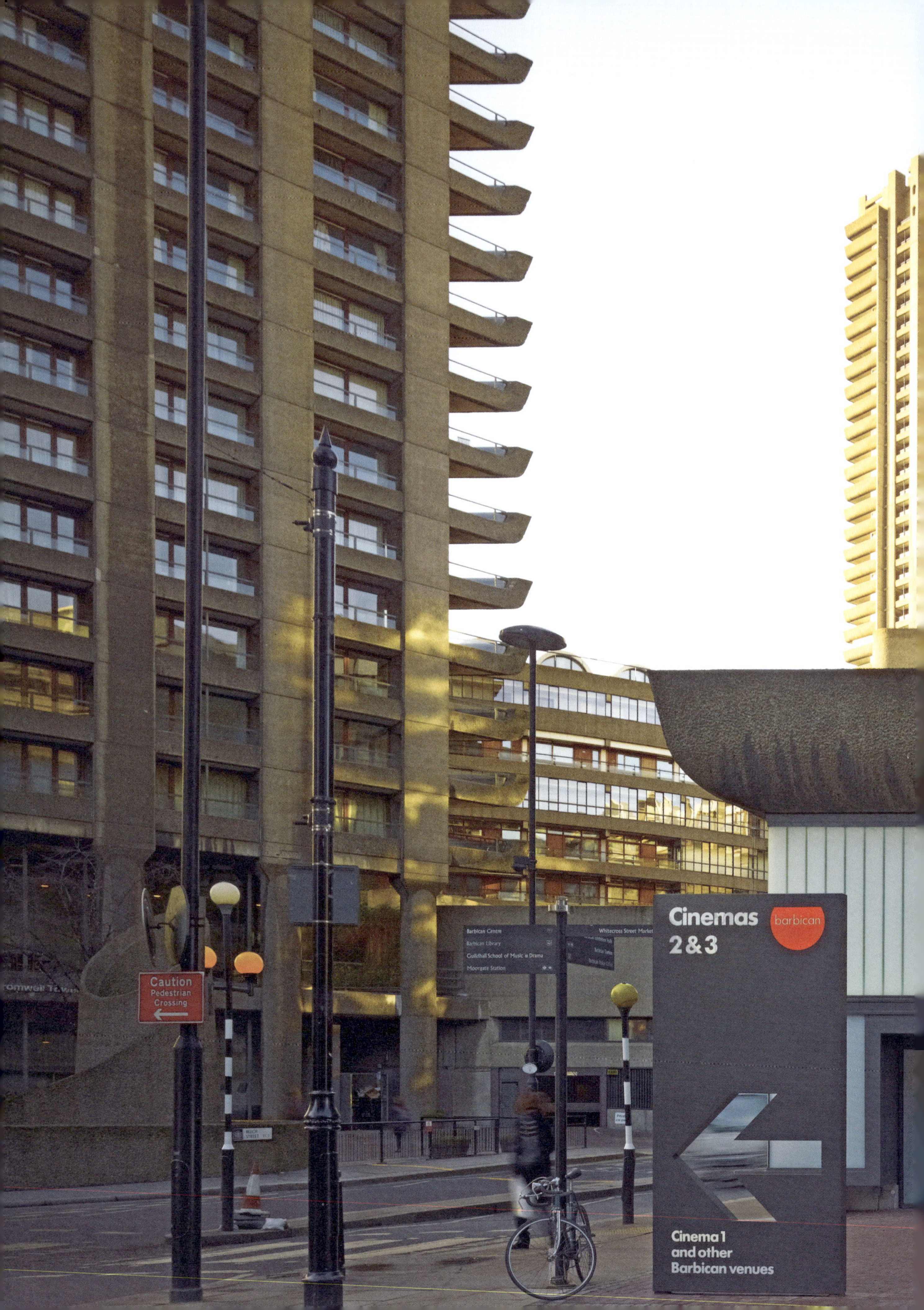
Caution
Pedestrian
Crossing
Barbican Centre
Barbican Library
Guildhall School of Music & Drama
Moorgate Station
Whitecross Street Market
Cinemas
2&3
barbican
Cinema 1
and other
Barbican venues

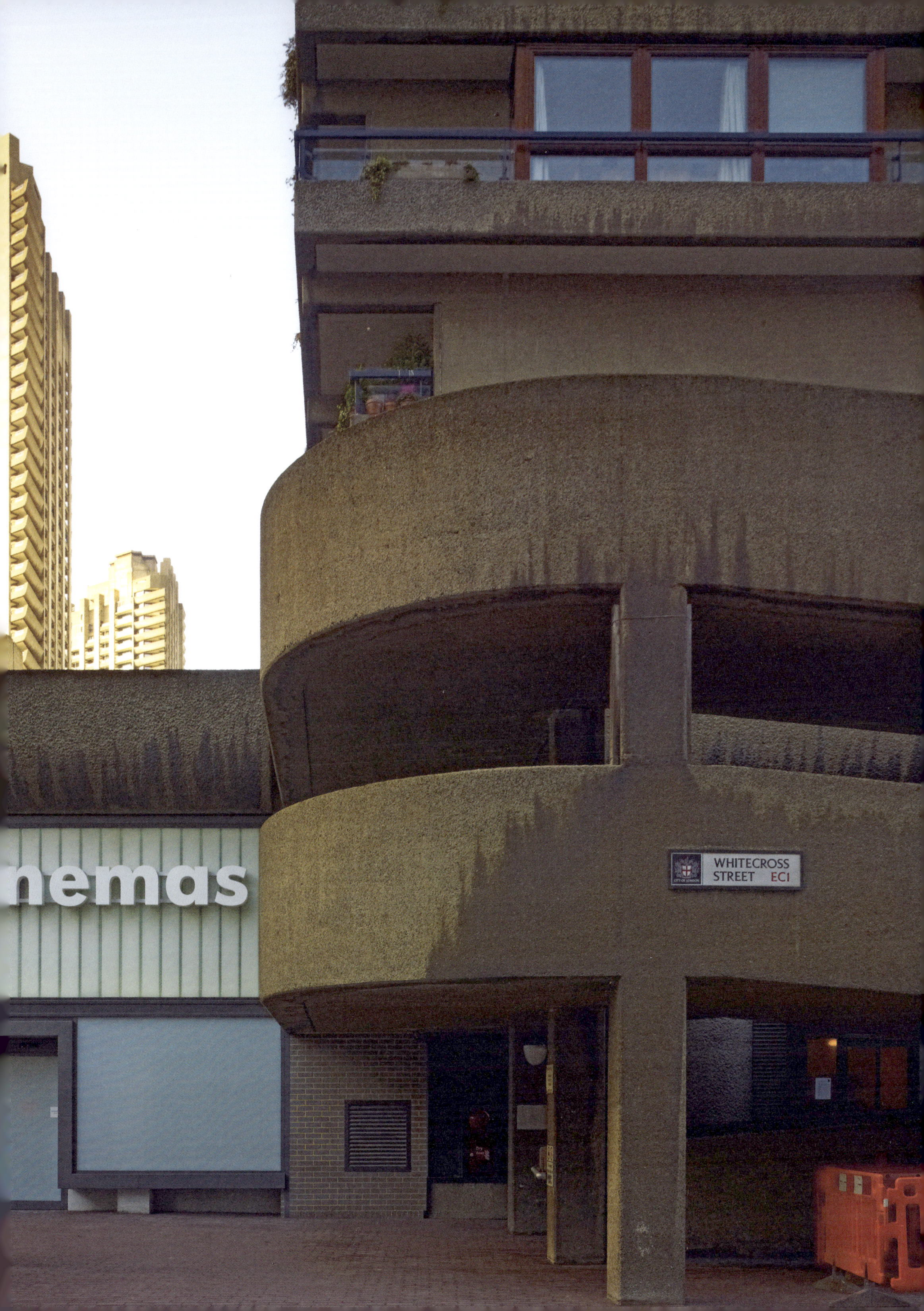
nemas
WHITECROSS
STREET EC1

pre-talkies. In 2003 he established a monthly Silent and Live Music series, in no small part because he wanted to champion 'a new group of silent film pianists – including Neil Brand, John Sweeney and Stephen Horne – that was coming to the fore'. Brand believes that Rider's commitment to silent cinema, evident even in his earliest programming at the Barbican, communicated itself to audiences. 'In my experience, venues only really push silent film when there's an influential personality. Robert would take risks, pay performers properly and take real care with the presentations. The Steinway grand piano alone would have cost serious money. Plus it's a lovely auditorium and a beautiful acoustic space. The Barbican took over from the National Film Theatre as the premier venue for silent cinema. He got terrifically good houses for pretty much everything he did.'

Rider was unusual in taking children's cinema seriously. In 1991 he staged a 26-film season, Through the Eyes of a Child, which featured not only classics such as Volker Schlondorff's *The Tin Drum* and Satyajit Ray's *Pather Panchali*, but lesser known works by Burkinabe director Idrissa Ouédraogo's *Yaaba* and Chinese-born Hou Xiaoxian's *Summer at Grandpa's*. In 2001, he organised a Studio Ghibli Art of Japanese Animation series which, two years before the release of Hiyao Miyazaki's breakthrough success *Spirited Away*, he remembers as being 'almost unknown to the West outside of animation circles'.

The Children's Cinema Club had been started in 1984, but, according to current curator Suzie Evans, it really came into its own under Rider. 'He revived the Saturday cinema club which had fallen out of fashion. It's unusual for a head of cinema to be so invested in children's programming but he loved it.' Evans herself has memories of seeing *Who Framed Roger Rabbit* and *Indiana Jones and the Last Crusade* at the Barbican – and of hanging around the centre with friends. 'We'd slide down the golden bannisters and get told off by the stewards. For us, the building was a wonderful labyrinth to get lost in.' Robert translated the grown-up programme into a version for children, she believes. 'Lots of research, very international, lots of activities surrounding the screenings. We became so popular we had to repeat screenings on Saturdays.' At one point it had 2,000 members. While the club's name was changed in 2001 to the Family Film Club, its idealism and ambition are still intact. It screens silent films ('there's something so special about that; young kids are just so spongy and open to everything'), films on celluloid ('I got the projectionist to come out into the auditorium and show the kids what a piece of film looks like'), and sees children's cinema as a crucial element in its efforts to expand community engagement.

Film-goers with a passion for mid-century British cinema were well-served in the 1990s with retrospectives on studios and production companies such as Ealing, Elstree and Pinewood. Space was also made for more left-field artists such as Derek Jarman and Powell & Pressburger. There were some raised eyebrows for Carry On Up the Barbican, a 30-film series in 1995 on the popular British series that the academic Andy Medhurst, writing in praise of them just three years earlier, had claimed were 'irreducibly vulgar, inescapably Not Art' and definitely not 'recuperable for proper culture'. A series on Hammer horror the following year also drew sizeable audiences during the traditionally quiet summer months. According to Helen Simmons, who worked in the film department from 1994 to 2011, 'These more populist cinema seasons caused

Previous pages
In the 2010s, underused spaces in the Barbican's Exhibition Halls in Beech Street were repurposed to create two new cinemas to replace those hidden in Frobisher Crescent. Cinemas 2 and 3 were opened in 2013 and have provided a welcome visibility on the street front for the Barbican's activities; they were updated in 2021.

quite a stir. Remember this was before nostalgia became culturally cool. In the 90s, the cinema was the wayward child of the centre, which was, let's face it, quite stuffy!'

Rider was hugely popular with colleagues who still talk about how he would chat at length with regular film-goers, attend lots of screenings to check their projections were optimal, and happily collaborate with other units within the Barbican to ensure his cinema team could contribute to programming planning. In 1998, the Barbican hosted *Inventing America*, a year-long festival devoted to a broad spectrum of American art. Initially there was no coverage of experimental film, but Rider was receptive to a proposal from Mark Webber, guitarist in the band Pulp, to address that void. His Underground America was the largest survey of US avant-garde film ever to be staged in the UK and presented rarely seen works by key figures such as Jonas Mekas, Harry Smith, the Kuchar brothers and Carolee Schneemann.

According to the curator, the response was rapturous apart from one notable star of the underground. 'Some months later I got a letter in the post from Kenneth Anger. It said: "Dear Mark Webber — How you could schedule a survey of Underground America and omit SCORPIO RISING is beyond me! A deliberate slap in the face perhaps? Both Marty Scorsese and Paul Schrader consider it THE MOST IMPORTANT American Underground film!!! I am beside myself with rage and anger."' This letter is one of my most treasured possessions.'

To complement the Barbican's Stockhausen season, Webber later curated Cinema Auricular: Cinema of the Ear, which explored connections between abstract film and early electronic music. The titles of individual programmes alone — Transcendent Power: Electronic Elevation and System Stimulation, Currents of Chaos: Electro-Shock Cinema, Ohm Taping: Tape Compositions & Musique Concrete — give a sense of their volatile originality. Over the next few years the Barbican was to become a significant venue for the cross-pollination of music and the moving image with live soundtracks being performed by the likes of Asian Dub Foundation (to *La Haine*, 2001), Saint Etienne (Paul Kelly's *What Have You Done Today Mervyn Day?*, 2005), and members of Godspeed You! Black Emperor and Fugazi (Jem Cohen's *We Have an Anchor*, 2014). Nitin Sawhney provided music for Hitchcock's 1927 silent film *The Lodger* in the main concert hall (p.131).

Barbican cinema was always busy, always ambitious. Apart from three days at Christmas it was programming three cinemas every day of the year. But that kind of productivity took its toll. 'There were occasional frustrations in negotiating and sharing inter-department staffing, such as technical support,' reflects Rider. In 2010 the opportunity arose to transform the under-used exhibition hall in Beech Street into two new cinemas to replace the hidden Cinemas 2 and 3. This was an ambitious project in line with the centre's desire to make more of its work visible, but like many such projects was delayed — it was meant to take one year, but dragged on for another two. 'It was a turbulent time. Some staff were laid off during the building works and some altogether. But the new cinemas proved to be a building triumph in the end, with an attractive layout, good accessibility and a visible street presence, which was the intention. We were also afforded from their launch, greater flexibility in our programming, keeping up with successful mainstream screenings alongside

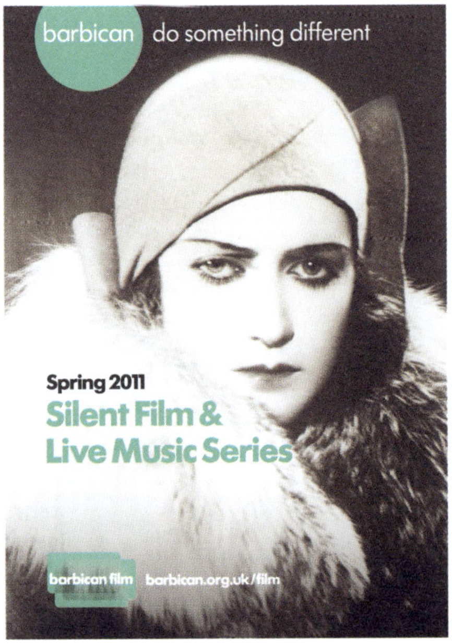
barbican
do something different
Spring 2011
Silent Film &
Live Music Series
barbican film
barbican.org.uk/film

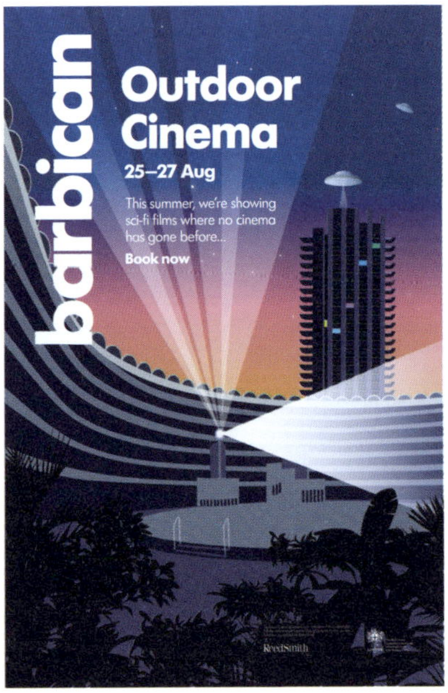
barbican
Outdoor
Cinema
25–27 Aug
This summer, we're showing
sci-fi films where no cinema
has gone before...
Book now

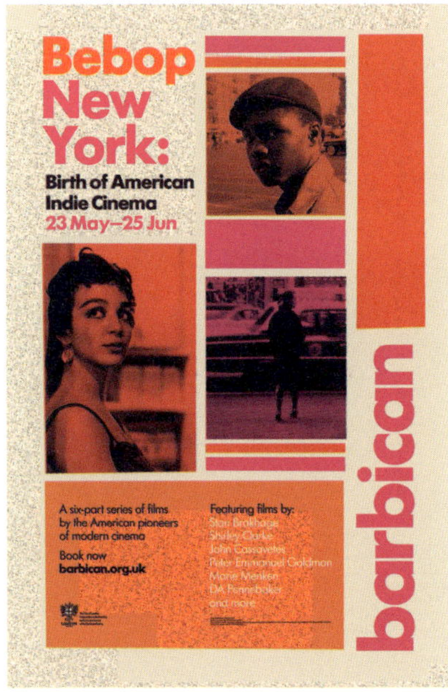
Bebop
New
York:
Birth of American
Indie Cinema
23 May–25 Jun
A six-part series of films
by the American pioneers
of modern cinema
Book now
barbican.org.uk
Featuring films by:
Stan Brakhage
Shirley Clarke
John Cassavetes
Peter Emmanuel Goldman
Marie Menken
DA Pennebaker
and more
barbican

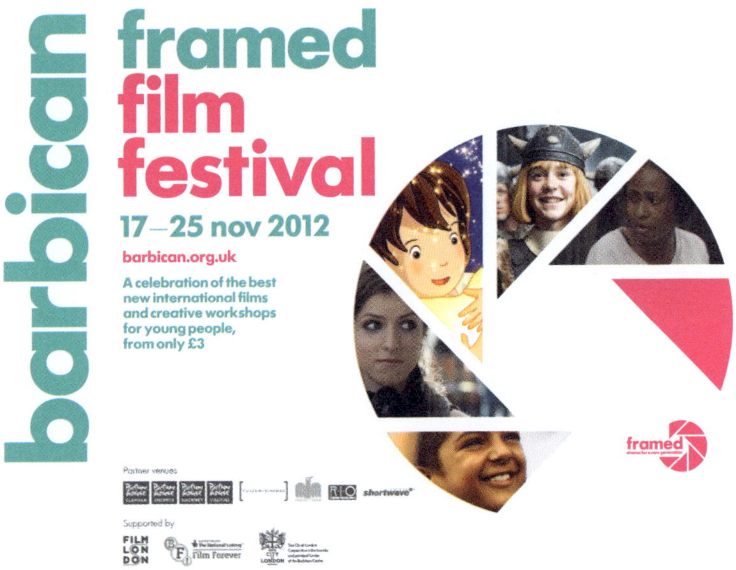
barbican
framed
film
festival
17–25 nov 2012
barbican.org.uk
A celebration of the best
new international films
and creative workshops
for young people,
from only £3
framed
Partner venues
Supported by
FILM
LON
DON
Film Forever

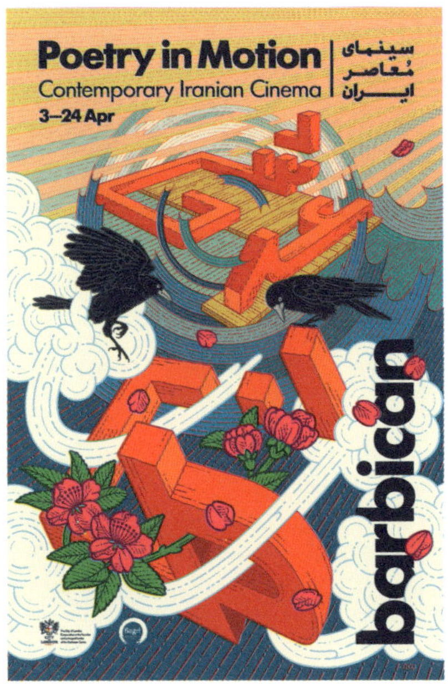
Poetry in Motion
Contemporary Iranian Cinema
3–24 Apr
سینمای
معاصر
ایران
barbican

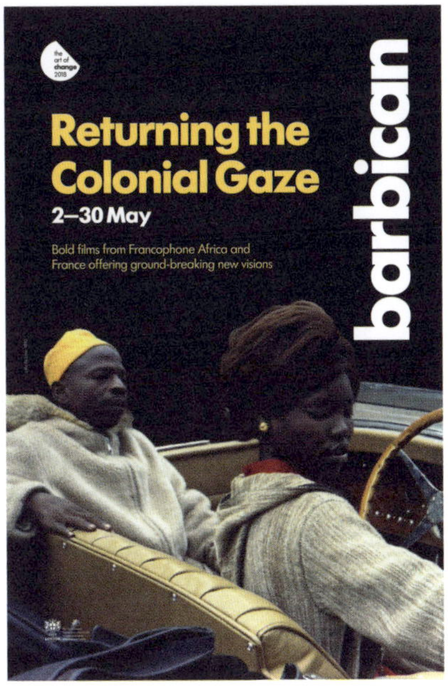

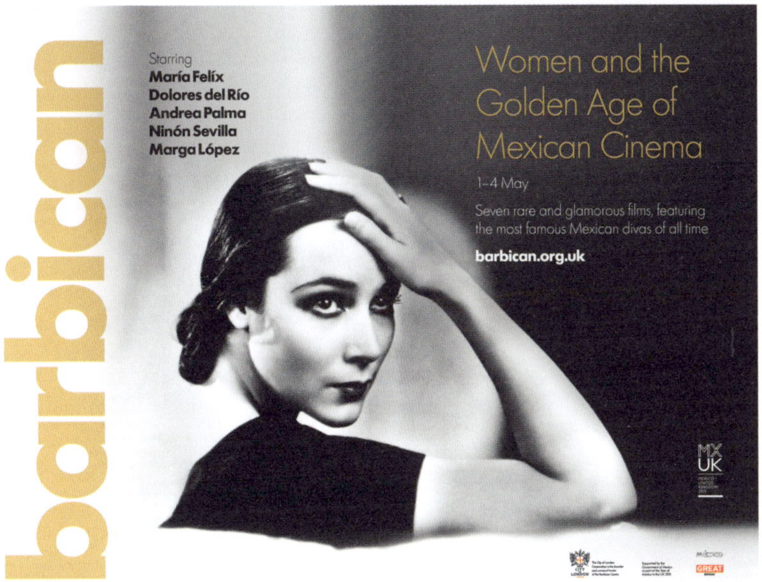

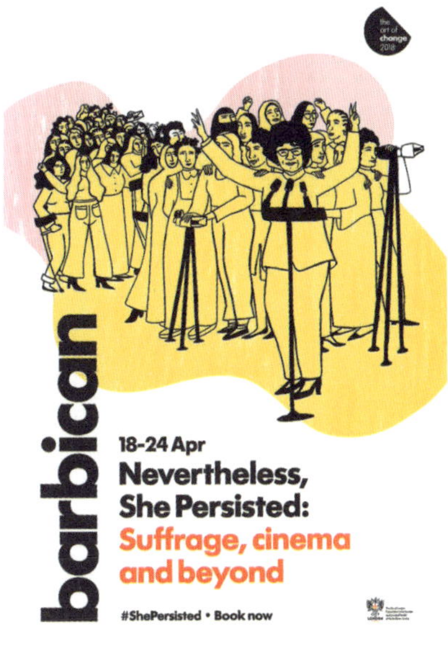

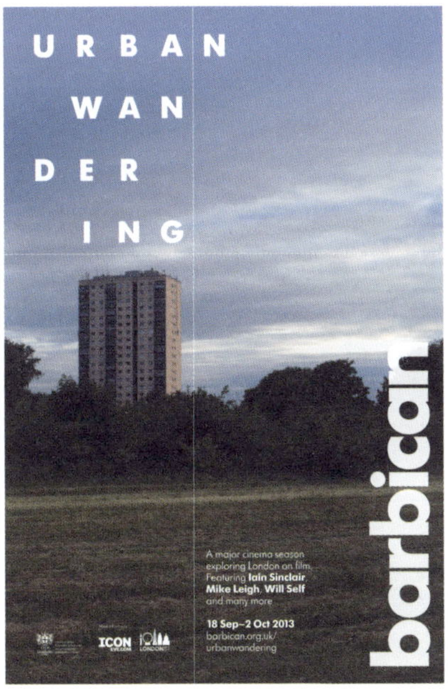

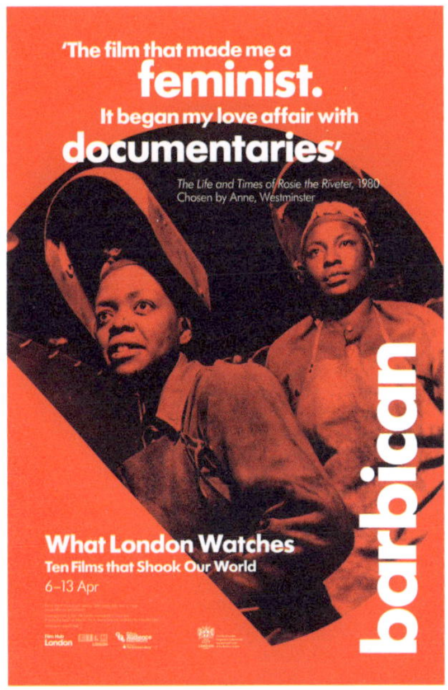

The look of cinema: posters and brochures illustrating the evolution of the Futura-dominated style to a freer concept in Women and the Golden Age of Mexican Cinema and then Urban Wandering.

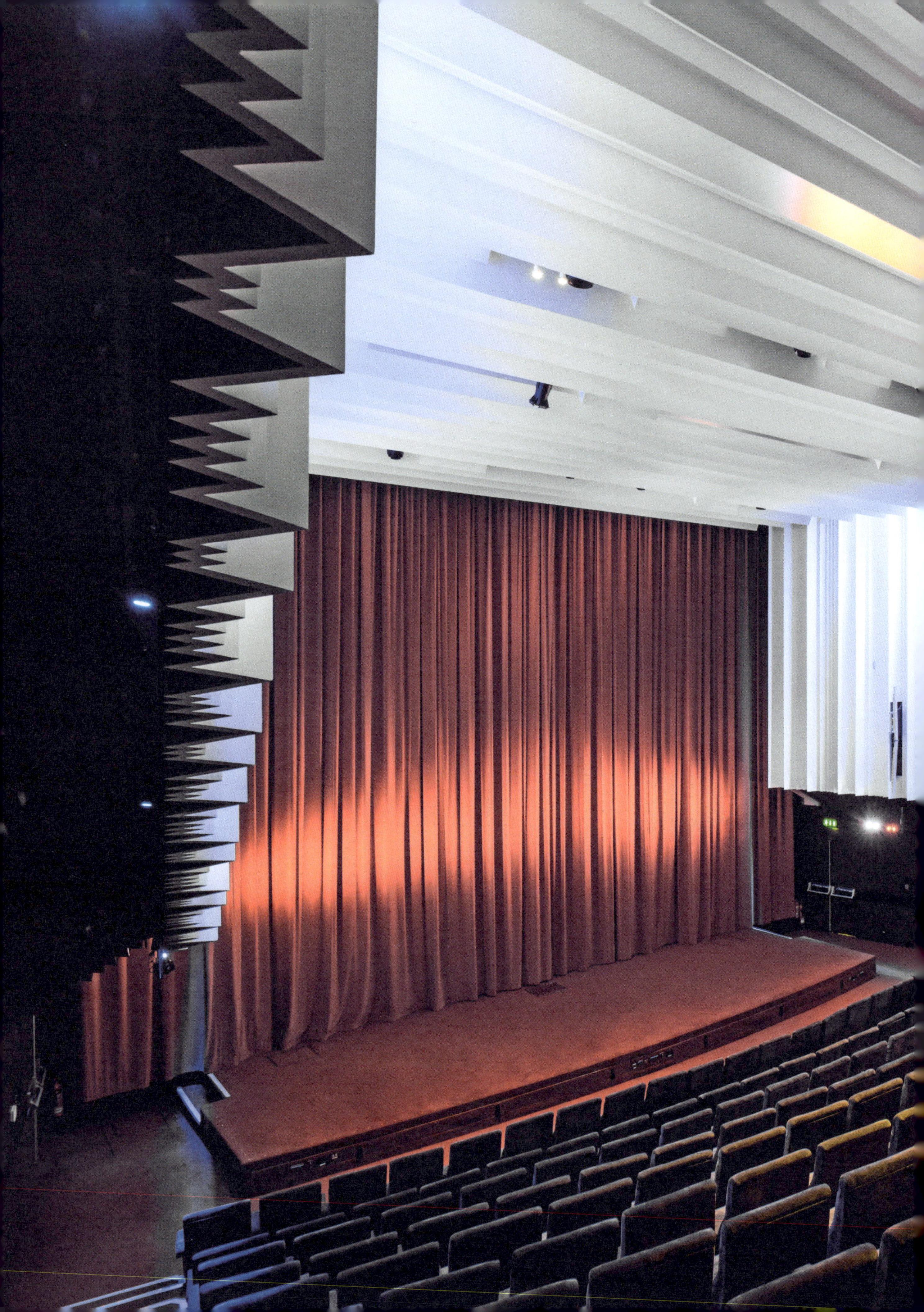

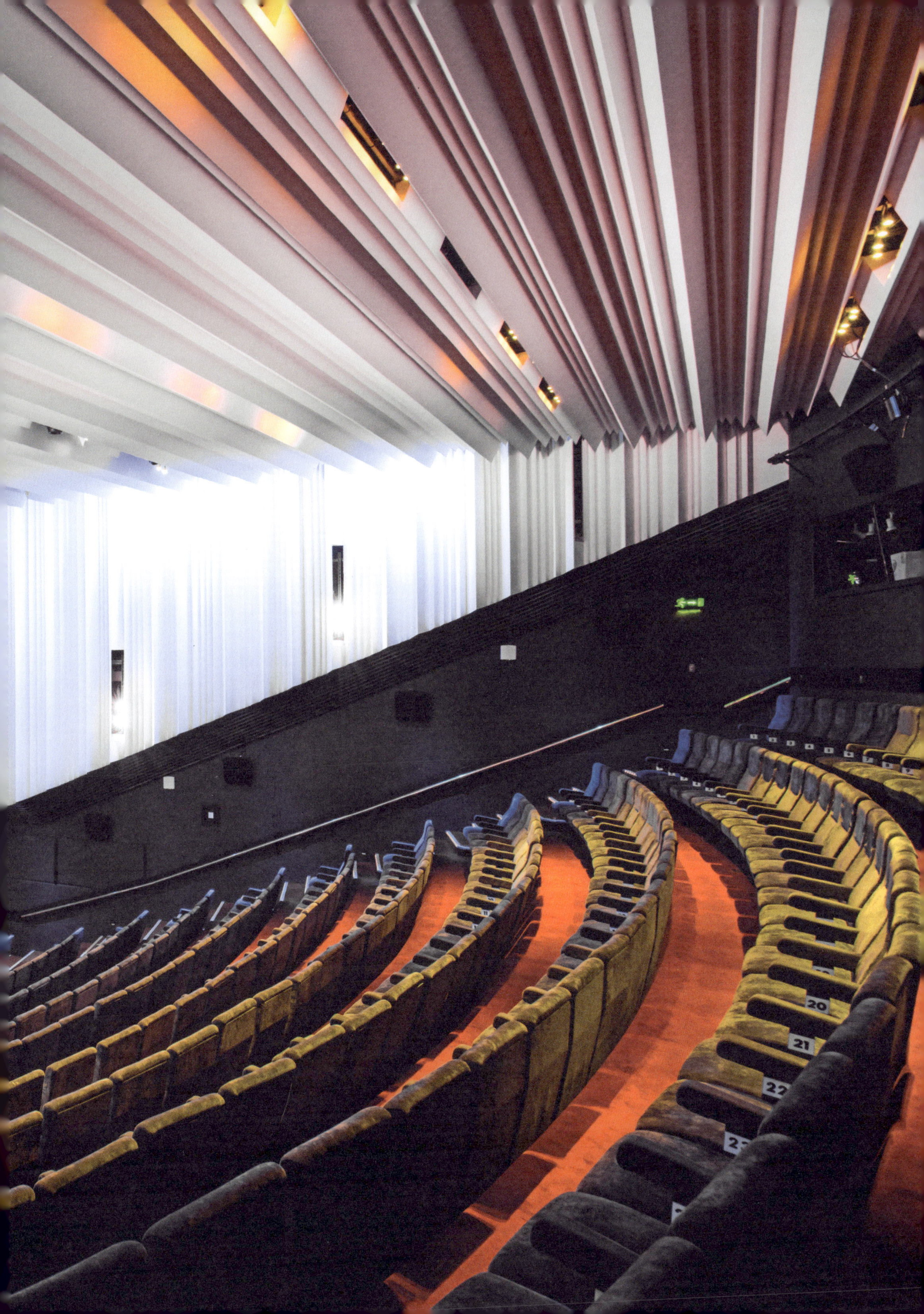

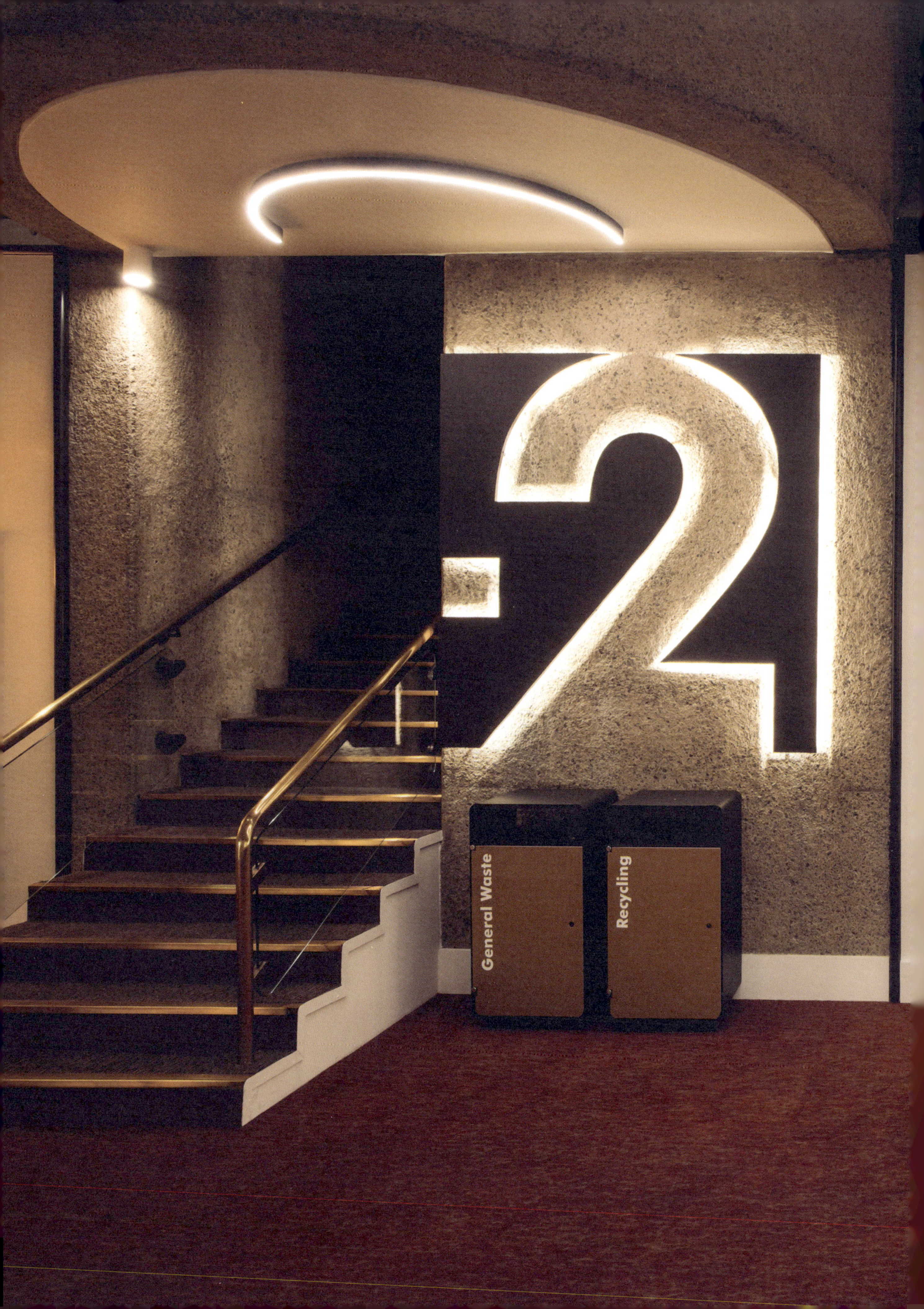
2
General Waste
Recycling

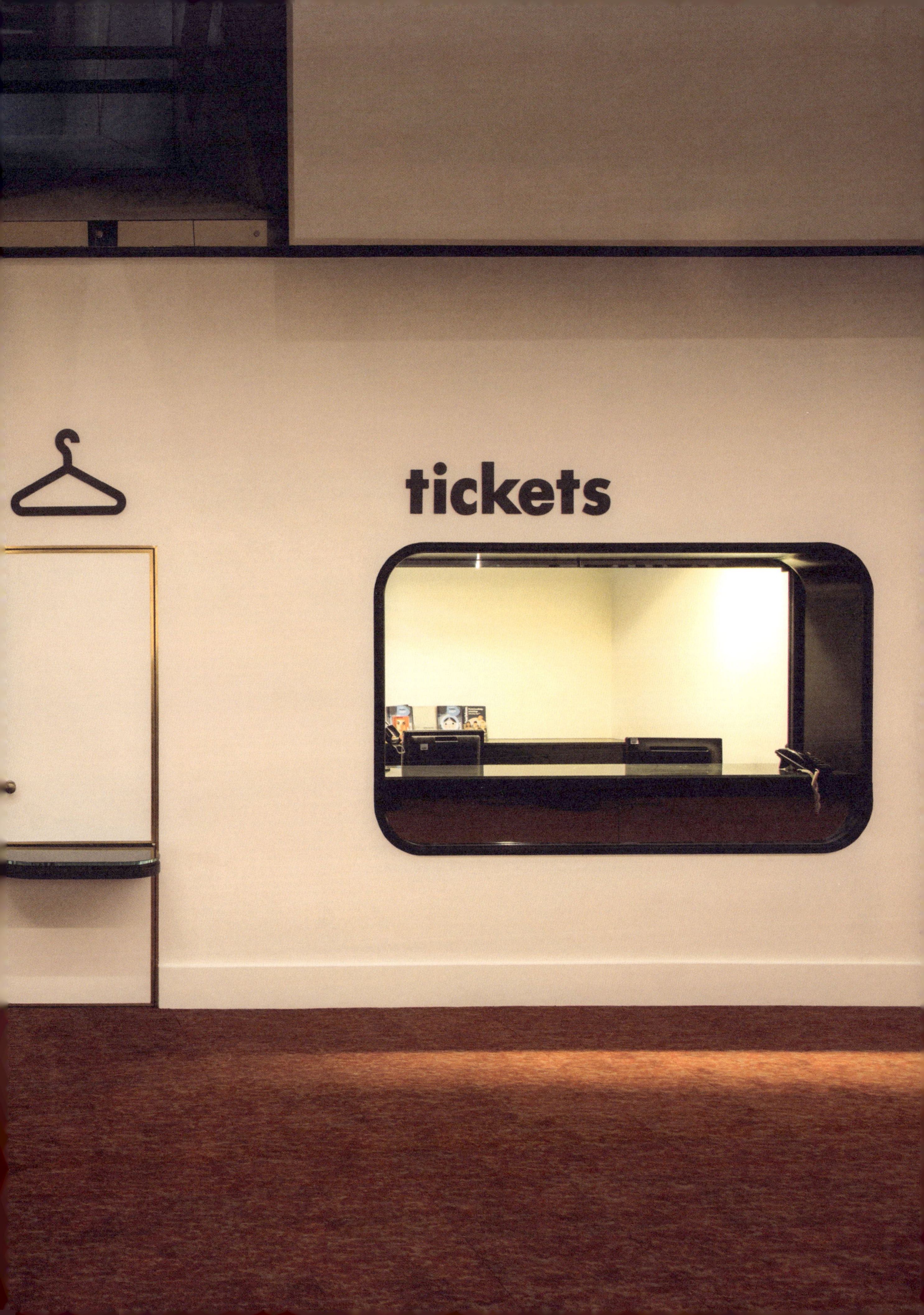
tickets

our more diverse programmes. Over my 29 years as head of cinema at the Barbican, I was driven by my two chief aims of raising and maintaining the profile of cinema alongside the other art forms, as well as bringing international and diverse films to UK audiences, alongside the mainstream.' In both, Rider succeeded handsomely.

Rider's successor as head of cinema, Gali Gold, initially came to London to do a PhD on female Israeli documentarians. She worked at the UK Jewish Film festival, taught at the University of East London, and joined the Barbican as a programmer in 2012. In March 2020, when she was less than two years into her job and the global Covid pandemic led to the closing down of the centre, the cinema had just marked its most successful year in terms of audience numbers and income. The ensuing months saw many international movie houses shut forever, films both major and independent migrate to online platforms, and a broad range of often agonised conversations about the role cinema might play in relation to the questions of social justice and racial diversity thrown up after the murder in the United States of George Floyd.

Gold believes in paying closer attention to the polyglot character of London. 'Coming as I did from a very segregated country you go around here on walks and the streets are not going to be segregated. There's mixture everywhere. You see diversity everywhere. I strongly believe that this has to be represented in the culture we put out — not just for the audiences who are enjoying it and engaging with it, but also in the statement it makes internationally.'

The cinema, as with other parts of the centre, has had to think more deeply and broadly than ever before in its history — the racial and class backgrounds of its curatorial staff, its relationship with audiences not just in EC2 but in East London, ways to enhance the visibility of under-represented groups. In summer 2020 an Emerging Film Curators' Lab was created to help train young people with limited experience or access to a gilded organisation such as the Barbican. Live events now have gender parity on stage. Programming increasingly engages with social and political themes. There is a growing focus on documentaries, on non-canonised directors, on a cinephilia that is as much about cultural critique as auteur reverence.

In the early days of the centre in the 1980s, there was a feeling that cinema was an afterthought at the Barbican and that its screening rooms were primarily there to be used for commercial conferences. That perception has been gradually dissipated with its success in attracting (along with the other art forms, especially the galleries) new and younger audiences to the centre, and in shaping the ecology of UK's arthouse cinema (as replicated by commercial operations such as Curzon). And with the attraction to passers-by of the new Cinemas 2 and 3 on Beech Street, the place of cinema in the Barbican's offer, so often invisible, was now significantly strengthened.

Now, entering its fifth decade, the Barbican is home to one of the few genuinely independent cinemas left in London. Cinema 1 is famed for the size of its screen, its excellent sightlines and sounds, its willingness to screen films on celluloid as well as digitally. It has scope to encourage more cross-disciplinary and cross-departmental projects, to use its magnificent buildings for outdoor- and site-specific screenings that feel like genuine events to which

Pages 248–251
Cinema 1 and the Cinema 1 foyer today. In 2021, during the closure of the building to the public, improvement works were undertaken to the Cinema 1 foyer on level -2, and Cinemas 2 and 3 in Beech Street, redesigning their spaces and bringing their visual styles closer together.

streaming-tempted audiences will want to travel, to be more ambitious and playful in the ways that it seeks to choreograph aura and affect. Says Gold: 'Ultimately we are about bringing people together in front of a big screen to experience what I think is one of the strongest kinds of experience you can have.' Cinema at Barbican can still represent a city within a city, another London, a locus of possibility.

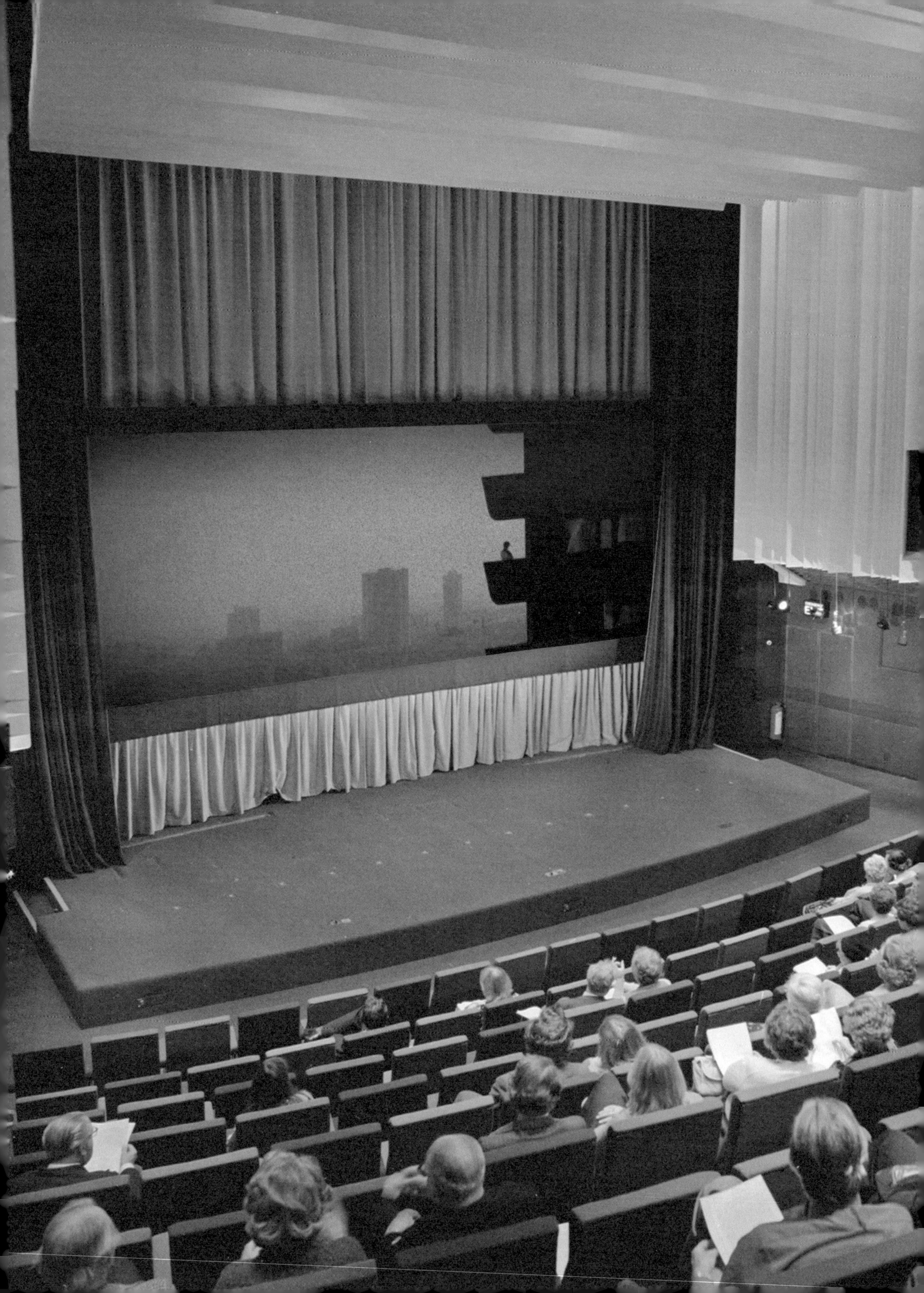

Barbican Filmography

This select filmography shows that the Barbican's story on film is, in part, a changing narrative of London's architecture on screen, captured within a single acre. It traces London's rebuild: from John Betjeman's portrait of the site as a vast post-war ruin in his 1959 Monitor episode 'A Poet in London', to the newly constructed and commercialised London Wall, which appeared in a variety of Swinging Sixties films including 1966's *Blow Up*, where David Hemmings drives his open-top Rolls-Royce down the new dual carriageway. It then signals the vilification of the high-rise in the 1980s, where Cromwell Tower offers a crepuscular retreat for Susan Sarandon in horror-noir *The Hunger* (pictured) and is the location for an police getaway in the eco-thriller *Edge of Darkness*. The reappraisal of brutalism in the 2000s saw the Barbican become a regular filming location, standing in for an Eastern European government centre with Judi Dench as M in the James Bond film *Quantum of Solace*, while the residents were profiled in their own documentary, *Barbicania*, in 2014.

Monitor, 'John Betjeman: A Poet in London', 1959
Barbican Regained, 1963
Blow-Up, 1966
Sebastian, 1968
The London Nobody Knows, 1969
The Rise and Rise of Michael Rimmer, 1970
McVicar, 1980
The Hunger, 1983
The Ploughman's Lunch, 1983
Edge of Darkness, 1985
Gangster No. 1, 2000
Rocknrolla, 2008
Quantum of Solace, 2008
Sherlock Holmes, 2009
The Day of the Triffids, 2009
I, Anna, 2012
Barbicania, 2014
The Barbican Mixtape, 2019

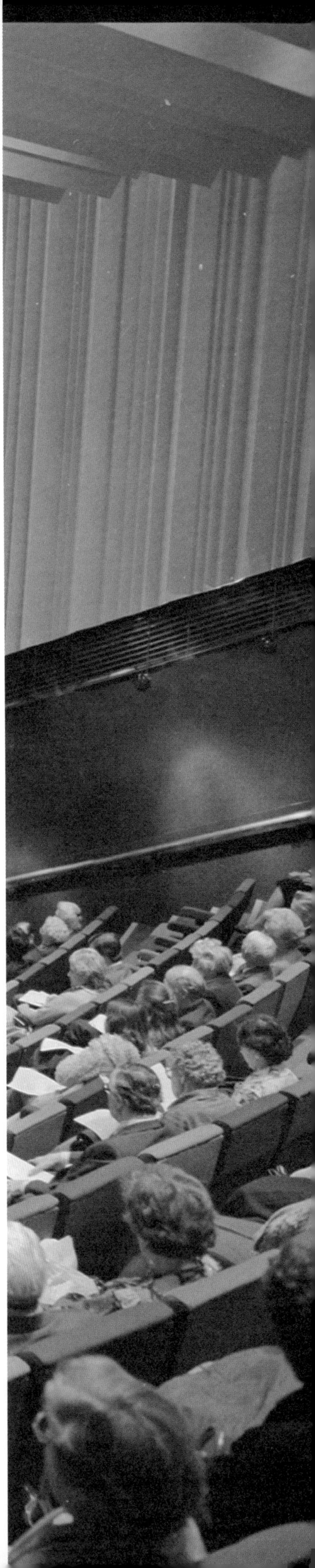

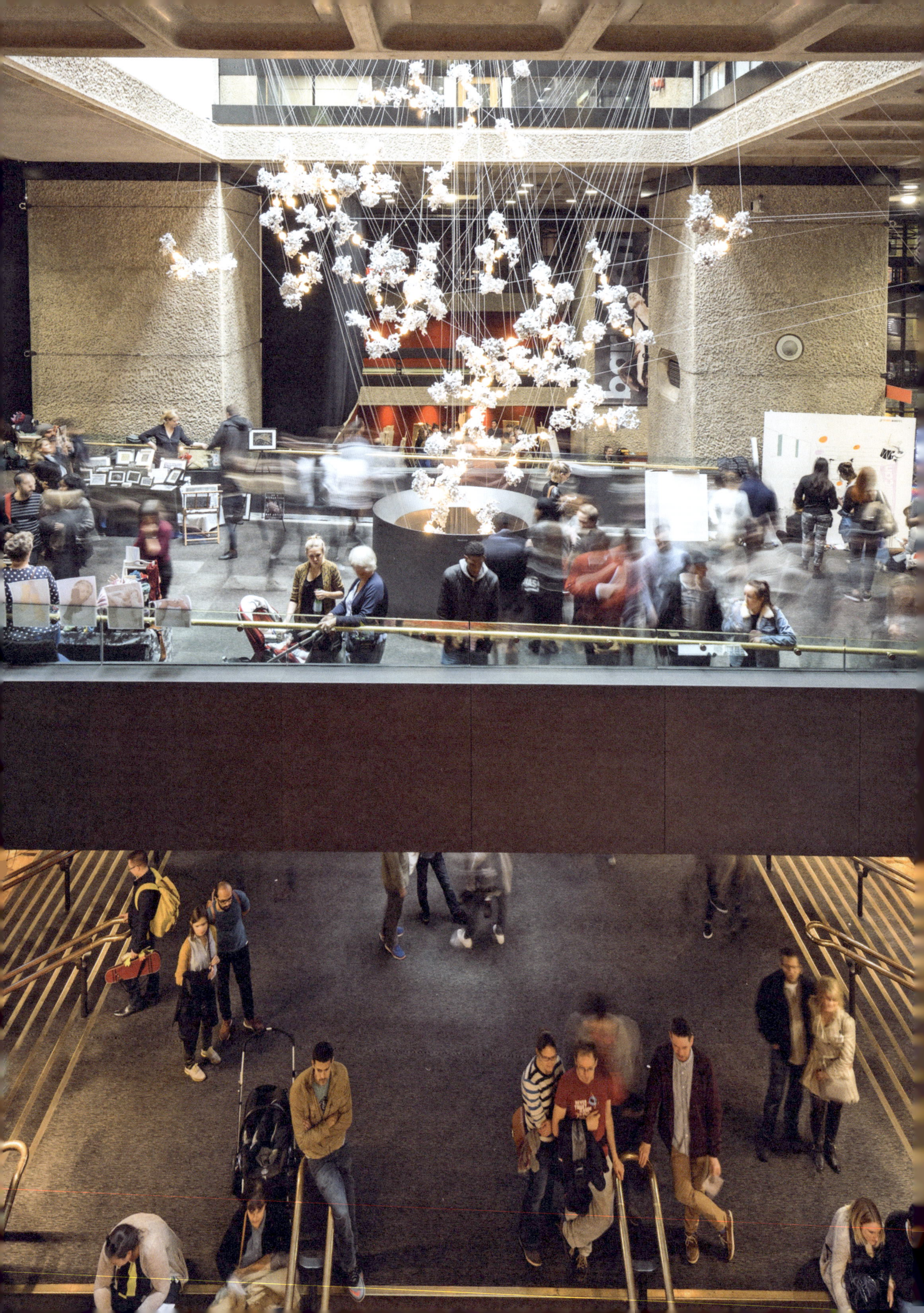

Running the Barbican 3
A conversation with Philip Dodd

Nicholas Kenyon, Louise Jeffreys and Sean Gregory

Succeeding John Tusa, Nicholas Kenyon arrived at the Barbican in October 2007. He had been director of the BBC Proms from 1996 to 2007, and controller of BBC Radio 3 from 1992–8. He left in September 2021. Louise Jeffreys was head of theatre during the years of John Tusa and Graham Sheffield; she became director of programming and then artistic director from 2010 until 2020. Sean Gregory came from the Guildhall School of Music and Drama as director of the newly formed joint Department of Creative Learning in 2009.

PD *Nick, you arrived at the Barbican at both an auspicious and a threatening moment: cuts in City funding were likely, the financial crash battered the West the year after you arrived, but the Olympics were already on the horizon. What was your priority?*

NK The one thing I really wanted to do — inheriting a really excellent arts programme as I did — was to turn the place outwards. That was why the relationship with East London, with the Olympics, was the way forward. I wanted to redefine the Barbican as not just a semi-detached part of the West End that was a bit difficult to find, but as the gateway to the east. We knew the Olympics were coming; and we knew it was a huge opportunity.

LJ Yes, the winning of the Olympics was one of the biggest game changers for us. There may have been a lot of cynicism around it, but I never for a moment felt cynical. It was shifting London to the east, and we were part of that.

PD *It changed your programme?*

LJ Totally. We had already been working in East London for several years and were ready to enhance and expand this work. We had presented a circus in Victoria Park, produced an immersive piece of theatre on Stratford Station and commissioned an installation for the Curve in Dalston. We had also begun to produce festivals which showcased international artists alongside local artists, the first was in Gillett Square, Hackney, and was gradually developed into a model which eventually led to the Walthamstow Garden Party.

NK Some of those pieces were so brilliant just because they were free from the constraints of the building we normally operated in. There we were in Stratford Station, sitting perched above the concourse, wearing headphones, trying to spot the actors in the melée below us. The city garden in Dalston — I remember one note pinned up from the audience: 'Why not move the Barbican here?' And the one that gave such pleasure to so many because it was so simple but so sophisticated was Leandro Erlich's Dalston House on a disused lot in Hackney, a house façade on the ground with a giant mirror, on which young and old could create gravity-defying illusions: a hit on Instagram!

PD *Did it shift the brand?*

NK I inherited a thriving institution whose mantra was 'Do something different'. That was very communicative for a particular period. It managed to articulate the distinctiveness of the Barbican brand really well. But we had to move to the next stage.

I think one of the huge successes over the succeeding years has been to expand outwards beyond the walls, by being genuinely inclusive, both reaching out and welcoming people in. There has always been the danger that the Barbican becomes a separate city, cut off from its surroundings, not really integrated with the community. One way to counter this was through the development of a Creative Learning programme.

My ambition was to move from being the world-class arts centre my predecessors had achieved, to being a world-class arts and learning centre — we expressed that in terms of inspiring people to engage with and love the arts, to innovate with outstanding artists and performers, and to create an international programme that crosses art forms. This was a shared ambition across the organisation, and was re-articulated as 'Arts without boundaries' — an important move.

SG At the risk of being over-semantic, but words are important here: we transformed what had been defined as education into what we called Creative Learning. We focused on that word 'learning' in creative terms. It's not done to you, it is an *active* activity, something that you do, and it's connected with what we are doing artistically.

I came from the Guildhall School and when I arrived at the Barbican we further developed the alliance with the School, which had begun with sharing finance and HR, with a new Barbican Guildhall Creative Learning division, which was the first outward-facing expression of our two organisations working together. This was a really exciting shift, both for me personally and in terms of the output, working across the art forms. This led to Creative Learning beginning to integrate itself with the Arts programme. With Louise and her team in 2012, we did a great performance in the main theatre (not in the foyers!) called *Unleashed*, created by young people about their experience of London, in partnership with a lot of Louise's associate companies. That was a landmark moment and catalysed a continuing, longer-term commitment to connected arts and learning.

LJ It absolutely proved that young people, with the right support, can create a work of the highest quality. The production values were the same as for everything else we did. We gave it the same respect and valued it in the same way. The support of our Associates, Boy Blue Entertainment, working alongside the international director, Walter Meierjohann, meant that the young people knew that we were taking them seriously. There was a standing ovation on every night — it is one of the productions I am proudest of — right up there with the international programme.

NK … and what was also important was the visibility of our commitment to that kind of work. As Sean says, when I arrived there was an education department. We moved beyond 'education' to something much broader and more integrated with the arts. And now there needs to be an even broader brief in terms of communities, inclusion, participation and engagement.

PD *Any regrets from your time, Louise, both before and during this period?*

LJ Looking back, I wish I had done more about the diversity of the programme when I was head of theatre. I made the mistake of believing that because we were producing an international programme it was inherently diverse, and that wasn't true. I programmed work by far too many white men, albeit fantastic and brilliant white men. The fact that this reflected what was happening at the time is no excuse.

During my time as artistic director, we worked hard to diversify the programme, we really focused on that and made a difference. However, we should have done more about diversity in the workplace too. That work still remains to be done.

PD *In the earlier interviews I have talked about the Barbican's internationalism. Were you filling a gap in the market or was this a matter of aesthetic, social and political imperatives?*

LJ There were other people presenting international work in London at the time — not least LIFT

(London International Festival of Theatre) and Dance Umbrella. But I think there was a gap in terms of seeing work of scale. We were able to bring work that others could not. Aesthetically, the work we presented tended to be director-led — in the European auteur tradition. This was a different style of production from much of what was seen in this country at the time. Towards the end of my time as head of theatre, I began to discover socially engaged projects that I thought were important to be seen and which I thought we could learn from.

NK It's important to stress that the international work has been about collaborations as well, learning from one another. I remember, Louise, your bringing Afro-Reggae here. The quality of the work and the leadership and the context that the Afro-Reggae project in Brazil resonated with our local ongoing work. It brought a whole new energy and quality which led to the establishment of DrumWorks and the way we approached some of our work in East London.

LJ Afro-Reggae changed me. I'd never met people who were more convinced about the social value of the arts. Their mantra was 'culture is our weapon' — they used art to bring about social change and they were successful.

When I went to Brazil to meet them, hosted by Paul Heritage of People's Palace Projects, there was a riot taking place so I couldn't see them perform. I spent the time when the gig was meant to be happening in a caravan with the band who somehow managed to persuade me to bring them to London sight unseen. When I got back home, I thought it was the most stupid thing I had ever done. Actually, it was the best thing I have ever done.

PD *Nick, how did you navigate initiatives such as Afro-Reggae with the Corporation? Were they happy?*

LJ They didn't know! But I don't think they would have found anything to object to. It was a high-quality project with a legacy that lives on today.

NK Well on the whole, the degree of artistic independence which John and Graham had negotiated — and indeed Henry Wrong had insisted on from the beginning — had become the tradition of the place, and it continued. As long as we were able to deliver something within a coherent narrative and within the financial resources we had available, we were reasonably free to do what we wanted. As Louise says, some of the really adventurous stuff that went on — which we knew would draw in audiences — wasn't closely scrutinised by the Corporation.

However, that's half the story. The other half is that that freedom had to be earned through trust. It is true that when I arrived there was a perception in the City that what the Barbican was doing was becoming more and more separate. Not quite that it had declared UDI, but that was the underlying fear. That was something which together we tried to repair over the years and show what the Barbican was doing actually matched the agenda of the City. Now we can demonstrate in detail how what the Barbican brings to the City Corporation in terms of its aims and objectives both mesh completely with what the City wants to achieve, and equally brings something totally distinctive of international reputation and importance; that is valued.

LJ In the early days, we would simply present our programme to the Board and they would respond personally — they would tell us what they liked and what they didn't like. Not the most useful of discussions!

More recently, and gradually, what's happened is that we have got better at expressing our strategic purpose and agreeing objectives with the Board. We explain our programme choices as a response to that strategic plan and we have also learned to be more reflective and self-critical.

SG For example, if you go back to the earliest days of the Barbican, and to the vision behind it, there were strong beliefs around civic urbanism and utopian visions of the wider community: we really wanted to connect that back into the thinking of the Board and of the City's members. I really think that is now understood, but it has taken some time!

PD *Clearly the Barbican / Corporation relationship is an interesting part of the centre's history, in all kinds of ways. But I think it illuminates a bigger issue — the relationship and conflict between commerce and culture which runs through European history for the last 200 years and more. It was an old lefty, Manny Farber, who once said that Hollywood was the biggest experiment in history, testing the relationship between art and big business. Clearly the Barbican is not on that scale. But in Britain, where most arts centres and museums are funded by public bodies — whether the State or the Arts Council — the Barbican is a fascinating test case of whether art and big business can understand one another.*

The Barbican has Barbican International Enterprises, the commercial arm of your visual arts programme. How does this sit in the Barbican brand?

NK It was since its inception a very clear part of the organisation's commercial activities and had a primary mandate to earn money for the Barbican. There was always an issue with it: as its exhibitions tour internationally, do they match our brand and our values? That it generated income meant that the gallery itself could have more freedom for its more purely artistic aspirations. However we're now clear that the two should work together more closely, and BIE is coming into our Arts division.

PD *Oddly enough, my view is that certain of the Enterprise's exhibitions such as the recent AI exhibition are more interesting and more risky than some in the gallery.*

NK That's interesting but unfair. Both have naturally had their share of great successes and shows that haven't quite worked, but when you think of how the gallery's path-breaking Basquiat show completely transformed our audience in that period, and the really quite edgy and commercially oriented things the gallery has done, Jean Paul Gaultier for instance, and how it now partners and earns income from its work abroad, the picture is much more overlapping. And we are now bringing together the two organisationally, so any dissonance can be resolved.

LJ We shouldn't be embarrassed about the 'commercial offerings' — they are a vital part of everything the centre does. But the gallery has increasingly been earning income too through sharing its shows abroad. I remember the interesting internal debate that happened when we staged the James Bond exhibition in 2012. My only concern is that we should do it well — if we did, I was fine about it.

NK In that Olympics year, we did James Bond and we did Bauhaus. BIE did Bond and the gallery did Bauhaus. Both great shows. And, perhaps oddly, they sat perfectly well next to each other in the centre, creating an incredibly lively atmosphere across the spaces — while there was *Einstein on the Beach* in the theatre and Wynton Marsalis with Simon Rattle in the concert hall: an unforgettable mix!

LJ Exactly. All sold out. Lots of people decided to see both exhibitions. I remember bringing *Les Misérables* back to the theatre — the first commercial musical we brought into the programme — and why not, it was hugely successful; it had premiered at the Barbican; it was associated with the RSC; and the rental income contributed to making the season balance financially. In the same way, other high-quality musicals have continued to underwrite our more adventurous work. It's now an established part of our business model.

PD *As the artistic programme evolved during this period, I sense you bringing more joined-up coherence through the use of some annual themes, and also trying to bring some of the spirit of the work beyond the walls back into the foyers and spaces of the centre?*

LJ When I became artistic director I moved from being a programmer to being a convenor. It was a great privilege to work with such a talented team across so many disciplines and I want us to learn from each other and collaborate more closely — to make real sense of the arts centre context. So, we worked on annual themes such as The Art of Change and Life Rewired — they provided coherence to the programme and enabled us to engage with urgent contemporary issues. We also began to commission new work for the foyers and expand our offsite offer because it helped us to support more new and emerging artists, and connect with different audiences.

PD *Can we turn finally to the future before I ask Nick to say something about how Covid will change the Barbican. In the interview with John Tusa and Graham Sheffield, Graham mentioned that he thought technology such as VR and more generally immersive experiences will transform the Barbican over the next ten years — where the actor is as much the viewer as the performer.*

LJ I may be incredibly naïve but I think there will still be desire for the live and the real. It's a cliché but when football was first put on television, everyone said it will kill the live experience of the game. In fact, the live audience increased.

NK The same applied in a previous generation to putting concerts on the radio! The latest technology must drive our development of live arts. We must get our work out there as much as we can, but Graham's right that it may transform what we do in here as well.

SG I don't think it's either/or. I think it's both. A key part of the next iteration of the strategy is about the environment we want to create in and immediately around the Barbican as well as our relationship with communities: an increasingly blended, sophisticated approach to live and on-line audience/user experience of the Barbican that is enabling us to do both.

NK Another comment from a different angle. I think from the moment I arrived here, we talked about participation, the whole Creative Learning push has been towards participation. We are not, except in some areas of the programme, quite as far as we might be with what can be called co-creation, but the ambition that everyone can have a sense of ownership about work created here is still there — and that can be done in all sorts of different ways.

PD *Nick, in certain ways, the Covid virus, on a worst-case scenario, may challenge or oblige arts institutions to reinvent themselves. Grayson Perry said it might prompt the arts world to dispense with some dead wood. If repentance is unlike innocence, and there is no way back to pre-Covid days, how does the Barbican live in a post-Covid world? Financially, artistically and socially?*

NK Well, first we should be clear that we are talking at a time when the virus is still with us and indeed we have had closures of the centre during 2020 and into 2021, restrictions which have been very painful and disappointing for everyone, and very damaging for our talent and artists. Second, I do not think reinventing ourselves is in any sense a worst-case scenario as you describe it, it's an opportunity to move things on: as we've seen during the pandemic, some things that might have taken an age to achieve in normal times have been achieved overnight against an imperative. So yes, we will adapt positively: improving our climate regime, less international travel, for example, an increased emphasis on working with our local communities, a much more radical and engaged approach to equality and inclusion — and you haven't even mentioned Brexit … By the time anyone reads this we will have recreated our very strategic plan for the new times, and it will be for my successor to take us forward into the next 40 years!

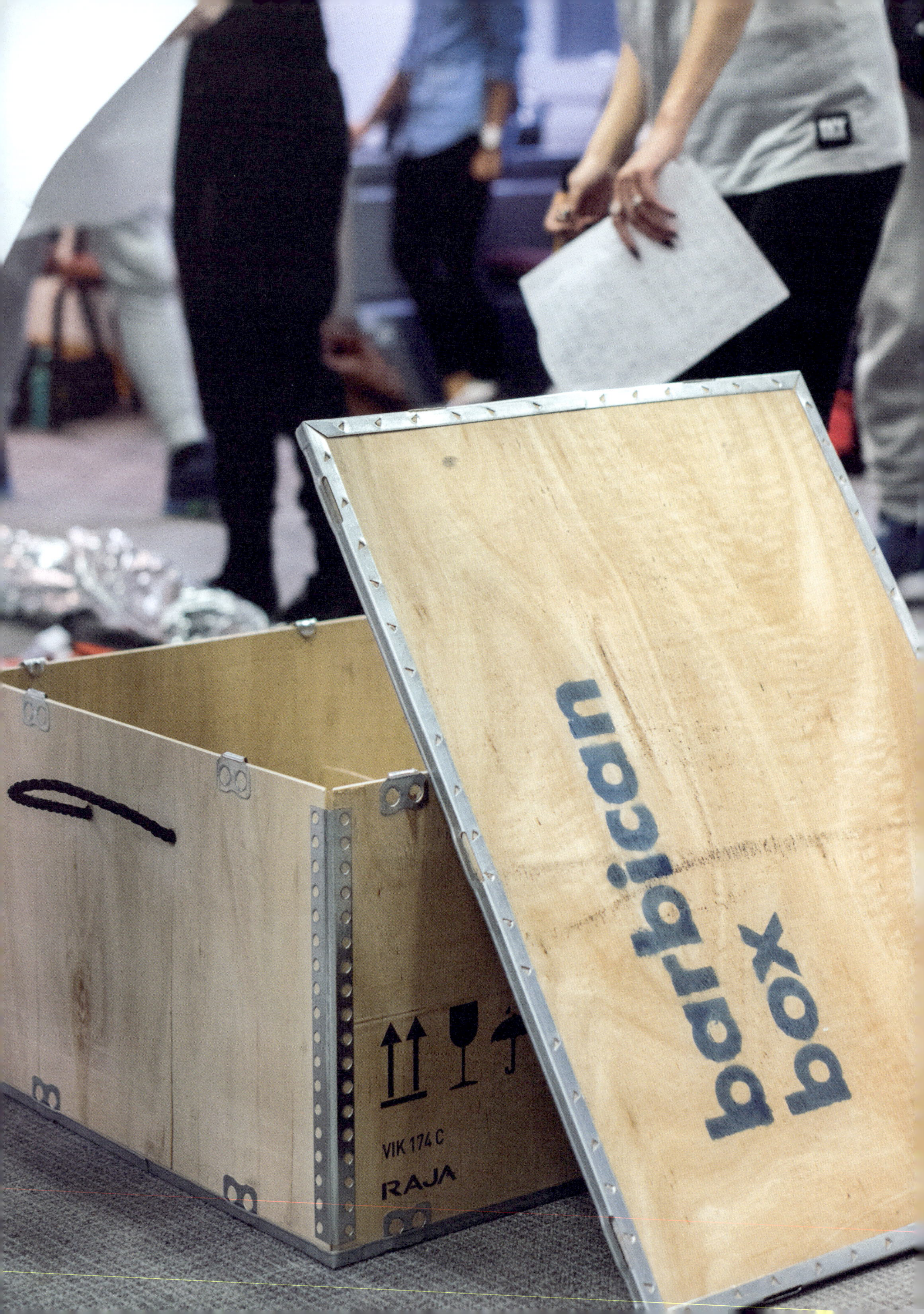
barbican
box
VIK 174 C
RAJA

Jenny Mollica

In 2019 Barbican Guildhall Creative Learning celebrated its own anniversary – ten years of supporting people of all ages and backgrounds to access and engage with the arts. Ten years of delivering its mission, Creative Skills for Life, with over 100,000 people. And this mission continues to thrive and flourish today, with Creative Learning working with partners locally, nationally and internationally across the three core pillars of its programme: Education, Employability and Enrichment.

I vividly recall the inception of Creative Learning in 2009 as a unique moment in time, heralding the beginning of an outward-facing 'creative alliance' between an arts centre and a conservatoire, pioneering new approaches to creative and cultural learning across film, music, theatre, dance, visual arts and poetry. From my time at the Barbican and Guildhall School, I remain particularly proud of a flagship schools programme that emerged early on in the life of Creative Learning, Barbican Box. To this day, Barbican Box continues to represent the depth and richness of Creative Learning's wider story: a dynamic arts and learning process that aims to provide a catalyst for young people's creativity, supporting and empowering students to create original creative work inspired by the Barbican's programme. Launched in September 2011 in 12 secondary schools across Hackney, the first Barbican Box was developed with the theatre company Told by an Idiot. The programme has been a trailblazer ever since: we launched the Visual Art Box in 2012, the Music Box in 2014, and in 2016 we were proud to both expand the programme nationally, and to develop a new version for primary schools.

More recently we have been able to develop a network of partners across England who collaborate with us on Barbican Box. A total of 6,300 students have taken part in a Barbican Box project to date, and that number continues to grow year on year. It's not about numbers, though, it's about organic engagement that gives young people the opportunity to unlock their creativity. At its heart, Barbican Box aims to leave a positive, sustainable legacy of arts-based learning in the classroom. This is underpinned by continuing professional development sessions for teachers, which focus on the development of their skills to ensure the Box has a lasting impact. Some of the extraordinary artistic partners involved so far include: Åbäke, Bellatrix curated by Serious, Complicité, Holly Casio, Hunt and Darton, Internationaal Theater Amsterdam, Laura Braun, Marcus du Sautoy, Max Richter, Michael Rosen, Native Instruments, One of My Kind, Sam Mumford, Slung Low, Soweto Kinch curated by Serious, and Tamasha Theatre Company.

Jenny Mollica was theatre and cross-arts producer, head and then director of creative learning from 2008 to 2020; she is now director of the Baylis Programme at English National Opera.

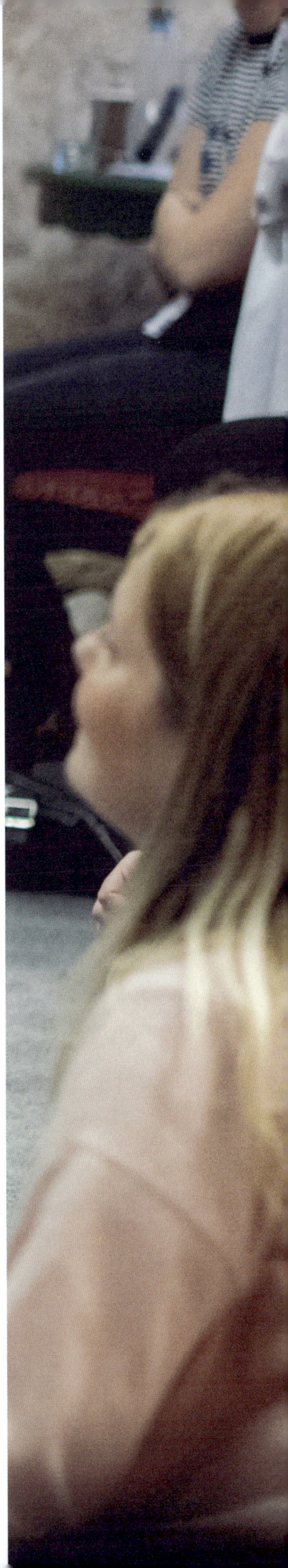

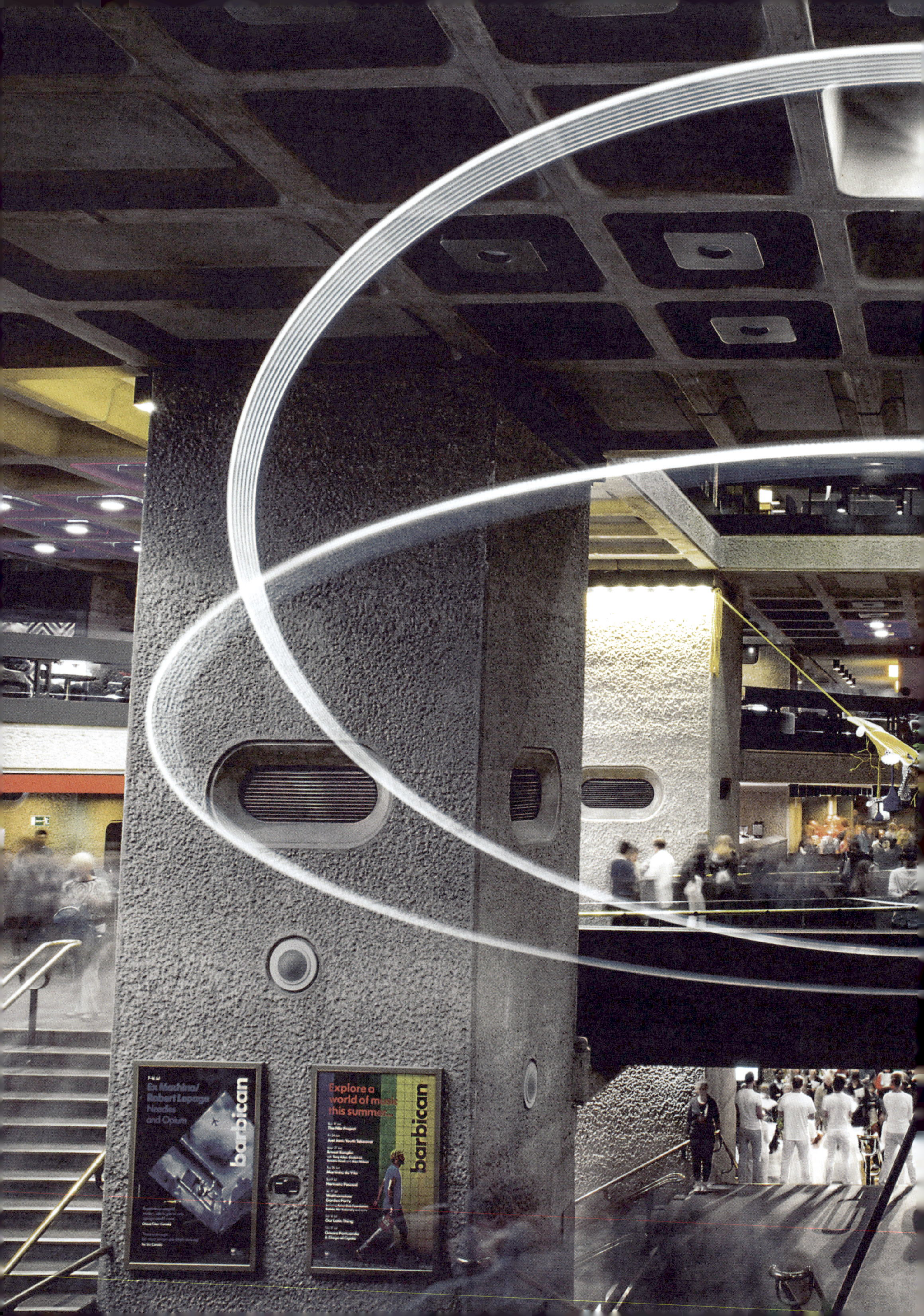
Ex Machina/
Robert Lepage
Needles
and Opium
barbican
Explore a
world of music
this summer...
barbican

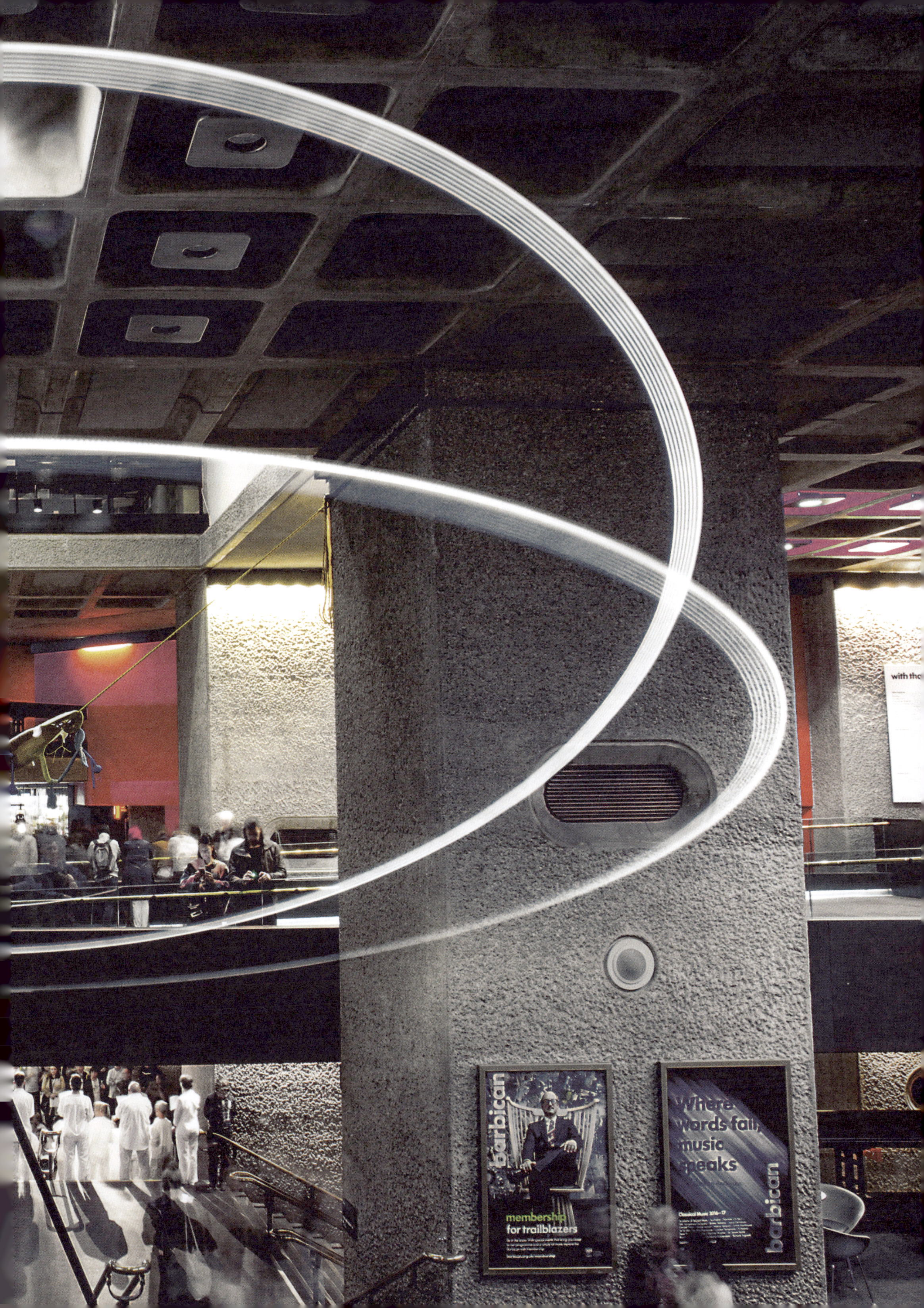
barbican
membership
for trailblazers
Where
words fail,
music
speaks
Classical Music 2016–17
barbican

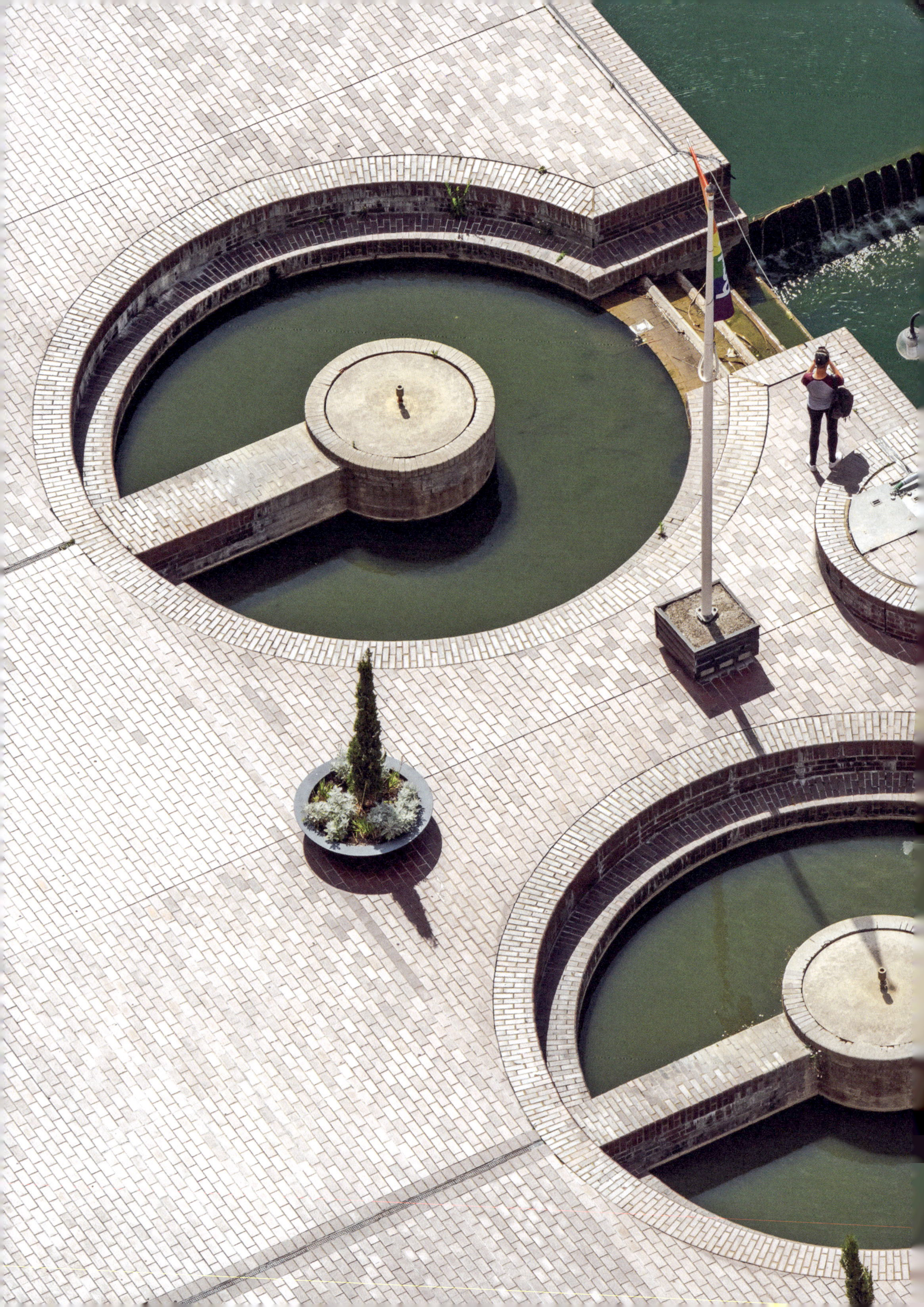

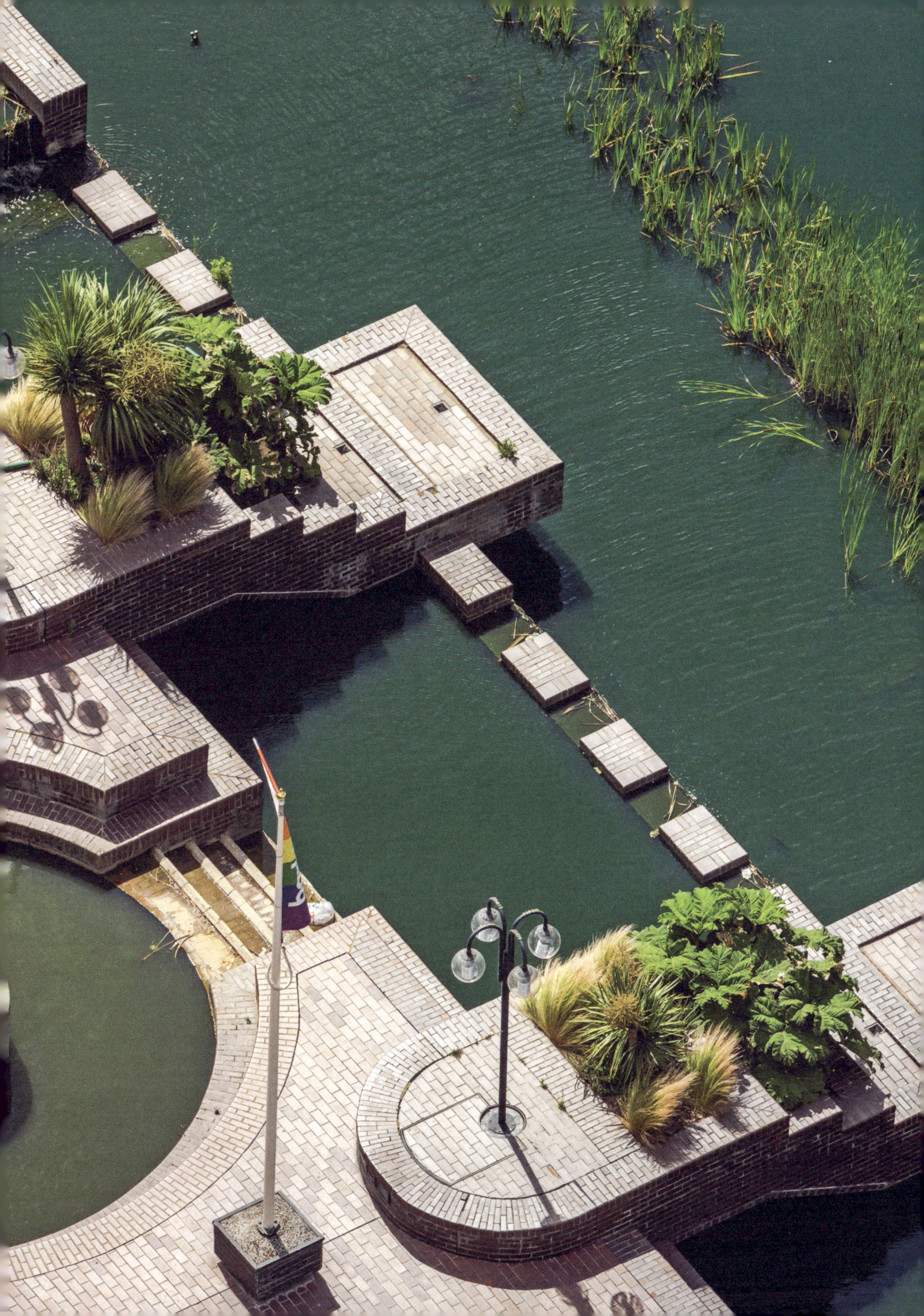

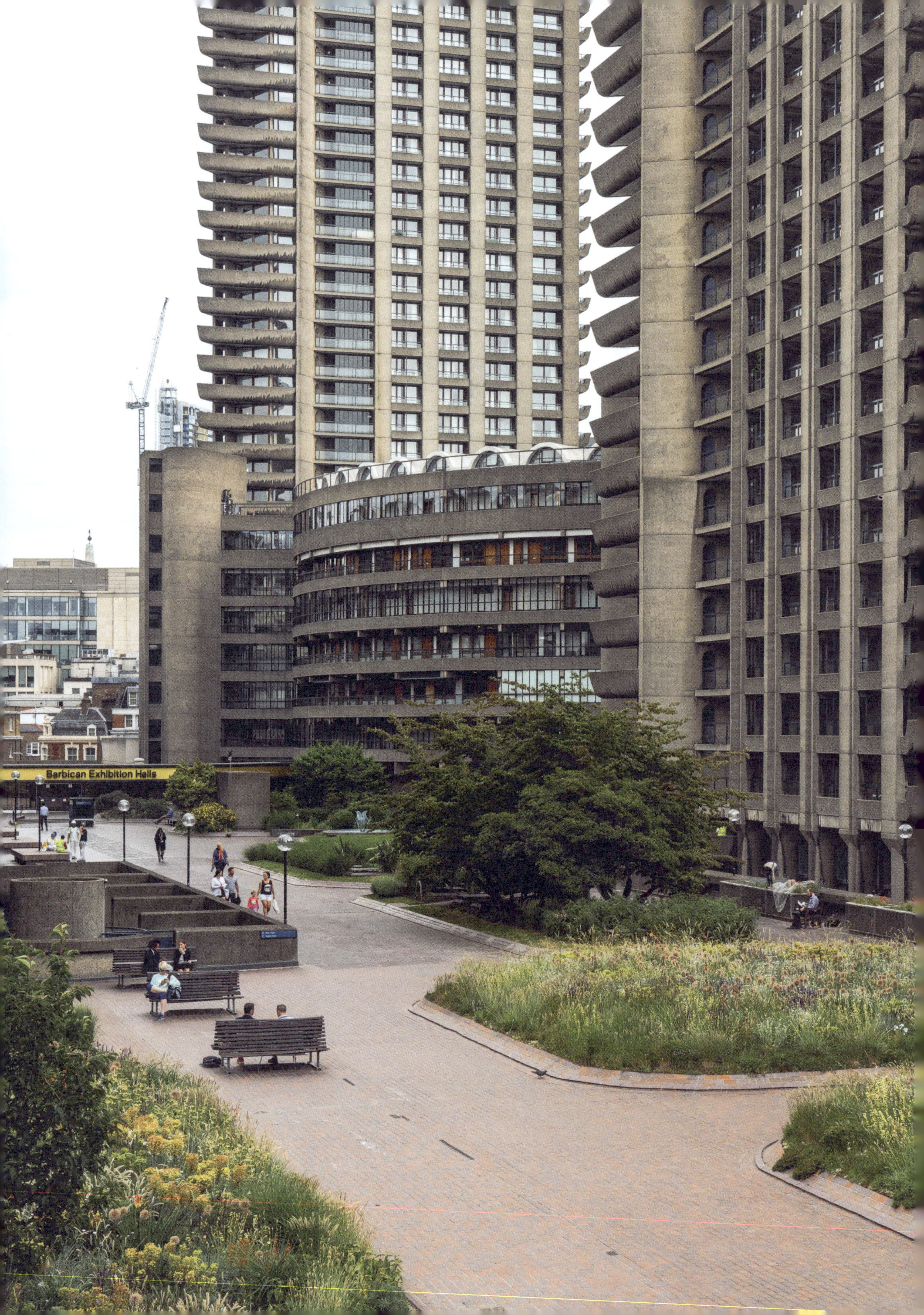
Barbican Exhibition Halls

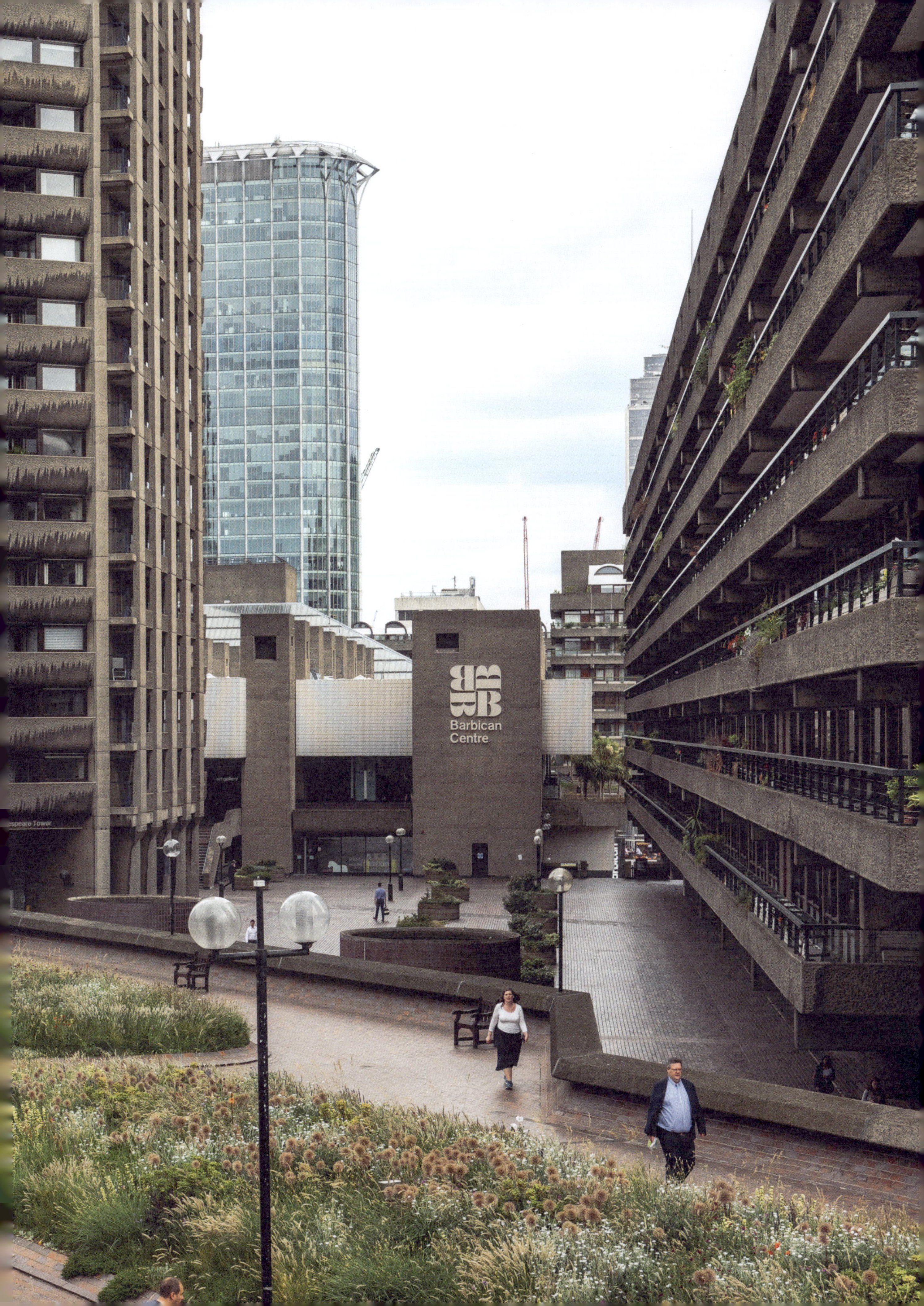
Barbican
Centre

Chronology

1982

Opening event in Hall and Theatre, LSO/Claudio Abbado, RSC

Aftermath: France, 1945–54 — New Images of Man, Gallery

Barbican Library opens, 1 April

Max Ophul's *La Ronde*, first film in Cinema

RSC: *Henry IV Parts I and II*, dir. Trevor Nunn, Theatre

Eric Sykes and Friends, Hall

LSO: William Walton 80th birthday concert, Hall

RSC: Peter Flannery *Our Friends in the North*, dir. John Caird, Pit

Nina Simone, Hall

Contemporary Canadian Tapestries, Concourse

Aditi: Indian visual culture and dance, Gallery

Abel Gance's *Napoleon* with live orchestra, Hall

Basil Brush stage show, Hall

Tippett-Berlioz festival, LSO/Colin Davis, Hall

RSC: *All's Well that Ends Well*, Peggy Ashcroft, dir. Trevor Nunn, Theatre

1983

Asger Jorn/Rodin and his contemporaries, Gallery

Hundertwasser/Carpet Magic, Gallery

Mostly Mozart Festival, AAM/Christopher Hogwood

RSC: *King Lear*, Michael Gambon and Anthony Sher, dir. Adrian Noble, Theatre

Summer in the City, Cross-Centre Festival

LSO/Rafael Kubelik residency, Hall

RSC: *The Tempest*, Derek Jacobi, dir. Ron Daniels, Theatre

1984

BBCSO: Haydn and Schumann/ John Pritchard, Hall

American Folk Art: Expressions of a New Spirit, Gallery

Family Film Club launched, Cinema

Montreal Symphony Orchestra, Hall

Woody Allen Retrospective, Cinema

RSC: *Mother Courage*, Judi Dench, dir. Howard Davies, Theatre

1985

BBC: *Stockhausen, Music and Machines*, Hall, Cinema

Tradition and Renewal, Contemporary Art in the German Democratic Republic, Gallery

LSO/Abbado: *Mahler, Vienna and the 20th Century*, concert series, Hall

The American Festival, Hall, Gallery, Cinema

RSC: *Les Misérables*, English–language premiere, Theatre

Mostly Mozart Festival/Christopher Hogwood, Hall

Toki: Tradition in Japan Today, Gallery

1986

The Bernstein Festival inc. Royal Gala LSO/Bernstein, Hall

Cecil Beaton, Gallery

Eugene Smith/Rabindranath Tagore, Gallery

RSC: *Les Liaisons Dangereuses*, Lindsay Duncan, Alan Rickman, Juliet Stevenson, Pit

Beethoven piano sonata cycle, John Lill, lunchtimes, Hall

Kurosawa Retrospective, Cinema

1987

LSO/Rozhdestvensky: *Stravinsky Plus:* Hall, GSMD

Russian Style 1700–1920: Court and Country Dress from the Hermitage, Gallery

Ansel Adams: Classic Images/A Paradise Lost, Gallery

RSC: *Richard II*, Jeremy Irons; *Macbeth*, Jonathan Pryce, Theatre

The Gershwin Years LSO/Tilson Thomas, Hall

Summer in the City Festival: Academy of St Martin in the Fields/Neville Marriner, Hall

RSC: *The Wizard of Oz*, dir. Ian Judge

1988

BBCSO: *Endless Parade*, Harrison Birtwistle, Hall

A Theme with Variations: British Music, LSO, GSMD, and others, Hall

LSO Summer Pops, Randy Crawford, Billy Connolly, Val Doonican, Timmy Mallet, Hall

Images de France: Cross-Centre

RSC: *The Merchant of Venice*, Anthony Sher as Shylock, dir. Bill Alexander, Theatre

LSO: Michael Tilson Thomas becomes principal conductor, Hall

Shostakovich: Music from the Flames, LSO/Rostropovich, RPO, Hall and South Bank Centre

RSC: Howard Brenton *The Churchill Play*, Colin Welland, dir. Barry Kyle

1989

Great Orchestras of the World series, Hall

RSC: *The Plantagenets*, dir. Adrian Noble, Theatre

LSO/Tilson Thomas: *The Flight of the Firebird*, Hall

100 Years of Russian Art 1889–1989: from private collections in the USSR, Gallery

A Golden Age: Art and Society in Hungary 1896–1914, Gallery

Summer in the City/The King's Singers, Hall and Cross-Centre

Magyarok: Britain Salutes Hungary, Cross-Centre and other venues

Through the Looking Glass: Photographic Art in Britain 1945–1989, Gallery

Chamber Orchestra of Europe series, Hall

RSC: *Hamlet*, Mark Rylance, dir. Ron Daniels, Theatre

1990

BBCSO: Berio at the Barbican, Hall

Easter Jazz Festival with Acker Bilk, Hall

Friends of the Earth: The Rainforest Festival, Cross-Centre

RSC: *A Clockwork Orange*, dir. Ron Daniels, Theatre

Pursuit of the Real: British Figurative Painting from Sickert to Bacon, Gallery

Daniel Barenboim plays Bach's Goldberg Variations, Hall

Israel: State of the Arts, inc. Israel Philharmonic Orchestra/Mehta, Hall

Chagall to Kitaj: Jewish Experience in 20th Century Art, Gallery

1991

LSO/Tilson Thomas: Childhood Festival, Hall

BBCSO: Henze Festival, Hall

Mozart 200, English Chamber Orchestra, Hall

Stanley Spencer: The Apotheosis of Love/Man Ray in Fashion, Gallery

Chamber Orchestra of Europe: Tenth Anniversary Season, Hall

True North: Canadian Landscape Painting 1896–1939, Gallery

Caribbean Carnival Extravaganza, Summer in the City, Cross-Centre

Japan and Britain: An Aesthetic Dialogue 1850–1930, Gallery

1992

Looking Forward Looking Back, celebration of 10th Birthday, Cross-Centre

LSO/Colin Davis, Michael Tilson Thomas; BBCSO/Pierre Boulez, Hall

Top Ten Films presented by Barry Norman, Cinema

Willard White sings Gershwin and Tippett with LSO, Hall

Van Gogh in England/William Eggleston: Ancient and Modern, Gallery

RSC: *Hamlet*, Kenneth Branagh, dir. Adrian Noble

Tender is the North, major Cross-Centre celebration of Nordic art and music

Beacon Europe Day, closing event of the European Arts Festival

1993

Eric Gill: Sculpture/Border crossings: Fourteen Scandinavian Artists, Gallery

The Ultimate Ealing Film Season, Cinema

RSC: *Macbeth* with Derek Jacobi, Theatre

Alphonse Mucha/Bill Brandt: Photographs, Gallery

LSO/Bernard Haitink, Hall

1994

London Australian Film Festival, Cinema

Evelyn Glennie in Celebrity Recitals Series, Hall

Evolving Tradition — British & Irish folk, Altan and the Kathryn Tickell Trio, Hall

Who's Looking at the Family? Gallery

A Bitter Truth: Avant-Garde and the Great War, Gallery

1995

Carry On Up the Barbican! season, Cinema

RSC: *Coriolanus* with Toby Stephens, dir. David Thacker, Theatre

CBSO/Simon Rattle: Beethoven Symphony Cycle, Hall

The Art of Dora Carrington/African Textiles, Gallery

1996

Barbican Jazz launched: Oscar Peterson, Hall

Sibelius Season, Gothenburg Symphony Orchestra, Hall

Evolving Tradition 2: World/Roots festival, Hall

Hammer at the Barbican, Cinema

JAM: Style + Music + Media, Gallery

1997

Modern Art in Britain 1910–1914/Lucie Rie and Hans Cooper, Gallery

Don McCullin: Sleeping with Ghosts, Gallery

1998

Inventing America: major year-long Cross-Centre season

The Art of Harley/Shaker: The Art of Craftmanship, Gallery

Monsters of Grace Robert Wilson and Philip Glass, Theatre

Tharp! Twyla Tharp Dance Company, Theatre

Maly Drama Theatre of St Petersburg, *The Possessed*, Theatre

Merce Cunningham Dance Theatre, Theatre

Postman Pat, Theatre

The Ninagawa Company, *Hamlet*

BITE (Barbican International Theatre Events) launched

1999

Wizadora, Theatre

Gate Theatre, Dublin, Samuel Beckett Festival, Theatre

Martha Graham Dance Company, Theatre

Twyla Tharp *Diabelli*, Hall

David Bailey. Archive One/New Art for a New era: Malevich's Vision of the Russian Avant-Garde, Gallery

Ensemble Modern, *Black on White*, Theatre

Ellington Sacred Songs with Jessye Norman, Hall/Theatre

2000

The Art of Star Wars, start of international BIE touring programme, Curve, Centre

Boulez 2000 LSO/Pierre Boulez season, Hall

Berlin to Broadway: the Music of Kurt Weill, BBCSO weekend, Hall; Weill season, Cinema

Africa: Roots and Shoots: Miriam Makeba, Ali Farka Toure and King Sunny Ade, Hall and foyers

Back to the Future, with Anne-Sophie Mutter/LSO, Hall

The 1000 Year Journey: A Celebration of Gypsy Music and Arts, Centre

Patience Agbabi: Transformatrix, with Lemn Sissay, Cinema

Hugh Masekela, Hall

Laurie Anderson, *Songs and Stories from Moby Dick*, Theatre

New York Philharmonic and Pittsburgh Symphony Orchestra, Hall

Ravi & Anoushka Shankar, Hall

Femi Kuti, Hall

Andy Goldsworthy, *Snowballs in Summer*, Curve

Aaron Copland centenary, BBC SO Hall, Guildhall and Cinema

Billy Bragg and the Blokes, Hall

LSO/Dave Brubeck band, Hall

Steppenwolf Company, *One Flew Over the Cuckoo's Nest*, with Gary Sinise, Theatre

2001

Lincoln Center Jazz Orchestra/Wynton Marsalis, Louis Armstrong Series, Hall

Ornette Coleman Trio: *Global Expressions*, Hall

Manu Dibango and The Afro-Funk Big Band, with Richard Bona and Tony Allen, Hall

RSC: Shakespeare History Plays, with Samuel West, David Tennant, Theatre

Only Connect launched

Women in Iranian Cinema, Cinema

The Films of Milos Forman, Cinema

Rokia Traoré, Hall

Peter Hall's *Tantalus: a Festival*, Theatre

Complicité/Emerson String Quartet, *The Noise of Time*, Theatre

Hungarian Literature in Focus

A Tribute to Pinewood Studios, Cinemas

Studio Ghibli Retrospective, Cinema

Andres Serrano, Curve

elektronic festival with Talvin Singh, Aphex Twin, Conservatory

Harry Potter Family Festival weekend

RSC: *Hamlet*, Samuel West, Theatre

2002

John's Earbox: The Music of John Adams, BBCSO weekend, Hall

Brad Mehldau Trio, Hall

Barbican: This Was Tomorrow, curated by David Heathcote, Curve

LSO: Mstislav Rostropovich 75th Birthday Series, Hall

RSC: David Edgar *The Prisoner's Dilemma*, dir. Michael Attenborough

Afel Bocoum and Damon Albarn, *Mali Music*, Hall

Kronos Quartet play Steve Reich, Hall

Game On: The History and Culture of Video Games, touring exhibition

Gilberto Gil: Bob Marley Tribute, Hall

Herbie Hancock, Hall

ENO: Wagner's *Ring Cycle* in concert, Hall

Grayson Perry: *Guerilla Tactics*, Curve

New Europe Film Season, Cinema

Orchestra Baobab & Orquesta Aragon, Hall

Kirov Opera/Valery Gergiev, Hall

Pina Bausch & Tanztheater Wuppertal, *Kontakthof*, Theatre

South African Gospel Singers, Hall

2003

RSC: *Midnight's Children*, Theatre

LSO: Colin Davis 75th birthday series, Hall

Laurie Anderson, *Happiness*, Theatre

Lincoln Center Jazz Orchestra/Wynton Marsalis residency, Hall

Complicité, *The Elephant Vanishes*, Theatre

Duckie, *C'est Barbican*, Pit

Robert Lepage, *the far side of the moon*, Theatre

Deborah Colker Dance Company, *4 por 4*, Theatre

2004

Ukulele Orchestra of Great Britain, Pit

Mikhail Baryshnikov, *Solos With Piano or Not*, Hall

Helen Chadwick/Tina Modotti and Edward Weston, first shows in refurbished Gallery

Billie and Me tribute to Billie Holliday with Neneh Cherry, Fontella Bass and Amy Winehouse, Hall

BITE: Robert Wilson/Tom Waits/William Burroughs *The Black Rider*, Marianne Faithfull, Theatre

Les arts florissants/Compagnie Montalvo-Hervieu: Rameau, *Les paladins*, Theatre

LSO: Centenary season celebrations begin

10 Years of South African Democracy: LSO and KwaZulu-Natal Philharmonic, Hall

2005

Steve Reich *You Are*, UK premiere, Hall

Ladysmith Black Mambazo, Hall

Abbey Theatre, Dublin, *The Plough and the Stars*, Theatre

Mikhail Pletnev conducts Sergey Taneyev, Russian National Orchestra, Hall

Julius Caesar, dir. Deborah Warner with Ralph Fiennes, Simon Russell Beale, Theatre

London Children's Film Festival launched with Film London, Cinema

Royal Gala performance for LSO Centenary, Hall

Laurie Anderson, *The End of the Moon*, Theatre

Jeremy Deller and Alan Kane, *Folk Archive*, Curve

Jenny Holzer text projections, Centre

Tintin in Tibet, Rufus Norris directs Russell Tovey, Hall with Young Vic

Yo-Yo Ma plays Bach, Hall

2006

Shostakovich symphony cycle: Valery Gergiev/LSO/Marinsky Theatre/Rotterdam PO/Vienna PO

Tropicalia, A Revolution in Brazilian Culture, Cross-Centre season

Joan Baez, Hall

LSO/Nitin Sawhney, soundtrack to Franz Osten's *A Throw of Dice*, Hall

Future City: Experiment and Utopia in Architecture 1956–2006, Gallery

Phases: Steve Reich 70th Birthday season, Hall, Theatre, LSO St Luke's

In the face of history: European Photographers in the 20th Century, Gallery

Robert Lepage: *The Andersen Project*, Theatre

Maly Theatre of St Petersburg, *King Lear*, Theatre

Michael Clark Dance Company, *Stravinsky Project Part 2,* Theatre

Mark Ravenhill, *Dick Whittington and his Cat*, Theatre

Duckie, *The Class Club*, Pit

2007

Maly Theatre of St Petersburg, *Platonov,* Theatre

Ninagawa Company, *Coriolanus,* Theatre

Lone Twin, *Spiral,* around the Barbican Estate

London Children's Film Festival, Cinema

Los Angeles Philharmonic/Esa-Pekka Salonen, *Sibelius Unbound*, Hall

Christopher Green and Ursula Martinez, *Office Party Xmas 2007*, Pit

AfroReggae, *From the Favela to the World*, Gilberto Gil and Lula da Silva, Gallery, Hall

Ian Bostridge, *Homeward Bound* concert series, Hall

Complicité, *A Disappearing Number,* Theatre

Michael Clark Dance Company, *Stravinsky Project,* Theatre

Jack and the Beanstalk, Theatre

Seduced: Art and Sex from Antiquity to Now, Gallery

2008

Dee Dee Bridgewater, Hall

Met Opera Live, Cinema

National Theatre of Scotland, *Black Watch*, Theatre

Laurie Anderson, *Homeland,* Theatre

Blaze, Victoria Park, Hackney Empire, Dalston Vortex

Antony and the Johnsons with the LSO, Hall

Toumani Diabate with the LSO, Hall

Drifting and Tilting — Songs of Scott Walker, Hall

London South African Film Festival, Cinema

2009

Radical Nature: Art and Architecture for a Changing Planet 1969–2009, Gallery

Boy Blue Entertainment, *Pied Piper*, Theatre

Beyond the Wall: Contemporary Chinese Culture, Gallery

Shah Jo Raag Fakirs, Hall

Toneelgroep Amsterdam, *Roman Tragedies*, Theatre

2010

Céleste Boursier-Mougenot, installation with zebra finches, Curve

Tanztheater Wuppertal Pina Bausch, *Kontakthof*, Theatre

The Surreal House: Architecture of Desire, Gallery

Boy Blue Entertainment, *A Nite with Da Bratz,* Theatre

Staff Benda Bilili, Hall

You Me Bum Bum Train, LEB Building, Bethnal Green

Cameron Mackintosh, *Les Misérables,* Theatre

Merce Cunningham Dance Company, *Nearly Ninety,* Theatre

Future Beauty: 30 Years of Japanese Fashion, Gallery

2011

Pioneers of the Downtown Scene: New York 1970s, Gallery

National Theatre of Scotland, *Black Watch*, Theatre

Reverberations: The Influence of Steve Reich, 75th Birthday Celebration, Hall

Watch me Move: The Animation Show, BIE touring exhibition

OMA/Progress, Rem Koolhaus and partners, Gallery

Lincoln Center New York Production: *South Pacific,* Theatre

A Night in Tahrir Square, Hall

Duckie, *Copyright Christmas,* Pit

Random International, *Rain Room*, Curve

2012

Hofesh Shechter and Antony Gormley, *Survivor*, Theatre

BBCSO Total Immersion weekend: Arvo Pärt, Hall

Botho Strauss's *Big and Small (Gross und Klein)*, with Cate Blanchett, Theatre

Robert Wilson & Philip Glass, *Einstein on the Beach,* Theatre

Vienna Philharmonic/Simon Rattle, Hall

Wynton Marsalis, LSO/Simon Rattle, *Swing Symphony,* Hall

Africa Express, Cultural Olympiad, Hall, UK venues

Britten Sinfonia, 20th Anniversary Concert, Hall

Complicité/Simon McBurney, *The Master and Margarita*, Theatre

Aphex Twin, *Remote Orchestra,* Hall

2013

Juan Diego Flórez and Friends, Hall

Open East Festival, Queen Elizabeth Olympic Park

Robert Wilson/Ruhrtriennale Festival, *John Cage Lecture on Nothing,* Theatre

Everything was Moving: Photography from the 60s and 70s, Gallery

The Bride and the Bachelors: Duchamp with Cage, Cunningham, Rauschenberg and Johns, Gallery

Pop Art Design, Gallery

Cabaret Duchamp, Theatre

Cheek by Jowl, *Ubu Roi,* Silk Street Theatre

Dance Nations Dalston, Gillett Square

Shoreditch Festival, Shoreditch Trust

Urban Wandering, Cinema

Digital Revolution, BIE, Curve and Pit

Curlew River, part of Barbican Britten, St Giles Cripplegate

Transcender season, Hall

Boy Blue Entertainment, *The Five and the Prophecy of Prana,* Theatre

Toneelgroep Amsterdam, *Scenes from a Marriage*, Theatre

2014

Maxim Vengerov, Artist Spotlight, Hall

Colm Tóibín *The Testament of Mary:* Fiona Shaw, dir. Deborah Warner, Theatre

Wynton Marsalis and Jazz at Lincoln Center Orchestra residency with Sachal Jazz Ensemble, Hall

Explorations: The Sound of Nonesuch Records, Kronos Quartet, Britten Sinfonia, Hall

Theo Parrish *Teddy's Get Down,* Pit

Circa – Opus, *Debussy String Quartet,* Theatre

The Miners' Hymns, Johann Johannsson and Bill Morrison, Hall

The Fashion World of Jean Paul Gaultier: From the Sidewalk to the Catwalk, Gallery

The Film World of Jean Paul Gaultier, Cinema

English National Ballet, *Lest we Forget,* Theatre

RSC return to the Barbican: *Richard II* with David Tennant, Theatre

Walthamstow Garden Party, Walthamstow

International Ibsen season, Thomas Ostermeier and others, Theatre

Constructing Worlds: Photography and Architecture in the Modern Age, Gallery

City Visions, Cinema

2015

London International Mime Festival, Theatre

Berliner Philharmoniker residency/Young Orchestra for London/Simon Rattle, Hall

Magnificent Obsessions: The Artist as Collector, Gallery

Ivo van Hove, *Antigone*, Juliet Binoche, Theatre

Ninagawa Company, *Hamlet*, Theatre

Barking Town Square Street Party, Barking

International Beckett Season, Theatre

Sonia Friedman Productions, *Hamlet,* Benedict Cumberbatch, Theatre

Doug Aitken, *Station to Station: a 30 Day Happening*, Cross-Centre

Touretteshero, *Backstage in Biscuit Land,* Pit

The Colour of Money, Cinema

Sound Unbound Classical Weekender, Hall, foyers and Cross-Centre

EFG London Jazz Festival: Kamasi Washington, Hall

The World of Charles and Ray Eames, Gallery

2016

LSO/ Simon Rattle: Debussy, *Pelléas et Mélisande*, dir. Peter Sellars, Hall

Complicité, *The Encounter,* Theatre

Los Angeles Philharmonic residency: Gustavo Dudamel / Young Orchestra East, Hall

Toneelgroep Amsterdam: *Kings of War,* Theatre

Odéon—Théâtre de l'Europe, *Phaedra(s),* with Isabel Huppert, Theatre

Nils Frahm curates *Possibly Colliding*: Anna von Hausswolff, Penguin Café, Hall

Ragnar Kjartansson, Gallery

Terry Riley *In C,* London Contemporary Orchestra, Hall

The Vulgar: Fashion Redefined, Gallery

Royal Concertgebouw Orchestra of Amsterdam/Daniele Gatti, Hall

Academy of Ancient Music, associate ensemble, Purcell cycle, Hall

2017

Boy Blue Entertainment, *Blak Whyte Gray,* Theatre

Complicité and Schaubühne Berlin, *Beware of Pity,* Theatre

Richard Mosse, *Incoming,* Curve

Ballet Black, *Triple Bill, Theatre*

Toneelgroep Amsterdam, *Roman Tragedies,* Theatre

The Japanese House: Architecture and Life after 1945, Gallery

Room 29: Jarvis Cocker and Chilly Gonzales, Hall

What London Watches: Ten Films That Shook Our World, Cinema

Barbican/Toneelgroep Amsterdam: *Obsession,* Jude Law and Halina Reijn, dir. Ivo van Hove, Theatre

Toots and the Maytals headline Walthamstow Garden Party, Lloyd Park

Into the Unknown: A Journey through Science Fiction: Curve, Pit

Trajal Harrell: Hoochie Koochie, Gallery

LSO and Barbican: *This is Rattle,* inaugural season of Simon Rattle as music director, Hall, GSMD

Michael Clark Company, *to a simple rock 'n' roll ... song*, Theatre.

Touretteshero Pit Party: Brewing in the Basement, Pit

Basquiat: Boom For Real, Gallery

RSC: *Julius Caesar, Antony and Cleopatra, Titus Andronicus,* Theatre

2018

Art of Change season, Cross-Centre

Helen Plumb, *A Prickly Subject*, film on Barbican YouTube

Studio 3 Arts Pit Party: Meat Raffle, Pit

Nevertheless, She Persisted: Suffrage, Cinema and Beyond, Cinema

Barbican Young Poets, *A Change is Gonna Come*, Pit.

Taylor Mac, *A 24-Decade History of Popular Music: The First Act,* Theatre

Barry Humphries' Weimar Cabaret, Theatre

Generations: Russian Cinema of Change, Gallery

Anthony Joseph & Friends, *Windrush: A Celebration,* Hall

Inua Ellams Pit Party: Poetry + Film/ Hack and Open Lab Rhythm and Poetry, Pit

Storme Toolis, *Redefining Juliet,* Pit

Jóhann Jóhannsson, *Last and First Men*, narrated by Tilda Swinton, Hall

The Wooster Group, *The Town Hall Affair,* Theatre

RSC: *Macbeth, Merry Wives of Windsor,* Theatre

2019

Wayward Productions/Complicité, *Grief is the Thing with Feathers,* Theatre

Love and Anarchy: The Films of Lina Wertmüller, Cinema

David Lang with 500-voice choir, *the public domain,* Foyers

Toneelgroep Amsterdam, *Medea,* Theatre

Ballet Black, *Double Bill*, Theatre

Moscow Pushkin Drama Theatre, *The Cherry Orchard, The Good Person of Szechwan,* Theatre

Maxine Peake in Julia Leigh's *Avalanche: A Love Story,* Theatre

Serge Aimé Coulibaly, *Kalakuta Republik*, Theatre

Merce Cunningham Trust, *Night of 100 Solos, a centennial event,* Theatre

Britten Sinfonia/Thomas Adès, Beethoven Symphony Cycle, Hall

Lee Krasner: Living Colour, Gallery

Janáček, *The Cunning Little Vixen*, LSO/Simon Rattle, Peter Sellars, Hall

Art Ensemble of Chicago 50th Anniversary, Hall

Cheek by Jowl/Moscow Pushkin Drama Theatre, *The Knight of the Burning Pestle,* Theatre

RSC: *Measure for Measure*, dir. Gregory Doran, Theatre

2020

Toyin Ojih Odultola, *A Countervailing Theory,* Curve

LSO/Pappano, Vaughan Williams, Hall

[Centre closed to the public from March]

Live from the Barbican, Bryn Terfel, Sarah Connolly, Kanneh-Masons, Hall and online

Academy of Ancient Music, Handel *Messiah,* online

2021

[Centre re-opened May]

Live from the Barbican: Paul Weller, Nadine Shah, George the Poet, Moses Boyd

LSO/Rattle, Hall and online

Jean Dubuffet, *Brutal Beauty,* Gallery

Claudia Andujar, *The Yanomami Struggle*, Curve and Pit

Bibliography

Archives and Reports

Arts Council for Great Britain, *Plans for an Arts Centre* (London: ACGB, 1945)

Arts Council of Great Britain, *Housing the Arts, Part 1 'The Needs of the Metropolis'* (London: ACGB, 1959)

Barbican Stories, Anon., June 2021

Besch, Anthony, 'Report to the Corporation of the City of London on the subject of the proposed concert hall and theatre to be built in the Barbican area with recommendations for their design, administration and finance', typescript, 1964

Cement and Concrete Association / Corporation of London, *Barbican: Detailed description* (1970)

Chamberlin, Powell and Bon, *Barbican Redevelopment*, May 1956

Chamberlin, Powell and Bon, *Barbican Redevelopment 1959: Report to the Court of Common Council of the Corporation of the City of London on residential development within the Barbican area, prepared on the instructions of the Barbican Committee by Chamberlin, Powell and Bon, architects*

Corporation of London, Joint Report of the Rates Finance, Music and Barbican Committees, Barbican Redevelopment – Concert Hall, March 1965

Corporation of London, Joint Report of the Barbican, Music and Library Committees, Barbican Redevelopment – Arts Centre, December 1968

Corporation of London, Joint Report of the Barbican, Music and Library Committees, Barbican Arts Centre, April 1971

Lee, Jennie, *A Policy for the Arts: The First Steps* (London: HMSO, 1965)

Williams, W E, *A Brighter Prospect*, 17th Annual Report of the Arts Council of Great Britain (London: ACGB, 1962)

Wrong, Henry, 'A Policy for the Future of the Barbican; The Management of the Barbican Arts, Conference and Exhibition Centre', typescript, 10 January 1978

Books and Articles

Bradley, Simon, and Pevsner, Nikolaus, *The Buildings of England, London 1: The City of London* (New Haven: Yale UP, 2002)

Chambers, Colin, *Inside the Royal Shakespeare Company: Creativity and the Institution* (London: Routledge, 2004)

Chamberlin, Powell & Bon, *Architects' Journal*, Vol. 117, No. 3020, 15 January 1953, p.72

Clapson, Mark and Larkham, Peter J (eds.), *The Blitz and its Legacy: Wartime Destruction to Post-War Reconstruction* (London: Routledge, 2013)

Clarke, Jennifer, *The Barbican: Sitting on History* (London: Corporation of London, 1990)

Darley, Gillian, 'Uneasy new warmth in a concrete overcoat', *The Observer*, 12 September 1993, p.51

Esher, Lionel, *A Broken Wave: The Rebuilding of England 1940–1980* (Harmondsworth: Allen Lane, 1981)

Fair, Alistair, 'British Theatres, 1926–1991: an architectural history', PhD, University of Cambridge, 2008

Goodwin, John, ed., *Peter Hall's Diaries: The Story of a Dramatic Battle* (London: Hamish Hamilton, 1983)

Grafe, Christopher, *People's Palaces: Architecture, culture and democracy in post-war Western Europe* (Amsterdam: Architectura & Natura, 2014)

Grindrod, John, *How to Love Brutalism* (London: Batsford, 2018)

Grylls, Vaughan, Geoffrey Powell obituary, *The Guardian*, 20 December 1999, p.18

Hall, Peter, *Making an Exhibition of Myself* (London: Sinclair-Stevenson, 1993)

Harwood, Elain, *Chamberlin, Powell & Bon: The Barbican and Beyond* (London: RIBA, 2011)

Heathcote, David, *Barbican: Penthouse over the City* (Chichester: Wiley-Academy, 2004)

Hebbert, Michael, 'The City of London Walkway Experiment', *Journal of the American Planning Association*, Vol. 59 No. 4, Autumn 1993

Hewison, Robert, 'Embattled Bastion', *The Sunday Times*, 1 March 1992

Hewison, Robert, 'How to update a utopian vision in concrete', *The Art Newspaper*, No. 233, March 2012

Hutchison, Robert, *The Politics of the Arts Council* (London: Sinclair Browne, 1982)

Kennedy, Maev, 'Farewell to lost visitors at Barbican mark two', *The Guardian*, 17 October 2000, p.8

Keynes, Henry Maynard, 'The Arts Council: Its Policies and Hopes', *The Listener*, XXXIV, No. 861, 12 July 1945, pp.31–2

Kynaston, David, ed. David Milner, *City of London: The History* (London: Vintage Books, 2011)

Morrison, Richard, *Orchestra: The LSO: A Century of Triumph and Turbulence*, (London: Faber & Faber, 2004)

Orazi, Stefi, *The Barbican Estate* (London: Batsford, 2018)

Pick, John, *Managing The Arts? The British Experience* (London: Rheingold, 1986)

Powell, Geoffry, 'Peter Chamberlin', *RIBA Journal*, Vol. 85, No. 8, August 1978, p.347

Shaughnessy, Adrian, *Ken Garland: Structure and Substance* (London: Unit Editions, 2012)

Smith, Deborah, 'Barbican Complete', *Architects' Journal*, Vol. 175, No. 10, 10 March 1982, p.19

Tusa, John, *Making a Noise: Getting It Right, Getting It Wrong in Life, the Arts and Broadcasting* (London: Weidenfeld & Nicolson, 2018)

Wright, Harry Cory, *Barbican Centre* (London: Thames & Hudson, 2019)

Contributors' biographies

Roma Agrawal MBE is an award-winning engineer, author and broadcaster. From footbridges and sculptures, to train stations and skyscrapers — including The Shard — she has left an indelible mark on London's landscape during her 15-year career in construction.

Tony Chambers is the founder of creative agency TC & Friends and co-founder, with artist Ryan Gander, of OTOMOTO — a design, art and ideas platform. He is the former Editor-in-chief of *Wallpaper** magazine, Art Director of British *GQ* and Art Editor of *The Sunday Times Magazine*.

Philip Dodd is a former Director of London's ICA, and an award-winning BBC broadcaster and author, including the recently republished *Englishness: Politics and Culture*. Since 2004 he has worked between the UK and China, curating exhibitions including Sean Scully and Hsiao Chin.

Lyn Gardner is an award-winning journalist, critic and novelist who has written for many national and international publications including *The Guardian* and *The Stage*, and has written novels for children.

Elain Harwood is an architectural investigator with Historic England and author of *Chamberlin, Powell & Bon* (2011), *Space, Hope and Brutalism* (2015) and *Mid-Century Britain* (2021). She is currently writing a book on brutalism
Robert Hewison is a writer, journalist and consultant in the field of cultural policy. An authority on John Ruskin, he has published more than 20 books on aspects of 19th and 20th century British cultural history, and wrote on theatre and the arts for *The Sunday Times* from 1981 to 2016. His latest book is *Passport to Peckham: Culture and Creativity in a London Village*.

Theo Inglis is a freelance graphic designer, writer and design historian. He is a graduate of the Royal College of Art's Critical Writing in Art & Design MA programme and his first book *Mid-Century Modern Graphic Design* was published in 2019.

Nicholas Kenyon was Managing Director of the Barbican Centre from 2007 to 2021. He was previously a music critic, Controller of BBC Radio 3 1992–8 and Director of the BBC Proms 1996–2007. He is the author of *The Life of Music* and editor of *The City of London: a Companion Guide*.

Fiona Maddocks is chief music critic for *The Observer*, and is the author of *Hildegard of Bingen, Harrison Birtwistle* and *Music for Life*.

Sukhdev Sandhu was Chief Film Critic for the *Daily Telegraph* between 2002 and 2011. He currently directs the Colloquium for Unpopular Culture at New York University.

Contributors' acknowledgements
The editor and researchers would like to thank John Kelly, Sidd Khajuria, Libby Rice, William Allen, Peter Hope-Parry, Sharon Kent and their colleagues at the Barbican Centre for all their input.

Elain Harwood would like to thank Polly Powell, Frank Woods and Alistair Fair.

Theo Inglis would like to thank Jim Northover, Richard Hollis, Ian McLaren, Angus Watson, William Allen, Sean Perkins, Ian Cartlidge, Stephen Gilmore, Sarah Boris, Bryan Clark, Mafalda Spencer and Graeme Jones.

Fiona Maddocks would like to thank Antony Lewis-Crosby and Clive Gillinson.

Sukhdev Sandhu would like to thank Robert Beeson, Don Boyd, Neil Brand, Ray Diehl, Gareth Evans, Suzie Evans, Jane Giles, Gali Gold, Antony Lewis-Crosby, Robert Rider, Sue Rider, Jonathan Romney, Beverley Silverstone, Helen Simmons, Mark Webber and Liz Wrenn.

Image credits

pp. 4–5 Russell Bell
pp. 9, 14, 17, 48, 72, 78, 108, 136, 168, 194, 234, 248–249, 250–251 Harry Cory Wright
p. 10 Poster for the Barbican Centre for the Arts, 1982 using David Hockney's 'Cubistic Bar' from 'Les Mamelles de Tirésias' 1980 (detail) 37 ½ × 28 ½" © David Hockney
pp. 12–13, 34 (top), 34 (bottom), 47 (left), 47 (right), 64–65, 96–97, 111 (top), 111 (bottom), 120, 135, 158, 170, 171, 174–175, 177, 179, 180, 184–185, 190, 192–193, 203, 204, 207, 238, 246–247 Barbican Archive
pp. 18, 30, 42, 45, 56–57, 68–69, 70–71, 74, 75, 76–77, 81, 86–87, 88–89, 90, 91, 92–93, 94, 100, 113, 140–141, 172, 197, 198–199, 200, 232–233, 254–255 Peter Bloomfield
p. 21 Arcaid Images/Alamy
p. 24 London Metropolitan Archives/Heritage Images
p. 29 Arthur Cross and Fred Tibbs, London Metropolitan Archives
p. 33 (top), 33 (bottom), 50 RIBA Collections
p. 36 London Metropolitan Archives
pp. 37, 51, 52 From the collection of Polly Powell
pp. 38, 39 Norah Glover/Barbican Archive
p. 50 Frank Woods
p. 55 Harry Todd/Getty Images
p. 58 (top), 58 (bottom) Elain Harwood
p. 61 © Historic England Archive. John Laing Photographic Collection
pp. 62–63 Terry Fincher/Getty Images
pp. 73, 264–265, 266–267, 268–269 Neil Perry
pp. 82–83 © John Maltby/RIBA Collections
pp. 98–99, 256 Sidd Khajuria
pp. 106–107 Stefi Orazi
pp. 114 Courtesy of the LSO archive
p. 116 Keystone Press/Alamy
p. 118 Robbie Jack
p. 119 Suzie Maeder/LSO Archive
pp. 122, 124–125, 128, 132, 160–161 Mark Allan
p. 123 Matt Kent/Getty Images
p. 127 Peter Williams
pp. 130–131 Hayley Madden/Getty Images
p. 139 Lucie Jansch
p. 143 (top) Donald Cooper/Alamy Stock Photo
p. 143 (bottom) Johan Persson/ArenaPAL
pp. 144–145 Tristram Kenton
p. 146 Overtures Archive
p. 147 Donald Cooper/Alamy
p. 149 © Hugo Glendinning. All rights reserved, DACS/Artimage 2021
p. 152 Sakura Hutari
p. 153 Robbie Jack/Getty Images
p. 154–155 Matt Crossick/Alamy
p. 156 Robbie Jack
p. 162, 181 Studio Myerscough and Cartlidge Levene Photography: Richard Learoyd
p. 176 Pentagram
pp. 182–83, 242–243 Tim Soar
pp. 186 (top), 186 (bottom), 188–189 courtesy of North
p. 205, 218–219 Oli Scarff/Getty Images
p. 208 Photography Michael Wicks
p. 211, 214–215 Lyndon Douglas
p. 212–213 Miles Willis
p. 216 Luke Hayes, courtesy A Practice for Everyday Life
pp. 220–221 Matthew Lloyd/Getty Images
p. 222 Courtesy A Practice for Everyday Life
p. 225 Architectural Press Archive/RIBA Collections
pp. 226–227 Rachel Williams
p.228 John Phillips/Getty Images
p.229 Robert Alexander/Getty Images
pp. 230–231 Max Colson
pp. 237 John Maltby/RIBA Collections
pp. 262–263 Camilla Greenwell

Index

First published in the United Kingdom in 2022 by

Batsford
43 Great Ormond Street
London
WC1N 3HZ

Design: Stefi Orazi Studio

ISBN 978-1-84994-681-0

A CIP catalogue record for this book is available from the British Library.

10 9 8 7 6 5 4 3 2 1

Reproduction by Rival Colour Ltd, UK
Printed and bound by Toppan Leefung, China

Acknowledgements
I am extremely grateful to Polly Powell, daughter of one of the Barbican's trio of architects and owner of Batsford, for seeing the potential importance of the book as we approach our 40th anniversary; to Matthew Harle and Thomas Overton, intrepid archivists at the Barbican for their constant research input, all the authors for their writing against unforgiving deadlines, Nicola Newman for her skilled editorial guidance, and Stefi Orazi who has designed the book with such flair and sensitivity. It has been a very happy project with which to conclude my 14 years at the service of the Barbican, and with which to entrust its legacy to my successors.

NK